WORLD TRADE ORGANIZATION

Dispute Settlement Reports

2002
Volume IX

Pages 3595-4077

CAMBRIDGE
UNIVERSITY PRESS

CAMBRIDGE UNIVERSITY PRESS

Cambridge, New York, Melbourne, Madrid, Cape Town, Singapore, São Paulo

Cambridge University Press
The Edinburgh Building, Cambridge CB2 2RU, UK

Published in the United States of America by Cambridge University Press, New York

www.cambridge.org
Information on this title: www.cambridge.org/9780521854689

First published 2005

Printed in the United Kingdom at the University Press, Cambridge

A catalogue record for this book is available from the British Library

ISBN-13 987-0-521-85468-9 hardback
ISBN-10 0-521-85468-7 hardback

THE WTO DISPUTE SETTLEMENT REPORTS

The *Dispute Settlement Reports* of the World Trade Organization (the "WTO") include panel and Appellate Body reports, as well as arbitration awards, in disputes concerning the rights and obligations of WTO Members under the provisions of the *Marrakesh Agreement Establishing the World Trade Organization*. The *Dispute Settlement Reports* are available in English, French and Spanish. Starting with 1999, the first volume of each year contains a cumulative index of published disputes.

This volume may be cited as DSR 2002:IX

TABLE OF CONTENTS

UNITED STATES – PRELIMINARY DETERMINATIONS WITH RESPECT TO CERTAIN SOFTWOOD LUMBER FROM CANADA

Report of the Panel
WT/DS236/R

Adopted by the Dispute Settlement Body on 1 November 2002

TABLE OF CONTENTS

Page

Page

Page

Page

LIST OF ANNEXES

I. INTRODUCTION

A. *Complaint of Canada*

1.1 On 21 August 2001, Canada requested consultations with the United States pursuant to Article 4 of the Dispute Settlement Understanding ("the DSU"), Article XXII of the General Agreement on Tariffs and Trade 1994 ("GATT 1994") and Article 30 of the Agreement on Subsidies and Countervailing Measures ("the *SCM Agreement*" or "the Agreement"), with regard to the preliminary countervailing duty determination and the preliminary critical circumstances determination made by the US Department of Commerce ("USDOC") on 9 August 2001, with respect to certain softwood lumber from Canada, and with regard to US measures on company-specific expedited reviews and administrative reviews.[1]

1.2 On 17 September 2001, Canada and the United States held the requested consultations, but failed to reach a mutually satisfactory resolution of the matter.

1.3 On 25 October 2001, Canada requested the establishment of a panel to examine the matter.[2]

B. *Establishment and Composition of the Panel*

1.4 At its meeting of 5 December 2001, the Dispute Settlement Body ("the DSB") established a Panel in accordance with Article 6 of the DSU and pursuant to the request made by Canada in document WT/DS236/2.

1.5 At that meeting, the parties to the dispute also agreed that the Panel should have standard terms of reference. The terms of reference therefore are the following:

> "To examine, in the light of the relevant provisions of the covered agreements cited by Canada in document WT/DS236/2 the matter referred to the DSB by Canada in that document, and to make such findings as will assist the DSB in making the recommendations or in giving the rulings provided for in those agreements."

---

[1] WT/DS/236/1.

[2] WT/DS/236/2.

1.6 On 22 January 2002, Canada requested the Director-General to determine the composition of the Panel, pursuant to paragraph 7 of Article 8 of the DSU. This paragraph provides:

> "If there is no agreement on the panelists within 20 days after the date of the establishment of a panel, at the request of either party, the Director-General, in consultation with the Chairman of the DSB and the Chairman of the relevant Council or Committee, shall determine the composition of the panel by appointing the panelists whom the Director-General considers most appropriate in accordance with any relevant special or additional rules or procedures of the covered agreement or covered agreements which are at issue in the dispute, after consulting with the parties to the dispute. The Chairman of the DSB shall inform the Members of the composition of the panel thus formed no later than 10 days after the date the Chairman receives such a request."

1.7 On 1 February 2002, the Director-General accordingly composed the Panel as follows:

Chairman: Mr. Dariusz Rosati

Members: Mr. Robert Arnott

Mr. Gonzalo Biggs

The European Communities, India and Japan reserved their third party rights.

C. *Panel Proceedings*

1.8 The Panel met with the parties on 24-25 April 2002 and 4 June 2002. The Panel met with third parties on 24 April 2002.

1.9 On 26 July 2002, the Panel provided its interim report to the parties.

II. FACTUAL ASPECTS

2.1 This dispute concerns the preliminary countervailing duty determination and the preliminary critical circumstances determination made by the USDOC on 9 August 2001 in respect of certain softwood lumber imports from Canada, classified under headings 4407.1000, 4409.1010, 4409.1020, and 4409.1090.[3] This dispute also concerns US law on expedited and administrative reviews in the context of countervailing measures.

2.2 On 2 April 2001 an application for countervailing duties was filed with the USDOC by the Coalition for Fair Lumber Imports Executive Committee; the United Brotherhood of Carpenters and Joiners; and the Paper, Allied-Industrial, Chemical and Energy Workers International Union. On 20 April 2001, the application was amended to include as applicants Moose River Lumber Co., Inc.; Shearer Lumber Products; Shuqualak Lumber Co.; and Tolleson Lumber Co., Inc. On 30 April 2001, the USDOC published a notice of initiation of a countervailing duty investigation in the US Federal Register.

[3] The countervailing duty investigation concerned in this dispute is sometimes referred to as the "*Lumber IV*" investigation.

2.3 In May 2001, the US International Trade Commission ("ITC") published its preliminary affirmative determination that there was a reasonable indication that the US industry was threatened with material injury by reason of imports from Canada of softwood lumber, which were alleged to be subsidized by the Government of Canada.

2.4 On 27 July 2001, the USDOC amended the initiation of the investigation, to exempt from investigation imports of certain softwood lumber produced in the Maritime Provinces from timber harvested in the Maritime Provinces.[4]

2.5 On 17 August 2001, the USDOC published in the Federal Register a notice of preliminary affirmative countervailing duty determination, preliminary affirmative critical circumstances determination, and alignment of final countervailing duty determination with final antidumping duty determination. Provisional measures (withholding of appraisement and posting of cash deposit or bond) were imposed on the basis of a preliminary subsidy rate of 19.31 per cent, applicable to all producers/exporters, and applied to all entries of the subject merchandise from Canada entered, or withdrawn from warehouse, for consumption on or after 90 days prior to the date of publication of the notice.

III. PARTIES' REQUESTS FOR FINDINGS AND RECOMMENDATIONS

A. *Canada*

3.1 Canada requests the Panel to:

- find that the Preliminary Countervailing Duty Determination of the United States in the softwood lumber case violates Articles 10, 14, 17.1, 17.2, 17.5, 19.4 and 32.1 of the *SCM Agreement* and Article VI:3 of GATT 1994;
- find that the Preliminary Critical Circumstances Determination of the United States in the softwood lumber case violates Article 17.1(b), 17.3, 17.4, 17.5, 19.4 and 20.6 of the *SCM Agreement* and Article VI:3 of GATT 1994;
- find that US countervailing duty law regarding expedited and administrative reviews and the application of that law in the *Lumber IV* investigation violate Articles 10, 19.3, 19.4, 21.2 and 32.1 of the *SCM Agreement* and that as a result, the United States has failed to ensure that its laws, regulations and administrative procedures are in conformity with its WTO obligations as required by Article XVI:4 of the WTO Agreement and Article 32.5 of the *SCM Agreement*; and
- recommend that the United States bring its measures into conformity with the *SCM Agreement* and the WTO Agreement, including by lifting the suspension of liquidation for the period of 19 May through 16 August 2001, and making company-specific expedited and administrative reviews available to exporters and producers subject to any coun-

[4] US Department of Commerce, *Notice of preliminary affirmative countervailing duty determination, preliminary affirmative critical circumstances determination, and alignment of final countervailing duty determination with final antidumping duty determination: Certain softwood lumber products from Canada*, Exhibit CDA-1, p. 43,188.

tervailing duty order that may be issued as a result of the *Lumber IV* investigation.

B. United States

3.2 The United States requests that the Panel reject Canada's claims in their entirety.

IV. ARGUMENTS OF THE PARTIES

4.1 The arguments of the parties are set forth in their written and oral submissions to the Panel, and in their answers to questions. The parties' arguments as presented in their submissions are summarized in this section. Summaries of the parties' written answers to questions are set forth in the Annexes to this report (*see* list of annexes at page).

A. First Written Submission of Canada

4.2 The following are Canada's arguments in its first written submission.

4.3 At issue in this dispute are the preliminary countervailing duty determination (the "preliminary determination") and the preliminary critical circumstances determination made by the USDOC on 9 August 2001, with respect to certain softwood lumber from Canada, which violate US obligations under the *SCM Agreement* and GATT 1994. Also at issue is the denial of company-specific expedited reviews and administrative reviews under US countervailing duty law, which violates US obligations under the *SCM Agreement* and the WTO Agreement.

1. The Preliminary Countervailing Duty Determination

4.4 In the preliminary countervailing duty determination, the USDOC concluded that "provincial stumpage programmes" in Quebec, British Columbia, Ontario, Alberta, Manitoba and Saskatchewan are countervailable subsidies. It determined (a) that stumpage is the "provision of a good or service", (b) based on a "cross-border" analysis of "benefit", that the stumpage programmes were subsidies to softwood lumber producers, and (c) that the alleged subsidies were specific. It assumed that the benefit was passed through to certain producers. Of the 19.31 per cent country-wide subsidy rate calculated by the USDOC, a full 19.21 per cent is attributed to these "stumpage programmes".

4.5 The USDOC's findings and determinations and the provisional measures imposed as a result are inconsistent with US obligations under the *SCM Agreement* and GATT 1994. Specifically: (a) the Canadian practices in question are not "subsidies" as defined in Article 1 of the *SCM Agreement*, (b) the USDOC impermissibly inflated the alleged subsidy rate by calculating a country-wide rate based on only a portion of Canadian production and exports of softwood lumber; and (c) the USDOC impermissibly inflated the provisional measures imposed by applying them on an entered value after having calculated the subsidy rate using a first mill value. Although Canada is not making submissions regarding the USDOC's preliminary finding of specificity, Canada does not accept that finding as correct[5].

4.6 The Canadian practices are not "subsidies" because: (a) "stumpage" is not a "financial contribution" within the meaning of Article 1.1(a) of the *SCM Agreement*; (b) the USDOC's determination and measurement of a "benefit" is based on a "cross-border" methodology that is not permitted by the *SCM Agreement*; and (c) the USDOC's determination assumes holders of harvesting rights pass through an alleged benefit to softwood lumber producers, without any basis for the assumption.

4.7 *"Stumpage" is not a "financial contribution"*. Most forest land in Canada is publicly owned "Crown" land. As stewards of this land, Federal and provincial governments manage forestry resources not for the benefit of specific users, but for the country as a whole, and with a view to conservation and preservation of Canada's natural heritage for future generations. Forest resource management is, therefore, concerned with a range of economic and public interests and activities associated with forest lands. These include timber, trapping, fishing, recreation, water quantity and quality, wildlife habitat, wilderness and aesthetics and erosion control. The management of forestry resources related to timber harvesting is characterized by a system of interlocking rights and obligations between provincial and federal governments, and timber harvesters. This system of resource management is based most frequently on tenure and licensing agreements.

4.8 Tenure and licensing agreements vary from province to province, but they are all similar in that they are a complex bundle of rights and obligations, containing at a minimum: (a) the right to harvest standing timber on Crown land or "stumpage"; (b) service and maintenance obligations on the part of the concern, such as road-building and maintenance, and protection against fire; (c) implementation of forestry management and conservation measures, including silviculture and reforestation; and (d) payment of a volumetric "stumpage charge ", levied upon the exercise of the harvesting right.

4.9 "Stumpage", as a right to exploit an *in situ* natural resource, takes two forms in Canada: a servitude referred to as a *profit à prendre* and a licence to harvest standing timber. Both rights are in respect of specified provincial Crown lands. A *profit à prendre* is a form of property right that conveys a non-possessory interest in the land to the recipient. Similarly, a licence is a revocable right to do something on, or to the detriment of, the land of another that would otherwise not be permitted – in this case, the right to harvest standing timber. Other related forms of rights include: mineral servitudes, mineral entry, timber easements, licensing quotas to harvest fish, and rights of access to exploit inland water currents for use in irrigation or electrical power generation.

4.10 By the terms of Articles 10 and 32.1 of the *SCM Agreement*, to be countervailable a practice must satisfy the definition of "subsidy" in Article 1.1. Where an investigating authority determines the existence of a subsidy in respect of a measure that does not fit within the terms of Article 1, that determination is not in accordance with the terms of the *SCM Agreement* and is, accordingly, in violation of Articles 10 and 32.1 of the Agreement. Article 17.1(b) specifically provides that provisional

[5] In response to a question from the Panel, Canada stated that it was not pursuing a claim pertaining to specificity in this dispute. (Canada's Answers to Questions from the Panel after the Second Meeting with the Panel, answer to question 36 from the Panel following the second meeting, Annex B-1.)

measures may be imposed only if "a preliminary affirmative determination has been made that a *subsidy* exists". (emphasis added).

4.11 Article 1 of the *SCM Agreement* sets out an *exclusive* definition for what constitutes a subsidy for the purposes of the *SCM Agreement*. The Appellate Body recognized in *Brazil – Export Financing Programme for Aircraft* that a subsidy as defined by Article 1 has two discrete elements: (i) a financial contribution that (ii) confers a benefit. The panel in *Export Restraints* noted that the definition of "subsidy" in Article 1 reflects the Members' agreement not only as to the types of government action subject to the *SCM Agreement*, but also that not all government actions that may affect the market come within the ambit of the *SCM Agreement*.

4.12 Under Article 1.1(a)(1)(iii) of the *SCM Agreement*, a financial contribution exists where a government provides *goods*. The ordinary meaning of "goods" is "tangible or movable personal property other than money; [especially] articles of trade or items of merchandise ‹goods or services›". Nothing in the context of the *SCM Agreement* in any way detracts from or expands this ordinary meaning. A good is a good, a product, something on the cross-border trade of which tariffs may be imposed.

4.13 This is confirmed by the negotiating history related to the measurement of a benefit. On 4 September 1990, the Chairman of the Negotiating Group on Subsidies and Countervailing Measures circulated seven "informal discussion papers" in preparation for issuing a revised version of the Chairman's text. Discussion Paper No. 6 dealt with the measurement of the amount of a subsidy and offered draft language for the current Article 14. Draft Article 14.4(a), as set out in Discussion Paper No. 6, reflects an understanding at the time of the negotiations on the *SCM Agreement* of the fundamental difference between tangible commercial inputs and intangible real property rights. This draft provided in relevant part that "the amount of subsidy arising from government provision of goods, services, *or extraction/harvesting rights ...* " (emphasis added). The terms "or extraction/harvesting rights" are nowhere found either in the final text of Article 1.1(a)(1)(iii) or in the final text of Article 14(d) of the *SCM Agreement*. This confirms that rights, such as *profits à prendre*, are not included within the scope of the Agreement.

4.14 The USDOC simply asserted that stumpage is a financial contribution in the form of a provision of goods or services. It did not declare itself as to whether, in its view, stumpage is the provision of "goods" or "services". The petitioner in *Lumber IV*, however, has argued that stumpage is the provision of goods ("wood fiber") in the form of timber or logs. Canada therefore understands the USDOC to have determined that stumpage is "the provision of goods".

4.15 The USDOC also made no attempt to examine the evidence on the record and did not analyse how property rights, such as *profits à prendre* and timber harvesting licenses, are a "financial contribution" under Article 1.1. Properly understood, *profit à prendre* and the license to harvest standing timber is not the provision of "goods" within the meaning of Article 1. These rights are not in themselves goods or services. As a simple factual matter, "stumpage" – the right to harvest standing timber – is not a log. "Stumpage" is instead the right to exploit an *in situ* natural resource, akin to the right to extract oil and minerals from public lands, quotas to harvest fish from a country's territorial waters, or the right of access to exploit inland water and water currents for use in irrigation or electrical power generation. To determine otherwise is to expand the scope of "provides goods" and, therefore, the *SCM Agreement* beyond all recognition.

4.16 Timber harvesters have the right to harvest timber from Crown lands by virtue of their tenures or licenses; they do not pay stumpage charges as remuneration to acquire this right. Rather, a "stumpage charge" is a levy on the exercise of an existing right to harvest timber. It is properly viewed as a form of revenue collection by the government and is the economic equivalent of a tax.

4.17 The USDOC erred in determining that "stumpage" is a "financial contribution". On a plain reading of Article 1.1(a)(1)(iii), the term "provides goods" cannot be interpreted to include the granting of rights such as "stumpage". Since stumpage is not a "financial contribution" and, therefore, not a subsidy as defined in Article 1.1, the determination by the USDOC that it is a subsidy and the imposition of provisional countervailing measures as a result, violates Articles 10, 17.1(b), 17.5, 19.4 and 32.1 of the *SCM Agreement* and Article V1:3 of GATT 1994.

4.18 *The USDOC's use of "cross-border" benchmarks to find and measure "benefit" violates the SCM Agreement.* Nothing in the *SCM Agreement* permits the USDOC to do so; indeed, the text, context, and Appellate Body interpretations of Articles 1 and 14 indicate that such an analysis violates the *SCM Agreement.*

4.19 The USDOC purported to establish that Canadian stumpage practices conferred a benefit by comparing: stumpage charges levied by Canadian provinces with stumpage prices on selected state lands in the *United States*, on the basis that such prices are "commercially available world market prices..." to softwood lumber producers in Canada. The USDOC found US stumpage prices to be higher than the charges levied by Canadian provinces. the USDOC then multiplied this difference by what it considered the portion of the provinces' harvest consumed in sawmills to arrive at the calculated amount of the "stumpage subsidy". The "stumpage subsidy" was wholly derived from the comparisons of stumpage charges in Canada and cross-border prices for stumpage in the United States.

4.20 Article 1.1 of the *SCM Agreement* provides that a subsidy exists where there is a financial contribution by a government and "a benefit is thereby conferred". In *Canada – Aircraft*, the Appellate Body stated that "the word 'benefit', as used in Article 1.1(b), implies some kind of comparison... [since] there can be no "benefit" to the recipient unless the "financial contribution" makes the recipient "better off" than it would otherwise have been, absent that contribution." In the case of a government provision of goods, the question is therefore whether the purchaser of a good from the government is "better off" than other purchasers who buy the same good from other sellers in the country subject to the investigation.

4.21 This is confirmed by Article 14(d), which sets out guidelines to calculate the amount of a subsidy based on a "benefit to the recipient" test in cases of an alleged government provision of goods. It provides in particular that, "[t]he adequacy of remuneration shall be determined *in relation to prevailing market conditions* for the good or service in question *in the country of provision or purchase*" (emphasis added). The words of Article 14(d) are unambiguous. "In the country of provision or purchase" means "in the country of provision or purchase." It does not mean adequacy can be determined as against prevailing market conditions in *some other country* or *internationally*. Nothing in the context, object and purpose or the negotiating history of Article 14 permits reading "in" as anything other than "in"; "in the country" does not admit of "cross-border" analysis. A cross-border analysis using transactions in another country to determine the existence of and measure a "benefit" is thus inconsistent with Article 1 and Article 14 as interpreted by the Appellate Body, and viewed in context and in the light of the object and purpose of the *SCM Agreement*.

4.22 The USDOC's cross-border analysis is illogical even in the context of its own previous determinations. In each of the prior lumber cases – *Lumber I*, *Lumber II* and *Lumber III* – the USDOC rejected the use of cross-border comparisons for a number of reasons, including the USDOC's view that they are "arbitrary and capricious".

4.23 By using a benchmark in the United States, outside the country of the alleged provision of goods, the United States breached its obligations under Article 14 of the *SCM Agreement*. The USDOC's finding of a subsidy based on criteria not permitted by the *SCM Agreement* is also inconsistent with US obligations under Articles 10, 17.5, 19.4 and 32.1 of the *SCM Agreement* and Article VI:3 of GATT 1994. Furthermore, the United States violated Article 17.1 of the *SCM Agreement* by imposing provisional measures with respect to a practice that is not a subsidy.

4.24 *The USDOC also impermissibly assumed a pass-through of an alleged benefit.* In the preliminary determination, the USDOC found that the alleged "financial contribution" to timber harvesters conferred a benefit on softwood lumber producers. This presumption that the alleged benefit to timber harvesters passes through to lumber producers, without a determination that this did, in fact, occur, is inconsistent with the *SCM Agreement*.

4.25 In Canada, standing timber is harvested and processed into logs. Logs are then usually processed in sawmills and pulp mills to produce a wide variety of products including softwood lumber. Lumber may be sold as an end product or sold to remanufacturing industries that make a vast array of products. Both softwood lumber and remanufactured products, but not logs, are subject to the US investigation. A significant portion of harvesting is done by entities operating at arm's-length from lumber producers; in these instances, logs are sold to lumber producers and other industries in arm's-length transactions.

4.26 A countervailing duty may be imposed only where all the elements of a subsidy have been established. A subsidy is exhaustively defined in Article 1 of the *SCM Agreement*. A direct subsidy exists where a financial contribution confers a benefit to the recipient of that contribution. The criteria for an *indirect* subsidy are found in Article 1.1(a)(1)(iv) of that Agreement. In the context of Article 1.1(a)(1)(iii), *i.e.* where the alleged financial contribution is the government provision of goods, an indirect subsidy may be found *only* where a private entity is entrusted or directed by government to provide these goods in a manner that confers a benefit. Thus, where the recipient of a subsidy (whose products are not subject to the investigation) enters into transactions with other entities, an investigating authority may not assume that the subsidy has been passed on, or if so, that the recipient was entrusted or directed by government to pass it on. Rather, the authority must establish the existence of a subsidy in respect of the entity being investigated. This is especially the case where the transaction is at arm's-length.

4.27 The findings of the Appellate Body in *British Steel* are particularly relevant in this instance. There, the Appellate Body agreed with the Panel that "in order to determine whether any subsidy was bestowed on the production [of the subject merchandise], it is necessary to determine whether there was any "benefit" to [the recipient]." This included examining, on administrative review, the continued existence of any "benefit" already found to have been conferred by "financial contributions" predating the privatization of the original recipient of those contributions. Moreover, this had to be done from the perspective of the producers of the imports subject to the review, not the producer that had been privatized prior to the review (i.e. whose imports were not subject to the review). Finally, in that case, the Appellate Body confirmed that where fair market value is paid on privatization, no previously conferred benefit could be passed through to the acquiring entity.

4.28 The Appellate Body's analysis in *British Steel* is even more apt in respect of *original* determinations where an investigating authority has the duty to establish *each element* of a subsidy. In such cases, the authority may find an "indirect" subsidy only where an indirect financial contribution has been found in the sense of Article 1.1(a)(1)(iv). The reason is simple. Where transactions take place in the market and at arm's-length, and where there has been no "direction" or "entrustment", the original recipient of a subsidy must be presumed to have retained the benefit. Conversely, to assume pass-through in such arm's-length transactions without establishing "direction" or "entrustment" in the sense of Article 1.1(a)(1)(iv) would nullify the clear meaning of that Article.

4.29 Since the USDOC did not do any indirect subsidy or pass-through analysis, its finding of "benefit" is, on its face, incorrect and illegal. In the current investigation there are no allegations of direct stumpage subsidies to the subject merchandise, softwood lumber. Softwood lumber is *processed* from logs, and logs from standing timber; neither logs nor timber are within the scope of the investigation. Logs result from the harvesting of timber – the subject matter of stumpage, which is the allegedly subsidized economic activity. The alleged subsidies therefore are on log production.

4.30 Lumber producers may not legally be *deemed* to be subsidized simply because of a finding of subsidization to upstream producers. Rather, to find that the downstream industries are subsidized, the USDOC must first establish an indirect financial contribution, and then demonstrate a benefit conferred *upon the recipient* by that contribution. The USDOC did not establish, as is required by the *SCM Agreement*, that any "financial contribution" by the government to timber harvesters had been "entrusted" or "directed" to be passed through to lumber producers or remanufacturers. It did not find that the alleged benefit of the financial contribution in question was also passed through to and conferred upon lumber producers or remanufacturers (the producers of the subject merchandise within the scope of the investigation). The USDOC did not provide any analysis of either requirement of Article 1 in respect of the merchandise on which it imposed a countervailing duty. *A fortiori*, remanufacturers who buy lumber from lumber producers may not legally be presumed to have benefited from an alleged stumpage subsidy two transactions away.

4.31 The USDOC has failed to establish the elements of a subsidy in respect of the subject merchandise by failing to demonstrate a pass-through of financial contribution and benefit. In imposing provisional measures on practices not properly found to be a subsidy, the United States has violated Articles 10, 17.1(b), 19.4 and 32.1 of the *SCM Agreement* and Article VI:3 of GATT 1994.

4.32 The USDOC also impermissibly inflated the subsidy rate by calculating a "weighted-average country-wide rate" based upon only a portion of Canadian production and exports. Having determined that various federal and provincial programmes were subsidies, the USDOC calculated the subsidy rate by 1) for each provincial stumpage programme, dividing the total calculated stumpage benefit by the total value of the province's production of softwood lumber and co-products by sawmills; and 2) for other provincial and federal programmes found to be countervailable, dividing the total calculated benefit by the value of sales (or exports, for an alleged export subsidy) of softwood lumber and co-products by sawmills for the relevant jurisdiction. In each case, the alleged benefit was the numerator, and the shipment value was the denominator of the calculation. The USDOC then weight-averaged the resulting provincial rates by the provinces' relative shares of exports to the United States to arrive at a "country-wide" rate. In these calculations, the USDOC impermissibly excluded Maritime shipments from the total Canadian shipments used as the denominator for calculating certain federal programme rates and excluded Maritime exports in weight averaging provincial rates to construct a country-wide rate.

4.33 Articles 17.2 and 19 (through Article 17.5) of the *SCM Agreement*, and Article VI:3 of GATT 1994 require the USDOC to estimate "the amount of the subsidy found to exist" so as to ensure it is representative of the actual subsidization. Accordingly, a "country-wide" countervailing duty rate must approximate the average rate of subsidization of the subject merchandise. This means that shipments of subject merchandise by any company in the country under investigation (including those companies that have been excluded from the investigation or countervailing duty order) must be included in calculating a country-wide rate. Exclusion of the Maritime Provinces' shipments and exports from the calculation results in imposition of provisional measures "in excess of the amount of the subsidy found to exist."

4.34 The impropriety of the USDOC's country-wide subsidy rate calculation becomes all the more evident when it is considered that the USDOC relied on import statistics that included imports from the Maritimes to find evidence of causation of material injury or threat of material injury sufficient to initiate the investigation. The USDOC cannot now credibly exclude these Maritime shipments from the subsidy calculation. Likewise, the International Trade Commission based its preliminary determination of threat of material injury on its analysis of total imports of softwood lumber from Canada, including the Maritime Provinces. Article 17.1(b) of the *SCM Agreement* requires that provisional measures may be applied only if "a preliminary affirmative determination has been made that a subsidy exists and that there is injury to a domestic industry caused by subsidized imports." Here, the ITC made no finding of injury based solely on the subnational group of imports on which the USDOC calculated provisional duties.

4.35 Since the preliminary determination inflates the weighted average country-wide subsidy rate in violation of Article 19.4 of the *SCM Agreement* and Article VI:3 of GATT 1994, the United States is also in violation of Articles 10 and 32.1 of the *SCM Agreement*.

4.36 *The USDOC also impermissibly applied provisional measures in excess of the subsidy preliminarily found to exist.* In its preliminary determination, the USDOC found a net subsidy rate of 19.31 per cent *ad valorem* and stated that it was directing the US Customs Service ("Customs") to suspend liquidation of entries of subject merchandise and to require a cash deposit or bond *in the amount of the subsidy found*. It did not in fact do so, however. Instead, the USDOC calculated the subsidy rate on a *first mill* basis, but applied it on an *entered value* basis, with the effect of significantly increasing the provisional measures applied to a considerable portion of Canadian exports of softwood lumber to the United States.

4.37 In all of the USDOC subsidy calculations, described above, the denominator of the calculation was the value of *sawmill* shipments or exports, *i.e.*, the "first mill" value. Sawmills ("first mills") produce lumber from logs. They ship lumber to end users, and also sell some quantity of lumber to downstream value-added remanufacturers ("final mills") that use lumber inputs, produce further processed lumber products (of which some are within the scope of the investigation).

4.38 A USDOC decision memorandum subsequently claimed that "[t]he record for the Preliminary Determination supports the collection of CVD deposits on an entered value basis" and the USDOC instructions to Customs referenced in the preliminary determination instructed Customs to require countervailing duty cash deposits or the posting of a bond without specifying that such provisional measures applied to the first mill value, thus ensuring application on an entered value basis. Thus, for example, where a 19 per cent duty calculated on first mill value is applied to the entered value (and, for illustration, assuming an import with first mill value of $100 and final mill or entered value of $125), the importer of the value-added product faces an actual duty not of 19 per cent but of 23.75 per cent of the first mill value.

4.39 Articles 17.2 and 19.4 (through 17.5) of the *SCM Agreement* and Article VI:3 of GATT 1994 establish the fundamental obligation that a duty may not exceed the subsidy found to exist. In applying the preliminary determination on an entered value basis, the United States significantly increased the provisional measures in violation of Articles 17.2 and 19.4 of the *SCM Agreement* and Article VI:3 of GATT 1994.

2. *The Preliminary Critical Circumstances Determination*

4.40 Commerce also made a preliminary critical circumstances determination as a result, the United States retroactively applied the provisional measures to entries occurring within 90 days prior to the date of publication of the preliminary determinations, *i.e.* entries from May 19 through 16 August 2001. The retroactive application of provisional measures is inconsistent with US obligations under the *SCM Agreement*. Even if such action were permitted under the Agreement, Commerce's preliminary critical circumstances determination is itself inconsistent with US obligations under the *SCM Agreement* and GATT 1994.

4.41 Under Article 20.6, "critical circumstances" exist only where four conditions are satisfied: (1) there is injury to the domestic industry that is difficult to repair; (2) such injury is caused by massive imports in a relatively short period; (3) such imports are of a product benefiting from subsidies paid or bestowed inconsistently with the provisions of GATT 1994 and of the *SCM Agreement*; and (4) retroactive assessment of definitive countervailing duties on those imports is necessary to preclude the recurrence of such injury.

4.42 Even where these elements are present, Article 20.6 states that the type of duties that may be assessed are "definitive", not "provisional". The term "definitive" is defined as "having the function or character of finality" or "decisive", "conclusive" and "finally settled." Accordingly, the ordinary meaning of the provision prohibits any retroactive application of countervailing measures under the Article until after a final determination is made. This understanding of the meaning of the word "definitive" in Article 20.6 of the *SCM Agreement* is reinforced by the consistent distinction in the Agreement, for example in Articles 20.1 and 20.3, and 22.4 and 22.5, between "provisional measures" on the one hand and "countervailing duties" or "definitive duties" on the other hand. Despite the clear application of Article 20.6 to definitive countervailing duties and not provisional measures, Commerce acted otherwise.

4.43 In its preliminary critical circumstances determination and related analysis, Commerce preliminarily determined that there had been "massive imports" of a product benefiting from a prohibited export subsidy. For Commerce, this was a sufficient basis to apply countervailing measures retroactively. Commerce recognized that the ITC had not considered (even preliminarily) the injury factors required to be considered under Article 20.6 of the *SCM Agreement*, and that "[f]or purposes of a final determination whether retroactive relief is warranted, other factors are considered by the ITC in its final determination". Nonetheless, Commerce applied its preliminary critical circumstances determination on a provisional basis. Since Article 20.6 permits the retroactive application of only definitive countervailing duties, and not provisional measures, for the reasons set out above, the United States has violated this provision.

4.44 Moreover, since the investigation was initiated on 23 April 2001, Article 17.3 requires that provisional measures in this case not be applied sooner than 22 June 2001. However, the United States applied provisional measures as of 19 May 2001. Article 17.3 thus not only confirms that Article 20.6 does not permit the retroactive application of provisional measures, but to the extent the United States has applied such measures sooner than 22 June 2001, it has also violated Article 17.3 outright.

4.45 Similar inconsistencies result under Article 17.4. This provision states that "[t]he application of provisional measures shall be limited to as short a period as possible, not exceeding four months." Pursuant to the preliminary determination, the United States has applied provisional duties to imports of softwood lumber from Canada for a period of four months, beginning on the date of publication of the determination on 17 August 2001 and ending 14 December 2001. However, in also retroactively applying provisional measures for the period from 19 May 2001 to 17 August 2001, the United States has applied provisional measures for a total of nearly 7 months. Here again, not only does Article 17.4 confirm that Article 20.6 does not permit the retroactive application of provisional measures, but to the extent the United States has applied such measures from 19 May 2001 through 14 December 2001, the United States has also violated Article 17.4 on its face.

4.46 Even if provisional measures could be applied retroactively under Article 20.6, Commerce did not establish that "critical circumstances" exist in its preliminary critical circumstances determination. **First**, the IQ SMB Guarantee programme upon which the determination is based is not a prohibited export subsidy and even if it were, the amount of subsidy found for the programme was *de minimis* and thus did not provide the basis for a determination under Article 20.6. Assuming, *arguendo*, that the IQ SMB Guarantee loan guarantees programme conferred a "benefit", the programme itself is not contingent on exports from Canada. Record information demonstrated that the programme is contingent on developing markets outside *Quebec*, not outside *Canada*. Accordingly, for the purposes of Commerce's investigation, the IQ SMB Guarantee programme is not "contingent on export performance" under Article 3.1(a) and the determination that the "massive imports" in question have benefited from "subsidies paid or bestowed inconsistently with the provisions of GATT 1994 and of [the SCM] Agreement" is flawed.

4.47 Furthermore, a critical circumstances determination cannot be based on a prohibited subsidy of a negligible amount. Commerce found that the benefit from this programme was less than 0.005 per cent, *i.e.* a rate that is *de minimis*. A *de minimis* rate is insufficient to provide a basis for applying any countervailing measure (provisional or final). By its own terms, Article 11.9 of the *SCM Agreement* applies to any part of a countervailing duty investigation. Therefore, a determination under Article 20.6 is governed by the *de minimis* threshold under Article 11.9, since action under the former is based solely on a subsidy that is "paid or bestowed inconsistently with the provisions of GATT 1994 and of this Agreement" and not *all* alleged subsidy programmes under investigation. Since Commerce's preliminary critical circumstances determination is based solely on the SMB Guarantee programme, which was not an export subsidy and was found to be *de minimis*, the United States has taken action under Article 20.6 in the absence of "critical circumstances", *i.e.* in violation of that provision.

4.48 **Second**, even if the SMB Guarantee programme had correctly been found to be a prohibited export subsidy, the rate applicable to the retroactive measures should have been the rate attributed to this programme – less than 0.005 per cent – and not the rate attributable to all other alleged subsidies taken together – 19.3 per cent. The text of Article 20.6 does not refer to "massive imports" of a product benefiting from "any or all of the subsidies under investigation". The provision specifically refers to "subsidies paid or bestowed inconsistently with the provisions of GATT 1994 and of this Agreement". The text of Article 20.6 of the *SCM Agreement* and the logic behind it allow the retroactive application of only the rate that is commensurate with the benefit bestowed by the alleged prohibited subsidy. Furthermore, any countervailing measures applied under Article 20.6 must conform to the basic requirement under Articles 17.5 and 19.4 of the *SCM Agreement* and Article VI:3 of GATT 1994 that they may not exceed the amount of the subsidy found to exist, i.e. such measures can be in an amount no greater than that needed to offset the benefit conferred by the alleged prohibited subsidies found to exist. To do so at a higher rate would countervail in an amount in excess of that required to "preclude the recurrence of [the] injury" caused by such subsidies in "critical circumstances", the object and purpose of Article 20.6. In the instant case, the applicable rate was less than 0.005 per cent as opposed to 19.31 per cent.

4.49 In applying provisional measures retroactively in the amount of 19.31 per cent, the United States has violated Article 20.6 of the *SCM Agreement*, as well as Articles 17.5 and 19.4 of the *SCM Agreement* and Article VI:3 of GATT 1994.

4.50 **Third**, no countervailing measure, whether provisional or final, can be applied retroactively under Article 20.6 without the requisite injury findings and no such findings were made by US authorities. There is no dispute that the USDOC's determination contains no finding on the two injury elements set out in Article 20.6 of the Agreement. First, neither the USDOC nor the ITC had found "injury which is difficult to repair" and neither the USDOC nor the ITC had determined that retroactive application of definitive countervailing duties was necessary "in order to preclude the recurrence of such injury". There can be no dispute on this point because the USDOC itself expressly stated that these determinations would be made by the ITC when the ITC made its final determination. Accordingly, in applying such countervailing measures retroactively under Article 20.6 without first making the requisite injury findings, the United States violated outright Article 20.6 of the Agreement.

4.51 **Fourth**, the USDOC's finding of "massive imports" (1) incorrectly attributed to all imports from Canada the alleged benefit conferred by the IQ SMB Guarantee programme, which applies only to shipments from Quebec and (2) attributed to an alleged export subsidy an increase in imports resulting from the impending and then actual expiration of the *Canada-United States Softwood Lumber Agreement* (SLA).

4.52 The USDOC determined that imports of softwood lumber from Canada had increased by 23.34 per cent in the three months following the filing of the petition compared to the previous three months and on this basis that the requirement of "massive imports" over a "relatively short period" of time had been satisfied. The SLA expired two days before the petition was filed, *i.e.* at the end of the first quarter of 2001. Its impending expiration sharply reduced exports in the first quarter of 2001 and its actual expiry led to an increase in the second quarter. These dramatic and well-documented trade trends were nonetheless attributed by the USDOC to the existence of a *de minimis* alleged export subsidy.

4.53 Even assuming that the SMB Guarantee programme were a prohibited export subsidy, it is patently impossible to attribute the "massive imports" finding in this case, an increase of 23.34 per cent, to a programme that did not benefit any exports during the period of investigation – and in any event could have benefited only a small fraction of exports and only in an amount of less than 0.005 per cent. Since the United States has applied provisional measures retroactively in the absence of a valid finding of "massive imports", it has violated Article 20.6.

4.54 **Fifth**, the USDOC's finding of "massive imports" improperly excludes imports from the Canadian Maritime Provinces. If it is permissible, as the USDOC did, to include shipments that have not benefited from the prohibited subsidy, then it should include all such shipments and not simply the portions of those shipments that suit its needs. In this respect, the USDOC's "massive imports" finding is defective also because it was "net of the Maritime Provinces", *i.e.* the USDOC excluded from any of its calculations imports from the Canadian Maritime provinces. Under various methods of calculating "massive imports", inclusion of exports from the entirety of Canada, including the exports from the Maritime Provinces, would have resulted in a negative "massive imports" finding under the *SCM Agreement*. There is no basis in Article 20.6 of the *SCM Agreement* for making a "massive imports" finding on the basis of only a segment of total imports.

3. *US Law is Inconsistent with US Obligations on Expedited and Administrative Reviews*

4.55 Article 19.3 of the *SCM Agreement* expressly requires Members to grant an expedited review to those exporters that were not individually investigated who have requested such a review, in order to establish an individual countervailing duty rate for that exporter. Article 21.2 requires the same for any interested party in cases of administrative review. The Agreement thus ensures that exporters and producers not individually investigated will nevertheless be able to obtain an individual countervailing duty rate if they so request. It also ensures that each exporter and producer is not subject to a duty rate higher than that called for in its individual circumstances. The United States has failed to implement these obligations in US law.

4.56 Section 777A(e)(1) of the *Tariff Act of 1930* establishes the general rule that the USDOC will determine an individual subsidy rate for each known exporter or producer of the subject merchandise. Where the application of the general rule is not practicable because of the large number of exporters or producers involved in the investigation, exception to this rule can be made under section 777A(e)(2)(A) and

(B) of the Tariff Act of 1930 ("the Act"), as interpreted by the SAA. Under subparagraph (A), the USDOC can limit its examination to a statistically valid sample of exporters or producers or limit its examination to those exporters and producers accounting for the largest volume of exports of the subject merchandise that the USDOC determines can reasonably be examined. Under subparagraph (B), the USDOC can determine a single country-wide rate to be applied to all exporters and producers.

4.57 The regulations implementing US obligations under the *SCM Agreement* regarding individual expedited and administrative reviews limit the availability of such reviews to instances where the USDOC has undertaken its investigation according to subsection (A) of section 777A(e)(2). The regulations limit the availability of expedited reviews and company-specific administrative reviews in cases where the USDOC elects to conduct its investigation on an aggregate "country-wide" basis. In such cases, the USDOC *must* deny individual exporters the benefit of company-specific expedited reviews and administrative reviews.

4.58 In the case of individual expedited reviews, section 351.214(k)(l) provides for a request for individual expedited review only if "the Secretary limited the number of exporters or producers to be individually examined under section 777A(e)(2)(A) of the Act" (i.e. by sample or by taking account of those exporters and producers accounting for the largest volume of exports). Significantly, this is the case as soon as the initial decision is made as to *how* the investigation is to be conducted. In the case of administrative reviews, subparagraphs (1), (2) and (3) of section 351.213(b) each expressly bar the request by an foreign government, exporter, or importer of record for an individual administrative review where the "investigation or prior administrative review was conducted on an aggregate basis". Moreover, the only requests the USDOC will consider for an individual administrative review in cases where administrative reviews are conducted on a country-wide basis are those for individual assessment and cash deposit rates of zero under subparagraph (1) of section 351.213(k) and then, "only to the extent practicable." Section 351.213(k)(2) provides, however, that if, in the review, the USDOC calculated a country-wide rate, "that rate will supersede, for cash deposit purposes, all rates previously determined in the countervailing duty proceeding in question."

4.59 This result is inconsistent with the obligations of the United States under the *SCM Agreement*. Article 19.3 provides that exporters not "actually investigated" are entitled upon request *in all cases* to an expedited review "in order that the investigating authorities promptly establish an individual countervailing duty rate for that exporter". Article 21.2 entitles exporters and producers to a company-specific administrative review upon request *in all cases*. This ensures that exporters and producers not given an individual rate during the countervailing duty investigation will be given one in an administrative review. This also means that exporters and producers already given an individual rate during the investigation, may be given an individual rate again in an administrative review. Nothing in the context or object and purpose of these provisions or indeed the *SCM Agreement* in any way modifies the nature of these obligations. Accordingly, section 351.214(k)(l) of the regulations violates Article 19.3 of the Agreement and section 351.213(b) violates Article 21.2.

4.60 Section 351.213(b) on administrative reviews also violates US obligations regarding expedited reviews under Article 19.3. Under the US retrospective duty system, final liability for countervailing duties is not determined until the administrative review. Section 351.213(b) specifically denies exporters and producers an administrative review if the investigation was conducted on an aggregate basis. This means that an exporter or producer would still be denied the opportunity to obtain a final individual countervailing duty rate contrary to Article 19.3, even if it were given the right to an expedited review to establish an individual cash deposit rate.

4.61 Finally, since section 351.213(k)(2) mandates that the single country-wide countervailing duty rate calculated by the USDOC in an administrative review must supersede all individual rates previously determined, this provision violates both Article 19.3 and Article 21.2. First, mandating that a single country-wide rate supersedes all individual rates effectively undoes the benefit of any expedited review that an exporter or producer may have been granted by the USDOC pursuant to an investigation conducted under section 777A(e)(2)(A). Second, it prevents exporters and producers from obtaining an individual rate in an administrative review if that review is conducted on an aggregate basis.

4.62 The USDOC decided to conduct the *Lumber IV* investigation on a country-wide basis. Three consequences flow from this decision. First, by operation of the regulations, exporters and producers involved in the investigation are denied expedited reviews and company-specific administrative reviews, in violation of Articles 19.3 and 21.2 of the *SCM Agreement*. Second, in this case, the USDOC will, as a result, impose a countervailing duty in excess of the amount of the subsidy found. This is because a country-wide rate necessarily imposes a duty on some exporters and producers in excess of what would be their individual duty rate. The United States therefore also violates Article 19.4. Third, as a consequence, the United States also violates Articles 10 and 32.1 of the *SCM Agreement*.

4.63 The US failure to provide for expedited reviews and company-specific administrative reviews in all cases means that the United States has failed to ensure the conformity of its laws, regulations and administrative procedures with its obligations under the *SCM Agreement*. Thus the United States should also be found in violation of its obligations under Articles XVI:4 of the WTO Agreement and Article 32.5 of the *SCM Agreement*.

B. First Written Submission of the United States

4.64 The following are the arguments of the United States in its first written submission.

1. Introduction

4.65 "No Member should cause, through the use of any subsidy ... , adverse effects to the interests of other Members, i.e ... injury to the domestic industry of another Member ... "[6] That obligation is the core of the dispute now before the Panel. When one Member causes injury to the domestic industry of another Member through the use of *any* subsidy, the injured Member has the right to take countervailing measures.

4.66 The United States has acted entirely within its rights under the *SCM Agreement* in this case by taking provisional countervailing measures to offset the injurious subsidies that Canada provides to its lumber mills. Canada's claims to the contrary are without merit. Canada is asking this Panel to ignore the text of the *SCM Agree-*

[6] Article 5 of the *SCM Agreement*.

ment and create exceptions to the subsidy disciplines for Canada's decades-old system of subsidies to its lumber industry. In addition, Canada's claims of WTO-inconsistent US laws are, in reality, an effort to resolve a future dispute that may never occur. Therefore, consistent with the *SCM Agreement* and the DSU, the United States asks the Panel to reject Canada's claims.

2. *Statement of Facts*

4.67 On 17 August 2001, the USDOC published its preliminary determination, which contained a preliminary affirmative countervailing duty determination and a preliminary affirmative finding of critical circumstances. In the preliminary determination, the USDOC preliminarily found that provincial stumpage programmes in Canada provided a countervailable subsidy to Canadian lumber producers. In addition, the USDOC found reasonable cause to believe or suspect that critical circumstances existed based on evidence that lumber producers received prohibited export subsidies and that there were massive imports of the subject merchandise over a relatively short period of time.

4.68 Accordingly, the USDOC imposed provisional measures (i.e., suspension of liquidation and posting of security in the form of cash deposits or bonds), effective on the date of publication of the preliminary determination, i.e., 17 August 2001. In light of the affirmative finding of critical circumstances, the USDOC ordered provisional measures applied to entries of the subject merchandise made during the period 90 days prior to the date of the publication of the preliminary determination.

3. *Standard of Review*

4.69 Article 11 of the DSU requires a panel to make an objective assessment of the matter before it and determine whether the identified measure is consistent with the provisions of the *SCM Agreement* upon which the claim is based. Panels cannot add to or diminish the rights and obligations provided in the *SCM Agreement*.

4.70 A panel does not conduct a *de novo* review of the evidence nor substitute its judgment for that of the competent authority. Moreover, the sufficiency of the evidence in this case should be judged in relation to the particular measure that Canada has challenged. It is important to bear in mind the preliminary nature of the determination at issue. The consistency of a preliminary determination with the obligations imposed on Members should be based on the record evidence before the authority at the time the determination was made.

4. *Argument*

(a) Canada Bears the Burden of Proving Its Claim

4.71 Canada, as the complainant, bears the burden of coming forward with evidence and argument that establish a *prima facie* case of a violation. If the balance of evidence is inconclusive with respect to a particular claim, Canada must be held to have failed to establish that claim.

(b) The Preliminary Countervailing Determination Is Consistent With the *SCM Agreement*

(i) Provincial Stumpage Programmes Constitute a "Financial Contribution"

4.72 The Canadian provincial governments own approximately 90 per cent of the forested land in Canada ("Crown land"), and the provincial governments control access to the timber on Crown land. The provinces enter into contractual arrangements that allow companies to harvest the timber on Crown land in exchange for an administratively set stumpage fee and the assumption of certain forest management obligations associated with harvesting operations. To be awarded such a contract, normally the company must either have a Canadian lumber mill, or have an agreement with a Canadian lumber mill to process all of the harvested timber. The vast majority of the Crown timber is awarded under long-term contracts that are not subject to competition (these contracts are usually referred to as tenures), with the fees set administratively by the provincial government.

4.73 In the preliminary determination, the USDOC concluded that these Canadian provincial "stumpage programmes" constitute a financial contribution because they provide a good to lumber producers within the meaning of Article 1.1(a)(1)(iii) of the *SCM Agreement*. That good is timber.

4.74 Article 31 of the *Vienna Convention on the Law of Treaties*, which reflects customary rules of interpretation of public international law, states that a treaty shall be interpreted "in accordance with the ordinary meaning to be given to the terms of the treaty in their context and in the light of its object and purpose." Article 1.1 of the *SCM Agreement* defines a subsidy as a "financial contribution" by a government that confers a benefit. Article 1.1(a)(1)(iii) states that a financial contribution shall be deemed to exist where, *inter alia*, the government "provides goods or services other than general infrastructure." The *SCM Agreement* does not specifically define the meaning of "provides" or "goods." The Panel should look to the ordinary meaning of these terms.

4.75 The New Shorter Oxford English Dictionary defines "provides" as meaning, among other things, to "supply or furnish for use." Black's Law Dictionary defines "goods" as specifically including "growing crops, and other identified things to be severed from real property." Provincial stumpage programmes therefore constitute a "financial contribution" because they "supply or furnish" an "identified thing to be severed from real property," i.e., timber.

4.76 The text of Article 1.1(a)(1)(iii) does not contain any exclusions for natural resources, nor can such an exclusion be read into the text. To the contrary, the Members evidently considered exceptions, and the sole exclusion from the phrase "goods and services" that they agreed on is reflected in Article 1.1(a)(1)(iii) itself, i.e., general infrastructure. It would be extraordinary if the Members intended *sub silentio* to provide a safe harbour for a broad group of government subsidies. Rather, this sole, express exclusion demonstrates that the Members intended to include all other goods and services.

4.77 Canada argues that provincial governments are not providing timber to lumber producers, but rather are merely granting the right to harvest the timber. There is, however, no meaningful distinction between providing the right to harvest timber and providing the timber itself. The provincial stumpage systems are designed for one purpose: to provide timber to Canadian mills that make lumber or wood pulp. Participation in these programmes is restricted to Canadian sawmills or pulpmills, or companies that have contracts with Canadian mills to process the harvested timber. Furthermore, each of the provincial stumpage programmes charges the tenure holder on a "volumetric" basis. Tenure holders do not pay stumpage fees for timber that they do not harvest. In light of these facts, it is obvious that the provincial governments are providing timber through these stumpage systems.

4.78 Moreover, the New Shorter Oxford English Dictionary defines "provides" as meaning to "make available" in addition to "supply or furnish for use." Thus, even if provincial tenures are viewed as simply providing the right to take timber off the land rather than providing the timber itself, such a provision would still constitute the "provision of a good" within the meaning of Article 1.1(a)(1)(iii) of the *SCM Agreement* because the government is making the timber available. Therefore, the USDOC's preliminary determination that provincial stumpage programmes constitute the provision of a good is entirely consistent with the text of Article 1.1(a)(1)(iii) of the *SCM Agreement*.

4.79 The USDOC's Preliminary Determination is also consistent with the context, object and purpose of Article 1.1(a)(1)(iii). The object and purpose of the SCM is to impose multilateral disciplines on subsidies because of the "the trade-distorting potential" of government largesse. It is evident from Article 1.1 that the Members recognized that governments have a variety of mechanisms at their disposal to confer an advantage on specific domestic enterprises or industries and that they intended to bring those mechanisms within the disciplines of the Agreement. Article 1.1(a)(1)(iii) should be interpreted in that context.

4.80 If the major input for a product is a natural resource – timber, bauxite, iron ore – a government that provides the natural resource to producers has the ability, depending upon the price charged, to provide an advantage that would not otherwise be available in the market. Canada's attempt to exempt such potentially market-distorting government practices from the disciplines of the *SCM Agreement* has no basis in the text of the Agreement and is entirely at odds with its object and purpose.

(ii) Provincial Stumpage Programmes Provide a "Benefit"

4.81 The *Canada Aircraft* panel stated that authorities must "determine whether the financial contribution places the recipient in a more advantageous position than would have been the case but for the financial contribution."[7] In this case, the USDOC used market stumpage prices from comparable regions of the United States, adjusted as appropriate, as the benchmark price to determine whether the stumpage programmes administered by the Canadian provincial governments provided timber to lumber producers on a more favorable basis than the marketplace would provide. The USDOC declined to use non-government prices between buyers and sellers within each province as the benchmark prices because provincial government sales constitute the overwhelming majority of timber sales in each of the provinces. As a result of the provincial governments' dominance of the timber market, the USDOC could not conclude that non-government prices within the provinces were unaffected

7 *Canada Aircraft - Measures Affecting the Export of Civilian Aircraft*, WT/DS70/R, Report of the Panel, as affirmed by the Appellate Body, adopted 20 August 1999, para. 9.112.

by the very distortion a market benchmark price is intended to measure, i.e., that they reflected the market "but for" the government financial contribution.

4.82 The USDOC's decision to use a US benchmark is consistent with Article 14 of the SCM, which sets forth guidelines for measuring the amount of the benefit to the recipient of a government's financial contribution. Article 14(d) states that "the provision of goods ... by a government shall not be considered as conferring a benefit unless the provision is made for less than adequate remuneration ... The adequacy of remuneration shall be determined *in relation to prevailing market conditions* for the good or service in question in the country of provision ... (including price, quality, availability, marketability, transportation and other conditions of purchase or sale)."[8]

4.83 The dictionary definition of "in relation to" is "with reference to." Thus, under Article 14(d), the prevailing conditions in the country of provision are a reference point, not necessarily an end point, for the market benchmark. The proper benchmark measures the market but for the financial contribution. Thus, the issue is finding a market benchmark with reference to what the "in country" market would be but for the subsidy. It would therefore be improper to look outside a country simply to determine what the market value of a good is elsewhere in the world. It is, however, entirely proper to do so if one can use such prices, properly adjusted, to determine the market value of the good in the country under investigation.

4.84 Moreover, Article 14(d) states that the "prevailing market conditions" to be taken into account are the conditions of purchase or sale. Therefore, when read in context, "in relation to prevailing market conditions" requires the authority to determine the adequacy of remuneration with reference to market prices for transactions that, while not necessarily between buyers and sellers within the country of provision, are (or could be adjusted to be) comparable to the government transactions at issue with respect to the conditions of purchase or sale in the market.

4.85 The "in relation to" language in Article 14(d) demonstrates the Members' intent to provide more flexibility in the selection of market benchmarks for determining the adequacy of remuneration for the provision of goods and services. This flexibility is evident elsewhere in the Agreement. The "market," as generally referred to in the Agreement, is not restricted to the exporting country, but rather encompasses the entire market available to the subsidized producer or exporter. For example, Article 14(b) refers to comparable commercial loans available to the firm "on the market." In *Canada Dairy*, the Appellate Body recognized this flexibility, confirming that "[w]orld market prices do ... provide one possible measure of value of milk to producers" in Canada.[9]

4.86 Limiting the benchmark to the exporting country's market would also seriously undermine the object and purpose of the *SCM Agreement* generally, and Articles 1.1(b) and 14(d) specifically. If the government were the sole provider of a good in the exporting country, for example, there would be no non-government benchmark prices in the exporting country to use as a point of reference and it therefore would be impossible to determine that the government had provided a benefit – even if it provided the good for a fraction of its value.

4.87 The trade-distorting potential of the government's provision of a good can be identified only by reference to an independent market price, i.e., a price that is unaf-

[8] Emphasis added.

[9] *Canada - Measures Affecting the Importation of Milk and the Exportation of Dairy Products*, WT/DS103/AB/RW, Report of the Appellate Body, adopted on 3 December 2001, para. 84.

fected by the very trade distortion the test is designed to identify. If the comparison price were entirely, or almost entirely, dependent upon the government price, as in the case where the government sales overwhelmingly dominate the market, the analysis would become circular because the benchmark price would reflect the very market distortion that the comparison is designed to detect. Using prices largely dictated by the government to measure the adequacy of government prices would therefore defeat the purpose of Article 14.

4.88 Whether a particular market benchmark price for the adequacy of remuneration is consistent with Article 14(d) must depend upon the facts of the particular case. Canada has failed to make a *prima facie* case that the USDOC's use of stumpage prices for comparable US forests, adjusted to take into account differences in the conditions of sale (i.e., in relation to prevailing market conditions) in the Canadian timber market, is *per se* inconsistent with Article 14(d) where the government sales dominate the Canadian market. To the contrary, the USDOC properly determined that US stumpage prices, as adjusted, represent prices under prevailing market conditions in Canada. The adjusted US prices represent an appropriate measure of what Canadian prices would be but for the subsidy.

(iii) The Calculation Did Not Overstate the Subsidy Found to Exist

Exclusion of Maritime Lumber

4.89 The investigation in this case initially covered softwood lumber products from all Canadian provinces. After receiving comments from Canada, however, the USDOC subsequently excluded from the investigation imports of softwood lumber products produced in the Canadian Provinces of New Brunswick, Nova Scotia, Prince Edward Island and Newfoundland (the "Maritime Provinces") from timber harvested in the Maritime Provinces ("Maritime Lumber").

4.90 In accordance with its aggregate methodology, the USDOC then calculated a single, country-wide rate based on the ratio of the total subsidy provided to producers of the subject merchandise to the total sales of the subject merchandise. In this calculation, neither the numerator nor the denominator included the excluded Maritime Lumber because Maritime Lumber was not subject merchandise, i.e., it was not within the scope of the investigation. Canada's alternative methodology would require the USDOC to allocate some portion of the aggregate subsidy found for subject merchandise to non-subject merchandise. The result of such a calculation would be a rate that would require the United States to impose duties in an amount *less* than the subsidy found to exist with respect to the subject merchandise. Articles VI:3 and 19.4 do not require such a result.

Total Value of All Sales that Canada Provided

4.91 The Panel should review the WTO consistency of the USDOC's preliminary determination based on the record before the Department at the time the determination was made. The record at the time of the preliminary determination establishes that the USDOC used in the denominator of its subsidy calculations the amount that Canada reported in its questionnaire response as the total value of softwood lumber sales, including all sales of first-mill lumber products and remanufactured products.

4.92 *After* the publication of the preliminary determination, Canada asserted, *for the first time,* that the total amount reported in its questionnaire response as the total value of softwood lumber sales did not, as indicated in its questionnaire response, include the value of remanufactured lumber shipments. Whatever the merits of this late claim by Canada that the data it submitted did not include sales of "remanufactured" products, that question is not before this Panel. Factual determinations should be reviewed "as perceived by the [administering authority] at the time it made its determination based upon the record before it ... "[10]

(iv) Canada's "Pass-through" Argument Is Inapposite

4.93 The stumpage subsidies at issue in this case are direct subsidies. As noted above, the provincial governments enter into tenure contracts with producers of the subject merchandise. As a general matter, there is no "private body" intermediary between the government and the recipient, as that term is used in Article 1.1(a)(1)(iv). Therefore, the provisions of Article 1.1(a)(1)(iv) do not apply to this case.

4.94 Furthermore, nothing in the *SCM Agreement* precludes a Member from issuing a preliminary determination and imposing provisional measures based on data establishing the total amount of the subsidy that the government provides to the subject merchandise. Although company-specific subsidy calculations may be preferred, they are not required. Canada does not contest this point.

4.95 The *SCM Agreement* simply requires that the countervailing duty rate applied not exceed the subsidy found to exist. As explained above, the USDOC in this case properly determined that Canadian federal and provincial governments provided subsidies to producers and exporters of softwood lumber, and properly calculated a country-wide subsidy rate based on the total amount of the subsidy preliminarily found to exist for the subject merchandise.

4.96 The Panel should reject Canada's argument that the USDOC should have conducted a "pass-through" analysis. While such an analysis might be relevant for purposes of determining the level of subsidy received by a specific producer or exporter, no producer or exporter-specific subsidy rates are calculated in an aggregate investigation. The USDOC did not collect company-specific information, and Canada neither objected to the aggregate approach taken in this case nor recommended a company-specific approach. Nor did Canada supply any company-specific data to support is claim of the necessity of a "pass-through" analysis.

(c) The Preliminary Critical Circumstances Finding Is Consistent with the *SCM Agreement*

(i) Judicial Economy

4.97 As an initial matter, the United States notes that the USDOC issued a final negative critical circumstances finding in this case. The USDOC's preliminary critical circumstances finding is no longer of any practical consequence; retroactive provisional measures have been terminated and no retroactive assessment will be im-

[10] *United States - Antidumping Measures on Stainless Steel Plate in Coils and Stainless Steel Sheet and Strip from Korea*, WT/DS179/R, Report of the Panel, adopted 2 February 2001, para. 6.29.

posed. The Panel therefore should not address Canada's critical circumstances claim because it is not "necessary to resolve the particular matter."[11] In this case, the normal course of the investigative process has resolved Canada's critical circumstances claim and has provided Canada with the relief it seeks.

4.98 If the Panel decides to resolve this issue on the merits, it should conclude that Canada has failed to make a *prima facie* case that the USDOC's preliminary critical circumstances finding was inconsistent with the *SCM Agreement.*

(ii) Authority to Impose Provisional Measures Retroactively

4.99 The USDOC's imposition of provisional measures on merchandise entered during the 90-day period prior to the publication of the preliminary determination is consistent with the text of Article 20 of the *SCM Agreement*, as well as with its object and purpose. Article 20.1 generally provides that provisional measures and final countervailing duties shall only be applied prospectively, i.e., to products that enter for consumption after the date of the preliminary determination under Article 17.1 or the final determination under Article 19.1, respectively. This rule, however, is not absolute. Article 20.1 expressly provides that the prospective application of provisional measures and final duties is "subject to the exceptions set out in this Article."

4.100 Article 20.6 of the *SCM Agreement* provides that a Member may assess final, definitive duties retroactively for a period "not more than 90 days prior to the date of application of provisional measures," if critical circumstances are present. Article 20.6 is intended specifically to provide retroactive relief in a "critical" situation. At the time of the preliminary determination, there may be a reasonable basis to believe or suspect that such a situation exists. However, retroactive assessment of definitive duties cannot be ordered until a final determination has been made many months later, following a full investigation. Absent suspension of liquidation, entries made 90 days prior to the preliminary determination might be liquidated during the intervening period. If the entries are liquidated, the possibility of retroactive relief, even though fully warranted, no longer exists.

4.101 Articles 17 and 20 of the *SCM Agreement* do not intend such an outcome. Article 17 of the *SCM Agreement* provides for the imposition of provisional measures to preserve a Member's right to relief once there is sufficient evidence to determine preliminarily that such relief is warranted. Retroactive provisional measures are essential to enable a Member to avail itself of the special remedy provided under Article 20.6. Therefore, Article 20.1 should be interpreted as providing for retroactive provisional measures where there is preliminary evidence of critical circumstances. A contrary interpretation would render Article 20.6 a nullity.

(iii) Basis for Critical Circumstances Findings

4.102 In order to find critical circumstances pursuant to Article 20.6 of the *SCM Agreement*, the authority must determine that there have been "massive imports" within a relatively short period, and that the imported product benefitted from "sub-

[11] *United States - Measures Affecting Imports of Woven Wool Shirts and Blouses from India*, WT/DS33/AB/R, Report of the Appellate Body, adopted 23 May 1997, page 18; *E.C. - Measures Concerning Meat and Meat Products (Hormones)*, WT/DS26,48/AB/R, Report of the Appellate Body, adopted 13 February 1998, para. 250.

sidies paid or bestowed inconsistently" with the *SCM Agreement*. The USDOC's preliminary finding of critical circumstances satisfied each of these requirements. An objective review of the facts in this case demonstrates that the USDOC had a reasonable factual basis to preliminarily determine that a Canadian province provided an export subsidy, which is prohibited under Article 3.1 of the *SCM Agreement*, and that imports of softwood lumber from Canada had increased more than 23 per cent over the base period. Moreover, the ITC preliminarily found that imports of softwood lumber from Canada were injuring the US industry before the USDOC made its preliminary critical circumstances determination. This preliminary injury determination, together with the evidence concerning prohibited subsidies and massive imports described above, constituted sufficient evidence to take the limited step of imposing provisional measures retroactively, pending the outcome of the full investigation.

(d) Expedited and Administrative Reviews

4.103 Under established WTO jurisprudence, a Member's law violates that Member's WTO obligations only if the law *mandates* action that is inconsistent with those obligations. If the law provides discretion to authorities to act in a WTO-consistent manner, the law, as such, does not violate a Member's WTO obligations.

4.104 None of the US laws that Canada challenges mandates that the United States take action inconsistent with its obligations under the *SCM Agreement*. US law gives the USDOC broad discretion to conduct reviews. Until the USDOC exercises that discretion in a particular case, any exploration of the issues raised by Canada would be hypothetical. That is particularly true in this case because aggregate cases are extremely rare.

(i) Section 777A(e)(2)(A) and (B) of the Tariff Act of 1930

4.105 Section 777A of the Tariff Act of 1930, as amended (the "Act") implemented several changes to US law to meet obligations under the *SCM Agreement* by eliminating the presumption in favor of country-wide rates and establishing a general rule in favor of company-specific rates. Section 777A(e)(2) contains two exceptions to the general rule to address cases, such as the lumber case, where there is such a large number of exporters and producers that it is not practicable to investigate each company individually.

4.106 Canada has not cited a single provision in the *SCM Agreement* that prohibits the investigative procedures set out in Section 777A(e)(2), and nothing in Section 777A(e)(2) limits the USDOC's broad authority to conduct reviews. Canada has therefore failed to establish a *prima facie* case of a violation because it has utterly failed to establish that Section 777A(e)(2) is inconsistent with any provision of the *SCM Agreement*.

(ii) Expedited Reviews

4.107 The USDOC's regulations governing expedited reviews do not cover aggregate cases. As noted above, aggregate cases are rare and, because they have only been used in cases involving industries with an extremely large number of producers and exporters, they present unique issues with respect to expedited reviews. Because these cases are so rare, the USDOC has not yet addressed these issues, by regulation or in practice.

4.108 Section 751 of the Act gives the USDOC broad authority to conduct reviews. The fact that the USDOC has not elected to promulgate specific regulations for handling what could potentially be an extremely large number of expedited reviews in an aggregate case does not in any way diminish the Department's statutory authority to conduct such reviews. Statutory authority is sufficient; regulations are not essential. Therefore, the fact that 19 C.F.R. § 351.214(k)(1) does not cover expedited reviews in aggregate cases does not in any way prohibit such reviews. The Panel therefore should reject Canada's claim that 19 C.F.R. § 351.214(k)(1) mandates that the United States violate its obligation to provide expedited reviews.

(iii) Administrative Reviews

4.109 Section 751 of the Act also provides broad authority for the USDOC to conduct administrative reviews. Again, Canada erroneously concludes that the USDOC's regulations limit that authority and require the Department to deny administrative reviews in aggregate cases.

C. First Oral Statement of Canada

4.110 In its first oral statement, Canada made the following arguments.

4.111 The complaint of Canada before this Panel involves three distinct sets of claims:

- first, the preliminary countervailing duty determination made by the US USDOC is inconsistent with US obligations;
- second, there is no basis in the *SCM Agreement* for retroactive application of provisional measures under a preliminary critical circumstances determination, and
- third, the denial of expedited reviews and company-specific administrative reviews where the USDOC conducts a country-wide investigation violates US obligations.

4.112 These actions stem primarily from two US interpretations of the *SCM Agreement* that Canada believes are fundamentally wrong, and that have immense implications for Members' rights to manage their natural resources. The first is an unwarranted reading by the USDOC of the agreed definition of "financial contribution". The second is the US determination that Canadian provincial stumpage programmes confer a "benefit".

4.113 The repeated US assertion that the appropriate comparison for determining "benefit" is between provincial and selected US jurisdictions demonstrates that the US measures are a demand that Canadian forest management practices mimic their own. The United States assumes that any public ownership of forestry resources is subsidised and argues that only by auction is there any assurance that this will not occur. The WTO Agreement does not direct Members to abandon public ownership of their natural resources.

4.114 The repeated references to the alleged "market distorting" effects of "stumpage" also indicate that the United States is arguing that any government action that

might have the potential to distort trade is a subsidy under the *SCM Agreement*. This interpretation, however, was expressly rejected by the panel in *Export Restraints*.
4.115 The panel in *Export Restraints* also found that the definition of "subsidy" in Article 1.1 reflects the Members' agreement not only as to the types of government action subject to the *SCM Agreement*, but also that not all government action that may affect the market comes within its ambit.

1. The Preliminary Countervailing Duty Determination

(a) Stumpage is not a "financial contribution"

4.116 As noted in the first written submission "stumpage" is a right to harvest standing timber. Provinces grant these rights through tenures or through licences. Tenures and licences both carry with them a broad range of forest management responsibilities and significant in-kind costs.
4.117 Timber harvesters have the right to harvest timber from Crown lands by virtue of their tenures or licences; they do not pay stumpage charges as remuneration to acquire this right. Rather, a "stumpage charge" is a levy on the exercise of an existing right to harvest timber. Stumpage charges are properly viewed as a form of revenue collection that is the economic equivalent of a tax.
4.118 Tenures and licences both confer real property rights – the right to exploit a natural resource on public land. They are comparable in this respect to the licensing of quotas to harvest fish or the leasing of the right to extract oil or minerals from public lands. The United States nevertheless treats these rights to harvest standing timber as a financial contribution in the form of a "provision of goods". In so doing, the United States makes two fundamental errors.
4.119 First, the ordinary meaning of the term "goods" refers to "articles of trade or items of merchandise <goods or services>" or "saleable commodities." The United States misinterprets the term "goods" by confusing it with the term "property". The United States found that property in its widest sense, includes all a person's legal rights of whatever description. The issue, however, is not what property means – and certainly not what the term property might be construed to include in its widest meaning – but rather what "goods" means in the context of the *SCM Agreement*. The right to exploit an *in situ* natural resource – the right to harvest standing timber – is not a saleable commodity. It is not an article of trade or an item of merchandise and therefore it does not come within the meaning of "goods". The right to harvest standing timber is not "wood fibre" or logs, any more than a lease to develop petroleum resources is gas at the pump or the right to catch fish is tuna in a can.
4.120 Indeed, this meaning of the term "goods" as articles of trade or saleable commodities is the only meaning that could have been intended by the negotiators of the WTO Agreements. As evidenced by the "General interpretative note to Annex 1A" to the WTO Agreement "goods" subject to GATT 1994 are those things in respect of which a tariff binding may be negotiated: in other words, tradable things. It follows that things that are inherently incapable of being traded across borders are not "goods". Accordingly, standing timber cannot be considered "goods" as it cannot be traded across borders.
4.121 The second US error relates to the determination that a "financial contribution" occurs when a tenure holder exercises its right to harvest timber. This is confirmed by the USDOC's finding in the preliminary determination that benefits con-

ferred by the provinces' administered stumpage programmes had been expensed in the year of receipt or when the timber was harvested. The USDOC has thus found that the "goods" were provided during the period of investigation when timber was harvested. The United States erred in its finding that a "financial contribution" under Article 1.1(a) occurred through the action of the alleged recipient, rather than in the action of a government as required.

4.122 In addition, the claim by the United States that Canada has requested the panel to read a "safe harbour" into subparagraph (iii) misses the entire point to having an agreed definition of "subsidy" to define the scope of Members' obligations under the *SCM Agreement*. The claim of the United States has no support in either the text of Article 1.1 or the negotiating history of Article 14. This confirms that real property rights were not intended to be included within the scope of the Agreement.

(b) The USDOC's Use of "cross-border" Benchmarks to Find and Measure "benefit" Violates the *SCM Agreement*

4.123 There are three fundamental problems with the USDOC's use of cross-border price comparisons to determine whether a benefit has been conferred, and to calculate the alleged subsidy.

4.124 First, Article 14(d) of the *SCM Agreement* requires that the adequacy of remuneration be determined in relation to prevailing market conditions for the good or service in question in the country of provision. This direction is unambiguous and nothing in the context, object and purpose or the negotiating history of Article 14 permits reading "in the country" in any other manner. In addition, the ordinary meaning, in context, of "prevail" is "exist". The reference to "prevailing market conditions" is, therefore, to conditions that actually exist in the country of provision and not to conditions that would exist only under hypothetical circumstances.

4.125 The United States offers a number of interpretations of the term "in relation to" that would effectively read out the phrase "in the country", and would turn the mandatory "shall" into the discretionary "may". The United States also attempts to justify using prices in the United States as a benchmark by suggesting that US stumpage is available "in" Canada. It is clear that US stumpage is not available in Canada, because producers can harvest this timber only in the United States

4.126 Second, Article 14(d) was drafted in this manner because cross-border comparisons make no economic sense. The mere fact that the domestic price in one country is lower than the price in another does not mean that the first country is providing a subsidy, because a wide range of complex political and economic factors may account for differences in prices between countries. These border-related differences make valid international comparisons substantially more difficult than comparisons within a province or a country. As well, the USDOC itself has repeatedly recognised the vast differences in natural and timber conditions that exist. These differences are so great that the USDOC rejected this methodology in all three of the previous *Lumber* cases, finding in one instance that such an analysis would be "arbitrary and capricious". These determinations were factual and all of the factors that led the USDOC to reject the use of cross-border comparisons in the past still exist today.

4.127 Third, the USDOC's reliance on cross-border benchmarks was based on unsubstantiated assertions that no in-country benchmarks were available. The USDOC asserted this without bothering to demonstrate that no valid benchmark existed "in"

Canada. It simply presumed that provincial stumpage charges are distorted because most standing timber is harvested on provincial lands.

4.128 In fact, the USDOC had compelling evidence before it related to private sales of timber harvesting rights, competitive tenures in certain provinces, and other evidence that provinces operate their stumpage systems on market terms. Instead of addressing this evidence, the USDOC simply asserted that stumpage fees on private lands are largely derivative of the public land prices. In the USDOC's opinion this meant that stumpage fees on private lands were distorted by that very fact. Moreover, the USDOC's purported rationale for moving to cross-border benchmarks, i.e., that there is distortion if the government does not auction timber harvesting rights, does not reflect its obligations under Article 14(d) – to determine if remuneration is "adequate".

4.129 If cross-border comparisons were permitted, then the only way Canada would ever know whether it was conferring a "benefit" would be to examine prices and market conditions in other countries. This interpretation is unreasonable and unduly onerous. It would also be impossible for Canada to be certain that the benchmark examined would be acceptable to the investigating authority. The *SCM Agreement* contemplates no such thing.

(c) The USDOC Impermissibly Presumed a Pass-Through of an Alleged Benefit

4.130 Under Article 1.1(a)(1)(iv), the USDOC must establish that any "financial contribution" by the government to timber harvesters had been "entrusted" or "directed" to be passed through to lumber producers. It also must establish that the alleged benefit of the alleged financial contribution was passed through to and conferred upon lumber producers and remanufacturers. It is not sufficient for the United States to simply assert, as it did here, that the subsidies at issue in this case are direct subsidies.

4.131 In this case, there is no allegation of direct subsidisation in respect of the subject merchandise, which is softwood lumber. Softwood lumber is produced from logs, and logs are made from standing timber; neither logs nor standing timber are within the scope of the investigation. In fact, a significant amount of harvesting is done by independent entities operating at arm's-length from lumber producers.

4.132 The United States argues that it does not matter if some producers do not receive direct benefits because it is conducting a country-wide investigation. It is Canada's position that lumber producers legally may not be deemed to be subsidised simply because of a finding of subsidisation to producers of the input product.

(d) The USDOC Impermissibly Inflated the Subsidy Rate by Calculating a "weighted-average country-wide rate" Based Upon Only a Portion of Canadian Production and Exports[12]

4.133 This issue concerns two problems with the USDOC's determination of the rate of subsidisation. The first is the effect of the exclusion of goods from Maritime

[12] In response to a question from the Panel, Canada indicated that it was no longer pursuing this claim. (Canada's response to Question 37 from the Panel following the second meeting, Annex B-1.)

Provinces in the preliminary determination on the calculation of a "country-wide" subsidy rate.

4.134 A "country-wide" rate is precisely that: the average rate of subsidisation of the exported product. It is the total amount of a subsidy in a country divided by all shipments or exports to the investigating Member. When the USDOC disregarded unsubsidised Maritime shipments in calculating the country-wide duty rate, it calculated a country-wide duty exceeding the average country-wide level of subsidisation. The *SCM Agreement* requires that a countervailing duty rate not exceed the amount of the subsidy.

4.135 The United States attempts to excuse its calculation by claiming, first, that its Maritime exclusion was a product exclusion for certain lumber produced in the Maritimes. In fact, the lumber is indistinguishable from other lumber and the exclusion was of the "Maritime provinces". More specifically, the exclusion is a partial exclusion of Maritime companies for lumber they produce from Maritime timber. This exclusion does not alter the proper method for calculating a country-wide weighted average subsidy rate.

4.136 The United States' second argument – that Canada simply misunderstood the US calculation methodology – is even further from the mark. This methodology is clearly flawed as it places the country-wide benefit in the numerator and only a portion of total shipments in the denominator.

(e) The USDOC Impermissibly Applied Provisional Measures in Excess of the Subsidy Preliminarily Found to Exist

4.137 This is the second problem relating to the application of the effective rate of duty. The United States determined a subsidy rate of 19.31 per cent *ad valorem*, but it employed a different basis for calculating this rate than it later used in applying the duties. Accordingly, the provisional measures were effectively applied at a higher rate than 19.31 per cent.

4.138 As stated in the preliminary determination, the United States calculated the amount of subsidy on a "first mill" basis. This means that the denominator of the calculation was the value of sawmill shipments, that is, the "first mills" that produce lumber from logs. The denominator did not include the value of shipments by secondary value-added producers of merchandise, or "final mills", that are also covered by the investigation.

4.139 The United States now claims that, at the time of the preliminary determination, it did not know that the data that it used was first mill data. It further argues that statements by the USDOC indicating that it had used first mill data were "inadvertent" and that it was surprised to find out later that the data was first mill data. Finally, the United States asserts that that the panel must limit its analysis to evidence used by the importing Member in making its determination to impose the measure.

4.140 These arguments are factually incorrect and cannot relieve the United States of its obligation, not to apply a duty that exceeds the subsidy found to exist. The data reported in the investigation was the same sawmill ("first mill") data that were provided and relied upon in all previous lumber investigations. Furthermore, by the time the USDOC issued its instructions to impose duties, it had received substantial information from Canada confirming that the data used was first mill data. Indeed, the United States acknowledges that Canada made this clarification, but it did not act upon the information. The US application of duties was inconsistent with its preliminary determination, and resulted in application of provisional measures in excess of the subsidy found to exist. As such, it violated Articles 17.2 and 19.4 of the *SCM Agreement* and Article VI:3 of GATT 1994.

2. *The Preliminary Critical Circumstances Determination*

4.141 The preliminary critical circumstances determination imposed a retroactive duty liability going back 90 days that amounting to $300 million and violated the obligations of the United States under Article 20.6 of the *SCM Agreement*. This provision permits the retroactive application of "definitive duties" following a critical circumstances finding. Article 20 and the *SCM Agreement* both indicate that "definitive duties" are distinct from preliminary or provisional measures. In the proper context, the term "definitive duties" plainly refers to countervailing duties imposed following a final determination. Consequently, the United States may apply measures retroactively under a critical circumstances finding after it has made a final countervailing duty determination.

4.142 The United States argues that it is permitted to make a preliminary critical circumstances determination and impose provisional measures retroactively. In support of its position, it relies on the findings of the *Hot Rolled Steel* panel and the object and purpose of Articles 17 and 20.

4.143 The *Hot Rolled Steel* panel report concerned a preliminary determination of critical circumstances under Article 10.7 of the *Antidumping Agreement*. The panel confirmed the limited scope of its own findings by observing that measures taken under Article 10.7 were not based on the evaluation of the same criteria as final measures that may be imposed at the end of the investigation. As there is no provision that corresponds to Article 10.7 in the *SCM Agreement*; the *Hot Rolled Steel* panel report is not relevant.

4.144 The plain text of Article 20.6 also belies the arguments of the United States concerning the object and purpose of this provision. The term definitive means definitive; it does not mean preliminary. The United States concedes as much, as it too equates definitive with final determination. The United States also invokes the object and purpose of Article 17, but neglects consideration of the specific provisions of that Article. Article 17.3 requires that a Member may not impose provisional measures sooner than 60 days after the date of initiation of the investigation. The preliminary critical circumstances determination imposed measures soon after the date of initiation, immediately violating this provision. Similarly, within a month of the preliminary critical circumstances determination the measures had violated Article 17.4 that limits the application of provisional measures to four months.

4.145 A "critical circumstances" measure must satisfy several requirements under the provisions of Article 20.6; this measure violated all of these requirements.

3. *US Law is Inconsistent with US Obligations on Expedited and Administrative Reviews*

4.146 The United States violates Articles 19.3 and 21.2 because it does not provide for company-specific reviews where it determines an "aggregate" subsidy level. It also violates Article 19.4, as exporters that would have benefited from these reviews pay more in countervailing duties. Finally, the United States proceeded with the investigation on an "aggregate" basis thereby denying exporters expedited and individual administrative reviews in violation of Articles 19.3 and 21.2.

4.147 Article 19.3 requires WTO Members to provide an expedited review when an exporter requests a review. The United States provides for expedited reviews only in non-country-wide cases. The United States argues that the regulations do not mandate a violation because the USDOC has broad discretion to conduct reviews and has only neglected to promulgate regulations. The United States position is untenable, for four reasons:

- First, the United States has the burden of establishing that the measure at issue is "discretionary". It asserts that the USDOC may conduct reviews, but it failed to create regulations. This explanation is insufficient to discharge this burden.
- Second, these regulations are procedural rules relating to every aspect of countervailing proceedings. The neglect of any right as fundamental as an individual review in aggregate cases would be deliberate. The preamble to the US regulations reinforces this conclusion, stating that the USDOC will not individually review firms when it uses a country-wide rate.
- Third, it is a basic principle of statutory construction that if a right is provided for in certain circumstances, its deliberate exclusion in other circumstances must be given meaning: that is, that no such right exists in those other cases. In this respect, the practice of the USDOC and its analysis of its own discretion with respect to the regulations concerning voluntary respondents demonstrates that it also interprets US law in this manner.
- Finally, the United States argues that it has broad authority under section 751 of the Tariff Act to conduct expedited reviews. This provision relates to annual administrative reviews and other forms of review, but is silent with respect to expedited reviews.

4.148 The United States argues that Article 21.2 does not create an obligation to conduct company-specific administrative reviews. In this instance, the US regulations also expressly prohibit company-specific administrative reviews in aggregate cases. In contrast, the text of Article 21.2 clearly requires company-specific administrative reviews. In *British Steel* the Appellate Body found that Article 21.2 required a Member to review the need for continued imposition of a countervailing duty when appropriate. The Appellate Body also indicated that this provision was designed to ensure that countervailing duties only remained in force long enough to counteract the injury caused by the subsidisation.

4.149 The administrative review provisions also violate Article 19.3 as the single country-wide rate arrived at in an administrative review supersedes all individual rates. Therefore, even if the United States had discretion to grant expedited reviews, in country-wide cases the benefits of those reviews vanish as soon as there is a country-wide rate on an administrative review. Finally, the regulations demonstrate that the discretion provided under s. 751 does not extend to individual administrative reviews. In fact, these regulations specifically deny the USDOC the discretion to grant individual administrative reviews.

4.150 The United States has argued that a violation of Articles 19.3 and 21.2 exists only where it has expressly refused to grant these reviews. This is not correct. Once the decision had been made to make an aggregate assessment, Canadian exporters could not secure a different form of assessment. Consequently, exporters were effectively denied these reviews as soon as the decision to make an aggregate assessment was made thereby breaching Articles 19.3 and 21.2.

D. *First Oral Statement of the United States*

4.151 In its first oral statement, the United States made the following arguments.

4.152 Although some of the facts of this case are technically complex and can be confusing, in the end the issues are simple. The preliminary record indicates that the Canadian provincial governments provide timber to lumber producers at less than market prices. Under Article 1 of the WTO *Agreement on Subsidies and Countervailing Measures* ("*SCM Agreement*"), that is a subsidy.

4.153 Article 5 of the *SCM Agreement* states that "No Member should cause, through the use of any subsidy ... , adverse effects to the interests of other Members, i.e ... injury to the domestic industry of another Member ..." When one Member causes injury to the domestic industry of another Member through the use of *any* subsidy, the injured Member has the right to take countervailing measures. The United States' preliminary decision to exercise that right was fully warranted in this case.

1. *Preliminary Subsidy Determination*

4.154 Article 1.1 of the *SCM Agreement* defines a subsidy as a financial contribution by the government that confers a benefit. Thus, there are two elements to a subsidy: financial contribution and benefit.

(a) Financial Contribution

4.155 The USDOC preliminarily determined that the system of timber contracts administered by the Canadian provincial governments constitutes a financial contribution within the meaning of Article 1.1(a)(1) of the *SCM Agreement*. Although Canada focuses on the complexities of these arrangements, none of those complexities alters the fundamental fact that these provincial programmes provide timber to lumber producers.

4.156 Over 90 per cent of the forested land in Canada is held by the provincial governments ("Crown timber"). Each province administers a system of contracts called tenures or licenses ("timber contracts") that allow the tenure holder or licensee to harvest the Crown timber.

4.157 There is no dispute that lumber producers participate in provincial timber contracts for one reason – to obtain timber. The definitions discussed in the US first submission leave no doubt that timber is a good within the ordinary meaning of Article 1.1(a)(1)(iii). Nevertheless, Canada argues that when the provinces issue these contracts they are not providing a good – timber – to lumber producers, but the *right to take* timber off the land. Neither the *SCM Agreement* nor the facts of this case support Canada's claim.

4.158 Although there are some variations across the provinces, the core elements of all timber contracts are the same, that is, the lumber producer obtains the right to cut timber in a specified area in exchange for an administratively set fee, the "stumpage" fee, and the assumption of certain forest management obligations. The lumber producer knows the specific area in which it will be able to harvest and knows the timber, that is, the species and quality of the trees. The producer pays stumpage fees only for the volume of timber actually harvested. The lumber producer is therefore obtaining a specifically identified good – timber.

4.159 Moreover, the ordinary meaning of "provide" includes "make available." Thus, the fact that a lumber producer has to get the timber off the stump is irrelevant. The economic consequences of providing a good or a right to a good are the same. To treat them as distinct would invite circumvention of the subsidy disciplines and seriously undermine their purpose.

4.160 Given the ample evidence that the provinces are providing lumber producers with timber, Canada's only hope is that the Panel will read into the *SCM Agreement* an exemption for all extraction and harvesting rights. There is no support in the text for such an exemption, and a treaty interpreter may not read into the *SCM Agreement* what is not there.

(b) Benefit

4.161 The USDOC preliminarily determined that the provincial governments provide timber for less than adequate remuneration, within the meaning of Article 14(d) of the *SCM Agreement*, thereby conferring a benefit.

(c) Cross-Border Benchmark

4.162 As the Appellate Body has confirmed, a benefit is conferred when the government's financial contribution places the recipient in a more advantageous position than would have been the case absent the financial contribution. Moreover, the Appellate Body has recognized that the marketplace provides an appropriate basis for comparison. In the underlying investigation, the USDOC preliminarily determined that no market benchmarks existed in Canada, and therefore used stumpage prices in US states with comparable forests, adjusted to reflect prevailing market conditions in Canada.

4.163 Article 14(d) states that: "The adequacy of remuneration shall be determined in relation to prevailing market conditions for the good or service in question in the country of provision or purchase (including price, quality, availability, marketability, transportation and other conditions of purchase or sale)." Canada ignores most of that language and argues, in effect, that Article 14(d) says: "The adequacy of remuneration shall be determined in the country of provision or purchase." The treaty interpreter, however, must give meaning to all the words in the Agreement.

4.164 World market prices can constitute part of the "market conditions in the country of provision." As the European Communities ("EC") points out, the relevance of world market prices is recognized in item (d) of the Illustrative List of Export Subsidies in Annex I of the *SCM Agreement*.

4.165 Therefore, the question is not whether Article 14(d) permits a Member to use something other than a domestic benchmark price, but when it is appropriate to do so. The facts more than adequately support the USDOC's preliminary decision to do so in this case.

4.166 As noted previously, 90 per cent of the forested land in Canada is held by the Crown. The market for timber is therefore dominated by the provincial governments.

The impact of the governments' administratively set prices on the very small residual market is virtually inescapable. Nevertheless, the USDOC did request information on private prices in each of the provinces. Only three of the provinces responded, and the USDOC determined that the prices provided were not market-based. For example, the record contained statements by a Quebec official and a Canadian forestry expert acknowledging that private timber prices in Quebec are suppressed by the overwhelming market power of low-cost Crown timber.

4.167 It is evident why Canada would insist that the United States use prices in Canada despite the evidence of a market dominated by the provincial governments. Canada would require the United States to measure the governments' prices against prices that reflect the very distortion that we are attempting to measure. Article 14(d) does not require such an obviously flawed and circular methodology.

(d) Benefit Calculation - Indirect Subsidies (Pass-Through)

4.168 The USDOC determined the total amount of the subsidy provided to Canadian producers of the subject merchandise based on aggregate data from the provincial governments. The Department then divided the total subsidy by total sales of the subject merchandise to obtain the subsidy rate. Canada claims that this calculation improperly assumed that benefits to tenure holders passed through to lumber producers. The United States does not, as the EC suggests, concede that this is the case. Some clarification of the facts is necessary to better understand the basis for the USDOC's subsidy calculation and shed light on the flaws in Canada's claim.

4.169 First, an input subsidy under Article 1.1(a)(1)(iii) is a direct subsidy. Under Canada's interpretation, all financial contributions through the provision of a good are transformed into an indirect subsidy under Article 1.1(a)(1)(iv). Canada's submission suggests that there are three distinct industries in Canada: loggers, lumber producers and remanufacturers. This is not the case. The vast majority of the Crown softwood timber is harvested under timber contracts held by integrated producers.

4.170 The vast majority of the timber contracts in Canada are directly between the provincial governments and Canadian forest products producers, or wood processing facilities. In most instances, only wood processing facilities, such as sawmills that produce lumber, are eligible to obtain a timber contract. Thus, Canada's alleged middleman between the provincial governments and the lumber producers is largely a myth.

(e) Benefit Calculation - Denominator

4.171 Canada also claims that the USDOC should have included non-subject merchandise in the calculation of the subsidy. The United States excluded certain Maritime lumber from the scope of the investigation, not producers. Canada nonetheless argues that the calculation of the benefit must exclude Maritime lumber, but the denominator must include Maritime lumber. Canada's reasoning would result in a rate less than the subsidy found to exist with respect to the subject merchandise.

4.172 Canada also argues that the USDOC calculated the subsidy on the basis of the total value of first milled lumber products, but then applied the subsidy rate to the entered value of subject merchandise. Canada's claim ignores the fact that the Department's calculation and application of the subsidy rate was entirely consistent with the preliminary record before the Department at the time of the preliminary determination. As previous panels have stated, the consistency of an authority's decisions must be assessed based on an objective assessment of the facts before the authority at the time the decision was made.

2. *Critical Circumstances*

4.173 Canada's claims relating to the USDOC's imposition of retroactive provisional measures rest on an interpretation of Article 20.6 that would render the retroactive remedies provided for a nullity. It is beyond dispute that the general principles of treaty interpretation preclude such a reading of the Agreement.

4.174 The general rule in Article 21 that provisional measures and definitive duties are applied prospectively is expressly made "subject to the exceptions set out in [Article 20]." Nothing in Article 20.1 limits the applicability of those exceptions to definitive countervailing duties.

4.175 Article 20.6 defines a set of exceptional circumstances that warrant retroactive relief. Under the text of Article 20.1 those exceptional circumstances apply to provisional measures.

3. *Reviews*

4.176 Finally, Canada claims that various provisions of US law are inconsistent with its obligations under the *SCM Agreement* because they preclude reviews in aggregate cases. Under established WTO jurisprudence, a Member's law breaches that Member's WTO obligations only if the law *mandates* action that is inconsistent with those obligations. If the law provides discretion to authorities to act in a WTO-consistent manner, the law, as such, does not breach a Member's WTO obligations.

4.177 US law provides the USDOC with discretion to conduct expedited and administrative reviews in all cases, including aggregate cases. Nothing in the regulations cited by Canada limits that discretion. Thus, US law does not mandate action that is inconsistent with US WTO obligations. The United States is entitled to the presumption that it will implement its obligations in good faith.

E. *Second Written Submission of Canada*

4.178 In its second written submission, Canada made the following arguments.

1. *Introduction*

4.179 This submission responds to the incorrect factual assertions and legal arguments that the United States has continued to make in its Oral Statement and in its Answers ("Answers") to the Panel's 26 April 2002 questions. Canada will demonstrate that: the United States misunderstands the "financial contribution" requirement of Article 1.1(a); its cross-border analysis of "benefit" is not permitted by Article 14(d); its response to the "pass-through" question is flawed and exhibits lack of comprehension of the "benefit" analysis that is required; in respect of critical circumstances, it continues to make implausible arguments. As well, Canada seeks to clarify US admissions concerning expedited reviews and will demonstrate that the US position on administrative review misstates US law and *SCM Agreement* obligations.

2. *The Preliminary Countervailing Duty Determination*

(a) "Financial Contribution"

4.180 In its Answers, the United States asserts that, "Canada claims that the *benefit* is received when the timber is harvested." From this faulty premise, the United States wrongly attributes to Canada the argument that, "the act of harvesting (which is not performed by the government) is the financial contribution." It then argues that, "[t]he provincial governments provide the timber by placing it at the lumber producer's disposal under the tenure contract."

4.181 The US argument distorts Canada's submission and conflates a series of distinct relationships into one transaction. A right to cut a tree is not the same thing as a log; nor are timber harvesters the same as lumber producers.

4.182 Under tenure agreements, timber harvesters have the right to harvest standing timber and undertake a number of forest management obligations. These obligations, such as fire protection and pest control, constitute their share of a fiduciary duty for the public good. Indeed, tenure holders must undertake such costly obligations regardless of whether they harvest any trees. The bundle of rights and obligations that a tenure represents does not admit of simplification into "provision of goods".

4.183 The right to harvest trees is, in law and in fact, distinct from trees themselves (standing timber), which is a physical thing attached to the land. Standing timber is, in turn, different from logs. The cutting down of timber is the point at which "goods" – logs – are produced from natural resources; this is similar to when fish are caught, or water is bottled. Logs are input goods into the production of lumber, which is the subject matter at issue. The right to harvest a tree is, therefore, different from the end results of harvesting (the cutting down of standing timber to produce logs) and processing (turning logs into lumber); this right does not amount to "goods" or "services" within the meaning of Article 1.1(a)(1)(iii). In fact, even the thing in which provincial governments convey an interest – standing timber – is not "goods" or "services".

4.184 The United States attempts to rebut this reading by relying on two arguments, neither of which has merit.

4.185 First, it states that "from the reference in Article 1.1(a)(1)(iii) to goods and services other than 'general infrastructure,' it follows *a contrario* that any specific immovable object may be a covered good." The conclusion in no way follows the premise. The converse of "general infrastructure" is not "any specific immovable object". In any event, "general infrastructure" is an *exception* to "services".

4.186 Second, the United States argues that "the economic consequence of providing a good and providing a right to a good are exactly the same." This argument follows the same faulty logic of the US argument in *Export Restraints* that, "an export restraint is 'functionally equivalent' to an entrustment of or direction to a private body to provide goods domestically." The panel in that case rejected the "functional equivalence" argument on the grounds that the verbs "entrust" and "direct" implied "an explicit and affirmative action of delegation or command." The panel also held that the "financial contribution" element of Article 1 was concerned with actions of governments and not the effects of those actions. The term "provides goods" implies a positive action on the part of the government in respect of the goods themselves.

4.187 The United States then relies on one of several definitions of "provide" set out in one dictionary, to try to persuade the Panel that the term "provide" should be interpreted to mean "make available" in the broadest sense of the phrase.

4.188 The US position is untenable as the more common meaning of "provide" is "supply". As well, the proposed US interpretation encompasses a range of government action that goes far beyond those actions contemplated under Article 1.1(a). To "*make available* services", for example, would include any circumstance in which a government action makes possible the receipt of services.
4.189 Finally, throughout the WTO Agreement, the word "provide" is used to indicate the giving of something rather than the more generally enabling someone to obtain or produce something. For example, the word "provide" in Articles 3.2 and 8 of the Agreement on Agriculture refers not to the availability of subsidies or support to potential recipients, but rather the giving of such support or of subsidies. This is also the case in respect of Article XV:1 of the GATS.
4.190 The US argument also ignores the distinction: between timber harvesters and lumber producers. Timber harvesters produce *logs* from trees; and logs are not subject to the investigation. Timber harvesters "provide" these logs to their own mills or to other mills for the production of lumber or other products. This equation of timber harvesting and production of lumber has serious consequences in two respects.
4.191 First, the repeated and erroneous reference to "lumber producers" diverts attention from the issue before the Panel: the provision of a right to harvest to timber harvesters. Second, it ignores the nature of the rights and obligations contained in tenure agreements. The US assertion is based on its contention that the laws of each province "require the tenure holders be sawmills." This is simply incorrect.
4.192 In B.C. a tenure holder is not required to build a sawmill. The major forms of tenure may require an applicant to maintain a "timber processing facility," but that facility can be any of a wide variety of facilities, such as pulp mills, waferboard plants, etc. Moreover, the relevant provisions in the *Forest Act* are more discretionary. Section 13(3)(c) has provisions regarding timber processing facilities, but only if they are required in the invitation for application.
4.193 The United States also argues that in B.C. most loggers operate as employees or contractors for tenure holders rather than as independent entities. There are thousands of Crown tenure holders, unaffiliated with any sawmill, that independently harvest standing timber, produce logs, and either use or sell the logs at arm's-length to sawmills and other kinds of processors. The record prior to the preliminary determination (PD) documented that of 5,932 Crown tenure holders in B.C. during the POI, only 105, or 1.8 per cent, owned sawmills.
4.194 In Quebec, there are two common forms of tenure. The dominant form of tenure, the TSFMA, can be and is held by any primary processing mill (for example, pulp mill, panel mill, veneer mill, etc.) and is not limited to sawmills. The second common form, the forest management contract ("FMC"), is rarely held by sawmills or even primary processing mills.
4.195 The United States further confuses the issues by leaving out two central facts in its discussion of Ontario tenures. Ontario, like other provinces, routinely grants export licenses for the export of logs. Indeed, Ontario granted export licenses pursuant to all requests.
4.196 Alberta also does not "generally require the tenure holders be sawmills." The United States misrepresents Alberta's questionnaire response that "[a]ll forms of commercial tenure own and operate sawmills". There, Alberta was indicating that when all sawmills are considered together, one will find among them all the types of

tenures that exist in the province. Alberta at no point suggested that all tenures were held only by sawmills, or that only sawmills could get a tenure.

(b) "Benefit"

4.197 A benefit analysis under Articles 1.1(b) and 14(d) of the *SCM Agreement* must use benchmarks "in the country of provision". Canada's submissions in this regard are based on three complementary points: first, that the text of Article 14(d) did not permit "cross-border" comparisons; second, that the injunction in Article 14(d) is based on sound economic principles; and third, that, in any event, there were ample benchmarks *inside* Canada that the United States could have used to determine "adequacy of remuneration".

4.198 The United States argues that the concept of "commercial availability" is incorporated in Article 14(d). Article 14(d) does not refer to "commercial" availability of goods, much less "prices commercially available" for those goods. The term "availability", read in context, refers not to the price of a good, or commerciality of that price, but whether the goods are available in the country in question. Article 14(d) reflects a simple economic reality: the availability of a product – its "supply" – has an impact on its price.

4.199 In any event, even if the United States were correct in its interpretation, its conclusions do not follow. The existence of imported goods in a market does not make the price of those goods the "prevailing market condition". Imported goods may, and often do, command premium prices on domestic markets.

4.200 The United States rejects the use of benchmarks reflecting market conditions prevailing in Canada and justifies the use of US benchmarks on grounds of subsidization and price suppression. The United States then proceeds to "prove" such subsidization and suppression solely on the basis of the US benchmark. Under this standard, any country enjoying a natural comparative or competitive advantage over the United States in anything would automatically be found to be giving countervailable subsidies.

4.201 The United States is also not correct in citing item (d) of Annex I as support for its proposition that "in the country of provision" means outside the country of provision. Item (d) identifies the elements of a specific practice that is considered in itself to constitute a prohibited export subsidy. It in no sense suggests that world prices can be used as a measure of benefit to domestic producers. Item (d) is framed in a way consistent with other items in Annex I, and it has the same relationship to Article 1 of the *SCM Agreement* as those other items. For example, the first paragraph of item (k) refers to lending at rates below the government's cost of borrowing. However, that does not mean that a "financial contribution" analysis must always find a cost to government.

4.202 The United States argues that it can do what the specific text of Article 14(d) does not allow, because forestry resources are for the most part owned by the Crown. It asserts that the only way it can determine "benefit" independently of the alleged distortion is to look beyond the borders of the "country of provision". The arguments of the United States must not prevail, for two reasons.

4.203 First, a "benefit" analysis seeks to identify whether a government practice has had "trade-distorting effects" but only in the sense of Article 1.1(b). The question is whether as a result of the financial contribution by the government, the recipient has got something it could not otherwise have got on its own in the market. Article 14(d), in turn, sets out the benchmark that can be used to determine the existence of "benefit" when the financial contribution in question is in the form of provision of goods. Neither Article 1 nor Article 14 *presumes* the existence of "distortion" because there is a financial contribution by the government. Furthermore, neither of these provisions permits dismissing benchmarks because of a presumption that these benchmarks might be "distorted" by a financial contribution.

4.204 The US argument is circular: market prices can be "suppressed" – driven below "normal" levels – by dominant government prices only if those government prices are below that "normal" level. However, that is the very point a benefit analysis must demonstrate.

4.205 Article 14(d) requires an investigating authority to use in-country benchmarks to determine and measure an alleged benefit. The finding of government dominance in the alleged supply of goods does not establish that the remuneration it receives is not adequate. And the United States did not make such a finding; it only asserted it. A Member also may not short-circuit the "in-country" requirement of Article 14(d) by a finding regarding the market share of the government. Market share does not equal market dominance; and neither may give rise to a presumption of price suppression.

4.206 Second, nothing in Article 1.1(a)(1) or in the jurisprudence of the WTO mentions alleged "price suppression" as a reason for dispensing with the market benchmarks set out in Article 14(d) in favour of US benchmarks. The benchmark under Article 1.1(b) is not the highest price the recipient might have liked to get, but rather the price prevailing in the market.

4.207 There are good reasons why Article 14(d) was written the way it was: cross border comparisons make no economic sense. The use of US stumpage prices as a benchmark rests on the wholly unsupported premise that "there should be no difference between the private prices in the country of exportation and world market prices, except for import taxes." In concluding this, the USDOC implicitly made an incorrect assumption that stumpage is a commodity product with negligible transportation and transactions costs.

4.208 In particular, borders affect prices and "thick border effects" are substantial and notoriously difficult to quantify. The border is highly relevant as political boundaries drive differences in government regulatory regimes, tax regimes, investment regimes, currency, banking and financial systems, business practices, and business climate. Government policies and other factors in different jurisdictions may affect economic conditions, including wage rates, taxes, capital costs, and exchange rates.

4.209 A wide variety of complex factors also affect stumpage rates. These factors include locational characteristics, timber characteristics, measurement systems, operating costs, government regulation, economic conditions, and tenure holders' obligations and responsibilities. Adjustments for these factors are difficult or even impossible to quantify for the following reasons:

- **Locational differences**: The PD assumes that tree-growing and harvesting conditions are "comparable" (an ambiguous term the USDOC never bothered to define) between the Canadian and US comparison areas. The USDOC addressed none of the contrary evidence in the record that significant differences in topography, soil conditions, climate, availability of ground and water transport, and distance to mills and to markets differentiate the Canadian and US market conditions.

- **Timber differences**: Differences in timber characteristics such as quality and stand density affect stumpage values but the USDOC made no adjustment for these differences
- **Differences in Measurements**: Differences in measurement conventions between the scales used to measure timber volumes in the United States and Canada and in the way in which timber is classified as "sawtimber" make cross-border comparisons impossible.
- **Differences in economic conditions**: Economic conditions such as wages, capital costs, taxes, and governmental regulatory policies affect stumpage values, and cross border comparisons must take into account these differences. The only economic condition that the USDOC made an adjustment for was in the PD exchange rates.
- **Differences in rights and obligations of timber harvesters**: The bundle of rights and obligations under any harvesting programme affects stumpage values. Canadian tenure holders obtain harvesting rights through tenures effectively of indefinite duration. This differs from the transactions used by the USDOC that consisted of short-term timber harvesting rights in US sales. Similarly, the lump-sum payments to obtain timber harvesting rights in the United States are not equivalent to stumpage charges in Canada levied on a volumetric basis that were previously conferred. With only limited exceptions, the USDOC did not attempt adjustments for these differences.

4.210 While Canada believes that the Panel need not address the issue of adjustments, the United States advised the Panel that the USDOC made adjustments. It further asserted that the USDOC examined the obligations that Canadian tenure holders were legally obligated to assume, and calculated a per unit amount for each category, which it then added to the stumpage fee to arrive at a total "price" for stumpage in Canada. The USDOC did not make or even attempt any adjustments for almost all of these factors. Where it did, it did so incorrectly, including as follows:

- the USDOC refused to make adjustments for the costs Canadian timber harvesters incur scaling (measuring) provincial logs, because it claimed that "costs related to scaling are not mandatory and are not borne exclusively by tenure holders....". Provincial regulations across Canada require tenure holders to scale timber to the provinces' requirements.
- the USDOC's claim that it calculated "a per-unit amount for each category of Canadian obligations that was above and beyond obligations incurred by parties paying stumpage charges in the United States" is equally without foundation. The USDOC did not examine US costs and did not compare US and Canadian obligations, but simply asserted that, where similar costs existed in the United States, no adjustments were necessary.
- In Quebec, the USDOC made an adjustment for primary and secondary roads, but refused to make an adjustment for the costs of haulage roads, rather than measuring the difference between haulage road costs in Quebec and Maine. In Ontario, the USDOC used a different methodology, measuring road costs by

their in-kind revenue to the Crown, rather than by the actual costs incurred by harvesters.

- In relation to B.C., the USDOC refused to adjust for timber sale costs incurred by B.C. licensees, such as the engineering and layout costs incurred to design and layout the appropriate contours and areas for harvesting. In Washington State lands (the benchmark the USDOC used) these costs are not imposed on the tenure holder.

4.211 One of the most significant errors made by the USDOC was the conversion factor it used to compare the stumpage rates in different jurisdictions. Comparing US and Canadian stumpage rates involves different measures of log volumes. Log volumes in several of the US comparison areas used by the USDOC are measured in thousand board feet (MBF) whereas stumpage in Canada is measured in cubic metres (m^3) using a metric scale designed to measure the total volume of solid wood in logs..

4.212 The issue of conversion rates arises because cubic log scales attempt to measure the total content of each log while the US log scales attempt to measure only that portion of total log volume that would be contained in the lumber produced from each log. This portion varies with the diameter, taper, and length of the log. Further, that portion will vary with which US log scale is being converted (and the United States has many different scales) the scale's log measurement conventions, and the scale's allowances for volume deductions for log defects. To accurately compare stumpage rates, the conversion factor must also account for differences in timber size and the utilization standards of the jurisdictions being compared.

4.213 Taken together this means that there is no such thing as a constant log scale conversion factor. Instead, the conversion factor must be specifically chosen to reflect differences in the log scales, the measurement conventions, the current timber profiles and the utilization standards of the jurisdictions being compared. The USDOC did not do this. Instead it took a "national" average factor and applied it across all provinces. The application of a proper conversion factor would have resulted in a rate substantially less than was calculated by the USDOC in the PD.

4.214 The United States continues to assert that "only the governments of Alberta, Quebec and Ontario provided any information" in response to the USDOC's request for in-country benchmarks, and that only "Quebec and Ontario actually provided private prices."

4.215 To the contrary, Alberta answered every US question and provided all documentation requested by the United States Alberta discussed and provided information on wood volumes. Further, Alberta responded fully to a series of follow up questions regarding Alberta's "private market stumpage figure." The USDOC's questions did not include any requests for further documentation of the stumpage value data.

4.216 Ontario provided the USDOC with a study entitled "Ontario's Private Timber Market" prior to the PD. The study was conducted by Resource Information Systems Inc. and explained that:

The results of the survey suggest that the market for private timber in Ontario appears to be both competitive and efficient. Buyers and sellers have the same information about market conditions, sellers produce homogeneous products, they are price-takers and they can enter and exit the market easily. Hence the market meets the classic definition of a competitive market. The market can also be classified as efficient given its low transaction costs and low level of government involvement.

4.217 Quebec submitted to the USDOC the results of the private forest stumpage surveys conducted annually for the three years preceding the period of investigation and explained that these surveys are used to determine stumpage rates on public land under the *Forest Act*. Quebec reminded the USDOC that it had accepted earlier versions of the same private forest surveys in *Lumber III* as a benchmark. Quebec also submitted a lengthy study demonstrating that the private forest in Quebec, is an open, competitive, and functioning market. This study analysed the conditions and circumstances of the private forest and found that it exhibited all the indicia of a competitive market.

4.218 Finally, the United States states that B.C. did not provide private stumpage rates. However, B.C. explained on the record before the PD that most private timber transactions are for logs, and log price data was provided.

4.219 The four primary exporting provinces also provided the USDOC with information demonstrating that they were operating their stumpage systems consistently with market principles. This information established that each of these provinces earned substantial profits from timber harvesting rights.

4.220 Finally, B.C. put on the record extensive economic analysis that established that B.C.'s price setting practices were consistent with market principles. This was because provincial stumpage charges were equal to, or even higher, than the prices that would prevail in a competitive market and prices for logs were no lower and quantities no higher than what would prevail in a competitive market. As well, B.C. provided the USDOC with information on competitive sales of stumpage in B.C. through the Small Business Forest Enterprise Programme sales.

4.221 The USDOC rejected the above evidence on the basis that private stumpage prices in Canada were not valid benchmarks for determining and measuring benefit. It stated in the PD:

> "Since the stumpage fees on public lands are the price driver for the stumpage market in those provinces, we conclude that the stumpage fees on private lands are largely derivative of the public land prices and are therefore distorted".

and later,

> "Because of the provincial government's control of the market through a system of administratively-set prices and other market distorting measures, there is no market-determined price for stumpage that is independent of the distortion caused by the government's interference in the market".

4.222 The USDOC cited the petition in support of its position. In particular, it relied on a letter of the Quebec Minister of Natural Resources to the President of the Wood Producer's Federation of Quebec (an association of private land owners). The United States now argues that this letter, and other outdated and anecdotal evidence, "[indicates] that private stumpage prices were depressed by the overwhelming majority of government-supplied timber in the market."

4.223 The letter is a Government response to the private land owners' association's criticisms of the cost adjustments used to make public and private timber comparable in Quebec's parity system, which itself is used for setting public land stumpage rates. The relevant portion of the letter relied upon by the USDOC states:

> "Toutefois, je suis conscient que la tarification des bois des forêts publiques puisse avoir une influence indirecte sur le marché privé".

4.224 The verb "puisse," as used in the letter, translated means "could" or "might". It does not translate into "does". Therefore, the above sentence, translated, reads:

> "However, I am aware that public land stumpage charges [*could* or *might*] have an indirect influence on the private market".

4.225 This in itself demonstrates the United States' gross mischaracterization of the value and import of the letter. However, the context of the above passage is equally revealing: the statement is simply the reason given by the Minister as to why the Government of Quebec continues to undertake meaningful dialogue with Quebec private landowners.

4.226 The United States also relies on a 1995 paper for its conclusion that Quebec private stumpage prices are distorted. The 1995 paper cites earlier studies (published between 1972 and 1985) that spoke to the Quebec stumpage regime that was replaced in 1989 as support for the relevant passage used by the United States In *Lumber III*, the Coalition made the same "distortion" argument regarding Quebec private stumpage prices. The USDOC addressed the argument and the evidence at that time as follows:

> "The Coalition contends the entire provincial stumpage system in Québec is not "market-based" because private prices in Québec are distorted and depressed by decades of artificially cheap provincial stumpage, and these prices are used to set public stumpage.
>
> Citing a study published in 1988 of the "20 quality zones" in Québec ... , the Coalition asserts the "cost adjustments" which Québec used to make public and private timber comparable are utterly fanciful and lead to anomalous results. Respondents point out that the Aktrin study cited by the Coalition is completely outdated and irrelevant since it examined a system that was replaced in 1989 by Québec's current system of 28 'biophysically and geologically homogeneous tariffing zones.'
>
> We agree with Respondents that private prices in Québec collected under Québec's own contracted out surveys, which we examined in depth at verification, are a viable benchmark. The evidence cited by the Coalition is either outdated and irrelevant or anecdotal..."

4.227 In *Lumber III* the USDOC, therefore, rejected evidence that was arguably more current, reliable and relevant than the material it is now relying on to arrive at the opposite conclusion.

(c) Pass-Through

4.228 Evidence on the record at the PD demonstrated that some lumber producers had purchased log inputs at arm's-length from timber harvesters; the alleged recipients of the "stumpage" subsidy. The USDOC failed to consider or even acknowledge that evidence and proceeded to grossly overstate the alleged benefit to lumber producers.

4.229 The United States now attempts to argue that it had, in fact, made a finding of no arm's-length transactions in respect of such downstream producers; and that no such analysis was necessary. This attempt must fail, for two reasons.

4.230 First, the US position is internally illogical and contradictory. If it was not necessary to make a finding, then the USDOC presumably did not make such a finding; and if it did make such a finding, it was because it found that the analysis was necessary. Second, the US assertion is simply untrue. The determination does not contain a "pass-through" analysis. In fact, there is no mention of the issue anywhere in the determination. The USDOC undertook no factual enquiry into the question of pass-through; it simply presumed that all lumber producers benefited from alleged subsidies.

4.231 Given the evidence on the record of arm's-length transactions between downstream producers of lumber and timber harvesters, the United States was under an obligation to establish an *indirect* subsidy in the sense of Article 1.1(a)(1)(iv) for all those transactions. In the absence of any such findings, even recognition of the evidence, the United States must be found in violation of its obligations under the *SCM Agreement* not to impose countervailing measures without first establishing the existence of a subsidy.

4.232 If the United States had examined the evidence on the record, it would have – indeed, should have – determined that, *first*, there were arm's-length transactions in which the pass-through of a subsidy may not be presumed; and *second*, that no subsidy was in fact passed-through from timber harvesters to arm's-length lumber producers. The United States now concedes that, if there were in fact independent loggers who sell logs in arm's-length transactions, then those sales cannot be countervailed, or at the very least, that a pass-through analysis must be conducted. To counter this, the United States claims that it "preliminarily concluded that the overwhelming majority of Crown timber is provided directly to sawmills."

4.233 The following examples provide a sampling of the evidence on the record on this issue. In B.C., more than 30 per cent of the timber harvested on Crown lands is harvested by entities that do not own sawmills. Similarly, in Ontario "approximately 30 per cent of the softwood timber harvested from Crown land during the USDOC's period of investigation was sold by tenure holders to third parties who subsequently processed this timber into forest products." Further, forest management contracts ("FMCs") in Quebec are typically held by municipalities, communities, or non-profit organizations and rarely held by primary processing mills.

4.234 This evidence was not considered by the USDOC and it made no finding on "pass-through" at the PD. The United States has now proceeded, for the first time, to counter the evidence on the record. It claims that there were no "true" independent loggers and cites evidence regarding the harvesting of timber in each province. The attempt by the United States to justify its failure to analyse evidence on the record must fail, for four reasons.

4.235 First, the facts presented by the United States do not support its conclusions. For example, the United States expressly admits that approximately 17 per cent of B.C. Crown timber is "provided under licenses that are normally reserved to entities not owning timber processing facilities," and that, in Saskatchewan, approximately 14 per cent "of the harvest was provided to smaller licenses... some of whom have their own sawmills." The United States also does not claim that all stumpage benefits are direct benefits, only that an "overwhelming majority" of Crown timber is provided directly to sawmills. Thus, notwithstanding that the United States' belated factual conclusion is incorrect, there was uncontroverted evidence on the record demonstrating arm's-length transactions between independent loggers and lumber.

4.236 Second, contrary to the United States's claim, the presence of domestic processing requirements or other regulations in no way preclude arm's-length transactions. The United States rests on the existence of an additional element in determining what constitutes an "arm's-length" transaction: the concept of an absence of "outside control or influence" For there to be an arm's-length transaction, there is no requirement that the Parties must operate independently of all other external influences.

4.237 Third, the US attempt to dismiss the evidence on the record after the fact only further highlights the USDOC's unjustifiable failure to undertake an indirect subsidy analysis in the preliminary determination . For example, the United States argues that in B.C., most loggers operate as employees or contractors for tenure holders rather than as independent entities. However, as noted above, the evidence on the record indicates otherwise.

4.238 Finally, the United States is simply incorrect to suggest that no pass-through analysis is necessary with respect to arm's-length purchasers who produce some merchandise that is subject to the investigation. Unaffiliated remanufacturers purchase lumber in arm's-length transactions from lumber producers. In those arm's-length transactions, any alleged benefit to the lumber producers would not be passed through to the remanufacturers.

4.239 The United States insists that no analysis of pass-through was necessary in a country-wide investigation. According to the United States, in such cases, "[t]he precise amount of the benefit received by any specific producer would only be determined in a company-specific review." An investigation undertaken on a country-wide basis does not relieve the United States of its obligation to establish the existence and amount of a subsidy. The effect of the US' failure to analyse the pass-through of alleged benefits was to countervail in instances where no benefit was received and to sharply increase the countervailing duty rate.

(d) First Mill

4.240 Although the calculation methodology in the survey makes clear that the data provided were from a survey of "sawmills" (also noted as "first mills"), the discussion of the methodology further intended to explain that the data also included a small portion of remanufactured products that were produced by the sawmills. Thus the statement - " [b]ecause the MSM does not collect commodity data, it was not possible to exclude 'remanufacturers' from its results" - intended to say that "it was not possible to exclude 're-manufactures' from its results." Canada explained this clearly in its August 21 and August 27 submissions, prior to the time at which the USDOC issued its Customs instructions implementing the decision.

3. The Preliminary Critical Circumstances Determination

4.241 The United States argues that it is not possible for the United States to apply definitive countervailing duties retroactively, if it were not permitted to suspend liquidation *provisionally* with respect to entries made before the PD that may later be subject to a definitive critical circumstances determination. This position is untenable for three reasons.

4.242 First, the essence of the US argument appears to have become this: the only way, under US law, the United States may exercise its right under Article 20.6 to make a definitive critical circumstances determination, is for it to breach that Article by imposing provisional measures not provided for by the Article, to preserve this right. At issue is not what the United States may or may not do under US law, but rather what are the United States's obligations under Article 20.6. If the United States is concerned about its ability to preserve retroactive imposition of definitive countervailing duties pursuant to a critical circumstances determination, it should ensure that its laws provide for this.. The United States does not lose its ability to impose duties retroactively by virtue of making a final determination of critical circumstances.

4.243 Second, the United States misinterprets Article 20.3 of the *SCM Agreement*. Article 20.3 in no way limits, or in fact speaks to, the right of Members under Article 20.6 to impose definitive duties retroactively pursuant to a critical circumstances determination. Rather Article 20.3 addresses the *amount* of countervailing duties that may be collected with respect to provisional measures imposed pursuant to a preliminary countervailing duty determination.

4.244 Third, Canada reiterates its position that the United States' reliance on *Hot Rolled Steel from Japan* is misplaced. Article 10.7 of the AD Agreement has no analogue in the *SCM Agreement*. Further, Article 20.6 does not permit a *preliminary* critical circumstances finding.

4. US Law on Expedited Reviews and Administrative Reviews

4.245 On the basis of the United States' replies, Canada understands US to have confirmed that:

- it has an unconditional obligation under Article 19.3 of the *SCM Agreement* to provide expedited reviews to any exporter not actually investigated for reasons other than a refusal to cooperate who requests such a review and in doing so promptly establish an individual countervailing duty rate for that exporter; and
- it has the discretion to grant such reviews when such a request is made.

4.246 In the light of these statements, Canada further understands that the United States does not propose to argue that its discretion to grant a review includes the discretion to *reject* such a review. Any such argument would directly contradict the US acceptance of its obligation under Article 19.3.

4.247 Canada is not convinced that US law provides the United States with the discretion to meet its obligations under Article 19.3. Nevertheless, its statements to the Panel represent declarations by the United States of both its understanding of its obligations under the WTO Agreement and also the operation of its laws. Therefore, Canada requests that the Panel find that the United States:

- has failed to fully implement its obligation under Article 19.3 to provide for expedited reviews in case of specific requests to do so in country-wide cases;
- now asserts that it has the lawful "discretion" to conduct such reviews despite the absence of specific statutory or regulatory provisions;
- may not exercise its "discretion" to *deny* any request for an expedited review; and
- must promptly grant all such requests made in *Lumber IV*, and in any other investigation.

4.248 It is critical that the USDOC give exporters subject to the country-wide countervailing duty rate in *Lumber IV* expedited reviews "promptly," as Article 19.3 requires. Within a few days, these exporters will be required to pay cash deposits at a country-wide CVD rate of 18.8 per cent. Moreover, expedited reviews provided months or years from now cannot, by definition, constitute the "expedited" reviews that Article 19.3 requires.

4.249 With respect to administrative reviews, the United States's responses effectively concede that Canada's understanding that US law prohibits granting exporters individual rates in country-wide cases is correct. In paragraph 67 of its answers, for example, the United States confirms that Section 351.213(b) of the Regulations does not provide for individual reviews in country-wide cases.

4.250 By relying on this section of the regulations, the United States asserts that its obligations with respect to administrative reviews are not to determine individual rates so as to ensure that individual companies are not paying more than the extent of the subsidy they actually receive. Rather, the United States argues that it is required to provide for individual rates only if such a rate turns out to be zero. This interpretation turns Articles 19.3 and 21.2 on their head. If adopted, the US interpretation would result in these provisions being read in a manner that would reduce the scope of their application far beyond that intended by drafters of the *SCM Agreement*, something a treaty interpreter must not do.

4.251 Furthermore, if the Panel does not find that the United States must conduct individual administrative reviews in country-wide cases, any relief granted regarding expedited reviews is virtually moot. Exporters and producers would obtain individual cash deposit rates that would be in effect only until completion of the first administrative review, given that the regulations mandate that a single country-wide rate calculated in an administrative review supersedes any individual rate previously determined.

F. Second Written Submission of the United States

4.252 In its second written submission, the United States made the following arguments.

1. Introduction

4.253 Over the course of this proceeding, the issues have been focused and the facts clarified. If there was ever a doubt, the United States has now demonstrated that the Canadian provincial governments provide timber to lumber producers – that is a financial contribution under the WTO *Agreement on Subsidies and Countervailing Measures* ("*SCM Agreement*").

4.254 The United States and the European Communities ("EC") also share the view that, in appropriate circumstances, the benefit from the government's provision of a good may be measured by comparison to commercially available world market prices, consistent with Article 14(d) of the *SCM Agreement*. Even Canada agrees that the use of import prices may be appropriate in certain circumstances. Therefore Article 14(d) does not prohibit the use of world market prices in appropriate circumstances.

4.255 There has, however, been much debate over whether the USDOC's recourse to such prices in this case was appropriate. In the end, as discussed below, the evidence demonstrates that the USDOC's use of US stumpage prices commercially available to Canadian lumber producers was entirely consistent with the *SCM Agreement*.

4.256 The United States has also amply rebutted Canada's claim that the USDOC inflated the amount of the subsidy benefit by failing to take into account so-called "independent loggers." The USDOC's preliminary determination that the Canadian provincial stumpage systems provide a subsidy to lumber producers was therefore entirely consistent with US obligations under the *SCM Agreement*.
4.257 Thus, we come full circle to where we began. "No Member should cause, through the use of any subsidy ..., adverse effects to the interests of other Members, i.e ... injury to the domestic industry of another Member."[13] When one Member causes injury to the domestic industry of another Member through the use of *any* "specific" subsidy, the injured Member has the right to take countervailing measures. The US right to impose provisional measures to counteract the injurious effects of billions of dollars of imports of subsidized Canadian lumber should therefore not be denied.

2. *Argument*

(a) The USDOC's Preliminary Determination that the Canadian Provincial Governments Provide a Good to Lumber Producers Is Consistent with Article 1.1(a)(1)(iii) of the *SCM Agreement*

4.258 It should be beyond dispute that the provincial governments are providing a good – timber – to lumber producers, within the meaning of Article 1.1(a)(1)(iii) of the *SCM Agreement*. This conclusion is inescapable under any definition of "good" in any language. It should also be beyond dispute that when a government gives a company the right to take a good, whether it is the right to take widgets from a government warehouse or timber from government land, the government is "providing" that good within the meaning of Article 1.1(a)(1)(iii). The Canadian provincial governments give tenure holders the right to take timber off Crown land and, thus, give them the timber itself. The only logical conclusion is that, in doing so, the provincial governments are providing a good within the meaning of Article 1.1(a)(1)(iii).
4.259 Canada's attempts to obfuscate this simple fact rely on logically flawed arguments, and ignore the basic principles of treaty interpretation reflected in Article 31 of the *Vienna Convention on the Law of Treaties*. For example, Canada asks the Panel to infer from the use of the phrase "imported goods" in Article 3.1(b) of the *SCM Agreement* and the word "products" in Parts III and V of the *SCM Agreement*, that "goods" can only mean traded goods that fall within the GATT 1994 Article II schedules. The fact that "products" are goods and "imported goods" are goods does not, however, logically give rise to the inference that nothing else can come within the meaning of "goods."
4.260 To sustain its strained interpretation, Canada simply ignores the most relevant aspect of the ordinary definition of "goods" in the source it relies upon, which is the inclusion of "growing crops, and other identified things to be severed from real property." Moreover, Canada's attempt to narrow the ordinary meaning of "goods" would render superfluous the only express limitation in the text itself, i.e., the exclusion for "general infrastructure." If "goods" were intended to be read as narrowly as Canada suggests, it could never encompass *any* infrastructure (e.g., a building, road, etc.), let

[13] Article 5, *SCM Agreement*.

alone general infrastructure. "Goods" must include some infrastructure, otherwise the specific exclusion in Article 1.1(a)(1)(iii) is superfluous. Thus, the very existence of that express limitation demonstrates that the Members intended "goods" to be read in accordance with its ordinary meaning and therefore to include things other than those listed in the GATT 1994 tariff schedule.

4.261 In addition, Canada's arguments are premised on the notion that the only thing at issue here is an intangible "right" granted by the provincial governments, which Canada then proceeds to totally divorce, analytically, from the object of the right granted. Under Canada's theory, form is everything: what something is called (e.g., an "exploitation right") is more important than what it actually is. In Canada's truncated analysis, if the government has granted a right, the inquiry stops, regardless of what the "right" entitles the holder of the right to do. By ignoring substance, Canada concludes that, while granting a right may constitute a financial contribution, it can never constitute the provision of a good. However, as the *Export Restraints* panel stated:

> We believe, in particular, that the appropriate way to conceive of a "financial contribution" is purely as a transfer of economic resources by a government to private entities in the market, without regard to the *terms* of the transfer.

4.262 Thus, it is in fact the "right," i.e., the terms under which the provinces transfer timber to lumber producers, that is irrelevant. To determine whether there is a financial contribution, the treaty interpreter should look at the reality of what actually occurs. In the case of provincial tenures, what actually occurs is that the provincial governments grant tenure holders the right "to take" a tangible good – timber – off the land. The right "to take" is, in fact, the mechanism (or terms) by which the government "provides" the timber, i.e., places the timber at the disposal of the lumber producer. The provincial governments are therefore providing goods within the meaning of Article 1.1(a)(1)(iii) of the *SCM Agreement*.

4.263 Canada concedes that offering steel producers the opportunity to load and haul (i.e., "to take") iron ore from a government stockpile would constitute the provision of goods. In reality, there is no meaningful difference between giving lumber producers the right to take trees off Crown land and giving steel producers the right to take iron ore from a government stockpile. While Canada may disagree, the United States is confident that the steel producers and the lumber producers would not.

4.264 The reality of the provincial tenure systems is readily apparent. The evidence demonstrates that companies obtain tenures for the sole purpose of obtaining timber, not to manage the forest. Tenure holders acquire nothing under the tenure but timber, and pay stumpage fees only on the amount of timber actually harvested. These facts leave no doubt that through the tenure systems the provincial governments are "providing" a "good" – timber.

(b) The USDOC Properly Measured the Benefit from Provincial Stumpage Systems Under Article 14(d) of the *SCM Agreement*

4.265 Canada has made several claims with respect to the USDOC's measurement of the benefit from provincial stumpage systems. In this section, the United States will address Canada's claims concerning the USDOC's selection of a market benchmark for stumpage.

(i) The Use of Commercially Available World Market Prices Is, in Appropriate Circumstances, Consistent with Article 14(d) of the *SCM Agreement*

4.266 As discussed in the US prior submissions, Article 14 of the *SCM Agreement* sets forth guidelines for determining the benefit conferred by a financial contribution. Prior panel and Appellate Body reports have defined a benefit as some form of advantage that would not otherwise be available in the marketplace, absent the financial contribution. The guidelines in Article 14(d) should therefore be interpreted to achieve an appropriate comparison of the financial contribution to the marketplace, i.e., a comparison that would identify the artificial advantage resulting from the government's financial contribution.

4.267 Article 14 does not purport to address every conceivable scenario in which a benefit must be determined. For instance, some types of financial contributions are not addressed at all in Article 14 (e.g., grants and debt forgiveness). Thus, authorities have the discretion to develop appropriate methodologies. It is the view of the United States that an appropriate methodology is one that is consistent with the guidelines in Article 14, considered in light of the object and purpose of Article 14 to compare the financial contribution to what would be available to the recipient in the market absent the financial contribution.

4.268 With respect to the provision of a good, Article 14(d) of the *SCM Agreement* states that the comparison should be made "in relation to prevailing market conditions for the good [] in question in the country of provision ... ". There is no dispute that the basis for the comparison described in Article 14(d) is the prevailing market conditions in the country under investigation. What constitutes prevailing market conditions is also described in Article 14(d), i.e., "price, quality, availability, marketability, transportation and other conditions of purchase or sale." Where the United States and Canada disagree is in defining what constitutes the universe of permissible market benchmarks that could be used to measure the adequacy of remuneration "in relation to prevailing market conditions" in the country under investigation, consistent with Article 14(d).

4.269 As the EC stated: "[t]he expression 'market conditions in the country of provision' in Article 14(d) of the *SCM Agreement* is sufficiently broad to allow the consideration of world market prices." In particular, as noted above, the concept of commercial "availability" is expressly incorporated in Article 14(d). The use of "commercially available" world market prices is also expressly sanctioned in item (d) of the Illustrative List of Export Subsidies, and has been endorsed by the Appellate Body. Prevailing market conditions in the country of provision may therefore encompass prices commercially available on the world market to purchasers in the country under investigation. Commercially available world market prices can therefore be used as a market benchmark, in appropriate circumstances, consistent with Article 14(d).

4.270 As the EC points out, the issue therefore is not whether Article 14(d) permits the use of commercially available world market prices (such as US stumpage prices) *per se*, but rather whether it was appropriate to do so in this case. The facts discussed below demonstrate that the USDOC's use of commercially available US stumpage prices was appropriate in this case and therefore consistent with Article 14(d) of the *SCM Agreement*.

(ii) There Is No Evidence of a Market Benchmark in Canada

4.271 When considering the entire universe of potential market benchmarks, the United States agrees that prices within the country under investigation should be used whenever possible. Use of prices within the country under investigation is, however, not always possible. The obvious example, which the EC noted, is the case of a government monopoly for the good in question. In such a case there is no "market" benchmark price. That example is no different in principle from the circumstances of this case. The provincial governments control 85 to 95 per cent of the market for timber. There is extremely limited information on non-government prices and the evidence indicates that non-government prices are suppressed by government prices. There is therefore no "market" benchmark price in Canada that could measure the benefit. That conclusion is not based on theory, it is based on the record evidence.

4.272 First, only three provinces provided any private price data in response to the USDOC's questionnaire. Canada's claim that there was "extensive evidence" related to private markets in those provinces is simply not supported by the record. The limited data provided by the provinces was inadequate for purposes of establishing a market benchmark. For example, as the United States explained in its response to the Panel's questions, Alberta stated that it does not have any data on private timber used in sawmills. The so-called "extensive" data provided by Alberta was a two-page excerpt from a KPMG survey, which contained a single estimated stumpage value derived from some price data for log sales. Moreover, Alberta acknowledged that the estimated value was based on information that did not distinguish between private and *Crown* timber.

4.273 Ontario and Quebec submitted market surveys. However, the Ontario survey was flawed in several respects (e.g., it provided no information on quality or grade). Moreover, there was substantial evidence on the record, including statements by an official in Quebec's Ministry of Natural Resources, that government prices suppressed private prices in the provinces. In fact, one Canadian group said that "downward pressure on the price of private wood is built into the system." The influence of a dominant owner has been recognized in other markets as well. A study of stumpage trends in South Australia notes:

> Of the total [productive forest land] ... [a]bout 70 per cent of the resource is publicly owned. The percentage of the publicly owned resource was even higher in the past. Hence it is likely that stumpage for public pine logs has held a dominating influence on stumpage for similar logs sold by private growers in [South Australia].

4.274 The remainder of the evidence that Canada cites consists of evidence that does not actually pertain to private prices. That evidence instead largely pertains to whether the provinces recover their costs and earn a profit when they sell timber. The government's profitability is, however, not the issue. It is now well settled that the cost to the government is irrelevant in measuring benefit. Moreover, the purported fact that the provincial governments made a profit does not establish that they sold Crown timber at market prices. The information provided therefore does not address the relevant inquiry, i.e., whether provincial prices for timber are more advantageous than those that would have been available to lumber producers on the market absent the provincial governments' financial contribution.

4.275 As the above analysis of the record demonstrates, there was insufficient evidence of "market" prices in Canada to form a benchmark. As the EC asked, "which other benchmark should be used in [such a case]?" The United States agrees with the EC that, in the absence of market prices in Canada, the use of other prices commercially available to Canadian lumber producers on world markets is a reasonable alternative. As demonstrated below, stumpage prices for comparable timber in the United States are commercially available to lumber producers in Canada.

(iii) US Stumpage Prices Are Commercially Available to Canadian Lumber Producers

4.276 Canada agrees that some prices commercially available on the world market, specifically import prices, can provide a benchmark consistent with Article 14(d). Canada argues, however, that it is impossible for there to be import prices in this case. Canada does not claim that Canadian producers cannot or do not harvest timber in the United States, or that US timber cannot be imported into Canada. Canada simply reverts to its argument that the provincial governments are providing a "right," not timber, and that a "right" cannot be imported. Once again, in Canada's view, form is all that matters. As the United States has amply demonstrated above, the provincial governments are not merely providing rights, they are providing timber. US timber can be, and in fact is, imported into Canada.

4.277 More importantly, Canadian lumber producers can and do purchase US timber on the stump for harvesting and import into Canada. The *SCM Agreement* states that "commercially available means that the choice between domestic and imported products is unrestricted and depends only on commercial considerations." Canadian lumber producers have virtually unrestricted access to US stumpage for import into Canada. US stumpage is therefore commercially available to Canadian lumber producers. Because US stumpage prices are commercially available to Canadian lumber producers, they fall within the universe of benchmarks that can be considered for purposes of measuring the benefit from provincial stumpage, consistent with Article 14(d) of the *SCM Agreement*.

4.278 In fact, based on commercial considerations, US stumpage prices are the most reasonable world market prices to use because the terrain, topography and species mix for US timber in border states are most comparable to those in Canada, and because the record shows that Canadian companies do in fact purchase US timber. In fact, virtually all of Canada's timber imports come from the United States.

4.279 Furthermore, it is reasonable to conclude that US stumpage prices represent appropriate market-based benchmark prices to measure whether provincial prices confer an artificial advantage. The observed price difference for Canadian and US stumpage does not reflect differences in inherent market characteristics in Canada versus the United States. Rather, it reflects the fact that the Canadian system precludes price arbitrage for timber. There is a fully integrated North American *lumber* market that coexists with a largely segregated North American *timber* market. Canada exports over half of its total lumber production to the United States, but only three per cent of its timber production. The United States exports little lumber to Canada, but exports nearly six times as much timber. The low volume of timber trade between the two countries is the result of domestic processing requirements in Canada that limit the flow of Canadian logs southward, and the advantageous stumpage prices in Canada inhibit the flow of US logs northward. The segregated timber market in North America allows for virtually no price arbitrage in timber markets across the border.

4.280 The unusual nature of the situation in the North American market is evident when compared to the substantial amounts of lumber and timber exports from other countries with major timber and lumber industries. More importantly, the data indicates that US stumpage prices are comparable to prices in Australia, New Zealand, Finland and Chile.

4.281 The USDOC's use of prices for comparable US timber that is commercially available to lumber producers in Canada was therefore appropriate in this case. Moreover, in establishing the market benchmark, the USDOC took into account other market conditions prevailing in Canada for timber, such as species, quality and tenure obligations. The market benchmark that the USDOC used in the preliminary determination was therefore consistent with Article 14(d).

(c) The USDOC Properly Calculated the Total Amount of the Subsidy to Producers of the Subject Merchandise

4.282 Canada alleges that the USDOC improperly assumed that the benefit from a financial contribution to one entity accrued to another entity. These allegations pertain to three distinct situations: (1) logs harvested by one sawmill and then sold in arm's-length transactions to other sawmills; (2) lumber sold in arm's-length transactions to companies that produce remanufactured lumber products; and (3) timber harvested by independent loggers who sell at arm's-length to lumber mills. In each case, the allegations do not withstand close scrutiny.

4.283 In the first two situations, all of the alleged recipients of the financial contribution and the benefit are producers of the subject merchandise. As discussed previously, in an aggregate case no further analysis of these situations is necessary to perform the aggregate calculation. The numerator (total benefit to the subject merchandise) is properly matched to the denominator (total sales of the subject merchandise). The precise amount of the benefit received by a specific producer would only be determined in a company-specific review.

4.284 Canada's claim with respect to the third situation rests on the assertion that the provincial governments provide a significant volume of Crown timber to independent loggers who then sell the timber at arm's-length to lumber mills. In response to the Panel's questions on this issue, the parties have provided record evidence concerning the operation of provincial tenures, and, in particular, the restrictions that the provinces impose on who may acquire a tenure and what the tenure holder may do with the harvested timber. While it is not the Panel's task to conduct a *de novo* review of those facts, a careful analysis of this evidence demonstrates that it does not support Canada's claim that lumber producers acquire a significant volume of timber from independent loggers.

4.285 First, as the United States has previously demonstrated, the potential volume of timber provided by so-called "independent" loggers is small. Canada's "evidence" to the contrary relies in large part on confusing or irrelevant statistical data. For example, Canada claims that "large numbers of harvesters" are independent loggers. The number of harvesters is, however, irrelevant. The issue is not how many independent loggers there are, but rather whether they provide a significant *volume* of Crown timber to lumber producers. Moreover, it is irrelevant if the harvester is "independent" if the mill owns the license (or is tied to the license contractually, as in Ontario).

4.286 The record demonstrates that the vast majority of the Crown softwood sawlog harvest is, in fact, under tenure to sawmills. This fact is obscured by Canada's province-specific data. For example, instead of estimating the volume of softwood sawlogs harvested by independent loggers in British Columbia, which is the relevant data, Canada estimates the volume of "timber" harvested by companies "not owning sawmills." "Timber" includes hardwood as well as softwood, and pulpwood as well as sawlogs. Moreover, it is completely irrelevant that some portion of the Crown timber was harvested by a tenure holder owning a pulpmill rather than a sawmill, if that timber was not used to make subject merchandise. The relevant fact is that more than 83 per cent of the British Columbia Crown softwood timber harvest is provided under tenures that require the tenure holder to own a sawmill.

4.287 Canada's statements with respect to the potential universe of "independent loggers" in Quebec are perhaps the most difficult to understand because they are almost entirely irrelevant. The issue is the percentage of the *Crown* harvest of softwood sawlogs that is provided to lumber mills by independent harvesters. In Quebec, 99 per cent of the Crown harvest is provided under Timber Supply and Forest Management Agreements ("TSFMA"). The Quebec Forest Act states that "[n]o one except a person authorized under Title IV to construct or operate a wood processing plant is qualified to enter into" a TSFMA. The harvest from Federal lands, which is minuscule (less than 1 per cent), and private lands is irrelevant to the benefit calculation, as is the fact that there are 40,000 registered woodlot owners. Given the TSFMA requirements, it is virtually impossible to have a significant percentage of independent loggers harvesting Crown timber in Quebec.

4.288 Similarly, in Saskatchewan, more than 86 per cent of softwood sawlogs were harvested by tenure holders that own sawmills and process their own timber, and in Manitoba, approximately 95 per cent of the softwood sawlogs were provided directly to sawmills. Alberta also stated that "[a]ll forms of commercial tenure own and operate sawmills."

4.289 Second, to the extent there may be a small portion of Crown timber harvested by entities that do not own processing facilities, transactions between those entities and the lumber mills are not at "arm's-length." A truly arm's-length negotiation is one where neither party is under any outside control or influence, either from the party with whom they are bargaining, or other parties.

4.290 Canada claims that tenure holders are free to sell their logs to unrelated mills. In fact, the record evidence demonstrates the contrary. For example, Quebec indicated that there were essentially no arm's-length transactions involving Crown timber sold by independent loggers to sawmills. Moreover, the record establishes that all of the provinces generally require that Crown timber be processed in a mill within the province. Each province also imposes other restrictions that impede a harvester's ability to negotiate freely and that compel the harvester to sell to particular customers. For example, in Ontario, as a condition of the license, tenure holders are required to sign "wood supply agreements," in which they agree to supply specific quantities of wood to specific mills. The licenses also provide that the Ministry of Natural Resources can direct excess log production to specific mills. In British Columbia, major licensees are required by law to process their logs or an "equivalent volume" of wood in their mills. Similarly, in Alberta, all licenses on the record specify a particular fixed volume that must be processed in a specific mill. Moreover, the evidence shows that the so-called independent loggers often operate as employees or contractors for tenure holders. In addition, Canada's claim of significant "sales" by independent harvesters includes transactions that are, in fact, "swaps."

4.291 In light of this evidence, the only reasonable conclusion is that there are no true arm's-length transactions for Crown timber between independent loggers and lumber mills. There is therefore no basis for Canada's claim.

(d) The Preliminary Critical Circumstances Finding Is Consistent with the *SCM Agreement*

4.292 As fully discussed in the US prior submissions, Canada has failed to make a *prima facie* case that the USDOC's preliminary critical circumstances finding was inconsistent with the *SCM Agreement.* The USDOC's imposition of provisional measures in this case on merchandise entered during the 90-day period prior to the publication of the preliminary determination was in fact fully consistent with the text of Article 20 of the *SCM Agreement*, as well as with its object and purpose.

4.293 Article 20.1 expressly provides that the prospective application of provisional measures and final duties is "subject to the exceptions set out in this Article." Article 20.6 provides such an exception, stating that a Member may assess final, definitive duties retroactively for a period "not more than 90 days prior to the date of application of provisional measures" if critical circumstances are present. As discussed in the US prior submissions, retroactive provisional measures (including suspension of liquidation and cash deposits or bonds) are essential to enable a Member to avail itself of the special remedy provided under Article 20.6. It is therefore the view of the United States that a Member may impose retroactive provisional measures if there is a reasonable basis to believe or suspect at the time of the preliminary determination that critical circumstances exist.

4.294 With respect to Canada's remaining critical circumstances claims, the United States will, at this time, rely on its prior submissions.

(e) US Laws Governing Reviews Are Consistent with the *SCM Agreement*

4.295 No reviews have been requested, much less denied, in this case because the United States has not yet imposed definitive countervailing duties. Canada simply claims that the US laws governing such reviews are inconsistent with the *SCM Agreement.* Under established WTO jurisprudence, however, a Member's law breaches that Member's WTO obligations only if the law *mandates* action that is inconsistent with those obligations. If the law provides discretion to authorities to act in a WTO-consistent matter, the law, as such, does not breach a Member's WTO obligations.

4.296 For the reasons fully discussed in the US prior submissions, the US laws that Canada challenges clearly do not mandate action inconsistent with US WTO obligations. US law instead gives the USDOC broad discretion to conduct reviews in a WTO-consistent manner.

3. *Conclusion*

4.297 For the reasons set forth above, the United States requests that the Panel reject Canada's claims in their entirety.[14]

G. *Second Oral Statement of Canada*

4.298 In its second oral statement, Canada made the following arguments.

1. *Introduction*

4.299 We are here because the United States, in violation of its WTO obligations, is imposing duties on Canadian softwood industries that are crippling our forest industries. This dispute is not just about trees or logs or lumber. It is, rather, about how the WTO Agreement applies to a Member's management of its natural resources. The United States claims a right to countervail the products of Members who manage their natural resources in a way that differs from the way chosen by the United States. Ignoring the *SCM Agreement*, the United States simply presumes that the difference between Canadian stumpage fees and US prices is a countervailing subsidy. In effect the US view is that where a government owns natural resources, it may exploit those resources only by auctioning them off in the US style. Of course this is not the way Canada manages its timber resources. And it is not the way the United States manages its natural resources, such as fisheries and mineral rights.
4.300 The US approach is also neither logical nor consistent with economic theory. For example, it is not at all evident that auctioning off stumpage in Canada would result in higher returns than those prevailing under Canada's current systems. However, where there is an abundance of resources and a small market, one would expect prices to be lower. And, the owner of those resources might well command a higher return by setting rates administratively.
4.301 The United States has imposed provisional countervailing measures against practices that are not subsidies within the meaning of the *SCM Agreement*. The United States has, also, impermissibly imposed retroactive provisional measures pursuant to a "preliminary" critical circumstances determination. Finally, in countrywide cases, the United States does not provide for expedited reviews as required by Article 19.3, and outright prohibits company-specific administrative reviews contrary to Article 21.2 of the *SCM Agreement*.

2. *Subsidy*

(a) Financial Contribution

4.302 The distinction between the right to harvest trees, standing timber, and logs, and the distinction between timber harvesters and lumber producers, are at the heart of this dispute. They are as follows:

- **the right to harvest trees** is a form of property interest. The owner of this right may go on someone's land and cut down the trees on that land;

---

[14] Canada asserts violations of Articles 10 and 32.1 of the *SCM Agreement*, which are dependent on the more specific claims addressed herein. The dependent claims are therefore also without merit for the reasons stated above.

- **standing timber** refers to trees in the forest, that are incapable of being traded; and
- **logs** are what is produced when trees are cut down and prepared for transportation;
- Sawmills, in turn, process logs into lumber, which is the subject merchandise.

The second set of distinctions relate to the different players.

- provinces own most forests in Canada;
- timber harvesters enter into agreements with provinces to manage these forestry resources. Under these agreements, the tenure holder has the right to harvest trees, but also incurs obligations (including reforestation, and the like), regardless of the quantity of trees harvested. The tenure holder may or may not own a mill; or if it has a mill, it may not be able to process all of the logs that result from its own harvest of standing timber. So the tenure holder could sell logs, process logs itself, or export them; and
- lumber producers are the sawmill operators that process logs into lumber. They are also secondary manufacturers that buy lumber from sawmills for further processing.

4.303 The United States assertion that provinces provide "timber" to lumber producers is, therefore, incorrect as a matter of fact, and its assertion that provinces "provide goods" when they enter into tenure agreements is incorrect as a matter of law.

4.304 The ordinary meaning of "provide" is to "supply", in the sense of to "give".

4.305 The United States proposes an alternative meaning, to "make available", in the sense of to "make it possible to obtain". The verb "provide", however, does not have such a wide scope:

- in subparagraph (iii), the converse of "provide" is "purchase". Properly construed, therefore, "provide" must mean "give" or "sell"; and
- elsewhere in the WTO Agreement, the verb "provide" is used when the drafters intended to denote "give".

4.306 If the negotiators had wanted to say, "make it possible to obtain", they would have said so in Article 1. In the light of its context, "provide" means to "give" or to "sell".

4.307 The term "goods" has the same meaning in Article 1 as elsewhere in the *SCM Agreement* and the WTO Agreement. "Goods" in Article 1 are the "goods" to which the modifier "imported" is applicable in Article 3; they are the same "goods" that are the subject of Article II of GATT 1994 and the Customs Valuation Agreement. "Goods" are tradable items – products – that are capable of bearing a tariff, and exclude real property, intellectual property and other property interests.

4.308 Moreover, the terms "goods" and "products" are used interchangeably in the WTO Agreement. Article II of GATT 1994 refers to "products" in paragraph 1(b) and "goods" in paragraph 1(c) – and both refer to items that may be subject to tariff bindings. The term "goods" is translated into "*biens*" and "*bienes*" in Article 1 of the French and Spanish versions of the *SCM Agreement*, and "*produits*" and "*productos*" in Article 3. The term "goods" is also translated into "*marchandises*" and "*mercancías*" in the French and Spanish versions of the Customs Valuation Agreement.

"Goods", "*biens*", "*bienes*", "*produits*", "*productos*", "*marchandises*", "*mercancías*" – all mean the same thing: tradable items, or *products* in the sense of Article II of GATT 1994.

4.309 The United States persists in its argument that providing the right to produce goods is in effect the same as providing goods. In this respect, the United States is rehashing its failed "functional equivalence" arguments from *United States – Export Restraints*. Subparagraph (iii) does not refer to the *effects* of a government action, but the action itself. This government action is entering into a tenure agreement, one element of which is a right to harvest trees.

4.310 The question before you is the scope of the phrase "provides goods" and not Article 1.1(a) of the *SCM Agreement* more generally. The United States tries to justify its stretching of "provides goods" by saying that Canada's objections elevate form over substance. On the contrary, it is evident that the drafters of the *SCM Agreement* made conscious and careful choices in defining "financial contribution" under the *SCM Agreement*, and we ask the Panel to give effect to those choices.

(b) Benefit

4.311 The Parties agree: that there is a "benefit" where "the recipient has received a 'financial contribution' on terms more favourable than those available to the recipient in the market"; where the alleged financial contribution is a government provision of goods, Article 14(d) of the *SCM Agreement* is the relevant guideline; and that Article 14(d) requires an investigating authority to determine adequacy of remuneration in relation to prevailing market conditions in the country of provision of the goods. The United States now concedes that "[t]here is no dispute that the basis for the comparison described in Article 14(d) is the prevailing market conditions in the country under investigation."

4.312 This is a significant departure from the USDOC's position in the preliminary determination (PD) and from the position the United States took earlier in this case. In the PD, the USDOC found that in-country benchmarks were not required. In its First Written Submission, the United States argued that Article 14(d) "requires [an] authority to determine the adequacy of remuneration with reference to market prices for transactions that, while not necessarily between buyers and sellers within the country of provision, are (or could be adjusted to be) comparable to the government transactions ... ".

4.313 The United States now argues that out-of-country benchmarks are "commercially available" in Canada. For the United States, it is no longer the case that "in" means "out" – rather, it is that "out" really means "in": that is to say the prevailing market conditions in the United States are somehow "available" in Canada, the appropriate benchmarks *in* Canada are those to be found in the United States

4.314 Moreover, Article 14(d) does not refer to "commercial" availability of the goods in question, much less "prices commercially available" for those goods. Rather, "availability", read in context, refers to whether the *goods* are available in the country of provision.

4.315 The United States argues that the US stumpage prices from selected lands it used as benchmarks in this case are "world market prices". This is untenable. Goods that are capable of having a "world market price" are essentially homogeneous commodities or ones whose characteristics can be defined so that they are interchangeable. Standing timber is not such a commodity. This is why the USDOC used six different US benchmarks

4.316 The United States also argues that US stumpage prices are comparable to stumpage prices in other parts of the world and are, therefore, "appropriate" and consistent with Article 14(d). It asserts that support for its position can be found in item (d) of the Illustrative List of Export Subsidies and case law - *Canada – Dairy*.

4.317 With respect to item (d), Canada has explained that its only possible relevance to this dispute is that it equates "goods" with "products". Further, *Canada – Dairy* is not relevant because the phrase "commercial availability" relates only to item (d) and there was no decision concerning this provision, as the Panel's findings were rendered moot and of no legal effect by the Appellate Body (AB). If anything, the significance of this decision is limited to the conclusion of the AB that world market prices did not provide a valid basis for determining whether there were "payments" under Article 9.1(c) of the Agreement on Agriculture. The AB found that a comparison between commercial export milk prices and world market prices gave no indication as to whether Canadian export production had been given an advantage.

4.318 Not only are US prices not "world market prices", they are also not "available" in Canada. According to the United States, US stumpage is commercially available "in" Canada for two reasons: (1) because Canadian producers can purchase US timber on the stump for harvesting, and (2) because logs produced from timber harvested in the United States can be exported to Canada. Neither reason is valid.

4.319 First, the fact that a Canadian can bid on timber in the United States does not make that standing timber available in Canada. Second, that some Canadian firms can use logs produced from US timber does not mean that they can use US timber harvesting rights in Canada. Rights to harvest timber in the United States are available only in the United States

4.320 Moreover, US law prohibits the export of logs from the public lands in the western US that the USDOC used as benchmarks for B.C. (Washington), Alberta (Montana) and Saskatchewan (Montana). Thus, the United States has used as benchmarks, stumpage from public lands where the export of logs is prohibited.

4.321 At the time of the PD the USDOC had before it ample evidence of benchmarks in Canada that it chose to ignore. The United States initially asserted that the in-country benchmarks were unusable because they were artificially suppressed by government involvement in the marketplace. However, the rejection of an in-country benchmark as "distorted" because of government involvement is not supported by the *SCM Agreement*.

4.322 The United States now argues that the evidence was inadequate to establish a market benchmark. Yet the USDOC did no analysis of this evidence. Alberta, Ontario and Quebec all provided evidence on private sales of timber harvesting rights. B.C. provided private log price data. Alberta and B.C. also provided information on competitive tenures.

4.323 In addition, these four provinces, which represent 96 per cent of softwood lumber exports from Canada provided the USDOC with information demonstrating that they were operating their stumpage systems consistently with market principles. The United States attempts to dismiss this evidence on the basis that "cost to government" is irrelevant in determining benefit. But the point has nothing to do with "cost to government". Rather, the substantial profits show that the provinces are acting consistently with market behaviour.

4.324 Moreover, the US position cannot be reconciled with the USDOC's own regulations, which provide for analysing consistency with market principles as a way to evaluate adequacy of remuneration. The USDOC has consistently determined adequacy of remuneration using this benchmark where it has found that the government played a dominant role in the market. Finally, the USDOC ignored evidence that there is no benefit to lumber producers when the situation in Canada is compared with results that would be produced in a competitive market. Regardless of what the United States now says respecting the adequacy of this evidence, the USDOC had an obligation to analyse it. It did not do so.

(c) Pass-through

4.325 The United States has not demonstrated that a subsidy exists in this case. Rather, it has improperly *presumed* the existence of a "subsidy" to producers of subject merchandise that buy their inputs at arm's-length.

4.326 The United States has admitted that *at least* 17 per cent of Crown timber harvest is done by independent harvesters in B.C., 14 per cent in Saskatchewan, and 5 per cent in Manitoba, and that a pass-through analysis is required at least in respect of companies that do not produce subject merchandise. Prior to the PD, the record evidence indicated even higher percentages. The requirement for a pass-through analysis, however, goes beyond this and includes instances of arm's-length transactions for inputs (logs or lumber) into the production of the subject merchandise. In all these cases, the United States has failed to demonstrate the existence of a subsidy because it has not undertaken the required pass-through analysis.

4.327 The United States now attempts to justify this violation by arguing that it does not need to undertake a pass-through analysis in countrywide cases. This argument is not relevant because it ignores the required elements of Article 1. More specifically, the United States has failed to establish that governments have made a financial contribution or that the financial contribution confers a benefit on a recipient. In arm's length transactions the profit maximizing recipient of an alleged subsidy must be presumed to have retained subsidies it received. Under the *SCM Agreement*, there are *no* exceptions to the obligation to establish the existence of a subsidy.

(d) First Mill

4.328 The USDOC calculated the subsidy rate on a first-mill basis, but applied it on an entered-value basis, with the effect of significantly increasing the countervailing measures applied. There is no dispute that the data used was first mill data. Therefore, there should be no dispute that the United States violated its obligations. The United States has attempted to excuse its violation, claiming that the USDOC did not know that the data it used was first mill data. This claim is not credible. The United States has acknowledged that the USDOC received clarification of the information provided to it before it made its decision to impose measures on a final mill basis.

3. Critical Circumstances

4.329 The United States argues that the term "definitive duties" in Article 20.6 also refers to preliminary measures, because, first, Article 20.1 refers to both definitive duties and preliminary measures. And second, Article 20.3 prohibits the collection of preliminary duties in an amount greater than definitive duties. The United States then argues that it must be permitted to breach Article 20.6 in order to be able, under its domestic law, to exercise the right to collect retroactive duties.

4.330 Article 20.1 prohibits retroactive application of preliminary measures and countervailing duties subject to exceptions listed in the rest of the Article. Each of the exceptions is applicable only to the extent relevant; Article 20.6 refers to definitive duties and not preliminary measures; it does not, therefore, create an exception in respect of preliminary measures.

4. *Expedited Review and Administrative Review*

4.331 The USDOC has posted a notice indicating that it will accept requests for expedited reviews in the *Lumber IV* case. The notice contains no information on timelines or procedures for these reviews or whether the reviews will actually be conducted for all requesting companies.

4.332 In the light of these considerations, and to ensure that there is no doubt as to the substance of the obligations under Article 19.3, Canada requests the following findings:

- First, that the United States is required under Article 19.3 to grant expedited reviews upon request and to establish an individual countervailing duty rate;
- Second, as the United States has repeatedly stated, nothing in US law or regulations prohibits the United States from granting expedited reviews in all instances upon request and establishing individual countervailing duty rates for requesting exporters; and
- Third, that the United States has *no* discretion to refuse to grant expedited reviews upon request or to establish an individual countervailing duty rate for the requesting exporter.

4.333 Accordingly, Canada asks that the Panel recommend that the United States may conform to its obligations under Article 19.3 only where it grants expedited reviews upon request and establishes individual countervailing duty rates for requesting exporters in countrywide cases at least in accordance with the timetable and procedures applicable to other expedited review requests.

4.334 The United States continues to deny its obligations under Article 21.2 of the *SCM Agreement* and maintains that it has provided for some form of administrative review in countrywide cases. US arguments in respect of Article 21.2 ignore two critical points.

4.335 First, the first sentence of Article 21.2 refers to "the duty". This can only mean the "countervailing duty" mentioned in Article 21.1. Accordingly, Article 21.2 should be read in the light of the preceding paragraph, which reads, "A countervailing duty shall remain in force only as long as and to the extent necessary to counteract subsidization which is causing injury." This means that the review must also consider the level of the countervailing duties. Second, there are *three* elements in Article 21.2. Article 21.2 requires that a Member review, "the need for the continued imposition of the duty ... upon request by any interested party which submits positive information substantiating the need for a review". It gives a right to an interested party to request such reviews in respect of "whether the continued imposition of the duty is necessary to offset subsidization" and whether injury would continue if the duty were removed *or varied.* And it requires that the authorities terminate the duty if it is no longer warranted.

4.336 Read together, in the light of Article 21.1, the obligation becomes clear: the United States must provide for, and conduct, administrative reviews upon request to determine not only whether countervailing duties are necessary at all, but also to establish company-specific rates.

4.337 The United States is in breach of Article 21.2 because it expressly denies administrative reviews in countrywide cases. The United States persists in arguing that it has the "discretion" to grant administrative reviews in certain limited circumstances and subject to certain qualifications. This is not enough. The "discretion" in question is to grant an administrative review only "where practicable" and then only when there is a request for a "zero rate".

4.338 Finally, if individual administrative reviews are not necessary in aggregate cases, any relief relating to expedited reviews becomes moot. This is because the aggregate rate determined at the first administrative review supersedes all other previously determined rates.

H. Second Oral Statement of the United States

4.339 In its second oral statement, the United States made the following arguments.

1. Financial Contribution

4.340 The provincial governments identify specific stands of timber and enter into tenure agreements that allow companies to harvest that timber, that is, to take the timber off the land, in exchange for a fee based on the volume of timber harvested. The provincial governments are therefore providing a good within the meaning of Article 1.1(a)(1)(iii) of the *Agreement on Subsidies and Countervailing Measures* ("*SCM Agreement*").

4.341 Canada's attempts to argue to the contrary defy general principles of treaty interpretation, the rules of logic and common sense. The essence of Canada's argument is that when the provincial governments grant lumber producers the right to take timber from government land, the producers actually provide *themselves* with a good when they cut down a tree. To support this rather extraordinary proposition, Canada ignores the ordinary meaning of "goods," which includes things to be severed from the land, such as timber. In Canada's view, a government can identify a whole forest of trees and give a specific lumber company the right to take those trees for free. The violence such a theory does to the subsidy disciplines is obvious.

4.342 Canada's strained interpretation is not supported by the text of the *SCM Agreement*. Based on the ordinary meaning of the text, when the provincial governments grant companies the right to take an identified good – timber – from government land, the government makes a financial contribution within the meaning of Article 1.1(a)(1)(iii) of the Agreement.

2. Benefit

4.343 A financial contribution confers a benefit if it provides some form of artificial advantage that would not otherwise be available in the marketplace absent the government's financial contribution. Under the guidelines in Article 14(d), the benefit from a government's provision of goods is to be determined in relation to the prevailing market conditions for the good in the country of provision. The United States shares the view of the European Communities that the concept of "prevailing market conditions in the country of provision" is sufficiently broad to permit consideration of prices for competitive goods commercially available on the world markets to purchasers in the country of provision.

4.344 That interpretation is firmly grounded in the text of the *SCM Agreement* and commercial reality. "Commercially available," as defined in the *SCM Agreement*, means that the choice between domestic and imported goods is unrestricted and depends solely on commercial considerations. Commercially available goods, both imported and domestic, compete in the domestic market and constitute the supply available to purchasers in the country of provision, that is, goods that the purchasers could obtain in the market absent the government's financial contribution.

4.345 Canada has acknowledged that "prevailing market conditions" in the country of provision include the available supply and that imports, which are part of the available supply, can, in appropriate circumstances, provide a market benchmark consistent with Article 14(d). Even under Canada's reading of Article 14(d), therefore, prices for competitive goods commercially available on world markets fall within the universe of potential market benchmarks in certain cases. Because prices for competitive goods commercially available on world markets fall within the ordinary meaning of the terms used in Article 14(d), there is no basis to interpret that provision as precluding the use of such prices, under any circumstances.

4.346 As the Canada Aircraft panel stated, the purpose of a benefit analysis is to determine whether the financial contribution places the recipient in a more advantageous position than would have been the case *but for* the financial contribution. Likewise, the Appellate Body stated that the analysis is to determine whether the recipient is better off than it would otherwise have been *absent the financial contribution*. Private prices for a good that are driven by government prices for that good do not represent prices that would otherwise have been available in the market *absent* the government financial contribution. The USDOC's preliminary investigation indicates that such is the case with respect to private stumpage prices in Canada.

4.347 The USDOC found that the provincial governments control approximately 90 per cent of the softwood timber supply. Moreover, tenure holders consistently harvest less than their annual allowable cut ("AAC") and, if necessary, a tenure holder may harvest in excess of its AAC. These undisputed facts indicate that Canadian lumber producers would have no incentive to purchase private stumpage unless the private seller was willing to meet, or better, the government's administratively set stumpage price. The record facts, when taken as a whole, support the USDOC's conclusion that private stumpage prices in Canada are integrally linked to the government prices and therefore could not logically serve as a benchmark.

4.348 Stumpage prices in contiguous US states were the most logical choice. US stumpage is commercially available to Canadian producers and the contiguous forests are generally comparable. The United States is the only country from which Canada obtains significant amounts of softwood timber. Canadian companies own timberland in the United States, bid on US stumpage and regularly import US timber.

4.349 In sum, the Panel should find that Article 14(d) permits the use of prices commercially available on world markets in appropriate circumstances. The Panel should also find that the use of such a benchmark was appropriate under the specific facts of this case.

3. *Critical Circumstances*

4.350 Canada argues in its second submission that, if the United States wishes to preserve the possibility of retroactively imposing definitive countervailing duties pursuant to a critical circumstances determination, it should provide in its laws for retroactive assessment. That is, however, precisely what suspension of liquidation does. Furthermore, Canada's assertion that US Customs' practice resolves this issue is incorrect. Under US law, an entry that is not liquidated within one year from the date of entry is deemed liquidated by operation of law at the rate of duty in effect at the time of entry. Countervailing duty investigations frequently take more than a year to complete; the *SCM Agreement* permits the investigation to go as long as 18 months. Entries during the 90-day retroactivity period would, in such cases, be liquidated by operation of law and no retroactive countervailing duties could be imposed.

4.351 The United States also notes that Canada's flexible interpretation of Article 20.3 stands in stark contrast to its restrictive reading of Article 20.1. The United States therefore takes little comfort in Canada's assertion that Article 20.3, which on its face does not contain the limitations assumed by Canada, would not be interpreted as precluding the imposition of retroactive duties where the amount of the duties has not been guaranteed by cash deposit or bond.

4. *Expedited Reviews*

4.352 The United States has demonstrated that US law provides the USDOC with discretion under section 751 of the statute to implement the United States' obligations under Article 19.3. Canada nonetheless asks the Panel to find "for the sake of clarity" that the United States has failed to implement its obligations under the *SCM Agreement*. Moreover, Canada even goes so far as to ask the Panel to make findings that the United States must implement its obligations in a specific fashion, not just in this case, but "in any other investigation." Such a request is, to say the least, inappropriate.

4.353 Where a Member's laws do not mandate WTO-inconsistent action, the Member is accorded the presumption that it will implement its obligations in good faith. The United States has demonstrated that the laws and regulations at issue do not mandate WTO inconsistent action or preclude it from implementing the obligations in Article 19.3 of the *SCM Agreement*. Therefore, the measures are not inconsistent with the *SCM Agreement*. No further findings or recommendations are necessary or appropriate.

4.354 Canada has also misstated the United States' position with respect to administrative reviews. Canada notes that the United States stated that Section 351.213(b) of the USDOC's regulations does not apply to aggregate cases. Canada fails to note, however, that the United States also stated that the regulation does not restrict the USDOC's authority to conduct reviews. More importantly, however, the regulations cited by Canada govern only assessment proceedings and Article 21.2 does not address assessment proceedings.

5. *Factual Support for the Preliminary Determination*

4.355 The factual record at the time of the preliminary determination consists largely of the information that Canada submitted in its initial responses to the USDOC's questionnaire. The United States has provided the Panel with a great deal of that information. The United States therefore finds very disturbing Canada's serious and entirely baseless accusation that the United States has wilfully misrepresented certain facts concerning tenures in Alberta. The documents provided by the United States speak for themselves.

4.356 Canada also argues at length in its second submission about the USDOC's preliminary adjustments. Although the United States could refute those claims, they are not before the Panel for the simple reason that Canada has not challenged those adjustments in this proceeding. Canada's eleventh hour attempt to expand the Panel's terms of reference is improper and should, therefore, be rejected.

4.357 Moreover, Canada cites its criticisms of the adjustments in an attempt to bolster its argument that the use of a cross-border comparison is prohibited *per se*. In doing so, Canada attempts to give the impression that the study relied upon by Canada to support this argument is the only record evidence on this issue. In fact, the record at the time of the preliminary determination contains extensive evidence that the US stumpage prices in contiguous states provide a very reasonable and logical basis for determining the market value of Canadian timber.

4.358 Canada also accuses the United States of engaging in post hoc rationalizations. Canada has not, however, claimed that the preliminary determination is inconsistent with Article 22 of the *SCM Agreement* regarding public notice and explanation of determinations.

4.359 The United States would now like to turn the Panel's attention to certain record facts before the USDOC at the time of the preliminary determination. The debate over the record facts has primarily centered on two issues: processing requirements imposed on tenure holders by the provincial governments and private stumpage prices in Canada.

(a) Processing Requirements - Independent Loggers

4.360 With respect to tenure processing requirements and the existence of so-called independent loggers, the United States would stress at the outset that the benefit calculation was based solely on the volume of Crown timber that went into the production of softwood lumber. Data pertaining to other tenure types, to timber from private lands or to timber going to the production of other types of products are entirely irrelevant.

4.361 In addition, the record at the time of the preliminary determination indicates that the vast majority of Crown timber obtained by lumber producers was provided by the provinces directly to those producers. The record also indicates that, due to the restrictions imposed by the provinces, any truly arm's-length transactions for the small amount of timber that a lumber producer may have acquired outside its own tenure are insignificant. In short, the record at the time of the preliminary determination does not indicate that pass-through is an issue, nor did Canada raise it as an issue until the day before the preliminary determination.

(b) Private Prices

4.362 Canada attempts to argue around the fact that only three provinces provided any information concerning non-government prices for stumpage. The fact remains that Alberta provided a single estimated stumpage value for all species and quality of trees; a value that is calculated by the province for the purpose of settling disputes over damaged timber. The United States provided the Panel with a copy of the Resource Information Systems study, which Ontario submitted to the USDOC. I refer the Panel to the United States' previous comments on the study and to the study itself, which we believe confirm the validity of the USDOC's assessment. With respect to Quebec, the United States notes that the record evidence of suppression of private stumpage prices that the United States has cited is only a sample of the record evidence.

4.363 Moreover, as discussed previously, this was not the only evidence on the record. Other facts concerning the governments' position as the dominant supplier of timber are consistent with the various statements on the record concerning price suppression. All of the evidence of the dominant influence of the provincial government on private stumpage prices, taken together, is more than sufficient to support the USDOC's preliminary determination that private prices could not logically serve as a valid market benchmark.

6. *Standard of Review*

4.364 As previous panels have recognized, what constitutes sufficient evidence to support a determination varies depending on the nature of the determination in question. At the time of the preliminary determination the investigation was, of course, incomplete. Canada appears to be asking the Panel to resolve the outstanding issues and render its own findings of fact. Accordingly, Canada has spent a great deal of time explaining the facts and statements it provided to the USDOC prior to the preliminary determination and even supplementing those facts with references to evidence submitted *after* the preliminary determination. In this proceeding, however, the preliminary record must speak for itself.

4.365 The question in this proceeding is whether Canada has established, based on the evidence before the USDOC at the time of the preliminary determination, that there is a breach of the cited WTO provisions. If there is a reasonable basis for the preliminary determination, as there is in this case, there can be no breach of the *SCM Agreement*. Moreover, Canada, as the complainant, bears the burden of establishing a *prima facie* case of a breach. Therefore, if the balance of evidence is inconclusive with respect to a particular claim, Canada must be held to have failed to establish that claim.

4.366 It is the view of the United States that an objective assessment of this matter, as presented here and in our prior submissions, and a proper application of the standard of review will lead the Panel to conclude that Canada has not established a breach of the cited WTO provisions.

V. ARGUMENTS OF THE THIRD PARTIES

5.1 The arguments of the third parties, the European Communities, India and Japan, as contained in their written submissions and oral statements are summarized below.

A. *Third Party Written Submission of the European Communities*

5.2 In its written submission, the European Communities made the following arguments.

1. *Scope of the Term "good" under Article 1.1(a)(1)(iii) of the SCM Agreement*

5.3 The question whether stumpage is covered by the term "goods" can be determined at least in two different ways:

5.4 First, stumpage presupposes the provision of land on which the harvester exercises its right. As "land" is an "immovable" good, Article 1.1(a)(1)(iii) of the *SCM Agreement* may apply. The term "good" is commonly defined as, *inter alia*, "property or possessions; esp. movable property, saleable commodities, merchandise, wares" or "tangible or moveable personal property, other than money; esp., articles of trade or items of merchandise". The French text of the *SCM Agreement* uses the term "biens", which is defined as, *inter alia*, "domaine, possession, propriéte". Finally, the Spanish version refers to the word "bienes", which encompasses "inmobiliario" as well as "mobiliario". Therefore, from the ordinary meaning of the word the term "goods" can not only apply to "movable" but also to "immovable" objects, including "land".

5.5 Contextually, such an understanding is corroborated by Article 1.1(a)(1)(iii) of the *SCM Agreement,* which refers to "(...) goods or services *other than general infrastructure* (...)" (emphasis added). According to this wording even streets, railways or channels - which are all immovable objects – are to be considered as a "good" to the extent that they are not "general". It follows *a contrario* that any "individual" immovable object may also be covered by Article 1.1(a)(1)(iii) of the *SCM Agreement.*

5.6 Second, stumpage gives a right to harvest a movable "good", i.e. the log, but it does not provide the object as such. In the EC's view even a "right to a good" might be sufficient for Article 1.1(a)(1)(iii) of the *SCM Agreement* because if one were to deny such a possibility Members could easily circumvent the obligations of the Agreement. As the economic consequences would be the same in both instances, the *SCM Agreement* should apply equally to both cases.

5.7 In the light of the complex nature of stumpage, the EC cautions that it would be necessary to carefully assess all the rights and obligations related to stumpage in the light of Article 1.1(a)(1)(iii) of the *SCM Agreement.* This is especially true because each province maintains a specific stumpage system. In this respect, the EC notes that all of the Canadian stumpage programmes appear to provide the beneficiary with the right to cut trees on certain "land". Furthermore, stumpage seems to be closely related to a defined movable good, which is the actual log to be harvested. In that respect, the EC finds it pertinent that, according to the main parties, the stumpage fee is calculated on the basis to the volume of the trees cut down and that applicants for stumpage are usually required to own a wood-processing facility.

2. *Determination of a "benefit" under Article 1.1(b), 14(d) of the SCM Agreement*

5.8 The starting point for the benefit analysis under Article 14(d) of the *SCM Agreement* should be the prices in the country of provision, here Canada. This is not contested by the main parties.

5.9 The term "distortion", which is used by the United States, is not mentioned in Article 14(d) of the *SCM Agreement* as being relevant to the benefit analysis. The EC considers that much care should be paid in determining the correct benchmark for the existence and amount of a benefit. As Article 14(d) of the *SCM Agreement* does not set explicitly forth a hierarchy of methodologies, the Panel should refrain from imposing any such hierarchy.

5.10 Article 14(d) of the *SCM Agreement* requires investigating authorities to use domestic price information as long as these prices are *market*-driven and *prevailing*. The notion of market implies "an opportunity for buying and selling", "a place or group with a demand for a commodity or service or sale as controlled by supply and demand". Indeed, where prices are controlled or imposed by the government and not market-driven, i.e., not freely negotiated between suppliers and purchasers, such prices would not fulfil the key "market" criterion under Article 14(d) of the *SCM Agreement*. In that respect, the EC would agree with the United States that in case of a state monopoly, there would be no *market* conditions in the country of provision.

5.11 Yet, this might be a rather exceptional situation. In the case at hand, the United States has not shown that the price for private stumpage in Canada is not market-driven. The United States has not demonstrated that the prices paid for stumpage rights on private lands, which may amount to 10 – 30 per cent of the provincial markets in Canada, are no longer determined by supply and demand.

5.12 Where the government manages the supply of natural resources from state owned property, it may be that the domestic industry satisfies additional demands from the private market or through the importation of additional resources. The EC fails to see why those domestic prices should *not* be assumed to be driven by supply and demand. Also, the EC does not understand why those private stumpage prices are not *prevailing*.

5.13 Thus, the mere assumption that prices on the private stumpage market are affected by the governmental stumpage system is not sufficient to establish that no domestic *market* within the meaning of Article 14(d) of the *SCM Agreement* exists.

5.14 Regarding the consideration of world market prices in the benefit determination under Article 14(d) of the *SCM Agreement*, the EC suggests to distinguish two situations. First, imports at world market prices may form part of the domestic market conditions. Second, world market prices may be a last resort where no domestic market exists.

5.15 The expression "market conditions in the country of provision" in Article 14(d) of the *SCM Agreement* is sufficiently broad to allow the consideration of world market prices. The term "market" defined as "an opportunity for buying and selling" suggests that world market prices may be relevant if the product at hand is commercially available to the recipient in the country of provision.

5.16 The consideration of all commercially available prices is clearly allowed in the benefit analysis under Article 14(b) and (c) of the *SCM Agreement* which only refer to "the market" but do not contain any territorial restriction. The principal relevance of world market prices is also recognised in the benchmark for export subsidies defined in item (d) of the Illustrative list of export subsidies in Annex I of the *SCM Agreement*. There, the domestic market price is only a relevant benchmark "provided such terms or conditions are more favourable than those commercially available on world markets to their exporters".

5.17 A proper analysis of the "market conditions in the country of provision" may thus include all commercially available alternative sources for the recipient, including the price for imports into that market.

5.18 The EC considers that the United States did not sufficiently explain why prices for imports from the United States into Canada are not "distorted" by the Canadian stumpage schemes or by the different market conditions in the United States Where imports take place, the respective prices form part of the "prevailing market conditions in the country of provision", i.e., Canada, and should have been considered together with the price information on private stumpage.

5.19 If the Panel found that the US correctly dismissed all price information relating to the domestic market, including also the prices in Canada's maritime provinces, the EC takes the view that world market prices may serve as a subsidiary means of establishing the existence of a benefit.

5.20 As shown above, the text of Article 14(d) of the *SCM Agreement* does not exclude the recourse to world market prices as a benchmark. The alternative use of the cost to government standard does not necessarily measure the price at which the private recipient could have obtained the good or service in the marketplace absent the financial contribution. According to Appellate Body jurisprudence, the existence of a benefit must be measured from the perspective of the recipient. To serve that purpose, there is a logical preference for taking account of actual prices at which the recipient might have obtained the good, because a cost to government standard appears to be a less precise measure whether the recipient is better off.

5.21 Finally, the EC emphasises that price information is not the sole criterion to determine the prevailing market conditions in the country of origin. Article 14(d) of the *SCM Agreement* requires the investigating authority to assess the adequacy of the remuneration in relation to all factors affecting the "prevailing market conditions for the good in question in the country of provision". These include not only the price, but according to Article 14(d) of the *SCM Agreement* also "quality, availability, marketability, transportation and other conditions of purchase or sale".

5.22 A high standard of demonstration is placed on the investigating authority through the introductory sentence of Article 14(d) of the *SCM Agreement*. Thus, great care should be taken before rejecting benchmarks in the country of exportation, particularly if this ultimately leads to the use of the petitioner's prices in the country of exportation.

3. The Determination of a "pass-through" Benefit

5.23 The EC reserves its position on this claim because it is linked to Canada's allegation that no expedited reviews are foreseen under US law where the investigation has been conducted on an aggregate basis.

4. No Application of Article 20.6 of the SCM Agreement to Provisional Countervailing Duties

5.24 A critical circumstances determination under Article 20.6 of the *SCM Agreement* cannot apply to a provisional countervailing duty. Apart from the plain language of Article 20.6 of the *SCM Agreement*, which only relates to "definitive" countervailing duties, the context as well as the purpose of this provision prevent any other approach.

5.25 Article 20.1 of the *SCM Agreement* provides for the general rule that neither provisional nor definitive duties shall be applied retroactively. This concept reflects a fundamental WTO principle. Therefore, exceptions to this rule should be stated *expressis verbis* in the Agreement and they should be interpreted narrowly. Article 20.6 of the *SCM Agreement* is such an exception regarding definitive countervailing duties. Thus, any extension of this provision to provisional countervailing duties by way of analogy would run counter to this general principle.

5.26 Furthermore, the retroactive application of provisional measures under Article 20.6 of the *SCM Agreement* would contradict the time constraints set out in Article 17.3 of the *SCM Agreement*. Under this provision provisional measures shall not be applied any earlier than 60 days from the date of initiation of the investigation. Yet, if Article 20.6 of the *SCM Agreement* were applicable to provisional measures, provisional duties could be imposed 90 days before the application of a provisional measure, thus, even to imports that enter before the time of the initiation of the investigation. While it is true that Article 20.6 of the *SCM Agreement* provides exactly for this consequence in case of a definitive countervailing duty, it has also to be born in mind that Article 17.3 of the *SCM Agreement* contains a specific time frame for provisional measures. What is more, by its very nature provisional measures may be reversed in the final determination. Yet, a retroactive application of a provisional measure would place an additional burden on the exporter if this provisional duty would be reversed in the final definitive determination.

5. *Requested Recommendation*

5.27 Canada's requested recommendation would involve an element of retroactivity, which is contrary to the general prospective nature of WTO remedies.

B. *Third Party Oral Statement of the European Communities*

5.28 The European Communities, in its oral statement, made the following arguments.

1. *Introduction*

5.29 In its written submission, the EC has already addressed certain legal issues, in particular on:

- the interpretation of the term "good" under Article 1.1(a)(1)(iii) of the *SCM Agreement*;
- the determination of a "benefit" in the meaning of Article 14(d) of the *SCM Agreement*;
- the restricted application of Article 20.6 of the *SCM Agreement* to "definitive" countervailing duties.

5.30 In its oral statement, the EC does not intend to dwell further on these aspects, but rather address two equally important questions of the case, i.e.:

- Canada's claim on the impermissible "pass through" determination of the benefit, and
- The scope of Article 19.3 of the *SCM Agreement* in view of an expedited review.

2. *A "pass-through" Benefit Determination*

5.31 In its first written submission, Canada takes issue with the US determination that the "financial contribution" to timber harvesters conferred a "benefit" on softwood lumber producers. In Canada's view, the United States incorrectly concluded that the benefit to harvesters "passes through" to softwood lumber producers. Such a determination could according to Canada only be made under Article 1.1(a)(1)(iv) of the *SCM Agreement*, which conditions were not fulfilled in the case at hand[15].

(a) Article 1.1(a)(1)(iv) of the *SCM Agreement* not the Relevant Benchmark for a "pass through" Benefit Determination

5.32 In the EC's view, Canada erred in its assumption that the determination of a "pass through" benefit must be based exclusively on Article 1.1(a)(1)(iv) of the *SCM Agreement*.

5.33 First, Canada's position conflicts with the circumstance that under Article 1 of the *SCM Agreement* the term "financial contribution" and the notion of a "benefit" have to be clearly distinguished. Article 1.1(a)(1)(iv) of the *SCM Agreement* is only relevant with regard to the "financial contribution", as is evidenced by the chapeau of Article 1.1(a)(1) of the *SCM Agreement*. Furthermore, in the case *Brazil – Aircraft* the Appellate Body considered it as a "mistake" to "import the notion of benefit into the definition of a financial contribution"[16].

5.34 Article 1.1(a)(1)(iv) of the *SCM Agreement* cannot, therefore, be relevant for the determination of whether a "benefit" "passes through" from one recipient to another. The EC would underline that, in particular, there is no requirement of identity between the recipient of a "financial contribution" and the "benefit" thereby conferred. For instance, the case *Brazil – Aircraft* involved an export credit programme where the government issued bonds to a financing bank. The beneficiary, and therefore, recipient of the benefit, however, was the aircraft manufacturer.

5.35 Second, the EC notes that the purpose of Article 1.1(a)(1)(iv) of the *SCM Agreement* is to clarify under which conditions payments made by private bodies can be imputed to governments. Governments do not escape their obligations under the *SCM Agreement* by using a private entity to confer a "financial contribution".

5.36 Yet, the case at hand differs from this scenario. The Canadian government does not use timber harvesters to distribute "financial contributions". Timber harvesters rather act autonomously when entering into contractual relationships with lumber producers.

5.37 The EC, therefore, considers that Article 1.1(a)(1)(iv) of the *SCM Agreement* is not relevant in this case.

(b) Determination of a "benefit" According to Article 1.1(b) of the *SCM Agreement*

5.38 In the EC's view any "benefit" determination, including a case of an alleged "pass through", has to abide by the normal rules as laid down in Article 1.1(b) and 14 of the *SCM Agreement*. Therefore, it is essential to determine whether the downstream producer has received a "benefit" and whether a causal link between the "financial contribution" and the "benefit" exists.

15 Canada's first written submission, paras. 54 to 68.

16 Appellate Body Report, *Brazil – Export Financing Programme for Aircraft*, WT/DS46/AB/R, adopted 20 August 1999, para. 157.

5.39 In this context, the EC would recall the jurisprudence on Article VI:3 of GATT 1947, which might give further guidance on this issue. In *United States – Pork from Canada*, the panel explicitly stated that a countervailing duty may only be imposed on a downstream product "if a subsidy has been determined to have been bestowed on the production of [that product]".[17] It further held that any subsidy granted to the upstream producer could only be considered to be bestowed on the downstream producer if this has led to a decrease in the level of prices for the primary product below the level that would be commercially available from other sources of supply.[18]

5.40 The EC considers that in the case at hand, the United States appears not to have carried out a proper "pass through" analysis with respect to those producers operating at arm's length from Canadian harvesting companies. It has also not correctly determined the existence of a "benefit" for downstream producers under Article 14(d) of the *SCM Agreement*[19] nor established a causal linkage between the "financial contribution" and the "benefit".

3. *The Scope of Article 19.3 of the SCM Agreement for an "expedited review"*

5.41 Canada claims that the United States implemented incorrectly Article 19.3 of the *SCM Agreement* by denying the possibility of an individual expedited review in case of an investigation that was conducted on a country-wide basis.[20] Canada argues that Article 19.3 of the *SCM Agreement* applies also to provisional measures by virtue of Article 17.5 of the *SCM Agreement*.[21]

5.42 Article 19.3 second sentence of the *SCM Agreement* refers only to a "definitive countervailing duty". Yet, as Article 17.5 of the *SCM Agreement* provides that "the *relevant* provisions of Article 19 shall be followed in the application of provisional measures" (emphasis added) the key issue before the Panel is to determine whether Article 19.3 second sentence of the *SCM Agreement* is pertinent.

5.43 In the EC's view, Article 19.3 second sentence of the *SCM Agreement* does not apply to provisional countervailing duties. The EC basis its conclusion on the following reasons:

5.44 First, the plain language of Article 19.3 second sentence of the *SCM Agreement* refers, *expressis verbis*, only to a "definitive" countervailing duty. This restriction is all the more significant as Article 19 of the *SCM Agreement* elsewhere uses the broader notion of "countervailing duties" without any further indication whether this encompasses "provisional" as well as "definitive" duties. The explicit limitation in Article 19.3 therefore strongly indicates that Article 19.3 second sentence of the *SCM Agreement* applies only to "definitive" countervailing duties and cannot be one of the "relevant provisions" under Article 17.5 of the *SCM Agreement*.

5.45 Secondly, the predecessor to Article 19.3 of the SCM Agreemen6t, Article 4.3 of the Tokyo Round Subsidies Agreement, did not mention the requirement of

---

[17] GATT Panel Report, *United States – Countervailing Duties on Fresh, Chilled and Frozen Pork from Canada*, DS7/R, adopted 11 July 1991, BISD 38/30, para. 4.5.

[18] *Ibid.*, para. 4.9.

[19] EC third party submission, paras. 10 to 35.

[20] Canada' first written submission, paras. 147 to 178.

[21] *Ibid.*, footnote 87.

expedited review. Article 5.4 of the Tokyo Round Subsidies Agreement, which is the predecessor to Article 17.5 of the *SCM Agreement*, could therefore not refer to such an obligation simply because it did not exist. To restrict Article 19.3 second sentence of the *SCM Agreement* to "definitive" countervailing duties (as the language indicates) would thus be in line with the legal situation, which existed already under the Tokyo Round Subsidies Agreement. Indeed, if the drafters of the *SCM Agreement* had intended to broaden the scope of Article 17.5 one would have expected to do so explicitly.

5.46 Finally, the EC considers that the restriction of an expedited review to "definitive countervailing duties" is also justified in view of the specific nature of a provisional measure. In fact, every provisional measure is by itself subject to a review because the investigating authorities will always have to determine whether or not they impose a definitive countervailing duty. In this respect, the EC notes that Article 17.4 of the *SCM Agreement* limits the application of a provisional measure to a maximum of four months. Thus, extending Article 19.3 second sentence of the *SCM Agreement* to provisional measures would place a heavy burden on the investigating authorities as they were at the same time obliged to complete the normal countervailing duty investigation.

4. *Conclusion*

5.47 To sum up, the EC considers that

- the determination of a "pass through" benefit has to establish, first, a benefit within the meaning of Article 14(d) of the *SCM Agreement* and, second, a causal link between the "financial contribution" and the "benefit".
- Article 19.3 second sentence of the *SCM Agreement* does not apply to "provisional" countervailing duties.

C. *Third Party Oral Statement of India*

5.48 India did not make a written submission. In its oral statement, India made the following arguments.

5.49 This dispute raises several issues of systemic interest. One such issue is whether the *SCM Agreement* permits the use of "cross-border" benchmarks to find and measure "benefit".

5.50 In this dispute, the USDOC sought to establish that Canadian stumpage practices "conferred" a benefit by comparing stumpage charges levied in Canada with stumpage prices levied in certain parts of the United States, on the basis that such prices are "commercially available world market prices..." to softwood lumber producers in Canada. Finding the US stumpage prices to be higher than the charges levied in Canada, the USDOC concluded that Canadian stumpage charges conferred a benefit. The USDOC thus derived the "stumpage subsidy" from the comparisons of stumpage charges in Canada and cross-border prices for stumpage in the United States.

5.51 India does not consider that the *SCM Agreement* permits such comparison.

5.52 Article 1.1 of the *SCM Agreement* provides that a subsidy exists where there is a financial contribution by a government and "a benefit is thereby conferred". The Appellate Body considered the meaning of "benefit" in Article 1 of the *SCM Agree-*

ment in the dispute, *Canada – Aircraft* (DS70). According to the Appellate Body, "the word 'benefit', as used in Article 1.1(b) implies some kind of comparison. This must be so, for there can be no 'benefit' to the recipient unless the 'financial contribution' makes the recipient 'better off' than it would otherwise have been, absent that contribution. In our view, the marketplace provides an appropriate basis for comparison in determining whether a 'benefit' has been 'conferred', because the trade-distorting potential of a 'financial contribution' can be identified by determining whether the recipient has received a 'financial contribution' on terms more favourable than those available to the recipient in the market".[22]

5.53 In the case of a government provision of goods, the question is therefore whether the purchaser of a good from the government is "better off" than other purchasers who buy the same good from other sellers in the country subject to the investigation. This is confirmed by Article 14(d) of the *SCM Agreement*, which sets out guidelines to calculate the amount of a subsidy based on a "benefit to the recipient" test in cases of an alleged government provision of goods. It provides that:

> "(d) the provision of goods or services or purchase of goods by a government shall not be considered as conferring a benefit unless the provision is made for less than adequate remuneration, or the purchase is made for more than adequate remuneration. The adequacy of remuneration shall be determined *in relation to prevailing market conditions* for the good or service in question *in the country of provision or purchase* (including price, quality, availability, marketability, transportation and other conditions of purchase or sale)". (Emphasis added.)

5.54 The words or Article 14(d) are clear and unambiguous. The expression "in the country of provision or purchase" means "in the country of provision or purchase". It does not mean prevailing market conditions in *some other country*. Similarly, Article 14(d) does not allow adequacy to be determined as against market conditions *internationally*. We agree with Canada that nothing in the text, context, object and purpose of Article 14(d) of the *SCM Agreement* permits reading "in" as anything other than "in"; "in" manifestly does not mean "out"; "in the country" does not admit of "cross-border" analysis. Therefore, it is not open to an investigating authority to look outside the country of provision.

5.55 For the purposes of Part V of the *SCM Agreement*, the proper benchmark in a provision of goods context is therefore the home market price of a good, and not its price in some other market. A cross-border analysis using transactions in another country is thus inconsistent with Articles 1 and 14 as interpreted by the Appellate Body, and viewed in context and in the light of the object and purpose of the *SCM Agreement*.

D. *Third Party Written Submission of Japan*

5.56 In its third party written submission, Japan made the following arguments. Japan did not make an oral statement.

---

[22] Appellate Body Report, *Canada – Measures Affecting the Export of Civilian Aircraft*, WT/DS70/AB/R, adopted 20 August 1999, para. 157.

1. *Introduction*

5.57 A standing timber price, which is included in log production cost, generally forms a part of production cost of lumber. Assuming that the cost of processing logs into lumber is fixed, when a standing timber price gets higher, the production cost of lumber using that standing timber as raw material would rise, and it works on the direction where production of lumber is discouraged. On the contrary, when the standing timber price is set significantly low, the production cost of lumber would also remain low, and it works on the direction that production of lumber is encourage. It can also lead to lowering a price of lumber by producers.

5.58 The issue before this Panel, however, is not the adequacy of Canadian lumber export pricing itself. Issues presented in this proceeding are whether the United States may countervail the stumpage programmes of Canadian provinces in accordance with the provisions of the *SCM Agreement* and Article VI:3 of GATT 1994.

5.59 Japan has no intention to argue whether assessment of underlying facts in the specific circumstances of this case is consistent with the *SCM Agreement*. This case, however, raises certain important systemic issues. In the interests of the sound interpretation of the *SCM Agreement*, Japan respectfully submits the following comments.

2. *Arguments*

(a) Indirect Subsidies

5.60 According to Canada, provincial stumpage programmes are granted to timber harvesters, and timber is further processed by downstream producers in Canada into lumber, some of which in turn are exported to the United States.

5.61 Article VI:3 of GATT 1994 and footnote 36 of the *SCM Agreement* provide that an importing Member may impose countervailing duties on a product for the purpose of offsetting any subsidy granted (or bestowed), "directly or *indirectly, on* the manufacture, production or export of" such product. (Emphasis added.)

5.62 Article VI:3 and footnote 36 also provide that in order to be countervailable a subsidy does not have to be granted directly on manufacture of a product. Such subsidy may be granted on exported products "indirectly". A subsidy may be countervailable even if the subsidy is granted on manufacture of exported products through something else. For example, a subsidy may be countervailable when the subsidy is granted to the raw material supplier upon its sales of its raw material to producers of an exported product, if a benefit accrues to such producers by the subsidy. But it should be noted that the term "indirectly" may not be construed beyond its meaning.

5.63 Japan respectfully requests that this Panel make its finding on the countervailability of the Canadian stumpage programme based on our consideration stated above.

(b) Existence of a Financial Contribution by a Government

5.64 Canada claims that stumpage programmes are not governmental provision of "goods or services other than general infrastructure" in Article 1.1(a)(1)(iii) of the *SCM Agreement*, and thus the provincial governments have not provided "a financial contribution" under Article 1.1(a)(1) of the *SCM Agreement*. Canada further claims that the stumpage is a right to exploit an *in situ* natural resource, and therefore, this right is not a good or service within the meaning of Article 1.1(a)(1)(iii) of the *SCM Agreement*[23].

5.65 Canada explained in paragraph 33 of its first submission that timber harvesters are given the right to harvest standing timber under stumpage programmes. These harvesters pay actual stumpage charges to provincial governments not when they acquire and maintain the right to harvest standing timber, but when they cut and acquire the timber. The amount of consideration is decided by multiplying the wood volume by unit prices defined by the provincial government. Although stumpage could be a "right" instead of "good" itself as Canada mentioned, a person given such a right will acquire the timber after all.

5.66 Japan respectfully requests that this Panel provide its finding of whether this stumpage should be distinguished from governmental provision of "goods or services other than general infrastructure".

(c) Benefits Conferred

5.67 The other question that Japan wishes to address in this submission is how "financial contribution" of a good should be adequately measured. This question is equivalent to whether the provision of a good is made for less than adequate remuneration "in relation to *prevailing market conditions* for the good or service in question *in the country of provision or purchase* (including price quality, availability, marketability, transportation and other conditions of purchase or sale)" (emphasis added) under Article 14(d) of the *SCM Agreement*.

5.68 The USDOC found in its preliminary determination that the financial benefit conferred by the Canadian provincial governments be valued by comparing the stumpage charge with stumpage prices in the United States with comparable forests[24]. Canada claims that this "cross-border" analysis is inconsistent with Article 14(d) of the *SCM Agreement* because the Article does not mean that adequacy can be based on prevailing market conditions in some other country or internationally[25].

5.69 In Japan's view, this Article means that the adequacy of remuneration be based, in principle, on prevailing market conditions in the territory of the exporting Member. Firstly, the text of Article 14(d) does not explicitly permit "cross-border" analysis. Secondly, the interpretation by the United States of Article 14(d) would create incongruous results. When the interpretation by the United States is strictly followed, in order to avoid granting a subsidy, a Member would be required to review prices in all foreign markets, to which a product would be exported, when the Member sells or purchases the product. This interpretation imposes an unreasonable burden on Members.

5.70 However, the question whether "cross-border" analysis has no ground for justification under any circumstances, or if it is ever permissible, and what are the conditions for a Member to use such an analysis, still remains. Japan hopes this question would be properly addressed in this Panels findings.

---

23 Canada's first written submission, at para. 34.

24 US first written submission at para. 50.

25 Canada's first written submission at para. 44.

VI. INTERIM REVIEW

6.1 On 19 August 2002, the United States submitted a written request for review by the Panel of particular aspects of the interim report issued on 26 July 2002. Canada did not provide any comments on the interim report. Canada commented on the United States' request for interim review on 26 August 2002. Neither party requested an additional meeting with the Panel.

6.2 We have reviewed the comments presented by the United States and the reaction thereto by Canada and have finalized our report. We note that in response to the comments received, the Panel corrected typographical and other clerical errors throughout the interim report.

6.3 The United States requested changes to the last sentence of paragraph 7.59 of the interim report. The United States posited that the Panel should have declined to consider the issue of adjustments to the benchmark price used by the USDOC, as this issue did not form part of the Panel's terms of reference. Canada urged the Panel to reject the United States' suggestion. Canada argued that its claim relating to the USDOC's determination and measurement of benefit was sufficiently identified in its request for establishment of a panel. According to Canada, the US was confusing "claims" and "legal arguments". We considered that paragraph 7.59 of the interim report referred to certain *arguments* which had been developed by Canada before us as part of its *claim* relating to the measurement of benefit by the USDOC. In particular, we were of the view that Canada's arguments concerning the appropriateness of the adjustments used by the USDOC to calculate the benchmark stumpage price formed part of Canada's claim concerning the benchmark for measuring the benefit, as set forth in its panel request. Canada developed a number of arguments under this claim, and as we had already found against the US on this claim on the basis of other more principal arguments, we saw no reason to address this additional Canadian argument in support of its claim. We have adjusted the drafting of paragraph 7.59 to clarify this point.

6.4 The United States further took issue with the Panel's statement in the first sentence of paragraph 7.74. According to the US, it had not conceded, as the Panel suggested, that in a certain number of cases the lumber producers were independent from the tenure harvesters and may have had to pay an arm's-length price to obtain the allegedly subsidized logs from the harvesters. The US also commented that the last sentence of the preceding paragraph 7.73 referred to arm's-length purchases of timber from private lands or from US suppliers, not purchases of Crown timber. The US therefore requested the Panel to revise the first sentence of paragraph 7.74. Canada commented that in its view the Panel's factual conclusion in paragraph 7.74 was correct and that the US was simply disagreeing with the Panel's appreciation of the evidence on the record. Moreover, Canada argued that the passage quoted by the Panel in the last sentence of paragraph 7.73 also referred to lumber producers purchasing logs at arm's-length in addition to lumber producers purchasing logs from private lands and US suppliers. We considered that the facts set out in paragraph 7.73, which had been confirmed by the US in its answers to questions from the Panel, were not contested. According to these uncontested facts, a certain percentage of Crown timber harvest is done by independent harvesters (i.e. harvesters that are not related to lumber producers). As the evidence on the record showed, this percentage differed from province to province. In the first sentence of paragraph 7.74, we only summarized that the factual information provided to us by the US in the course of the proceedings showed that in a certain number of cases, the lumber producers were independent from the tenure harvesters and may have had to pay an arm's-length price to obtain the logs from the harvesters. We acknowledge that the US has on various occasions during the proceedings argued that the evidence does not support Canada's claim that there is a significant volume of Crown timber that the provincial governments provide to truly independent loggers who then sell the timber at arm's-length to the lumber mills. However, as paragraph 7.74 did not state that the US conceded that there was a significant number of such transactions nor that the US conceded that these transactions were "actual" arm's-length transactions between "truly" independent harvesters, we saw no reason to amend the text of paragraph 7.74 as suggested by the US.

6.5 The United States finally requested a change to footnote 146 regarding the US position. We decided to amend this sentence taking into account the comment made.

VII. FINDINGS

7.1 Canada is challenging the imposition of provisional measures by the United States on imports of softwood lumber from Canada on the basis of the United States Department of Commerce (USDOC) Preliminary Countervailing Duty Determination (hereafter: the "Preliminary Determination") and the USDOC Preliminary Determination of Critical Circumstances (hereafter: the "Preliminary Critical Circumstances Determination"). In addition, Canada is challenging certain provisions of the US laws and regulations concerning expedited and administrative reviews. We will discuss these three sets of claims in the order in which they were presented to us by Canada. We will therefore first address the first set of claims which relates to the preliminary findings and determinations of the USDOC concerning subsidization of softwood lumber from Canada as set out in the USDOC Preliminary Determination. We will then discuss the second set of claims which concerns the USDOC's preliminary determination of the existence of critical circumstances which formed the basis for the retroactive application of provisional measures in this case. Finally, we will examine the third and final set of claims which refers to the consistency of the US legislation with the WTO Agreement, in particular, US countervailing duty laws and regulations on expedited and administrative reviews as well as the application of the legislation in the challenged investigation of softwood lumber from Canada.

7.2 As a preliminary matter, we note that in the course of these proceedings, we decided to accept for consideration one unsolicited *amicus curiae* brief from a Canadian non-governmental organization, the *Interior Alliance*. This brief was submitted to us prior to the first substantive meeting of the Panel with the parties and the parties and third parties were given an opportunity to comment on this *amicus curiae* brief. After this meeting, we received three additional unsolicited *amicus curiae* briefs. For reasons relating to the timing of these submissions, we decided not to accept any of these later briefs.

A. *Claims Relating to the Preliminary Countervailing Duty Determination*

1. *Introduction*

7.3 Canada is challenging the USDOC's Preliminary Countervailing Duty Determination with respect to certain softwood lumber from Canada of 9 August 2001. Canada argues that the USDOC preliminary findings and determinations and the imposition of provisional measures by the US are inconsistent with its obligations under the Agreement on Subsidies and Countervailing Measures ("*SCM Agreement*") because:

(a) the Canadian "stumpage"[26] practices in question are not "subsidies" as defined in Article 1 of the *SCM Agreement*. Specifically:

- "stumpage" is not a "financial contribution" within the meaning of Article 1.1(a) of the *SCM Agreement,*
- even if stumpage were a financial contribution, the USDOC's determination and measurement of a "benefit" is based on a "cross-border" methodology that is not permitted by the *SCM Agreement*, and
- even if a cross-border methodology were permitted, the USDOC's determination assumes holders of harvesting rights pass through an alleged benefit to softwood lumber producers, without any basis for the assumption;

(b) the USDOC impermissibly inflated the alleged subsidy rate by calculating a country-wide rate based on only a portion of Canadian production and exports of softwood lumber[27], and

(c) the USDOC impermissibly inflated the provisional measures imposed by applying them on an entered value basis after having calculated the subsidy rate using first mill value.

7.4 Canada therefore requests that the Panel find that the Preliminary Countervailing Duty Determination of the United States in the softwood lumber case violates Articles 10, 14, 17.1, 17.2, 17.5, 19.4 and 32.1 of *SCM Agreement* and Article VI:3 of the GATT 1994.

7.5 The United States asserts that the USDOC correctly determined the existence of a subsidy to Canadian softwood lumber producers in accordance with the *SCM Agreement* as it found that the Canadian provincial stumpage programmes conferred a benefit on Canadian softwood lumber producers. The US therefore requests the Panel to reject all of Canada's claims relating to the Preliminary Countervailing Duty Determination.

---

26 Canada uses this term to refer to the "right to harvest standing timber on Crown land". Canada's First Written Submission, para. 18.

27 This claim by Canada related to the exclusion of the Maritime provinces from the country-wide duty rate. In response to a question from the Panel after the second meeting, Canada stated that it was "no longer pursuing its claims in respect of the "Maritimes" question in this proceeding". Canada's Answers to Questions from the Panel after the Second Meeting, para. 69. In light of this statement, we consider that there is no need for us to address this claim, and neither will we make any ruling in respect of this claim.

2. *Claim 1: Inconsistent Finding of the Existence of a Financial Contribution.*

(a) Arguments of the Parties

(i) Canada

7.6 Canada considers that the USDOC erred in determining that "stumpage" is a financial contribution in the form of the provision of a good by the government.[28] Canada argues that the practice of stumpage, which it views as a right to exploit an in situ natural resource, or more specifically, the right to harvest standing timber, is not a financial contribution. According to Canada, it is a form of a property right which cannot be equated to the provision of a good or a service by the government as required by Article 1.1(a)(1)(iii) *SCM Agreement*.[29] In Canada's view, rights such as *profits à prendre* and licences (two different forms of stumpage) are not included within the scope of the Agreement.[30] In Canada's view, the ordinary meaning of a "good" in the SCM and GATT/WTO context is tangible or movable personal property; and as an intangible real property right, stumpage is thus not a good. Canada also refers to the negotiating history of Article 14 *SCM Agreement* in support of its argument that harvesting rights like stumpage are not "goods".[31] Canada submits that even if one were to consider that in fact it is standing timber, rather than harvesting rights, which is made available through the tenure or licence agreements, standing timber is not a "good" in the sense of Article 1.1(a)(1)(iii) *SCM Agreement*. Furthermore, in Canada's view, the term "goods" in Article 1.1(a)(1)(iii) *SCM Agreement* has the same meaning and scope as "products" used elsewhere in the *SCM Agreement* and the WTO Agreement, in particular Article II of GATT 1994, i.e. tradeable items with an actual or potential customs classification. According to Canada, standing timber which cannot be traded across borders is, for this reason as well, not a "good" in the sense of Article 1.1(a)(1)(iii) *SCM Agreement*.

---

[28] The USDOC Preliminary Determination equates stumpage to the provision of a good. See USDOC Preliminary Countervailing Duty Determination ("USDOC Preliminary Determination"), 66 Fed. Reg., p. 43,192. (Exhibit CDA-1). Canada submits that Commerce's legal analysis and conclusion with respect to the requirement of a "financial contribution" consists, in its entirety, of two sentences:

> "We preliminarily determine that the provision of stumpage by the provincial governments constitutes the provision of a good or service under section 771(5)(D)(iii) of the [Tariff Act of 1930, as amended]. Thus, we preliminarily determine that the provincial governments have provided a financial contribution as defined under section 771(5)(D) of the Act to Canadian softwood lumber producers."

[29] In Canada's view, the cutting down of timber is the point at which the "goods" – logs- are produced from natural resources.

[30] Canada notes that a stumpage charge is not money paid to obtain the right to harvest timber, but rather a levy on the exercise of the existing right to harvest timber. According to Canada, it should be viewed as a form of revenue collection by the government and the equivalent of a tax. Canada's Oral Statement at the First Meeting of the Panel with the Parties (hereafter: "Canada's First Oral Statement"), para. 13.

[31] Canada's First Written Submission, para. 30. According to Canada, an earlier draft of what later became Article 14 *SCM Agreement* mentions harvesting rights separately from "goods or services". This, in Canada's view, demonstrates that harvesting rights are a category separate from goods. Canada argues that, as harvesting rights are not mentioned in Article 1.1(a)(1) (iii) *SCM Agreement*, but only "goods or services", the granting of harvesting rights cannot constitute the provision of a financial contribution under subparagraph (iii) of Article 1.1 *SCM Agreement*. Exhibit CDA-20, p.17.

7.7 In addition, Canada submits, to "provide goods" implies a positive action on the part of the government in respect of the goods themselves, and not any other action that merely allows someone to obtain goods or which has the same economic effect as the government action which consists of providing goods.[32] Canada asserts that the United States' broad interpretation of the word "provide" as "to make available" is untenable, for it offers an interpretation of the term "provide" that makes little sense in context and that is not consistent with the way that term is used throughout the WTO Agreement. Throughout the WTO Agreement, the word "provide" is used to indicate the giving of something, rather than more generally enabling someone to obtain or produce something. According to Canada, the more common meaning of "provide" is "supply".[33] Canada argues that, given the use of the word "purchase" as an opposite of "provide" in subparagraph (iii), this sense of provide, implying to give or to sell, is far more contextually logical than the general term "make available". Canada further asserts that the proposed United States interpretation encompasses a range of government actions that go far beyond those contemplated under Article 1.1(a)(1)(iii) *SCM Agreement*. According to Canada, to "*make available* services", for example, would include in the US interpretation any circumstance in which a government action makes possible the receipt of services. Canada submits that the financial contribution test is not concerned with the *consequences* of a government action, however, but with those actions themselves.[34]

7.8 Canada submits therefore that the USDOC Preliminary Determination that the right to harvest standing timber (stumpage) constitutes a "financial contribution" is inconsistent with Article 1.1(a) *SCM Agreement* and as a result violates Articles 10, 17.1(b), 17.5, 19.4 and 32.1 of the *SCM Agreement* and Article VI:3 of GATT 1994.

(ii) United States

7.9 The United States is of the view that the Canadian provincial stumpage programmes provide a financial contribution, in the form of a good, standing timber, to the softwood lumber producers in Canada. The United States argues that the ordinary meaning of a "good" includes an "identified thing to be severed from real property".[35] According to the United States, Canada is elevating form over substance when it argues that stumpage only confers the *right to harvest* timber. In the view of the United States, there is no meaningful distinction between providing standing timber as such or providing the right to harvest standing timber as the clear purpose of the stumpage programmes is to provide timber to Canadian mills that make lumber or wood pulp. According to the United States, the ordinary meaning of "to provide", the

[32] Canada rejects the United States argument that "the economic consequence of providing a good and providing a right to a good are exactly the same." In Canada's view, this argument follows the same faulty logic of the earlier argument of the United States before the *Export Restraints* panel that, "an export restraint is 'functionally equivalent' to an entrustment of or direction to a private body to provide goods domestically." Canada's Second Written Submission, para. 12, referring to *United States – Measures Treating Export Restraints as Subsidies*, Report of the Panel, WT/DS194/R, adopted 23 August 2001, at para 8.22.

[33] Canada points out that the Concise Oxford Dictionary does not list "make available" as a meaning for "provide". See *The Concise Oxford Dictionary of Current* English, 8th ed. (Oxford: Clarendon Press, 1990), at 962. (Exhibit CDA-79)

[34] Canada's Second Written Submission, para. 13.

[35] *Black's Law Dictionary*, 7th ed. (St. Paul: West, 1999), p. 701 –702. Exhibit CDA-17.

verb used in Article 1.1(a)(1)(iii) *SCM Agreement*, is "to make available".[36] In the US view, Canada is certainly making the standing timber available to the loggers by providing the right to harvest the timber standing on Crown land.

7.10 The US argues that there is no "natural resources" exception in the *SCM Agreement*, and that the provision of a good, like timber, thus constitutes a financial contribution in the sense of Article 1.1(a)(1)(iii) *SCM Agreement*. The only exception provided for in the Article is for general infrastructure. The United States asserts that the context, object and purpose of Article 1 *SCM Agreement* confirm that if the government provides a good in the form of a natural resource which constitutes the major input for a product, this practice is covered by Article 1 *SCM Agreement* as it is a practice through which the government has the ability to provide an advantage that would not be available on the market. According to the US, the "negotiating history" to which Canada refers in support of its argument that harvesting rights are excluded from the scope of Article 1 *SCM Agreement* is an informal discussion paper which does not shed light on the consensus view. The United States therefore requests the Panel to reject Canada's claim concerning the USDOC's Preliminary Determination of the existence of a financial contribution.

(b) Analysis

7.11 Canada claims that the USDOC Preliminary Determination that the Canadian provincial stumpage programmes constitute a financial contribution in the form of the provision of a good is inconsistent with Article 1.1 (a) *SCM Agreement*. Article 1.1 *SCM Agreement* provides as follows:

Article 1

Definition of a Subsidy

"1.1 For the purpose of this Agreement, a subsidy shall be deemed to exist if:

(a)(1) there is **a financial contribution by a government** or any public body within the territory of a Member (referred to in this Agreement as "government"), i.e. where:

(i) a government practice involves a direct transfer of funds (e.g. grants, loans, and equity infusion), potential direct transfers of funds or liabilities (e.g. loan guarantees);

(ii) government revenue that is otherwise due is foregone or not collected (e.g. fiscal incentives such as tax credits);

(iii) a government provides goods or services other than general infrastructure, or purchases goods;

(iv) a government makes payments to a funding mechanism, or entrusts or directs a private body to carry out one or more of the type of functions illustrated in (i) to (iii) above which would normally be vested in the government and the practice, in no real sense, differs from practices normally followed by governments;

[36] The US argues that according to the *New Shorter Oxford English Dictionary*, "provides" means to "make available" in addition to "supply or furnish for use." Exhibit US-5.

or

(a)(2) there is any form of income or price support in the sense of Article XVI of GATT 1994;

and

(b) a **benefit** is thereby conferred." (emphasis added)

7.12 Article 1.1 *SCM Agreement* defines a subsidy as a financial contribution by the government which confers a benefit. An investigating authority, in a countervailing duty (CVD) investigation will thus as a first step need to establish the existence of a financial contribution by the government. Subparagraph (iii) of Article 1.1(a)(1) *SCM Agreement* states that a financial contribution exists if the government provides "goods or services other than general infrastructure". In its Preliminary Determination, the USDOC stated that :

> "We preliminarily determine that the provision of stumpage by the provincial governments constitutes the provision of a good or service under section 771(5)(D)(iii) of the [*Tariff Act of 1930*]. Thus, we preliminarily determine that the provincial governments have provided a financial contribution as defined under section 771(5)(D) of the Act to Canadian softwood lumber producers."[37]

7.13 In order to determine whether the USDOC correctly concluded that "stumpage" by the government constitutes the "provision" to the Canadian softwood lumber industry of a "good", in the sense of the *SCM Agreement*, we consider that it is important to first clarify the exact meaning and operation of the Canadian provincial stumpage programmes in question. We will then examine whether these stumpage programmes constitute the "provision of a good" in the sense of Article 1.1(a)(1)(iii) *SCM Agreement*. We recall that in the interpretation of this provision we are guided by the customary rules of interpretation of public international law, as laid down in Articles 31 and 32 of the Vienna Convention on the Law of Treaties. Article 31 of the Vienna Convention on the Law of Treaties provides that "a treaty shall be interpreted in good faith in accordance with the ordinary meaning to be given to the terms of the treaty in their context and in light of its object and purpose".

(i) How do the stumpage programmes operate?

7.14 On the basis of the information and documents on the record of the investigation concerning the operation of stumpage programmes, including the forest legislation and various timber sales agreements submitted by Canada[38], and as clarified by the parties before us, we understand that most forest land in the covered provinces[39] of Canada is Crown land[40] and that interested persons who want to harvest on such Crown land have to enter into tenure or licensing agreements with the provincial

[37] USDOC Preliminary Determination, p. 43,192.

[38] Exhibits CDA-63, 64, 67and 68 are some examples of such provincial tenure agreements which, according to Canada, are generally representative of the long term and short term tenures found in Canada.

[39] We recall that the USDOC Preliminary Determination excluded softwood lumber from the Maritime provinces.

[40] The term Crown land refers to land that is not privately owned.

governments.[41] In general, such tenure and licensing agreements, the terms of which may vary slightly from province to province, allow the licensee or tenure holder (hereafter referred to as the "tenure holder") to harvest the standing timber on a particular parcel of Crown land. In return, the tenure holders commit themselves to a number of obligations, including at a minimum (i) service and maintenance obligations, such as road-building and maintenance, and protection against fire, disease, and insects; (ii) implementation of forestry management and conservation measures, including silviculture and reforestation; and (iii) payment of a volumetric "stumpage charge " that is levied upon the exercise of the harvesting right.

7.15 The Canadian provinces as the owners of the land and the trees standing thereon typically employ these tenure arrangements or licenses to confer rights to harvest standing timber. Canada agrees that if any company wants to log trees standing on Crown land for *inter alia* further processing or sale, it will have to enter into tenure or license stumpage agreements with the provincial government. Canada further acknowledges that the tenure agreements contain various processing requirements as well as certain minimum and maximum cut requirements. For example, tenure agreements in Alberta, Ontario and Québec contain maximum cut limits. According to Canada, Ontario and Québec have no minimum cut requirements. Canada further asserts that some of Alberta's tenures also contain minimum cut requirements, but that they are not enforced. In British Columbia, licensees under certain designated types of tenures are subject to minimum cut requirements, which require the harvester to harvest plus or minus 50 per cent of the annual allowable cut for that licensee in any given year, and plus or minus 10 per cent over a five year period.[42]

(ii) Do stumpage programmes provide standing timber?

7.16 Canada seems to suggest that a distinction should be made between a government extending a right to take the trees from its land, and that government selling the trees as such. In our view, however, and according to the record, the trees which grow on the publicly owned Crown land are government owned.[43] We consider that there are a number of ways in which the government may be providing timber, by auctioning off the trees as such, by entering into short term tenure agreements or by concluding long term tenure or licence agreements. The conclusion of tenure or licence agreements is in our view one way in which the government supplies timber. When the government enters into a contract with a harvesting company whereby it allows this company to exercise this right and to cut the trees, it is in fact supplying trees, standing timber, to such companies.[44] The fact that the main purpose of the

---

[41] Exhibit CDA-69 for example includes Alberta's Forest Act. Under this Act, the Crown may provide the exploitation of timber in one or more of the following ways: through forest management agreements; through the sale of timber quota certificates; and through the issuance of timber permits.

[42] Canada's Answers to Questions from the Panel after the Second Meeting, paras. 33 –36.

[43] Canada states that "the Canadian provinces have title to the majority of public property and exercise exclusive jurisdiction to legislate in relation to the development, conservation and management of" *inter alia* forestry resources. According to Canada, "In the various provincial systems, the provinces retain ownership of the land, typically employing tenure agreements or licences that confer rights to exploit the resource". Canada's Answers to Questions from the Panel after the First Meeting, paras. 21 -22.

[44] It is interesting to note in this respect that a Canadian court has recognized that "Stumpage is the price a licensee must pay the Crown for its timber". *British Columbia v. Canadian Forest Products*

stumpage programmes is to provide trees to harvesting companies is confirmed by the various processing requirements as well as the minimum and maximum cut requirements in most stumpage agreements.[45] In fact, if a company does not cut and process a certain number of trees for a determined period of time, it risks losing the licence. We wish to note that we do not deny that the Canadian provinces may well be pursuing broader forestry management policy goals in addition to ensuring the appropriate exploitation of the forestry resources when entering into stumpage arrangements with the harvesting companies. Indeed, it is normal that when a government makes a financial contribution, including where it provides a subsidy, that there is a mix of policy objectives. However, the fact of the matter remains that, from the harvesting company's point of view, the only reason to enter into such tenure or licensing agreements is to cut trees for processing or sale. As Canada acknowledged, the main interest of tenure holders is the end-product of the harvest.[46] Ultimately, and in this context, from the tenure holder's point of view, there is no difference between receiving from the government the right to harvest standing timber and the actual supply by the government of standing timber through the tenure holder's exercise of this right.

7.17 Canada argues that even if one were to accept that the issuance of harvesting rights by the provincial governments is equal to the provinces making standing timber available to the loggers, this still does not qualify as the "provision" of a good. According to Canada, "to provide" means "to give" or "to sell" and not just "to make available". We note that both parties agree that the ordinary meaning of the verb "to provide" is "to supply".[47] Canada is right that the provinces do not provide logs to lumber producers when they make it possible for timber harvesters to harvest trees.[48] In our view, however, the issue is whether the provinces supply standing timber, not logs, to the tenure holders who harvest the trees and turn the timber into logs. In our view the only way to supply *standing* timber to harvesting companies is by allowing them to harvest the timber. We consider that this is precisely what the stumpage agreements do. We therefore find that standing timber is provided to the tenure holders through the provincial stumpage programmes.

7.18 In sum, and in the context of Article 1.1(a) (1)(iii) *SCM Agreement*, we are of the view that where a government allows the exercise of harvesting rights, it is providing standing timber to the harvesting companies.[49] From the perspective of the harvesting company the situation is clear: most forest land is Crown land, and if the company wants to cut the trees for processing or sale, it will need to enter into a stumpage contract with the provincial government, under which it will have to take on a number of obligations in addition to paying a stumpage fee for the trees actually harvested. We thus view the service and maintenance obligations, the obligations to

---

(8 February 1998). US Answers to Questions from the Panel after the First Meeting, para.13, footnote 31.

[45] A discussion of the minimum and maximum cut requirements per province may be found in Canada's Answers to Questions from the Panel after the Second Meeting, paras. 33 –36.

[46] Canada's Answers to Questions from the Panel after the Second Meeting, para. 37.

[47] *The Concise Oxford Dictionary*, ninth edition, Clarendon Press, Oxford p. 1102. See US Second Written Submission, footnote 5; Canada's Second Written Submission, para 13.

[48] Canada's Oral Statement at the Second Substantive Meeting of the Panel with the Parties, para 22.

[49] We note that of course there will be technical differences between the various ways of supplying timber, which will no doubt be reflected in for example the costs for obtaining the timber.

undertake various forestry management, conservation and other measures, combined with the stumpage fees required by the stumpage agreements, as the price the tenure holder has to pay for obtaining and exercising its harvesting rights.

(iii) Is standing timber a "good"?

7.19 We recall that Article 1.1 (a) (1) (iii) *SCM Agreement* provides that:

> "1.1 For the purpose of this Agreement, a subsidy shall be deemed to exist if:
>
> (a)(1) there is **a financial contribution by a government** or any public body within the territory of a Member (referred to in this Agreement as "government"), i.e. where: ...
>
> **(iii) a government provides goods or services other than general infrastructure, or purchases goods;**

7.20 We concluded above that when a provincial government enters into tenure or licence stumpage agreements, it is in fact "providing" the trees that stand on Crown land. The question we will need to answer next is whether the USDOC correctly determined that the supply of standing timber through the provincial stumpage programmes constitutes the provision of a good under Article 1.1(a)(1)(iii) *SCM Agreement*, in short, whether standing timber is a "good" in the sense of this provision.[50]

7.21 The term "goods" has been defined in many ways in various dictionaries. Black's Law Dictionary, for example, defines "goods" as "tangible or movable personal property other than money; especially articles of trade or items of merchandise ‹goods and services›".[51] Black's Law Dictionary adds that "[g]oods means all things, including specially manufactured goods, that are movable at the time of identification to a contract for sale and future goods. The term includes the unborn young of animals, growing crops, and other identified things to be severed from real property ... "[52].

7.22 Other dictionaries define a "good" as "personal property having intrinsic value but [usually] excluding money, securities, and negotiable instruments."[53] The ordinary meaning of the word "goods" is thus very broad and in and of itself does not seem to place any limits on the kinds of "tangible or movable personal property, other than money" that could be considered a "good".

7.23 In Article 1.1(a)(1)(iii) *SCM Agreement*, "goods" is used in the context of "goods or services other than general infrastructure". We consider that the context in which the term "goods" is used in Article 1.1(a)(1)(iii) *SCM Agreement* confirms the broad ordinary meaning of "goods" as tangible or movable personal property, other than money. In our view, the sentence "goods or services other than general infra-

---

[50] We recall that Article 3.2 DSU requires a panel to interpret the Agreement in accordance with customary rules of interpretation of public international law, as laid down in Articles 31 and 32 of the Vienna Convention on the Law of Treaties. Article 31 of the Vienna Convention on the Law of Treaties provides that "a treaty shall be interpreted in good faith in accordance with the ordinary meaning to be given to the terms of the treaty in their context and in light of its object and purpose".

[51] *Black's Law Dictionary*, p. 701 (Exhibit CDA-17). See also *New Shorter Oxford English Dictionary* (Oxford: Clarendon Press, 1993), p. 1116 ("Saleable commodities; merchandise, wares; [in singular] a type of merchandise") (Exhibit CDA-18).

[52] *Black's Law Dictionary*, p. 701 (Exhibit CDA-17).

[53] *Webster's Ninth New Collegiate Dictionary* (Markham: Merriam-Webster, 1991), p. 527. (Exhibit CDA-19).

structure" refers to a very broad spectrum of things a government may provide. The fact that the only exception provided for in subparagraph (iii) is general infrastructure reinforces our view concerning the unqualified meaning of the term goods as used in this provision.

7.24 The object and purpose of Article 1.1 *SCM Agreement* is to provide a definition of a subsidy for the purposes of the *SCM Agreement*. Article 1.1(a)(1) *SCM Agreement* provides that the first element of a subsidy is a "financial contribution by the government". Subparagraphs (i) through (iv) then explain that a financial contribution can exist in a wide variety of circumstances including, of course, the direct transfer of funds. But subparagraphs (ii) and (iii) show that a financial contribution will also exist if the government does not collect the revenue which it is entitled to or when it gives something or does something for an enterprise or purchases something from an enterprise or a group of enterprises. Subparagraph (iv) ensures that government directed transfers effected through a private entity do not thereby cease to be government transfers.[54] In other words, Article 1.1(a)(1) *SCM Agreement* provides that a *financial* contribution can exist not only when there is an act or an omission involving the transfer of money, but also in case goods or certain services are provided by the government. In short, Article 1.1(a)(1)(iii) *SCM Agreement* in its context and in light of its object and purpose establishes that a *financial* contribution also exists in case *goods* or *services* are provided which can be valued and which represent a value to the beneficiary in question. The word "goods" in this context of "goods or services" is intended to ensure that the term financial contribution is not interpreted to mean only a money-transferring action, but encompasses as well an in-kind transfer of resources, with the exception of general infrastructure.

7.25 Canada argues that rights to exploit *in situ* natural resources are not covered by Article 1.1(a)(1) (iii) *SCM Agreement*. Canada can not point to any provision in particular in the Agreement in support of this view, but instead reaches this conclusion on the basis of a working paper from the time of the Uruguay Round negotiations which explicitly mentioned *harvesting rights* separately from goods or services.

7.26 We note that the text of the *SCM Agreement* does not in any way provide an exception for the right to exploit natural resources.[55] The only exception from the term "goods or services" provided for in Article 1.1(a)(1)(iii) *SCM Agreement* is general infrastructure, not natural resources. Moreover, the paper referred to by Canada in support of its argument that harvesting rights are not covered by Article 1.1(a)(1)(iii) *SCM Agreement*, called Discussion Paper No. 6, is an "informal discussion paper" from the Chairman of the Negotiating Group on Subsidies and Countervailing Measures dated 4 September 1990, which together with six other "informal discussion papers" was circulated in preparation for the issuance of a revised version of the Chairman's draft text of the *SCM Agreement*.[56] Canada argues that this Discus-

---

[54] We note here the finding of the Panel in the case *United States – Measures Treating Export Restraints as Subsidies*, that "Subparagraph (iv) ensures that the same kinds of *government* transfers of economic resources, when undertaken through explicit *delegation of those* functions to a private entity, do not thereby escape disciplines". Panel Report, *United States – Measures Treating Export Restraints as Subsidies*, WT/DS 194/R, adopted 23 August 2001, para. 8.73.

[55] We agree with the Appellate Body that "a proper interpretation is first of all a textual interpretation". Appellate Body Report, *Japan – Taxes on Alcoholic Beverages*, WT/DS8/AB/R, WT/DS10/AB/R, WT/DS11/AB/R, adopted 1 November 1996, page 17.

[56] In particular Canada relies on the proposed draft for Article 14 .4 (A) which read in relevant part:

sion Paper reflects an understanding at the time of the *SCM Agreement* negotiations of the fundamental difference between tangible commercial inputs and intangible real property rights.[57] We note however that, as stated in the Chairman's Note accompanying the discussion paper, this paper was circulated solely to "facilitate" discussions and that it did not reflect the Chairman's view of "what may be included in the subsequent revision", nor did it "have any status relating [it] to the Chairman's paper."[58] The Note further states that some of the views expressed in the discussion papers "are purposefully provocative in order to make evident technical complexities and/or workability (or its lack) of certain approaches."[59] In our view, this Discussion Paper thus has little if any probative value, especially in light of the fact that the reference to "harvesting rights" as separate from "goods" was not included in the final text of the Agreement.[60]

7.27 Canada further argues that the reference in Article 1.1(a)(1)(iii) *SCM Agreement* to the provision of "goods" is to be interpreted as referring to tradable products for which there is a tariff line. Canada's argument in favour of such a very narrow interpretation of the word *goods* is basically that, in Canada's view, it is used throughout the GATT and WTO Agreements as an equivalent of *products* on which tariff concessions may be given under Article II GATT 1994.[61] Canada thus submits that standing timber which is not capable of being traded across borders is not a "good".

7.28 In our view however, although in many cases the general word "good" may indeed be used as an equivalent of the term "products", this does not imply that this necessarily is always so, precisely because "goods" is a term with a broad and general meaning. Canada refers to certain provisions which contain the term "imported goods", and concludes on that basis that wherever the term "goods" is used in the Agreement, it refers to products which are capable of being imported and traded across borders. We find no basis for such a conclusion in the text of the *SCM Agreement*. Although "goods" in Article 1.1(a)(1)(iii) *SCM Agreement* certainly includes tradable products, there is no reason to limit its meaning to only such products, par-

---

"(a) the amount of subsidy arising from government provision of goods, services, *or extraction/harvesting rights* shall be determined by comparing the difference between prices charged by the government to certain enterprises within its jurisdiction and the benchmark price ... "

[57] "Article 14: 'Criteria for the calculation of the amount of a subsidy'," Informal Discussion Paper No. 6, Negotiating Group on Subsidies and Countervailing Measures, 4 September 1990, p. 17 (Exhibit CDA-20). Discussion Paper No. 6 was based on US practice in subsidy calculation. See T.P. Stewart, ed., *The GATT Uruguay Round: A Negotiating History (1986-1992)* (Boston: Kluwer, 1993), p. 935 (Exhibit CDA-21).

[58] Informal Discussion Paper: Note by the Chairman, Negotiating Group on Subsidies and Countervailing Measures, 4 September 1990 (Exhibit CDA-20).

[59] *Ibid.*

[60] Neither do we consider that it is our task to guess what the drafters could have meant, if anything, by not explicitly mentioning harvesting rights alongside of "goods or services" in Article 1.1(a)(1)(iii) *SCM Agreement*. What is clear from the text of this provision of the *SCM Agreement* is that harvesting rights are not excluded in the same way as general infrastructure is.

[61] Canada argues that "this meaning of the term "goods" as articles of trade or saleable commodities is the only meaning that could have been intended by the negotiators of the WTO Agreements. The term "goods" is used throughout the Agreements, yet is nowhere defined. As evidenced by the "General interpretative note to Annex 1A" to the WTO Agreement "goods" subject to the GATT 1994 are those things in respect of which a tariff binding may be negotiated: in other words, tradable things. Accordingly, things that are inherently incapable of being traded across borders are not "goods" *for the purposes of the WTO Agreements*." Canada's First Oral Statement, para. 21.

ticularly where the immediate context in which the term is used does not suggest such a limitation. In particular, this provision states that when the government provides "goods or services", this constitutes a financial contribution. The "goods" in question are not imported or exported, simply provided by the government, and nothing suggests therefore that the goods in question need to be tradeable products with a potential or actual tariff line. Goods in this context are distinguished from services, and in our view the two cover the full spectrum of in-kind transfers the government may undertake by providing resources to an enterprise. Our view is reinforced by the fact that there is only one exception among all possible goods and services that could be provided by the government - general infrastructure – which is explicitly defined as not constituting a financial contribution. We thus find that there is no basis in the text of the *SCM Agreement* to conclude that "goods" in Article 1.1 is limited to products with an actual or potential tariff line.

7.29 In sum, we find that through the Canadian provincial government stumpage programmes, Crown timber is being supplied to the tenure holders. Standing timber is the valuable input for logs which may be processed by sawmills into softwood lumber.[62] In light of our finding that there is no basis in the text of the *SCM Agreement* to limit the term "goods" to tradeable products with a potential or actual tariff line, we consider that standing timber, trees, are goods in the sense of Article 1.1(a)(1)(iii) *SCM Agreement.*[63]

(c) Conclusion

7.30 We therefore conclude that the Canadian provincial stumpage programmes involve the provision by the government of standing timber and, as such, the provision of a good in the sense of Article 1.1(a)(1)(iii) *SCM Agreement.* We therefore find that the USDOC determination that the provision of stumpage constituted a financial contribution, in the form of the provision of a good or service, is not inconsistent with Article 1.1 *SCM Agreement*, and therefore reject Canada's claims in this respect.

3. *Claim 2: Inconsistent Determination of Benefit*

(a) Arguments of the Parties

(1) Canada

7.31 Canada argues that, even if one were to accept that the provision of stumpage constitutes a financial contribution in the form of the provision of a good under Article 1.1(a)(1)(iii) *SCM Agreement*, the USDOC erred in finding that the Canadian provincial stumpage programmes *conferred a benefit*. The USDOC compared the Canadian stumpage prices to those charged in the United States, which, in the USDOC's view, correspond with "commercially available world market prices". Canada is of the view that the USDOC's use of a benchmark for determining benefit based

[62] We note that even Canada seems to acknowledge that "goods" in subparagraph (iii) refers to "inputs". Canada's Answers to Questions from the Panel after the First Meeting, para. 7.

[63] We note that in its Sale of Goods Act, the Canadian province of British Columbia, the prime exporter of softwood lumber to the US, defines "goods" as including "growing crops, [...], and things attached to or forming part of the land that are agreed to be severed before sale or under the contract of sale". This definition seems to include standing timber as a good.

on conditions outside the country of the alleged provision of goods, was inconsistent with Article 14(d) *SCM Agreement*. Canada asserts that whether a "benefit" is conferred by the alleged provision of goods by the government (stumpage) depends on whether the Canadian producers were better off than other purchasers who buy the same good from other sellers *in the country subject to the investigation*.[64] Canada argues that a cross-border analysis using transactions in another country to determine the existence of a benefit, and to measure it, is inconsistent with Article 1 and Article 14 (d) *SCM Agreement*.[65]

7.32 Canada further asserts that there was sufficient information on the record concerning private stumpage prices in Canada that could have been used by USDOC in determining the amount of the alleged benefit.[66] Canada submits that neither Article 1 nor Article 14 *SCM Agreement* presumes the existence of "distortion" of any kind simply because there is a financial contribution by the government, nor does either permit dismissing an in-country benchmark because of a presumption that that benchmark is or might be "tainted" or "distorted" by the financial contribution in question.[67]

7.33 In addition, Canada argues, there are a number of factual differences between the rights and obligations involved in acquiring harvesting rights in the United States and in Canada which invalidate the use of the United States' system as a benchmark and which demonstrate that cross-border comparisons make no economic sense.[68] Canada asserts that a wide variety of complex factors affect stumpage rates, such as locational characteristics, timber characteristics, measurement systems, operating costs, differences in economic conditions and tenure holders' rights and obligations. In Canada's view, the USDOC failed to make proper adjustments and ignored other obvious differences between the two markets.

7.34 Canada, therefore, claims that the USDOC Preliminary Determination which measured the benefit under the "adequacy of remuneration standard" by reference to conditions in another country rather than the prevailing market conditions in Canada is inconsistent with Articles 1 and 14 *SCM Agreement*.

---

64 Canada's First Written Submission, para. 43.

65 Canada also refers to the protocol of accession of China which explicitly, and in its view, exceptionally allows for the use of a benchmark outside of China. In Canada's view, there would be no need to include such a provision in a protocol of accession if, as the US is arguing, the language of Article 14 already allows for the use of cross-border benchmarks.

66 Canada provides a complete discussion of the data provided by the Canadian provinces in this respect in its Second Written Submission, paras. 53 –62.

67 Canada's Second Written Submission, para. 35. Canada notes that the USDOC did not have any evidence of alleged price suppression, but simply relied on a erroneous translation of a letter of the Quebec Minister of Natural Resources which formed part of the petition, which in fact merely stated that public land stumpage charges could have an indirect influence on the private market. Canada argues that a doctoral thesis further relied on in this respect by the United States before the Panel is outdated and the information on which it is based has earlier been rejected by the USDOC in the earlier investigation of imports of lumber from Canada (*Lumber II*) as evidence of alleged price suppression.

68 This, Canada argues, USDOC recognized in the first three investigations on imports of lumber from Canada (*Lumber I –III*) in which, in an identical factual setting, it rejected the use of cross-border benchmarks. Canada discusses the practical problems relating to the use of US benchmarks in this case in its Second Written Submission paras. 44 – 52.

(ii) United States

7.35 The United States observes that, in accordance with Article 14 (d) *SCM Agreement*, the adequacy of the remuneration and the existence of a benefit must be determined "*in relation to* the prevailing market conditions in the country under investigation" and not necessarily "*in* the country under investigation".[69] The US argues that this "market" benchmark may refer to the entire market available to the subsidized producers.[70] According to the US, the concept of "prevailing market conditions in the country of provision" is sufficiently broad to permit consideration of prices for competitive goods commercially available on the world markets to purchasers in the country of provision.[71] The US argues that commercially available goods, both imported and domestic, compete in the domestic market and together constitute the supply available to purchasers in the country of provision, that is, goods that the purchaser could obtain in the market absent the government's financial contribution.[72]

7.36 According to the US, in this particular case, the provincial governments completely dominate the market in those provincial markets and are virtually the sole providers of timber. In the US' view, the evidence indicates that Canadian provincial governments so dominate the Canadian market for timber[73] that below–market government prices suppress prices in the small private market for timber in Canada. Therefore, the US submits, in the absence of market prices in Canada, the use of other prices commercially available to Canadian lumber producers on world markets is the only reasonable alternative. In light of the object and purpose of Article 14 *SCM Agreement* it would not make sense to use prices determined or influenced by the government to measure the adequacy of the remuneration for the goods. According to the US, the comparison in Article 14 (d) *SCM Agreement* is intended to identify the potentially trade-distorting artificial advantage resulting from the government's provision of a good, and the market conditions referred to in Article 14 (d) *SCM Agreement* thus relate to what the market price would have been absent the financial contribution. The US asserts that the USDOC used stumpage prices in various US states with comparable forests and adjusted such prices to reflect prevailing market conditions in Canada.[74] According to the US, the USDOC's use of US prices is supported by ample record evidence indicating that many Canadian companies do, in fact, import US logs and bid on US stumpage.[75] The US submits that US timber is

---

[69] According to the US, "in relation to" means "with reference to" and thus, under Article 14 (d) the prevailing conditions in the country of provision are a reference point, not necessarily an end point, for the market benchmark. US First Written Submission, para. 43

[70] The US refers to the Appellate Body report in the case *Canada – Measures Affecting the Importation of Milk and the Exportation of Dairy Products* ("*Canada –Dairy*"), *Recourse to Article 21.5 DSU* (DS103AB/RW, para 84) and item (d) of the Illustrative List of Export Subsidies in Annex I *SCM Agreement*.

[71] US Oral Statement at the Second Meeting of the Panel with the Parties ("US Second Oral Statement"), para. 7.

[72] US Second Oral Statement, para. 8.

[73] In para. 26 of its Answers to Questions from the Panel after the First Meeting, the US argues that the Canadian provincial governments' share of the market was 90 per cent or more.

[74] The US refers to the Report of the Panel in *Canada-Dairy* in support of its argument in this respect. Panel Report, *Canada – Dairy*, WT/DS103/R, adopted as modified by WT/DS103/AB/R on 27 October 1999, para. 7.54.

[75] US Second Written Submission, para. 27; US Second Oral Statement, para. 18.

therefore "commercially available" to Canadian lumber mills, and in light of the specific facts of this case, the USDOC's use of US prices for stumpage that is commercially available to lumber producers in Canada was appropriate and consistent with Article 14(d) *SCM Agreement*.

7.37 In any case, the US submits, only three provinces (Alberta, Quebec and Ontario) provided any information on private stumpage prices and such limited information was inadequate to serve as a benchmark for those provinces. Similarly, the US notes that it had no or insufficient information on stumpage prices in the Maritime provinces, the lumber originating from which the USDOC excluded from the investigation on the grounds that it was not subsidized.

7.38 For all these reasons, the US requests the Panel to reject Canada's claim concerning the inconsistency of the use of US stumpage prices as a benchmark to measure the amount of benefit conferred on Canadian lumber producers through the provincial stumpage programmes.

(b) Analysis

7.39 Article 1.1 *SCM Agreement* provides that a subsidy in the sense of the *SCM Agreement* shall be deemed to exist when a financial contribution confers a benefit. In light of our findings above concerning the USDOC Preliminary Determination that the provision of stumpage by the Canadian provincial governments constitutes a financial contribution by the government under Article 1.1(a)(1)(iii) *SCM Agreement*, we will therefore need to examine whether the USDOC determination that this financial contribution conferred a benefit was made in a manner consistent with the US obligations under the Agreement. The issue before us is whether the USDOC determined the existence and amount of benefit to the Canadian softwood lumber producers in a manner consistent with Articles 1.1 and 14 of the *SCM Agreement*. We recall that Canada raises two claims relating to the USDOC's benefit determination. First, Canada challenges the use of US stumpage prices as the benchmark to assess the adequacy of the remuneration and thus the existence and amount of the benefit. We will discuss this claim in this section. Second, Canada claims that the USDOC failed to properly examine and properly determine that the benefit was conferred on the producers of the subject merchandise, softwood lumber. This claim will be discussed in the following section.

7.40 In its Preliminary Determination, the USDOC compared the stumpage fees set by the Canadian provincial governments with stumpage sales prices in the United States in order to determine the amount of benefit to Canadian lumber producers. According to the USDOC, "The point of comparison for measuring the benefit from these types of subsidies is the market-place free of government interference".[76] The USDOC concluded that:

> "there is no market determined price for stumpage within Canada that is independent of the distortion caused by the government's interference in the market. Therefore we preliminarily determine that we cannot use private transaction prices provided by the provincial governments.
>
> Information on the record of this investigation indicates that there are prices from the world market for comparable goods which can be used

[76] USDOC Preliminary Determination, p. 43193.

> to determine whether the provincial stumpage programmes provide a good or service to softwood lumber producers for less than adequate remuneration. For the reasons detailed below, we preliminarily determine that stumpage prices from the United States qualify as commercially available world market prices because it is reasonable to conclude that US stumpage would be available to softwood lumber producers in Canada at the same prices available to US lumber producers".[77]

7.41 Canada argues that as a matter of principle a cross-border price analysis is not permitted under Article 14 (d) *SCM Agreement*. Even if it were in theory permitted, Canada submits that there was sufficient evidence on the record of private stumpage prices in Canada which, in accordance with Article 14 (d) *SCM Agreement* could have and should have been used by the USDOC in determining benefit. In addition, Canada argues that in any event, under the facts of this case, the specific US benchmark used, was not an appropriate benchmark because of the factual difficulty in comparing prices for standing timber in the US and Canada.

7.42 The US argues that the benchmark used by the USDOC is consistent with the guidelines of Article 14 (d) *SCM Agreement* since the US stumpage prices are commercially available to Canadian lumber producers and, therefore, constitute part of the prevailing market conditions for the sale of stumpage in Canada.[78] The US submits that the USDOC properly rejected private prices for domestic timber as a benchmark because the weight of the evidence at the time of the Preliminary Determination indicated that such prices were driven by the government-provided timber, the financial contribution at issue.[79] Thus, in the US view, such prices are uninformative as to the adequate remuneration inquiry, i.e., a comparison of the government price to prices otherwise available in the market *absent* the financial contribution.

7.43 Article 14 (d) is the relevant provision in the *SCM Agreement* for measuring the amount of benefit to the recipient by determining whether the government has provided a good or service, within the meaning of Article 1.1(a)(1)(iii) *SCM Agreement*, for less than adequate remuneration. Article 14 (d) *SCM Agreement* provides as follows:

Article 14

Calculation of the Amount of a Subsidy in Terms of the Benefit to the Recipient

For the purpose of Part V, any method used by the investigating authority to calculate the benefit to the recipient conferred pursuant to paragraph 1 of Article 1 shall be provided for in the national legislation or implementing regulations of the Member concerned and its application to each particular case shall be transparent and adequately explained. Furthermore, any such method shall be consistent with the following guidelines:

(a) government provision of equity capital shall not be considered as conferring a benefit, unless the investment decision can be regarded as inconsistent with the usual investment practice (including for the provi-

77 USDOC Preliminary Determination, p. 43195.

78 US Answers to Questions from the Panel after the Second Meeting, para. 85

79 US Answers to Questions from the Panel after the Second Meeting, para. 92.

sion of risk capital) of private investors in the territory of that Member;

(b) a loan by a government shall not be considered as conferring a benefit, unless there is a difference between the amount that the firm receiving the loan pays on the government loan and the amount the firm would pay on a comparable commercial loan which the firm could actually obtain on the market. In this case the benefit shall be the difference between these two amounts;

(c) a loan guarantee by a government shall not be considered as conferring a benefit, unless there is a difference between the amount that the firm receiving the guarantee pays on a loan guaranteed by the government and the amount that the firm would pay on a comparable commercial loan absent the government guarantee. In this case the benefit shall be the difference between these two amounts adjusted for any differences in fees;

(d) the provision of goods or services or purchase of goods by a government shall not be considered as conferring a benefit unless the provision is made for less than adequate remuneration, or the purchase is made for more than adequate remuneration. The adequacy of remuneration shall be determined in relation to prevailing market conditions for the good or service in question in the country of provision or purchase (including price, quality, availability, marketability, transportation and other conditions of purchase or sale). (emphasis added)

7.44 Article 14 (d) *SCM Agreement* thus provides that the provision of goods by a government shall not be considered as conferring a benefit unless the provision is made for less than *adequate remuneration*. The adequacy of the remuneration charged by the government shall be determined "**in relation to the prevailing market conditions for the good or service in question in the country of provision or purchase (including price, quality, availability, marketability, transportation and other conditions of purchase or sale)**". We find that the text of Article 14 (d) *SCM Agreement* is very clear: the adequacy of remuneration is to be determined in relation to *prevailing market conditions* for the good or service in question *in the country of provision or purchase*. It further specifies market conditions that have to be taken into account: price, quality, availability, marketability, transportation and other conditions of purchase or sale. The text of the Agreement thus clearly requires that the prevailing market conditions to be used as a benchmark are those in the country of provision of the goods, in this case Canada. The words "in relation to" in our view, mean "on the basis of" or "in comparison with" and indicate in this context that the adequacy of the remuneration charged by the government is to be compared with the prevailing market conditions in the country of provision. We therefore disagree with the US that "the prevailing market conditions in the country of provision are a reference point, not necessarily an end-point for the market benchmark".[80] The prevailing market conditions in the country of provision *are* the benchmark and operate as the reference point or the point of comparison for the adequacy of the remu-

[80] US First Written Submission, para. 43.

neration. We therefore find, on the basis of a plain reading of Article 14 (d) *SCM Agreement*, that the ordinary meaning of this provision excludes an analysis based on market conditions other than those in the country of provision of the goods, i.e. Canada.

7.45 We note that, in its arguments before us, the US "agree[d] with Canada that, as the text of Article 14 (d) states, the relevant 'prevailing market conditions' are those in the country of provision, not some other country".[81] The US argues however that "[b]ecause US stumpage prices are commercially available to Canadian lumber producers, they fall within the universe of benchmarks that can be considered for purposes of measuring the benefit from provincial stumpage, consistent with Article 14(d) of the *SCM Agreement*."[82] The issues in dispute are thus (i) whether the concept of "prevailing market conditions in the country of provision" includes *world market prices*, as the US is suggesting, and hence whether US stumpage prices are part of the prevailing market conditions in Canada, and, if so, whether a price benchmark for the purposes of Article 14 (d) *SCM Agreement* can be *exclusively* based on such prices; and (ii) whether the USDOC had valid reasons in this case to disregard Canadian private stumpage prices.

(i) Are US prices part of the prevailing market conditions in Canada?

7.46 In our view, there is no basis in the text of the *SCM Agreement* to conclude that the market conditions in the country of provision could mean anything else than the conditions prevailing in the market of that country, and not those prevailing in some other country. Article 14 (d) *SCM Agreement* does not just refer to "market conditions" in general, but explicitly to those prevailing "in the country of provision" of the good. The US argues, that because "conditions of purchase or sale" and "availability" are listed as market conditions in Article 14 (d) *SCM Agreement*, US stumpage which is available to Canadian producers and which may be purchased by Canadian producers is part of the market conditions in Canada. However, the fact that a good may also be bought on a market outside the country of provision, does not, in our view, imply that the prices for those goods in that other country become part of the market conditions "in the country of provision". To accept the US argument would imply that the phrase "prevailing market conditions in the country of provision" in fact refers to the world market conditions for the good in question, which is not what the text of the *SCM Agreement* says. In light of the clear language of Article 14 (d) *SCM Agreement*, the "availability" of the good, the "conditions of purchase or sale", the "price", are various aspects of the market conditions existing in the country of provision, and refer to the price for the good in that country, its availability in that country, the conditions of sale as they are prevailing in that country. In our view, the bracketed language in Article 14 (d) *SCM Agreement* specifies what the market conditions referred to in the preceeding sentence are, and, as is the case for the "market conditions", they also all relate to the country of provision, and not some other country.

7.47 We consider that a proper interpretation is one which gives meaning to all the terms in the treaty and does not reduce certain parts of the treaty to redundancy or

---

81 US Answers to Questions from the Panel after the Second Meeting, para. 82

82 US Second Written Submission.

inutility.[83] We consider that the US is reading Article 14 (d) *SCM Agreement* to mean that the benchmark to be used should be "market conditions" in general. In our view, to adopt the US approach that the market refers to the entire market available to the allegedly subsidized producers, would effectively read out of the *SCM Agreement* the explicit reference to the country of provision, as the country the prevailing market conditions of which have to be used as a benchmark.

7.48 In support of its argument that the "market", as generally referred to in the *SCM Agreement*, is not restricted to the exporting country, but rather "encompasses the entire market available to the subsidized producer or exporter", the US refers to item (d) of the Illustrative List of Export Subsidies of Annex I of the *SCM Agreement*. We note that item (d) of the Illustrative List establishes conditions under which certain instances of provision of goods constitute *export* subsidies. Thus, item (d) is concerned with a significantly different situation from that addressed by Article 14 (d). While it is true that item (d) of the Illustrative List contains explicit language requiring as a second part of the test that it establishes that the terms of provision of the good be more favourable "than those commercially available *on world markets*", we recall that item (d) of the Illustrative List is not before us in this dispute. The text of Article 14 (d) *SCM Agreement*, the provision that is before us, does not provide for such a world market test. The fact that in the different context of criteria for a similar measure to constitute a prohibited export subsidy there is an explicit requirement to look at commercially available world market prices, cannot mean that any reference to the "market" in the *SCM Agreement* necessarily refers to the world market, or some portion thereof, particularly when the language in the provision clearly states otherwise.[84] We note that the prices of *imported* goods in the market of provision can indeed form part of the prevailing market conditions in the sense of Article 14 (d) *SCM Agreement*.[85] But this is not the same as the price for those goods prevailing in the country of export. Nor does this imply that import prices necessarily can be the exclusive basis to determine prevailing market conditions. To us, the US chain of reasoning seems to be the following: Canadian lumber producers can purchase standing timber and logs in the United States, and some do, therefore, the prevailing US stumpage prices form "part of" the prevailing market conditions for stumpage in Canada, and therefore US stumpage prices represent and can be used as the exclusive benchmark for the prevailing market conditions for stumpage in Canada. For the reasons set forth above, we cannot accept such reasoning. In sum, we find that US

---

[83] As the Appellate Body stated in the *United States – Standards for Reformulated and Conventional Gasoline* case: "... One of the corollaries of the 'general rule of interpretation' in the Vienna Convention is that interpretation must give meaning and effect to all the terms of the treaty. An interpreter is not free to adopt a reading that would result in reducing whole clauses or paragraphs of a treaty to redundancy or inutility." Appellate Body Report, *United States – Standards for Reformulated and Conventional Gasoline* case, WT/DS2/AB/R adopted on 20 May 1996, p.23.

[84] The US has also referred to various statements of the Panel and the Appellate Body in the *Canada – Dairy* case. We are of the view that these reports are of little, if any relevance to the case in question as both dealt with certain provisions concerning export subsidies under the Agreement on Agriculture. We note that the Panel report was overturned on appeal, and that the Appellate Body itself rejected the use of world market prices as a benchmark. See Appellate Body Report, *Canada – Dairy*, WT/DS103/AB/RW, adopted on 18 December 2001, para. 84.

[85] We note that in its Third Party submission, the European Communities submits that "a proper analysis of the "market conditions in the country of provision" may include all commercially available alternative sources for the recipient, including the price for imports into that market". European Communities Third Party Submission, para. 26.

stumpage prices cannot be considered to constitute prevailing market conditions in Canada, the country of provision of the good (standing timber).

(ii) Did there exist valid reasons not to use Canadian private stumpage prices?

7.49 The US justifies its reliance on US prices as the benchmark by arguing that, although the use of Canadian private stumpage prices would have been the preferred option to calculate the amount of benefit, in this particular case it was not possible to use such prices as the benchmark because they were distorted and suppressed by the very large number of government sales. According to the US, the trade-distorting potential of the government's provision of a good can be identified only by reference to an independent market price, i.e., a price that is unaffected by the very trade distortion the test is designed to identify.[86]

7.50 In our view, however, the "prevailing market conditions" of Article 14 (d) *SCM Agreement* do not refer to a theoretical market free of government interference as the US seems to be suggesting. Article 14 (d) *SCM Agreement* provides that the "prevailing" market conditions in the country of provision of the goods are to form the basis for the comparison. The ordinary meaning of the term "prevailing" market conditions is the market conditions *"as they exist"* or *"which are predominant"*.[87] Considering that the only qualifier used to the "market conditions" in question is that they be "prevailing", we are of the view that the text of Article 14 (d) *SCM Agreement* does not in any way require the "market" conditions to be those of a hypothetical undistorted or perfectly competitive market.

7.51 Moreover, the chapeau of Article 14 *SCM Agreement* clearly states that Article 14 *SCM Agreement* establishes guidelines for the calculation of "benefit" *to the recipient*.[88] We are of the view that in order to calculate the benefit to the recipient, an authority is to compare the price the recipient paid the government with the prices prevailing in other market transactions. We do not consider that the goal of the examination of the benefit enjoyed by the recipient is to determine what the market price would have been absent the government's financial contribution, as the US is suggesting[89], or to measure the trade distorting potential of the government's financial

[86] We note, however, that, as mentioned earlier (para. 7.36 of our Report), the United States has recognised that US timber is commercially available to Canadian lumber mills. This assertion would contradict the US rejection of the existence of a competitive timber and /or lumber market in Canada.

[87] Concise Oxford Dictionary, Ninth Edition, p. 1084.

[88] We note that the US agrees that "As stated in the chapeau to Article 14, and confirmed by the Appellate Body, the benefit for purposes of paragraph 1 of Article 1 is the benefit to the recipient." US Answers to Questions from the Panel after the First Meeting, para. 41. The Appellate Body in the *Canada – Measures Affecting the Export of Civilian Aircraft* case interpreted the term "benefit" in the *SCM Agreement* in the following manner:

> "157. We also believe that the word "benefit", as used in Article 1.1(b), implies some kind of comparison. This must be so, for there can be no "benefit" to the recipient unless the "financial contribution" *makes the recipient "better off" than it would otherwise have been, absent that contribution.* In our view, the marketplace provides an appropriate basis for comparison in determining whether a "benefit" has been "conferred", because the trade-distorting potential of a "financial contribution" can be identified by determining whether the recipient has received a "financial contribution" *on terms more favourable than those available to the recipient in the market*." (emphasis added)
>
> Appellate Body Report, *Canada – Measures Affecting the Export of Civilian Aircraft,* WT/DS70/AB/R, adopted 20 August 1999, para. 157.

[89] US Answers to Questions from the Panel after the First Meeting, paras. 23 – 24.

contribution.[90] The text of Article 14 *SCM Agreement* does not require a general "*but for*" test to the prevailing market conditions. We are thus of the view that Article 14 (d) *SCM Agreement* does not require that the authority construct a market price that could have existed but for the government's involvement, nor does it allow the authority to decline to use in-country prices because they may be affected by the government's financial contribution.

7.52 We consider that if the drafters of the *SCM Agreement* had wanted to exclude the use of market prices in case of price suppression due to the government's involvement, they would have explicitly provided so, but they have not. The opposite is the case. As we found above, when it comes to the market conditions, the only qualifier in the text of the Agreement is "prevailing". Thus, the market conditions are those that are actually existing in the country and are those faced by the recipient of the financial contribution. The reference prices are those that the producer would have had to pay if it had to buy the goods now provided by the government from a different and independent seller.

7.53 We wish to note that even if in certain exceptional circumstances it may prove difficult in practice to apply Article 14 (d) *SCM Agreement*, that would not justify reading words into the text of the Agreement that are not there or ignoring the plain meaning of the text. In our view, the text of Article 14 *SCM Agreement* leaves no choice to the investigating authority but to use as a benchmark the market, for the good (or service) in question, *as it exists* in the country of provision.

7.54 Canada also argues that the USDOC was not justified in rejecting private stumpage sales in Canada as providing a benchmark for market conditions in Canada. We note that the USDOC in its preliminary CVD determination found that

> "the softwood harvest from Crown lands accounts for approximately 70 to 90 per cent of the stumpage sold in each province. Therefore, between 70 and 90 per cent of the good or service within each of the provinces is provided by the government."[91]

7.55 We conclude from this statement in the Preliminary Determination that between 10 and 30 per cent of the good within each province was not provided by the government. In the course of the proceedings before us, we requested further clarification from the parties as to the record evidence on the percentage of softwood lumber harvest in each province in Canada that took place on Crown land versus private land. The US stated that the evidence on the record at the time of the Preliminary Determination indicated that private stumpage sales represented 2 per cent in Alberta, 6 per cent in Manitoba, 8 per cent in Ontario, 10 per cent in British Columbia, 10 per cent in Saskatchewan and 17 per cent in Quebec.[92]

---

[90] We thus disagree with the US that the market conditions referred to in Article 14 (d) *SCM Agreement* relate to what the market price would have been absent the financial contribution.

[91] USDOC Preliminary Determination, p. 43195.

[92] US Answers to Questions from the Panel after the First Meeting, para. 39. At the second meeting, we asked both parties the similar question of what percentage of the softwood harvest for sawmills took place on Crown land. Both parties provided essentially the same figures as in the US response at the first meeting. The one significant difference is that Canada reported that in respect of Quebec, 77 per cent of the logs processed in sawmills came from Crown land, and 23 per cent came from private land or from outside Quebec. The difference between the 23 per cent figure reported by Canada and the 17 per cent reported by the United States as the non-Crown timber harvest is accounted for by timber from outside Quebec that was processed in Quebec. US and Canada's answers to question 1 of the second set of questions. Exhibits US-55 and CDA-107.

7.56 Finally, the US argues that as a practical matter, the USDOC could not have calculated the benefit on the basis of the private sales prices even if it had wanted to, since the Canadian provinces failed to provide the necessary information. We note first of all that, while the US has argued before us that private sales data were not provided, it is clear from the Preliminary Determination that this was not an element in the USDOC's decision to use a cross-border price analysis. In fact the USDOC clearly acknowledged that the Canadian provinces reported private stumpage prices but that "an examination of the information on the record demonstrates that the private stumpage prices reported by the Provinces do not constitute market determined prices ... ".[93] The alleged lack of information is thus not mentioned by the USDOC as a consideration which led to its decision to use a cross-border price analysis. In any case, even the US acknowledges that at least two provinces (Quebec and Ontario) did provide private market standing timber prices.[94] Nevertheless, even for those two provinces no private stumpage sales data were used as a benchmark, because of the alleged price suppression.[95]

7.57 Accordingly, based on our interpretation of the text of Article 14(d) *SCM Agreement*, which does not require the prevailing market conditions to be those of an "undistorted" market, we consider that the USDOC provided no rationale in the context of Article 14 (d) *SCM Agreement* for rejecting Canadian private stumpage prices as the basis for calculating the benefit.[96]

7.58 We note, moreover, that the domestic markets of the member countries of the WTO are not identical – nor are they expected to be – and that there is nothing in the WTO or *SCM Agreement* indicating that, in order to qualify as such, markets must meet specific qualitative requirements, as the US would seem to suggest. A contrary conclusion would lead to a result in which the importing country would have a very broad scope to choose another market, including its own, in order to determine benefit. Such a result would clearly distort the letter and purpose of Article 14 (d) and vitiate its intended application. We further note that using the US methodology for determining a benefit from the provision of government-owned resources that are not in themselves tradable across borders and not sold at public auction would lead to the virtual automatic determination of the existence of subsidization in a resource-rich

---

93 USDOC Preliminary Determination, p. 43194.

94 US Answers to Questions from the Panel after the First Meeting, para 29. In fact the US admits that a third province, Alberta also provided some private sales information, but asserts that "the only information Alberta provided was a two page excerpt from a KPMG survey" without any supporting evidence or source information. US Answers to Questions from the Panel after the First Meeting , paras. 30 -31

95 US Answers to Questions from the Panel after the First Meeting, para. 40. In addition, Canada notes that the four primary exporting provinces, among which British Columbia - which represents about 60 per cent of Canada's softwood lumber production according to the US - provided information to the USDOC demonstrating that they were operating their stumpage systems consistently with market principles. Canada adds that the information that for example British Columbia provided consisted of data on the volume and value of competitive sales of stumpage, sold through a competitive auction on the basis of price. Canada's Answers to Questions from the Panel after the First Meeting, paras. 62 –67.

96 The USDOC determined that "since stumpage fees on public lands are the price driver for the stumpage market in those Provinces, we conclude that the stumpage fees on private lands are largely derivative of the public land prices and are therefore distorted", and for that reason decided that they could not be used as a benchmark to determine the amount of benefit to the lumber producers. USDOC Preliminary Determination, p. 43195.

exporting country, even where the perceived price difference was simply a reflection of the exporting country's comparative advantage in the product

(c) Conclusion

7.59 We therefore find that by using prevailing *US* stumpage prices, which by definition do not constitute the prevailing market conditions in *Canada*, the USDOC acted inconsistently with Article 14 and 14 (d) *SCM Agreement* in determining the benefit to the recipient, and therefore also acted inconsistently with Article 1.1 *SCM Agreement* in determining the existence of a subsidy. As for the issue of the appropriateness of the actual adjustments used to calculate the benchmark stumpage prices in this case, our understanding is that Canada raised this point as factual support for its basic legal argument that the cross-border methodology used by the USDOC was invalid, and that Canada has raised no separate claim in this regard. Given this, and given our conclusion above, we do not need to consider this issue.

4. *Claim 3: Failure to Examine and Determine the Existence of Benefit to the Producers of the Subject Product*

(a) Arguments of the Parties

(i) Canada

7.60 Canada asserts that the USDOC impermissibly assumed that the alleged financial contribution to timber harvesters through the stumpage rights conferred a benefit on the downstream producers of softwood lumber. Canada notes that standing timber is harvested and processed into logs which are then processed in sawmills and pulp mills to produce a wide variety of products including softwood lumber, and that the lumber may then be sold at arm's-length as an end-product or sold to remanufacturing industries that make a vast array of products. Canada argues that it is not the case, as the US is suggesting, that all tenure or licence agreements require tenure/licence holders to own a sawmill. Nor are there in general any requirements either by law or by the terms of tenure that require tenure holders to sell to specific mills or to sell at specific prices or under specific terms and conditions. Canada argues that only in certain cases are tenure holders required to construct or maintain a facility with the ability to mill harvested timber.[97] Stumpage tenure holders are therefore in general free to sell their logs to unrelated sawmills.[98]

7.61 Canada asserts that the evidence on the record demonstrates that a significant portion of harvesting is done by entities operating at arm's-length from lumber producers, and logs produced by such independent entities are sold to lumber producers in arm's-length transactions. In such cases, according to Canada, the USDOC should have conducted a pass-through analysis to determine whether the alleged benefit from the stumpage programmes was passed through to the lumber producers.

7.62 Canada argues that the record indicates that for British Columbia, 30.09 per cent of timber from Crown licenses was harvested by companies that do not have sawmills (33.0 per cent if private land logging is included); in Quebec, apart from a

[97] Canada's Answers to Questions from the Panel after the First Meeting, para. 33.

[98] Canada's Answers to Questions from the Panel after the First Meeting, para. 34. According to Canada, the exception is Quebec where under the Timber Supply Forest Management Agreement mills hold the tenure and timber harvested under that tenure must be processed at that mill.

certain type of tenures (Timber Supply Forest Management Agreement (TSFMA) tenures in particular), 27 per cent of the provincial harvest was sold through arm's-length transactions from private lands and Forest Management Contracts (FMC); in Ontario, 30 per cent of harvested timber from Crown land was sold to third parties who processed it into forest products; in Alberta, 6 per cent of total softwood logs harvest were sold at arm's-length in the sense that the transactions were between totally unrelated parties. Canada argues in addition that at least 8 primary mills requested an exclusion as they purchased all their log inputs in arm's-length transactions. Canada further asserts that a large number of unaffiliated remanufacturers purchase lumber in arm's-length transactions from lumber producers. Canada argues that in those arm's-length transactions, any alleged benefit to the lumber producers would not be passed through to the remanufacturers and that, therefore, remanufactured products cannot be presumed to be subsidized.[99] In any case, Canada submits, even prices between related parties may and often are also arm's-length prices because they are freely negotiated without regard to any relationship of the parties.[100]

7.63 According to Canada, when transactions take place at arm's-length, the recipient of a subsidy is presumed to have retained the benefit. Canada submits that since the USDOC failed to conduct an analysis of whether any benefits were passed along in such arm's-length transactions in the case at hand, its finding of a benefit conferred to the Canadian softwood lumber producers by the alleged provision of stumpage to the upstream log producers is inconsistent with the *SCM Agreement*.[101]

(ii) United States

7.64 The United States proffers two main arguments against the need for a pass-through analysis for determining benefit to the lumber producers. First, the US argues that no truly arm's-length transactions between independent harvesters and independent lumber mills existed. Second, the US asserts that a pass-through analysis was not required in this case as the investigation was conducted on an aggregate basis.

7.65 Concerning the first point, the US argues that no pass-through analysis was required because the subsidies were bestowed directly on the producers of the subject merchandise, since the entity receiving the financial contribution (standing timber) and the entity receiving the benefit (a below-market stumpage price) are "generally one and the same".[102] The United States asserts that a very significant number of tim-

---

99 Canada's Second Written Submission, para. 83.

100 Canada's Answers to Questions from the Panel after the First Meeting, para. 49 –61.

101 Canada argues that a subsidy is either direct in the case it confers a benefit on the recipient thereof (Article 1.1(a)(iii)), or is indirect in case a private entity is entrusted or directed by government to provide goods in a manner that confers a benefit (Article 1.1 (a) (iv)). In Canada's view, since in this case the alleged financial contribution (standing timber) was provided to the log producers and not to the downstream lumber producers, Article 1.1(a)(iv) SCM concerning indirect subsidies applies. In such a case, Canada argues, an investigating authority must also always establish both elements of a subsidy as regards a downstream producer that has allegedly been subsidized: a financial contribution to that downstream producer, and a benefit. According to Canada, in addition to failing to determine any benefit, the USDOC failed to establish that the lumber producers received a financial contribution, as it did not demonstrate that the Canadian provinces directed the log producers to provide a financial contribution (logs) to the lumber producers. Canada's Answers to Questions from the Panel after the First Meeting, para. 81.

102 US Answers to Questions from the Panel after the First Meeting , para. 43.

ber harvesters also own sawmills and are therefore at the same time producers of softwood lumber. In other words, according to the US, most lumber producers are also harvesters of standing timber, which they obtain through the conclusion of tenure agreements with the Canadian provincial governments. The United States asserts that in fact each Canadian province generally requires that tenure holders be sawmills or own a sawmill.[103] The small portion of Crown timber harvested by tenure holders that do not own sawmills is subject to restrictions that tie the timber to specific sawmills in Canada.[104] In such circumstances, the US argues, the loggers and the lumber producers (sawmills) are thus not operating at arm's-length with each other[105], and there is no need to examine the pass-through issue. Thus, according to the US, the evidence indicates that there are virtually no truly arm's-length transactions between harvesters and lumber mills, and the independent logger is therefore "largely a myth".[106]

7.66 The US argues that, in Canada's view, in two other situations involving arm's-length transactions a pass-through analysis was required:(i) in case logs are harvested by one sawmill and then sold at arm's-length to another sawmill, and (ii) when lumber is sold at arm's-length to companies that produce remanufactured lumber products. The US submits that in those two situations, no pass-through analysis is required in an aggregate case as all of the entities involved are producers of the subject merchandise.[107] The US is of the view that for remanufacturers who produce merchandise within the scope of the investigation, it is only in the context of determining a company-specific subsidy rate that a pass-through analysis may be necessary.[108] The US asserts that, as a result, the USDOC did not request any information on these types of transactions. According to the US, the precise amount of the benefit received by individual producers (for example, whether the benefit stayed with the original recipient or "travelled to" the purchaser) would only be determined in a company-specific review.

7.67 In sum, the US argues that, given this evidence, it was not necessary for the USDOC to conduct a pass-through analysis in order to determine the existence of benefit to Canadian softwood lumber producers by the government provision of stumpage.[109]

---

[103] US Answers to Questions from the Panel after the First Meeting, para. 1.

[104] US Answers to Questions from the Panel after the First Meeting, para. 9.

[105] US Answers to Questions from the Panel after the First Meeting, para. 87.

[106] US Answers to Questions from the Panel after the First Meeting, para. 44.

[107] US Answers to Questions from the Panel after the First Meeting, para. 48. According to the US, "in an aggregate case, the Commerce Department determines the total amount of the subsidy to producers of the subject merchandise and allocates that amount over all sales of the subject merchandise. Thus, when all of the alleged recipients of the financial contribution and the benefits are producers of the subject merchandise, no further analysis is required to perform the aggregate calculation. Benefits that potentially shift from one producer to another in an arm's-length transaction would still be part of the overall numerator (either remaining with the original recipient or "traveling to" the purchaser), as long as both companies produce subject merchandise". US Answers to Questions from the Panel after the First Meeting, para 76.

[108] US Answers to Questions from the Panel after the First Meeting, para. 50.

[109] The US argues that if the government made the financial contribution to an entity that does not produce the subject merchandise, it would be necessary to analyse whether that financial contribution benefited another entity that does produce the subject merchandise. In this case, according to the US, the only allegation of a financial contribution to an entity that does not produce the subject merchandise is Canada's claim that there is a significant volume of Crown timber that the provincial govern-

(b) Analysis

7.68 Article 1.1 (b) *SCM Agreement* establishes that a subsidy shall be deemed to exist if there is a financial contribution by the government and a benefit is thereby conferred on the producers of this subject product, in this case softwood lumber. The USDOC determined that the provision of stumpage, standing timber, constituted a financial contribution by the government. However, the subject product of the USDOC's countervailing duty investigation is the downstream product, softwood lumber, which is processed from logs, which in turn have been processed from standing timber. The various forms of stumpage agreements in the form of tenures or licenses are all concluded between timber harvesting companies/loggers and the provincial governments.

7.69 We consider that the question before us is whether under the facts of this case, the USDOC was required to examine whether, in certain transactions covered by the investigation, some or all of the alleged benefit to the tenure holders from the stumpage programmes was passed through to the producers of the subject merchandise exported to the US. These transactions were not only the case where a sawmill buys logs in an arm's-length transaction but also where a re-manufacturer buys lumber for further processing in an arm's-length transaction. Thus, conceptually, for some remanufactured products that are subject merchandise the issue of quantifying pass-through of benefit could involve two separate arm's-length transactions.

7.70 We note that the US agrees that if a government makes a financial contribution to an entity which does not produce the subject merchandise, it would be necessary to analyze whether that financial contribution benefitted another entity that does produce the subject merchandise.[110] The US also acknowledges that, in theory, an arm's-length transaction between an independent tenure holder and an unrelated lumber mill may give rise to the issue of whether the financial contribution to the tenure holder conferred a benefit on the lumber producer.

7.71 We are of the view that an authority may not assume that a subsidy provided to producers of the "upstream" input product automatically benefits unrelated producers of downstream products, especially if there is evidence on the record of arm's-length transactions between the two.[111] Rather, we consider that in such circumstances the investigating authority should examine whether and to what extent the subsidies bestowed on the upstream producers benefited the downstream producers. In this respect, we recall that in the *US – Lead and Bismuth II* case (WT/DS138/AB/R) the Appellate Body concluded in a different context involving subsidies provided to entities subsequently privatized, that an entity other than the original recipient of the subsidy should not be deemed to have received a benefit in

ments provide to independent loggers who then sell the timber at arm's-length to lumber mills. However, the US submits, the evidence does not support Canada's claim. The US refers to its discussion in paras. 1–11 of its answers to questions from the Panel. US Answers to Questions from the Panel after the First Meeting, paras. 46 –47.

[110] US Answers to Questions from the Panel after the First Meeting, para. 46.

[111] We note that in the *United States - Pork* case, the Panel stated that the parties "did not dispute that Canada had granted subsidies to swine producers, that swine producers and pork producers are separate industries operating at arm's-length and that the subsidies granted to swine producers could have indirectly bestowed a subsidy on the production of pork". For all these reasons, the Panel concluded that the DOC should have examined whether and to what extent the subsidies bestowed on the upstream producers benefited the downstream producers. Panel Report, *United States, Countervailing Duties on Fresh, Chilled and Frozen Pork from Canada*, DS7/R, adopted on 11 July 1991, 38S/45.

the case where an arm's-length price was paid to acquire the entity that had received the subsidies:

> "68. The question whether a "financial contribution" confers a "benefit" depends, therefore, on whether the recipient has received a "financial contribution" on terms more favourable than those available to the recipient in the market. In the present case, the Panel made factual findings that UES and BSplc/BSES paid fair market value for all the productive assets, goodwill, etc., they acquired from BSC and subsequently used in the production of leaded bars imported into the United States in 1994, 1995 and 1996. *We, therefore, see no error in the Panel's conclusion that, in the specific circumstances of this case, the "financial contributions" bestowed on **BSC** between 1977 and 1986 could not be deemed to confer a "benefit" on UES and **BSplc/BSES**.* (emphasis added)[112]

7.72 Canada and the US agree that the evidence on the record demonstrates that a large number of tenure holders own a sawmill and are thus at the same time softwood lumber producers. It is clear that in such circumstances of complete identity between the tenure holder/logger and the lumber producer, no pass-through analysis is required. Canada argues however that in a significant number of cases, lumber producers purchase logs at arm's-length from unrelated tenure holders. In addition, Canada argues that logs are traded at arm's-length between lumber producers and that lumber is sold at arm's-length by sawmills to remanufacturers who also produce the subject merchandise. According to Canada, in all these situations, USDOC failed to examine whether the subsidy passed through to the producers of the subject merchandise, softwood lumber. The US submits that the evidence does not support Canada's argument concerning independent loggers. As far as the two other categories is concerned, the US submits that the question of pass-through is moot in an aggregate investigation since all of the entities concerned are also producers of the subject merchandise.

7.73 We first examine the evidence on the record with regard to the relationship between the lumber producers and the tenure holders/loggers. The USDOC Preliminary Determination and additional clarifying statements of the US in the current proceedings reveal that not all logging companies are at the same time softwood lumber producers. For Ontario, the USDOC states in its Preliminary Determination that lumber producers may obtain the forest products they need in five ways. One such way is to pay the government stumpage fees and harvest the timber themselves, but another way is to purchase logs at arm's-length from a company that harvested them from

---

[112] Appellate Body Report, *United States – Imposition of Countervailing Duties on Certain Hot-Rolled Lead and Bismuth Carbon Steel Products Originating in the UK*, ("*US - Lead and Bismuth II*"), WT/DS138/AB/R, adopted on 7 June 2000, para. 68. We further note that the Panel in the *US – Lead and Bismuth II* case (WT/DS138/R) observed in a footnote that:

> fn 69. " ... a "financial contribution" does not have to be bestowed directly on a company in order to confer a "benefit" on that company. For example, one company may be found to "benefit" from a "financial contribution" conferred on another company. Furthermore, in certain circumstances an untied, non-recurring "financial contribution" bestowed directly on, and benefiting, a prior company may be deemed to have been bestowed indirectly on the successor company".
>
> Panel Report, *US - Lead and Bismuth II*, WT/DS138/R, adopted as upheld by the Appellate Body Report WT/DS138/AB/R on 7 June 2000, footnote 69.

Crown lands.[113] As the US clarified before the Panel, the record shows that for British Columbia, between 9 and 17 per cent of Crown timber harvest is done by independent harvesters.[114] For Alberta, the US states that 95 per cent of softwood timber was provided to tenure holders who own sawmills. This suggests that some 5 per cent of the timber provided would have been sold to sawmills by unrelated loggers. For Saskatchewan and Manitoba, the US gives a similar figure of 95 per cent of softwood timber which was provided to entities that also hold provincial licences to operate sawmills.[115] The USDOC also acknowledged that it received a number of company specific requests for exclusion, thirteen of which from companies "purchasing logs at arm's-length, from private lands, or from US suppliers".[116]

7.74 We find that the US has thus conceded before us that in a certain number of cases, the lumber producers were independent from the tenure harvesters and may well have had to pay an arm's-length price to obtain the allegedly subsidized logs from the harvesters. Nothing in the record indicates, and the US does not argue, that in such cases where the harvesters and lumber producers are unrelated, the USDOC examined whether the prices charged between the harvester and its customer, the unrelated lumber producer, were at arm's-length, and hence whether any benefit passed through. We find that in such circumstances, where a downstream producer of subject merchandise is unrelated to the allegedly subsidized upstream producer of the input, an authority is not allowed to simply assume that a benefit has passed through. We further consider that conducting the investigation on an aggregate basis versus a company-by-company basis is irrelevant to this issue. The fact that in the large majority of cases the lumber producers and the harvesters are related, does not imply that it is no longer necessary in cases where there is no such relationship to examine and determine whether a benefit existed for the independent producers of the subject merchandise including independent re-manufacturers. By failing to examine whether the independent lumber producer paid arm's-length prices for the logs that they purchased, the USDOC determined the benefit to the producers of the subject merchandise inconsistently with the *SCM Agreement.*

7.75 The US argues, with regard to the situations of sawmills buying logs from other sawmills at arm's-length and of remanufacturers purchasing lumber from unrelated sawmills, that no pass-through analysis was required as all of the entities involved are producers of the subject merchandise. In sum, the US position, both in the investigation and before us, is that in an aggregate case, no pass-through analysis is necessary where all of the entities involved are producers of the subject merchandise. We find no basis in the *SCM Agreement* for this argument, however. In our view, the purpose of the original investigation is precisely to determine whether and to what extent a subsidy has been granted to the producer of the subject merchandise. An authority cannot simply assume the existence of such a benefit in the original investigation. As the Appellate Body in the *Lead and Bismuth* Case stated:

[113] USDOC Preliminary Determination, p. 43203

[114] US Answers to Questions from the Panel after the Second Meeting, para. 18.

[115] US Answers to Questions from the Panel after the Second Meeting, paras. 21-23.

[116] USDOC Preliminary Determination, p. 43188

> "In an original investigation, the investigating authority must establish that *all* conditions set out in the *SCM Agreement* for the imposition of countervailing duties are fulfilled."[117]

7.76 Here we recall that any calculation of the rate of subsidization in a countervailing duty investigation involves three distinct steps. First is the calculation of the total amount of the subsidy provided during the period of investigation (the establishment of the numerator of the equation). Second is the calculation of the total amount of relevant sales to which the subsidy amount can be attributed (the establishment of the "sales denominator"). Third is the calculation of the rate of subsidization, by dividing the subsidy amount numerator by the denominator of relevant sales. The result is an *ad valorem* rate of subsidization of the subject merchandise.[118]

7.77 In this dispute, the US seems to be approaching the issue of pass-through of benefits as if it can be resolved solely by correctly identifying the value of relevant sales of the subject merchandise (softwood lumber) to be used as the denominator. This appears to be the reasoning behind the US position that a pass-through analysis for the purchases of inputs by unrelated producers of softwood lumber would be unnecessary where the calculation is performed on an aggregate basis. We disagree. In our view, the issue of pass-through has to do in the first instance with correctly establishing the amount of the subsidy benefiting the producers of the subject merchandise, i.e. the numerator. That is, alleged benefits from the stumpage programmes can only be included in the total subsidy amount to the extent that they benefit the producers of the subject merchandise, softwood lumber. Where a given producer of the subject merchandise itself harvests logs, and thus itself is the recipient of the alleged benefit, the entire amount of the alleged benefit to that recipient can be included in the subsidy amount (numerator) without further analysis. Where, however, a producer of softwood lumber does not itself harvest logs, but instead buys logs or lumber from unrelated suppliers, any alleged benefit from the stumpage programmes that may have benefitted the producer of the logs or lumber involved could only be included in the total subsidy amount to the extent that it has been established as a factual matter that the purchaser has received some or all of the benefit.

7.78 We find particularly important in this respect that, as Canada pointed out[119], prior to the Preliminary Determination, the USDOC had applications for exclusion from 98 producers who purchased logs or lumber from unrelated suppliers.[120] Of these, 78 were remanufacturers unrelated to firms with harvesting rights and at least 8 were first mills that purchased all of their log inputs from unrelated suppliers. In light of the fact that, at the Preliminary Determination, the USDOC had knowledge of a sizeable number of lumber producers purchasing log and lumber inputs from unrelated suppliers allegedly at arm's-length, the USDOC should have examined, in

---

117 Appellate Body Report, *US - Lead and Bismuth II*, WT/DS138/AB/R, adopted on 7 June 2000, para. 63.

118 This is of course without prejudice to other bases for calculating the rate for the levying of countervailing duties such as on a per unit basis, by using as the denominator the number of units of relevant sales.

119 Canada's Answers to Questions from the Panel at the First Meeting, para. 60.

120 *See* Letter to the Honourable Donald L. Evans from Weil, Gotshal & Manges, Certain Softwood Lumber From Canada: Company Exclusions, p. 3-4 and appendices A-F (August 8, 2001) (Exhibit CDA-44).

calculating the total amount of the alleged subsidy, whether and to what extent any benefit passed through to those lumber producers.

(c) Conclusion

7.79 In sum, we find that in this case, there was evidence on the record of a certain amount of sales by producers of logs that did not own a lumber-processing facility, and were not related to the downstream lumber producers to which they sold their logs. In addition, there is evidence on the record that USDOC was aware of the fact that a number of lumber producers buy logs or lumber inputs from unrelated sawmills We therefore find that, given such record evidence, the absence of any examination of these transactions by the USDOC was not consistent with the *SCM Agreement.* The USDOC should have examined, in the original investigation, whether, in cases where the tenure holders were not at the same time processing the logs in their own sawmills, the lumber producers benefited from the financial contribution given to the tenure holders. We therefore conclude that the USDOC imposed a provisional countervailing duty without determining the existence and amount of the benefit conferred on the allegedly subsidized product, and, therefore, in a manner inconsistent with the *SCM Agreement.*[121]

5. *Claim 4: Impermissible Application of a Provisional Duty in Excess of the Subsidy Rate*

(a) Arguments of the Parties

(i) Canada

7.80 Canada argues that the US *calculated* the subsidy rate of 19.31 per cent *ad valorem* on a *first mill* basis, but *applied* it on *an entered value* basis with the effect of significantly increasing the provisional measures applied to a considerable portion of Canadian exports of softwood lumber to the United States. Canada argues that in all of the subsidy calculations, the denominator was the value of sawmill (first mill)[122] exports. Nevertheless, in a decision memorandum[123] accompanying the USDOC's instructions to Customs, the USDOC claims that the record for the Preliminary Determination supports the collection of countervailing duty deposits on an entered value basis. Canada submits that this practice implies that the importer of the value added product faces an actual duty of above 19 per cent of the first mill value. This application of a duty in excess of the rate is inconsistent with the *SCM Agreement*.

7.81 Canada asserts that the statement by Statistics Canada on which the USDOC based its decision in this regard, which stated that the data provided related to both first-mill and "re-manufactu*rers*" reflects a typographical error. Canada argues that, in actuality, the statement which caused the alleged confusion intended to say that "it

[121] In light of this finding, we see no need to address the issue raised by Canada in footnote 101.

[122] Sawmills produce lumber from logs and ship the lumber to either end-users or downstream value-added re-manufacturers (final mills) that use lumber inputs and produce further processed lumber products..

[123] Memorandum from M.G. Skinner, Director, Office of AD/CVD Enforcement VI to B.T. Carreau, Deputy Assistant Secretary, AD/CVD Enforcement, re "Basis of the Countervailing Duty Deposit Rate," dated 31 August 2001, p. 3. (Exhibit CDA-31)

was not possible to exclude 're-manufactu*res* from its results." Canada argues that the actual calculation methodology in the survey makes clear that the data provided were in fact from a survey of "sawmills" (also noted as "first mills"), and that the discussion of the methodology further intended to explain that the data also included a small portion of remanufactured products that were produced *by the sawmills*. According to Canada, this is because Statistics Canada stated that it was unable to isolate the small portion of further millwork or value added that was performed *within* the sawmills, and therefore, such values were included in the reported data. Canada argues that it explained this clearly in its 21 August and 27 August submissions to the USDOC, *prior to* the time at which the USDOC issued its Customs instructions implementing the decision on a final mill basis.[124] However, Canada submits, even though Canada had fully explained that the data used in the preliminary calculations did not contain any final mill sales, the United States applied provisional measures on a final mill basis.

(ii) United States

7.82 The United States submits that the USDOC calculated the duty based on the total value of all sales (first mill and remanufactured) which was the information requested from and provided by Canada in the Questionnaire.[125] The US argues that the Canadian argument is flawed since the USDOC at the time of making its determination did not know and could not know that the information provided by Canada only referred to first mills, since Canada only informed the USDOC of this for the first time after the Preliminary Determination. As this is evidence and information

[124] *See, e.g.,* Letter from Weil, Gotshal & Manges, counsel for the Government of Canada, to the Department of Commerce regarding Certain Softwood Lumber Products from Canada: StatsCan Data Based on "First Mill" Values, dated 21 August 2001 (Exhibit CDA-96), where Canada explained:

> Confusion on this issue arose as a result of a statement in the GOC Questionnaire Response that, "[b]ecause the MSM does not collect commodity data, it was not possible to exclude 're-manufacturers' from its results." *See* Questionnaire Response on Behalf of the GOC, Volume I, Exhibit GOC-GEN-2 ("Calculation Methodology Summary") (28 June 2001) [Exhibit US-13]. As was explained in the meeting with the Department, however, this statement does not mean that the data on the record relate to any manufacturers other than "sawmills." Rather, when read in context (*i.e.*, in relation to the Monthly Survey of Manufacturing for the Sawmills industry), the explanation simply indicates that, if a primary sawmill performed additional manufacturing within its own mill, such additional millwork would be included in the data, because commodity details on the production of sawmills are not broken out in the survey. Any such further processed products of the sawmills would, moreover, be "first mill" products. As is demonstrated in the Attachment to this letter, the reported StatsCan data, which was limited to NAICS subsection 321111, do not contain any sales or production information for "remanufacturers."

See also Letter to the Honourable Donald L. Evans from Weil Gotshal and Manges (27 August 2001) (Exhibit CDA-46) ("As explained in [Canada's August 15, 2001 (Exhibit CDA-45) and 21 August 2001 (Exhibit CDA-96)] submissions, with the exception of insignificant amounts for first-mill further manufactured products, these data do not include shipments made by 'remanufacturers.'")

[125] The US argues that the USDOC asked for information on total value of sales and specifically requested to include information on remanufactured products, and that Canada replied that the information provided included both. US First Written Submission, footnotes 84 -85; Exhibit US-12 and US -13.

not before the USDOC at the time of the determination, the Panel cannot take it into account when reviewing the USDOC's Preliminary Determination.[126]

(b) Analysis

7.83 In light of our finding above concerning the USDOC's incorrect determination of the amount of benefit which formed the basis for the calculation of the countervailing duty rate, we consider that it is not necessary for us to address this claim in order to resolve the dispute before us and we therefore decide to apply judicial economy in respect of this claim.

6. *Conclusion on Canada's Claims Relating to the Preliminary Countervailing Duty Determination.*

7.84 In light of our conclusions above that the USDOC Preliminary Countervailing Duty Determination

- was not inconsistent with Article 1.1(a) *SCM Agreement* when it found that the provision of stumpage constituted a financial contribution, in the form of the provision of a good or service;
- failed to determine the existence and amount of benefit to the producers of the subject merchandise on the basis of the prevailing market conditions in Canada as required by Article 1.1 (b) and Article 14 and 14(d) *SCM Agreement*; and
- failed to establish that a benefit in the sense of Article 1.1 (b) *SCM Agreement* was conferred to certain producers of the subject merchandise, since the USDOC did not examine whether a benefit was passed through by the unrelated upstream producers of log inputs to the downstream producers of the subject merchandise;

we conclude that the USDOC' s imposition of provisional countervailing measures was inconsistent with the US' obligations under Articles 1.1 (b), 14, 14 (d) *SCM Agreement* as well as Articles 10 and 17.1 (b) of the *SCM Agreement*, as these provisional measures were imposed on the basis of an inconsistent preliminary determination of the existence of a subsidy.[127] We do not consider it necessary to address Can-

---

126 The US refers to the Panel report in *US – Measure Affecting Imports of Woven Wool Shirts and Blouses from India*, which stated that: "When assessing the WTO compatibility of the decision to impose national trade remedies, DSU panels do not reinvestigate the market situation but rather limit themselves to the evidence used by the importing Member in making its determination to impose the measure. In addition, such DSU panels, contrary to the TMB, do not consider developments subsequent to the initial determination. In respect of the US determination at issue in the present case, we consider, therefore, that this Panel is requested to make an objective assessment as to whether the United States respected the requirements of Article 6.2 and 6.3 of the ATC at the time of the determination". Panel Report, *US – Measure Affecting Imports of Woven Wool Shirts and Blouses from India,*WT/DS33/R, adopted as modified by Appellate Body Report WT/DS33/AB/R on 23 May 1997, para. 7.21.

127 Article 10 *SCM Agreement* provides that "Members shall take all necessary steps to ensure that the imposition of a countervailing duty on any product of the territory of any Member imported into the territory of another Member is in accordance with the provisions of Article VI of GATT 1994 and the terms of this Agreement. Countervailing duties may only be imposed pursuant to investigations initiated and conducted in accordance with the provisions of this Agreement and the Agreement on Agriculture".

ada's additional claims regarding the consistency of USDOC' s actions with Articles 17.2, 17.5, 19.4 and 32.1 of the *SCM Agreement* and Article VI:3 of GATT 1994. In light of our conclusions above, we do not find it necessary either to rule on Canada's claim that the USDOC instructions transmitted to the United States Customs Service on 4 September 2001, imposed provisional measures in excess of the subsidy preliminarily found to exist in a manner inconsistent with Articles 10, 17.2, 17.5, 19.4 and 32.1 of the *SCM Agreement* and Article VI:3 of GATT 1994.

B. Claims Relating to the Preliminary Critical Circumstances Determination and the Retroactive Application of Provisional Countervailing Measures

7.85 The second set of claims of Canada relates to the USDOC Preliminary Critical Circumstances Determination which formed the basis for the retroactive application of provisional measures in this case. Canada argues, first , that the *SCM Agreement* does not under any circumstances allow for the retroactive application of provisional measures, and thus considers that the USDOC Preliminary Critical Circumstances Determination is inconsistent with the *SCM Agreement.* In addition, Canada argues that the retroactive application of the provisional measures violated the disciplines of Article 17 *SCM Agreement*. Finally, Canada submits that, in any event, and even if we were to find that the *SCM Agreement* would in certain circumstances allow for the retroactive application of provisional measures, the USDOC failed to establish the existence of critical circumstances which would have justified the retroactive application of the provisional measures in question.

1. Claim 1: Retroactive Application of Provisional Measures is Inconsistent with Article 20.6 SCM Agreement and Violates Article 17.3 and 17.4 SCM Agreement.

(a) Arguments of the Parties

(i) Canada

7.86 Canada is challenging the USDOC Preliminary Critical Circumstances Determination on the basis of which the United States retroactively applied the provisional measures to entries occurring 90 days prior to the date of publication of the preliminary determinations, *i.e.* entries occurring in the period of May 19 through August 16, 2001.

7.87 According to Canada, a retroactive application of provisional measures inevitably violates Article 20.6 *SCM Agreement* as this provision only allows for the retroactive application of *definitive* duties. Canada argues that the plain and ordinary meaning of the terms of Article 20.6 *SCM Agreement*, read in context and in the light of the object and purpose of the provision, make clear that only definitive countervailing duties, if warranted, can be applied retroactively, and that retroactive application of provisional measures is simply not permitted. In addition, Canada argues that Article 17.3 *SCM Agreement* provides that provisional measures shall not be applied

---

Article 17.1 (b) *SCM Agreement* states that "provisional measures may be applied only if:

(b) a preliminary affirmative determination has been made that a subsidy exists and that there is injury to a domestic industry caused by subsidized imports;"

sooner than 60 days from the date of initiation of the investigation. Due to the Preliminary Critical Circumstances Determination, provisional measures in this case were applied to entries occurring within 90 days prior to the date of publication of the Preliminary Determination (17 August 2001), i.e. as of 19 May 2001. As a consequence, the date of application of provisional measures in this case was less than a month after the initiation (23 April 2001), thereby violating Article 17.3 *SCM Agreement*, which provides that provisional measures shall not be applied sooner than 60 days from the date of initiation of the investigation. In addition, Canada submits that Article 17.4 *SCM Agreement* provides that the maximum period of application of provisional measures is 4 months following the Preliminary Determination. According to Canada, as the US applied provisional duties retroactively for 90 days in addition to the 4 month period following the Preliminary Determination, provisional measures were applied for almost 7 months thereby violating Article 17.4 *SCM Agreement*. Accordingly, Canada argues, not only is the retroactive application of provisional measures not permitted under Article 20.6 *SCM Agreement*, but any such action by the United States also constitutes a violation of Article 17.3 and 17.4 of the *SCM Agreement*.

7.88 Canada therefore considers the USDOC's Preliminary Critical Circumstances Determination to be inconsistent with Articles 17.1(b), 17.3, 17.4, 17.5, 19.4 and 20.6 of the *SCM Agreement*.

(ii) United States

7.89 The United States is of the view that the retroactive application of provisional measures, in this case in the form of suspension of liquidation and the posting of a bond or cash deposits, is allowed under Article 20 *SCM Agreement*. The United States argues that both suspension of liquidation of import entries and the posting of bonds or cash deposits are necessary to ensure that it retains the possibility of exercising the right to retroactive relief provided for in Article 20.6 *SCM Agreement*. Suspension of liquidation alone would not be sufficient, the United States asserts, since, if no amount is guaranteed by a cash deposit or bond, Article 20.3 *SCM Agreement* would, on its face, preclude the collection of duties retroactively. The retroactive application of provisional measures is thus necessary, according to the US, to preserve the possibility and the ability to exercise the retroactive definitive remedy.[128] According to the United States, Article 20 *SCM Agreement* provides an exception to the timing provisions of Article 17.3 and 17.4 *SCM Agreement* relating to the maximum duration of the provisional measures and the earliest possible date of application of such measures. The US argues that Article 20.1 and 20.6 *SCM Agreement* establish an exception which, although not altering the date when provisional

[128] The United States acknowledges that there is no equivalent to the early measures provision of Article 10.7 Anti-Dumping Agreement, but argues that this only implies that a critical circumstances determination in the countervailing duty context may not be made as early as in the anti-dumping context where Article 10.7 Anti-Dumping Agreement allows Members to take precautionary measures "after initiation of the investigation". US Answers to Questions from the Panel after the Second Meeting, para. 57.

measures may be imposed, expands the universe of "entries" of the subject merchandise to which those measures apply.[129]

7.90 In sum, according to the United States, where provisional measures are imposed in accordance with the requirements of Article 17 *SCM Agreement* (i.e. after preliminary determinations of subsidization and injury), Article 20.1 *SCM Agreement* permits a Member to expand the scope of these provisional measures to encompass entries during the 90 days prior to the preliminary determination if there is sufficient evidence that the circumstances described in Article 20.6 *SCM Agreement* exist.

(b) Analysis

(i) Does Article 20.6 *SCM Agreement* Allow for the Retroactive Application of Provisional Measures?

7.91 The USDOC made a preliminary determination of the existence of critical circumstances on the basis of which it ordered the retroactive application of provisional measures. The USDOC accordingly directed the US Customs Service to suspend liquidation of all entries of the subject merchandise from Canada, entered or withdrawn from warehouse for consumption on or after 90 days prior to the date of publication of the Preliminary Determination, and instructed Customs to require a cash deposit or bond for such entries of the subject merchandise.[130] The US argues that both suspension of liquidation and the posting of bonds or cash deposits are necessary to ensure the possibility of exercising the right to retroactive definitive relief provided for in Article 20.6 *SCM Agreement*. Thus, for the US, the USDOC Preliminary Critical Circumstances Determination is consistent with Article 20.6 *SCM Agreement*.

7.92 Article 20 *SCM Agreement* provides as follows:

> Article 20
>
> *Retroactivity*
>
> 20.1 Provisional measures and countervailing duties *shall only be applied to products which enter for consumption after the time when the decision under paragraph 1 of Article 17 and paragraph 1 of Article 19, respectively, enters into force, subject to the exceptions set out in this Article.*
>
> 20.2 Where a final determination of injury (but not of a threat thereof or of a material retardation of the establishment of an industry) is made or, in the case of a final determination of a threat of injury, where the effect of the subsidized imports would, in the absence of the provisional measures, have led to a determination of injury, countervailing duties may be levied retroactively for the period for which provisional measures, if any, have been applied.

[129] US First Written Submission, footnote 103. Thus, according to the US, in a case of retroactive application, the period of 4 months during which the provisional measures are applied remains the same, but the amount of entries covered becomes larger.

[130] USDOC Preliminary Determination, p. 43215

20.3 If the definitive countervailing duty is higher than the amount guaranteed by the cash deposit or bond, the difference shall not be collected. If the definitive duty is less than the amount guaranteed by the cash deposit or bond, the excess amount shall be reimbursed or the bond released in an expeditious manner.

20.4 Except as provided in paragraph 2, where a determination of threat of injury or material retardation is made (but no injury has yet occurred) a definitive countervailing duty may be imposed only from the date of the determination of threat of injury or material retardation, and any cash deposit made during the period of the application of provisional measures shall be refunded and any bonds released in an expeditious manner.

20.5 Where a final determination is negative, any cash deposit made during the period of the application of provisional measures shall be refunded and any bonds released in an expeditious manner.

20.6 In critical circumstances where for the subsidized product in question the authorities find that injury which is difficult to repair is caused by massive imports in a relatively short period of a product benefiting from subsidies paid or bestowed inconsistently with the provisions of GATT 1994 and of this Agreement and where it is deemed necessary, in order to preclude the recurrence of such injury, to assess countervailing duties retroactively on those imports, *the definitive countervailing duties may be assessed on imports which were entered for consumption not more than 90 days prior to the date of application of provisional measures."* (emphasis added)

7.93 As its text indicates, Article 20.1 *SCM Agreement* provides that provisional measures and countervailing duties shall only be applied to products entering the country following the imposition of such measures, "*subject to the exceptions set out in this Article*". While Article 20.2 and Article 20.6 *SCM Agreement* provide for explicit exceptions in the case of the *definitive* countervailing duties, we find no similar exceptions relating to provisional measures. Article 20.2 *SCM Agreement* sets forth the circumstances in which definitive countervailing duties may be applied retroactively for the period during which provisional measures were applied.[131] Similarly, in critical circumstances, Article 20.6 *SCM Agreement* allows for the definitive duties to be assessed on imports which entered the country from 90 days prior to the date of application of the provisional measures.

7.94 Pursuant to the Preliminary Critical Circumstances Determination, the USDOC ordered the retroactive imposition of provisional measures in the form of the suspension of liquidation and a cash deposit or bond requirement. The US acknowledges in this dispute that such measures constitute provisional measures within the

[131] We note that the use of the term "countervailing duties" in Article 20.2 *SCM Agreement* reflects the distinction made in Article 20.1 *SCM Agreement* between "provisional measures" on the one hand and "countervailing duties" on the other. It is clear from the immediate context of the term "countervailing duties" in Article 20.2 *SCM Agreement* that this term refers to definitive duties, as the text of the provision juxtaposes the terms countervailing duties and provisional measures. "Countervailing duties" in the context of Article 20.2 *SCM Agreement* thus refers to definitive duties only.

meaning of Article 17 *SCM Agreement*.[132] We are of the view that the only two exceptions to the general rule of non-retroactivity of Article 20.1 *SCM Agreement* as set forth in Article 20.2 and 20.6 *SCM Agreement* do not apply to provisional measures, but concern definitive countervailing duties only. On the basis of the clear language in the *SCM Agreement*, we therefore consider that the general rule of non-retroactivity applies to provisional measures, without exceptions. We therefore find that the retroactive application of the provisional measure imposed by the USDOC is inconsistent with Article 20.6 *SCM Agreement*.

7.95 We agree with the United States that a Member is allowed to take measures which are necessary to preserve the right to later apply definitive duties retroactively. In our view, an effective interpretation of the right to apply definitive duties retroactively requires that a Member be allowed to take such steps as are necessary to preserve the possibility of exercising that right. What kind of measures may thus be taken by the Member concerned will have to be determined on a case-by-case basis. In this case, the US argues that both suspension of liquidation and the posting of a cash deposit or bond are necessary for the US authorities to be able to collect the duties retroactively. According to the United States, without suspension of liquidation, the products will have definitively entered the country and no duties can be assessed on such entries after liquidation. The United States further argues that the posting of a bond or a cash deposit is equally necessary because Article 20.3 *SCM Agreement* would not allow the retroactive duty collection beyond the amount guaranteed by the cash deposit or bond. In the view of the United States, if no cash deposit or bond is required, Article 20.3 *SCM Agreement* would imply that no definitive countervailing duty for the period preceding the Preliminary Determination could be levied either.

7.96 We are not convinced by the US argument in respect of the posting of cash deposits or bonds. We consider that Article 20.3 *SCM Agreement* states that if the amount guaranteed by the cash deposit is lower than the definitive countervailing duty, the difference shall not be collected. If the reverse is true, the excess amount shall be reimbursed and the bond released in an expeditious manner. Article 20.3 *SCM Agreement* thus concerns the wholly different issue of how to deal with a discrepancy between the provisional and the final rates of the countervailing duty. It does not address the retroactive imposition and collection of definitive duties for the period before the application of provisional measures. Article 20.6 *SCM Agreement* provides that definitive duties may in certain circumstances be assessed on imports which were entered for consumption from 90 days *prior to the date of application of provisional measures*.

7.97 The text thus clearly indicates that the Agreement allows for the retroactive application of definitive duties at a time when *no* provisional measures were in place and thus *no* provisional duties were collected. To accept the US argument that Article 20.3 *SCM Agreement* would preclude a Member from collecting definitive duties for the period prior to the date of application of provisional measures, would mean that a Member doing what Article 20.6 *SCM Agreement* expressly allows for, would be violating the Agreement nevertheless. We cannot accept an interpretation which leads to this contradictory result. We consider that the principle of effective treaty

132 United States Answers to Questions from the Panel after the First Meeting, para. 52.

interpretation requires the treaty interpreter to "read all applicable provisions of a treaty in a way that gives meaning to *all* of them, harmoniously."[133]

7.98 We therefore find that the USDOC retroactive application of provisional measures is inconsistent with Article 20.6 *SCM Agreement*, as this provision allows for the retroactive application of *definitive* duties only. In our view, and leaving aside the question which sorts of actions of a conservatory nature a Member would be allowed to take in order to preserve the right to apply definitive duties retroactively, provisional measures such as the requirement of a cash deposit or the posting of a bond are not necessary to preserve the right to apply definitive duties retroactively under the *SCM Agreement*.[134]

(ii) Does the Retroactive Application of Provisional Measures Also Violate the Disciplines of Article 17 *SCM Agreement*.

7.99 We next turn to Canada's claim pursuant to Article 17.3 and 17.4 *SCM Agreement* in respect of the date of application and the duration of the provisional measures in this case. These provisions read as follows:

> "17.3 Provisional measures shall not be applied sooner than 60 days from the date of initiation of the investigation.
>
> 17.4 The application of provisional measures shall be limited to as short a period as possible, not exceeding four months".

7.100 In our view, Article 17.3 and 17.4 *SCM Agreement* are unambiguous, clearly specifying that provisional measures shall not be applied sooner than 60 days after initiation and their application shall be limited to maximum 4 months. Article 20.1 *SCM Agreement* provides that provisional measures may be applied only to products which entered the country after the time when the decision under paragraph 1 of Article 17 *SCM Agreement* was taken, subject to the exceptions set out in that Article. In respect of the starting-point for the application of provisional and final measures, Article 20 *SCM Agreement* thus establishes two exceptions to the general rule of non-retroactivity of final countervailing duties and no exceptions to the general rule of non-retroactivity of provisional measures. Nothing in Article 20 *SCM Agreement* provides an exception to the rules relating to the minimum period between initiation and application of provisional measures or the maximum period of application of such measures as provided for in Article 17.3 and 17.4 *SCM Agreement*.

7.101 The USDOC initiated its countervailing duty investigation on 23 April 2001, and applied retroactive provisional measures on imports entering from 19 May 2001, i.e. less than 60 days after initiation. The USDOC applied provisional measures on imports entering from 19 May 2001, until 14 December 2001, which is 4 months after the Preliminary Determination. In total, the provisional measure thus covered imports for a period of almost 7 months. We therefore find that the US application of

---

[133] Appellate Body Report, *Korea- Definitive Safeguard Measure on Imports of Certain Dairy Products*, WT/DS98/AB/R, adopted on 12 January 2000, para. 81.

[134] We consider that the US argued before us that both the suspension of liquidation and the bond or cash deposit requirement are necessary conservatory measures, and we therefore have treated them jointly. We note on the other hand that Canada recognised that in a retrospective duty assessment system, Members "may keep liquidation open for a long enough period that would allow the retroactive imposition of definitive duties following a critical circumstances determination". Canada's Answers to the Questions from the Panel after the Second Meeting, para. 65.

provisional measures during the period prior to the 60 days after initiation, and for longer than 4 months is inconsistent with Article 17.3 and 17.4 *SCM Agreement*.

7.102 We consider that the US argument that the period of application in Article 17.4 *SCM Agreement* refers to the period during which cash deposits or bonds are taken rather than the period during which the affected imports enter for consumption would have the effect of nullifying the provision, particularly in light of Article 20.1 *SCM Agreement*. We cannot accept such an interpretation which would reduce a provision of the treaty to redundancy or inutility.[135] The US interpretation would allow significantly more than 4 months worth of entries to be covered by a provisional measure. For example, under this interpretation, a decision under Article 17.1 *SCM Agreement* could be taken after 60 days, following which the importing country would wait say 3 months before "applying" the provisional measures for 4 months, including retroactively to imports entering after the date of the decision. In our view this would render meaningless the disciplines imposed by Article 17 *SCM Agreement*.

(c) Conclusion

7.103 In sum, we find that the United States' application of provisional measures in the form of cash deposits or bonds under the USDOC Preliminary Critical Circumstances Determination is inconsistent with Article 20.6 *SCM Agreement*, as this provision does not allow for the retroactive application of provisional measures. In addition, we find that the provisional measures at issue were applied in violation of Article 17.3 and 17.4 *SCM Agreement* as they were imposed less than 60 days after initiation and covered imports for a period of more than four months.

2. *Claim 2: USDOC Failed to Establish Critical Circumstances under Article 20.6 SCM Agreement*

(a) Arguments of the Parties

(i) Canada

7.104 Canada argues that even if, in theory, retroactive application of provisional measures were permitted under Article 20.6 *SCM Agreement*, the USDOC Preliminary Critical Circumstances Determination is still inconsistent with Article 20.6 *SCM Agreement* since the USDOC failed to establish the existence of critical circumstances.

7.105 Canada asserts that the Investissement Quebec Small and Medium Businesses Guarantee programme (the "IQ SMB" programme) upon which the USDOC Preliminary Critical Circumstances Determination was based is not a prohibited export subsidy, as it is contingent upon developing markets outside Quebec, not outside Canada. Therefore the determination that the alleged massive imports have benefitted from subsidies bestowed inconsistently with the provisions of GATT 1994 and of the *SCM Agreement* is, in Canada's view, flawed. In any case, Canada submits, even if the IQ SMB programme were a prohibited subsidy, the amount of the subsidy found (0.005 per cent) is *de minimis*. Canada argues that Article 11.9 *SCM Agreement* pro-

135 Appellate Body Report, *United States – Standards for Reformulated and Conventional Gasoline*, WT/DS/2/AB/R, adopted on 20 May 1996, p. 23.

vides that a *de minimis* rate is an insufficient basis for applying any countervailing measure whether final or provisional, and the determination was thus made in the absence of any critical circumstances in the sense of Article 20.6 *SCM Agreement*.[136]

7.106 Canada argues that even if the IQ SMB Guarantee programme were a prohibited export subsidy, Articles 17.5 and 19.4 *SCM Agreement*, as well as Article 20.6 *SCM Agreement*, require that the rate to be applied retroactively to this programme should have been no more than the rate of subsidization under this programme, i.e. 0.005 per cent rather than the country-wide rate of 19.3 per cent. Canada argues that the text of Article 20.6 *SCM Agreement* allows for the retroactive application of only the rate that is commensurate with the benefit bestowed by the alleged prohibited subsidy. By applying a duty at this higher rate, the US countervailed to an amount in excess of that required to "preclude the recurrence of the injury" caused by such subsidies in "critical circumstances", which is the object and purpose of Article 20.6 *SCM Agreement*. The US thus violated Article 20.6 *SCM Agreement* as well as Articles 17.5 and 19.4 *SCM Agreement*.

7.107 Canada further asserts that countervailing measures were applied retroactively without a finding by USDOC or USITC of "injury which is difficult to repair" or that the retroactive application of the duties was "necessary to preclude the recurrence of such injury" in violation of the explicit requirements of Article 20.6 *SCM Agreement*. Canada adds that the USDOC itself admitted as much, as it acknowledged that these findings would have to be made by the USITC at the time of the final critical circumstances determination.[137]

7.108 Canada submits that the USDOC's finding of "massive imports" is flawed as it is based on all imports from Canada while the SMB subsidy programme applies only to shipments from Quebec. Moreover, in Canada's opinion, the increase in imports of 23.34 per cent following the petition was not due to the alleged export subsidy of a *de minimis* level but rather to the anticipated and then actual expiration of the Softwood Lumber Agreement between the US and Canada, which first sharply reduced exports in the first quarter of 2001 and whose actual expiry led to an increase in the second quarter. Canada submits that the retroactive application of provisional measures in the absence of "massive imports of a product benefitting from subsidies paid or bestowed inconsistently with the GATT 1994 and the *SCM Agreement*" is in violation of Article 20.6 *SCM Agreement*.

7.109 Canada finally argues that if it is permissible to include for purposes of determining massive imports, shipments that have not benefitted from the prohibited subsidy, an authority should include *all* such shipments and not just the portion of such shipments that an authority needs in order to find a high rate of subsidization. Canada asserts that the finding of "massive imports" violates Article 20.6 *SCM Agreement*, as it did not include all shipments from Canada, but rather excluded imports from the Maritime provinces, which would have resulted in a negative "massive imports" finding under the *SCM Agreement*.

[136] Canada asserts that the USITC recognized as much in a case involving certain steel products from Korea (Exhibit CDA – 36).

[137] USDOC Preliminary Determination, p. 43189.

(ii) United States

7.110 The United States argues that there existed a sufficient basis for a preliminary critical circumstances determination, especially as in its view the evidentiary standard in the case of a preliminary determination should be lower than in case of a final determination.

7.111 According to the US, one Canadian provincial subsidy programme was an Article 3- inconsistent export subsidy which was meant to promote economic development in Quebec by encouraging growth of exports. The US argues that the existence of a prohibited export subsidy suffices to preserve the possibility of retroactive application later, and the fact that this programme's subsidy rate was *de minimis* is not relevant in this respect.

7.112 The US further submits that, as no methodology is prescribed in the *SCM Agreement* for determining the existence of "massive imports", it was reasonable for the USDOC to consider an increase of 23 per cent as massive. The US notes that the USDOC's analysis in this respect took the expiration of the Softwood Lumber Agreement between Canada and the US into account and came to the conclusion that it did not have the distorting effect Canada is alleging.

7.113 The US finally notes that the USITC had already made a preliminary finding of injury before the USDOC made its Preliminary Critical Circumstances Determination. According to the US, the remaining conditions for the retroactive application of definitive duties, relating to injury which is difficult to repair, are necessarily determinations that can only be made at the time of the final determination. For the purpose of the Preliminary Critical Circumstances Determination and the retroactive application of provisional measures, the preliminary determination of injury by the USITC was sufficient.

(b) Analysis

7.114 Canada argues that "[e]ven if the Panel found that provisional measures could be applied retroactively under Article 20.6, Commerce had not established the existence of any or all of the elements required under that provision".[138] In light of the fact that we uphold Canada's principal claim by finding that the Agreement does not allow for the retroactive application of provisional measures, we do not consider it necessary for the resolution of the dispute before us to address the arguments made by the parties concerning the specific hypothetical conditions that would need to be met for such inconsistent measures to be applied. For this reason we apply judicial economy and do not rule on this claim.

3. *Conclusion on Canada's Claim Concerning the USDOC Preliminary Critical Circumstances Determination*

7.115 In light of the conclusions above, we find that the United States' retroactive imposition of provisional measures on the basis of the USDOC Preliminary Critical Circumstances Determination is inconsistent with Article 20.6 *SCM Agreement*, as there does not exist a basis for the retroactive application of provisional measures in the *SCM Agreement*. Moreover, the retroactive application of provisional measures in the form of a cash deposit or bond in this case violated Article 17.3 and 17.4 *SCM*

---

[138] Canada's First Written Submission, para. 116.

Agreement, as the measures covered imports for a period of almost seven months and were applied before sixty days after the initiation of the investigation. In light of this finding, we do not consider it necessary or appropriate to examine Canada's claims with regard to a violation of Articles 17.1 (b), 17.5 and 19.4 *SCM Agreement* and Article VI:3 GATT 1994.

C. *Claim of Inconsistent CVD Law Concerning Expedited and Administrative Reviews*

(a) Arguments of the Parties

(i) Canada

7.116 Canada claims that US countervailing duty law[139] violates the United States' obligations under the WTO because it fails to provide for company-specific expedited reviews and "administrative reviews"[140] in countervailing duty cases in which the investigation was conducted on an aggregate basis[141], and because it mandates that a single country-wide duty rate calculated in an administrative review supersedes all individual rates previously determined in the countervailing duty proceeding.[142] Canada considers that these measures are inconsistent with US obligations under Article VI:3 of GATT 1994 and Articles 10, 19.3, 19.4, 21.2 and 32.1 of the *SCM Agreement.*[143]

7.117 In particular, Canada submits that the US legislation is in violation of Article 19.3 SCM, which according to Canada provides that exporters "not actually investigated" are entitled upon request, with "no exceptions" to an "expedited review" to establish an individual countervailing duty rate for that exporter.[144] Canada further submits that the US legislation is in violation of Article 21.2 *SCM Agreement*, which in Canada's view entitles exporters and producers to a "company-specific administrative review" upon request, again with "no exceptions".[145]

---

[139] The relevant US law is found in Section 777 A (e) (2) (A) and (B) Tariff Act of 1930 and USDOC Regulations at 19 C.F.R. Sections 351.214 (k) (1) with regard to expedited reviews and section 351.213 (b) and (k) concerning administrative reviews.

[140] Canada does not define the term "administrative review", which is not a term found in the *SCM Agreement*. From its arguments before us, we understand Canada uses this term to refer to the reviews conducted to finalize the rate of duty collection under the retrospective duty assessment system used by the United States in applying countervailing duties. This is the meaning that we ascribe to this term in our findings.

[141] We understand Canada to use the term "aggregate" to refer to an investigation where instead of individual rates of subsidization being calculated, an overall average rate or "country-wide" rate is calculated, for the purpose of applying countervailing duties.

[142] Canada asserts that under US law the only exception is for requests for administrative review concerning zero or *de minimis* subsidies, and even there, only where practicable.

[143] In its Request for Establishment of a Panel (WT/DS236/2), Canada also cites Article 21.1 *SCM Agreement* in connection with its claims concerning US legislation. Canada does not pursue an allegation of a violation of this provision in its submissions in this dispute, however. Rather, it argues in its oral statement at the first meeting that Article 21.2 *SCM Agreement* should be read in conjunction with Article 21.1 *SCM Agreement* as meaning that the review obligations in Article 21.2 *SCM Agreement* relate not only to whether countervailing duties should continue, but also to the level at which duties should continue to be imposed. Canada's First Oral Statement, para. 106. We therefore do not address any allegation of violation of Article 21.1 *SCM Agreement* in our findings.

[144] First Written Submission of Canada, paras. 163 - 165.

[145] First Written Submission of Canada, paras. 166 - 168.

7.118 Canada submits that by maintaining legislation which is inconsistent with the *SCM Agreement*, the US also failed to ensure the conformity of its laws, regulations and administrative procedures with its obligations under the *SCM Agreement* in violation of Article XVI:4 WTO Agreement and Article 32.5 *SCM Agreement*.

7.119 Canada further submits that, since the USDOC conducted the softwood lumber investigation on a country-wide basis, the cited US legislation denies expedited reviews and company specific administrative reviews to the exporters concerned in the investigation, which in turn will necessarily amount to a duty being applied to certain exporters in excess of their individual duty rate. This, Canada argues, is in violation of Articles 19.3, 21.2 and 19.4 *SCM Agreement*.

7.120 According to Canada, the US statute, Section 777A(e)(2)(B), by failing to explicitly provide for company-specific expedited and administrative reviews where an investigation has been conducted on an aggregate basis, makes such reviews impossible. Canada further submits that Section 351.213(b) of the USDOC Regulations specifically denies exporters and producers an "administrative review" if the investigation was conducted on an aggregate basis. Finally, Canada argues, the requirement of Section 351.213 (k) (2) of the Regulations, that a single country-wide duty rate calculated in an administrative review supersede all individual rates previously established through expedited reviews, undoes the benefit of the expedited review under Article 19.3 *SCM Agreement*, and prevents exporters from obtaining an individual rate in an administrative review.

(ii) United States

7.121 The US argues that the US laws and regulations referred to by Canada do not constitute mandatory legislation, and therefore cannot be challenged as such before a WTO panel.[146]

7.122 In particular, the US argues, US law does not prohibit the conduct of such reviews. The United States maintains that the USDOC Regulations cited in Canada's claim do not apply to cases in which investigations are conducted on an aggregate basis – a very rare situation - and the fact that no regulations concerning expedited or administrative reviews have yet been promulgated for this situation does not mean that such reviews are prohibited. Rather, the US submits, Section 751 of the US Tariff Act provides for a broad authority to conduct reviews, and does not require further regulations to be implemented by the USDOC. The US further notes its view that Article 21.2 *SCM Agreement* in any case does not imply an unfettered right to a review in all cases upon request as Canada seems to be suggesting. The US asserts that Canada also is mistaken when it claims that a decision by USDOC to conduct an investigation on an aggregate basis necessarily implies the denial of an expedited review or a company-specific "administrative review".

[146] The United States further considers that the Panel should decline to address Canada's challenge to these laws and regulations as applied because, in the absence of any final measures at the time of the request for establishment of this case, no reviews have been initiated yet. Canada is thus, in the US view, seeking an advisory opinion from the Panel. US First Written Submission, para. 102.

(b) Analysis

7.123 Canada argues that the US laws and regulations are inconsistent with Articles 19.3 and 21.2 *SCM Agreement* relating to expedited and administrative reviews respectively.

7.124 With regard to expedited reviews, Article 19.3 *SCM Agreement* provides as follows:

> "When a countervailing duty is imposed in respect of any product, such countervailing duty shall be levied, in the appropriate amounts in each case, on a non-discriminatory basis on imports of such product from all sources found to be subsidized and causing injury, except as to imports from those sources which have renounced any subsidies in question or from which undertakings under the terms of this Agreement have been accepted. *Any exporter whose exports are subject to a definitive countervailing duty but who was not actually investigated for reasons other than a refusal to cooperate, shall be entitled to an expedited review in order that the investigating authorities promptly establish an individual countervailing duty rate for that exporter*". (emphasis added)

7.125 Article 21.2 *SCM Agreement* concerning certain kinds of reviews provides that:

> "The authorities shall review the need for the continued imposition of the duty, where warranted, on their own initiative or, provided that a reasonable period of time has elapsed since the imposition of the definitive countervailing duty, upon request by any interested party which submits positive information substantiating the need for a review. Interested parties shall have the right to request the authorities to examine whether the continued imposition of the duty is necessary to offset subsidization, whether the injury would be likely to continue or recur if the duty were removed or varied, or both. If, as a result of the review under this paragraph, the authorities determine that the countervailing duty is no longer warranted, it shall be terminated immediately".

7.126 Due to the US laws and regulations' alleged inconsistencies with Articles 19.3 and 21.2 *SCM Agreement*, Canada also alleges that the US violates Article 32.5 *SCM Agreement*, which provides as follows:

> "Each Member shall take all necessary steps, of a general or particular character, to ensure, not later than the date of entry into force of the WTO Agreement for it, the conformity of its laws, regulations and administrative procedures with the provisions of this Agreement as they may apply to the Member in question."[147]

7.127 Canada further, and finally, alleges that because exporters in the lumber case are denied by *US law* the possibility of expedited reviews and company-specific administrative reviews, the United States also violates Articles 10, 19.4 and 32.1 *SCM Agreement* and Article VI:3 of GATT 1994. Article 19.4 *SCM Agreement* provides that no countervailing duty shall be levied in excess of the amount of the subsidiza-

[147] Canada also alleges on the same basis a violation of Article XVI:4 of the WTO Agreement.

tion found to exist, calculated per unit of the subsidized exported product. Canada argues that the legislatively required denial of the reviews at issue will necessarily result in a violation of Article 19.4 *SCM Agreement* as certain exporters will be subject to countervailing duties in excess of their rates of subsidization. As a consequence, according to Canada, Articles 10 and 32.1 *SCM Agreement* are violated, as these provisions require Members to ensure conformity with the *SCM Agreement* and Article VI:3 of GATT 1994 in conducting investigations and applying countervailing duties.

(i) Mandatory Versus Discretionary Legislation

7.128 We consider that it is a well established GATT/WTO practice that legislation can only be challenged as such before a WTO panel, when it is mandatory in nature and *requires* the violation of the Agreement. As the Appellate Body in the *United States – 1916 Act* stated:

> "88. As indicated above, the concept of mandatory as distinguished from discretionary legislation was developed by a number of GATT panels as a threshold consideration in determining when legislation as such – rather than a specific application of that legislation – was inconsistent with a Contracting Party's GATT 1947 obligations. The practice of GATT panels was summed up in *United States – Tobacco* as follows:
>
> ... panels had consistently ruled that legislation which mandated action inconsistent with the General Agreement could be challenged as such, whereas legislation which merely gave the discretion to the *executive authority* of a contracting party to act inconsistently with the General Agreement could not be challenged as such; only the actual application of such legislation inconsistent with the General Agreement could be subject to challenge. (emphasis added)
>
> 89. Thus, *the relevant discretion, for purposes of distinguishing between mandatory and discretionary legislation, is a discretion vested in the executive branch of government"*. (footnotes omitted) (emphasis added)[148]

7.129 We thus consider that legislation which merely gives the executive authority the discretion, either through silence or otherwise, to act inconsistently with the Agreement cannot as such be challenged before a Panel, i.e. independent of its actual application in a particular case.

7.130 The question before us is thus whether the US laws and regulations on administrative and expedited reviews are inconsistent with the *SCM Agreement* by mandating a violation of the relevant provisions of the *SCM Agreement*. Canada challenges the following US legislative provisions as inconsistent with the obligations of the United States under the *SCM Agreement*:

- Section 777A(e)(2)(A) and (B) of the Tariff Act of 1930, as interpreted by the Statement of Administrative Action (SAA)(pages 941-942); and

[148] Appellate Body Report, *United States – Anti-Dumping Act of 1916*, WT/DS136/AB/R and WT/DS162/AB/R, adopted 26 September 2000, paras. 88 – 89.

- the Department of Commerce Regulations at 19 C.F.R. Section 351.214(k) and Section 351.213(b) and (k)[149]

(ii) The US Statute and the Statement of Administrative Action

7.131 Sections 777A(e)(2)(A) and (B) of the US Tariff Act provide as follows:

" (e) Determination of Countervailable Subsidy Rate.

. . .

(2) Exception. If the administering authority determines that it is not practicable to determine individual countervailable subsidy rates under paragraph (1) because of the large number of exporters or producers involved in the investigation or review, the administering authority may

(A) determine individual countervailable subsidy rates for a reasonable number of exporters or producers by limiting its examination to

(i) a sample of exporters or producers that the administering authority determines is statistically valid based on the information available to the administering authority at the time of selection, or

(ii) exporters and producers accounting for the largest volume of the subject merchandise from the exporting country that the administering authority determines can be reasonably examined; or

(B) determine a single country-wide subsidy rate to be applied to all exporters and producers."

7.132 The relevant part of the SAA reads as follows:

"Section 265 (1) of the implementing bill repeals section 706 (a)(2). It eliminates the presumption in favor of a single country-wide CVD rate and amends section 777A of the Act to establish a general rule in favor of individual CVD rates for each exporter or producer individually investigated. [...] In addition, instead of examining a limited number of individual exporters and producers, section 777 A (e)(2)(B) would permit Commerce to calculate, on the basis of aggregate data, a single country-wide subsidy rate to be applied to all exporters and producers of the subject merchandise."[150]

7.133 Section 777 of the US Tariff Act of 1930 does not deal with the conduct of administrative or expedited reviews as such, but merely provides for the possibility in investigations and reviews to calculate the rate of subsidization on an aggregate basis and to determine a country-wide subsidy rate. In our view, the SAA[151] only confirms

149 19 C.F.R. §§ 351.213(b) and (k) and 351.214(k). (Exhibit CDA-39)

150 "Statement of Administrative Action" in *Message from the President of the United States Transmitting the Uruguay Round Agreements, Texts of Agreements Implementing Bill, Statement of Administrative Action and Required Supporting Statements*, H.R. Doc. No. 103-316, vol. 1, p. 941 (1994). (Exhibit CDA-38)

151 We note that as was recognized by the Panel in the *United States – Anti-Dumping Measures on Certain Hot-Rolled Steel Products from Japan* case, the SAA is "an authoritative expression by the Administration concerning its views regarding the interpretation and application of the Uruguay

that although no longer the rule, it remains possible to conduct an investigation or a review on an aggregate basis and determine a country-wide duty rate. Nothing in the statute or the SAA indicates that expedited reviews or company-specific administrative reviews are necessarily excluded where an investigation has been conducted on an aggregate basis. In other words, neither the statute nor the SAA on its face appears to prohibit the USDOC from conducting such reviews where the investigation has been conducted on an aggregate basis.

(iii) USDOC Regulations

7.134 We now consider whether the US Department of Commerce Regulations cited by Canada prohibit the USDOC from conducting either expedited reviews or company-specific "administrative reviews", and if so, whether any such prohibition would violate Articles 19.3 or 21.2 *SCM Agreement*, as Canada alleges.

(a) Expedited reviews

7.135 With regard to expedited reviews, Canada alleges that USDOC Regulations Section 351.214(k)(l) prohibits the conduct of expedited reviews where an investigation has been conducted on an aggregate basis.

7.136 We recall the relevant part of Article 19.3 *SCM Agreement*, namely that any exporter whose exports were not actually investigated for reasons other than a refusal to cooperate is "*entitled*" to an expedited review to establish an individual countervailing duty rate. To us, this text makes clear that an expedited review to establish an individual countervailing duty rate must be conducted, upon request, for any exporter of the type referred to in Article 19.3 *SCM Agreement*. Thus, the question before us is whether the relevant regulations prohibit the USDOC from conducting such reviews in aggregate cases.

7.137 Section 351.214(k)(1) of the USDOC Regulations provides in relevant part:

> (k) *Expedited reviews in countervailing duty proceedings for non-investigated exporters*. (1) *Request for review*. If, in a countervailing duty investigation, the Secretary limited the number of exporters or producers to be individually examined under section 777A(e)(2)(**A**) of the Act, an exporter that the Secretary did not select for individual examination or that the Secretary did not accept as a voluntary respondent (*see* § 351.204(d)) may request a review under this paragraph (k).

7.138 Canada argues that because this regulation refers only to expedited reviews in the case of investigations conducted on the basis of the exception set forth in Section 777A(e)(2)(**A**) of the Act (sampling), it is impossible for the USDOC to conduct such reviews in investigations conducted on the basis of the *other* exception in the statute (aggregate cases), which is provided for in Section 777A(e)(2)(**B**) of the Act. Canada bases this argument on the fact that expedited reviews are expressly provided for in the Regulations, except in respect of aggregate cases. In Canada's view, it is a basic principle of statutory construction that if a right is provided for in certain circumstances, its deliberate exclusion in other circumstances must be given meaning,

Round agreements, both for purposes of US international obligations and domestic law". Panel Report, *United States – Anti-Dumping Measures on Certain Hot-Rolled Steel Products from Japan*, WT/DS184/R, adopted as modified by Appellate Body Report WT/DS184/AB/R on 23 August 2001, para. 7.198.

in particular, that no such right exists in those other cases. Thus, Canada argues, Section 351.214(k)(1), by providing for expedited reviews for cases other than aggregate cases, precludes the possibility of such reviews in aggregate cases.

7.139 The United States responds that Section 351.214(k)(1) does not cover aggregate cases. According to the United States, the fact that the USDOC has not issued regulations to cover such cases, which are rare, does not justify Canada's conclusion that US law prohibits expedited reviews in aggregate cases. The United States further argues that the USDOC has broad discretion under the statute, in particular Section 751 of the US Tariff Act (which is not before us in this dispute), to conduct the kinds of reviews required by the *SCM Agreement*.[152] According to the US, Section 751 of the Tariff Act provides the USDOC with ample authority to fulfil all of the United States' obligations under the *SCM Agreement*, with regard to expedited and administrative reviews alike.

7.140 We note that the regulation at issue in respect of Canada's claim concerning expedited reviews, Section 351.214(k)(l) USDOC Regulations, addresses only one of the two situations identified in the US statute as an exception to the general rule of company-specific rates of subsidization. Namely, this regulation addresses the exceptional situation of an investigation conducted on the basis of some sort of a sample. Canada would have us infer, *a contrario*, that the silence of this regulation and the absence of any other in respect of the other exceptional situation – an investigation conducted on an aggregate basis – means that the USDOC is prohibited by law from conducting expedited reviews in such a situation. We find Canada's *a contrario* argument to be unjustified. We consider that the fact that no regulation exists regarding the apparently rare case of aggregate investigations does not imply that the USDOC is required by law to deny any requests for expedited review where an aggregate countervailing duty rate has been applied. In other words, the USDOC Regulations are simply silent on the issue.

7.141 We thus agree with the US that the fact that the USDOC has not elected to codify specific rules for handling what could potentially be an extremely large number of expedited reviews in an aggregate case does not in any way diminish the Department's statutory authority to conduct such reviews.[153] We therefore find that the fact that 19 C.F.R. § 351.214(k)(1) does not specifically address the possibility of expedited reviews in aggregate cases does not prohibit such reviews. In fact, as Canada acknowledged in the course of the second meeting with the Panel, "with respect to expedited reviews, we note that the United States has in fact posted a notice indi-

[152] The US argues that Section 751 of the US Tariff Act authorizes reviews to "determine the amount of any net countervailable subsidy" at least annually, upon request. It also authorizes reviews of "new shippers," defined as exporters and producers that did not export the subject merchandise to the United States during the period of investigation and were not affiliated with exporters or producers who did. In addition, the United States argues, the statute authorizes the USDOC to conduct a review "whenever [Commerce or the ITC] receives information concerning, or a request from an interested party for a review ... which shows changed circumstances sufficient to warrant a review of," *inter alia*, a countervailing duty order. US First Written Submission, para. 110.

[153] The US asserts that it is a long-established principle of US law that administrative agencies have the discretion to promulgate formal procedures or to proceed on a case-by-case basis, especially when the agency has not had sufficient experience with a particular issue to formulate binding regulations. *See Securities & Exchange Commission v. Chenery Corporation,*, 332 US 194, 202-203 (1947). US First Written Submission, para. 112.

cating that it will accept requests for such reviews in the *Lumber IV* case."[154] We consider that this is further evidence of the fact that the US laws and regulations challenged by Canada do not require the authority to deny any expedited reviews in case of an aggregate investigation. We consider that the fact that no regulation exists regarding the apparently rare case of aggregate investigations, does not imply that exporters are denied by law the right to an expedited review where an aggregate countervailing duty rate was applied. The US laws and regulations cited by Canada thus do not mandate a violation of the requirement under Article 19.3 *SCM Agreement* to conduct an expedited review in order that the authority promptly establish an individual countervailing duty rate for any exporter whose exports are subject to a definitive countervailing duty but who was not actually investigated for reasons other than a refusal to cooperate. For this reason also, we do not find that the USDOC is required by law to violate Article 19.4 *SCM Agreement* in the softwood lumber case by inevitably levying countervailing duties in excess of the amount of the subsidy found.

7.142 In sum, we find that the above-cited US laws and regulations concerning expedited reviews do not mandate a violation of Article 19.3 *SCM Agreement*, or thereby, of Article 19.4 *SCM Agreement*, and thus reject Canada's claims in this respect.

(b) Company specific "administrative reviews"

7.143 Canada submits that Article 21.2 *SCM Agreement*, read in the light of Article 21.1 *SCM Agreement*, contains the clear obligation to provide company-specific "administrative reviews" i.e., calculation of duty rate for a given period, upon request, without exceptions. Thus, Canada argues, the United States must provide for, and conduct, administrative reviews *upon request* to determine not only whether countervailing duties are necessary at all, but also to establish company-specific rates. Canada asserts that there are no exceptions to the US obligation to provide for administrative reviews.[155]

7.144 According to Canada, under US law, contrary to the clear obligation in Article 21.2 *SCM Agreement*, an administrative review is not available to an exporter (nor to a producer, domestic interested party, foreign government, or importer) where the USDOC has conducted its investigation or prior administrative review under Section 777A(e)(2)(B) of the Act (*i.e.* where the USDOC has established a country-wide rate).

7.145 Canada further argues that because US law prohibits such company-specific administrative reviews, it also violates the requirement in Article 19.3 *SCM Agreement* to conduct expedited reviews upon request. Here, Canada argues, because exporters and producers are denied an administrative review (to finalize the rate of duty collection) if the investigation was conducted on an aggregate basis, this means that an exporter or producer would still be denied the opportunity to obtain a *final* individual countervailing duty rate, contrary to Article 19.3 *SCM Agreement*, even if that exporter or producer were given the right to an expedited review to establish an individual *cash deposit* rate. Canada further argues that, as a result, Article 19.4 *SCM*

---

[154] Canada's Oral Statement at the Second Meeting, para. 71 referring to USDOC , *Countervailing Duty Order on Softwood Lumber Products from Canada: Request for Expedited Review*, available online at http://www.ia.ita.doc.gov/lumber/expedite/ index.html (posted 24 May 2002). (Exhibit CDA-103).

[155] Canada's Oral Statement at the Second Meeting, para. 78

Agreement is also violated, as the legislatively required denial of the reviews at issue will necessarily result in a violation of 19.4 *SCM Agreement* since certain exporters will be subject to countervailing duties in excess of their rates of subsidization.

7.146 The United States argues, in the first instance, that Article 21.2 *SCM Agreement* does not contain the obligation asserted by Canada. The United States notes that what its law refers to as "administrative reviews" are the annual reviews that it conducts to finalize the duty collection rate under its retrospective duty assessment system. In the US view, these sorts of reviews are not covered by Article 21.2 *SCM Agreement*. Rather, according to the United States, Article 21.2 *SCM Agreement* provides for, and requires, three completely different types of review: reviews to determine (1) whether the continued imposition of the duty is necessary to offset subsidization; (2) whether the injury would be likely to continue or recur if the duty were removed or varied; or (3) both.[156] Furthermore, the United States argues, even if Canada were correct that Article 21.2 *SCM Agreement* does require administrative reviews in the US sense of the term, Section 751(a) of the Tariff Act gives the USDOC ample discretion to conduct administrative reviews.

7.147 The legislative provisions cited by Canada as violating US obligations in respect of administrative reviews are Section 351.213(b) subparagraphs (1) and (2), and Section 351.213(k) subparagraph (2) of the USDOC Regulations.

7.148 Section 351.213(b) subparagraphs (1) and (2) of the USDOC Regulations provide as follows:

> (b) *Request for administrative review.* (1) Each year during the anniversary month of the publication of an antidumping or countervailing duty order, a domestic interested party or an interested party described in section 771(9)(B) of the Act (foreign government) may request in writing that the Secretary conduct an administrative review under section 751(a)(1) of the Act of specified individual exporters or producers covered by an order (*except for a countervailing duty order in which the investigation or prior administrative review was conducted on an aggregate basis*), if the requesting person states why the person desires the Secretary to review those particular exporters or producers.
>
> (2) During the same month, an exporter or producer covered by an order (except for a countervailing duty order in which the investigation or prior administrative review was conducted on an aggregate basis) may request in writing that the Secretary conduct an administrative review of only that person.
>
> (3) During the same month, an importer of the merchandise may request in writing that the Secretary conduct an administrative review of only an exporter or producer (*except for a countervailing duty order in which the investigation or prior administrative review was conducted on an aggregate basis*) of the subject merchandise imported by that importer. (emphasis added)

7.149 Section 351.213(k) subparagraph (2) on administrative review provides:

[156] According to the United States, the USDOC has the discretion under US law to conduct the first type of review, while the second type of review, falls under the authority of the US International Trade Commission.

> (2) *Application of country-wide subsidy rate.* With the exception of assessment and cash deposit rates of zero determined under paragraph (k)(1) of this section, if, in the final results of an administrative review under this section of a countervailing duty order, the Secretary calculates a single country-wide subsidy rate under section 777A(e)(2)(B) of the Act, *that rate will supersede, for cash deposit purposes, all rates previously determined in the countervailing duty proceeding in question.* (emphasis added)

7.150 Canada further asserts that the only requests the Secretary of the USDOC will consider for an individual administrative review in cases where administrative reviews are conducted on an aggregate (country-wide) basis, are those for individual assessment and cash deposit rates of zero under subparagraph (1) of Section 351.213(k) and even then, "only to the extent practicable." This regulation provides in relevant part as follows:

> "(k) *Administrative reviews of countervailing orders conducted on an aggregate basis* – (1) *Request for a zero rate.* Where the Secretary conducts an administrative review of a countervailing duty on an aggregate basis under section 777A(e)(2)(B) of the Act, the Secretary will consider and review requests for individual assessment and cash deposits of zero to the extent practicable...."

7.151 In view of the nature of Canada's claim the first question that we must address is the nature of the obligations under Article 21.2 *SCM Agreement*, and in particular, whether that provision requires "administrative reviews" as that term is used in this dispute, i.e. the yearly review procedure undertaken by the United States in its retrospective duty assessment system. Here, we agree with the United States that Article 21.2 *SCM Agreement* deals with different kinds of review mechanisms, requiring the authority to provide for the right of interested parties to request the authorities to examine whether the continued imposition of the duty is necessary to offset subsidization, whether the injury would be likely to continue or recur if the duty were removed or varied, or both. Thus, the first type of review addresses the question of whether subsidization is present at all, while the second type of review, by its very terms, has to do primarily with injury questions, that is, the effect on the domestic industry of changing or removing entirely the countervailing duty. This second type of review thus does not have to do with finalizing the rate of countervailing duty during a particular period for which estimated duties have been collected, but rather with the underlying need and rationale, from the standpoint of the affected domestic industry, for maintaining a countervailing duty. In short, Article 21.2 *SCM Agreement* is silent on the question of "administrative reviews".

7.152 In the USDOC Regulations, Section 351.213 quoted above deals with administrative reviews under Section 751 (a) of the US Tariff Act entitled "periodic review of amount of the duty" and sets forth the yearly duty assessment and review mechanism as part of the US retrospective duty assessment system. Section 751 (b) of the Tariff Act entitled "reviews based on changed circumstances" provides that the US International Trade Commission shall upon receipt of a substantiated request from an interested party review whether revocation of the order is likely to lead to the continuation or recurrence of injury.[157] In our view, Section 751 (b) of the Tariff Act is

[157] Section 751 (a) (1) and 751 (b) (1) of the US Tariff Act of 1930, as amended, provide as follows:

the relevant provision of the US legislation implementing the US obligations under Article 21.2 *SCM Agreement* to review the need for continued imposition of the duty, *inter alia* upon request from an interested party to examine whether injury would be likely to continue or recur if the duty were removed or varied. Leaving aside the question of whether the US legislation provides for detailed regulations to deal with all the rights exporters are entitled to in this context, we find that the US statute allows the investigating authority to provide for and conduct reviews consistently with the *SCM Agreement*.

7.153 In addition, we consider that although Section 351.213 (b) states that the rules relating to administrative duty assessment reviews are not applicable to cases where the original investigation or the prior administrative review was conducted on an aggregate basis, it does not restrict the USDOC 's authority to conduct reviews, nor does it require the authority to deny interested parties the right to request reviews in the sense of Article 21 *SCM Agreement*. We further note that subparagraph (k) of the same Section 351.213 provides an opportunity for exporters to request reviews where their subsidy rates are zero.[158] We consider that this review possibility tracks Article

---

SEC. 751. ADMINISTRATIVE REVIEW OF DETERMINATIONS

(a) PERIODIC REVIEW OF AMOUNT of DUTY. -

(1) IN GENERAL. - At least once during each 12-month period beginning on the anniversary of the date of publication of a countervailing duty order under this title or under Section 303 of this Act, an anti-dumping duty order under this title or a finding under the Anti-Dumping Act, 1921, or a notice of the suspension of an investigation, the administering authority, if a request for such a review has been received and after publication of notice of such review in the Federal Register, shall

(A) review and determine the amount of any net countervailable subsidy,

(B) review, and determine (in accordance with paragraph (2)), the amount of any anti-dumping duty, and

(C) review the current status of, and compliance with, any agreement by reason of which an investigation was suspended, and review the amount of any net countervailable subsidy or dumping margin involved in the agreement, and shall publish in the Federal Register the results of such review, together with notice of any duty to be assessed, estimated duty to be deposited, or investigation to be resumed.

[...]

(b) REVIEWS BASED ON CHANGED CIRCUMSTANCES. -

(1) IN GENERAL. - Whenever the administering authority or the Commission receives information concerning, or a request from an interested party for a review of -

(A) a final affirmative determination that resulted in an anti-dumping duty order under this title or a finding under the Anti-Dumping Act, 1921, or in a countervailing duty order under this title or Section 303,

(B) a suspension agreement accepted under Section 704 or 734, or

(C) a final affirmative determination resulting from an investigation continued pursuant to Section 704(g) or 734(g), which shows changed circumstances sufficient to warrant a review of such determination or agreement, the administering authority or the Commission (as the case may be) shall conduct a review of the determination or agreement after publishing notice of the review in the Federal Register.

We note that the relevant section in the USDOC Regulations dealing with changed circumstances reviews is Section 351.216 which has not been challenged by Canada.

[158] US Answers to Questions from the Panel after the First Meeting, para. 63.

21.2 *SCM Agreement* which provides for reviews to determine *inter alia* whether the continued imposition of the duty is necessary to offset subsidization.[159]

7.154 We conclude that with regard to "administrative reviews", the challenged USDOC Regulations specify the rules that apply to a certain kind of review, and do not on their face alter the general statutory requirement to conduct reviews in the sense of Article 21 *SCM Agreement*. In our view, and in light of the broad statutory authority for the US authorities to conduct administrative reviews under Section 751 of the Tariff Act, and the specific provision in the Regulations which allows for review requests in case of a zero duty rate, we do not consider that the US laws and regulations mandate the executive authority to deny interested parties the opportunity to request a review of the need for the continued imposition of the duty under Article 21.2 *SCM Agreement*. In the absence of provisions in the legislation which require the executive authority to act in violation of the *SCM Agreement*, we reject Canada's claim in this respect.

7.155 We next consider Canada's claim that the alleged prohibition under US law of company-specific administrative reviews in aggregate cases also violates Article 19.3 *SCM Agreement*, by foreclosing the possibility in such cases that the results of expedited reviews would ever give rise to company-specific final countervailing duty rates, and Article 19.4 *SCM Agreement*, as certain exporters will be subject to countervailing duties in excess of their rates of subsidization. As we have found that the legislation challenged by Canada does not mandate a violation of Article 21.2 *SCM Agreement*, and that the USDOC has broad discretion to conduct reviews under Article 21 *SCM Agreement*, we also reject this claim. In addition, and more specifically, we note that Section 351.213(k) subparagraph (2), cited by Canada in connection with this claim, does not directly address the situation alluded to by Canada, and thus does not mandate the violation alleged by Canada. In particular, this regulation provides that where an administrative review is conducted on an aggregate basis, the final results of that review will supersede the previously-established countervailing duty rates. This regulation therefore does not address, or contain any requirements regarding, the circumstances under which an administrative review will be conducted on an aggregate basis.

7.156 Finally, Canada challenges what it views as the inevitable denial of expedited reviews and company-specific "administrative reviews" in the current softwood lumber investigation as a necessary result of the USDOC's decision to conduct this countervailing duty investigation on an aggregate basis. In light of the fact that at the time of the Preliminary Determination which is under review by the panel, no final determination had yet been made, no reviews of such a determination could have actually been requested, let alone denied, nor has Canada argued that this has happened.

7.157 Therefore, given our finding that the laws and regulations cited by Canada do not preclude the USDOC acting consistently with the US' obligations under Articles 19.3 and 21 *SCM Agreement* with respect to expedited and administrative reviews, we consider that it is not appropriate to rule on a potential denial of a request for review if no such request has even been made. The WTO dispute settlement system allows a Member to challenge a law as such or its actual application in a particular case, but not its possible future application.

---

[159] We note that the second leg of the review under Article 21.2 *SCM Agreement* relates to the injury analysis which in the US is not performed by the USDOC, but by the US International Trade Commission (USITC). We note that Canada is not challenging the USITC Regulations.

7.158 In sum, we find that the US laws and regulations challenged by Canada do not require the executive authority to violate Articles 19.3 and 21.2 *SCM Agreement* in respect of the reviews required thereby, and are therefore not inconsistent with the *SCM Agreement*.

(c) Conclusion

7.159 For the reasons set forth above, we find that the US laws and regulations on Expedited and Administrative Reviews as challenged by Canada do not constitute a violation of the provisions of Articles 19 and 21 *SCM Agreement* in respect of the reviews required thereby, and we therefore reject all of Canada's claims in this respect.

VIII. CONCLUSIONS AND RECOMMENDATIONS

8.1 In light of the findings above that the USDOC Preliminary Countervailing Duty Determination

(a) was not inconsistent with Article 1.1 (a) *SCM Agreement* when the USDOC found that the provision of stumpage constituted a financial contribution, in the form of the provision of a good or service;

(b) failed to determine the existence and amount of benefit to the producers of the subject merchandise on the basis of the prevailing market conditions in Canada as required by Article 1.1 (b) and Article 14 and 14 (d) *SCM Agreement*; and

(c) failed to establish that a benefit was conferred to certain producers of the subject merchandise as the USDOC did not examine whether a benefit was passed through by the unrelated upstream producers of log inputs to the downstream producers of the subject merchandise;

we conclude that the USDOC's imposition of provisional measures based on the preliminary countervailing duty determination was inconsistent with the US obligations under Articles 1.1 (b), 10, 14, 14 (d), and 17.1(b) *SCM Agreement*. In light of our conclusion, we apply judicial economy, and therefore do not rule on Canada's claim that the USDOC instructions transmitted to the United States Customs Service on 4 September 2001, imposed provisional measures in excess of the subsidy preliminarily found to exist in a manner inconsistent with Articles 10, 17.2, 17.5, 19.4 and 32.1 of the *SCM Agreement* and Article VI:3 of GATT 1994.

8.2 In light of the findings above concerning the USDOC Preliminary Critical Circumstances Determination, we conclude that the retroactive imposition of a provisional measure on the basis of the USDOC Preliminary Critical Circumstances Determination is inconsistent with Articles 20.6, 17.3, and 17.4 *SCM Agreement*. In light of this conclusion, we decide to apply judicial economy and therefore do not rule on Canada's claim that the USDOC failed to establish the existence of critical circumstances under Article 20.6 *SCM Agreement* in its Preliminary Critical Circumstances Determination.

8.3 Finally, in light of the findings above concerning the US countervailing duty laws and regulations, we conclude that the US laws and regulations challenged by Canada on expedited and administrative reviews are not inconsistent with the *SCM Agreement* as they do not require the executive authority to act in a manner inconsistent with the US obligations under Articles 19 and 21 of the *SCM Agreement* concerning expedited and administrative reviews. As a result we also reject Canada's claims that the United States has failed to ensure that its laws and regulations are in conformity with its WTO obligations as required by Article 32.5 of the *SCM Agreement* and Article XVI:4 of the WTO Agreement.

8.4 Under Article 3.8 of the DSU, in cases where there is infringement of the obligations assumed under a covered agreement, the action is considered *prima facie* to constitute a case of nullification or impairment of benefits under that agreement. Accordingly, we conclude that, to the extent the United States has acted inconsistently with the provisions of the *SCM Agreement*, it has nullified or impaired benefits accruing to Canada under that Agreement. We recommend that the Dispute Settlement Body request the United States to bring its measure into conformity with its obligations under the *SCM Agreement*.

ANNEX A

Parties Responses to Questions – First Meeting of the Panel

ANNEX A-1

Responses of Canada to Questions Posed in the Context of the First Substantive Meeting
(21 May 2002)

1. *In situ* natural resources are not "goods" within the meaning of the *SCM Agreement*. Accordingly, the right of exploitation of such resources does not come within the meaning of "provision of goods" in Article 1.1(a)(1)(iii). This does not mean that the consequences flowing from real property rights in general, and resource exploitation rights in particular, cannot come within the scope of other parts of Article 1.1.

A land grant, or the grant of a building, may come within Article 1.1. However, such a grant would not constitute the provision of "goods". Land, as an asset, is often a source of revenue. A land grant, therefore, can constitute the foregoing of revenue that the owner might expect from its rental or sale. Whether a 99-year lease comes within the terms of Article 1.1 depends on the terms of the lease and, as mentioned above, the prevailing legal regime for leasing of publicly-owned land.

Finally, for the purpose of Article 1.1, real property rights such as those in land, leases or *in situ* natural resources are no different from property rights in patents or copyrights (or other intangibles). It is not that the "granting" of these rights in each instance can never amount to a financial contribution, but that such grants do not amount to the provision of "goods".

2. (a) Yes. The term "goods" in Article 1.1(a)(1)(iii) has the same meaning and scope as "products" used elsewhere in the *SCM Agreement* and the WTO Agreement. The ordinary meaning of "goods" is "tangible or movable personal property other than money; (especially) articles or items of merchandise (goods or services)".

The context for this term in the *SCM Agreement* is highly instructive as to its scope and confirms the ordinary meaning of "goods" as tradable items with an actual or potential customs classification.

- First, in Part II, Article 3.1(b) refers to "the use of domestic over imported *goods*." Evidently, "goods" refers to tradable items: rights to *in situ* natural resources cannot be "imported" or "used".
- Second, Parts III and V of the *SCM Agreement* refer to "products". There is no indication anywhere in the text that the "product" or "imports" referred to in these Parts is different from the "goods" referred to in Article 1 or 3.

Other agreements in the WTO Agreement are also particularly useful as context.

- First, countervailing measures are provided for in Article VI of the GATT 1994, as an exception to Article II. Therefore, the coverage of Part V of the *SCM Agreement* and that of Article II of the GATT 1994 must be the same.
- Second, the interpretative note to Annex 1A of the *Marrakesh Agreement* provides a rule of conflict between the GATT 1994 and the covered agreements. The logical conclusion of the note is that the agreements set out in

Annex 1A apply to the same products, or "goods" as those subject to the GATT 1994.

- Third, Article 1 of the TRIMs Agreement (TRIMS) provides that the TRIMs "applies to investment measures related to trade in *goods* only." Article 2 requires that, "... no Member shall apply any TRIM that is inconsistent with the provisions of Article III or Article XI of GATT 1994." The unambiguous implication is that the "goods" referred to in Article 1 of the TRIMs are the same as the "products" covered by Articles III and XI of the GATT 1994.
- Fourth, the *Agreement on Implementation of Article VII of the GATT 1994* refers to imported or exported "goods". There is no indication that the term has a different meaning in this agreement than the same word in other agreements in Annex 1A, or indeed the term "product" in the GATT 1994.
- Fifth, the *Agreement on Rules of Origin* also refers to "goods" in the context of Articles I, II, III, XI and XIII of the GATT 1994.

Finally, nothing in the object and purpose of the *SCM Agreement* suggests that the term "goods" in Article 1.1 should be read as anything other than tradable items with an actual or potential customs classification. To the extent that there is a concern that certain forms of government largesse may not be captured by definition of "goods", the Panel may consider the following:

- First, as the panel in *United States – Export Restraints* noted, Article 1.1(a)(1) does not cover *all* government actions that may affect the market, but only those that fall within the definition of "subsidy".
- Second, land or lease grants may well be covered by other provisions in Article 1.1(a)(1). It is not, however, necessary for this Panel to define the precise scope of that Article to arrive at the conclusion that real property rights are not "goods".

The Spanish and French versions of the WTO Agreement are useful in confirming the meaning of the term "goods". In both texts, the word "goods" is translated into both "bienes" and "productos" as well as "biens" and "produits" in the Spanish and French versions, respectively. For the purposes of the other two official versions of the *SCM Agreement*, the term "goods" in Article 1.1 has the same meaning and scope as "products".

The Appellate Body also uses the terms "goods" and "products" interchangeably as reflected in their decisions in both EC – Bananas (para. 221) and Canada – Autos (para. 140).

(b) No. A building that is affixed to the land is not "goods" for the purposes of Article 1.1 of the *SCM Agreement*. Such a building would be real property.

(c) Heading 0602 covers "live trees ... of a kind commonly supplied by nursery gardeners or florists for planting or for ornamental use." Live firs of small dimensions that are fully transportable are properly considered as goods since they fall under the Harmonized System. Fully-grown live firs in the form of standing timber are not "goods" for the purposes of the WTO Agreement.

(d) The fact that "services" are mentioned in the first half of Article 1.1(a)(1)(iii) does not in any way affect the scope of "goods". Goods are those tradable items that come or may come under the coverage of the GATT 1994, while services are those economic activities that would fall within the scope of the GATS. Other assets or property – such as intellectual property rights – do not fall within Article 1.1(a)(1)(iii) at all.

3. Where a private party produces a product from natural resources in which it has property interests, the "goods" so produced are *not* provided by government. Where, however, a lorry-full of iron-ore is delivered by the government to a processor, this constitutes the provision of goods. If the government produces the iron ore and offers it to a steel producer willing to load and haul the ore to its mill the government would also be providing goods. However, granting exploitation rights to a resource that is part of the land and that cannot be traded, does not constitute the provision of goods.

4. Under the Canadian constitution, provinces have title to the majority of public property and exercise exclusive jurisdiction to legislate in relation to the development, conservation, and management of non-renewable natural resources and forestry resources.

5. Yes. The text of Article 14(d) unambiguously requires that a Member determine the adequacy of remuneration "in relation to prevailing market conditions for the good or service in question in the country of provision". The ordinary meaning of "prevail", read in context, is "exist". The reference to "prevailing market conditions" is, therefore, to conditions that actually exist in the country of provision. There is nothing in the context, object and purpose or the negotiating history of Article 14 that would permit reading this as "in another country".

Further contextual evidence may be found in the Accession Protocol of China. The Protocol specifically permits the use of "methodologies for identifying and measuring the subsidy benefit which take into account the possibility that prevailing terms and conditions in China may not always be available as appropriate benchmarks." If Article 14(d) permitted Members to consider conditions outside "the country of provision", this exceptional treatment would not have been necessary.

Market benchmarks can also still exist where there is a government monopoly. For instance, if the government's monopoly was over domestic production of the goods in question then the government price could be compared to the price of imports of the same good. Even where there are no imports, remuneration is "adequate" where the government operates on a market basis. All of the provinces submitted substantial and unrebutted, factual evidence and economic analyses demonstrating that they were acting in a manner consistent with market principles.

6. The requirements for entering into tenures vary substantially, but before tenures are granted, provinces will require a demonstration of forest management expertise and financial capabilities sufficient to undertake required obligations. Subject to the qualifications, there are no limitations on who can enter into these agreements.

The responsibilities that a long-term tenure holder must agree to undertake generally include: sustainable forest management, forest management, development and operational planning, public consultations, silviculture prescriptions, construction or maintenance of wood processing facilities, preparation of forest inventories, pest and disease control, timber cruises, scaling, firefighting and forest research activities.

In most cases, tenure holders are free to sell their logs to unrelated sawmills. There are generally no requirements either by statute or by the terms of tenures that require tenure holders to sell to specific mills or to sell at specific prices or under specific terms and conditions.

7. The log price data provided to Commerce prior to the PD is described by province below. Logs are highly heterogeneous and prices differ by species, size and quality. As with stumpage rates, any comparison of average prices must at a minimum include adjustments for these characteristics. As well, log prices reflect the value of a delivered good; that is, they include the cost of harvesting and transporting the good as well as all tenure obligation costs borne by the harvester. Accordingly, log prices are not the same as stumpage rates

B.C. is home to the most organized log exchanges in Canada. B.C.'s information is summarized in the following table:

	Volume (m^3)	**Value ($)**	**Average Value ($\$/m^3$)**
Vancouver Log Market (2000/2001)	6,559,073	655,366,782	99.92
Log transactions in BC Interior (1999)	11,309,545	782,088,207	69.15
Vernon Log Yard (2000/2001)	54,907	3,632,694	66.16
Revelstoke Log Yard (2000/2001)	28,754	3,157,601	109.81

The VLM is an informal arrangement amongst the log supply departments of various coastal B.C. licencees, the log buyers for small companies or their agents, and the traders employed by log brokers who buy and sell logs. The VLM does not distinguish between logs originating from privately owned, federally owned or provincially owned land.

There is no similarly organized log market in the interior of B.C.. It consists of a series of small, separate local markets. The Vernon log yard was established in March 1993 and obtains its logs from timber sales harvested in local districts from a variety of tenure arrangements. The Revelstoke log yard is extremely small and the logs sold through it are mainly high-value cedar sawlogs.

Alberta provided survey information it collects in the ordinary course of business on average log prices paid by purchasers. The following table shows the calendar year volume and value (FOB purchasing mill) of these transactions. This data does not break out private land sourced logs from logs harvested on provincial lands and also does not provide information on species type or quality.

Excerpted from Table 32 - Exhibit AB-LER-5 Volume and Value of Domestic Arm's-length Log Sales from Survey

	Total Softwood Log Harvest m^3	**Total Arm's-length Transaction Softwood Log Volumes m^3**	**Percent Arm's-length Transaction Softwood Log Volumes**	**Arm's-length logs sales prices (FOB purchasing mill) $\$/m^3$**
2000	14,168,657	884,552	6.24%	50.40

In its initial questionnaire response, Ontario provided Commerce with the results of a survey and a report done by the independent accounting firm of KPMG. The first schedule in the survey itemized the costs of SPF (spruce, jack pine and fir) logs from Crown lands delivered to the mill gate. KPMG reported that total weighted average costs of delivered SPF logs cut from Crown land of \$50.42 m^3. The second schedule in the survey reported purchases of timber in Ontario by third parties of timber harvested from several jurisdictions. The prices for these purchases were established by negotiation between buyer and seller. Weighted average market prices reported by KPMG ranged from \$47.36 m^3 for timber harvested from Ontario private land and \$49.15 m^3 for timber harvested from Ontario Crown land.

There are two separate and distinct markets for the supply of standing timber in Québec: the public forest and the private forest. The only private forest prices obtained by Québec are through annual market surveys and a tri-annual census. Québec uses these market prices to set public forest stumpage rates. Québec provided the Department of Commerce with private stumpage price data for the three years 1998, 1999 and 2000.

8. By "arm's-length" prices, Canada means prices of log sales between a willing seller and a willing buyer that are not related, i.e. market prices freely negotiated between independent parties. Such sales include both sales for a specific price and sales transacted by means of "swapping" a bundle of different types of logs between unrelated tenure holders.

An estimate of the volume of timber harvested in B.C. by companies operating at arm's-length from sawmills can be obtained by analysing the timber harvested under specific licences and permits separately for companies that have and do not have sawmills. This analysis, based on information on the record prior to the PD, indicates that 30.09 per cent of the timber from Crown licences was harvested by companies that do not have sawmills. In the aggregate (including private land), 33.0 per cent of timber harvested in the province during the POI was harvested by entities that did not have sawmills.

Québec's TSFMA tenures require the tenure holder to process the public timber they harvest. Forest management contracts (FMC) do not require tenure holders to process timber. Sales from Federal lands are largely stumpage sales done by sealed bid tender. None of the 40,000 registered private woodlot owners is required to process timber. The tenure data submitted prior to the PD shows that up to 27 per cent of the provincial harvest will be sold through arm's-length transactions from private lands and FMC tenures. In addition, almost 35 per cent of the total log supply comes from arm's-length transactions from private lands, FMC tenures and log imports.

Approximately 30 per cent of the softwood timber harvested from Ontario's Crown land during Commerce's period of investigation was sold by tenure holders to third parties who subsequently processed this into forest products.

Alberta indicated to Commerce that it had survey data (both price and volumes) on arm's-length transactions in volumes that represented approximately 6 per cent of the total softwood log harvest in Alberta. A sample of a substantial portion of the forest industries in Alberta was used to develop these data. "Arm's-length" transactions in this survey were defined as transactions entered into freely between totally unrelated parties. Further, this sample was limited to transactions where the cash price was the only consideration exchanged.

In addition to the survey data giving volumes and prices, Alberta also has data on the volume of logs delivered to mills from sources other than from their own forestry tenures. Alberta's records show that volumes of timber traded or swapped for other logs or woodchips and purchased in cash transactions or in exchange for other consideration comprised 3,900,000 m^3 in the period of investigation or slightly more than 30 per cent of the total softwood sawlog harvest.

Prior to the PD, Canada submitted to Commerce applications for exclusion from 98 producers who purchased logs or lumber at arm's-length. Of these, 78 were remanufacturers unrelated to firms with harvesting rights and at least 8 were primary mills that purchased all of their log inputs in arm's-length transactions.

9. The programmes and policies investigated by Commerce were provincial stumpage programs, not the sale of logs. Indeed, the US used state stumpage programmes as benchmarks rather than log sales. There was a significant amount of information on the record at the time of the PD regarding a variety of sources of data that might have been used by Commerce as benchmarks. This information included data on private stumpage, competitive tenures in certain provinces and other evidence that provinces operate their stumpage systems on market terms. Three provinces – Alberta, Ontario and Québec – provided extensive evidence related to private markets operating within their provinces. Alberta also provided Commerce with data broken out for its competitively sold tenures. The four primary exporting provinces, representing 96 per cent of the exports of softwood lumber, provided information demonstrating that they operated their stumpage systems in a manner consistent with market principles.

The size of the available in-country benchmark market should not determine the adequacy of the data. Rather, adequacy should be assessed taking into account other factors, including the existence of willing buyers and sellers and other indicia of a viable market. For example, arbitrage works between different timber supply sources to ensure that stumpage rates derived from the sale of a relatively small volume of harvesting rights from one source can represent a valid basis for comparison with stumpage rates from other sources.

One example of arbitrage is found in Québec, where the majority of timber on private forestlands is sold as delivered logs; that is, the owner undertakes the logging himself, or contracts with a logger to do the harvesting. A smaller portion of Québec's private harvest is sold as sales of harvesting rights. Both of these sale prices represent valid competitive market prices because the opportunity for arbitrage between the private log and private stumpage markets exists.

10. The factual determinations by Commerce in the three previous lumber cases are highly relevant in establishing that cross-border benchmarks are inherently arbitrary and capricious. In these cases, Commerce made specific factual findings and concluded that so many factors affect the comparability of adjacent US and Canadian timber that valid cross-border comparisons are impossible. The facts underlying Commerce's findings have not changed since then and the findings still hold true today, regardless of the change in the legal regime.

Accordingly, Commerce's finding in *Lumber I* that no unified North American market for stumpage existed is valid today. For example, the wide differences between the US and Canada in terms of species composition; size, quality, and density of timber; and terrain and accessibility, remain unchanged.

As for the factors that can be influenced by government, these also have remained unchanged. For example, supply of timber from public lands in the US is still limited, and, as referred to by Commerce in *Lumber III*, variations in exchange rates and other factors tied to the existence of the political border between the two countries remain.

In *Lumber III* Commerce relied on private forest surveys in Québec because it found these surveys accurately reflected market driven prices in Québec. Québec's system has not changed since. Yet, in *Lumber IV*, not only did Commerce ignore such surveys that were on the record prior to the PD, it ignored every other possible in-country benchmark put on the record by the other provinces.

11. (a) No. Under Part V of the *SCM Agreement*, a Member may impose a countervailing measure only where it has established that a subsidy exists in respect of each entity producing or exporting the subject merchandise subject to the measure. Specifically, the investigating authority must establish a "financial contribution" by government that confers a "benefit". Nothing in the *SCM Agreement* permits an investigating authority to presume the existence of a subsidy simply because the original recipient provides inputs to a downstream producer.

Where the subject merchandise is not produced or exported by the original recipient of an alleged subsidy, the investigating authority must establish the existence of a subsidy in respect of the downstream producer. That is, it must establish that a financial contribution by government has conferred a benefit on that producer. In the absence of a direct relationship between the downstream producer and the government, Article 1.1(a)(1)(iv) sets out the criteria for determining when a government has made an indirect financial contribution to that downstream producer.

The EC argues that an "effects" test should be incorporated into the subsidy definition. However, Article 1.1 does not include such a test. The enquiry under Article 1.1 of the *SCM Agreement* is whether a government has made a "financial contribution" that confers a "benefit". The panel in United States – Export Restraints summarized this analysis:

> We believe ... that the appropriate way to conceive of "financial contribution" is purely as a transfer of economic resources by a government to private entities in the market, without regard to the *terms* of that transfer. Such a transfer can be effected either by a government directly (subparagraphs (i)-(iii)) or indirectly through private bodies (subparagraph (iv)). The question of the terms on which the transfer is made does not have to do with the existence of a financial contribution but rather goes to the separate issue of benefit, as Article 14 makes clear, by providing that to determine whether a benefit exists, the terms of the financial contribution need to be compared with the market terms. [emphasis in original]

The panel went on to state:

> In short, the negotiating history confirms that the introduction of the two-part definition of subsidy, consisting of "financial contribution" and "benefit", was intended specifically to prevent the countervailing of *benefits* from any sort of (formal, enforceable) government measures, by restricting to a finite list the *kinds* of government measures that would, if they conferred benefits, constitute subsidies. The negotiating history confirms that items (i)-(iii) of that list limit these kinds of measures to the transfer of economic resources from a government to a private entity. Under subparagraphs (i)-(iii), the government act-

> ing on its own behalf is effecting that transfer by directly providing something of value – either money, goods, or services – to a private entity. Subparagraph (iv) ensures that the same kinds of *government* transfers of economic resources, when undertaken through explicit *delegation of those* functions to a private entity, do not thereby escape disciplines. [emphasis in original]

The EC argument does not, therefore, have support in either the text or in the negotiating history of Article 1. A subsidy exists where there is a financial contribution by government that confers a benefit. An investigating authority must always establish both elements of a "subsidy" as regards a downstream producer.

(b) No. In an original investigation an investigating authority may never assume that any of the requirements of the subsidy definition have been met. This is true for upstream producers as it is in respect of an alleged subsidy to downstream producers. Thus a subsidy to upstream producers cannot be presumed to be passed through to downstream producers in any circumstances. This is especially the case regarding arm's-length transactions where, under fundamental principles of economics, an upstream recipient of a subsidy would not normally subsidize a downstream producer.

(c) Yes. Article 1.1 requires in all instances that for a given recipient, a subsidy exists only where there has been a financial contribution and a benefit. In the context of allegations of indirect subsidies, in order to determine that the downstream producer is "subsidized", it must be found that: (1) a government entrusts or directs the original recipient of a financial contribution to itself make a financial contribution to the downstream producer under subparagraph (iv); and (2) that such subsequent financial contribution be made on terms such that it thereby confers a benefit to the downstream recipient.

12. Where the harvester is not free to: process the logs it harvests itself; sell to whomever it wishes on whatever terms and conditions that are mutually agreed; swap logs with other timber harvesters; or obtain permits to export, then a government requirement that the logging company contract to provide logs to a sawmill for processing may constitute the government directed provision of logs by the logging company to the sawmill.

13. With few exceptions, tenure agreements do not contain requirements that tenure holders have contracts with unrelated sawmills.

14. Canada does not wish, at this point, to add to its submissions on this subject

15. The issue of liquidation of entries is a red herring, because in the US the entries in the 90 days prior to a PD would rarely if ever be liquidated before a final determination (including, if appropriate, a final critical circumstances determination) was made. At that point, once there is a critical circumstances finding, the liquidation of unliquidated entries may be suspended.

Under US Customs regulations, entries are to be liquidated within one year after entry, but Customs may extend that period by an additional two years. In practice, if the period is not extended, an entry will be liquidated on the 314th day after it was made. Thus entries potentially subject to retroactive application of definitive duties would not be liquidated by the time Commerce is required to complete an investigation.

16. Canada implemented its obligations under the *SCM Agreement* in the Special Import Measures Act (SIMA) and related regulations. In the Canadian system two

investigating authorities are involved in decision-making. Dumping and subsidy determinations are made by the Commissioner of the Canada Customs and Revenue Agency (CCRA). Injury decisions are made by the Canadian International Trade Tribunal (CITT).

Under section 41(1)(a)(iv)(C), in a final determination, the Commissioner makes a finding as to whether a particular investigation involves a prohibited subsidy. Where there is a finding of a prohibited subsidy or "specification", then in making its final injury inquiry under section 42, the CITT is directed, to determine whether the remaining criteria of Article 20.6 are satisfied. Where the CITT makes a positive determination under section 42(1)(c) (as reflected in section 6(a)), the Commissioner is directed by section 6(b) to assess "a countervailing duty in the amount equal to such of the amount of the subsidy on imported goods as is a prohibited subsidy". Consistent with Article 20.6, which allows for the retroactive assessment of "definitive countervailing duties", this provision is under the definitive "Antidumping and Countervailing Duty" heading of the Act (i.e., sections 3-7).

Pursuant to section 37.11 of the SIMA, imports considered would be those imported within a representative period within the period of investigation beginning ninety days before the date of initiation and ending on the date of the Commissioner's PD, which were "massive" relative to a preceding representative period of comparable duration also within the POI.

The retroactive application of final duties would be effected through a determination by a designated CCRA officer under section 55 of the SIMA. This determination is subject to re-determination by the Commissioner under section 59(1) of the Act. While the goods that these duties would be applied to would have been released (or in the US sense, "liquidated"), the record of their entry would still be in the CCRA records system and thus could be retrieved as necessary.

17. There is no basis in the *SCM Agreement* for the application of provisional measures pursuant to a PD of critical circumstances. Accordingly, no Member may take an action or impose a measure in respect of "critical circumstances" on a provisional basis. In this sense "suspension of liquidation" is no different than a bonding requirement.

18. (a) The relevant data for Canada as a whole is set out in Commerce's PD. There, based on a comparison of the three months preceding and the three months following initiation of the investigation, Commerce states that it found an increase in import levels of 23.34 per cent using import statistics net of the Maritime provinces, and found an increase of 19.02 per cent when it included imports from the Maritime provinces. Commerce decided that the "massive imports" element of Article 20.6 of the *SCM Agreement* had been satisfied since both rates of increase were above the regulatory 15 per cent threshold under US law. If Commerce had considered other comparison periods or approaches to seasonality adjustments, as Canada had argued were necessary to an objective assessment of "massive imports", the inclusion of Maritime shipments would have demonstrated an increase in shipments below the 15 per cent threshold.

(b) Québec's exports of softwood lumber to the US in FY 2000/2001 amounted to 21 per cent, or approximately one-fifth of total Canadian exports of softwood lumber to the US. Thus, in order for exports from Québec to have accounted for a 15 per cent increase in Canada-wide exports, exports from Québec would have had to increase by five times the 15 per cent amount, or by 75 per cent. There is nothing in the record indicating that exports from Québec followed any pattern different than exports from the rest of Canada.

However, since at most three Québec producers may have benefited from the alleged prohibited subsidy during the POI, any exports from these producers would have been minute relative to total exports from Canada (or even from Québec) and would not have resulted in a "massive imports".

19. The Canada-US Softwood Lumber Agreement (SLA) provides the background against which the US should have conducted its "massive imports" analysis. The CVD investigation was timed to coincide with the economic and trade consequences of the expiration of the SLA. A period of investigation adjusted for such consequences would have found normal trade patterns, rather than "massive imports".

In 1996, Canada implemented the SLA through quota-based export fees. The SLA expired on 31 March 2001. In anticipation of this expiration, and the consequent removal of the fees, Canadian exporters and US importers and purchasers of softwood lumber made a number of rational business decisions. Importers stopped purchasing Canadian lumber. This resulted in a drop in prices throughout March. Exporters, deterred by low prices and SLA fees alike, deferred exports to April. Placed in this context, it is hardly coincidental that exports to the US in April 2001 increased by 463 million board feet over total exports in the month of April 2000.

To Both Parties

1. When a timber harvester cuts down a tree, it produces goods – logs. The harvester may then use the goods as input into its own sawmill, pulp mill or other mill, if it has one; it may sell the goods in question to other users of logs; or export them. Goods are, accordingly, provided in the sense of Article 1.1 of the *SCM Agreement* where logs are given or sold from one party to another.

2. There is no "international market price" for softwood lumber, even though it is bought and sold internationally. Unlike commodities such as oil or minerals, softwood lumber is priced to specific domestic or regional markets. As well, because of the huge differences between different sorts of lumber, lumber prices vary depending on the species, dimension and grade of the lumber, whether the lumber has been air or kiln-dried, and whether the lumber has been mechanically stress rated. Different markets would have different requirements, thus making it difficult to have a single "international market price" for lumber.

3. Article 15(b) of the Accession Protocol of China establishes that under Article 14(d) of the *SCM Agreement* cross-border price comparisons are not permitted. If Article 14(d) permitted Members to consider conditions outside of China there would have been no reason to negotiate this provision. Article 15, unlike the other provisions, introduces special and additional rules. This is apparent from the following:

- the chapeau, which requires the *SCM Agreement* to be applied "consistent with the following listed considerations". If this were a reintroduction of the *SCM Agreement* into the Protocol, the form of wording would not be needed;
- Article 15(b) states that, "the relevant provisions of the *SCM Agreement* shall apply; *however* ..." This demonstrates that what follows the "however" is out-

side the normal rules, and that the subordinate clause provides for additional rules;

- when Members use the methodologies set out in 15(a) (antidumping) and 15(b) (CVD), they are required to notify the WTO. If these methodologies were the norm, no such notification would be required; and
- 15(a) expires once a market economy is established in China. However, Members realized that it would not be necessary to require 15(b) to expire, because once there is a market economy, there would be no "special difficulty" in establishing a market benchmark.

4. Attached as Exhibits CDA-63 to CDA-70 please find provincial forest tenure agreements and the relevant underlying legislation from B.C. and Alberta.

5. Commerce did not request any information related to the pass-through issue. Instead, Commerce simply presumed that any subsidy provided on the upstream input logs was automatically passed through in the arm's-length sale of those logs.

In its submissions, Canada demonstrated that it was impermissible for Commerce to presume benefits to subject merchandise without conducting an upstream subsidy analysis. Canada also demonstrated that in many instances any alleged subsidization would not be passed through from harvesters to arm's-length lumber producers. These submissions were also consistent with Commerce's pass-through determination in Lumber III.

Canada also submitted applications for exclusion from many producers who had purchased lumber at arm's-length from unrelated suppliers. It many instances, these producers were also independent remanufacturers (i.e., completely unrelated to firms with harvesting rights).

B.C. provided information on the purchase and sale of logs in the province. That information, set out in Question 7 above, included the volume and value of logs sold in each log market within the province, as well as detailed information describing the functioning and operation of each log market.

Furthermore, the B.C. log sales information contained sufficient detail to establish the total volume of softwood logs sold domestically to unrelated purchasers on the coast and in the interior. B.C.'s initial questionnaire response stated that, over the past three years, between 26 and 30 per cent of the timber harvested on the Coast was sold through the VLM. This response also demonstrated that between 22 and 25 per cent of the timber harvested in the interior was sold domestically rather than internally consumed by integrated companies.

Alberta stated unequivocally in its' Questionnaire Response to Commerce that it did not interfere in the disposition of logs harvested from Crown land. Alberta also stated that, "The Province of Alberta has no policies, regulations or statutes that require, encourage or discourage companies to produce certain products. The expectation is just that operators should make efficient use of the wood fibre." Alberta also provided extensive data on arm's-length log sales.

Ontario informed Commerce in its initial questionnaire response that timber is often obtained through an arm's-length purchase from the private party that acquired it from the Crown (resale). Ontario also provided Commerce with a report prepared by KPMG concerning Crown timber resold at arm's-length in an after-market. This report demonstrated that approximately 30 per cent of the softwood timber harvested from Crown land was sold by tenure holders to independent third parties who subsequently processed it into forest products.

ANNEX A-2

Responses of the United States to Questions Posed in the Context of the First Substantive Meeting of the Panel (21 May 2002)

Questions to the United States

1. Q1: At the time of the Preliminary Determination, the Commerce Department had extensive evidence on the record indicating that the vast majority of government timber in Canada was provided directly to tenure holders that owned sawmills or other wood processing facilities. Specifically, the laws and regulations of each Canadian province (with the partial exception of Ontario) generally require that tenure holders be sawmills. The evidence described below for each province consisted primarily of provincial legislation, sample tenure contracts and statistical data provided by the provincial governments.

2. More than 83 per cent of the B.C. Crown softwood timber harvest is provided to holders of four types of B.C. tenures. Each of these tenures *requires* the tenure holder to own a processing facility (for these purposes, a sawmill) and process the harvested timber (or an equivalent volume) in its own mill. The remaining B.C. Crown timber is provided under licences that are normally reserved to entities not owning timber processing facilities. However, the B.C. Forest Act requires that all timber harvested from Crown lands be processed in B.C. In addition, other legal restrictions apply to these forms of B.C. tenure, which indicate that transactions for the timber covered by these tenures are not at arm's-length.

3. Quebec ensures that only sawmills are permitted to harvest the vast majority of Crown softwood timber. For example, section 37 of the Quebec Forest Act states that "[n]o one except a person authorized under Title IV to construct or operate a wood processing plant is qualified to enter into" a Timber Supply and Forest Management Agreement, the virtually exclusive form of tenure in Quebec (covering 99 per cent of the Crown harvest).

4. In its questionnaire response, Ontario stated that "[g]enerally, in order to obtain any type of licence, an applicant must either own a forest resource processing facility (e.g., a sawmill, pulpmill, veneer mill, etc.) or must have a market to supply wood to some type of forest resource processing facility." Alberta stated that "[a]ll forms of commercial tenure own and operate sawmills".

5. In Saskatchewan, 86 per cent of softwood sawlogs were harvested by Forest Management Agreement holders, all of whom own sawmills and process their own timber. The remainder of the harvest was provided to smaller licencees under Forest Product Permits, some of whom have their own sawmills.

6. In Manitoba, 49 per cent of softwood sawlogs were provided to holders of Forest Management Licences, who by law are required to own timber processing facilities. Virtually all of the remaining 51 per cent of softwood sawlogs were provided under Timber Sales Agreements ("TSA"). The volume of softwood harvested by TSA holders owning sawmills amounted to 46 per cent of the total softwood saw-

log harvest. Thus, approximately 95 per cent of softwood sawlogs were provided directly to sawmills in Manitoba.

7. With respect to the obligations undertaken by the tenure holders, the Commerce Department examined the obligations that tenure holders were legally obligated to assume in Canada and compared them to those assumed by harvesters of the benchmark timber. The Commerce Department calculated a per-unit amount for each category of Canadian obligations that was above and beyond obligations incurred by parties paying stumpage charges in the United States. The Commerce Department used the values for each obligation provided by the Canadian provincial governments in their questionnaire responses, and considered the per-unit cost of these obligations as a form of "in-kind" payment, which it added to the stumpage fee.

8. Q2(a): Article 14(d) sets forth guidelines for determining whether the government has provided a good, within the meaning of Article 1.1(a)(1)(iii), for less than adequate remuneration. There should be no doubt that, through timber tenures, the provincial governments provide a good – timber – to lumber producers. Canada's claims to the contrary are contradicted by ordinary dictionary definitions and Canada's own laws. Because the provincial governments are unquestionably providing a good within the meaning of Article 1.1(a)(1)(iii), Article 14(d) provides the appropriate guidelines for determining the benefit.

9. Q2(b): The phrase "in relation to prevailing market conditions for the good ... in the country of provision" in Article 14(d) does not restrict the authority to using only prices between buyers and sellers in the country under investigation. The concept of commercial availability is expressly incorporated in Article 14(d), which defines "prevailing market conditions for the good" to include, *inter alia*, availability. Prevailing market conditions in the country of provision may therefore encompass prices commercially available on the world market to purchasers in the country under investigation. The flexibility to use commercially available world market prices in Article 14(d) is reflected in item (d) of the Illustrative List of Export Subsidies, and was confirmed by the panel and the Appellate Body in *Canada Dairy*.

10. The use of world market prices commercially available to producers in the country under investigation is therefore not *per se* inconsistent with Article 14(d). Canada has, in fact, conceded that world market prices can constitute an appropriate benchmark in certain situations. An obvious example of when commercially available world market prices may be an appropriate benchmark is where the government is the sole provider of the input in the country under investigation. The facts of this case present an analogous situation. Specifically, only two provinces provided any information on private stumpage prices, and that limited information was inadequate to serve as a benchmark for those provinces. Moreover, the evidence indicates that the Canadian provincial governments so dominate the market for timber that below-market government prices suppress prices in the small market for private timber in Canada.

11. The Commerce Department's use of US prices, as opposed to other world market prices, is supported by ample record evidence indicating that Canadian companies import US logs and bid on US stumpage. US timber is therefore "commercially available" to Canadian mills.

12. Q2(c): The US interpretation of Article 14(d) is consistent with the general meaning of "benefit" as previously articulated by panels and the Appellate Body, i.e.,

a benefit is some form of advantage that would not otherwise be available in the marketplace, absent the financial contribution. In *Canada Aircraft*, the panel stated that "[i]n order to determine whether the financial contribution ... confers a 'benefit', *i.e.*, an advantage, it is necessary to determine whether the financial contribution places the recipient in a more advantageous position than would have been the case *but for* the financial contribution. In our view, the only logical basis for determining the position the recipient would have been in absent the financial contribution is the market." (emphasis added). The Appellate Body in *Canada Aircraft* similarly stated that "there can be no 'benefit' to the recipient unless the 'financial contribution' makes the recipient *'better off' than it would otherwise have been, absent the contribution.* In our view, the marketplace provides an appropriate basis for comparison in determining whether a 'benefit' has been 'conferred', because the *trade-distorting potential* of a 'financial contribution' can be identified by determining whether the recipient has received a 'financial contribution' on terms more favourable than those available to the recipient in the market." (emphasis added).

13. Q2(d): The comparison in Article 14(d) is intended to identify the potentially trade-distorting artificial advantage resulting from the government's provision of a good. Commercially available prices in the country under investigation are normally the most appropriate benchmark. However, where the evidence indicates that the government so dominates the market that non-government domestic prices for the good in question are suppressed by the alleged below-market government prices for that good, the domestic prices cannot serve as a basis to measure the potential benefit. In such cases, other prices commercially available to producers in the country under investigation can provide an appropriate benchmark.

14. Q2(e): The purpose of the Article 14(d) comparison is to determine what, if any, advantage flows from the government's financial contribution at issue, not other government actions.

15. Q2(f): The only instance in which we might even inquire into whether prices in the country under investigation are below world market prices would be where there is other evidence indicating that the non-government prices in the country under investigation may be distorted by the government financial contribution at issue.

16. Q2(g)(i),(ii): In this case, and in the only other case in which the Commerce Department has addressed this issue, the government's share of the market was 90 per cent or more. However, each case must be evaluated on the basis of its particular facts. Normally, where the government dominates the market for a particular good and there is some evidence that government prices are suppressing the rest of the market, the non-government prices could not logically serve as a benchmark. However, that may not always be the case. For example, even where the government dominates the market, if there is an open and competitive auction for some significant portion of the market, those prices could serve as a benchmark. There may also be other instances in which the facts would indicate that the non-government portion of the market was undistorted by the government action. In such cases, the non-government portion of the market could also serve as a benchmark.

17. Q2(h): The Commerce Department requested information on private stumpage prices and prices in the spot market for logs in the Maritime Provinces. In their questionnaire response, the Maritime Provinces stated that they had no information on private stumpage prices, that "[t]here is no spot market price for harvested saw

logs from Crown land", that they do "not collect any data concerning spot market prices for ... logs harvested from private land", and that surveys of prices for logs harvested from private land "appear to be based on limited sampling". Given this limited and inadequate information, the Commerce Department was unable to consider whether Maritime prices could serve as an appropriate benchmark.

18. Q3: The Commerce Department asked a series of questions regarding private prices in each province or territory. Only the governments of Alberta, Quebec and Ontario provided any information in response to this request. And, as described below, only Quebec and Ontario actually provided private prices. This limited information was insufficient to form the basis for a benchmark for these provinces. In addition, there was information on the record indicating that these private stumpage prices were depressed by the government prices. The largest province in terms of softwood lumber production, British Columbia (representing approximately 60 per cent of Canada's softwood lumber production), did not provide any private prices for stumpage.

19. Alberta did not provide private prices. In its questionnaire response, it stated: "Alberta does not track private timber harvesting and does not have any data on any private timber used in mills." It also stated that it "does not collect spot price information for logs from provincial or private lands" and it therefore was "not providing such spot log price information" to the Commerce Department. The only information Alberta did provide was a two-page excerpt from a KPMG survey, which contained a single estimated stumpage value derived from some price data for log sales. No supporting evidence or source information for the estimate was provided.

20. In its questionnaire response, Quebec stated: "Private market standing timber prices are obtained through a market survey of forestry companies that trade standing timber for harvesting every year in Quebec." However, the Commerce Department also had evidence that private stumpage prices in Quebec are suppressed by the administratively-set price for Crown stumpage.

21. Ontario stated that over 10 per cent of the timber consumed in Ontario's "forest products industry" is harvested from private lands. However, that figure covers the entire forest products industry, including companies that do not produce the subject merchandise (e.g., pulp mills). Moreover, Ontario stated that it does not regulate or monitor the private timber market on an ongoing basis, and therefore does not collect these data in the course of normal operations. Ontario commissioned an independent forestry research firm to conduct a survey, but the Commerce Department found numerous flaws with this study.

22. The record also contained evidence indicating that private stumpage prices were depressed by the overwhelming majority of government-supplied timber in the market. For example, a Canadian forestry expert concluded that "[t]he *quasi-monopolistic importance of the State in the supply* of the industries *obligates the small producers to align their prices with those of the public forest*". (emphasis added). Even a provincial forestry official stated in writing that private stumpage prices were affected by the administratively-set price for public stumpage.

23. Q4: The statement the Panel refers to pertained to the small private market for stumpage, not log sales. The evidence at the time of the Preliminary Determination indicated that Crown and private stumpage sales were the following percentages of the harvest in each province:

	Crown Sales	*Private Sales*
British Columbia:	90 per cent	10 per cent
Quebec:	83 per cent	17 per cent
Ontario:	92 per cent	8 per cent
Alberta:	98 per cent	2 per cent
Manitoba:	94 per cent	6 per cent
Saskatchewan:	90 per cent	10 per cent

Only two of the provinces provided data on private stumpage prices, and record evidence indicated that those prices were suppressed by the governments' administratively-set prices.

24. Q5: As stated in the chapeau to Article 14, and confirmed by the Appellate Body in *Canada Aircraft*, the benefit for purposes of Article 1 is the benefit to the recipient. It is the artificial advantage – or benefit – that the Appellate Body in *Canada Aircraft* referred to as the "trade-distorting potential" of a financial contribution. It is to that trade-distorting artificial advantage that the United States was referring in the passage cited by the Panel.

25. Q6: *Lead and Bismuth II* concerned subsidies to a government-owned entity, British Steel, which was subsequently sold to private investors. The panel stated that the presumption that the benefit flowing from a financial contribution continues to flow, even after a change in ownership that created an apparently new and distinct producer, could not be irrebuttable. The panel found that the circumstances in that proceeding, in which British Steel's specialty steels business was first transferred to the partnership UES and then re-acquired by BSplc, rebutted the presumption that the benefit to British Steel continued in UES and BSplc. The panel also found that UES and BSplc were distinct legal persons which, because they had paid fair market value for the assets of British Steel, obtained no benefit from the prior subsidies to British Steel.

26. *Lead and Bismuth II* addressed circumstances that are not present in this case. Most significantly, in the present case the subsidies at issue were bestowed directly on the current producers of the subject merchandise. The evidence simply does not support Canada's claim of a significant volume of timber harvested by independent loggers who sell at arm's-length to lumber mills. The vast majority of Crown sawtimber is provided to Canadian lumber mills under tenures held directly by those mills. Record evidence also indicates that most "independent" loggers are in fact bound by law or by contract to those very same sawmill/tenure holders. Thus, the entity receiving the financial contribution (the provision of timber) and the entity receiving the benefit (below-market stumpage prices) are generally one and the same. As discussed below in response to question 7 to the United States, the other two situations in this case in which the issue of whether a financial contribution to one entity confers a benefit on another may arise – logs harvested by one sawmill and then sold in arm's-length transactions to other sawmills, and lumber sold in arm's-length transactions to companies that produce remanufactured lumber products – are not relevant in an aggregate case.

27. Q7: In an aggregate case, the Commerce Department determines the total amount of the subsidy to producers of the subject merchandise and allocates that

amount over all sales of the subject merchandise. When all of the alleged recipients of the financial contribution and the benefits are producers of the subject merchandise, no further analysis is required. The precise amount of the benefit received by any specific producer would only be determined in a company-specific review. However, if the government made the financial contribution to an entity that does *not* produce the subject merchandise, it would be necessary to analyze whether that financial contribution benefited another entity that *does* produce the subject merchandise. In this case, the only allegation of a financial contribution to an entity that does not produce the subject merchandise is Canada's claim that there is a significant volume of Crown timber that the provincial governments provide to independent loggers who then sell the timber at arm's-length to lumber mills. However, the evidence does not support Canada's claim.

28. Canada also argues that the Commerce Department was required to perform a pass-through analysis to address two other situations: (1) logs harvested by one sawmill and then sold in arm's-length transactions to other sawmills; and (2) lumber sold in arm's-length transactions to companies that produce remanufactured lumber products. However, in both of these situations, all of the entities involved are producers of the subject merchandise. Therefore, no further analysis is required in an aggregate case. Specifically, a separate benefit analysis is not required in an aggregate case for logs harvested by one sawmill and allegedly sold at arm's-length to another, as the full benefit is always enjoyed by a sawmill, i.e., a producer of the subject merchandise. Likewise, the remanufactured articles at issue are within the scope of the investigation. The Commerce Department therefore properly matched the total benefit received by producers of the subject merchandise (the numerator) to the total sales of the subject merchandise, including remanufactured products (the denominator), without determining any company-specific rates. If any individual producer of subject merchandise believes that it has not received any countervailable benefit, the procedures for review exist.

29. Q8: There seems to be no question that provisional countervailing duties would constitute a provisional measure within the meaning of Article 17. Although Article 17.2 is somewhat ambiguous, a cash deposit or bond requirement would also appear to constitute a provisional measure within the meaning of Article 17. While the United States did not impose a provisional duty, it did require security in the form of cash deposits or bonds.

30. There is no reference in Article 17.2 to withholding of appraisement, which is referred to in the United States as suspension of liquidation. Suspension of liquidation is merely a legal status that enables the assessment of additional duties when all of the issues related to final duty liability are resolved. Nevertheless, under the US countervailing duty law, suspension of liquidation is treated as a provisional measure.

31. Q9: Under US law, absent suspension of liquidation, final duties are assessed and no additional duties can be imposed on that entry. Suspension of liquidation is therefore essential to preserve the possibility of exercising the right under Article 20.6 to impose duties retroactively.

32. Q10: Suspension of liquidation would enable the Commerce Department to delay final determination of total duty liability. However, if no amount is guaranteed by a cash deposit or bond, Article 20.3 would, on its face, preclude the collection of duties retroactively.

33. The absence of an analogue in the *SCM Agreement* to Article 10.7 of the Anti-Dumping Agreement does not alter this analysis. Article 10.7 authorizes authorities to take measures even before there is a preliminary determination of dumping or injury. In the case concerning *Hot-Rolled Steel from Japan*, the panel viewed these special "precautionary measures" as something other than provisional measures. Because there is no analogue to Article 10.7 in the *SCM Agreement*, there is no exception to the requirements of Article 17.1 of the *SCM Agreement* that would permit early "precautionary measures". However, the Commerce Department did not take such measures in this case. Where, as in this case, provisional measures are imposed in accordance with Article 17 (i.e., after preliminary determinations of subsidization and injury), Article 20.1 permits a Member to expand the scope of those provisional measures to encompass entries 90 days prior to the preliminary determination if there is sufficient evidence that the circumstances described in Article 20.6 exist.

34. Q11: Both suspension of liquidation and the posting of bonds or cash deposits are necessary to ensure the possibility of exercising the right to retroactive relief provided for in Article 20.6. The reference to "suspension of liquidation" in the Preliminary Determination is a short form of reference sometimes used by the Commerce Department when discussing provisional measures generally, including posting of bonds or cash deposits.

35. Q12: Article 20.6 requires a finding of "injury which is difficult to repair," but does not contain an evidentiary standard for that determination. However, this issue was addressed by the panel in *Hot-Rolled Steel from Japan*, which concerned the evidentiary standard in the US anti-dumping law for a preliminary critical circumstances finding. That evidentiary standard is "a reasonable basis to believe or suspect" that critical circumstances exist. That is also the standard in the US countervailing duty law for a preliminary critical circumstances finding. The *Hot-Rolled Steel from Japan* panel found that in applying that standard, the Commerce Department has "made affirmative determinations when sufficient evidence was adduced that the conditions of application were satisfied." As the *Hot-Rolled Steel from Japan* panel noted, "sufficient evidence" refers to the quantum of evidence necessary to make a determination. What constitutes "sufficient evidence" varies depending on the nature of the determination in question. The approach taken by other panels "has been to examine whether the evidence before the authority at the time it made its determination was such that an unbiased and objective investigating authority evaluating that evidence could properly have made the determination".

36. Q13: Section 351.213(b) of the regulations does not apply to aggregate cases but it does not restrict the Commerce Department's authority to conduct reviews. The inquiry required in Article 21.2 of the *SCM Agreement*, on which Canada's claim is based, is whether continued imposition of the duty is necessary to offset subsidization. Under section 351.213(k) of the regulations, exporters have the opportunity for a review to determine whether imposition of a duty is necessary on future entries, i.e., whether their subsidy rate is zero. If no subsidy is found, the cash deposit and assessment rate on future entries will be zero, unless the results of a subsequent review demonstrate that subsidies have recurred. Section 351.213(k) therefore fulfills the requirements of Article 21.2.

Questions to Both Parties

37. Q1: While some financial contributions take place at a single point in time, that is not always the case. The Canadian timber tenures are long-term contracts that provide recurring subsidies. As long as the tenure contract remains in force the provincial government is providing the lumber producer with timber, and the producer receives a benefit each time it pays below-market prices for the timber.

38. Q2: While there is no uniform world market price for softwood lumber and softwood logs, lumber and logs are traded internationally in all regions of the world. It is possible to calculate average unit import values for lumber and logs in various countries based on either import or export statistics. However, because these statistics are kept on a broad product category basis, the average unit import values are not useful for comparison purposes.

39. Q3: The United States negotiated the language of Article 15(b) of the China Protocol, which was intended to clarify that Article 14 of the *SCM Agreement* allows authorities to measure the benefit on the basis of a benchmark outside the country of investigation when prevailing terms and conditions in the country of investigation are "not ... available as appropriate benchmarks." Although Article 14 of the *SCM Agreement* already allows Members to use such benchmarks, the Members incorporated this clarifying language into Article 15(b) of the China Protocol because they were concerned that prices in China would not be appropriate benchmarks while China was transitioning to a market economy and they wanted to leave no doubt that Article 14 allowed authorities to use external benchmarks in such instances. In addition, because Article 14 only addresses countervailing duty proceedings under Part V of the *SCM Agreement*, they wanted to make clear that external benchmarks would also remain available were a Member to pursue a WTO proceeding under Part II or III of the Agreement.

40. Article 15(b) is only one of several provisions of the China Protocol that simply restate and clarify existing WTO obligations that apply to all Members. Article 10.1 of the China Protocol, for example, restates existing obligations in Article 25 of the *SCM Agreement*. Several articles of the China Protocol also restate and clarify existing WTO most-favoured nation and national treatment obligations.

41. Q4: This information has been provided in response to question 1 to the United States.

42. Q5: In an aggregate case, the Commerce Department determines the total amount of the subsidy to producers of the subject merchandise and allocates that amount over all sales of the subject merchandise. When all of the alleged recipients of the financial contribution and the benefits are producers of the subject merchandise, no further analysis is required to perform the aggregate calculation. Benefits that potentially shift from one producer to another in an arm's-length transaction would still be part of the overall numerator, as long as both companies produce subject merchandise. Therefore, for two of the three categories that Canada claims a pass-through analysis was necessary – logs harvested by one sawmill and then sold to another, and lumber sold to remanufacturers – the question of pass-through is moot in an aggregate context and the Commerce Department did not request any information on these types of transactions.

43. For the remaining category where Canada claims a pass-through analysis is necessary – independent loggers selling to sawmills – the Commerce Department

asked questions about logs sold domestically at arm's-length prices. In response, Quebec indicated that there were essentially no arm's-length transactions involving Crown timber sold by independent loggers to sawmills. Ontario suggested that 30 per cent of Crown timber was sold in arm's-length transactions, but tenure holders who do not own a sawmill are limited with respect to where such harvested timber can be sold and evidence indicated that log swapping was common among large tenure holders. Alberta's questionnaire response suggested that only a small portion of the harvest was characterized by arm's-length transactions. B.C. suggested that as much as 30 per cent of Crown timber was sold in arm's-length transactions, but this figure is misleading because loggers operate as employees or contractors for tenure holders, various requirements serve to narrow the range of purchasers available to any harvester of Crown timber who is not a mill owner, and log swapping is a major part of the so-called arm's-length transactions. These factors combine to ensure that the great majority of Crown timber is force-fed to tenure-holding lumber producers. As such, the evidence does not support Canada's claim that a pass-through analysis is necessary or appropriate.

Questions to Canada

44. Q5: A Member is not always obliged to determine the benefit using as a benchmark market prices from the country under investigation. This is confirmed by numerous references in WTO agreements and prior WTO decisions. The United States also notes that the Panel's example of a government monopoly over the supply of a good is no different in principle from the circumstances of the instant case, where the provincial governments control 85 to 95 per cent of the market for timber. If it is shown that the government supply significantly distorts the market, the benchmark can be found outside the country, so long as a reasonable effort is made to measure the benefit provided in the country under investigation.

45. Q8: Given the ordinary meaning of "arm's-length," a so-called independent logger should only be viewed as operating at "arm's-length" from lumber producers if the harvester is freely negotiating, under no outside control or influence and under no compulsion to sell. The record establishes that not only are there very few transactions by independent harvesters, but even in such transactions, the provincial governments impose numerous restrictions and requirements on the transactions. In light of this evidence, the only reasonable conclusion is that there are no true arm's-length transactions for Crown timber.

46. Q10: Past determinations by the Commerce Department, which apply US law on the basis of different factual records, are of no relevance in determining whether the United States has acted consistently with its obligations in the present case. That is particularly true where, as here, the prior determinations at issue were decided under a different domestic legal standard, as well as different international obligations. At the time of the *Lumber III* determination cited by Canada, under US law the government provision of a good was deemed to provide a benefit if the good "was provided at preferential rates". That standard is fundamentally different than the current "adequate remuneration" standard and therefore the issue of an appropriate benchmark is fundamentally different as well. The Commerce Department rejected cross-border prices in *Lumber III* because it had "sufficient and reliable non-preferential price data" from within Canada. Other factors, such as comparability,

were therefore moot and were simply noted in passing to underscore the Commerce Department's primary rationale.

47. Q14(b): The Commerce Department did not investigate and, therefore, did not conclude that the Maritime Provinces received no support or that lumber sales from the Maritime Provinces were not subsidized.

48. Q14(e): Nothing in the *SCM Agreement* addresses the calculation of a "country-wide rate". The "country-wide rate" at issue is a creature of US law, not the WTO. Under current US law, the calculation of the country-wide rate is based on the total amount of the subsidy found to exist with respect to the *subject merchandise*, allocated across all sales of the *subject merchandise*. Nothing in US law or practice requires that non-subject merchandise be included in a country-wide rate calculation.

ANNEX B

Parties' Responses to Questions – Second Meeting of the Panel

ANNEX B-1

RESPONSES OF CANADA TO QUESTIONS POSED IN THE CONTEXT OF THE SECOND SUBSTANTIVE MEETING OF THE PANEL

(24 June 2002)

To Both Parties:

1. The evidence on the record related to softwood log harvest going to sawmills for processing into softwood lumber during the period of investigation is found in the following exhibits: CDA-104 (British Columbia); CDA-105 and CDA-106 (Alberta); CDA-107 and CDA-108 (Québec); and CDA-109 (Ontario). In addition, the percentage of Crown logs entering sawmills (as opposed to veneer mills, pulpmills, etc.) was as follows for each of the provinces: B.C. – 61.6 per cent on the Coast and 83.8 per cent in the Interior; Alberta – 59 per cent; Québec – 80 per cent; Ontario – 57 per cent. The record evidence does not always respond directly to the Panel's question. For example, British Columbia does not distinguish between logs from private lands and logs from Crown land entering sawmills, but did provide information to Commerce on the total percentages of logs entering sawmills. In addition, Alberta's figures are for all wood categories that could possibly have been made into softwood lumber products as Alberta does not track whether the softwood entering sawmills is used to make softwood lumber or other products such as pulp, chips, etc.

2. If by "tenure contract" the Panel means any form of tenure agreement including short-term licenses and permits, the answer to the question is yes. For trees to be cut on Crown land, a tenure contract is always required.

3. Canada elaborates on the processing requirements in existence in Canada, and the reasons for those requirements, in its response to Question 5, below. This answer describes the different types of tenure arrangements that exist in each province, the domestic processing requirements – if any – that attach to each arrangement, and the evidence on the record as to the percentage of total logs harvested that were subject to such requirements.

British Columbia - There are basically two types of tenures that have some form of processing requirement: Tree Farm Licenses and Forest Licenses. The vast majority of these types of tenures do *not* require the licensee to process harvested logs in a specific sawmill. Rather, the standard processing requirement requires only that the licensee process the timber harvested or an equivalent volume in a processing mill of any kind (sawmill, pulpmill, etc.) owned by the licensee. Harvesters frequently sell logs they harvest to third parties, and purchase logs they need from third parties to supplement their log supply for particular grades, species, etc. Only 11.5 per cent of the total harvest is subject to an appurtenancy clause, under which logs harvested by the licensee must be processed in a specific mill. Evidence on the record at the time of the CVD PD also indicates that 34 per cent of the total provincial Crown harvest (all tenure types) was harvested under tenures that were not subject to processing or appurtenancy requirements.

In addition, while part 10 of the *Forest Act* requires logs harvested from Crown land to be used or manufactured in the province, unless exempted, the record evidence indicates that more than 97 per cent of all applications to export logs from Crown land during the period of investigation were granted.

Alberta - There are three main tenure types: Forest Management Agreements (FMAs), Timber Quota Certificates and Commercial Timber Permits. With few exceptions, FMA holders in Alberta can use all the wood they harvest or sell all or a portion of the wood to third parties. Timber Quota Certificates and Commercial Timber Permits have no processing requirements. Harvesters in Alberta are also free to export their logs after obtaining export permits from the Alberta and Federal Governments. All export permits applied for by Alberta harvesters during the period of investigation were approved.

Ontario - There are two main types of tenure: Sustainable Forest Licenses and Forest Resource Licenses. License holders are not required to own or operate milling facilities. They are, however, required to indicate to the province that they have a market for the timber they intend to harvest. That market may be a facility in which they have an ownership interest or one in which they have no interest. In certain instances tenure holders and mills reach agreements that provide the opportunity for some forest resources to be committed to a specific facility or facilities. Actual supply of a facility pursuant to such an agreement is subject to the parties involved agreeing on the terms of the transaction. Approximately 30 per cent of Ontario's Crown timber is acquired by sawmills through arm's-length transactions with third parties who have their own licenses. While Ontario does have a requirement that its Crown timber be processed in the province unless an exemption is granted by the Minister, all permits to export logs from the province applied for were granted during the period of investigation.

Québec - There are two types of tenure arrangements: Timber Supply and Forest Management Agreements (TSFMAs) and Forest Management Contracts (FMCs). The timber harvested under TSFMAs (which represents 99.4 per cent of the softwood harvest in 2000-2001) must be processed in the mill holding the TSFMA. While Québec has a requirement that timber harvested be processed in the province, TSFMA holders may apply for authorization to export logs harvested under their tenure agreements rather than process them. All such applications were granted.

4. Timber refers to standing trees in the forest. In their natural state, trees are not capable of being traded because they are firmly rooted in the ground.

Logs are produced when standing timber is harvested and prepared for transportation.

Lumber is produced when logs are processed by sawmills. Logs are, therefore *input goods* into the production of lumber, which is the subject merchandise.

Sawlog refers to widely different things in Canada and the United States. Most Canadian provinces do not use the term "sawlog" other than to generally refer to logs of any size that enter a sawmill; therefore, in Canada the term refers to a particular *use* for logs. In the United States, however, "sawlog" refers to a *grade* of logs, rather than their intended *use*. There, "sawlogs" are defined as logs exceeding a minimum size requirement, while smaller logs are classified as "pulpwood".

"Pulpwood" prices are often less than half of "sawlog" prices in many US jurisdictions. Sawmills in the US can and do process both "sawlogs" and "pulpwood". In Canada, mills in several provinces use a significant amount of logs that would be classified as "pulpwood" in the United States. As well, in Canada, softwood stumpage charges are usually levied for the stand as a whole, rather than separately for the different log grades that can be produced from the stand. In contrast, US stumpage prices are specified for different log grades.

For the above reasons, which log classes are used in any calculation has an enormous impact on the resulting pricing benchmarks.

One of the several ways in which Commerce biased its preliminary determination calculations was by using United States price data that was explicitly based on "sawlog" and "pulpwood" grades, but then excluding all smaller "pulpwood" price data from its US calculations. In short, Commerce compared only the highest US prices to the stumpage charges it chose from Canada.

Stumpage is the right to harvest *timber*, or standing trees. It is a property interest in land. This right is normally accorded in return for a series of obligations related to the management of the resource, including management of the land and reforestation, and payment of a charge on the exercise of that right.

Stumpage programme or practice refers to provincial forestry management policies under which provinces enter into tenure agreements with or issue harvesting licenses to timber harvesters in return for the assumption of obligations, including forestry management and payment of charges, by the harvester.

Stumpage rate refers to the charge imposed on the volume of harvest.

There is a distinction between a standing tree in the forest that cannot be traded, and a log that results from the harvest of that tree. For the purposes of the WTO Agreement, standing trees, which cannot be traded, are not "goods". Also "timber" is simply not "goods" within the meaning of the *Black's Law Dictionary* definition, which is based on nearly two centuries of common law making a distinction between interests in land and "goods".

5. Canada adds the following to its discussion in answer to Question 3 above.

Domestic processing requirements are intended to ensure that tenure holders carry out their short and long term obligations under tenure agreements consistently with sound forestry and environmental objectives and that standing timber that is harvested is utilized fully and is not wasted.

Neither Alberta nor Ontario has appurtenancy requirements. In Québec, under the main type of tenure arrangement, agreement holders must process the timber they harvest in the facility that holds the TSFMA.

Tenure holders are free to apply to export the logs that they harvest from Canada. As noted above, permits to export are issued routinely by the Federal government and provincial governments in Alberta, Ontario and Québec for export from those provinces. In British Columbia permits to export are issued when various criteria are met. 97 per cent of all applications to export from the province during the POI were approved.

6. Commerce used public lands as benchmarks for British Columbia (Washington), Alberta (Montana) and Saskatchewan (Montana), that are subject to log export restrictions. Exports of softwood lumber from British Columbia, Alberta and Saskatchewan represented almost 61 per cent of Canadian exports subject to countervailing duties. The United States, therefore, used as benchmarks for 61 per cent of Canadian exports subject to the determination, stumpage from US public lands that have

export restrictions. This means that even if a Canadian could obtain the ability to harvest on these lands, he or she could *not* export the logs to Canada.

7. Import data relating to the imports of logs from the United States into Canada, by province, during the period of investigation was on the record at the time of the preliminary determination. No information on the re-export to the United States of lumber processed from those logs was asked for by Commerce nor provided to it. The import statistics consisted only of a basket category "wood in the rough" and so included imports of products other than rough logs such as poles, roughly squared timber and house logs. With the exception of imports of logs into Québec, the import of logs into Canada represent less than 1 per cent of the total annual harvest. With respect to log imports into Québec, these imports, from Maine into southern Québec, are not large in volume and relate to particular factors that are unique to this area. Imports of logs by volume by province are as follows: British Columbia - 593,760m^3; Alberta - 2,212m^3; Ontario - 272,385m^3; Québec - 2,910,929m^3.

8. Tenure agreements in British Columbia, Alberta, Ontario and Québec contain maximum cut limits. Ontario and Québec have no minimum cut requirements. Some of Alberta's tenures contain minimum cut requirements, but they are not enforced, as Alberta confirmed during the hearings before the US International Trade Commission in the *Lumber IV* injury proceeding. The Annual Allowable Cut (AAC) for each of these provinces and the volume of timber harvested for 1998, 1999 and 2000 was provided to Commerce and are set out in Exhibits CDA-125 (Alberta), CDA-126 (Ontario), CDA-127 (Québec) and CDA-128(British Columbia).

In British Columbia licensees under certain designated types of tenures are subject to minimum cut requirements, which require the harvester to harvest plus or minus 50 per cent of the annual allowable cut for that licensee in any given year, and plus or minus 10 per cent over a five year period. Information on the record reveals that in years 1998, 1999, and 2000/2001, the total timber harvest was less than the applicable total AAC allocation for those years. The record does not contain information on whether the 5-year limits were met or exceeded. Thus, it is not possible to determine from record evidence whether the cut requirements were satisfied. The *Forest Act* (Section 66) provides the Minister with discretion not to enforce those cut requirements in particular cases if the circumstances so warrant.

In B.C., the record evidence demonstrates that a significant portion of logs is purchased from third parties. Even if a tenure holder has an unused AAC, it will still supplement its input by purchasing logs of specific species, grade, etc., from third parties that are not available from its Crown holdings.

To Canada:

28. The main interest of tenure holders is the end product of the harvest. From the perspective of the tenure holder, however, the distinction between the *right to harvest* and that end product has significant legal and economic consequences . A long-term tenure represents current and future harvests, and also obligations. A simple sale of stumpage as is done in the United States, however, concerns a set harvest volume available today – only in this sense can it be argued that there is no real distinction between the right to harvest and the end result of the harvest. While the end result of each activity is the production of logs, the nature of economic interests timber har-

vesters acquire when entering into different types of arrangements is significantly different.

29. Whether stumpage is a price or tax was immaterial to the question at issue in *British Columbia* v. *Canadian Forest Products*. Instead, this case only considered whether a statutory appeal board had exceeded its jurisdiction.

Furthermore, other higher courts in Canada have described stumpage as a tax. In *Royal Bank of Canada* v. *The King*, the Supreme Court of Canada referred to stumpage as "being by definition 'a *tax* charged for the privilege of cutting timber on State lands'." Accordingly, to the extent that this US argument is at all relevant, the precedent of *this* court is controlling.

In any event, Canada's position in this respect is a matter of sound economics and WTO law. Stumpage is the right to harvest timber. This right is accorded by a province in exchange for obligations assumed by the tenure holder, one of which is the payment of a stumpage fee or charge on the timber cut and processed into logs. The nature of the volumetric stumpage charge as part of a broader bundle of rights and obligations underscores the inappropriateness of the comparison made by the United States of stumpage charges in Canada to lump-sum auction prices for short-term harvesting rights on public lands in the US to determine and measure a benefit.

30. Canada initially used the term "arm's-length" to make the point that Article 1 of the *SCM Agreement* does not permit an investigating authority to presume that a purchaser of a good from an allegedly subsidised entity is also subsidised. There are two elements in a subsidy determination, financial contribution by government that confers a benefit.

With respect to financial contribution, an alleged provision of goods by the government to a seller may not be *presumed* to be the provision of goods by the government to someone who purchases from that seller *at arm's-length*. Thus, for the United States to demonstrate, under Article 1, that a sawmill received "goods" from the *government* when it entered into an *arm's-length* transaction with a timber harvester, it must establish "entrustment" or "direction" under subparagraph (iv).

A similar analysis is applicable to the second element. Where two unrelated parties acting in their own self-interest enter into a transaction, an investigating authority may not *presume* that the allegedly subsidised seller has passed on a benefit to the purchaser. A "benefit" analysis looks at the terms of a sale available *to a recipient* and not those obtained in a previous transaction by the seller. Parties at arm's length act in their own self-interest, and a seller will not "pass on" a benefit willingly. An investigating authority must, accordingly, *demonstrate* that an arm's-length transaction is not at "fair market value", and may not presume that it is not.

(a) Canada has been consistent in defining what constitutes an "arms-length" transaction: it is the sale between unrelated parties where each is acting in its own self interest. An arm's-length transaction forms the basis to determine fair market value. Canada agrees with Black's definition of fair market value. However, the US conclusion from that definition that an arm's length transaction is one where neither party is under "any outside control or influence" from any person has no basis in anything other than its own assertion, and should be rejected. Contrary to what the US appears to argue, fair market value is not a required element of an arm's-length transaction. Where timber harvesters and sawmills are at arm's-length, an investigating authority must demonstrate government entrustment or direction in the sense of subparagraph (iv) and may not presume that a subsidised seller in an arm's-length transaction passes on the benefit to the purchaser.

(b) A government-directed sale may or may not constitute a subsidy *depending on the terms of the sale agreed by the parties*. Where the parties are at arm's-length, even where the goods are *provided* under instruction from the government, it may not be presumed that the goods are provided at *less than the market rate*. There are two elements in a subsidy determination and each must be demonstrated.

In the *Lumber IV* investigation there was no allegation or demonstration of a financial contribution within Article 1.1(a)(1)(iv). Commerce conducted no analysis and simply presumed a pass-through of alleged subsidies to timber harvesters to producers of softwood lumber despite the fact that Canada raised "pass-through" as a significant issue in the investigation even before the investigation was initiated. Indeed, the questionnaire responses of the provinces provided data demonstrating that a portion of logs entering sawmills were acquired in arm's-length transactions with timber harvesters.

(c) Canada's statement in paragraph 49 of its responses to the Panel's questions related to the market *prices* that are normally the product of an arm's-length transaction rather than to the hallmarks of an arm's-length transaction *per se*.

A transaction is considered to be at arm's-length where neither party controls the other in respect of its acceptance of the terms of the transaction. In this respect, both parties must be "willing" to enter into that transaction with the other. In such a case, an investigating authority may not simply *presume* that because the seller was allegedly subsidised, then the buyer is also subsidised. Indeed, since each party is acting "in his or her own self interest" and seeking to maximize profits, any presumption may *only* be that the transaction price is a market price.

31. To maximize efficiency, mills are designed to process a given species (or species group) and timber of a given size. Each mill owner, whether with or without tenure, will seek to ensure that the log supply for each mill best meets its species and dimension requirements. For example, an owner of a cedar mill may not have sufficient supply of cedar and will seek to purchase cedar logs from other sources of log supply. The same need to enter the log market occurs to ensure that the log dimension requirements of mill owners are met.

In many cases the log sales by tenure holders are on a cash basis, but in other cases they entail log trades or "swaps". That is, logs of a given species and/or size are traded to another mill in return for logs of a different species and/or size. There is no legal requirement for tenure holders to trade or "swap" logs. Log purchases, sales and trades result from the profit maximizing behaviour of tenure holders, and in any log transaction, both parties want to receive fair value. Indeed, the practice of partial cash settlements in log trades confirms the nature of the transaction: they would only occur if the value of the logs being traded were not equal and the cash settlement was required to equalize the value.

32. Where a government has given a harvester no choice but to harvest standing timber and enter into a contract with a sawmill to process the logs that result from the

harvest, this could constitute a government-directed provision of goods. The investigating authority would, of course, have to gather and analyse facts regarding whether the situation described in the question existed, and whether the other requirements of subparagraph (iv) were present.

There was no allegation in *Lumber IV* of government-directed provision of goods, and Commerce did not undertake any such analysis. It simply asserted that provinces directly provide goods to lumber producers under Article 1.1(a)(1)(iii) of the *SCM Agreement*. This, the provinces do not do.

33. With the exception of certain commitment letters in Ontario, tenured log harvesters in Canada who do not own sawmills are not required to contract with sawmills in the province for processing of the logs they harvest.

34. It is up to a WTO Member to structure its laws in such a way as to permit it to avail itself of rights it might have under the WTO Agreement. A WTO Member may not apply a measure in direct contravention of its obligations to "preserve" the rights the Agreement affords.

With respect to critical circumstances, a WTO Member has the *right* to impose *definitive* duties retroactively, subject to the requirements of Article 20.6. In the case of Members with retrospective systems, they may keep liquidation open for a long enough period that would allow the retroactive imposition of definitive duties following a critical circumstances determination or otherwise provide themselves with the legal authority to impose definitive countervailing duties retrospectively when the requirements of Article 20.6 have been met.

35. Yes. Opening an investigation would have commercial consequences for traders. However, opening an investigation that alleges the existence of critical circumstances merely implies the *possibility* of a retroactive imposition of duties *in the future* once there have been positive determinations both on the underlying action and with respect to critical circumstances. Suspension of liquidation specifically targets the traded goods at issue and results in an immediate chilling effect in the market.

36. Yes. Canada is not pursuing its claims in respect of "specificity" in this dispute. Canada has decided instead to pursue this claim in its WTO challenge to the US final countervailing duty determination (WT/DS257).

37. Yes. Canada is no longer pursuing its claims in respect of the "Maritimes" question in this proceeding.

To the United States:

12. Article 19.3 does not contain any exceptions, and the United States has *not*, in any of its submissions throughout this case, claimed the benefit of an exception to the obligation to grant expedited reviews and to establish an individual countervailing duty rate for requesting exporters.

14. While the United States has stated that it has discretion under US law to grant expedited reviews, it has not unequivocally stated, as Canada requested, that such "discretion" does *not* include discretion to *refuse* to grant an expedited review or to establish individual countervailing duty rates. Accordingly, the findings requested by Canada are necessary to resolve the other questions that are at the heart of the obligation in Article 19.3, and that remain in dispute.

16. Regarding the use of import log prices, neither the data nor the methodology necessary to estimate "adequate remuneration" based on log import data exists.

Further, logs are not a homogeneous good. The price of logs varies by species and quality. Comparing import log prices to domestic log prices is confounded by a number of practical matters including:

- The "wood in the rough" category in StatsCan's import data (Tariff Item 44.03) is a catch-all category that includes other, and frequently more valuable, products in addition to logs, and it is not possible to derive from the official customs data an import price for softwood logs only, the necessary first step in developing a log import benchmark.
- Export (import) prices may not be representative of domestic prices because exports are often higher in quality, and export price data are rarely collected with enough care to assure that there are not important quality differences between them.

Estimating "adequate remuneration" for vast reaches of any Canadian province based on prices of imported logs is an intractable problem. For example, the cost of harvesting different species may be different because of differences in the terrain on which those species are found or differences in the distance to mill or market for different species, and species-specific prices must be used because the species mix of imported and domestic logs may differ. There is therefore no valid means to estimate the harvesting and transportation costs that should be deducted from imported log prices as a measure of stumpage charges, even (incorrectly) assuming that in this case the necessary information about log imports were available by species, grade, and other relevant criteria.

17. For reasons that include the following, cross-border log price comparisons do not provide a valid in-market price benchmark:

- Differences in economic conditions: economic conditions such as wages, capital costs, taxes, and various governmental regulatory policies differ between countries and as such affect prices in each country.
- Trade distortions: Commerce's period of investigation coincided with the final year of the Canada/United States Softwood Lumber Agreement (SLA). The SLA restricted Canadian exports of lumber to the US and, as such, caused Canadian domestic lumber prices to fall relative to US lumber prices. As prices are set at the margin and as the demand for logs is a derived demand, derived from the demand for lumber, any fall in Canadian lumber prices relative to US lumber prices would cause Canadian log prices to fall relative to US log prices.
- Locational differences: A log price is the price of the log delivered to a specific location, typically a mill. For US log prices that location is not within Canada. At a minimum adjustments will be needed for both differences in log haul and lumber transportation costs. In addition, comparison of prices in one regional market to prices in another regional market, where the supply and demand conditions are different, would be invalid. This applies for comparisons made within US juris-

dictions let alone across international borders. This is illustrated by the table at paragraph 75 of Canada's responses to questions from the Second Substantive Meeting which reveals significant domestic Douglas fir log price variations among sub regions in western Oregon and Washington during the year 2000.

- Timber differences: Logs are not a homogenous product. They differ in species and quality. There are significant differences in timber species and quality (*i.e.*, diameter, length, taper, ring-width, defects, etc.) between Canada and the United States. Thus, any comparison of aggregate average log prices would need to account for the differences in species mix and quality which requires some standard set of log grading rules along with grade specific prices. No such standard grading system exists in the US, and the Canadian grading rules differ from those in the US
- Differences in Measurements: Log prices in the United States are measured in $/MBF while Canadian stumpage charges are measured in $/m^3. The near impossibility of finding appropriate conversion factors for converting US stumpage prices measured by antiquated US log scales to Canadian charges in cubic metres equally plagues comparisons of log prices.

18. The use of any benchmark that is not a benchmark in Canada (i.e. within the country of provision in this case) is inconsistent with the *SCM Agreement* and Article 14(d) in particular.

21. The fundamental US position at issue in this case is that the word "in" in Article 14(d) can be understood as meaning "out". The word "in" cannot be read as "out" and thus Article 14(d) cannot be found to permit using cross-border benchmarks in determining the adequacy of remuneration, i.e. in determining whether a benefit has been conferred. It is this fundamental point that Canada requests that the Panel confirm.

The "new" US position that "out" means "in" is also predicated on an erroneous reading of Article 14(d) – that "availability" means the "availability of commercial prices". It is clear from the separate inclusion of "price" and "availability" in the list of factors set out in Article 14(d) that it is a "good" and not a "price" that has to be available in Canada. Thus this US interpretation of Article 14(d) must also fall. Canada requests that the Panel confirm this.

The basic factual problems regarding Commerce's determination that have been discussed with the Panel underline why these US approaches to the "appropriate methodology" under Article 14(d) must fail and why Canada's interpretation is correct. Alberta, Ontario and Québec all provided evidence on private sales of timber harvesting rights and Alberta and B.C. provided information on competitive tenures. Québec also provided a comprehensive economic analysis showing Québec's private forest to be an open and competitive market free of government distortion. Ontario provided Commerce with a study that concluded that the market for private timber in Ontario was both competitive and efficient. Further, these provinces provided Commerce with evidence that provincial stumpage systems earned substantial profits and are operated consistently with market principles. Finally, evidence was presented that there is no benefit to lumber producers when the situation in Canada is compared with results that would be produced in a competitive market.

Commerce's own regulations provide for analysing consistency with market principles as a way to evaluate adequacy of remuneration. "Consistency with market principles" is the benchmark used by Commerce to determine adequacy of remuneration in cases where it has found that the government played a dominant role in the market. In a number of recent cases Commerce has clarified that government prices are consistent with market principles when the government earns a profit.

27. There were two *measures* applied pursuant to two *determinations*: the preliminary countervailing duties determination, and the preliminary critical circumstances determination. Absent a "critical circumstances" determination, provisional measures would have applied *only* to entries *within* the period in which provisional measures existed. The CC PD purported to permit the retroactive application of provisional measures to imports entered in the 90 days before the date of the determination. This is not permitted by Article 20.6 which allows only for the retroactive application of *definitive duties*.

Even if the Panel agrees that there was only one measure, it was applied to entries over approximately a seven-month period, i.e. four months under the CVD PD and 90 days under the CC PD. For this reason alone, that measure would be inconsistent with Article 17.4.

ANNEX B-2

Responses of the United States to Questions Posed in the Context of the Second Substantive Meeting of the Panel
(24 June 2002)

Questions to Both Parties

1. Q1: The record at the time of the Preliminary Determination clearly demonstrates that the vast majority of logs used to make softwood lumber in Canada during the period of investigation were harvested from Crown lands. British Columbia reported that exact figures regarding the volume of softwood logs sent to sawmills were unavailable. However, it stated that *89.5 per cent* of the softwood sawlog-grade logs that were harvested during the period of investigation were harvested from Crown land. Quebec reported that *84.7 per cent* of the softwood logs that were harvested and sent to sawmills during the period of investigation were harvested from Crown land. Ontario reported that *93.2 per cent* of softwood logs that were harvested and sent to sawmills during the period of investigation were harvested from Crown land. Alberta reported that *98.5 per cent* of softwood logs that were harvested and sent to sawmills during the period of investigation were harvested from Crown land. Saskatchewan reported that *88.5 per cent* of softwood logs that were harvested and sent to sawmills during the period of investigation were harvested from Crown land. Finally, Manitoba reported that 546,667.52 cubic meters of softwood logs were harvested and sent to sawmills from Crown land during the period of investigation. Manitoba indicated that it did not have data regarding the size of the harvest on private or federal land, but stated that Crown land accounted for *95 per cent* of the forested land in the province. In calculating the amount of the subsidy benefit, the Commerce Department only included those logs harvested from Crown land.

2. Q2: The record evidence at the time of the Preliminary Determination unequivocally demonstrates that the harvesting of Crown timber without a tenure contract or license is prohibited by law in each of the Canadian provinces producing lumber subject to the investigation. The British Columbia Forest Act provides that rights to harvest Crown timber may only be granted in accordance with the Forest Act and specifies the types of tenure contracts under which harvesting rights may be granted. The Quebec Forest Act forbids any person to "carry on a forest management activity" without a forest management permit, and defines these activities to include "timber felling and harvesting." The Ontario Crown Forest Sustainability Act provides that no person may conduct any forest operations except in accordance with a forest management plan approved by the Minister. The Alberta Forest Act provides that no person may cut "any forest growth on forest land" without the permission of the Minister, and that the Minister may dispose of Crown timber only under one of the three forms of tenure in Alberta. The Saskatchewan Forest Resources Management Act provides that no person may "harvest forest products except in accordance" with the Act and its regulations governing licenses required to harvest or operate a wood processing facility. Finally, the Manitoba Forest Act states that timber cutting

rights may only be granted under the authority of the Minister, and that no person may cut or remove timber without a license.

3. Q3: The record at the time of the Preliminary Determination demonstrated the following with regard to processing requirements imposed on tenure holders in British Columbia: (1) by law, all logs harvested from Crown land must be used in British Columbia or manufactured into lumber or another approved wood product in British Columbia; (2) by law, four tenure types are limited to licensees who own wood processing facilities. More than 83 per cent of the British Columbia softwood log harvest that was sent to sawmills was harvested under these four tenure types. Eight per cent of the Crown softwood timber harvest was provided to entities for which the evidence was not conclusive as to whether the tenure holders were required to own mills. Only 9 per cent of the British Columbia Crown softwood timber harvest was provided to licensees under tenures normally reserved for entities not owning wood processing facilities; and (3) the sample licenses provided by British Columbia indicate that all timber harvested under the license, or an equivalent volume, must be processed in the wood processing facility named in the license.

4. The record at the time of the Preliminary Determination demonstrated the following with regard to Quebec: (1) the Quebec Forest Act states that "[a]ll timber harvested in the public domain, whatever the nature or object of the management permit authorizing the harvesting, must be completely processed in Quebec;" (2) the same Act limits eligibility for Timber Supply and Forest Management Agreements ("TSFMAs") to entities authorized to construct or operate wood processing facilities, and timber harvested under TSFMAs accounts for 99 per cent of the Crown softwood timber harvest in Quebec; and (3) the sample TSFMA provided by Quebec states that the license holder is granted authority to harvest "for the purpose of supplying its plant," and that the tenure holder is required to "[p]rocess all wood harvested under its forest management permit with a view to using it at the plant identified in the preamble to this Agreement."

5. The record at the time of the Preliminary Determination demonstrated the following with regard to Ontario: (1) by law, all timber licenses are "subject to the condition that all trees harvested shall be manufactured in Canada into lumber, pulp, or other products;" (2) Ontario's questionnaire response stated that "[g]enerally, in order to obtain any type of license, an applicant must either own a forest resource processing facility or must have a market to supply wood to some type of forest resource processing facility;" and (3) Ontario's questionnaire response stated that the typical license "directs that the forest resources harvested pursuant to that license should be used to supply the forest resource processing facility owned by the license holder identified in the license, as well as other mills with commitments to receive wood from that license area." The Ministry of Natural Resources requires tenure holders to sign agreements (i.e., wood supply agreements) with the mills to supply the mills with timber.

6. The record at the time of the Preliminary Determination demonstrated the following with regard to Alberta: (1) by law, logs from public land may not be transported outside the province of Alberta without the permission of the Minister; (2) the sample tenure contract provided by Alberta requires the tenure holder to construct "a veneer plant within the vicinity of Rocky Mountain House, Alberta" within two years, to upgrade the plant within five years, to complete "the current expansion to its sawmill/planer mill at Sundre, Alberta" within 18 months and to expend a specified,

minimum sum on the veneer mill construction and upgrade and on the sawmill expansion; and (3) while there are no generally applicable legal requirements that tenure holders process the timber obtained under the tenure in their own facilities, provisions in individual tenure contracts are designed to achieve that objective.

7. The record at the time of the Preliminary Determination demonstrated that Saskatchewan limits harvesting rights and the right to operate wood processing facilities to holders of approved licenses for each, and Saskatchewan has entered into four forest management agreements with entities, all of which own sawmills. These four agreements account for 86 per cent of the Crown softwood sawlog harvest in Saskatchewan. Furthermore, 9 per cent of the Crown softwood sawlog harvest was provided to other tenure holders who own sawmills. Thus, as much as 95 per cent of Saskatchewan Crown softwood sawtimber was provided to entities that also hold provincial licenses to operate sawmills. While by law the agreements must include a requirement to "utilize the licensed volume or area," Saskatchewan did not provide any sample agreements.

8. The record at the time of the Preliminary Determination demonstrated that in Manitoba the Minister is authorized by law to grant Forest Management Licenses ("FMLs") "[w]here the investment in a wood-using industry established or to be established in Manitoba is sufficient to require the security of a continuous timber supply." In fact, all FMLs own sawmills, and FMLs account for 49 per cent of the softwood logs harvested in Manitoba. Furthermore, as much as an additional 46 per cent of the harvest was provided under other tenures to entities that do, in fact, own wood processing facilities.

9. Q4: The *New Shorter Oxford English Dictionary* defines "timber" as "[t]he wood of large growing trees able to be used for structural purposes" and "the trees themselves." The United States has used the term in both of these ways. "Logs" are felled trees or sections of felled trees that may have been delimbed or debarked, but have not been further processed into another end product. "Sawlogs " are logs that are suitable for sawing into lumber or logs that in fact are sawn into lumber. "Lumber" refers to sawn wood products (usually with at least two parallel sides) such as structural or framing lumber, flooring, or siding. The United States has used the term "softwood lumber" more precisely to refer to any lumber product within the scope of the subject merchandise in this investigation. "Stumpage" can mean: (1) "standing timber"; (2) "the value of standing timber"; (3) "a license to cut timber"; or (4) "the fee paid for the right to cut timber." The United States has used this term to refer to standing timber. "Stumpage rates" refers specifically to the fee paid for timber. The United States has used this term to refer to the rates charged by the provincial governments for Crown timber. "Stumpage programmes" are the legal regimes through which the provinces provide provincially owned timber. "Stumpage practices" is not a term used by the United States. As used by Canada, the term appears to be synonymous with stumpage programmes.

10. Q5: Ontario stated in its questionnaire response that "[g]enerally, in order to obtain any type of license, an applicant must either own a forest resource processing facility or must have a market to supply wood to some type of forest resource processing facility." Ontario also stated that the typical license "directs that the forest resources harvested pursuant to that license should be used to supply the forest resource processing facility owned by the license holder identified in the license, as well as other mills with commitments to receive wood from that license area." In

Ontario, in order to build a wood processing facility such as a sawmill, a mill must identify available timber on Crown lands and sign a wood supply commitment letter with the Ministry of Natural Resources to receive the timber. In turn, the Ministry requires tenure holders to sign agreements with the mills to supply the mills with timber. Since all tenure holders appear to be required by their licenses to use the harvested timber either in their own wood processing facility or in a defined wood processing facility within the license area for which a pre-existing contract exists, the evidence indicates that any "third party" purchases of logs are largely, if not entirely, mandated transfers of logs from tenure holders to the mills named in their license.

11. Q6: In the Preliminary Determination, benchmarks for three of the six provinces investigated by the Commerce Department were based entirely on stumpage rates from public lands where export restrictions apply. The Commerce Department found that (1) stumpage rates from public lands were based on open, competitive sales; (2) sales from public lands accurately reflected the market price available to US and Canadian purchasers because they constituted a minority of sales in the United States and were driven by the majority of sales in the United States, which consist of open, competitive sales from private lands; and (3) the Department would continue to seek private sales data as the investigation proceeded towards the final determination.

12. Q7: There is no record evidence on the volume of log imports from the United States that are processed in Canada and re-exported as lumber to the United States. US government statistics, however, demonstrate that US exports of softwood logs to Canada during 2000 totaled 2,476,000 cubic meters. The US statistics by port of exit indicate that a large majority of those exports (approximately 75 per cent) are from the Eastern United States. Data from Quebec companies that requested exclusion indicate that most of those exports likely went to mills in Quebec. With respect to lumber exports, approximately 50 per cent of Canada's lumber production is exported to the United States. No aspect of the Commerce Department's analysis was dependent on the level of Canadian imports of logs from the United States that was re-exported to the United States as lumber.

13. Q8: British Columbia reported that the total Crown harvest in fiscal year 2000-01 was 94 per cent of the annual allowable cut ("AAC "). By law, major licensees must ensure that between 50 per cent and 150 per cent of their allocated cut is harvested in any given year, and that between 90 per cent and 110 per cent of their allocated cut is harvested over a five-year period. Quebec reported that the total Crown harvest in fiscal year 2000-01 was 89.3 per cent of the AAC. By law, the Minister may reduce a tenure holder's AAC after a five-year interval if the tenure holder has not made full use of its prior allotment. Ontario reported that the total Crown harvest was 79.2 per cent of the AAC. By law, the Minister may amend the license based upon the "business requirement" of the licensee. The sample license provided by Ontario states that the amount of timber actually harvested shall be considered a "business requirement" for purposes of that statutory provision and explicitly states that the Minister may reduce a tenure holder's AAC after a five-year interval if the tenure holder has not made full use of its prior allotment. Alberta reported that the total Crown harvest in calendar year 2000 was 104.5 per cent of the AAC. According to Alberta, salvage operations following severe fires in 1998 and 1999 account for the temporary authority to harvest more in each of the years from 1998 to 2000 than would normally be allowed. By law, the Minister may suspend or cancel a

timber license or quota if the tenure holder harvests more or less timber than authorized during a five-year period. Saskatchewan reported that the total Crown harvest in fiscal year 2000-01 was 68.8 per cent of the AAC. Tenure holders are required by law to prepare plans describing the amount of timber to be harvested and to follow those plans as a condition of remaining in compliance with their licenses. Finally, Manitoba reported that the total Crown harvest in fiscal year 1999-2000 was 34.6 per cent of the AAC. The record evidence did not indicate what, if any, provincial cut requirements exist.

Questions to the United States

14. Q9: The Commerce Department rejected the use of stumpage prices for timber on private land in Canada because the evidence demonstrates that the provincial tenures drive the prices for those private timber sales. The impact of the provincial tenures on private prices was the only government action considered in this analysis.

15. Q10(i): The United States position is precisely as it was stated in the quoted US response, i.e., "if the government made the financial contribution to an entity that does *not* produce the subject merchandise, it would be necessary to analyze whether that financial contribution benefitted another entity that *does* produce the subject merchandise."

16. Q10(ii): The ordinary meaning of an "arm's-length" transaction is one in which the parties are unrelated and neither party is under any outside control or influence, either from the party with whom they are bargaining, or other parties.

17. Q10(iii): In an aggregate case, if there is a financial contribution to an entity that does not produce the subject merchandise, it would be necessary to analyze whether that financial contribution benefitted another entity that does produce the subject merchandise. Canada's allegation of a financial contribution to an entity that does not produce the subject merchandise is based on its unsubstantiated assertion that there is a significant volume of Crown timber that the provincial governments provide to independent loggers who then sell the timber at arm's-length to lumber mills. Canada's assertion concerning independent loggers is not, however, supported by the record at the time of the Preliminary Determination. Moreover, Canada did not assert this claim until one day before the Preliminary Determination.

18. Q10(iv): The United States agrees that countervailing duties may not be imposed in excess of the subsidy found to exist. The Commerce Department calculated the benefit on an aggregate basis and the record at the time of the Preliminary Determination did not indicate that any significant amount of Crown timber was provided to independent entities that did not produce subject merchandise. Canada did not argue to the contrary until one day prior to the Preliminary Determination. The Commerce Department did not, therefore, examine the issue of pass-through in the Preliminary Determination.

19. Q11: The US position is that, consistent with Article 19.3, "[a]ny exporter whose exports are subject to a definitive countervailing duty but who was not actually investigated for reasons other than a refusal to cooperate, shall be entitled to an expedited review in order that the investigating authorities promptly establish an individual countervailing duty rate for that exporter." The provision speaks for itself. The United States has established that Section 751 of the Tariff Act of 1930, as amended, provides the United States with ample discretion to implement its obliga-

tions under Article 19.3. Moreover, *even if* Canada's characterization of the Article 19.3 obligations were correct, Section 751 of the Act provides the United States with ample discretion to implement such obligations.

20. Q12: Article 19.3 speaks for itself. In addition, it is uncontested that *no expedited reviews have been requested or refused in any prior case*. Moreover, Canada has acknowledged that the Commerce Department has offered exporters an opportunity to request expedited reviews in this case; none of those requests has been denied. If a Member's law provides discretion to authorities to act in a WTO-consistent manner, established WTO jurisprudence dictates that the law, as such, does not breach the Member's WTO obligations. Refraining from further review in such cases avoids unnecessary adjudication and respects the presumption that Members will implement their obligations in good faith. This is Canada's third attempt to reverse that presumption in connection with the lumber dispute. US law, however, unquestionably provides the United States with ample discretion to implement its obligations under Article 19.3 of the *SCM Agreement*, even as those obligations are characterized by Canada. There is therefore no basis for Canada's claim that US law is inconsistent with the *SCM Agreement*, and the United States is entitled to the presumption that it will implement its obligations in good faith. In seeking to answer the question of whether the United States *would* breach Article 19.3 *if*, at some point in the future, it were to exercise its discretion in a specified manner, Canada is merely requesting an advisory opinion on a non-existent measure not before the Panel. The United States notes that this issue was central to the *Section 129* panel report, which was issued to the parties on June 12, 2002 but remains confidential. The United States urges the Panel to review the report when it becomes available.

21. Q13: What the United States refers to as an "administrative review" is an annual assessment proceeding. Section 751(a) of the Act states that the Commerce Department shall, upon request, conduct an annual administrative review to determine the rate of duty to be assessed on entries during the preceding year. US law requires such proceedings, upon request, in all cases, including aggregate cases. Article 21.2 of the *SCM Agreement* does not address assessment proceedings. It instead requires reviews to determine "whether the continued imposition of the duty is necessary to offset subsidization." The Commerce Department has the discretion to conduct reviews to determine whether continued imposition of the duty is necessary to offset subsidization and, if not, to revoke the countervailing duty order. While those provisions of the statute and regulations are not before the Panel, we note that they are applicable in all cases, including aggregate cases. Moreover, even if Canada were correct that Article 21.2 does require administrative reviews, Section 751(a) of the Act gives the Commerce Department ample discretion to conduct such reviews.

22. Q14: Canada's request that the Panel make the "findings" listed in paragraph 95 of its second submission amounts to no more than a request that the Panel issue an advisory opinion regarding hypothetical future requests for expedited reviews. The United States has demonstrated that the first requested finding is wrong as a matter of fact and Canada has failed to establish this alleged finding in this proceeding. The second finding the United States has already addressed and shown that it does have sufficient discretion under US law. The last two requested "findings" are prospective in nature and outside the terms of reference of this Panel.

23. Q15: The Commerce Department has the discretion to conduct administrative reviews or changed circumstances reviews on a company-specific basis and to estab-

lish duty rates on a company-specific basis. Any exploration of how the Commerce Department will exercise its discretion in a hypothetical future administrative or changed circumstances review would improperly go beyond the boundaries of the existing dispute. The United States respectfully requests that the Panel not address legal issues not implicated by measures in this dispute, and it again commends to the Panel the approach taken in the forthcoming *Section 129* panel report.

24. Q16: The Commerce Department's initial questionnaire asked each province to provide the "average prices paid for US-origin softwood logs ... by species ... and quality." The provincial governments, however, provide timber at the stump (i.e., standing trees), not "roadside" (i.e., as logs). A stumpage price is analogous to an ex-factory price. The benchmark must, therefore, also be an ex-factory (i.e., stumpage) price. One could derive a stumpage price from import prices for logs, but it would be far more complex and, in all likelihood, less accurate, than using an actual stumpage price. US timber is commercially available to Canadian lumber producers, and Canadian lumber producers may, and do, purchase US timber at the stump as well as in the form of logs. Furthermore, the United States is the only country from which Canada purchases a significant amount of timber, either standing timber or logs.

25. Q17: Provincial timber is provided at the stump. The most appropriate benchmark for provincial stumpage prices, therefore, is a market stumpage price. Log prices themselves could not be compared to stumpage prices, but log prices could possibly be used to derive a stumpage price. In this case, that is not necessary, because actual stumpage prices commercially available to Canadian lumber producers are available. The cost to the government of providing the timber is not an appropriate measure of the adequacy of the remuneration. WTO panels and the Appellate Body have repeatedly and properly rejected a cost to government benchmark. Canada also cited to three unique cases in which, because there were no commercially available market benchmark prices, the Commerce Department measured the adequacy of remuneration through an analysis of whether the government prices were consistent with market principles. Canada fails to note, however, that the Commerce Department conducted such an analysis in those cases only because there were *no* market benchmark prices available, from either domestic sources or commercially available imports.

26. Q18: The United States erroneously included a reference to subparagraph "(d)" in the first line of paragraph 15 of its second written submission. The United States was pointing out that Article 14 in its entirety (not Article 14(d) specifically) "does not purport to address every conceivable scenario in which benefit must be determined." The guideline in Article 14(d) establishes a criterion that any methodology for determining the adequacy of remuneration must meet. Any reasonable measure consistent with the stated guidelines is permissible. The United States agrees that the relevant "prevailing market conditions" are those in the country of provision, not some other country. Where the United States and Canada differ is over what type of evidence constitutes evidence of prevailing market conditions in the country of provision, which Article 14(d) does not address. In Canada's view, evidence of prevailing market conditions in Canada consists solely of transactions for domestic goods. The United States disagrees. "Prevailing market conditions" are the commercial conditions under which goods are bought and sold in the country of provision. A plain reading of the text would indicate that "prevailing market conditions" include the

existence of all sources for the good in question that are commercially available to purchasers in the country of provision, including imports. Since US stumpage is commercially available to lumber producers in Canada, it constitutes part of the prevailing market conditions in Canada.

27. Q19: The United States confirms the statement it made. A market may be small but nevertheless robust and driven by market forces. Such a market would produce prices that could serve as a benchmark for determining the adequacy of remuneration. The issue is not the size of the "market" *per se*, but rather what the "market conditions" encompass. In particular, "market conditions" encompass the total commercially available supply, including imports. In the Commerce Department's preliminary analysis, while the overall size of the market was not a consideration, the relative size of the government-controlled segment of the market for Canadian stumpage relative to the private segment of the market was a consideration. The provincial governments control approximately 90 per cent of the Canadian softwood timber supply. The relative size of the government's segment of the market is particularly significant because provincial tenure holders consistently harvest less than their AAC and, if necessary, a tenure holder may harvest in excess of its AAC. Canadian lumber producers, therefore, have little or no incentive to purchase private stumpage, unless the private seller is willing to meet, or better, the government's administratively set stumpage price. Thus, the government's overwhelmingly dominant share of the market for stumpage drives private stumpage prices toward an equilibrium with government prices. This was confirmed by other record evidence.

28. Q20: There does not appear to be any record evidence to support Canada's claim that swaps must be equivalent in value as well as volume. Tenure holders are generally not permitted to sell the timber they harvest. "Swaps" generally involve two mills that are required under their tenures to process all the timber they harvest or an "equivalent quantity" in their mill. Thus, the provincial laws themselves place a premium on the *quantity* exchanged, not the value. The existence of the "equivalent quantity" language in the provincial statutes is tacit recognition of the occasional need for swaps to meet specific input requirements. The primary factors in swaps are volume and the physical characteristics of the logs, not value. Moreover, swaps are between sawmills. In an aggregate benefit calculation, where both parties are producers of the subject merchandise, the value of the logs swapped and the nature of the transaction are irrelevant because the benefit is calculated based on the total volume of Crown timber going into lumber production, allocated over all sales of softwood lumber.

29. Q21: Adequate remuneration must be determined in relation to prevailing market conditions in the country of provision, consistent with Article 14(d). No amount of evidence could overcome this express requirement. If the Panel is asking what amount of evidence is needed in order for an investigating authority to reject prices for domestically produced goods in favor of prices available in the domestic market for foreign-produced goods, it is the view of the United States that Article 14(d) is not concerned with whether the benchmark is based on domestically produced goods versus commercially available imported goods, but rather with whether the benchmark reflects the prevailing market conditions facing the purchaser in the country of provision. It is purely an evidentiary matter whether domestically produced goods versus commercially available imported goods represent the appropriate benchmark.

30. There may be instances where a government has a monopoly on a particular good. In this instance, the logical alternative would be to test the government price against a commercially available import price. Even Canada concedes that import prices could be utilized in the case of a government monopoly. Where a government does not maintain a monopoly, but exercises overwhelming dominance in the market, the same considerations would apply. Across all of Canada, a *single* government supplier controls on average 90 per cent of the supply of timber. The remaining 10 per cent of supply is provided by *thousands* of small, private landowners. It is impossible to conclude that the private landowners have any market power whatsoever.

31. A benchmark based on foreign-produced goods must be *commercially available* to the domestic purchasers in the country of provision. Thus, it would be inappropriate to choose a world market price from Latvia, Russia, Japan, Europe or Chile as a benchmark for stumpage in Canada. Canadian lumber producers do not import timber from these countries, and only actual or potential import prices could conceivably satisfy the commercially available requirement. The only country that Canada does import timber from is the United States. Proof of actual imports is the strongest possible evidence that a price is commercially available to domestic purchasers in the country of provision.

32. Finally, the benchmark for measuring adequate remuneration must itself be a *market* price, whether the benchmark stems from domestically produced goods or from commercially available imported goods. Thus, the Commerce Department did not seek to demonstrate that the US market was "more competitive" than the Canadian market for stumpage. Rather, the Commerce Department found that the US stumpage market is open and competitive and the prices, therefore, are "market" prices.

33. Q22: Article 20.1 establishes a general rule of prospective application for both provisional measures and definitive duties, subject to the exceptions in Article 20. Article 20.6 defines a set of circumstances under which retroactive assessment is permitted. The reference to exceptions in Article 20.1, including the Article 20.6 exception, should, logically, be interpreted to include within the exception the provisional measures essential to preserving the possibility of such a remedy where there is evidence that the requisite circumstances exist. Nothing in Article 20.6 precludes such a reading of Article 20.1. The reference to "provisional measures" in Article 20.6 is used solely to fix a point in time from which to calculate the 90-day retroactivity period and thereby define a universe of entries that may be subject to retroactive assessment. The fact that the date on which provisional measures are applied is used to calculate the 90-day period does not preclude subjecting the universe of entries during that period to provisional measures.

34. Q23: The timing provisions of Article 17 address the point in a proceeding at which provisional measures can be imposed. That point occurs after affirmative preliminary determinations of subsidization and injury have been made, *and* no earlier than 60 days after initiation. Article 20 addresses the universe of entities to which those measures may be applied.

35. Q24: Provisional measures were imposed for 4 months, i.e., they were ordered on 17 August 2001 and terminated on 15 December 2001.

36. Q25: The US International Trade Commission ("ITC") does not conduct an analysis of "injury which is difficult to repair" until it makes the final injury determi-

nation. As the panel concluded in *Hot-Rolled Steel from Japan*, conducting such an analysis at the preliminary stage would be speculative. In contrast, the existence of massive imports and a subsidy inconsistent with the Agreement are comparatively straightforward analyses of facts. The ITC's preliminary injury determination, together with the evidence concerning prohibited subsidies and massive imports, constitutes sufficient evidence to take the limited step of imposing provisional measures retroactively, pending the outcome of the full investigation.

37. Q26: Article 20.3 states that "[i]f the definitive countervailing duty is higher than the amount guaranteed by the cash deposit or bond, the difference shall not be collected." If there is no cash deposit or bond, the amount guaranteed is zero. It follows that, absent provisional measures in the form of a deposit or bond for entries during the 90-day retroactivity period, no definitive duties may be collected on those entries. The conflict between Articles 20.3 and 20.6 does not exist if Article 20.1 is interpreted to permit provisional measures where there is sufficient evidence that critical circumstances exist.

38. Q27: In the Preliminary Determination, the Commerce Department issued a single order imposing provisional measures. The universe of entries subject to that order included all entries made or on after 90 days prior to the Preliminary Determination. Moreover, under US law, entries during the 90-day retroactivity period are subject to the provisional measures cap. If the Panel should find that there are two such periods, the rules governing provisional measures cannot apply to the 90-day retroactive assessment period. If Article 20.6 only addresses assessment, not provisional measures, then the 4-month limitation on provisional measures and the provisional measure cap do not apply to such assessments.

Questions to Canada

39. Q36: Canada has *de facto* abandoned its specificity claim in this proceeding. Any attempt by Canada to pursue its specificity claim at this late stage would deny the United States its right to defend its interest and the rights of third parties to be heard.

40. Q37: If Canada is still pursuing this claim, it would not be appropriate at this late stage for Canada to supplement its prior submissions with additional information or argument. The US right to defend its interest would be severely prejudiced in such a case.

UNITED STATES – COUNTERVAILING DUTIES ON CERTAIN CORROSION-RESISTANT CARBON STEEL FLAT PRODUCTS FROM GERMANY

Report of the Appellate Body

WT/DS213/AB/R*

Adopted by the Dispute Settlement Body on 19 December 2002

United States – *Appellant/Appellee*
European Communities – *Appellant/Appellee*
Japan – *Third Participant*
Norway – *Third Participant*

Present:
Taniguchi, Presiding Member
Ganesan, Member
Sacerdoti, Member

TABLE OF CONTENTS

* WT/DS213/AB/R and Corr.1.

TABLE OF CASES CITED IN THIS REPORT

Short Title	Full Case Title and Citation
Argentina – Textiles and Apparel	Appellate Body Report, *Argentina – Measures Affecting Imports of Footwear, Textiles, Apparel and Other Items*, WT/DS56/AB/R and Corr.1, adopted 22 April 1998, DSR 1998:III, 1003
Brazil – Desiccated Coconut	Appellate Body Report, *Brazil – Measures Affecting Desiccated Coconut*, WT/DS22/AB/R, adopted 20 March 1997, DSR 1997:I, 167
Canada – Autos	Appellate Body Report, *Canada – Certain Measures Affecting the Automotive Industry*, WT/DS139/AB/R, WT/DS142/AB/R, adopted 19 June 2000, DSR 2000:VI, 2995
Canada – Patent Term	Appellate Body Report, *Canada – Term of Patent Protection*, WT/DS170/AB/R, adopted 12 October 2000

Short Title	Full Case Title and Citation
EC – Bananas III	Appellate Body Report, *European Communities – Regime for the Importation, Sale and Distribution of Bananas*, WT/DS27/AB/R, adopted 25 September 1997, DSR 1997:II, 591
EC – Hormones	Appellate Body Report, *EC Measures Concerning Meat and Meat Products (Hormones)*, WT/DS26/AB/R, WT/DS48/AB/R, adopted 13 February 1998, DSR 1998:I, 135
EC – Sardines	Appellate Body Report, *European Communities – Trade Description of Sardines*, WT/DS231/AB/R, adopted 23 October 2002
Guatemala – Cement I	Appellate Body Report, *Guatemala – Anti-Dumping Investigation Regarding Portland Cement from Mexico*, WT/DS60/AB/R, adopted 25 November 1998, DSR 1998:IX, 3767
Japan – Alcoholic Beverages II	Appellate Body Report, *Japan – Taxes on Alcoholic Beverages*, WT/DS8/AB/R, WT/DS10/AB/R, WT/DS11/AB/R, adopted 1 November 1996, DSR 1996:I, 97
Korea – Alcoholic Beverages	Panel Report, *Korea – Taxes on Alcoholic Beverages*, WT/DS75/R, WT/DS84/R, adopted 17 February 1999, as modified by the Appellate Body Report, WT/DS75/AB/R, WT/DS84/AB/R, DSR 1999:I, 44
Korea – Dairy	Appellate Body Report, *Korea – Definitive Safeguard Measure on Imports of Certain Dairy Products*, WT/DS98/AB/R, adopted 12 January 2000, DSR 2000:I, 3
Mexico – Corn Syrup (Article 21.5 – US)	Appellate Body Report, *Mexico – Anti-Dumping Investigation of High Fructose Corn Syrup (HFCS) from the United States – Recourse to Article 21.5 of the DSU by the United States*, WT/DS132/AB/RW, adopted 21 November 2001

Short Title	Full Case Title and Citation
Thailand – H-Beams	Appellate Body Report, *Thailand – Anti-Dumping Duties on Angles, Shapes and Sections of Iron or Non-Alloy Steel and H-Beams from Poland*, WT/DS122/AB/R, adopted 5 April 2001

Short Title	Full Case Title and Citation
US – 1916 Act	Appellate Body Report, *United States – Anti-Dumping Act of 1916* WT/DS136/AB/R, WT/DS162/AB/R, adopted 26 September 2000
US – Carbon Steel	Panel Report, *United States – Countervailing Duties on Certain Corrosion-Resistant Carbon Steel Flat Products from Germany*, WT/DS213/R and Corr.1, 3 July 2002
US – DRAMS	Panel Report, *United States – Anti-Dumping Duty on Dynamic Random Access Memory Semiconductors (DRAMS) of One Megabit or Above from Korea*, WT/DS99/R, adopted 19 March 1999, DSR 1999:II, 521
US – FSC	Appellate Body Report, *United States – Tax Treatment for "Foreign Sales Corporations"*, WT/DS108/AB/R, adopted 20 March 2000, DSR 2000:III, 1619
US – Hot-Rolled Steel	Appellate Body Report, *United States – Anti-Dumping Measures on Certain Hot-Rolled Steel Products from Japan*, WT/DS184/AB/R, adopted 23 August 2001
US – Lead and Bismuth II	Appellate Body Report, *United States – Imposition of Countervailing Duties on Certain Hot-Rolled Lead and Bismuth Carbon Steel Products Originating in the United Kingdom*, WT/DS138/AB/R, adopted 7 June 2000, DSR 2000:V, 2601
US – Wheat Gluten	Appellate Body Report, *United States – Definitive Safeguard Measures on Imports of Wheat Gluten from the European Communities*, WT/DS166/AB/R, adopted 19 January 2001

US – Wool Shirts and Blouses	Appellate Body Report, *United States – Measure Affecting Imports of Woven Wool Shirts and Blouses from India*, WT/DS33/AB/R and Corr.1, adopted 23 May 1997, DSR 1997:I, 323

I. INTRODUCTION

1. The United States and the European Communities each appeal certain issues of law and legal interpretations in the Panel Report, *United States – Countervailing Duties on Certain Corrosion-Resistant Carbon Steel Flat Products from Germany* (the "Panel Report").[1] The Panel was established to consider a complaint by the European Communities against the United States regarding the continuation of countervailing duties on certain corrosion-resistant carbon steel flat products from Germany ("carbon steel") following the conduct of a five-year, or "sunset", review of those duties.

2. On 17 August 1993, the United States imposed definitive countervailing duties on carbon steel. The imposition of the duties was based on an investigation by the United States Department of Commerce ("USDOC") in which it determined that certain German producers of carbon steel benefitted, at a total rate of 0.60 percent *ad valorem*, from five countervailable subsidy programs.[2] On 1 September 1999, USDOC gave notice of the automatic initiation of a sunset review of these countervailing duties.[3] In the course of this review, USDOC determined that revocation of the countervailing duties "would be likely to lead to continuation or recurrence of a countervailable subsidy" with respect to carbon steel and transmitted this determination to the United States International Trade Commission ("USITC").[4] Based on its finding that two of the original five subsidy programs had been terminated, the likely rate of such continuation or recurrence of a countervailable subsidy was determined by USDOC to be 0.54 percent *ad valorem*.[5] Following an affirmative determination of the likelihood of continuation or recurrence of injury by USITC, USDOC published a notice of the continuation of the countervailing duties on 15 December 2000.[6]

---

1 WT/DS213/R, 3 July 2002, WT/DS213/R/Corr.1, 12 August 2002.

2 "Final Affirmative Countervailing Duty Determinations: Certain Steel Products From Germany", United States Federal Register, 9 July 1993 (Volume 58, Number 130), p. 37315; Exhibit EC-2 submitted by the European Communities to the Panel; and "Countervailing Duty Orders and Amendment to Final Affirmative Countervailing Duty Determinations: Certain Steel Products From Germany", United States Federal Register, 17 August 1993 (Volume 58, Number 157), p. 43756; Exhibit EC-4 submitted by the European Communities to the Panel.

3 "Initiation of Five-Year ('Sunset') Reviews of Anti-Dumping and Countervailing Duty Orders or Investigations of Carbon Steel Plates and Flat Products", United States Federal Register, 1 September 1999 (Volume 64, Number 169), p. 47767; Exhibit EC-5 submitted by the European Communities to the Panel.

4 Panel Report, para. 2.1.

5 *Ibid.*

6 "Continuation of Antidumping and Countervailing Duty Orders on Certain Carbon Steel Products from Australia, Belgium, Brazil, Canada, Finland, France, Germany, Japan, South Korea, Mexico, Poland, Romania, Spain, Sweden, Taiwan and the United Kingdom", United States Federal Reg-

3. The European Communities argued before the Panel that United States law relating to sunset reviews, as such, and as applied in the sunset review of countervailing duties on carbon steel in this case, was inconsistent with United States' obligations under the *Agreement on Subsidies and Countervailing Measures* (the "*SCM Agreement*"). The European Communities argued that the United States acted contrary to Article 21.3 of the *SCM Agreement* by automatically self-initiating sunset reviews and by failing to apply in sunset reviews the *de minimis* standard of 1 percent set out in Article 11.9 of that Agreement.

4. During the course of the Panel proceedings, the Panel was called upon to determine whether three further matters were within its terms of reference. First, the Panel granted a request by the United States for a preliminary ruling that the European Communities' claim relating to the United States' expedited sunset review procedure was outside the Panel's terms of reference.[7] The other two challenges to the terms of reference arose in connection with two questions put by the Panel to the European Communities following the second meeting of the parties with the Panel. In response to these questions, the European Communities responded affirmatively to the Panel that it was making claims with respect to United States law, as such, relating to the determination to be made in a sunset review[8], and United States law, as such, dealing with the opportunity to present evidence in a sunset review.[9] On 14 May 2002, the Panel issued its interim report to the parties. In its interim report, the Panel made findings on, *inter alia*, the claims asserted by the European Communities in its responses to the questions from the Panel.

5. On 23 May 2002, the United States submitted a request for interim review, *inter alia*, objecting to the Panel's interim findings with regard to United States law, as such, relating to the determination to be made in a sunset review[10], and with regard to the consistency of United States law, as such, and as applied, with the obligation to provide ample opportunity to submit evidence in a sunset review[11], as outside the terms of reference. The Panel rejected the first of these objections.[12] The Panel found, however, that the consistency of United States law, as such, and as applied, with the obligation to provide ample opportunity to submit evidence in a sunset review was outside its terms of reference.[13] As a consequence, certain reasoning and findings with respect to this claim, that appeared in the interim report, were not included in the Panel Report.

6. In the Panel Report, circulated to Members of the World Trade Organization ("WTO") on 3 July 2002, the Panel found that:

(a) US CVD law and the accompanying regulations are consistent with Article 21, paragraphs 1 and 3, and Article 10 of the *SCM*

---

ister, 15 December 2000 (Volume 65, Number 242), p. 78469; Exhibit EC-12 submitted by the European Communities to the Panel.

[7] Panel Report, paras. 8.5-8.12.

[8] See, European Communities' response to Question 51 posed by the Panel; Panel Report, para. 5.517.

[9] See, European Communities' response to Question 54 posed by the Panel; Panel Report, para. 5.522.

[10] Panel Report, para. 7.20.

[11] *Ibid.*, para. 7.24.

[12] *Ibid.*, paras. 7.21-7.23.

[13] *Ibid.*, paras. 8.137 and 8.145.

Agreement in respect of the application of evidentiary standards to the self-initiation of sunset reviews;

(b) US CVD law and the accompanying regulations are *inconsistent* with Article 21.3 of the *SCM Agreement* in respect of the application of a 0.5 per cent *de minimis* standard to sunset reviews, and therefore violate Article 32.5 of the *SCM Agreement* and, consequently, also Article XVI:4 of the WTO Agreement;

(c) the United States, in applying a 0.5 per cent *de minimis* standard to the instant sunset review, acted *in violation* of Article 21.3 of the *SCM Agreement*;

(d) US CVD law and the accompanying regulations and statement of policy practices are consistent with Article 21.3 of the *SCM Agreement* in respect of the obligation to determine the likelihood of continuation or recurrence of subsidisation in sunset reviews; and

(e) the United States, in failing to determine properly the likelihood of continuation or recurrence of subsidisation in the sunset review on carbon steel, acted *in violation* of Article 21.3 of the *SCM Agreement*.[14] (original underlining)

7. The Panel accordingly recommended that:

> ... the Dispute Settlement Body request the United States to bring its measures ... into conformity with its obligations under the WTO Agreement.[15]

8. On 30 August 2002, the United States notified the Dispute Settlement Body ("DSB") of its intention to appeal certain issues of law covered in the Panel Report and certain legal interpretations developed by the Panel, pursuant to paragraph 4 of Article 16 of the *Understanding on Rules and Procedures Governing the Settlement of Disputes* (the "DSU") and filed a Notice of Appeal pursuant to Rule 20 of the *Working Procedures for Appellate Review* (the "*Working Procedures*"). On 9 September 2002, the United States filed its appellant's submission.[16] On 16 September 2002, the European Communities filed an other appellant's submission.[17] On 24 September 2002, the European Communities and the United States each filed an appellee's submission.[18] On the same day, Japan and Norway each filed third participant's submissions.[19]

---

[14] Panel Report, para. 9.1. One member of the Panel dissented from the findings in paragraphs 9.1(b) and 9.1(c). That member found, at paragraph 10.15 of the Panel Report, that:

(a) US CVD law and the accompanying regulations are *consistent* with Article 21.3 of the *SCM Agreement* in respect of the application of a 0.5 per cent *de minimis* standard to sunset reviews; and

(b) The United States, in applying a 0.5 per cent *de minimis* standard to the instant sunset review, did *not* act in violation of Article 21.3 of the *SCM Agreement*. (original underlining)

[15] Panel Report, para. 9.2.

[16] Pursuant to Rule 21 of the *Working Procedures*.

[17] Pursuant to Rule 23 of the *Working Procedures*.

[18] Pursuant to Rule 22 of the *Working Procedures*.

[19] Pursuant to Rule 24 of the *Working Procedures*.

9. The oral hearing was held on 11 October 2002. The participants and third participants each presented oral arguments and responded to questions put to them by the Members of the Division hearing the appeal.

II. ARGUMENTS OF THE PARTICIPANTS AND THE THIRD PARTICIPANTS

A. *Claims of Error by the United States – Appellant*

1. *Article 21.3 of the SCM Agreement – Applicability of a de minimis Standard in Sunset Reviews*

10. The United States appeals the findings by the Panel that United States law, as such, and, as applied in the sunset review with respect to carbon steel, is inconsistent with United States' WTO obligations because it applies a *de minimis* standard of 0.5 percent. Both these findings flow from the Panel's erroneous conclusion that the less than 1 percent *de minimis* standard applicable to countervailing duty investigations in Article 11.9 of the *SCM Agreement* is implied in Article 21.3 of the Agreement as well. The United States submits that, by implying into Article 21.3 words that are not there, the Panel failed to act in accordance with customary rules of treaty interpretation.

11. The United States emphasizes that the text of Article 21.3 does not contain any *de minimis* standard for sunset reviews. The Panel failed to give meaning to the express absence of any textual reference to a *de minimis* requirement in Article 21.3, and improperly relied upon the Appellate Body Report in *Canada – Autos* as a basis for finding that textual silence in this case was not dispositive.

12. The United States refers to Article 21 of the *SCM Agreement* as immediate context to Article 21.3. Article 21 contains no cross-reference to Article 11.9, yet does contain specific cross-references to other provisions. In particular, Article 21.4 expressly makes the evidentiary and procedural provisions of Article 12 applicable to Article 21 reviews, while Article 21.5 expressly makes the provisions of Article 21 applicable to Article 18 undertakings. These cross-references demonstrate that where the drafters wanted the obligations set forth in one provision to apply in another context, they did so expressly. In this respect, the United States notes that the dissenting panelist found the omission of any express link between Article 21.3 and Article 11.9 to be dispositive on the issue of whether the Article 11.9 *de minimis* standard is applicable to sunset review.

13. The United States also disputes the Panel's analysis and understanding of the *de minimis* standard set out in Article 11.9 of the *SCM Agreement*. The United States points to the decision of the panel in *US – DRAMS*[20] and argues that the Panel in this dispute should have interpreted Article 11.9 in the same way as that panel interpreted Article 5.8 of the *Agreement on the Implementation of Article VI of the General Agreement on Tariffs and Trade 1994* (the "*Anti-Dumping Agreement*"). That panel found that the *de minimis* standard expressed in Article 5.8 of the *Anti-Dumping Agreement* does not apply beyond the investigative stage of anti-dumping proceedings.

[20] Panel Report, *US – DRAMS*, para. 6.87.

14. The United States objects to the Panel's reliance upon a 1987 Note by the Secretariat in order to find that the "sole or principal rationale for the *de minimis* standard set out in Article 11.9 is that a *de minimis* subsidy is considered to be non-injurious."[21] The United States further submits that recourse to the 1987 Note was inconsistent with the rules of treaty interpretation embodied in the *Vienna Convention on the Law of Treaties* (the "*Vienna Convention*").[22] That Note sets out two rationales for a *de minimis* concept, but all that the negotiating history demonstrates is that there was no consensus or single reason why the drafters established a *de minimis* standard for investigations. Finally, the United States contends that it is difficult to reconcile the Panel's finding that the *de minimis* standard relates to the question of whether there is injury with the fact that the *SCM Agreement* has not one, but three different, *de minimis* standards, depending on the level of economic development of the exporting country. The United States argues that it is difficult to see how injury from subsidized imports depends upon the level of economic development in the exporting Member.

2. *Article 6.2 of the DSU – Whether the Panel's Terms of Reference Included a Claim Against United States Law, As Such, Regarding the Determination to be Made in a Sunset Review*

15. The United States appeals the refusal by the Panel to dismiss the European Communities' claim regarding the consistency of United States law, as such, with the obligation to determine the likelihood of continuation or recurrence of subsidization in a sunset review established by Article 21.3 of the *SCM Agreement*. The United States argues that the European Communities' panel request failed to comply with the requirements of Article 6.2 of the DSU. The United States' appeal is *conditional* upon the Appellate Body first *reversing* the Panel's finding that United States law, as such, is not inconsistent with the obligation to determine the likelihood of continuation or recurrence of subsidization in sunset reviews. However, in response to questioning at the oral hearing, the United States indicated that this condition need not be fulfilled for the Appellate Body to consider this issue.

16. According to the United States, its written submissions to the Panel demonstrate its understanding that the European Communities' challenge to United States laws, *as such*, was limited to two issues only, namely, the automatic self-initiation of sunset reviews and the *de minimis* standard employed in sunset reviews. When, following the second meeting with the Panel, the European Communities purported to have included this additional challenge to United States law in its panel request, the United States promptly objected.

17. The United States insists that it was prejudiced by the European Communities' failure to comply with Article 6.2. The United States points out that, because it was unaware of any such claim until after the second meeting, its submissions to the Panel did not contain any arguments regarding the consistency of United States law, as such, with the obligation to determine the likelihood of continuation or recurrence of subsidization in sunset reviews. The United States adds that this prejudice was not

[21] Panel Report, para. 8.61.

[22] Done at Vienna, 23 May 1969, 1155 U.N.T.S. 331; 8 International Legal Materials 679.

mitigated by the fact that the Panel ruled in favour of the United States on the merits of this particular claim.

B. Arguments of the European Communities – Appellee

1. Article 21.3 of the SCM Agreement – Applicability of a de minimis Standard in Sunset Reviews

18. The European Communities requests the Appellate Body to uphold the Panel's findings with respect to the application of the *de minimis* standard under Article 21.3. The European Communities accepts that Article 21.3 does not contain any explicit textual reference to the *de minimis* standard established in Article 11.9, and that nothing in the text of Article 11.9 provides for its *de minimis* standard to be implied in Article 21.3. However, the European Communities notes that the text of Article 21.3 requires the domestic authorities to engage in a review to determine that the expiry of the countervailing duty would be likely to lead to "continuation or recurrence of subsidization and injury". These concepts are defined elsewhere in the *SCM Agreement* for the Agreement as a whole and are not repeated each time for individual articles. In particular, the reference to "continuation or recurrence" makes Article 11.9 and the original investigation relevant and applicable. Article 11.9 prevents the authorities from making a finding on subsidization and injury when the amount of subsidy is found in the investigation to be less than 1 percent *ad valorem*. Article 15.3 of the *SCM Agreement*, dealing with the determination of injury, also refers explicitly to Article 11.9 for the purpose of establishing the *de minimis* rule. According to the European Communities, these provisions demonstrate that subsidization of less than 1 percent is irrebuttably presumed not to cause injury. If a *de minimis* subsidization cannot cause injury in an original investigation, it must follow that it also cannot cause injury in a sunset review.

19. The European Communities argues, referring in particular to Article 21.2 of the *SCM Agreement*, that the object and purpose of the requirement to demonstrate subsidization and injury in a sunset review must be the same as when subsidization and injury were determined in the original investigation. It follows that, if the *de minimis* rule is applicable to original investigations, it must also be equally applicable to reviews generally and all the more so in the context of time-bound sunset reviews under Article 21.3. This analysis is further supported by one of the principal objectives of the *SCM Agreement* identified by the Panel, namely, the establishment of a "framework within which to offset *injurious* subsidisation".[23] As a result, the absence of cross-references in both Article 11.9 and Article 21.3 is explained by the drafters' belief that it is "obvious" that the same threshold of injurious subsidization should apply to investigations and sunset reviews.[24] The European Communities also defends, as justified under Article 32 of the *Vienna Convention*, the Panel's reference to the negotiating history of the *SCM Agreement*. In particular, the European Communities underlines that the interpretation of Article 21.3 proposed by the United States "produces a result which is 'manifestly absurd and unreasonable' with respect to the basic obligation".[25]

---

[23] Panel Report, para. 8.66. (original underlining)

[24] European Communities' appellee's submission, para. 29.

[25] *Ibid.*, para. 35.

20. The European Communities emphasizes that acceptance of the United States' position would allow countervailing duties based on a *de minimis* level of subsidization to remain *ad aeternum*. This would violate the text of Articles 21.3 and 21.1 of the *SCM Agreement* because it would allow the continuation of countervailing duties in blocks of five more years without there being any real need to counter subsidization which is likely to cause injury.

2. *Article 6.2 of the DSU – Whether the Panel's Terms of Reference Included a Claim Against United States Law, As Such, Regarding the Determination to be Made in a Sunset Review*

21. The European Communities submits that the matter of the consistency of United States law, as such, relating to the determination to be made in a sunset review with its obligations under Article 21.3 of the *SCM Agreement*, was within the Panel's terms of reference. The request for establishment of a panel explained the history and basic framework of the relevant United States laws, regulations and practices, and mentioned Article 21 of the *SCM Agreement*. The request identified the relevant measure, the *SCM Agreement* provisions claimed to have been violated, and the grounds on which this claim is based. The European Communities argues that it further developed this claim and all supporting arguments in each of its written and oral submissions to the Panel, and that the United States responded to such claims and arguments in its pleadings before the Panel. The European Communities adds that the late stage of the Panel proceedings at which the objection was raised indicates that the United States was not prejudiced by any lack of clarity in the panel request.

C. *Claims of Error by the European Communities – Appellant*

1. *Article 21.3 of the SCM Agreement – Self-Initiation of a Sunset Review by the Authorities*

22. The European Communities argues that the Panel erred in its interpretation of Article 21.3 with respect to the evidentiary standards applicable to the self-initiation of sunset reviews and requests the Appellate Body to find that the standards specified in Article 11.6 of the *SCM Agreement* apply equally to the self-initiation by authorities of sunset reviews. The European Communities contends that the Panel conducted only a partial interpretation of the text of Article 21.3, but failed to analyze the context of Article 21.3 and the object and purpose of the *SCM Agreement*.

23. In the view of the European Communities, no provision in the *SCM Agreement* can be read in isolation, and all provisions are potentially applicable, *mutatis mutandis*, to Article 21.3, to the extent that they are relevant to sunset reviews and that their application does not create a situation of conflict or is not specifically excluded. This is true in particular within Part V of the *SCM Agreement*. The European Communities thus disputes the significance of the omission from Article 21.3 of any explicit reference to the evidentiary standards for the self-initiation of sunset reviews. No such reference is necessary because it is "obvious from the overall context and

architecture of Part V of the *SCM Agreement*" that such evidentiary standards apply to the self-initiation of sunset reviews as well.[26]

24. The European Communities explains that, notwithstanding the lack of any explicit cross-reference to the evidentiary standard set out in Article 11.6 of the *SCM Agreement*, Article 21.3 requires domestic authorities that engage in a review to "determine" that the expiry of the countervailing duty would be likely to lead to continuation or recurrence of subsidization. The verb "to determine" means to find out, to ascertain, to establish, or to carry out all those activities necessary to reach a reasoned decision. Furthermore, Articles 11.2 and 11.6 prescribe the same evidentiary burden for both the domestic industry and the domestic authorities to initiate an investigation. It is difficult therefore to understand why, in a sunset review, the same evidentiary standard as set out in Article 11.2 applies only to initiation by the domestic industry, but not to self-initiation by the authorities.

25. The European Communities argues that the Panel also failed to consider Articles 22.1 and 22.7 of the *SCM Agreement*. It is clear from Article 22.7 that the same procedural guarantees that apply to the initiation of an original investigation also apply to the initiation of a sunset review. In particular, when read in conjunction with Article 22.1, Article 22.7 clearly requires domestic authorities to have "sufficient evidence" before self-initiating sunset reviews.

26. Lastly, the European Communities questions certain reasoning used by the Panel to support its finding that there is no evidentiary standard applicable to the self-initiation by the authorities of a sunset review. In particular, the European Communities questions the Panel's reliance on its own assessment that initiation is "merely the beginning of a process leading to a determination as to whether or not subsidisation and injury are likely to continue or recur."[27] The European Communities also takes issue with the Panel's reliance on concepts such as the "chilling effect [of countervailing duty actions] on trade in the product concerned"[28] and "trade harassment"[29], in order to distinguish the initiation of investigations from the regime applicable to sunset reviews. Such concepts are not found in the *SCM Agreement* and should not have formed a basis for the Panel's interpretation of Article 21.3.

2. *Article 11 of the DSU and Article 21.3 of the SCM Agreement – United States Law, As Such, Regarding the Determination to be Made in a Sunset Review*

27. The European Communities requests the Appellate Body to reverse the Panel's finding that United States law, as such, regarding the determination to be made in a sunset review, is consistent with Article 21.3 because no provision of United States law mandates WTO-inconsistent behaviour. In addition to its appeal regarding Article 21.3, the European Communities submits that in considering the relevant United States law, as such, the Panel failed to make an "objective assessment" of the matter before it, thus also violating its duty under Article 11 of the DSU.

28. The European Communities recalls that the Panel expressed doubts with respect to the conformity of United States law with United States' obligations regarding

[26] European Communities' other appellant's submission, para. 25.
[27] Panel Report, para. 8.42.
[28] *Ibid.*, para. 8.35.
[29] *Ibid.*, para. 8.34.

the determination to be made in a sunset review and considered that it did not have any information to resolve these doubts.[30] Yet the Panel did nothing to obtain such information. The European Communities argues that, in "wilfully" failing to analyze United States law[31], the Panel exceeded the bounds of its discretion, as the trier of facts, in its appreciation of the evidence. The Panel should have gathered further information and should have considered United States practice to resolve its doubts with respect to United States law.

29. The European Communities argues that a proper analysis of United States law and practice reveals that, in a sunset review, USDOC never considers any changes or terminations of subsidy programs, unless such changes or terminations were found by it in a previous review. This refusal to conduct a new investigation in a sunset review violates the requirements of Article 21.3 of the *SCM Agreement* because it contravenes the duty placed on domestic authorities to "determine" the likelihood of continuation or recurrence of a subsidy, and shifts the burden of proving a change in circumstances to the foreign exporter.

30. The European Communities also challenges the Panel's analysis of whether the law in question was mandatory or discretionary. According to the European Communities, the Panel found that, although the law allows WTO-inconsistent determinations, the law, as such, was not inconsistent because one interpretation could lead to WTO-consistent behaviour. The European Communities claims that upholding this Panel finding "would amount to a mockery of justice"[32], since the Panel in effect confirmed that USDOC's interpretation of United States law is WTO-inconsistent, but found that the law itself is not. The European Communities urges the Appellate Body to find that United States law "mandates" outcomes that are inconsistent with Article 21.3 of the *SCM Agreement*, and consequently that the law also violates Article 32.5 of the *SCM Agreement* and Article XVI:4 of the *Marrakesh Agreement Establishing the World Trade Organization* (the "*WTO Agreement*").

3. *Articles 6.2 and 11 of the DSU – The Opportunity to Submit Evidence in a Sunset Review*

31. The European Communities appeals the Panel's finding that the European Communities' claims that United States law was inconsistent with the obligation in Article 12.1 of the *SCM Agreement* to provide "ample opportunity to present ... evidence" were outside the Panel's terms of reference. The European Communities requests the Appellate Body to reverse the Panel's finding on this issue and either to reinstate and modify the substantive findings made by the Panel in its interim report, or to itself find the relevant United States law, as such, and as applied in this case, to be inconsistent with the obligation to afford ample opportunity to submit evidence in a sunset review.

32. The European Communities argues that the request for the establishment of a panel was sufficiently precise on this matter to comply with the requirements of Article 6.2 of the DSU. The panel request mentioned Article 21 of the *SCM Agreement* in its totality, and paragraph 4 of Article 21 applies Article 12 to sunset reviews. More-

[30] European Communities' other appellant's submission, paras. 43 and 45, referring to the Panel Report, para. 8.105.

[31] European Communities' other appellant's submission, para. 46.

[32] European Communities' other appellant's submission, para. 55.

over, the request identified the relevant United States laws and regulations. Before the Panel, the European Communities made arguments with regard to Articles 21.3, 21.4, as well as Article 12 of the *SCM Agreement.* The United States did not object to the claims regarding the opportunity to submit evidence until late in the proceedings, which suggests that the United States suffered no prejudice on account of any lack of clarity in the panel request.

33. The European Communities further contends that the Panel acted inconsistently with Article 11 of the DSU in its interpretation of Article 6.2. The Panel could not, on the basis of the request for the establishment of the Panel and the first written submission of the European Communities, objectively have concluded that the European Communities' claims were not sufficiently clear, nor that the United States was not aware that such claims were being made.

D. Arguments of the United States – Appellee

1. Article 21.3 of the SCM Agreement – Self-Initiation of a Sunset Review by the Authorities

34. The United States submits that the Panel's finding that no evidentiary standards are applicable to the self-initiation of sunset reviews under Article 21.3 of the *SCM Agreement* is correct and should be affirmed. The United States argues that, under Article 21.3, the right of the authorities to initiate a sunset review on their own initiative is unqualified. The use of disjunctive language in Article 21.3 is unambiguous. Under the customary rules of treaty interpretation of public international law, the provision must be read according to its ordinary meaning, namely that the authorities may either self-initiate a sunset review, or, initiate a sunset review in response to a duly substantiated request from the domestic industry. The fact that the text of Article 21.3 contains no reference to evidentiary requirements for self-initiation of sunset reviews must have some meaning. The United States asserts that the ordinary meaning of the absence of such a reference is simply that there is no requirement to apply the evidentiary requirements in Article 11.6 of the *SCM Agreement* (or any other evidentiary requirement) when authorities initiate sunset reviews on their own initiative.

35. The United States argues that analysis of the terms of Article 21.3 in their context and in light of the object and purpose of the *SCM Agreement* leads to the same conclusion. Article 21 contains no reference to Article 11.6, yet it does contain specific references to other provisions of the Agreement. The *SCM Agreement*, in general, also contains multiple instances where obligations set forth in one provision are made applicable in another context by means of an express cross-reference or by means of an explicit statement on the scope of application of the particular provision. The omission of any express link between Article 21.3 and Article 11.6 means that the Members chose not to apply the evidentiary requirements of Article 11.6 to Article 21.3. The United States argues that reading into Article 21.3 a cross-reference to Article 11.6 that is plainly not there would render these cross-references redundant.

36. The United States submits that nothing in the text of Article 11.6 supports the European Communities' assertion that the evidentiary requirements of that provision apply when authorities self-initiate sunset reviews under Article 21.3. To the contrary, the text of Article 11.6 unequivocally states that those evidentiary requirements are applicable when authorities decide to self-initiate an *investigation*.

37. In the view of the United States, because the functions of original investigations and sunset reviews are different, it is not unreasonable to find that the initiation requirements for investigations and sunset reviews are different. The purpose of an investigation is to determine whether the conditions necessary for the imposition of a countervailing duty currently exist. The purpose of a sunset review is to determine whether the conditions necessary for continued imposition of a countervailing duty exist. In contrast to the retrospective focus of an investigation, a sunset review is required to focus on likely future behaviour.

2. *Article 11 of the DSU and Article 21.3 of the SCM Agreement – United States Law, As Such, Regarding the Determination to be Made in a Sunset Review*

38. The United States argues that the Panel properly found that United States law, as such, is consistent with United States' obligations relating to the determination to be made in a sunset review. The United States dismisses the Panel's expression of doubt with respect to the conformity of one particular regulatory provision with such obligations[33] on the ground that the Panel drew an incorrect inference as to how that provision operates.

39. The United States submits that the European Communities misstates the standard for distinguishing between mandatory and discretionary legislation. The fact that a particular application of a law is found to be WTO-inconsistent does not mean that the law as such is automatically WTO-inconsistent. The European Communities has failed to identify and articulate how any provisions of the United States statute or regulations require USDOC to act inconsistently with obligations relating to the likelihood determination or preclude USDOC from acting consistently with such obligations. Nor has the European Communities articulated how particular text in the Statement of Administrative Action (the "SAA") or the Sunset Policy Bulletin[34] requires USDOC to interpret the statute or the regulations in a WTO-inconsistent manner in respect of the determination to be made in a sunset review.

40. As for the European Communities' argument that the SAA, in conjunction with the Sunset Policy Bulletin, establishes a practice which demonstrates that the United States statute violates Article 21.3, the United States puts forward two arguments. First, the European Communities misstates United States practice by suggesting that USDOC does not consider any changes or terminations of subsidy programs, unless such changes or terminations were found in a previous review of the order. In fact, United States law requires USDOC to consider whether any change to a subsidy program has occurred that is likely to affect the net countervailable subsidy. Second, noting, *inter alia*, the ruling of the Appellate Body in *US – Hot-Rolled Steel*[35], the United States argues that United States practice, even if it were WTO-inconsistent, could not render the United States statute and regulations, as such, WTO-inconsistent.

---

[33] Panel Report, para. 8.105.

[34] Policy Bulletin, "Policies Regarding the Conduct of Five-Year ('Sunset') Reviews of Antidumping and Countervailing Duty Orders", United States Federal Register, 16 April 1998 (Volume 63, Number 73), p. 18871.

[35] Appellate Body Report, *US – Hot-Rolled Steel*, para. 200.

3. Articles 6.2 and 11 of the DSU – The Opportunity to Submit Evidence in a Sunset Review

41. The United States submits that the Panel properly found that the European Communities' claims regarding the consistency of United States law, as such, and as applied, in respect of the opportunity to submit evidence in a sunset review, were not within its terms of reference. As the Panel found, the European Communities' panel request failed to identify the opportunity to submit evidence in a sunset review as a specific measure at issue. Moreover, the panel request also failed to identify the provisions of the *SCM Agreement* allegedly violated and failed to provide a brief summary of the legal basis of the complaint. Therefore, even if the Appellate Body should reverse the Panel's finding that the European Communities' panel request failed to identify the specific measure at issue, the United States urges the Appellate Body to affirm the Panel's finding that these matters were beyond the Panel's terms of reference on these additional grounds.

42. On the issue of whether the Appellate Body may reinstate or modify the Panel's interim findings, the United States submits that the interim findings have no legal status and could not, therefore, be reinstated.

E. Arguments of the Third Participants

1. Japan

(a) Article 21.3 of the *SCM Agreement* – Applicability of a *de minimis* Standard in Sunset Reviews

43. Japan submits that the *de minimis* standard under Article 11.9 of the *SCM Agreement* is applicable to sunset reviews as well, and supports the Panel's finding in this regard. Although Article 21.3 does not itself define the terms "subsidization" and "injury", the meaning of these terms can be determined from Articles 1, 14 and 15 of the *SCM Agreement*. A proper interpretation of Article 15 requires that only those subsidies that are more than *de minimis* be considered injurious and thus subject to countervailing duties. Article 11.9 supports this view as its second sentence refers not to "investigations", but rather to the broader concept of "cases" which must be read to include sunset reviews. Japan finds further support for its view in the language of Articles 21.1, 22 and 27 of the *SCM Agreement*.

44. Japan adds that the Panel's interpretation is consistent with the object and purpose of Article 21.3. In Japan's view, sunset reviews and original investigations both decide whether countervailing duties should apply. Both determinations should therefore apply the *de minimis* rule of Article 11.9 to determine the existence of a countervailable subsidy. Lastly, with respect to the reasoning of the panel in *US – DRAMS*, Japan argues that duty assessment reviews, which were at issue in that case, differ fundamentally from sunset reviews. Japan submits that the logic of the *US – DRAMS* panel supports the Panel's findings in the present proceedings.

(b) Article 21.3 of the *SCM Agreement* – Self-Initiation of a Sunset Review by the Authorities

45. Japan argues that the authorities must be in possession of "sufficient evidence" in order to self-initiate sunset reviews under Article 21.3 of the *SCM Agreement*. Japan submits that, in finding that authorities may automatically self-initiate

sunset reviews without *any* evidentiary basis, the Panel misread the text of Article 21.3. The absence of even a scintilla of evidence can never be considered "sufficient". Investigating authorities must have some factual basis in order to initiate a review. Japan points to Article 22 of the *SCM Agreement* as explicitly requiring authorities to satisfy themselves that there is "sufficient evidence" to justify the initiation of sunset reviews, and faults the Panel for not examining this provision. Japan emphasizes that Article 22.7 specifically states that Article 22.1 applies, *mutatis mutandis*, to sunset reviews under Article 21.3.

46. Japan also argues that Article 11.6 of the *SCM Agreement* requires that authorities have "sufficient evidence" to initiate sunset reviews under Article 21.3. Japan submits that Article 11 specifically applies to sunset reviews due to Article 22.7, which requires the *mutatis mutandis* application of Article 22.1 in such reviews. Japan argues that the Panel improperly focused its interpretation on Article 11.6 in isolation, without examining its relationship to Articles 22.1 and 22.7.

47. Japan submits that the Panel failed to focus on the purpose of initiation. In Japan's view, Article 21.3 contemplates that some countervailing duties may terminate without review. The duty may be continued beyond five years only when this is necessary to counteract injurious subsidization. Under Article 11.6, authorities must have sufficient evidence to self-initiate an original investigation. It makes no sense, in Japan's view, for the *SCM Agreement* to limit the discretion to self-initiate in some instances but allow unfettered discretion in other instances.

48. Japan adds that the *de minimis* rule under Article 11.9, and the obligation under Article 21.1 to continue the imposition of countervailing duties "only as long as" necessary to counteract injurious subsidization, also support an interpretation of Article 21.3 that would require authorities to be in possession of sufficient evidence to initiate sunset reviews under that provision.

2. *Norway*

(a) Article 21.3 of the *SCM Agreement* – Applicability of a *de minimis* Standard in Sunset Reviews

49. Norway argues that the Panel correctly found that the *de minimis* requirement of Article 11.9 also applies to sunset reviews. A proper analysis of the context of Article 21.3 reveals that all provisions of the *SCM Agreement* are applicable, *mutatis mutandis*, to Article 21.3, to the extent that they are relevant to sunset reviews. The immediate context of Article 21.3 is Article 21.1, which establishes that, where subsidization does not cause such injury, the Agreement does not authorize the imposition of countervailing duties. Furthermore, Article 11.9 requires that there shall be immediate termination in cases where the amount of subsidy is *de minimis*. There is no reason why the same *de minimis* standard should not apply to sunset reviews. Sunset reviews and the original investigation share the same object and purpose, and all impositions of countervailing duties must fulfil the same requirements. Finally, Norway attaches no significance to the absence in Article 21 of any mention of, or cross-reference to, Article 11.9. Norway argues that certain basic concepts such as "subsidy" and "injury", once defined, need not be repeated, and that Article 21.3 must be interpreted in good faith.

(b) Article 21.3 of the *SCM Agreement* – Self-Initiation of a Sunset Review by the Authorities

50. Norway argues that the Panel erred in finding that the United States standard of initiation for sunset reviews of countervailing duties is consistent with Articles 21 and 11 of the *SCM Agreement.* Article 11 applies to sunset reviews, as do all the provisions of Part V of the *SCM Agreement.* Norway finds support for this view in the reference made to Article 12 in Article 21.4 of the Agreement. Norway points to the context of Article 21.3, in particular paragraphs 1 and 2 of Article 21; as well as Article 11, which sets out evidentiary requirements for the initiation of countervailing duty investigations. According to Norway, the requirement of sufficient evidence in Article 11 is also clearly set forth in Article 22.1, which is explicitly applied to sunset reviews by virtue of Article 22.7.

(c) Article 11 of the DSU and Article 21.3 of the *SCM Agreement* – United States Law, As Such, Regarding the Determination to be Made in a Sunset Review

51. Norway submits that United States law violates Article 21.3 and 21.1 and the purpose of Part V of the *SCM Agreement* (and consequently also Article 32.5 of the *SCM Agreement* and Article XVI:4 of the *WTO Agreement*) by not requiring a new investigation in sunset reviews. Article 21.3 establishes a positive obligation upon the domestic authorities to "determine" the likelihood of continuation or recurrence of subsidization. This means that Article 21.3 requires the authorities to undertake an unbiased review, independent of the results of the original investigation, in full conformity with all the procedural and substantive requirements for an initial determination. There is no reason to understand the requirement of "determination" of subsidization and injury differently in Article 21.3 as compared to, *inter alia*, Articles 11 and 15. This is also sustained by Article 21.1 and the purpose of Part V of the *SCM Agreement.* United States law limits the ability of the authorities to conduct a proper determination in a sunset review. For this reason, Norway also supports the European Communities' argument that the Panel mischaracterized the distinction made in previous WTO rulings between discretionary and mandatory laws.

III. ISSUES RAISED IN THIS APPEAL

52. The following issues are raised in this appeal:

(a) as to the *de minimis* standard in sunset reviews:

whether the Panel erred in finding, in paragraphs 8.80, 8.81, 8.84, 9.1(b) and 9.1(c) of its Report that, in not applying a less than 1 percent *de minimis* standard in sunset reviews, United States law, as such, and as applied in the sunset review of countervailing duties on carbon steel, is inconsistent with Article 21.3 and, therefore, with Article 32.5, of the *Agreement on Subsidies and Countervailing Measures* (the "*SCM Agreement*"), and consequently is also inconsistent with Article XVI:4 of the *Marrakesh Agreement Establishing the World Trade Organization* (the "*WTO Agreement*");

(b) as to the evidentiary standards for the self-initiation of sunset reviews:

whether the Panel erred in finding, in paragraphs 8.49 and 9.1(a) of its Report, that United States law, as such, with respect to the automatic self-initiation by authorities of sunset reviews, is consistent with paragraphs 1 and 3 of Article 21, and with Article 10, of the *SCM Agreement*;

(c) as to the determination to be made in sunset reviews:

(i) whether the Panel erred in finding, in paragraph 7.23 of its Report, that the request for the establishment of the Panel satisfied the requirements of Article 6.2 of the *Understanding on Rules and Procedures Governing the Settlement of Disputes* (the "DSU") with respect to a claim regarding the consistency of United States law, as such, with the obligation to determine the likelihood of continuation or recurrence of subsidization in sunset reviews;

(ii) whether the Panel erred in finding, in paragraphs 8.106 and 9.1(d) of its Report, that United States law, as such, is not inconsistent with the obligation in Article 21.3 of the *SCM Agreement* to determine the likelihood of continuation or recurrence of subsidization in sunset reviews; and whether the Panel acted inconsistently with its duties under Article 11 of the DSU in so finding; and

(d) as to the opportunity to present evidence in sunset reviews:

whether the Panel erred in finding, in paragraph 8.145 of its Report, that the request for the establishment of the Panel failed to satisfy the requirements of Article 6.2 of the DSU with respect to claims regarding the consistency of United States law, as such, and as applied in the sunset review of countervailing duties on carbon steel, with obligations regarding the opportunity to present evidence in sunset reviews; and whether the Panel acted inconsistently with its duties under Article 11 of the DSU in so finding.

IV. BACKGROUND

53. This appeal raises a number of issues relating to Members' obligations under the *SCM Agreement* in the conduct of five-year, or "sunset", reviews of countervailing duties. We consider it useful, at the outset, to set out a brief overview of our understanding of the relevant United States' legal framework relating to sunset reviews, based on the explanations provided by the participants in the course of these proceedings.

54. In United States law, sunset reviews are governed primarily by Sections 751(c) and 752 of the Tariff Act of 1930, as amended (the "Tariff Act"), which correspond, respectively, to Sections 1675(c) and 1675a of Title 19 of the United States Code.[36] Pursuant to Section 751(c)(1), the United States Department of Commerce

[36] As the participants, and the Panel, have referred primarily to Sections 751(c) and 752 of the Tariff Act, rather than to Sections 1675(c) and 1675a of Title 19 of the United States Code, we will

("USDOC") is directed, in a sunset review, to "determine, in accordance with Section 752, whether revocation of the countervailing ... duty order ... would be likely to lead to continuation or recurrence of ... a countervailable subsidy".[37] Section 752 sets forth certain "special rules" that apply, *inter alia*, to the determination to be made by USDOC in sunset reviews. Specifically, Section 752(b)(1) provides that USDOC "shall consider":

> (A) the net countervailable subsidy determined in the investigation and subsequent reviews, and
>
> (B) whether any change in the program which gave rise to the net countervailable subsidy described in subparagraph (A) has occurred that is likely to affect that net countervailable subsidy.

55. Section 752(b)(2) of the Tariff Act provides that, "if good cause is shown", USDOC shall also consider, in certain circumstances and within specified limits, certain other subsidy programs that are either determined in other investigations or reviews to provide net countervailable subsidies, and certain programs newly alleged to provide countervailable subsidies. Section 752(b)(3) requires USDOC to provide to the United States International Trade Commission ("USITC") "the net countervailable subsidy that is likely to prevail if the order is revoked". It further stipulates that USDOC "shall normally" choose a net countervailable subsidy that was determined in the final determination made in an investigation[38], or in a subsequent review of the countervailing duty.[39]

56. These statutory provisions are implemented through additional provisions contained in the United States Code of Federal Regulations (the "Regulations"). Specifically, Part 351 of Title 19 of the Regulations sets forth regulations relating to anti-dumping and countervailing duties and related procedures as they relate to USDOC, and Section 218 of Part 351 deals with sunset reviews.

57. In their discussion of the framework governing the conduct of sunset reviews, the participants have also referred to the Statement of Administrative Action[40] (the "SAA") and USDOC's "Policies Regarding the Conduct of Five-year ("Sunset") Re-

also refer to the Tariff Act provisions in this Report. By way of background, Title 19 of the United States Code deals with matters relating to customs duties. Chapter 4 of Title 19 corresponds to the Tariff Act of 1930, as amended. Its Subtitle IV sets forth the legislative rules relating to anti-dumping and countervailing duties.

[37] Under United States law, USDOC is charged with responsibility for determinations relating to subsidization. A separate agency, the United States International Trade Commission, is responsible for injury determinations. None of the issues in this appeal relates to an injury determination.

[38] Pursuant to Section 705 of the Tariff Act.

[39] Pursuant to Section 751(a) or 751(b)(1) of the Tariff Act. We observe that in addition to sunset reviews, Section 751 of the Tariff Act provides for two other types of reviews, namely "periodic review of amount of duty", and "reviews based on changed circumstances". Periodic reviews, dealt with in Section 751(a), are sometimes referred to as "administrative reviews". Pursuant to Section 751(a), USDOC is required, upon request, to "review and determine the amount of any net countervailable subsidy" once a year, and then publish "the results of such review, together with notice of any duty to be assessed, estimated duty to be deposited, or investigation to be resumed." Paragraph (b) of Section 751 deals with "reviews based on changed circumstances", and applies to both USDOC and USITC. When USDOC or USITC receives information, or a request from an interested party, which "shows changed circumstances sufficient to warrant a review", then USDOC or USITC (as the case may be) must conduct a review of the relevant determination or agreement.

[40] H.R. 5110, H.R. Doc. 316, Vol. 1, 103d Congress, 2nd Session, 656 (1994).

views of Antidumping and Countervailing Duty Orders"[41] (the "Sunset Policy Bulletin"). The SAA, which was submitted to the United States Congress along with the proposed Uruguay Round Agreements Act[42] (the "URAA"), "represents an authoritative expression by the Administration concerning its views regarding the interpretation and application of the Uruguay Round agreements".[43] According to the URAA, the SAA is to be:

> ... regarded as an authoritative expression by the United States concerning the interpretation and application of the Uruguay Round Agreements and this Act in any judicial proceeding in which a question arises concerning such interpretation or application.[44]

The Sunset Policy Bulletin, issued by USDOC, is "intended to complement the applicable statutory and regulatory provisions by providing guidance on methodological or analytical issues not explicitly addressed by the statute and regulations".[45]

V. ARTICLE 21.3 OF THE *SCM AGREEMENT* – APPLICABILITY OF A *DE MINIMIS* STANDARD IN SUNSET REVIEWS (APPEAL BY THE UNITED STATES)

58. The Panel was of the view that, for sunset reviews, the "less than 1 percent" *de minimis* standard[46] specified, with respect to the amount of the subsidy, in Article 11.9 of the *SCM Agreement* is "implied in Article 21.3".[47] Based on this view, the Panel found that:

> US CVD law and the accompanying regulations are *inconsistent* with Article 21.3 of the *SCM Agreement* in respect of the application of a 0.5 per cent *de minimis* standard to sunset reviews, and therefore violate Article 32.5 of the *SCM Agreement* and, consequently, also Article XVI:4 of the WTO Agreement.[48] (original underlining)

---

41 Policy Bulletin, United States Federal Register, 16 April 1998 (Volume 63, Number 73), p. 18871.

42 Public Law 103-465, 108 Stat. 4809, which became law in the United States on 8 December 1994.

43 SAA, *supra*, footnote 40, p. 656.

44 URAA, Section 102(d); 19 U.S.C. § 3512(d).

45 Sunset Policy Bulletin, *supra*, footnote 41, p. 18871. In response to questioning at the oral hearing, the United States indicated that the Sunset Policy Bulletin represents a statement of existing USDOC practice. The United States explained that the Sunset Policy Bulletin, as such, is not binding upon USDOC, but that USDOC may not depart from it in an arbitrary or capricious manner. The European Communities submitted that the Sunset Policy Bulletin "contains a compendium of the DOC policies with regard to sunset reviews of AD and CVD orders, i.e. it illustrates the normal best practice of the domestic investigating authority on the issue under dispute". (European Communities' other appellant's submission, para. 47)

46 We observe that Article 11.9 of the *SCM Agreement* defines as *de minimis* an amount of subsidy of *less than* 1 percent *ad valorem*. For the sake of simplicity, we will refer to this standard as either the "1 percent *de minimis* standard" or as the "*de minimis* standard in Article 11.9".

47 Panel Report, para. 8.80.

48 *Ibid*., para. 9.1(b).

> [T]he United States, in applying a 0.5 per cent *de minimis* standard to the instant sunset review, acted *in violation* of Article 21.3 of the *SCM Agreement*.[49] (original underlining)

59. The United States appeals these findings. The United States argues that the Panel failed properly to apply the customary rules of treaty interpretation and wrongly "read into" Article 21.3 of the *SCM Agreement* words and obligations that simply do not exist under that provision. According to the United States, if the text of Article 21.3 is properly interpreted, in its context and in the light of the object and purpose of the *SCM Agreement* as a whole, it is clear that this provision does not require the application of any *de minimis* standard in a sunset review.[50] The United States underlines that one member of the Panel expressed that view in his separate dissenting opinion.[51]

60. This issue requires us to consider whether, as the Panel found, the *same* 1 percent *de minimis* standard that must be applied, pursuant to Article 11.9 of the *SCM Agreement*, in countervailing duty *investigations*, must also be applied in *sunset reviews* carried out pursuant to Article 21.3 of that Agreement. The issue arises because United States law does not require application of a 1 percent *de minimis* standard in sunset reviews. Rather, United States law prescribes a *de minimis* standard of 0.5 percent *ad valorem* for sunset reviews[52] In its legislation and regulations implementing the results of the Uruguay Round, the United States provided for a *de minimis* standard of 1 percent to be applied in *investigations*[53], but maintained its pre-existing *de minimis* standard of 0.5 percent for *reviews*.[54] These modifications reflected the view of the United States Administration, as expressed in the SAA, that the "*de minimis* requirements of Articles 11.9, 27.10 and 27.11 of the Subsidies Agreement are applicable *only* to initial CVD *investigations*. Thus ... these standards are *not applicable* to reviews of CVD orders."[55]

---

[49] *Ibid.*, para. 9.1(c).

[50] United States' appellant's submission, para. 33.

[51] One member of the Panel dissented from the findings of the Panel in paragraphs 9.1(b) and 9.1(c). That member found, at paragraph 10.15 of the Panel Report, that:

> (a) US CVD law and the accompanying regulations are *consistent* with Article 21.3 of the *SCM Agreement* in respect of the application of a 0.5 per cent *de minimis* standard to sunset reviews; and
>
> (b) The United States, in applying a 0.5 per cent *de minimis* standard to the instant sunset review, did *not* act in violation of Article 21.3 of the *SCM Agreement*. (original underlining)

[52] Section 752(b)(4)(B) of the Tariff Act provides that the same *de minimis* standard that applies in periodic reviews and changed circumstances reviews shall also apply to sunset reviews. This rate is not specified in the Tariff Act, but is set at 0.5 percent *ad valorem* in Section 351.106(c)(1) of Title 19 of the Regulations.

[53] Sections 703(b)(4) and 705(a)(3) of the Tariff Act.

[54] Sunset reviews did not exist under United States law prior to the passage of the URAA. By virtue of Section 752(b)(4)(B) of the Tariff Act, the same *de minimis* standard that applies in periodic reviews and changed circumstances reviews is also applied to sunset reviews. The SAA explains that:

> [in reviews of countervailing duty orders], the Administration intends that Commerce will continue its present practice of waiving the collection of estimated deposits if the deposit rate is below 0.5 percent *ad valorem*, the existing regulatory standard for *de minimis*.

(SAA, *supra*, footnote 40, p. 939)

[55] SAA, *supra*, footnote 40, p. 939. (emphasis added) These expressed views of the United States contrast with the practice of the European Communities. The European Communities' legislation

61. At the outset of our analysis, we recall that Article 3.2 of the DSU recognizes that interpretative issues arising in WTO dispute settlement are to be resolved through the application of customary rules of interpretation of public international law. It is well settled in WTO case law that the principles codified in Articles 31 and 32 of the *Vienna Convention on the Law of Treaties* (the "*Vienna Convention*") are such customary rules. Article 31(1) provides in relevant part that:

> A treaty shall be interpreted in good faith in accordance with the ordinary meaning to be given to the terms of the treaty in their context and in the light of its object and purpose.

62. Thus, the task of interpreting a treaty provision must begin with its specific terms. Accordingly, we turn, first, to Article 21.3 of the *SCM Agreement*, which deals with sunset reviews:

> Notwithstanding the provisions of paragraphs 1 and 2, any definitive countervailing duty shall be terminated on a date not later than five years from its imposition (or from the date of the most recent review under paragraph 2 if that review has covered both subsidization and injury, or under this paragraph), unless the authorities determine, in a review initiated before that date on their own initiative or upon a duly substantiated request made by or on behalf of the domestic industry within a reasonable period of time prior to that date, that the expiry of the duty would be likely to lead to continuation or recurrence of subsidization and injury.[52] The duty may remain in force pending the outcome of such a review.
>
> [52] When the amount of the countervailing duty is assessed on a retrospective basis, a finding in the most recent assessment proceeding that no duty is to be levied shall not by itself require the authorities to terminate the definitive duty.

63. Article 21.3 imposes an explicit temporal limit on the maintenance of countervailing duties. For countervailing duties that have been in place for five years, the terms of Article 21.3 require their termination *unless* certain specified conditions are met. Specifically, a Member is permitted *not* to terminate such duties only if it conducts a review and, in that review, determines that the prescribed conditions for the continued application of the duty are satisfied. The prescribed conditions are "that the expiry of the duty would be likely to lead to continuation or recurrence of subsidization and injury". If, in a sunset review, a Member makes an affirmative determination that these conditions are satisfied, it may continue to apply countervailing duties beyond the five-year period set forth in Article 21.3. If it does not conduct a sunset re-

does not deal explicitly with the *de minimis* standard to be applied in a sunset review (or, in European Communities' terminology, "Expiry Review"). (See Article 17 of Council Regulation (EC) 2026/97 of 6 October 1997 on the protection against subsidised imports of countries not members of the European Community, Official Journal L288/1 of 21 October 1997; Exhibit EC-26 submitted by the European Communities to the Panel) However, in a specific case where a subsidy granted by a developing country was found to be less than 2 percent, the European Commission terminated the duty at the expiry review stage as a consequence of its finding that the subsidy was *de minimis*. (EC Commission Decision of 12 June 1998, terminating the countervailing duty proceeding concerning imports of polyester fibres and polyester yarns originating in Turkey, Official Journal L168/46 of 13 June 1998; Exhibit EC-27 submitted by the European Communities to the Panel)

view, or, having conducted such a review, it does not make such a positive determination, the duties must be terminated.

64. As the Panel observed, and as all of the participants in this appeal agree, the text of Article 21.3 does not mention any *de minimis* standard to be applied in sunset reviews. Nor does it make any express reference to the *de minimis* standard set forth in Article 11.9 of the *SCM Agreement.*

65. We have previously observed that the fact that a particular treaty provision is "silent" on a specific issue "must have some meaning".[56] In this case, the lack of any indication, in the text of Article 21.3, that a *de minimis* standard must be applied in sunset reviews serves, at least at first blush, as an indication that no such requirement exists. However, as the Panel itself observed, the task of ascertaining the meaning of a treaty provision with respect to a specific requirement does not end once it has been determined that the text is silent on that requirement.[57] Such silence does not exclude the possibility that the requirement was intended to be included by implication.

66. With this in mind, we next consider Article 11.9 of the *SCM Agreement,* which sets forth, for original investigations, the *de minimis* standard that the Panel found to be "implied" in sunset reviews carried out pursuant to Article 21.3. Article 11.9 provides:

> An application under paragraph 1 shall be rejected and an investigation shall be terminated promptly as soon as the authorities concerned are satisfied that there is not sufficient evidence of either subsidization or of injury to justify proceeding with the case. There shall be immediate termination in cases where the amount of a subsidy is *de minimis*, or where the volume of subsidized imports, actual or potential, or the injury, is negligible. For the purpose of this paragraph, the amount of the subsidy shall be considered to be *de minimis* if the subsidy is less than 1 per cent ad valorem.

67. This provision is one of the eleven paragraphs of Article 11. The various paragraphs set forth rules of a mainly procedural and evidentiary nature. All of them relate to the authorities' initiation and conduct of a countervailing duty *investigation*, as would be expected given the overall title of Article 11 – "*Initiation and Subsequent Investigation*". Paragraph 9 of Article 11 requires authorities to terminate immediately investigative action in three situations. One of these is when the authorities are satisfied that the amount of the subsidy is less than 1 percent *ad valorem.*

68. Although the terms of Article 11.9 are detailed as regards the obligations imposed on authorities thereunder, none of the words in Article 11.9 suggests that the *de minimis* standard that it contains is applicable *beyond* the investigation phase of a countervailing duty proceeding.[58] In particular, Article 11.9 does *not* refer to Article 21.3, nor to reviews that may follow the imposition of a countervailing duty.

---

[56] Appellate Body Report, *Japan – Alcoholic Beverages II*, at 111. See also, Appellate Body Report, *Canada – Patent Term*, para. 78.

[57] Panel Report, paras. 8.27-8.30.

[58] We do not subscribe to the view, expressed by Japan, that the use of the word "cases" (rather than the word "investigation") in the second sentence of Article 11.9 means that the application of the *de minimis* standard set forth in that provision must be applied in *all* phases of countervailing duty proceedings—not only in investigations. The use of the word "cases" does not alter the fact that the terms of Article 11.9 apply the *de minimis* standard only to the investigation phase. We note further that the panel in *US – DRAMS* rejected a similar argument with respect to the meaning of the word

69. We observe, in this regard, that the technique of cross-referencing is frequently used in the *SCM Agreement*. Article 21.4 refers to the obligations set forth in Article 12, and Article 21.5 subjects undertakings given in accordance with Article 18 to the review mechanisms contemplated in Article 21. Similarly, Article 22.7 of the *SCM Agreement* explicitly applies the provisions of Article 22, entitled "*Public Notice and Explanation of Determinations*", to reviews carried out under Article 21. Furthermore, Article 11.9 is specifically referred to in Article 15.3 of the *SCM Agreement*, and the provisions of Article 11, more generally, are referred to in a number of other provisions of the *SCM Agreement*.[59] These cross-references suggest to us that, when the negotiators of the *SCM Agreement* intended that the disciplines set forth in one provision be applied in another context, they did so expressly. In the light of the many express cross-references made in the *SCM Agreement,* we attach significance to the absence of any textual link between Article 21.3 reviews and the *de minimis* standard set forth in Article 11.9. We consider this to be noteworthy, having regard to the fact that both the adoption of a *de minimis* standard for investigations, and the introduction of a "sunset" provision, were regarded as important additions to the Tokyo Round Subsidies Code for improving GATT disciplines on subsidies and countervailing duties.[60]

70. Turning to the immediate context of Article 21.3, we observe the title to Article 21 of the *SCM Agreement* reads "*Duration and Review of Countervailing Duties and Undertakings*". The first paragraph of Article 21 stipulates that a countervailing duty "shall remain in force only as long as and to the extent necessary to counteract subsidization which is causing injury". We see this as a general rule that, after the imposition of a countervailing duty, the continued application of that duty is subject to certain disciplines. These disciplines relate to the *duration* of the countervailing duty ("only as long as ... necessary"), its *magnitude* ("only ... to the extent necessary"), and its *purpose* ("to counteract subsidization which is causing injury"). Thus, the general rule of Article 21.1 underlines the requirement for periodic review of countervailing duties and highlights the factors that must inform such reviews. This does not, however, assist us in determining whether a specific *de minimis* standard is intended to be applied in an Article 21.3 review.

71. Continuing our examination of Article 21 with its second paragraph, we recall that, as we explained in *US – Lead and Bismuth II*, "Article 21.2 provides a review mechanism to ensure that Members comply with the rule set out in Article 21.1 of the

"cases" in Article 5.8 of the *Anti-Dumping Agreement*, a provision almost identical to Article 11.9 of the *SCM Agreement*. (Panel Report, *US – DRAMS*, para. 6.87)

[59] See, for example, Articles 12.13, 13.1, 17.1 and 22.1 of the *SCM Agreement*. Moreover, as the Panel noted that:

> [a] number of provisions in the *SCM Agreement* also apply independently of cross-references in that they contain explicit statements of their scope of application: definition of "subsidy" in Article 1 ("For the purpose of this Agreement"); definition of "interested parties" in Article 12.9 ("for the purposes of this Agreement"); calculation of the amount of a subsidy under Article 14 ("For the purpose of Part V"); definition of "initiated" in footnote 37 ("as used hereinafter"); definition of "injury" under Article 15 and in footnote 45 ("Under this Agreement"); definition of "like product" in footnote 46 ("Throughout this Agreement"); definition of domestic industry in Article 16 ("For the purposes of this Agreement"); and definition of "levy" in footnote 51 ("As used in this Agreement").

(Panel Report, footnote 261 to para. 8.26.)

[60] See *infra.*, para. 90.

SCM Agreement."[61] Moreover, the last sentence of Article 21.2 emphasizes the principle that the countervailing duty must be terminated "immediately" when "the authorities determine that the countervailing duty is no longer warranted". As we explained in our Report in *US – Lead and Bismuth II*, the determination made in a review under Article 21.2 must be a meaningful one:

> [o]n the basis of its assessment of the information presented to it by interested parties, as well as of other evidence before it relating to the period of review, the investigating authority must determine whether there is a continuing need for the application of countervailing duties. The investigating authority is not free to ignore such information. If it were free to ignore this information, the review mechanism under Article 21.2 would have no purpose.[62]

While the requirement of a rigorous review cannot be denied, Article 21.2 does not expressly establish a *de minimis* standard. Accordingly, its terms do not, in our view, shed light on whether such a standard must be "implied" either for reviews carried out pursuant to that provision or pursuant to Article 21.3.

72. The immediate context of Article 21.3 also includes paragraph 4 of Article 21, the first sentence of which provides that "[t]he provisions of Article 12 regarding evidence and procedure shall apply to any review carried out under this Article." Article 12 sets out obligations, primarily of an evidentiary and procedural nature, that apply to the conduct of an *investigation*. It comes immediately after Article 11, which sets forth a number of procedural, evidentiary as well as substantive rules related to the initiation and conduct of an *investigation*. Given that the requirements of Articles 11 and 12 are placed consecutively in the Agreement, and the fact that both Articles expressly set out obligations in relation to *investigations*, we read the express reference in Article 21.4 to Article 12, but not to Article 11, as an indication that the drafters intended that the obligations in Article 12, but not those in Article 11, would apply to reviews carried out under Article 21.3.

73. Looking beyond the immediate context of Article 21.3, we turn to the object and purpose of the *SCM Agreement*. We note, first, that the Agreement contains no preamble to guide us in the task of ascertaining its object and purpose. In *Brazil – Desiccated Coconut*, we observed that the "*SCM Agreement* contains a set of rights and obligations that go well beyond merely applying and interpreting Articles VI, XVI and XXIII of the GATT 1947."[63] The *SCM Agreement* defines the concept of "subsidy", as well as the conditions under which Members may not employ subsidies. It

---

[61] Appellate Body Report, *US – Lead and Bismuth II*, para. 53. Article 21.2 of the *SCM Agreement* provides that:

> The authorities shall review the need for the continued imposition of the duty, where warranted, on their own initiative or, provided that a reasonable period of time has elapsed since the imposition of the definitive countervailing duty, upon request by any interested party which submits positive information substantiating the need for a review. Interested parties shall have the right to request the authorities to examine whether the continued imposition of the duty is necessary to offset subsidization, whether the injury would be likely to continue or recur if the duty were removed or varied, or both. If, as a result of the review under this paragraph, the authorities determine that the countervailing duty is no longer warranted, it shall be terminated immediately.

[62] Appellate Body Report, *US – Lead and Bismuth II*, para. 61.

[63] Appellate Body Report, *Brazil – Desiccated Coconut*, at 181.

establishes remedies when Members employ prohibited subsidies, and sets out additional remedies available to Members whose trading interests are harmed by another Member's subsidization practices. Part V of the *SCM Agreement* deals with one such remedy, permitting Members to levy countervailing duties on imported products to offset the benefits of specific subsidies bestowed on the manufacture, production or export of those goods. However, Part V also conditions the right to apply such duties on the demonstrated existence of three substantive conditions (subsidization, injury, and a causal link between the two) and on compliance with its procedural and substantive rules, notably the requirement that the countervailing duty cannot exceed the amount of the subsidy.[64] Taken as a whole, the main object and purpose of the *SCM Agreement* is to increase and improve GATT disciplines relating to the use of both subsidies and countervailing measures.[65]

74. We thus believe that the Panel properly identified, as among the objectives of the *SCM Agreement*, the establishment of a framework of rights and obligations relating to countervailing duties[66], and the creation of a set of rules which WTO Members must respect in the use of such duties.[67] Part V of the Agreement is aimed at striking a balance between the right to impose countervailing duties to offset subsidization that is causing injury, and the obligations that Members must respect in order to do so. While we agree that Part V strikes such a balance, this alone does not assist us in the task of determining whether the 1 percent *de minimis* standard in Article 11.9 is intended to be applied in reviews carried out pursuant to Article 21.3.

75. This brings us to an examination of the reasoning used by the Panel to find that the *de minimis* standard of Article 11.9 "must be applicable to sunset reviews as it is to investigations".[68] The Panel was of the view that "the sole or principal rationale for the *de minimis* standard set out in Article 11.9 is that a *de minimis* subsidy is considered to be non-injurious."[69]

76. Using this rationale, the Panel reasoned that it would be "difficult to see how *de minimis* rate of likely subsidisation could be considered injurious at the stage of sunset review and continuation of a CVD, when the same rate is considered non-injurious at the stage of investigation and imposition of a CVD."[70] The Panel summarized its reasoning as follows:

> ... the rationale for the *de minimis* standard set out in Article 11.9 is clearly that CVDs are to be used to counter injurious subsidisation, and the threshold set out in this provision demarcates the level below

---

[64] See Article 19.4 of the *SCM Agreement*. We also note that Article 19.2 expressly states that "[i]t is desirable ... that the duty should be less than the total amount of the subsidy if such lesser duty would be adequate to remove the injury to the domestic industry".

[65] We recall that the 1986 Punta del Este Ministerial Declaration, which initiated the Uruguay Round, and charted the course of the negotiations, provided that:

> [n]egotiations on subsidies and countervailing measures shall be based on a review of Articles VI and XVI and the MTN agreement on subsidies and countervailing measures *with the objective of improving GATT disciplines relating to all subsidies and countervailing measures that affect international trade*. (emphasis added)

(Ministerial Declaration on the Uruguay Round, GATT Doc. No. MIN.DEC (20 September 1986), p. 7)

[66] Panel Report, para. 8.32.

[67] *Ibid.*, para. 8.68.

[68] *Ibid.*, para. 8.79.

[69] *Ibid.*, para. 8.61.

[70] *Ibid.*, para. 8.65.

> which subsidisation is deemed to be so small as to be non-injurious for purposes of the imposition of CVDs. Having found this to be the case, and having established that one of the objects and purposes of the *SCM Agreement* is to regulate the imposition of CVDs and to create a disciplinary framework therefor, we are of the view that the *de minimis* standard must be applicable to sunset reviews as it is to investigations. Finding otherwise would compromise the very object and purpose of the *SCM Agreement* and the disciplinary framework that the drafters sought to create through the Agreement.[71]

77. The Panel's approach was centered on the premise that the *de minimis* standard set forth in Article 11.9 represents a threshold below which subsidization is always *non-injurious*. The Panel formed this opinion after examining a 1987 Note prepared by the Secretariat for the Uruguay Round Negotiating Group on Subsidies and Countervailing Measures[72], which was brought to the Panel's attention by the European Communities.[73] The Panel cited part of the Note which recognized that there are two alternative (but not mutually exclusive) theoretical justifications for a *de minimis* rule.[74] The Panel continued:

> [w]hile it is not known which of the two rationales, if not both ("not mutually exclusive"), served as a basis for Article 11.9, the language of that provision suggests to us that it was the first rationale that was the basis for, or was at least paramount in, the drafting of that provision.[75]

78. We observe, first, that in taking this approach, the Panel did not explain why it thought that it was appropriate to rely on the 1987 Note, but simply stated that "it is useful to consider the rationale for the application of a *de minimis* standard to investigations, as reflected in a Note by the Secretariat prepared in April 1987".[76] In any event, it seems to us that the 1987 Note does not support the Panel's conclusion that the "rationale" for the *de minimis* standard in Article 11.9 is that a *de minimis* subsidy is considered to be non-injurious. As the Panel itself recognized, the 1987 Note sets forth *two* rationales for *de minimis* standards, but does not suggest which of them is more compelling or preferable. Nor was any evidence adduced before the Panel suggesting that the negotiators of the *SCM Agreement* considered these or other rationales and expressed a preference for any of them. The Panel chose to base its interpretation of Article 11.9 on only one of these rationales. Even if it were appropriate to

---

[71] Panel Report, para. 8.79.

[72] *Ibid.*, para. 8.60, referring in footnote 296 to MTN.GNG/NG10/W/4, 28 April 1987.

[73] The 1987 Note was first referred to by the European Communities in its comments on the responses of the United States to questions from the Panel following the first meeting of the Panel with the parties. (Panel Report, para. 5.320.) For further discussion of the Note by the parties, see also, Panel Report, paras. 5.464-5.466, 5.501-5.504 and 5.530-5.536. The 1987 Note was submitted by the United States to the Panel as Exhibit US-7.

[74] The first view that "no action should be taken … 'where the effect of the subsidy on the industry in the importing country is not such as to cause material injury'". The second was that "'*de minimis non curat lex*': the law does not take notice of minimal matters". (original underlining) (Panel Report, para. 8.60, quoting from the 1987 Note, MTN.GNG/NG10/W/4, p. 46)

[75] Panel Report, para. 8.60.

[76] *Ibid.*, para. 8.60. It is, for example, unclear to us whether the Panel considered the Note to form part of the preparatory work of the treaty and intended to use it as a supplementary means of treaty interpretation within the meaning of Article 32 of the *Vienna Convention*.

rely on the 1987 Note in interpreting the *SCM Agreement* in accordance with the rules of interpretation set forth in the *Vienna Convention*, selective reliance on such a document does not provide a proper basis for the conclusion reached by the Panel in this regard.

79. More importantly, leaving aside the 1987 Note, the *SCM Agreement* does not, in our view, support the "rationale" attributed by the Panel to the *de minimis* standard in Article 11.9. Article 15 of the *SCM Agreement*, which deals with injury and how it is to be determined, refers, in its paragraph 3, to the *de minimis* standard in Article 11.9 only for the purpose of cumulation of imports. Moreover, footnote 45 to Article 15 indicates that, in the *SCM Agreement*, the term "injury" is, "unless otherwise specified", to:

> ... be taken to mean material injury to a domestic industry, threat of material injury to a domestic industry or material retardation of the establishment of such an industry and shall be interpreted in accordance with the provisions of [Article 15].

In defining the concept of injury, footnote 45 does not make any reference to the amount of subsidy involved.

80. Similarly, Article 1 of the *SCM Agreement* sets out a definition of "subsidy" that applies to the whole of that Agreement. This definition includes *all* such subsidies, regardless of their amount. None of the provisions in the *SCM Agreement* that uses the term "subsidization" confines the meaning of "subsidization" to subsidization at a rate equal to or in excess of 1 percent *ad valorem*, or to any other *de minimis* threshold.[77] It is also worth noting that, under Part II of the *SCM Agreement*, prohibited subsidies are prohibited regardless of the amount of the subsidy.

81. Thus, in our view, the terms "subsidization" and "injury" each have an independent meaning in the *SCM Agreement* which is not derived by reference to the other. It is *unlikely* that very low levels of subsidization could be demonstrated to *cause* "material" injury. Yet such a possibility is not, *per se*, precluded by the Agreement itself, as injury is not defined in the *SCM Agreement* in relation to any specific level of subsidization.

82. We note, too, that Articles 27.10 and 27.11 of the *SCM Agreement* require termination of a countervailing duty *investigation* with respect to a developing country Member whenever "the overall level of subsidies granted does not exceed" 2 or 3 percent, depending on the circumstances. These provisions require authorities, in a countervailing duty investigation, to apply a higher *de minimis* subsidization threshold to imports from developing country Members. To accept the Panel's reasoning—that *de minimis* subsidization is non-injurious subsidization—would imply that, for the same product, imported into the same country, and affecting the same domestic industry, the *SCM Agreement* establishes different thresholds at which the same industry can be said to suffer injury, depending on the origin of the product. This unreasonable implication casts further doubt on the "rationale" attributed by the Panel to Article 11.9's *de minimis* standard.

83. To us, there is nothing in Article 11.9 to suggest that its *de minimis* standard was intended to create a special category of "*non-injurious*" subsidization, or that it reflects a concept that subsidization at less than a *de minimis* threshold *can never*

[77] The term "subsidization" is used in the following Articles of the *SCM Agreement*: 6.1(a); 8.3; 11.9; 12.10; 15.3; 17.2; 18.2; 18.4; 19.4; 21.1; 21.2; 21.3; as well as in Annex IV.

cause injury. For us, the *de minimis* standard in Article 11.9 does no more than lay down an agreed rule that if *de minimis* subsidization is found to exist in an original investigation, authorities are obliged to terminate their investigation, with the result that no countervailing duty can be imposed in such cases.

84. Accordingly, we do not believe that there is a clear "rationale" behind the 1 percent *de minimis* rule of Article 11.9 that must also apply in the context of reviews carried out under Article 21.3. However, the Panel reasoned that it would be "difficult to see how *de minimis* rate of likely subsidisation could be considered injurious at the stage of sunset review and continuation of a CVD, when the same rate is considered non-injurious at the stage of investigation and imposition of a CVD."[78] The Panel added that "[s]uch an interpretation would also yield irrational results".[79] For the reasons that follow, we are not persuaded that this is so.

85. Under the *SCM Agreement*, it is the *countervailing duty* that comes up for a review under Article 21.3. Once the Agreement has been in operation for a sufficient number of years, a countervailing duty subject to such a review will typically be a duty that was imposed after the entry into force of the *SCM Agreement*.[80] For this reason the underlying subsidy will have been found, in a proper investigation conducted in accordance with the requirements of the *SCM Agreement*, to be a subsidy that was in excess of the *de minimis* standard of Article 11.9 (or Article 27.10 or Article 27.11 as the case may be) at the time of imposition of the countervailing duty. There would be no countervailing duty to be reviewed where, in the original investigation, the amount of subsidy was found to be less than the *de minimis* standard. In that case, the investigation itself would have been terminated and no duty could have been imposed.[81]

86. We believe that the relevant question to be addressed is, therefore, what obligations the negotiators intended to apply in the case of a review of a countervailing duty where the underlying subsidy has fallen below the *de minimis* standard of Article 11.9 subsequent to the original investigation. It is not inconceivable that the negotiators of the *SCM Agreement* took the view that when a subsidy, originally found to

---

78 Panel Report, para. 8.65.

79 *Ibid.*, para. 8.69.

80 Articles 32.3 and 32.4 of the *SCM Agreement* provide:

> Subject to paragraph 4, the provisions of this Agreement shall apply to investigations, and reviews of existing measures, initiated pursuant to applications which have been made on or after the date of entry into force for a Member of the WTO Agreement.
>
> For the purposes of paragraph 3 of Article 21, existing countervailing measures shall be deemed to be imposed on a date not later than the date of entry into force for a Member of the WTO Agreement, except in cases in which the domestic legislation of a Member in force at that date already included a clause of the type provided for in that paragraph.

By virtue these provisions, even countervailing duties imposed as a result of investigations initiated prior to the date of entry into force of the WTO Agreement are subjected to sunset review in accordance with the requirements of Article 21.3. With the passage of time, however, countervailing duties reviewed under Article 21.3 will increasingly be countervailing duties that were imposed as a result of an investigation initiated after the date of entry into force of the WTO Agreement.

81 We note that in the instant case of carbon steel, the original countervailing duty was imposed in 1993, before the *SCM Agreement* came into force. Had this been a case where the original subsidy was the subject of an investigation under the *SCM Agreement*, the investigation would have been terminated under Article 11.9 as the original subsidy was below the 1 percent *de minimis* standard.

be in excess of the *de minimis* level and to be causing injury, has fallen below the *de minimis* level subsequent to the investigation stage, authorities conducting a sunset review should nevertheless determine whether revocation of the duty is still likely to lead to continuation or recurrence of the injury to the domestic industry. The automatic termination of the countervailing duty may not have been considered desirable in such a situation.

87. We further observe that original investigations and sunset reviews are distinct processes with different purposes. The nature of the determination to be made in a sunset review differs in certain essential respects from the nature of the determination to be made in an original investigation. For example, in a sunset review, the authorities are called upon to focus their inquiry on what would happen if an existing countervailing duty were to be removed. In contrast, in an original investigation, the authorities must investigate the existence, degree and effect of any alleged subsidy in order to determine whether a subsidy exists and whether such subsidy is causing injury to the domestic industry so as to warrant the imposition of a countervailing duty. These qualitative differences may also explain the absence of a requirement to apply a specific *de minimis* standard in a sunset review.

88. At the same time, we wish to underline the thrust of Article 21.3 of the *SCM Agreement*. An automatic time-bound termination of countervailing duties that have been in place for five years from the original investigation or a subsequent comprehensive review is at the heart of this provision. Termination of a countervailing duty is the rule and its continuation is the exception. The continuation of a countervailing duty must therefore be based on a properly conducted review and a positive determination that the revocation of the countervailing duty would "be likely to lead to continuation or recurrence of subsidization and injury." Where the level of subsidization at the time of the review is very low, there must be persuasive evidence that revocation of the duty would nevertheless lead to injury to the domestic industry. Mere reliance by the authorities on the injury determination made in the original investigation will not be sufficient.[82] Rather, a fresh determination, based on credible evidence, will be necessary to establish that the continuation of the countervailing duty is warranted to remove the injury to the domestic industry.

89. For these reasons, we consider that the non-application of an express *de minimis* standard at the review stage, and limiting the application of such a standard to the investigation phase alone, does not lead to irrational or absurd results. Accordingly, we do not consider it strictly necessary to have recourse to the supplementary means of interpretation identified in Article 32 of the Vienna Convention.

90. In any event, we consider that recourse to the negotiating history of the *SCM Agreement* tends to confirm our view as to the meaning of Article 21.3. We note that the two issues, namely the application of a specific *de minimis* standard in investigations, and the introduction of a time-bound limitation on the maintenance of countervailing duties, were considered to be highly important and were the subject of protracted negotiations. Specific provisions dealing with each of these two issues were viewed as necessary to improve the existing disciplines of the GATT and of the Tokyo Round Subsidies Code. The final texts of Article 11.9 and of Article 21.3 were the result of a carefully negotiated compromise that drew from a number of different proposals, reflecting divergent interests and views. We further note in this respect

[82] As we noted earlier, no issues relating to the injury determination are raised in this case.

that none of the participants in this appeal pointed to any document indicating that the inclusion of a *de minimis* threshold was ever considered in the negotiations on sunset review provisions leading to the text of Article 21.3.[83]

91. We are of the view that a finding on our part that the *de minimis* standard of Article 11.9 is implied in sunset reviews under Article 21.3 would upset the delicate balance of rights and obligations attained by the parties to the negotiations, as embodied in the final text of Article 21.3. Such a finding would be contrary to the requirement of Article 3.2, repeated in Article 19.2 of the DSU, that our findings and recommendations "cannot add to or diminish the rights and obligations provided in the covered agreements".

92. For the reasons set forth above, we are unable to conclude that the *de minimis* standard set forth in Article 11.9 of the *SCM Agreement* is implied in Article 21.3 of the Agreement. We, therefore, reverse the finding of the Panel that "the *de minimis* standard of Article 11.9 is implied in Article 21.3."[84]

93. Having found that there is no *de minimis* standard implied in Article 21.3 of the *SCM Agreement*, it follows that United States law as such is not inconsistent with Article 21.3 of the *SCM Agreement* on the ground that it does not require application of a 1 percent *de minimis* standard in sunset reviews. Accordingly, we also reverse the Panel's finding, in paragraph 9.1(b) of the Panel Report, that:

> US CVD law and the accompanying regulations are *inconsistent* with Article 21.3 of the *SCM Agreement* in respect of the application of a 0.5 per cent *de minimis* standard to sunset reviews, and therefore violate Article 32.5 of the *SCM Agreement* and, consequently, also Article XVI:4 of the WTO Agreement. (original underlining)

94. The Panel also found, at paragraph 9.1(c) of the Panel Report, that the United States acted inconsistently with Article 21.3 of the *SCM Agreement* in not applying a 1 percent *de minimis* standard in the sunset review of countervailing duties on carbon steel at issue in this case. The United States requests us to reverse this finding, for the same reasons that it requests reversal of the Panel's finding that the United States law, as such, relating to the *de minimis* standard to sunset reviews, is inconsistent with Article 21.3 of the *SCM Agreement*.

95. The Panel's reasoning on this issue consisted almost entirely of the following sentence:

> ... [h]aving found that the *de minimis* standard set out in Article 11.9 is applicable to sunset reviews and that US CVD law is inconsistent with the *SCM Agreement* in this respect, we find that the United States violated the *SCM Agreement* by failing to apply such a *de minimis* standard to the instant sunset review.[85]

---

[83] Having examined a number of proposals made by delegations, Notes by the Secretariat summarizing the discussions, and a succession of drafts of the Agreement, we are also unable to find any sign that this issue was addressed during the negotiations. (See, notably, the so-called "Cartland drafts" of 1990, MTN/GNG/NG10/W/38 and Rev. 1, 2 and 3; and the "Dunkel Draft" of 1991, Draft Final Act Embodying the Results of the Uruguay Round of Multilateral Trade Negotiations, MTN.TNC/W/FA, 20 December 1991). Our review of certain commentaries on and summaries of the negotiation of the *Anti-Dumping Agreement* and the *SCM Agreement* – the negotiations of which were in part closely linked – also gives no indication that the issue arose during the negotiations.

[84] Panel Report, para. 8.80.

[85] Panel Report, para. 8.84.

96. In other words, the Panel's finding that the United States acted inconsistently with its obligations under Article 21.3 of the *SCM Agreement* in its sunset review of carbon steel depended on, and was the inevitable consequence of its finding that United States law, as such, is inconsistent with those obligations. Logic compels us to take the same approach. Indeed, none of the participants suggests that we should reach a different conclusion regarding the consistency with Article 21.3 of USDOC's application of its *de minimis* standard in this case from the one we reach with respect to the consistency of United States law as such in this regard.

97. We therefore reverse also the Panel's finding, in paragraph 9.1(c) of the Panel Report, that:

> ... the United States, in applying a 0.5 per cent *de minimis* standard to the instant sunset review, acted *in violation* of Article 21.3 of the *SCM Agreement*.[86] (original underlining)

VI. ARTICLE 21.3 OF THE *SCM AGREEMENT* – SELF-INITIATION OF A SUNSET REVIEW BY THE AUTHORITIES (APPEAL BY THE EUROPEAN COMMUNITIES)

98. The Panel found that:

> ... no evidentiary standards are applicable to the self-initiation of sunset reviews under Article 21.3. We thus conclude that US CVD law and the accompanying regulations are consistent with the *SCM Agreement* in respect of the automatic self-initiation of sunset reviews, and accordingly reject the European Communities' claim in this regard.[87]

99. The European Communities asks us to reverse this finding on the ground that the Panel erred in its interpretation of Article 21.3. According to the European Communities, the evidentiary standards specified in Article 11.6 of the *SCM Agreement* for authorities to initiate an *investigation* on their own initiative also apply to the initiation by such authorities of a *sunset review* on their own initiative. Specifically, the European Communities considers that Article 21.3 requires investigating authorities, if they wish to self-initiate a sunset review, to be in possession of the same level of evidence as would be required in a "duly substantiated request" from the domestic industry.[88] Because United States law provides for the *automatic* self-initiation of sunset reviews by USDOC, in every case, regardless of whether USDOC is in possession of *any* evidence, the European Communities asks us to find that such law is inconsistent with Article 21.3 of the *SCM Agreement*, as well as with Article 32.5 of the *SCM Agreement* and Article XVI:4 of the *WTO Agreement*.

100. Japan supports the assertion of the European Communities that the Panel misinterpreted Article 21.3 of the *SCM Agreement* in finding that no evidentiary standard applies to the self-initiation of sunset reviews by the authorities. For Japan, however, the evidentiary standard that applies is not necessarily the same as would be required

---

[86] *Ibid*., para. 9.1(c).

[87] *Ibid*., para. 8.49. (footnote omitted)

[88] In footnote 9 to paragraph 13 of its other appellant's submission, the European Communities refers to paragraphs 8.15 and 8.16 of the Panel Report for details as to the type of evidence that it considers must be included in such a "duly substantiated request".

under Article 11.6 or as would be required in a request by the domestic industry under Article 21.3. Rather, Japan submits that the authorities must be in possession of "sufficient evidence". Although what constitutes "sufficient evidence" will vary from case to case, Japan insists that the automatic initiation of sunset reviews, "without even a scintilla of evidence" can never be considered "sufficient".[89]

101. Before commencing our analysis, we note that United States law provides for the automatic self-initiation of sunset reviews by the authorities in each and every case. Section 751(c)(2) of the Tariff Act directs USDOC to publish a notice of initiation of a sunset review no later than 30 days before, *inter alia,* the fifth anniversary of the date of publication of a countervailing duty order. Section 351.218(b) of Title 19 of the Regulations confirms that USDOC will conduct a sunset review of *each* countervailing duty order. Both the Sunset Policy Bulletin and the SAA describe the initiation of sunset reviews by USDOC as "automatic".[90]

102. We begin our consideration of this issue with the text of Article 21.3 of the *SCM Agreement*, the relevant part of which provides that:

> ... any definitive countervailing duty shall be terminated on a date not later than five years from its imposition ... unless the authorities determine, in *a review initiated before that date on their own initiative or upon a duly substantiated request made by or on behalf of the domestic industry* within a reasonable period of time prior to that date, that the expiry of the duty would be likely to lead to continuation or recurrence of subsidization and injury. (emphasis added)

103. As we have seen, Article 21.3 requires the termination of countervailing duties within five years unless the prescribed determination is made in a review. Article 21.3 contemplates initiation of this review in one of two alternative ways, as is made clear through the use of the word "or". Either the authorities may make their determination "in a review initiated ... on their own initiative"; *or, alternatively*, the authorities may make the determination "in a review initiated ... upon a *duly substantiated* request made by or on behalf of the domestic industry ...". The words "duly substantiated" qualify only the authorization to initiate a review upon request made by or on behalf of the domestic industry. No such language qualifies the first method for initiating a sunset review, namely self-initiation of a review by the authorities.

104. In principle, when a provision refers, without qualification, to an action that a Member may take, this serves as an indication that no limitation is intended to be imposed on the manner or circumstances in which such action may be taken. However, because the task of interpreting a treaty provision does not end with a bare examination of its text, the absence of an express limitation on Members' ability to take a certain action is not dispositive of whether any such limitation exists.[91]

105. Before leaving our analysis of the *text* of Article 21.3 of the *SCM Agreement*, we, lastly, note that the provision contains no explicit cross-reference to evidentiary rules relating to initiation, such as those contained in Article 11.6. We believe the absence of any such cross-reference to be of some consequence given that, as we have seen[92], the drafters of the *SCM Agreement* have made active use of cross-

[89] Japan's third participant's submission, para. 32.

[90] Sunset Policy Bulletin, *supra*, footnote 41, p. 18872; SAA, *supra*, footnote 40, p. 889.

[91] "[O]missions in different contexts may have different meanings, and omission, in and of itself, is not necessarily dispositive." (Appellate Body Report, *Canada – Autos*, para. 138)

[92] *Supra*, paras. 69 and 72.

references, *inter alia*, to apply obligations relating to *investigations* to review proceedings. In our view, the omission of any express cross-reference thus serves as a further indication that the negotiators of the *SCM Agreement* did not intend the evidentiary standards applicable to the self-initiation of *investigations* under Article 11 to apply to the self-initiation of *reviews* under Article 21.3.

106. We now turn to the immediate context of Article 21.3 of the *SCM Agreement*, namely the other paragraphs of Article 21.

107. Article 21.2 provides, in relevant part:

> The authorities shall review the need for the continued imposition of the duty, where warranted, on their own initiative or, provided that a reasonable period of time has elapsed since the imposition of the definitive countervailing duty, upon request by any interested party which submits *positive information substantiating the need for a review*. (emphasis added)

108. Article 21.2 differs from Article 21.3 in that the former identifies certain circumstances in which the authorities are under an *obligation* to review ("shall review") whether the continued imposition of the countervailing duty is necessary. In contrast, the principal obligation in Article 21.3 is not, *per se*, to conduct a review, but rather to *terminate* a countervailing duty *unless* a specific determination is made in a review. We note that Article 21.2 sets down an explicit evidentiary standard for requests by interested parties for a review under that provision. In order to trigger the authorities' obligation to conduct a review, such requests must, *inter alia*, include "positive information substantiating the need for review". Article 21.2 does not, on its face, apply this same standard to the initiation by authorities "on their own initiative" of a review carried out under that provision. Thus, Article 21.2 contemplates that, for reviews carried out pursuant to that provision, the self-initiation by the authorities of a review is not governed by the same standards that apply to initiation upon request by other parties.

109. As we have noted earlier, the fourth paragraph of Article 21 explicitly applies to Article 21.3 reviews the detailed rules set out in Article 12 of the *SCM Agreement* regarding evidence and procedure in the *conduct* of investigations.[93] However, the rules on evidence and procedure contained in Article 12 do not relate to the *initiation* of such investigations.[94] Rather, the rules relating to evidence needed to *initiate* an investigation are set out in Article 11, which is not referred to in Article 21.4. The fact that the rules in Article 11 governing such matters are not incorporated by reference into Article 21.3 suggests that they are not, *ipso facto*, applicable to sunset reviews.

110. Looking further into the context of Article 21.3, we turn to Article 22 of the *SCM Agreement*, which is entitled "*Public Notice and Explanation of Determinations*". Paragraph 1 of Article 22 provides:

> When the authorities are satisfied that there is sufficient evidence to justify the initiation of an investigation pursuant to Article 11, the

---

[93] *Supra*, para. 72.

[94] One provision in Article 12 of the *SCM Agreement* deals indirectly with the *initiation* of an investigation. Paragraph 12 reads, in relevant part:

> The procedures set out above are not intended to prevent the authorities of a Member from proceeding expeditiously with regard to initiating an investigation ... in accordance with relevant provisions of this Agreement.

> Member or Members the products of which are subject to such investigation and other interested parties known to the investigating authorities to have an interest therein *shall be notified and a public notice shall be given.* (emphasis added)

111. Article 22.1 imposes *notification and public notice obligations* upon Members that have decided, in accordance with all the requirements of Article 11, that the initiation of a countervailing duty investigation is justified. Article 22.1 does not itself establish any evidentiary rule, but only refers to a standard established in Article 11.9.

112. Article 22.7 applies the provisions of Article 22 "*mutatis mutandis* to the initiation and completion of reviews pursuant to Article 21". To us, in the same way that Article 22.1 imposes notification and public notice requirements on investigating authorities that have decided, in accordance with the standards set out in Article 11, to initiate an *investigation*, Article 22.1 (by virtue of Article 22.7) also operates to impose notification and public notice requirements on investigating authorities that have decided, in accordance with Article 21, to initiate a *review*. Similarly, in the same way that Article 22.1 does *not* itself establish evidentiary standards applicable to the initiation of an *investigation*, it does *not* itself establish evidentiary standards applicable to the initiation of sunset reviews. Such standards, if they exist, must be found elsewhere.

113. We, therefore, turn next to Article 11 of the *SCM Agreement* as possible relevant context in our interpretation of Article 21.3. It is, in fact, Article 11 that sets forth the evidentiary standards that apply to the *initiation* by authorities of a countervailing duty investigation.

114. We recall that Article 11 is entitled "*Initiation and Subsequent Investigation*". Paragraph 2 of Article 11 sets forth guidance as to what may constitute "sufficient evidence" for purposes of an application by or on behalf of domestic industry seeking initiation of an *investigation*. It provides, in part, that:

> An application under paragraph 1 shall include sufficient evidence of the existence of (a) a subsidy and, if possible, its amount, (b) injury within the meaning of Article VI of GATT 1994 as interpreted by this Agreement, and (c) a causal link between the subsidized imports and the alleged injury. Simple assertion, unsubstantiated by relevant evidence, cannot be considered sufficient to meet the requirements of this paragraph.

115. The remainder of Article 11.2 sets forth the type of evidence that should be included in the application. Article 11.3 directs the authorities to "review the accuracy and adequacy of the evidence provided in the application to determine whether the evidence is sufficient to justify the initiation of an investigation." Article 11.6 applies the "sufficient evidence" standard in Article 11.2 to the self-initiation of investigations by investigating authorities, and Article 11.9 requires the authorities to reject an application that does not contain "sufficient evidence of subsidization and injury".[95] Thus, Article 11 sets out a number of evidentiary requirements that must be satisfied in order to initiate a countervailing duty investigation.

---

[95] Article 11.6 of the *SCM Agreement* provides:

> If, in special circumstances, the authorities concerned decide to initiate an investigation without having received a written application by or on behalf of a domestic

116. In sum, our review of the context of Article 21.3 of the *SCM Agreement* reveals no indication that the ability of authorities to self-initiate a sunset review under that provision is conditioned on compliance with the evidentiary standards set forth in Article 11 of the *SCM Agreement* relating to initiation of investigations. Nor do we consider that any other evidentiary standard is prescribed for the self-initiation of a sunset review under Article 21.3.

117. This is not to say that authorities may continue the countervailing duties after five years in the absence of evidence that the expiry of the duty would be likely to lead to continuation or recurrence of subsidization and injury. Article 21.3 prohibits the continuation of countervailing duties unless a review is undertaken and the prescribed determination, based on adequate evidence, is made.[96]

118. For all of these reasons, we agree with the Panel that Article 21.3 of the *SCM Agreement* does not prohibit the automatic self-initiation of sunset reviews by investigating authorities.[97] Accordingly, we uphold the Panel's finding in paragraph 9.1(a) of the Panel Report that:

> US CVD law and the accompanying regulations are consistent with Article 21, paragraphs 1 and 3, and Article 10 of the *SCM Agreement* in respect of the application of evidentiary standards to the self-initiation of sunset reviews.

VII. THE DETERMINATION TO BE MADE IN A SUNSET REVIEW

A. *Article 6.2 of the DSU – Whether the Matter was Within the Panel's Terms of Reference (Appeal by the United States)*

119. The United States appeals the Panel's refusal to dismiss, as outside its terms of reference, the European Communities' claim under Article 21.3 of the *SCM Agreement* against United States law, as such, regarding the determination to be made in a sunset review.[98]

120. Before the Panel, this issue arose in the following manner. Following the second meeting of the Panel with the parties, the Panel posed a question to the European Communities asking whether it was to understand that the European Communities was "making a claim that US law as such violates the *SCM Agreement* in respect of

> industry for the initiation of such investigation, they shall proceed only if they have sufficient evidence of the existence of a subsidy, injury and causal link, as described in paragraph 2, to justify the initiation of an investigation.

[96] We note that, by virtue of the last sentence of Article 21.3, a countervailing duty "may remain in force pending the outcome of" an ongoing sunset review that was initiated before the five-year anniversary of the imposition of the countervailing duty. Moreover, Article 21.4 provides that such a review "shall be carried out expeditiously and shall normally be concluded within 12 months of the date of initiation of the review."

[97] Panel Report, para. 8.49.

[98] Panel Report, paras. 7.21 and 7.23. In its Notice of Appeal and appellant's submission, the United States has stated that its appeal on this issue is conditional upon our reversing the Panel's findings with regard to the consistency of United States law, as such, with the obligation to determine the likelihood of continuation or recurrence of subsidization in a sunset review. However, in response to questioning at the oral hearing, the United States withdrew this condition and suggested that we should consider this issue before turning to the substance of the European Communities' appeal. The European Communities objected to the withdrawal by the United States of this condition to its appeal, arguing that it was too late to do so.

the obligation to "'determine" the likelihood of continuation or recurrence of subsidization' contained in Article 21.3".[99] The European Communities responded in the affirmative.[100] In its comments on the responses of the European Communities to questions from the Panel, the United States asserted that any such claim was outside the Panel's terms of reference.[101] This assertion was reiterated in the United States' request for interim review, after the Panel had issued its interim report, which included findings on this matter.[102]

121. In addressing this issue, the Panel, first, stated that it would not address the objection because the United States could have, and should have, raised it at an earlier stage in the proceedings.[103] Nevertheless, the Panel went on to examine the request for establishment of the Panel, and stated that it did "not consider that the European Communities' claims regarding the obligation to determine likelihood of continuation or recurrence of subsidisation are outside the Panel's terms of reference."[104]

122. The United States disputes the Panel's rejection of the United States' objection as untimely, and submits that the panel request did not satisfy the requirements of Article 6.2 of the DSU with respect to the claim regarding the consistency of United States law, as such, with its obligations relating to the determination to be made in a sunset review.

123. In considering this issue, we recall that we have consistently held that, in the interests of due process, parties should bring alleged procedural deficiencies to the attention of a panel at the earliest possible opportunity.[105] In this case, we see no reason to disagree with the Panel's view that the United States' objection was not raised in a timely manner. At the same time, however, as we have observed previously, certain issues going to the *jurisdiction* of a panel are so fundamental that they may be considered at any stage in a proceeding.[106] In our view, the Panel was correct, therefore, in turning to consider its terms of reference and in satisfying itself as to its jurisdiction with respect to this matter.

124. We thus turn to consider the United States' assertion that the Panel erred in its finding that this matter was within its terms of reference.[107] We recall that, pursuant to Article 7 of the DSU, a panel's terms of reference are governed by the request for establishment of a panel. Article 6.2 of the DSU sets forth the requirements applicable to such requests. It provides, in relevant part:

---

[99] Question 51 posed by the Panel; Panel Report, para. 5.517.

[100] Panel Report, para. 5.517.

[101] *Ibid.*, para. 5.581.

[102] *Ibid.*, para. 7.20.

[103] *Ibid.*, para. 7.21.

[104] *Ibid.*, para. 7.23.

[105] Appellate Body Report, *Mexico – Corn Syrup (Article 21.5 – US)*, para. 50; Appellate Body Report, *US – FSC*, para. 166; and Appellate Body Report, *US – 1916 Act*, WT/DS136/AB/R, para. 54.

[106] Appellate Body Report, *Mexico – Corn Syrup (Article 21.5 – US)*, para. 36; and Appellate Body Report, *US – 1916 Act*, para. 54.

[107] As we have just stated, this jurisdictional issue is one that may properly be considered at any stage in the proceedings. In our view, irrespective of the condition initially placed by the United States upon its appeal, it is appropriate in this case to ascertain the scope of the Panel's terms of reference *before* turning to the merits of the European Communities' appeal with regard to the consistency of United States law, as such, with the obligation to determine the likelihood of continuation or recurrence of subsidization in a sunset review.

> The request for the establishment of a panel shall ... identify the specific measures at issue and provide a brief summary of the legal basis of the complaint sufficient to present the problem clearly.

125. There are, therefore, two distinct requirements, namely identification of *the specific measures at issue*, and the provision of a *brief summary of the legal basis of the complaint* (or the *claims*). Together, they comprise the "matter referred to the DSB", which forms the basis for a panel's terms of reference under Article 7.1 of the DSU.[108]

126. The requirements of precision in the request for the establishment of a panel flow from the two essential purposes of the terms of reference. First, the terms of reference define the scope of the dispute. Secondly, the terms of reference, and the request for the establishment of a panel on which they are based, serve the *due process* objective of notifying the parties and third parties of the nature of a complainant's case.[109] When faced with an issue relating to the scope of its terms of reference, a panel must scrutinize carefully the request for establishment of a panel "to ensure its compliance with both the letter and the spirit of Article 6.2 of the DSU."[110]

127. As we have said previously, compliance with the requirements of Article 6.2 must be demonstrated on the face of the request for the establishment of a panel. Defects in the request for the establishment of a panel cannot be "cured" in the subsequent submissions of the parties during the panel proceedings.[111] Nevertheless, in considering the sufficiency of a panel request, submissions and statements made during the course of the panel proceedings, in particular the first written submission of the complaining party, may be consulted in order to confirm the meaning of the words used in the panel request and as part of the assessment of whether the ability of the respondent to defend itself was prejudiced.[112] Moreover, compliance with the requirements of Article 6.2 must be determined on the merits of each case, having considered the panel request as a whole, and in the light of attendant circumstances.[113]

128. With these considerations in mind, we turn to the request for the establishment of the Panel to ascertain whether it satisfies the requirements of Article 6.2 of the DSU with respect to the claim that United States law, as such, regarding the determination to be made in a sunset review, is inconsistent with Article 21.3 of the *SCM Agreement*. The panel request states, in relevant part:

> Under Article 21.3 of the *SCM Agreement*, countervailing duties have to be terminated after five years, unless the investigating authorities determine that their expiry would be likely to lead to (i.e. cause), *inter alia*, the continuation or recurrence of subsidisation. It is therefore for the DOC to make a positive demonstration to this effect. In fact, the DOC has not made such a demonstration; it has merely found that

---

[108] Appellate Body Report, *Guatemala – Cement I*, paras. 69-76.

[109] Appellate Body Report, *Brazil – Dessicated Coconut*, at 186. See also, Appellate Body Report, *EC – Bananas III*, para. 142.

[110] Appellate Body Report, *EC – Bananas III*, para. 142.

[111] *Ibid*., para. 143.

[112] See, for example, Appellate Body Report, *Korea – Dairy*, para. 127; Appellate Body Report, *Thailand – H-Beams*, para.95.

[113] Appellate Body Report, *Korea – Dairy*, paras. 124-127.

> subsidies of less than the *de minimis* level provided for in Article 11.9 will continue. ...
>
> The EC consider that the US decision of 2 August 2000 not to revoke the countervailing duties imposed on imports of corrosion resistant steel (Issue No. 65 FR 47407), *as well as certain aspects of the sunset review procedure which led to it (regulated by Section 751 c) of the Tariff Act of 1930 and the implementing regulations and interim final rules issued by the DOC –see footnote 2) are inconsistent with the obligations of the United States under the SCM Agreement and, in particular, Articles 10, 11.9, 21 (notably paragraphs 1 and 3),* and 32.5 thereof, and under Article XVI:4 of the Agreement establishing the World Trade Organization.[114] (underlining added)

129. As observed by the Panel[115], the panel request expressly refers to the obligation to determine the likelihood of continuation or recurrence of subsidization in sunset reviews and to the need to make a "positive demonstration to this effect." In addition, the request mentions "certain aspects of the sunset review procedure which led to [the decision not to revoke countervailing duties on carbon steel]", and specifically refers to the United States statutory provision governing sunset reviews, to related regulatory provisions, and to the Sunset Policy Bulletin. Together, these provisions govern USDOC's conduct of a sunset review, including the determination that must be made in such a review.

130. Further, the panel request identifies obligations under, and alleges violation of, Article 21.3 of the *SCM Agreement*. This statement of the legal basis for the European Communities' claim is, indeed, very brief. But this alone does not mean that it falls short of the standard required by Article 6.2 of the DSU. As we have observed, although the listing of the treaty provisions allegedly violated is always a *necessary* "minimum prerequisite" for compliance with Article 6.2, whether such a listing is *sufficient* to constitute a "brief summary of the legal basis of the complaint sufficient to present the problem clearly" within the meaning of Article 6.2 will depend on the circumstances of each case, and in particular on the extent to which mere reference to a treaty provision sheds light on the nature of the obligation at issue.[116] In examining the provision at issue in this case, we note that Article 21.3 of the *SCM Agreement* is a relatively short provision, and the determination to be made in a sunset review is one of its central features. In addition, we read the words in the panel request that it is "for the DOC to make a positive demonstration to this effect" as further elaboration of the relevant obligation imposed on domestic authorities by Article 21.3.

[114] WT/DS213/3, pp. 2 and 3. Footnote 2 to the request for the establishment of the Panel refers to: Section 751 c) of the Tariff Act of 1930, in the Implementing Regulations on anti-dumping and countervailing duties issued by USDOC (F.R. Vol. 62 No. 96 Monday, May 19, 1997 p 27296 - 19 CFR Parts 351, 353, and 355 Antidumping Duties; Countervailing Duties Final rule) and in the USDOC's Interim final rules on procedures for conducting five-year ("Sunset") Reviews of Antidumping and Countervailing Duty Orders (19 CFR Section 351- FR Doc. 98-7165 Filed 3-19-98).

[115] Panel Report, paras. 7.22-7.23.

[116] Appellate Body Report, *Korea – Dairy*, para. 124.

131. Thus, although we agree with the Panel that "the European Communities could certainly have been more forthcoming in its request for establishment" [117], we find that the Panel did not err in concluding that the request for establishment of the panel satisfied the requirements of Article 6.2 of the DSU with respect to the European Communities' claim regarding the consistency of United States law, as such, with the obligation to determine the likelihood of continuation or recurrence of subsidization in a sunset review.

132. We are confirmed in this view by our reading of the European Communities' first written submission to the Panel. This submission clearly addresses United States law, as such, governing the likelihood determination. Section 6 of the submission, entitled "Claims", is divided into four subsections. Subsection 6.2 deals with the determination to be made in a sunset review, and in part 6.2.2 of that subsection, headed "US laws and practice", the European Communities alleges, *inter alia*, that United States law is inconsistent with the United States' obligations under Article 21.3 of the *SCM Agreement*. [118]

133. In the light of the references to the requirement to make a likelihood determination in the panel request, and the arguments elaborated in the European Communities' first written submission to the Panel, we believe that the United States was given adequate notice of the European Communities' claim. The absence of prejudice to the United States is also reflected in the fact that the Panel did not sustain the claim of the European Communities in relation to United States law, as such, regarding the likelihood determination, but rather found United States law in this regard to be consistent with the obligations in Article 21.3 of the *SCM Agreement*.

134. We therefore uphold the Panel's finding that:

> [w]e therefore do not consider that the European Communities' claims regarding the obligation to determine likelihood of continuation or recurrence of subsidisation are outside the Panel's terms of reference. [119]

B. *Article 11 of the DSU and Article 21.3 of the SCM Agreement – Whether the Panel Erred in its Assessment of United States Law (Appeal by the European Communities)*

135. The Panel found that:

> ... US law is not inconsistent with Article 21.3 of the *SCM Agreement* with respect to the obligation that the investigating authorities determine the likelihood of continuation or recurrence of subsidisation in a sunset review.
>
> ... Having found that US CVD law and the accompanying regulations are consistent with Article 21.3 of the *SCM Agreement* in respect of the obligation that the investigating authorities determine the likelihood of continuation or recurrence of subsidisation in a sunset review, we need not, and do not, consider whether US CVD law and the ac-

[117] Panel Report, para. 7.23.

[118] European Communities' first submission to the Panel, para. 76.

[119] Panel Report, para. 7.23.

companying regulations are inconsistent with Article 32.5 of the *SCM Agreement* and Article XVI:4 of the WTO Agreement.[120]

136. The European Communities requests us to reverse these findings and to find that United States law, as such, is inconsistent with Article 21.3 of the *SCM Agreement* in respect of the investigating authorities' obligation to determine the likelihood of continuation or recurrence of subsidization in a sunset review. The European Communities also asks us to make consequential findings that United States law, as such, is inconsistent with United States' obligations under Article 32.5 of the *SCM Agreement* and Article XVI:4 of the *WTO Agreement.*[121]

137. The Panel's analysis of this issue consists of two distinct parts. First, the Panel interpreted Article 21.3 to ascertain what that provision requires of investigating authorities making a "determination" in a sunset review.[122] In this part of its analysis, the Panel opined that "a determination of likelihood under Article 21.3 must rest on a sufficient factual basis"[123], namely "on the evaluation of the evidence that it has gathered during the original investigation, the intervening reviews and finally the sunset review."[124] Furthermore, according to the Panel:

> [w]hat the investigating authority must do under Article 21.3 is to assess whether subsidisation is likely to continue or recur should the CVD be revoked. This is, obviously, an inherently prospective analysis. Nonetheless, it must itself have an adequate basis in fact. The facts necessary to assess the likelihood of subsidisation in the event of revocation may well be different from those which must be taken into account in an original investigation. Thus, in assessing the likelihood of subsidisation in the event of revocation of the CVD, an investigating authority in a sunset review may well consider, *inter alia*, the original level of subsidisation, any changes in the original subsidy programmes, any new subsidy programmes introduced after the imposition of the original CVD, any changes in government policy, and any changes in relevant socio-economic and political circumstances.[125]

138. These Panel findings are *not* appealed by the European Communities. Accordingly, we are *not* called upon, in this particular appeal, to review the Panel's the *interpretation* of Article 21.3 and the obligations it sets forth with respect to the determination to be made in a sunset review.

139. It is, rather, the second part of the Panel's analysis of this matter that forms the subject of this appeal. The European Communities' appeal is limited to the find-

---

[120] Panel Report, paras. 8.106 and 8.107. See also, Panel Report, para. 9.1(d).

[121] We note that neither party has appealed the additional Panel finding, set out in para. 9.1(e) of the Panel Report, that the specific determination made in the sunset review of countervailing duties on carbon steel was inconsistent with the requirements of Article 21.3 of the *SCM Agreement*.

[122] See Section VIII.D(1)(b)(i) of the Panel Report, paras. 8.89-8.96.

[123] Panel Report, para. 8.94.

[124] *Ibid.*, para. 8.95.

[125] Panel Report, para. 8.96.

ings made by the Panel in its assessment of whether the relevant United States law, as such, conforms to the requirements of Article 21.3 of the *SCM Agreement*.[126]

140. In appealing this part of the Panel Report and the resulting finding that United States law "is not inconsistent with Article 21.3" of the *SCM Agreement* with respect to the likelihood determination, the European Communities argues that the Panel did not ascertain the meaning of United States law in accordance with its duty, under Article 11 of the DSU, to make an "objective assessment of the matter". The European Communities further contends that the Panel erred in its interpretation and application of the distinction between mandatory and discretionary laws. The European Communities' appeal rests upon both Article 11 of the DSU and Article 21.3 of the *SCM Agreement*.

1. *Article 11 of the DSU – Limitations Imposed by United States Law*

141. Article 11 of the DSU provides, in relevant part:

> ... a panel should make an objective assessment of the matter before it, including an objective assessment of the facts of the case and the applicability of and conformity with the relevant covered agreements, and make such other findings as will assist the DSB in making the recommendations or in giving the rulings provided for in the covered agreements.

142. We recall that "the standard of review set forth in Article 11 of the DSU [applies to disputes] arising under Part V of the *SCM Agreement*".[127] As we have observed previously, Article 11 requires panels to take account of the evidence put before them and forbids them to wilfully disregard or distort such evidence.[128] Nor may panels make affirmative findings that lack a basis in the evidence contained in the panel record.[129] Provided that panels' actions remain within these parameters, however, we have said that "it is generally within the discretion of the Panel to decide which evidence it chooses to utilize in making findings"[130], and, on appeal, we "will not interfere lightly with a panel's exercise of its discretion".[131]

143. In arguing that the Panel acted inconsistently with Article 11 of the DSU and "ignored the legal limitations imposed by United States law on investigating authorities [in making their determination in a sunset review]", the European Communities challenges: (i) the Panel's failure to accord sufficient weight to the Sunset Policy Bulletin and the SAA in determining the meaning of Sections 751(c) and 752 of the Tariff Act; (ii) the Panel's failure to draw the appropriate inferences from USDOC's "consistent practice" as to the meaning of United States law; and (iii) the Panel's failure to engage in the additional fact-finding necessary properly to appreciate the

---

[126] In response to questioning at the oral hearing, the European Communities confirmed that its appeal is limited to the reasoning and findings contained in Section VIII.D(1)(b)(ii) of the Panel Report, paras. 8.97-8.107.

[127] Appellate Body Report, *US – Lead and Bismuth II*, para. 51.

[128] Appellate Body Report, *EC – Hormones*, para. 133.

[129] Appellate Body Report, *US – Wheat Gluten*, paras. 161-162.

[130] Appellate Body Report, *EC – Hormones*, para. 135.

[131] Appellate Body Report, *US – Wheat Gluten*, para. 151.

meaning of Section 351.218(e)(2)(i) of the Regulations.[132] We will examine the Panel's treatment of each of these issues in turn.

144. With respect to the first point, we note that, before the Panel, the European Communities introduced the Sunset Policy Bulletin and the SAA into evidence.[133] In its arguments before the Panel, the European Communities cited certain provisions from the Sunset Policy Bulletin and the SAA, but did not make arguments as to the precise nature of the relationship between these instruments, on the one hand, and the relevant statutory and regulatory provisions, on the other hand.

145. In its analysis, the Panel reproduced the relevant portions of Sections 751(c) and 752 of the Tariff Act, referred to Section 315.218(a) of the Regulations, and observed that:

> [t]he Sunset Policy Bulletin and the Statement of Administrative Action ("SAA") basically elaborate further on the provisions of the Statute and the Sunset Regulations within the limits set out in the Statute.[134] (footnote omitted)

146. Thus, the Panel specifically referred to the Sunset Policy Bulletin and the SAA, and took the view that they operated "within the limits set out" in the legislation—namely Sections 751(c) and 752 of the Tariff Act.[135] The Panel also stated that these instruments did not "change" United States law as set forth in those statutory provisions.[136] It is clear, from these statements, that the Panel took account of, and did not disregard, the evidence placed before it by the European Communities. Accordingly, bearing in mind that Article 11 does not oblige panels to attach to a particular piece of evidence the same weight as the party submitting that evidence[137], we see no reason to disturb the Panel's treatment of the Sunset Policy Bulletin and the SAA in its assessment of the meaning of United States law.

147. The European Communities' second point alleges that, in considering United States law as such, the Panel did not draw the correct inferences from the "consistent practice" of USDOC. Specifically, the European Communities argues that such practice demonstrates that, under United States law, USDOC does not consider *any* changes or terminations of subsidy programs, unless such changes or termination were found in a previous review of the duty, and that this is tantamount to a "refusal to conduct any investigation in a sunset review".[138] Before the Panel, and on appeal, the European Communities referred to the sunset review of carbon steel at issue in this case as evidence of the "consistent practice" of USDOC.

148. We are not persuaded that the conduct of a single sunset review can serve as conclusive evidence of USDOC practice, and, thereby, of the meaning of United States law. This is particularly so in the absence of information as to the number of sunset reviews that have been conducted, the methodology employed by USDOC in

---

[132] European Communities' other appellant's submission, paras. 44-54.

[133] Exhibits EC-15 and EC-16 submitted by the European Communities to the Panel.

[134] Panel Report, para. 8.101.

[135] *Ibid.*, para. 8.101.

[136] *Ibid.*, para. 8.106.

[137] Appellate Body Report, *Korea – Alcoholic Beverages*, para. 164. Consequential changes should be made to the Table of Cases Cited in This Report on page iii, where the full case citation for this Report should read "Appellate Body Report, *Korea - Taxes on Alcoholic Beverages*, WT/DS75/AB/R, WT/DS84/AB/R, adopted 17 February 1999, DSR 1999:I,3".

[138] European Communities' other appellant's submission, para. 50.

other reviews, and the overall results of such reviews.[139] We also point out that, as the Panel noted, even in the sunset review at issue in this case, USDOC did make certain adjustments to the rate of subsidization determined in the original investigation, notwithstanding the absence of any intervening review of the duty.[140] Furthermore, the European Communities itself put evidence before the Panel, in the form of a decision by a United States domestic court, suggesting that USDOC's sunset review of countervailing duties on carbon steel in this case was not conducted in accordance with United States law.[141] Accordingly, the evidentiary foundation upon which the European Communities sought to have the Panel draw an inference from USDOC practice seem to us to have been a weak one. For all of these reasons, we believe that the Panel acted well within the scope of its discretion in its appreciation of the evidence relating to USDOC practice in its analysis of United States law relating to the likelihood determination.

149. The third point raised by the European Communities relates to the Panel's treatment of the phrase "extraordinary circumstances" in Section 351.218(e)(2)(i) of Title 19 of the Regulations, which provides, in relevant part, that:

> ... only under the most extraordinary circumstances will the Secretary rely on a countervailing duty rate or a dumping margin other than those it calculated and published in its prior determinations.

---

[139] We note that, although the European Communities does not seem to have submitted such evidence to the Panel, the United States provided, in response to a question from the Panel, a broader picture of the results of sunset reviews. (Panel Report, para. 5.274) The European Communities did refer, briefly, to three other sunset reviews conducted by USDOC, but did not introduce the text of the determinations made in those cases into the Panel record. (Panel Report, para. 5.218)

[140] Panel Report, para. 8.116.

[141] On 4 March 2002, after the parties had made their second written submissions to the Panel but before their second meeting with the Panel, the European Communities transmitted to the Panel a decision of the United States Court of International Trade dated 28 February 2002 (*AG der Dillinger Hüttenwerke v. United States* ("*Dillinger I*"), 193 F. Supp. 2d 1339 (Ct. Int'l Trade 2002); Exhibit EC-24 submitted by the European Communities to the Panel). By letter dated 5 March 2002, the Panel invited the United States to submit any comments on the European Communities' submission of that decision by 12 March 2002. The United States did not submit any comments. In its decision, the Court found that USDOC had not complied with its duties under United States statutory law in making its determination in the sunset review of carbon steel. The Court opined, *inter alia*, that United States law imposes a "fact-gathering" obligation on USDOC in a full sunset review. (*Dillinger I*, p. 1348) The Court also rejected USDOC's argument that, when no administrative review has been conducted, the SAA and the Sunset Policy Bulletin preclude USDOC, in a sunset review, from making adjustments to the countervailable subsidy rate determined in the original investigation. The Court stated that:

> ... the SAA indicates that Congress contemplated that Commerce is to engage in some fact gathering when conducting a full sunset review. ... Such fact gathering would be pointless if Commerce were prohibited from considering those facts in order to determine whether adjustments to the original CVD rate are warranted.
>
> ... the court finds no support for such a restriction in the statute, the regulations or the SAA. In fact, the court finds that such an interpretation ... would directly conflict with the SAA and the statutory scheme, and is therefore impermissible.

(*Dillinger I*, pp. 1353-1354). In this appeal, the European Communities also submitted, as exhibits to its appellee's submission, USDOC's redetermination pursuant to the Court's remand, together with a 5 September 2002 decision by the Court of International Trade with respect to this remand determination (*AG der Dillinger Hüttenwerke v. United States*, Slip Op. 02-107, Ct. No. 00-09-00437 (Ct. Int'l Trade, 5 September 2002)). At the oral hearing in this appeal, the United States stated that these decisions of the Court of International Trade are interlocutory in nature and may yet be appealed.

150. In considering whether United States law restricted the determination that authorities are to make in a sunset review, the Panel noted the similarity between the language of Section 751(c) of the Tariff Act and Article 21.3 of the *SCM Agreement*, and then summarized the provisions of Article 752 of the Tariff Act, which govern USDOC's assessment of the likely rate of subsidization in a sunset review. The Panel went on to express "some concern" about the possible limiting effects of the phrase "extraordinary circumstances" in Section 351.218(e)(2)(i) of Title 19 of the Regulations.[142]

151. In its challenge to the Panel's approach, the European Communities does *not* claim that the Panel failed to take account of relevant evidence submitted by the European Communities. Instead, the European Communities alleges that the Panel "failed" to engage in the fact-finding the European Communities thinks necessary to appreciate properly the meaning of the phrase "extraordinary circumstances".

152. We observe, in this regard, that although Section 351.218(e)(2)(i) of the Regulations was one of the many provisions submitted by the European Communities in Exhibit EC-14 to the Panel, the submissions made by the European Communities to the Panel do not specifically refer to Section 351.218(e)(2)(i) of the Regulations, much less elaborate its meaning. Nor did the European Communities explain how this provision operates to preclude USDOC from making a determination consistent with Article 21.3 of the *SCM Agreement*. In these circumstances, the European Communities has failed to make its case and we cannot fault the Panel for its treatment of Section 351.218(e)(2)(i).

153. We also wish to underline that although panels enjoy a *discretion*, pursuant to Article 13 of the DSU[143], to seek information "from any relevant source", Article 11 of the DSU imposes no *obligation* on panels to conduct their own fact-finding exercise, or to fill in gaps in the arguments made by parties. In consequence, given that the European Communities itself had submitted no evidence—other than the text of the provision—on this point, the Panel did not act inconsistently with Article 11 in refraining from seeking additional information on its own initiative.

2. *The Panel's Treatment of the Distinction Between Mandatory and Discretionary Legislation*

154. Turning to the part of the European Communities' appeal relating to the Panel's treatment of the distinction between mandatory and discretionary legislation, we recall that the Panel found that:

> [h]aving considered the provisions challenged by the European Communities, we find no provision in US law that *mandates* WTO-inconsistent behaviour. We also note that the Regulations, the Sunset Policy Bulletin and the SAA do not contain any provision that changes US law in this respect.[144] (original underlining)

155. The European Communities challenges this finding, arguing that the Panel could not properly have found that the United States law at issue in this case was a

---

142 Panel Report, para. 8.105.

143 As we have stated, "[t]his is a grant of discretionary authority: a panel is not duty-bound to seek information in each and every case or to consult particular experts under this provision." (Appellate Body Report, *Argentina – Textiles and Apparel*, para. 84)

144 Panel Report, para. 8.106.

"discretionary" law. The European Communities draws a distinction between a "genuinely discretionary law", where the authorities are afforded discretion of sufficient breadth and nature to allow for the law to be applied in a WTO-consistent manner, and a deliberately "complex and ambiguous web of provisions, such as the one at issue", which creates "a smoke screen of procedures in order to show a (*de facto* inexistent) discretion".[145] In short, the European Communities alleges that any discretion afforded to USDOC under United States law is illusory.

156. We note, first, that, in dispute settlement proceedings, Members may challenge the consistency with the covered agreements of another Member's laws, as such, as distinguished from any specific application of those laws. In both cases, the complaining Member bears the burden of proving its claim. In this regard, we recall our observation in *US – Wool Shirts and Blouses* that:

> ... it is a generally-accepted canon of evidence in civil law, common law and, in fact, most jurisdictions, that *the burden of proof rests upon the party, whether complaining or defending, who asserts the affirmative of a particular claim or defence*.[146] (emphasis added)

157. Thus, a responding Member's law will be treated as WTO-*consistent* until proven otherwise. The party asserting that another party's municipal law, as such, is inconsistent with relevant treaty obligations bears the burden of introducing evidence as to the scope and meaning of such law to substantiate that assertion.[147] Such evidence will typically be produced in the form of the text of the relevant legislation or legal instruments, which may be supported, as appropriate, by evidence of the consistent application of such laws, the pronouncements of domestic courts on the meaning of such laws, the opinions of legal experts and the writings of recognized scholars. The nature and extent of the evidence required to satisfy the burden of proof will vary from case to case.

158. In this case, the European Communities asserts that United States law has three main characteristics which effectively remove USDOC's discretion to make a determination consistent with the requirements of Article 21.3 of the *SCM Agreement* : first, "no change or termination of subsidy program can be considered unless such change or termination were found in a previous review of the order"; second, United States law establishes "a mechanism that results in a reversal of the presumption of termination of CVD orders"; and, third, the law generates "a consistent and persistent practice of WTO-inconsistent continuation of CVD orders".[148] We will consider each of the points raised by the European Communities.

159. First, we address the allegation that USDOC is precluded from considering any changes to or termination of subsidy programs when there has been no review of the duty between the time of the final determination in the original investigation and the sunset review. On this point, we recall that the Panel relied on the specific language in Section 752(b)(1) of the Tariff Act in order to dismiss the claim of the European Communities.[149] This provision, *inter alia*, mandates USDOC to consider "whether any change in the program that gave rise to such net countervailable sub-

[145] European Communities' other appellant's submission, para. 61.

[146] Appellate Body Report, *US – Wool Shirts and Blouses*, at 335. See also, Appellate Body Report, *EC – Hormones*, para. 98; and Appellate Body Report, *EC – Sardines*, para. 281.

[147] See, for example, Appellate Body Report, *US – Wool Shirts and Blouses*, at 335.

[148] European Communities' other appellant's submission, para. 60.

[149] Panel Report, para. 8.104.

sidy ... has occurred that is likely to affect that net countervailable subsidy." The Panel also noted that "the words of Section 751(c) of the Tariff Act reflect closely the language of Article 21.3 of the *SCM Agreement*."[150] We believe that it was appropriate for the Panel to rely on the express provisions of the statute. Furthermore, we have already noted that, in this case: (i) USDOC did make certain adjustments to the rate of subsidization determined in the original investigation, notwithstanding the absence of any intervening review of the duty[151]; and (ii) the European Communities itself introduced a decision by the United States Court of International Trade finding not only that United States law does not preclude USDOC from taking account of changes in subsidy programs when no review has been conducted, but that any interpretation of the law that would include such a restriction is "impermissible".[152]

160. Second, with respect to the alleged "reversal of the presumption of termination" of countervailing duties after five years, this argument also seems to depend on the premise that USDOC will not consider changes in subsidy programs. The European Communities seems to argue that when a subsidy program was found, in an original investigation, to provide countervailable subsidies, then United States law requires USDOC automatically to make the same finding in a sunset review. However, as we have just stated, the Panel properly held that United States law requires changes in a subsidy program to be taken into account in a sunset review.

161. Third, as to the argument that United States law generates a consistent practice of WTO-inconsistent continuation of countervailing duty orders, we recall that, in support of this assertion, the European Communities relied primarily on the conduct of the sunset review in this case. This was not sufficient to require the Panel to make any finding as to USDOC's "consistent practice".[153]

162. It follows that, in this case, the European Communities did not satisfy its burden of proving either that United States law mandates USDOC to act inconsistently with Article 21.3 of the *SCM Agreement*, or that such law restricts in a material way USDOC's discretion to make a determination consistent with Article 21.3 in a sunset review. Thus, we conclude that the Panel did not err in finding that United States law had not been shown to be inconsistent with Article 21.3 of the *SCM Agreement*. Given the evidence before it, the Panel was entitled to rely on the language of Sections 751(c) and 752 of the Tariff Act in finding that United States law, as such, is not inconsistent with the obligations that the Panel found to be contained in Article 21.3 of the *SCM Agreement*.[154]

163. Accordingly, we uphold the Panel's findings, at paragraph 8.106, that:

US law is not inconsistent with Article 21.3 of the *SCM Agreement* with respect to the obligation that the investigating authorities deter-

---

[150] *Ibid.*, para. 8.103.

[151] *Ibid.*, para. 8.116.

[152] *Dillinger I*, *supra*, footnote 141, p. 1354.

[153] In this regard, we recall our reasoning *supra* in paragraph 148 and the footnotes thereto.

[154] We also recall that the Panel's *legal interpretation* of the requirements imposed under Article 21.3—*inter alia*, that "a determination of likelihood under Article 21.3 must rest on a sufficient factual basis", and specifically "on the evaluation of the evidence that it has gathered during the original investigation, the intervening reviews and finally the sunset review"—has not been appealed. (Panel Report, paras. 8.94-8.96)

mine the likelihood of continuation or recurrence of subsidisation in a sunset review.[155]

VIII. ARTICLES 6.2 AND 11 OF THE DSU – THE OPPORTUNITY TO SUBMIT EVIDENCE IN A SUNSET REVIEW (APPEAL BY THE EUROPEAN COMMUNITIES)

164. The European Communities requests that we reverse the Panel's finding that the European Communities' claims with respect to the consistency of United States law, as such, and as applied in the case, with the obligation to provide "ample opportunity" to present evidence in a sunset review, were outside the Panel's terms of reference.[156]

165. Before the Panel, this issue arose in the following manner. Following the second meeting of the Panel, the Panel posed a question inquiring whether it was to understand that the European Communities was making claims, pursuant to Article 12.1 of the *SCM Agreement*, regarding the consistency of United States law with obligations with respect to the opportunity to present evidence in sunset reviews.[157] The European Communities responded in the affirmative.[158] The United States asserted, in its comments on the European Communities' response to this question, that such claims were outside the Panel's terms of reference.[159] This objection was reiterated in the United States' request for interim review, after the Panel had issued its interim report, which included findings on these matters.[160]

166. In its Report, the Panel found:

> ... that the European Communities has failed to set out a claim in its request for establishment with respect to the United States' CVD law in respect of the investigating authority's obligation to provide ample opportunity to interested members and parties to submit relevant evidence in a sunset review. This "measure" is therefore outside our terms of reference. Accordingly, we do not address the European Communities' claims under Article 12 of the *SCM Agreement*.[161]

167. As a consequence, the Panel omitted from its Report certain substantive findings and reasoning, which had appeared in the interim report.[162] On appeal, in addi-

---

155 See also, Panel Report, para. 9.1(d).

156 Panel Report, para. 8.145.

157 Question 54 posed by the Panel; Panel Report, para. 5.522.

158 Panel Report, para. 5.522.

159 *Ibid.*, para. 5.589.

160 *Ibid.*, paras. 7.24 and 8.133.

161 *Ibid.*, para. 8.145. See also, Panel Report, para. 8.137.

162 In its interim report, the Panel made the following findings in relation to these matters:

> 12.1 In conclusion, we: ...
>
> (f) reject the claim of the European Communities that US CVD law and the accompanying regulations and statement of policy practices are inconsistent with Article 12.1 of the *SCM Agreement* in respect of the obligation to provide ample opportunity to interested Members and all interested parties to present in writing all relevant evidence, and therefore violate Article 32.5 of the *SCM Agreement* and, consequently, also Article XVI:4 of the WTO Agreement; and

tion to asking us to reverse the Panel's finding on its terms of reference, the European Communities requests that we "reinstate and modify" these findings from the interim report, or issue our own substantive findings on the basis of material on the record.

168. The European Communities further asserts that, in considering whether these matters were within its terms of reference, the Panel committed "serious legal errors in its appreciation of the facts" [163] and thereby failed to make an objective assessment of the matter before it, as required by Article 11 of the DSU. In the view of the European Communities, the Panel could not reasonably have concluded that it was not clear that the European Communities was making claims regarding the opportunity to present evidence in sunset reviews.

169. In considering the European Communities' appeal, we first set out the portions of the request for establishment of the Panel that the European Communities asserts demonstrate its compliance with the requirements of Article 6.2 of the DSU to "identify the specific measures at issue and provide a brief summary of the legal basis of the complaint sufficient to present the problem clearly." The penultimate paragraph of the panel request sets forth the following summary of the preceding parts of the request:

> The EC consider that the US decision of 2 August 2000 not to revoke the countervailing duties imposed on imports of corrosion resistant steel (Issue No. 65 FR 47407), *as well as certain aspects of the sunset review procedure which led to it (regulated by Section 751 c) of the Tariff Act of 1930 and the implementing regulations and interim final rules issued by the DOC –see footnote 2) are inconsistent with the obligations of the United States under the SCM Agreement and, in particular, Articles 10, 11.9, 21 (notably paragraphs 1 and 3),* and 32.5 thereof, and under Article XVI:4 of the Agreement establishing the World Trade Organization. [164] (underlining added)

170. As the Panel noted, the panel request contains no explicit reference to the opportunity to present evidence in a sunset review. [165] Indeed, it does not contain the word "evidence" at all. Nor does the request give any indication as to *why* or *how* USDOC allegedly failed to afford sufficient opportunity to present evidence in the sunset review of carbon steel. Furthermore, the panel request does not cite any particular provisions of United States law, or other examples of United States practice, that relate specifically to the submission of evidence.

> (g) uphold the claim of the European Communities that the United States, in failing to provide ample opportunity to interested Members and all interested parties to present in writing all relevant evidence in the instant sunset review, acted in violation of Article 12.1 of the *SCM Agreement*.

[163] European Communities' other appellant's submission, para. 77.

[164] WT/DS213/3. Footnote 2 to the request for the establishment of the Panel refers to:

> Section 751 c) of the Tariff Act of 1930, ... the Implementing Regulations on anti-dumping and countervailing duties issued by USDOC (F.R. Vol. 62 No. 96 Monday, May 19, 1997 p 27296 - 19 CFR Parts 351, 353, and 355 Antidumping Duties; Countervailing Duties Final rule) and ... the USDOC's Interim final rules on procedures for conducting five-year ("Sunset") Reviews of Antidumping and Countervailing Duty Orders (19 CFR Section 351- FR Doc. 98-7165 Filed 3-19-98).

[165] Panel Report, para. 8.141.

171. In our view, the references in the panel request to "certain aspects of the sunset review procedure", to the United States statutory provisions governing sunset reviews, to related regulatory provisions, and to the Sunset Policy Bulletin, can be read to refer, generally, to United States law regarding the determination to be made in a sunset review.[166] However, we do not believe they can be read to refer to *distinct* measures, consisting of United States law, as such, and as applied, relating to the submission of evidence. Accordingly, we agree with the Panel that the matters relating to the submission of evidence in a sunset review were not within its terms of reference because the *specific measures at issue were not adequately identified* in the request for the establishment of the panel[167], as required by Article 6.2 of the DSU.

172. We would add that, in our view, the panel request also fails to comply with the second requirement of Article 6.2—to set out the legal basis of the European Communities' complaints with regard to these matters. The panel request does not refer to Article 12.1 of the *SCM Agreement*, which deals with the treatment of evidence in a sunset review. The panel request neither identifies the first paragraph of Article 12 of the *SCM Agreement* as relevant. Nor does it contain any language—such as the phrase "ample opportunity to present evidence"—that would at least suggest the legal basis of the claims. Nor does the request specifically identify Article 21.4, which applies the requirements of Article 12 to sunset reviews. We recall that the identification of the treaty provisions claimed to have been violated is a "minimum prerequisite" for stating of the legal basis of a complaint.[168] In this appeal, the panel request falls short of this minimum prerequisite with respect to the issue of submission of evidence.

173. Our view is confirmed by a review of the European Communities' submissions to the Panel. The *arguments* of the European Communities relating to the opportunity to present evidence were made *exclusively* in the context of its claims regarding the obligation to determine the likelihood of continuation or recurrence of subsidization.[169] However, as we have previously observed, it is important to distinguish between *claims*, which must be sufficiently identified in the panel request, and the *arguments* in support of those claims, which are set out in the written submissions and statements made by the parties during panel proceedings.[170] Here, the European Communities made *arguments* on the rules relating to the submission of evidence in support of *claims* concerning the determination to be made in a sunset review.

174. Accordingly, we uphold the Panel's finding that its terms of reference did not include claims against United States law, as such, and as applied in the sunset review of countervailing duties on carbon steel, relating to the obligation to provide "ample opportunity" to present evidence in a sunset review.[171]

175. Lastly, we consider the European Communities' assertion, invoking Article 11 of the DSU, that the Panel did not comply with its duty to make an objective assessment of the matter before it, by failing to find that the European Communities was

---

[166] *Supra*, paras. 129 to 134.

[167] Panel Report, para. 8.145.

[168] Appellate Body Report, *Korea – Dairy*, para. 124.

[169] See, European Communities' first submission to the Panel, paras. 99 and 101; European Communities' second submission to the Panel, paras. 40-44; European Communities' second oral statement to the Panel, para. 20. See also Panel Report, paras. 5.35, 5.412-5.415, and 5.454.

[170] Appellate Body Report, *EC – Bananas III*, paras. 141 and 143.

[171] Panel Report, para. 8.145. See also, Panel Report, para. 8.137.

making claims with respect to the opportunity to present evidence in a sunset review.[172]

176. In this case, we have upheld the Panel's finding that the request for the establishment of the Panel failed to comply with the requirements of Article 6.2 of the DSU in relation to matters regarding the opportunity to submit evidence in sunset reviews. We did so on the basis of our review of the reasoning upon which this finding of the Panel was based—with which we agree—as well as on the basis of our own examination of the panel request. In sum, we are satisfied that the Panel complied with its duties under Article 11 of the DSU in finding that its terms of reference did not include the European Communities' claims relating to the opportunity to submit evidence in a sunset review.[173]

IX. FINDINGS AND CONCLUSIONS

177. For the reasons set out in this Report:

(a) as to the *de minimis* standard in sunset reviews, the Appellate Body:

reverses the Panel's findings, in paragraphs 8.80, 8.81, 8.84, 9.1(b) and 9.1 (c) of its Report, that, in not applying a less than 1 percent *de minimis* standard in sunset reviews, United States law, as such, and as applied in the sunset review of countervailing duties on carbon steel, is inconsistent with Article 21.3 and, therefore, with Article 32.5, of the *SCM Agreement*, and consequently is also inconsistent with Article XVI:4 of the *WTO Agreement*;

(b) as to the evidentiary standards for the self-initiation of sunset reviews, the Appellate Body:

upholds the Panel's finding, in paragraphs 8.49 and 9.1(a) of its Report, that United States law, as such, with respect to the automatic self-initiation by authorities of sunset reviews, is consistent with paragraphs 1 and 3 of Article 21, and with Article 10, of the *SCM Agreement*;

(c) as to the determination to be made in sunset reviews, the Appellate Body:

(i) *upholds* the Panel's finding, in paragraph 7.23 of its Report, that the request for the establishment of the Panel satisfied the requirements of Article 6.2 of the DSU with respect to a claim regarding the consistency of United States law, as such, with the obligation to determine the likelihood of continuation or recurrence of subsidization in sunset reviews;

(ii) *upholds* the Panel's finding, in paragraphs 8.106 and 9.1(d) of its Report, that United States law, as such, is not inconsistent with the obligation in Article 21.3 of the *SCM Agreement* to determine the likelihood of continuation or recurrence of sub-

---

172 European Communities' other appellant's submission, para. 77.

173 As a result of our findings in this section, we are not required to, and do not, consider the European Communities' request that we "reinstate and modify" findings included in the interim report, but omitted from the Panel Report.

sidization in sunset reviews; and finds that the Panel acted consistently with its duties under Article 11 of the DSU in so finding;

(d) as to the opportunity to present evidence in sunset reviews, the Appellate Body:

upholds the Panel's finding, in paragraph 8.145 of its Report, that the request for the establishment of the Panel failed to satisfy the requirements of Article 6.2 of the DSU with respect to claims regarding the consistency of United States law, as such, and as applied in the sunset review of countervailing duties on carbon steel, with obligations regarding the opportunity to present evidence in sunset reviews; and finds that the Panel acted consistently with its duties under Article 11 of the DSU in so finding.

178. The Appellate Body *recommends* that the DSB request that the United States bring its measure found in the Panel Report, as modified by this Report, to be inconsistent with the *SCM Agreement* into conformity with its obligations under that Agreement.

UNITED STATES – COUNTERVAILING DUTIES ON CERTAIN CORROSION-RESISTANT CARBON STEEL FLAT PRODUCTS FROM GERMANY

Report of the Panel
WT/DS213/R*

Adopted by the Dispute Settlement Body
on 19 December 2002
as Modified by the Appellate Body Report

TABLE OF CONTENTS

* WT/DS213/R and Corr.1.

Page

Page

I. INTRODUCTION

A. *Complaint of the European Communities*

1.1 On 10 November 2000, the European Communities requested consultations[1] with the United States pursuant to Article 4 of the Understanding on Rules and Procedures Governing the Settlement of Disputes ("DSU"), Article XXII:1 of the General Agreement on Tariffs and Trade 1994 ("GATT 1994"), and Article 30 of the

[1] *See* WT/DS213/1.

Agreement on Subsidies and Countervailing Measures ("*SCM Agreement*"), regarding countervailing duties ("CVDs") imposed by the United States on imports of certain corrosion-resistant carbon steel flat products originating in Germany, in particular, the sunset review of these CVDs.

1.2 The European Communities and the United States held consultations on 8 December 2000, but failed to reach a mutually satisfactory solution.

1.3 On 5 February 2001, the European Communities requested further consultations[2] with the United States, regarding certain aspects of the procedure followed by the United States in sunset reviews, both as such and as applied in the sunset review in question, in particular, the evidentiary standards applied for the self-initiation of these reviews.

1.4 The European Communities and the United States held further consultations on 21 March 2001, but failed to reach a mutually satisfactory solution.

1.5 On 8 August 2001, the European Communities requested the establishment of a panel[3] pursuant to Article 6 of the DSU, Article XXIII of GATT 1994, and Article 30 of the *SCM Agreement*.

B. Establishment and Composition of the Panel

1.6 The Dispute Settlement Body ("DSB") established a panel on 10 September 2001, with standard terms of reference. The terms of reference of the Panel are:

> To examine, in the light of the relevant provisions of the covered agreements cited by the European Communities in document WT/DS213/3, the matter referred to the DSB by the European Communities in that document, and to make such findings as will assist the DSB in making the recommendations or in giving the rulings provided for in those agreements.

1.7 On 18 October 2001, the European Communities requested the Director-General to determine the composition of the Panel, pursuant to paragraph 7 of Article 8 of the DSU. This paragraph provides:

> If there is no agreement on the panelists within 20 days after the date of the establishment of a panel, at the request of either party, the Director-General, in consultation with the Chairman of the DSB and the Chairman of the relevant Council or Committee, shall determine the composition of the panel by appointing the panelists whom the Director-General considers most appropriate in accordance with any relevant special or additional rules or procedures of the covered agreement or covered agreements which are at issue in the dispute, after consulting with the parties to the dispute. The Chairman of the DSB shall inform the Members of the composition of the panel thus formed no later than 10 days after the date the Chairman receives such a request.

1.8 On 26 October 2001, the Director-General accordingly composed the panel as follows[4]:

---

2 *See* WT/DS213/1/Add.1.

3 *See* WT/DS213/3.

4 *See* WT/DS213/4.

1.9 Chairman: Mr. Hugh McPhail
Members: Mr. Ronald W. Erdmann
Mr. Wieslaw Karsz

1.10 Japan and Norway reserved their rights to participate in the panel proceedings as third parties.

C. *Panel Proceedings*

1.11 The Panel met with the parties on 29 January 2002, and on 19 March 2002. The Panel met with the third parties on 29 January 2002.

1.12 The Panel submitted its interim report to the parties on 14 May 2002. Comments were received from the parties on the interim report on 23 May 2002, and on each other's comments on 30 May 2002 (*See* Section VII, *infra*). The Panel submitted its final report to the parties on 14 June 2002.

II. FACTUAL ASPECTS

2.1 At issue in this dispute is the US law as such in respect of sunset reviews of CVDs, as well as its application in a sunset review carried out by the United States of a CVD order on imports of certain corrosion-resistant carbon steel flat products from Germany. The United States Department of Commerce ("DOC") determined that revocation of the order "would be likely to lead to continuation or recurrence of a countervailable subsidy".[5] The DOC transmitted this determination to the United States International Trade Commission ("ITC"), along with a determination regarding the magnitude of the net countervailable subsidy likely to prevail in case of revocation of the order – 0.54 per cent in the review at issue. The ITC determined that revocation of the order "would likely lead to continuation or recurrence of material injury to an industry in the United States within a reasonably foreseeable time".[6] Accordingly, the United States decided not to revoke the CVD order under review[7] on imports of the product in question.

2.2 The European Communities considers that the relevant US laws, regulations, administrative procedures, and statement of policy practices in respect of sunset reviews of CVDs, as well as their application in this instance, violates the *SCM Agreement* and the Marrakesh Agreement Establishing the World Trade Organization ("WTO Agreement"). The European Communities' claims therefore relate to the US sunset review system as such, as well as the specific sunset review determination by the DOC in respect of certain corrosion-resistant carbon steel flat products from Germany.

2.3 The measures that the European Communities challenges as violating Articles 10, 11.9, 21, and 32.5 of the *SCM Agreement*, and XVI:4 of the Agreement establishing the World Trade Organization are:

---

[5] Certain Corrosion-Resistant Carbon Steel Flat Products, etc.; Final Results of Full Sunset Reviews ("Commerce Sunset Final"), 65 FR 47407 (2 August 2000) (Exhibit EC-9).

[6] Certain Carbon Steel Products, etc.; Injury Determination, 65 FR 75301 (1 December 2000) (Exhibit EC-11).

[7] Countervailing Duty Orders and Amendment to Final Affirmative Countervailing Duty Determinations: Certain Steel Products from Germany, 58 FR 43756 (17 August 1993) (Exhibit EC-4).

1. the US CVD law in respect of sunset reviews: Section 751(c), as complemented by Section 752, of the Tariff Act of 1930 ("Tariff Act")[8], as amended;
2. the accompanying Implementing Regulations: Procedures for Conducting Five-year ("Sunset") Reviews of Anti-Dumping and Countervailing Duty Orders, or "Sunset Regulations"[9];
3. the accompanying statement of policy practices: Policies Regarding the Conduct of Five-year ("Sunset") Reviews of Anti-Dumping and Countervailing Duty Orders; Policy Bulletin, or "Sunset Policy Bulletin"[10]; and
4. their application in this instance, in the sunset review determination in respect of certain corrosion-resistant carbon steel flat products from Germany.[11]

III. PARTIES' REQUESTS FOR FINDINGS AND RECOMMENDATIONS

A. *European Communities*

3.1 The European Communities requests that the Panel find that the measures identified by the European Communities (*See* paragraph 2.3, *supra*):

1. infringe Article 21, paragraphs 3 and 1, as well as Article 10, of the *SCM Agreement*, by requiring that sunset reviews are automatically initiated for all existing CVD measures under the conditions specified therein;
2. violate Article 21, paragraphs 3 and 1, in conjunction with Articles 10 and 11, of the *SCM Agreement*, by applying expedited reviews, through automatic initiation and presumption of likelihood of continuation or recurrence;[12]
3. violate Article 21.3, in conjunction with Article 11, of the *SCM Agreement*, by requiring the automatic self-initiation of sunset reviews;
4. establish a standard of investigation for sunset reviews that violates the requirements of the *SCM Agreement*; and
5. violate Article 21.3, in conjunction with Article 21.1 and Article 11.9, of the *SCM Agreement*, by not requiring the application of the 1 per cent *de minimis* rule in sunset reviews and by enabling the continuation of CVDs for five more years in circumstances where there is no

[8] Codified in 19 USC 1675(c) (Exhibit EC-13).

[9] 63 FR 13516 (20 March 1998), codified in 19 CFR part 351 (Exhibit EC-14).

[10] 63 FR 18871 (16 April 1998) (Exhibit EC-15).

[11] Continuation of Antidumping and Countervailing Duty Orders on Certain Carbon Steel Products from [16 countries, including Germany], 65 FR 78469 (15 December 2000) (Exhibit EC-12). *See also* Certain Corrosion-Resistant Carbon Steel Flat Products, etc.; Final Results of Full Sunset Reviews ("Commerce Sunset Final"), 65 FR 47407 (2 August 2000) (Exhibit EC-9), and accompanying Decision Memorandum ("Commerce Sunset Final Decision Memorandum") (Exhibit EC-10).

[12] Please note that the United States made a request for a preliminary ruling in respect of this claim of the European Communities. *See* Section 8, infra.

need to counter subsidisation which is likely to cause injury, and, because, in the present instance, the US authority continued a measure despite having found that the rate of subsidisation likely to prevail was less than 1 per cent.

3.2 Accordingly, the European Communities requests the Panel to find the US CVD law, regulations, and statement of policy practices to be inconsistent with Article 32.5 of the *SCM Agreement* and, consequently, also inconsistent with Article XVI:4 of the WTO Agreement.

B. *United States*

3.3 The United States disputes the claims of the European Communities, and requests that the Panel find that:

6. the US procedure for the automatic self-initiation of sunset reviews by the DOC is not inconsistent with the *SCM Agreement*;
7. in not applying the 1 per cent *de minimis* standard of Article 11.9 of the *SCM Agreement* to sunset reviews, the United States has not acted inconsistently with its obligations under the *SCM Agreement*; and
8. the DOC sunset review determination in respect of certain corrosion-resistant carbon steel flat products from Germany is not inconsistent with US obligations under the *SCM Agreement*.

IV. REQUEST OF THE UNITED STATES FOR A PRELIMINARY RULING

A. *Request of the United States*

4.1 The United States requests that the Panel make a preliminary ruling that the European Communities' claims with respect to the expedited sunset review procedure are not before the Panel because this procedure is not a measure within the Panel's terms of reference.

4.2 The United States submits that the European Communities did not identify any measure or type of proceeding in consultations other than (i) the sunset review determination in carbon steel; (ii) the initiation of sunset reviews by the DOC; and (iii) the *de minimis* standard employed by the DOC in sunset reviews. Nor, argues the United States, did the European Communities identify the expedited sunset review procedure in its request for consultations or in its request for the establishment of a panel.

4.3 The arguments of the United States in this regard are reflected below (*See* Section V, *infra*).

B. *Response of the European Communities*

4.4 The European Communities disagrees with the United States, and submits that the European Communities' claims regarding the United States' expedited sunset review procedure are within the Panel's terms of reference. The European Communities asserts that, given the reference in its request for establishment to Section 751(c) of the Tariff Act, which contains procedural rules on sunset reviews, including expe-

dited sunset reviews, the issue of expedited reviews has also been raised by the European Communities and is therefore within the Panel's terms of reference.
4.5 The arguments of the European Communities in this regard are reflected below (*See* Section V, *infra*).

V. ARGUMENTS OF THE PARTIES

5.1 The arguments presented by the parties in their written submissions, oral statements, responses to questions, and comments on each other's responses to questions are reflected below.[13]

A. *First Written Submission of the European Communities*

1. *Introduction*

5.2 This dispute concerns the compatibility of the United States (the "US") basic countervailing duty law (Tariff Act of 1930)[14], its accompanying regulations (Sunset Regulations)[15] and policy practices (Sunset Policy Bulletin)[16], and their concrete application in the sunset review of countervailing duties on imports of certain corrosion-resistant carbon steel flat products ("corrosion resistant steel") from Germany. This decision violates the US WTO obligations in several ways.
5.3 First, the *Agreement on Subsidies and Countervailing Measures* (the "*SCM Agreement*") provides for a presumption of termination of countervailing duty measures after 5 years. In the EC's view, the *automatic* initiation of sunset reviews under US practice (without a requirement for any evidence to be produced) disregards this presumption for termination. As such, it contravenes Article 21.3 of the *SCM Agreement.*
5.4 Second, the *SCM Agreement* requires that an investigating authority determines that the expiry of the duty would be likely to lead to recurrence of subsidisation. In not considering changes or terminations in subsidy programmes in the course of the sunset review, the US Department of Commerce ("DOC") effectively refused to conduct a proper investigation of the likelihood or recurrence of subsidisation. Therefore, the US breaches Article 21.3 of the *SCM Agreement* also under this instance.
5.5 Third, the *SCM Agreement* provides that a level of subsidisation which is less than 1 per cent is *de minimis*. In this case, the investigation should be terminated without the imposition of measures. Under US law, this *de minimis* threshold does not apply in sunset reviews. Instead, the US practice is to apply a *de minimis* threshold of 0.5 per cent. In not applying the *de minimis* threshold provided for in the *SCM*

[13] Except in cases where parties submitted executive summaries of their written submissions, oral statements, responses to questions, and comments on each other's responses, the texts – rather than executive summaries – of such documents have been incorporated into this section. In cases where the executive summaries were submitted, however, such summaries have been incorporated in place of the original documents.
[14] Codified in 19 USC 1675(c) (Exhibit EC-13).
[15] Implementing Regulations on anti-dumping and countervailing duties issued by DOC, Section 351 of Title 19 of the US CFR (Exhibit EC-14).
[16] DOC Policies Regarding the Conduct of Five-year ("Sunset") Reviews of Antidumping and Countervailing Duty Orders (Exhibit EC-15).

Agreement, DOC effectively imposes and collects countervailing duties which are below the *de minimis* level. As a result, these provisions are in violation of Article 21.3, in conjunction with Articles 21.1 and 11.9, of *the SCM Agreement*.

5.6 Finally, for the same reasons identified above, the US has failed to ensure that its laws, regulations and administrative procedures are in conformity with and Article 32.5 of the *SCM Agreement* and consequently with its WTO obligations under Article XVI:4 of the *Marrakesh Agreement Establishing the World Trade Organization* (the "WTO Agreement").

2. *Factual Background*

5.7 Following the initiation of an investigation on 24 July 1992, DOC issued, on 9 July 1993, its final affirmative determination that exports of corrosion resistant steel from Germany were subsidised. DOC found that 5 subsidy programmes conferred a benefit to the German exporters. The subsidy level was determined at 0.60 per cent[17]. DOC found that two of the above programmes, the Capital Investment Grants ("CIG") and the Aid for Closure of Steel Operations (which account for 0.45 per cent of the total subsidy amount), were *non-recurring grants* because the recipient could not be expected to receive benefits on an ongoing basis. On the basis of the US methodology for non-recurring grants, the benefit was allocated over a 15-year period.

5.8 Following the introduction of sunset provisions in the Uruguay Round, DOC was obliged to review all of its outstanding CVD orders by the end of 1999. On 1 September 1999, DOC automatically initiated a sunset review of the definitive countervailing duties on corrosion-resistant steel from Germany[18]. Following the publication of the notice, the domestic interested parties filed a notice of intent to participate. Subsequently, the foreign interested parties, i.e., the German producers, the Government of Germany and the European Commission filed substantive responses within 30 days after the publication of the Notice of Initiation.

5.9 Following the investigation, on 20 March 2000, DOC issued the *preliminary results* of the full sunset review[19]. DOC preliminary concluded that revocation of the CVD order was likely to lead to recurrence of continuation or recurrence of a countervailable subsidy at a net subsidy rate of 0.54 per cent. The German producers argued that the benefit stream would become *de minimis* after the sunset review. As regards the CIG programme, DOC stated that some payments were given up to 1990 and, based on DOC's 15-year allocation period, would continue to confer a benefit to the German producers beyond the end of the sunset review.[20] Only regarding the Structural Improvement Aids, DOC concluded that recurring benefits were granted up to 1986 and that no evidence was brought forward that benefits would occur after the sunset review.

5.10 In calculating the amount of benefit, DOC simply took the subsidy rate from the original investigation in 1993 and deducted the amounts related to the Structural Improvement Aid programme and the Zonal Area programme. Therefore, the origi-

---

[17] This amount was imposed as the final CVD rate on 17 August 1993, having been increased from 0.59 per cent to 0.60 per cent due to a "ministerial error".

[18] 64 FR 47767, 1 September 1999 (Exhibit EC-5).

[19] 65 FR 16176, 27 March 2000 (Exhibit EC-6).

[20] Exhibit EC-7, pages 24-25.

nal countervailing duty rate was decreased by the amount of 0.06 per cent resulting in a net subsidy rate of 0.54 per cent being reported to ITC as the rate likely to prevail.

5.11 On 2 August 2000, the DOC published the *final results* of its sunset review, in which the preliminary findings were confirmed.

3. *Standard of Review*

5.12 By virtue of Article 30 of the *SCM Agreement*, the provisions of the DSU are applicable to the settlement of disputes under the *SCM Agreement*, "except as otherwise specifically provided [t]herein." In the absence of any specific standard of review provided for in the *SCM Agreement* on the issues raised in the present dispute, the EC considers that the standard of review set forth in Article 11 of the DSU is applicable in this case. The same has already been held by the panel and the Appellate Body reports in the United States – Leaded Bars case.[21]

5.13 As regards the standard of review contained in Article 11 of the DSU, in the *European Communities – Hormones* case, the Appellate Body stated that "the applicable standard is neither *de novo* review as such, nor 'total deference', but rather the 'objective assessment of the facts' ".[22] This does *not* mean that panels must simply *accept* the conclusions of the competent authority. To the contrary, a panel can assess whether the US competent authority's explanation for its determination under Article 21.3 is reasoned and adequate *only* if the panel critically examines that explanation, in depth, and in the light of all the facts before the panel. Panels must, therefore, review whether the competent authority's explanation fully addresses the nature, and, especially, the complexities, of the data, and responds to other plausible interpretations of that data.[23]

5.14 The Panel is required to "make an objective assessment of the matter before it", including an objective assessment of the applicability of and conformity with the *SCM Agreement* of the US laws and regulations that are the subject matter of the present proceedings.[24] For the purposes of interpreting the *SCM Agreement*, therefore, Article 11 of the DSU imposes upon panels a comprehensive obligation to make an "objective assessment of the matter" as a whole, an obligation which embraces all aspects of a panel's examination of the "matter", both factual and legal. Thus, panels

---

[21] See Panel Report, *United States – Imposition of Countervailing Duties on Certain Hot-Rolled Lead and Bismuth Carbon Steel Products Originating in the United Kingdom ("United States – Leaded Bars")*, WT/DS138/R, adopted 7 June 2000, at para. 6.18, as upheld by the Appellate Body Report, WT/DS138/AB/R, adopted 7 June 2000, at para. 51. These cases have also established that the standard of review set out in Article 17.6 of the *Anti-Dumping Agreement* is not applicable in the context of the *SCM Agreement*.

[22] Appellate Body Report, *EC Measures Concerning Meat and Meat Products (Hormones) ("European Communities – Hormones")*, WT/DS26/AB/R-WT/DS48/AB/R, adopted 13 February 1998, para. 117.

[23] Appellate Body Report, *United-States – Safeguard Measures on Imports of Fresh Chilled or Frozen Lamb Meat from New Zealand and Australia ("United-States – Lamb Safeguards")*, WT/DS177/AB/R, WT/DS178/AB/R, adopted 16 May 2001, para. 106.

[24] This approach is entirely consistent with statements made by the Appellate Body in the *European Communities – Hormones* case, cit. *supra*, para. 118. In that report (at para. 133) the Appellate Body said:

> "The duty to make an objective assessment of the facts is, among other things, *an obligation to consider the evidence presented to a panel* and to make factual findings on the basis of that evidence". (emphasis added)

should make an "objective assessment of the facts", of the "applicability" of the covered agreements, and of the "conformity" of the measure at stake with those covered agreements. Therefore, the text of Article 11 DSU and of the *SCM Agreement* clearly necessitate an *active* review or examination of all the pertinent facts.[25]

5.15 The requirement to conduct an "objective assessment" of a claim has, in principle, two elements. First, a panel must review whether competent authority has evaluated *all the relevant factors*[26] and, second, a panel must review whether the authority has provided a *reasoned and adequate explanation* of how the facts support their determination.[27] Thus, the panel's objective assessment involves a *formal* aspect and a *substantive* aspect.[28]

5.16 The relevant provisions of the DSU and *SCM Agreement* and the Appellate Body findings in the above cases require that the Panel in the present case is obliged to examine *all* the relevant facts and evidence presented to it by the parties to this dispute or obtained through the Panel's own initiative. It follows that the Panel is obliged to assess whether the national authority provided a *reasoned and adequate explanation* of how the facts in the record or otherwise available to the US competent authority supported the determinations that were made by them in the contested measure. Obviously, this goes to the heart of the panel's role in a dispute settlement case, as it relates to the panel's discretionary authority to examine and weigh all factual evidence and to assess the applicability of and conformity with the relevant covered agreements of the measure under consideration.

---

[25] Appellate Body Report, *United States – Anti-Dumping Measures on Certain Hot-Rolled Steel Products from Japan*, WT/DS184/AB/R, adopted 23 August 2001, paras. 54 and 62.

[26] The Appellate Body clarified the appropriate standard of review, in particular the quantitative aspect of the assessment, in Appellate Body Report, *Korea – Definitive Safeguard Measure on Imports of Certain Dairy Products ("Korea – Dairy Safeguards")*, WT/DS98/AB/R, adopted 12 January 2000, at para. 137, as follows:

> "...However, under Article 11 of the DSU, a panel is charged with the mandate to determine the facts of the case and to arrive at factual findings. In carrying out this mandate, a panel has the duty to examine and consider *all* the evidence before it, not just the evidence submitted by one or the other party, and to evaluate the relevance and probative force of *each piece* thereof." (emphasis added).

[27] In the context of the *Safeguards Agreement*, the Appellate Body clarified the concept of "objective assessment" in Appellate Body Report, *Argentina – Safeguard Measures on Imports of Footwear ("Argentina – Footwear Safeguards")*, WT/DS121/AB/R, adopted 12 January 2000, at para. 121 in fine, as follows:

"... [T]o determine whether the safeguard investigation and the resulting safeguard measure applied by Argentina were consistent with Article 4 of the *Agreement on Safeguards*, the Panel was obliged, by the very terms of Article 4, to assess whether the Argentine authorities *had examined all the relevant facts and had provided a reasoned explanation of how the facts supported their determination*". (emphasis added).

[28] Appellate Body Report, *United-States – Lamb Safeguards*, cit. *supra*, para. 103.

4. *Legal Arguments*

(a) The Standards of Initiation of Sunset Review Lead to a Violation of Article 21.3 of the *SCM Agreement*

(i) Initiation

5.17 Under US law, sunset reviews are automatically and initiated by DOC on its own initiative five years after the publication of the CVD order[29]. Under Article 21.3 *SCM Agreement*, WTO Members have an unequivocal obligation to terminate countervailing measures on a date no later than 5 years from their imposition, unless it is determined, following a review, that the expiry of the duties would be likely to lead to continuation or recurrence of subsidisation and injury. The rationale of this provision should be read in conjunction with Article 21.1 *SCM Agreement* which provides that a countervailing duty shall remain in force only as long as necessary and to the extent to counteract subsidisation which is causing injury. Therefore, Article 21.3 reinforces the requirement of Article 21.1 by creating a presumption that duties lapse after 5 years. These provisions provide that the continuation of measures beyond the five years is an exceptional situation (demonstrated by the term "unless"). This corresponds to the object and the purpose of Part V of the *SCM Agreement* to guarantee that trade defence measures are to be imposed and maintained only if they are necessary to offset injurious subsidisation.

5.18 By requiring that sunset reviews are automatically initiated, the US effectively transforms this exception into a general rule, thus infringing Article 21, paragraphs 1 and 3, of the *SCM Agreement*.

(ii) Expedited reviews will "normally" result in the continuation of countervailing duties

5.19 The automatic initiation under US law is also biased towards the continuation of countervailing duties and not towards the presumption of their termination. This is clear in the case of "expedited" sunset reviews. Under this procedure, if domestic interested parties file a "notice of intent to participate", the sunset procedure continues and interested foreign parties, i.e., exporters and the foreign government, are required to file substantive responses. If the foreign government, or exporters accounting for at least 50 per cent of exports, do not file substantive responses, DOC will shorten the timeframe for the review and normally presume that subsidisation continues.[30] Therefore, the US procedure of expedited reviews, through automatic initiation and presumption of likelihood of continuation or recurrence, is clearly biased towards continuation of countervailing duties, in violation of the duty to terminate them set in Article 21 of the *SCM Agreement*.

(iii) The self-initiation of sunset reviews requires sufficient evidence of continuation or recurrence of subsidisation

5.20 Article 21.3 *SCM Agreement* states that a sunset review can be initiated either on the initiative of the domestic producers or upon a duly substantiated request made

[29] 19 USC §1675(c)(1).

[30] 19 C.F.R. §351.218(e)(1)(ii)(B) and (C).

by or on behalf of the industry. In the first case, the EC considers that Article 11 of the *SCM Agreement* on the initiation and conduct of the original subsidy investigation is of application in the case of sunset review as context to Article 21.3 of the same Agreement. It results from Article 11.2 that the initiation of an investigation to determine the existence of subsidisation should normally be based on the existence of a substantiated request made by or on behalf of the domestic industry. On the contrary, self-initiation by the domestic authority is the exception, which is justified only if domestic authority have the *same level* of sufficient evidence of subsidisation, injury and causal link (Article 11.6). In the same way, it follows that in order to initiate a sunset review on its own initiative, the domestic authority should be in possession of the same level of evidence that would be required in a "duly substantiated request" from the domestic industry. The automatic initiation requirement under US law converts the exception into a general rule, thus leading to the violation of Article 21.3 *SCM Agreement*.

(b) The Domestic Authority is under an Obligation to "determine" the Likelihood of Continuation or Recurrence of Subsidisation

(i) The requirements of the *SCM Agreement*

5.21 Article 21.3 *SCM Agreement* set out the requirements under which the investigating authority can deviate from the presumption of termination of CVD orders after five years. It requires that authorities *determine* that the expiry of the duty would be likely to lead to continuation or recurrence of subsidisation and injury. The Appellate Body in the case *United States – Leaded Bars,* considered that in a review under Article 21.2 the domestic authorities are required to make a finding of subsidisation during the period of review[31]. If this applies for Article 21.2 reviews, a *fortiori* a positive finding that all the conditions are fulfilled is necessary in the context of an Article 21.3 investigation. The parallel drawn between sunset reviews and original investigations is confirmed by the findings of the Panel in *Brazil – Desiccated Coconut*. There, called to judge of the applicability of the *SCM Agreement* to measures taken prior to the entry into force of the WTO Agreement, the Panel recognised that:

> even measures maintained and imposed under the pre-WTO regime, and not subject to a review under Article 21.2 of the *SCM Agreement*, will ultimately be brought under WTO disciplines under this sunset provision[32].

(ii) US law and practice

5.22 US law, however, requires the DOC to consider (a) the net countervailable subsidy determined in the investigation or a review and (b) whether any changes in the subsidies occurred that may affect the countervailing duty. This is clearly stated in Section 752(b)(1) of the Tariff Act, URAA Statement of Administrative Action and Paragraph III.B.1 of the *Sunset Policy Bulletin.* In practice, DOC normally se-

[31] Appellate Body Report, *United States – Leaded Bars*, para. 54

[32] Panel Report, *Brazil - Measures Affecting Desiccated Coconut ("Brazil - Desiccated Coconut")*, WT/DS22/R, adopted 20 March 1997, as upheld by the Appellate Body Report, WT/DS22/AB/R, para. 277.

lects the CVD rate from the original investigation or a review, on the basis that it is the only rate that reflects the behaviour of governments and exporters without the discipline of an order in place. In the EC's view, this provision establishes a standard for sunset reviews that violates the *SCM Agreement*. This is clearly demonstrated in the case of corrosion resistant steel from Germany. Since there have not been any administrative reviews since the original investigation, the only available subsidisation rate is the original 1993 subsidy rate. DOC refused, in the course of the sunset review, to consider changes or terminations of subsidy programmes despite the concrete evidence submitted by the German exporters in the sunset review. DOC justified this decision by stating that no full investigation is conducted in a sunset review and decisions should be based on investigated and verified results.

5.23 The EC considers that the DOC refusal to conduct any meaningful investigation in a sunset review is in violation of the requirements of Article 21.3 of the *SCM Agreement*. This practice not only contravenes the duty placed by Article 21.3 on the domestic authorities to "determine" the likelihood of continuation or recurrence of a subsidy, but it also shifts the burden of proving a change in circumstance on the foreign exporters and to a stage of the procedure, the administrative review, which is considered by the *SCM Agreement* as non-obligatory and which is in any event overtaken by the sunset review. The fact that a party did not request an administrative review cannot relieve the domestic authorities from their duties to "determine" the likelihood of continuation or recurrence of subsidisation. In any case, in the present case the German exporters did all they could to submit relevant information.

(iii) The US DOC refused to conduct a proper determination of the likelihood of continuation or recurrence of subsidization

5.24 In the sunset review concerning corrosion resistant steel from Germany, the German producers stated that the major subsidy programme involved in the original investigation, the CIG programme, had been terminated and did not provide any further benefits. In particular they claimed that this programme, which provided non-recurring benefits, applied only to investments made prior to 1 January 1986.[33] DOC had already determined in the original investigation that this programme applied in fact only to investments made prior to 1 January 1986.34 This was confirmed in the sunset review.[35]

5.25 Despite this evidence, DOC rejected the claims of the German exporters. It stated that since no administrative reviews of these orders had been conducted, it was unable to determine whether any additional benefits under these programmes were received subsequent to the period of investigation. It should be stressed that DOC had both the non-confidential version of the questionnaire response and the calculation memorandum as part of the record of the original investigation and could have easily verified whether the benefits received by the German manufacturers of the subject merchandise under the CIG after 1 January 1986 were *de minimis*. The fact that DOC referred back to the original subsidy rate for CIG, violated Article 21.3

[33] Exhibit EC-7, at p. 26-28.

[34] Exhibit EC-2, at pp. 37316-17.

[35] Exhibit EC-10, at p. 34

SCM Agreement because it did not take into consideration the termination of the CIG programme despite evidence on the record.

(iv) The CIG programme should have been considered as terminated

5.26 In the present case, the German producers claimed that the CIG programme , had been terminated and did not provide any further benefits. In particular they claimed that this programme, which provided nonrecurring benefits, applied only to investments made prior to 1 January 1986[36]. The calculation memorandum of the original investigation[37] shows that Thyssen last received payments under the CIG programme in 1989, and that the amount received after 1985 was so small that it would have been automatically expensed in the year of receipt under the DOC 0.5 per cent rule[38]. Therefore, in accordance with their obligations under Article 21.3, the DOC should have taken this into account. DOC had already determined in the original investigation that this programme applied in fact only to investments made prior to 1 January 1986.[39] DOC reaffirmed this finding in the final results of the sunset review, stating that: "We agree with Dillinger and the German Group's contention that ... the CIG is applicable only to investments made prior to January 1, 1986."[40]

5.27 Thus, the issue in the sunset review was not whether the programme continued to exist but whether any of the old benefit would continue after the end of the sunset review[41]. In their response, the US producers claimed that Preussag, the predecessor to Salzgitter AG, had received benefits under this programme as late as 1990[42]. In their rebuttal of 15 October 1999, the German producers clarified that 99.4 per cent of the CIG paid to Preussag were received prior to the end of the 1985/86 fiscal year.[43] Given that, using the 15-year allocation period applied by DOC, only 0.6 per cent of the original grants should have been considered by DOC as remaining to be countervailed after the end of the sunset review, the original subsidy rate for this programme of 0.39 per cent should have diminished to only 0.00234 per cent.[44] Because DOC only calculates subsidy rates to the second decimal place, a rate of 0.00234 per cent would have been equivalent to zero.

5.28 In its response, the US authorities did not directly discuss this evidence or respond in substance to the German producers' evidence and arguments submitted in this regard during the sunset review. In fact, DOC rejected the German producers claim on the basis that the record of these sunset reviews is not sufficient for us to definitely conclude whether the benefits received by the German manufacturers of the subject merchandise under the CIG and/or IPA after January 1, 1985 were less than 0.5 percent of the corresponding beneficiary's annual net sales and, conse-

---

36 *Ibid.* at p. 26-28.

37 Exhibit EC-20 (business confidential information).

38 See 19 C.F.R. § 351.524(b)(2).

39 Exhibit EC-2, at pp. 37316-17.

40 Exhibit EC-10, at p. 34.

41 *Ibid.*, footnote 34.

42 *Ibid.*, at p. 32-33. See also *U.S. Producers Substantive Response* of 1 October 1999, at p. 9-10 (Exhibit EC-17).

43 *German Producers Rebuttal* of 15 October 1999, at p.2 (Exhibit EC-18).

44 0.39 per cent (original subsidy rate) x 0.6 per cent (grant received after 1985/86 fiscal year) = 0.00234 per cent.

quently, whether the benefits should be expensed in the year they were received. Furthermore, since no administrative reviews of these orders were conducted, we are unable to determine whether any additional benefits under these programmes were received subsequent to the period of investigation. As a result, as we did in our preliminary results, we determine that benefit streams from the CIG and IPA continue beyond the end of these sunset reviews and that, therefore, a countervailable subsidy from the CIG and IPA to manufacturers of subject merchandise would be likely if the orders were revoked[45].

5.29 On the issue of the insufficiency of the record of the sunset review, it has to be noted that, on 28 April 2000, the US producers filed a submission containing a copy of the public version of Preussag's questionnaire response in the original investigation. Although the public version of the questionnaire response did not contain any payment amounts, it showed that of the fourteen CIG payments made to Preussag, only three were received after the end of the 1985/86 fiscal year.[46] DOC, however, had both the non-confidential version of the questionnaire response and the calculation memorandum as part of the record of the original investigation and could have easily verified whether the benefits received by the German manufacturers of the subject merchandise under the CIG after 1 January 1986 were *de minimis*. The German producers were, therefore, not asking the DOC to rely upon speculative, unverified information, but simply to acknowledge the evidence that it had collected and verified itself in the original investigation.

5.30 With regard to the argument that no administrative review had been conducted, DOC seems to argue that it was somehow prevented by law from considering the evidence because the German producers of corrosion-resistant flat products had not requested an administrative review.[47] As seen above, Section 752 of the Act specifically requires the DOC to consider "the net countervailable subsidy determined in the investigation and subsequent reviews, and whether any change in the programme which gave rise to the net countervailable subsidy ... has occurred that is likely to affect the net countervailable subsidy". There can be no doubt that the termination of a subsidy programme and the cessation of payments thereunder should be regarded as "change in the programme" that must be considered by the DOC. Moreover, while the relevant provisions of US law states that the DOC shall "normally" choose a net countervailable subsidy from the original investigation or an administrative review when determining the net countervailable subsidy that is likely to prevail if the order is revoked, this did not prohibit DOC from using in this case other rates or making adjustments to the rates found in an original investigation or an administrative review[48].

5.31 It follows from the above that the facts on record in this case require that the responsible US authorities should have adjusted the original subsidy rate to account for the termination of the CIG programme despite the fact that there were no administrative reviews of the countervailing duty order on corrosion-resistant flat products.

45 Exhibit EC-10, at pp. 34-35. DOC's reference to "January 1, 1985" is apparently a clerical error. There can be no dispute under DOC's declining balance methodology with a 15-year allocation period, any non-recurring assistance received in 1985 would be finally amortised no later than 1999 (i.e. before completion of the sunset review).

46 Letter from Dewey Ballantine LLP to Secretary of Commerce of 28 Apr 2000 (Exhibit EC-19).

47 See Exhibit EC-10, p. 18-22.

48 19 USC §1675a(b)(3).

In any case, the fact that the amount of the net countervailable subsidy likely to prevail was close to zero and, hence, *de minimis*, should have led the US authorities to terminate the duty in accordance with Article 21.3 of the *SCM Agreement*. The US has, therefore, erred in not accounting for the termination of the CIG programme, when it calculated the net countervailable subsidy that was likely to prevail if the countervailing duty order were revoked, and this is a violation of Article 21.3 of the *SCM Agreement*.

(v) Application of DOC's declining balance methodology

5.32 DOC should also have reached the conclusion that the effects of the CIG programme had ended on the basis of its *declining balance methodology*. Under this methodology, DOC allocates non-recurring subsidies over time and in order to account for the "time value of money", it "front-loads" the amounts allocated to the early years of the allocation period. This inevitably results in a gradual year-by-year decline of the subsidy amount. In the present case, even without any consideration of individual programmes being made, it would have taken the subsidy amount even further below *de minimis*.

(vi) Treatment of evidence

5.33 Finally, the EC considers that the US violated the standards of Article 21.3 *SCM Agreement* regarding the *treatment of evidence*. The German producers presented to DOC the reasons why the CIG programme should have been considered as terminated and as not providing any further benefits. Based upon this evidence, the German producers believed that DOC would find that subsidisation under the CIG programme would not be likely to continue or recur. However, in its preliminary results of 20 March 2000, DOC continued to assign a 0.39 per cent subsidy rate for this programme.

5.34 The counsel for the German producers contacted DOC and stated that, if there were any doubts about how much was paid under the CIG programme after 1986, then DOC should make its calculation memoranda from the original investigation part of the record in the sunset review. On 13 April 2001, the German producers made a written request that DOC places the calculation memoranda on the record of the sunset review.[49] DOC never took any action on the German producers' request concerning the calculation memoranda and, in its final results of 27 July 2000, it claimed that the German producers' request was untimely since it should have been submitted prior to 15 October 1999.[50] .

5.35 The EC considers that such a short deadline violates the provisions of Article 21.3, in conjunction with Articles 12.1 and 21.4, of the *SCM Agreement* because it fails to afford the producers with an "ample opportunity" to present in writing all evidence which they consider relevant in respect of the sunset review.

---

49 Letter from deKieffer & Horgan to Secretary of Commerce of 13 April 2000 (Exhibit EC-21).

50 Exhibit EC-10, at p. 18.

(c) The *de minimis* Rules Division

5.36 The EC considers that the U.S. interpretation and application of the sunset provisions in Article 21.3, as regards the *de minimis* requirement, is inconsistent with the *SCM Agreement.*

(i) The US law and practice

5.37 Under the Sunset Regulations[51] and the Sunset Policy Bulletin,[52] the US will treat as *de minimis* any countervailable subsidy rate that is less than 0.5 per cent. In initial investigations, the US applies a *de minimis* threshold of 1 per cent[53]. The US' Statement of Administrative Action made it clear that the US considers that the *de minims* requirements of Articles 11.9 of the *SCM Agreement* only apply to initial investigations.

(ii) Interpretation of the relevant provisions of the *SCM Agreement*

5.38 Article 21.3 of the *SCM Agreement* provides that any definitive countervailing duty shall be terminated not later than five years from its imposition, unless the authorities make a positive determination in a review that the expiry of the countervailing duty would be likely to lead to continuation or recurrence of subsidisation and injury. The continuation of the duty after a sunset review for five more years will be possible only if two conditions are met: a) *a review is initiated*; and b) *the determination is made that subsidisation and injury would be likely to continue or recur if the duty were to expire.* The Appellate Body in the *United States – Leaded Bars* case held that in order to establish the continued need for countervailing duties, an investigating authority will have to make a finding on *subsidisation*, i.e., whether or not the subsidy continues to exist. If there is no longer a subsidy, there would no longer be any need for a countervailing duty[54].

5.39 Therefore, in the context of a review under Article 21.2, the *object and purpose* of the requirement to demonstrate subsidisation and injury must be the same as when subsidisation and injury were determined in the original investigation. It follows then that if the *de minimis* rule is applied in original investigations, it must also remain applicable in reviews under Article 21.2. The EC submits that the above analysis in case of Article 21.2 reviews applies all the more so in the context of sunset reviews under Article 21.3. Indeed, there are compelling reasons to conclude that a countervailing duty, which is anyhow supposed to expire upon five years, will not be maintained without a clear demonstration of "*subsidisation*" and "*injury*". The Appellate Body further held that Article 21.2 sets out a review mechanism to ensure that Members comply with the rule of Article 21.1. The EC submits that the same reasoning applies *a fortiori* as regards the object and purpose of the sunset review mechanism laid down in Article 21.3 and renders sunset reviews similar to the original investigations, thus imposing on the authorities the burden of demonstrating the

---

51 Section 351.106(c)(1) of the *Sunset Regulations*

52 Section III.A.6.(b) of the *Sunset Policy Bulletin* provides that: In accordance with section 752(b)(4)(B) of the Act and 19 CFR 351.106(c)(1), the Department will treat as *de minimis* any countervailable subsidy rate that is less than 0.5 per cent ad valorem or the equivalent specific rate".

53 Section 703(b)(4)(a) of the Act

54 Appellate Body Report, *United States – Leaded Bars*, para. 54.

likelihood of a continuation or recurrence of *subsidisation* and *injury* (from a subsidy that is not *de minimis*), if the duty is not to expire.

5.40 The term "subsidisation", in Articles 21.1, 21.2 and 21.3, can only interpreted in a systematically coherent manner, in context and in the light of the other relevant provisions of the *SCM Agreement* as a whole. One of these relevant provisions is clearly Article 11.9. This is because Article 11.9, in the context of original investigations, *prevents* the authorities from making a finding on subsidisation and injury on the basis of an amount of subsidy that is less than 1 per cent *ad valorem*, since it requires "immediate termination" of investigations in such circumstances. In addition, the US practice of applying a *de minimis* rule of (albeit at a WTO-inconsistent rate of 0.5 per cent) in, *inter alia*, sunset reviews provides an implicit confirmation of the need to apply a *de minimis* rule in the context of Article 21.3. Indeed, it is inherently contradictory for the US to argue that the rule of Article 11.9 of the *SCM Agreement* does not apply to sunset reviews, but nevertheless continue applying such a *de minimis* rule in practice. The US inconsistent and contradictory approach may seem to reduce the legal debate from one of principle to one about the actual amount or level of subsidy that is considered to be *de minimis* (i.e., in practice to 0.5 instead of 1 per cent). However, a closer examination of the US law and practice, as applied to the facts of the present case, would demonstrate that it could produce very perverse and inconsistent results.

(iii) Application of the *de minimis* rule to the corrosion-resistant steel products case

5.41 In the case of corrosion resistant steel from Germany, the countervailing duty rate determined in the original investigation, which stemmed essentially from non-recurring subsidies allocated over time, was 0.59 per cent. This was only 0.09 per cent above the *de minimis* level of 0.50 per cent applied in the US before the entry into force of the WTO Agreements.[55] Thus, if the original investigation had been conducted under the currently applicable rules for *de minimis* subsidies, the investigation should have been immediately terminated without the imposition of any countervailing duties, in accordance with Article 11.9 of the *SCM Agreement.* In the sunset review, which was conducted under WTO rules, the US, despite finding that the subsidy rate likely to prevail would be 0.53 per cent, nevertheless continued the measure, since its practice is to apply a 0.5 per cent *de minimis* threshold in sunsets. The EC submits that, for the reasons stated above, this threshold is not appropriate, and that since 0.53 per cent is below the 1 per cent *de minimis* level which *should* apply in sunset reviews, the US was in breach of Article 21.3 in continuing the measure

(d) The Obligation to Bring its Law Into Conformity with the WTO Agreements

5.42 Article XVI:4 of the WTO Agreement and Article 32.5 of the *SCM Agreement* oblige Members to bring their domestic law into conformity with their obligations under the WTO Agreements. Indeed, as the panel report in Brazil – Desiccated Coconut has found,[56] countervailing duty measures applied before 1995 would have

[55] See Exhibits EC-7, at pp. 24-25, and EC-10, at pp. 12-16.

[56] Panel Report, *Brazil - Desiccated Coconut*, cit. *supra*, at para. 277.

to be brought under the disciplines of WTO over time pursuant to reviews under Article 21.2 or under the sunset provision of Article 21.3 of the *SCM Agreement*. The EC has demonstrated that the basic US law, the accompanying regulations and practices relating to sunset reviews of countervailing duties and their concrete application to the facts of the present case are inconsistent with a number of provisions of the *SCM Agreement*, i.e., Articles 21, paragraphs 1, 3 and 4, Article 10 and Article 11.9. For those reasons, the EC submits that the US failed to bring its domestic law in conformity with WTO obligations and, thereby, violating Article 32.5 of the *SCM Agreement* and Article XVI.4 of the WTO Agreement.

5. *Conclusions*

5.43 For these reasons, the EC respectfully requests that the Panel finds that the US basic countervailing duty law (Tariff Act of 1930), its accompanying regulations (sunset regulations) and policy practices (sunset policy bulletin) as such, and their concrete application to imports of certain corrosion-resistant carbon steel flat products from Germany in the present case are inconsistent with Article 21 paragraphs 3, 1 and 4, Article 10 and Article 11.9 of the *SCM Agreement*. For the above reasons, the US countervailing duty law, regulations and practice should also be considered to be inconsistent with Article 32.5 of the *SCM Agreement* and, consequently, should be found to violate also Article XVI.4 of the WTO Agreement.

B. *First Written Submission of the United States*

1. *Introduction*

5.44 The crux of the EC's case that is properly before the Panel consists of allegations that the US countervailing duty law, as well as the sunset review determination in certain corrosion-resistant carbon steel flat products from Germany based upon that law, are inconsistent with the *SCM Agreement* because: (1) Commerce automatically initiates sunset reviews without first gathering evidence regarding the continuation or recurrence of subsidization; and (2) Commerce does not apply the *SCM Agreement*'s *de minimis* standard for countervailing duty investigations to sunset reviews. The EC argues that the Panel should read into Article 21.3 – the provision of the *SCM Agreement* that deals with sunset reviews – the requirements of Articles 11.6 and 11.9.

5.45 The EC's claims, however, run afoul of a basic principle of treaty interpretation. As stated by the Appellate Body in *India Patent Protection*, "the principles of treaty interpretation set out in Article 31 of the *Vienna Convention* ... neither require nor condone the imputation into a treaty of words that are not there ...." This is precisely what the EC is asking the Panel to do here; impute into Article 21.3 of the *SCM Agreement* "words that are not there".

5.46 The EC tries to overcome this problem by repeatedly asserting that sunset reviews are "exceptions" to some other principle and, thus, must be interpreted in such a manner as to read into Article 21.3 "words that are not there." As discussed below, sunset reviews are not "exceptions" to something else, but instead are merely one part of an overall balance of rights and obligations negotiated during the Uruguay Round. However, even if one were to treat the provision on sunset reviews as an "exception" to something else, the EC's arguments run afoul of another principle, articulated in *EC Hormones*, which is that "merely characterizing a treaty provision as an 'exception' does not by itself justify a 'stricter' or 'narrower' interpretation of that provision than would be warranted ... by applying the normal rules of treaty interpretation."

2. *Factual Background*

(a) Sunset Reviews under US Law

5.47 Commerce and the USITC jointly conduct sunset reviews pursuant to sections 751(c) and 752 of the Act. Pursuant to section 751(d)(2) of the Act, a countervailing duty order must be revoked after five years unless both Commerce and the USITC make respective affirmative determinations that subsidization and injury would be likely to continue or recur. Under the statute, Commerce automatically initiates a sunset review on its own initiative within five years of the date of publication of a countervailing duty order.

5.48 Commerce has the responsibility of determining whether revocation of a countervailing duty order would be likely to lead to continuation or recurrence of subsidization, whereas the USITC has the responsibility of determining whether revocation of a countervailing duty order would be likely to lead to continuation or recurrence of injury. If Commerce's determination is negative – *i.e.*, if Commerce finds that there is no such likelihood – Commerce must revoke the order. If Commerce's determination is affirmative, Commerce transmits its determination to the USITC, along with a determination regarding the magnitude of the net countervailable subsidy that is likely to prevail if the order is revoked. Under US law, the applicable *de minimis* standard in sunset reviews is the same as the standard in other types of reviews (*e.g.*, duty assessment reviews) – 0.5 per cent.

5.49 Commerce's 1998 *Sunset Regulations* describe specifically the information to be provided by all interested parties in a sunset review and invite parties to submit, with the required information, "any other relevant information or argument that the party would like [Commerce] to consider." These regulations function as the standard questionnaire. The *Sunset Regulations* also provide that substantive responses to a notice of initiation are due 30 days after the date of publication in the *Federal Register* of the notice of initiation; rebuttals are due five days later. The regulations provide that Commerce normally will not accept or consider any additional information from a party after the time for filing rebuttals has expired.

5.50 On 14 May 1998, Commerce published the schedule for initiation of sunset reviews of pre-1995 anti-dumping and countervailing duty orders, indicating that the sunset review of the countervailing duty order on corrosion-resistant steel would be initiated in September 1999.

5.51 Thus, with the applicable information requirements, deadlines, and initiation schedule published in the *Federal Register* by May 1998, the EC and German producers had *over 15 months to prepare* for the sunset review of the countervailing duty order on certain corrosion-resistant carbon steel flat products from Germany.

(b) Certain Corrosion-Resistant Carbon Steel Flat Products from Germany

5.52 On 9 July 1993, Commerce published its final affirmative countervailing duty determination on certain corrosion-resistant carbon steel flat products from Germany.

Commerce calculated a country-wide total *ad valorem* countervailing duty rate of 0.59 per cent, based on the German producers receipt of countervailable benefits under the following five programmes: (1) Capital Investment Grants (hereinafter "CIG"); (2) Structural Improvement Aids; (3) Special Subsidies for Companies in the Zonal Border Area; (4) Aid for Closure of Steel Operations; and (5) ECSC Redeployment Aid Under Article 56(2)(b). On 9 August 1993, the USITC notified Commerce of its final affirmative injury determination. On 17 August 1993, Commerce amended its final determination to correct a ministerial error, which increased the *ad valorem* rate to 0.60 per cent, and issued the countervailing duty order.

5.53 On 26 August 1999, Commerce notified representatives of the EC, the German Government, and German producers, by mail, that the sunset review of the countervailing duty order on certain corrosion-resistant carbon steel flat products from Germany would be initiated on or about 1 September 1999 (consistent with the *Sunset Initiation Schedule*). On 1 September 1999, Commerce published its notice of initiation. In both its letters to German producers and the published initiation notice, Commerce highlighted the 30-day deadline for filing substantive responses, as well as the applicable information requirements.

5.54 By 4 October 1999, the EC, the German Government, German producers, and domestic interested parties filed their substantive responses. The EC, the German Government, the German producers, and the domestic interested parties filed rebuttal comments on 15 October 1999. On 20 October 1999, Commerce determined to conduct a full sunset review based on its receipt of complete substantive responses from the EC, the German Government, and German producers accounting for a significant portion of German exports to the United States.

5.55 On 27 March 2000, Commerce published its preliminary sunset determination finding likelihood of continuation or recurrence of subsidization. Based on its finding that benefit streams from non-recurring grants under the CIG programme would continue beyond the five-year mark and that the Aid for Closure of Steel Operations and ECSC programmes continue to exist, Commerce determined there was likelihood of continuation or recurrence of subsidization.

5.56 As required under US law, Commerce also determined the net countervailable subsidy likely to prevail if the order were revoked. As a general matter, and starting with the total *ad valorem* rate determined in the original investigation, Commerce considers whether, since the investigation, it has found subsidy programmes to be terminated and/or new programmes to be countervailable. Based on findings, which normally are made in the context of administrative reviews under section 751(a) of the Act, Commerce may adjust the rate determined in the original investigation to take these subsequent findings into account. Although no administrative reviews of the order on certain corrosion-resistant carbon steel flat products from Germany were ever conducted, Commerce agreed with the EC and the German producers that the Structural Improvement Aids and Special Subsidies for Companies in the Zonal Border Area programmes had been terminated with no continuing benefits and adjusted the net countervailable subsidy rate accordingly. Because no administrative reviews had been conducted, Commerce did not consider the domestic interested parties' allegations concerning additional countervailable subsidies. For the same reason, Commerce did not recalculate the subsidy rates determined in the original investigation. Based on this analysis, Commerce determined a net countervailable subsidy rate of 0.54 per cent.

5.57 In its final determination, published 2 August 2000, Commerce did not change the basis for its likelihood determination or its determination concerning the net countervailable subsidy likely to prevail. On 1 December 2000, the USITC published its determination that revocation of the countervailing duty order would be likely to lead to continuation or recurrence of injury. On 15 December 2000, the United States published notice of the continuation of the countervailing duty order on certain corrosion-resistant carbon steel flat products from Germany based on the decisions by Commerce and the USITC finding likelihood of continuation or recurrence of subsidization and injury.

3. *Standard of Review*

5.58 With respect to disputes involving a determination made by a domestic authority based upon an administrative record, the Appellate Body, in *US Cotton Yarn*, recently summarized the standard of review under DSU Article 11. The United States does not disagree with this standard. The EC erroneously argues, however, that the Panel cannot "disregard or refuse to consider facts and evidence *submitted to it*" by the parties to the dispute. The United States disagrees with the EC's implication that a panel has unfettered discretion to consider any evidence in deciding the issues before it and, as discussed below, the Panel should decline to consider the document submitted by the EC.

4. *Substantive Argument*

(a) Automatic Self-Initiation of Sunset Reviews is Consistent with the *SCM Agreement*

5.59 Article 21.3 authorizes authorities to initiate a sunset review "on their own initiative *or* upon a duly substantiated request made by or on behalf of the domestic industry" (emphasis added). This disjunctive language is unambiguous, and, under the customary rules of interpretation, must be read according to its ordinary meaning, which is that a Member may *either* self-initiate a sunset review or initiate a sunset review in response to a duly substantiated request. The right of an investigating authority to initiate a sunset review on its own initiative is unqualified and the Panel may not "diminish" this right. Despite the plain language of Article 21.3, the EC argues that the Article 11.6 requirements for self-initiation of an investigation are applicable to self-initiation of sunset reviews. The obvious flaw in the EC's argument is that there is no reference to the Article 11.6 requirements in the text of Article 21.3 or vice versa. Furthermore, the *SCM Agreement* itself distinguishes between the investigatory phase and the review phase of a countervailing duty proceeding, *e.g.*, Article 11 deals with investigations, while Article 21 deals with reviews.

5.60 The EC's arguments, therefore, find no support under customary rules of treaty interpretation. Article 21.3 explicitly provides for initiation of sunset reviews on an authority's own initiative. Furthermore, nothing in the text of Article 21.3, or Article 11.6, imposes any evidentiary requirements on authorities who initiate sunset reviews on their own initiative. It is impossible to violate an obligation that does not exist. Therefore, the United States' automatic initiation of sunset reviews is not inconsistent with the *SCM Agreement*.

(b) There is no *de minimis* Standard for Sunset Reviews

5.61 The focus of a sunset review under Article 21.3 is future behaviour, *i.e.*, the likelihood of continuation or recurrence of subsidization – not whether or to what extent subsidization currently exists. The analysis is perforce predictive. Under these circumstances, mathematical certainty or precision as to the exact amount of likely future subsidization is not necessarily practicable and certainly not required.

5.62 Under Article 11.9, Members must apply a one per cent *de minimis* standard in countervailing duty *investigations*. The EC erroneously argues that the Article 11. 9 *de minimis* standard is applicable in sunset reviews under Article 21.3. There is no textual or contextual support for the EC's claim.

5.63 In *Korea DRAMs*, Korea argued that the *de minimis* standard in Article 5.8 of the AD Agreement applied to reviews as well as to investigations. Article 5.8 of the AD Agreement is the parallel provision to Article 11.9 of the *SCM Agreement*. The panel rejected Korea's arguments, finding that "the term 'investigation' [used in the context of Article 5.8] means the investigative phase leading up to the final determination of the investigating authority." Thus, the *Korea DRAMs* panel found no textual or contextual support for Korea's claim that the *de minimis* standard applied beyond the investigative phase.

5.64 The EC's argument is not only devoid of support in the text of the *SCM Agreement*, it also fails to mention, much less reconcile, its position with relevant language in the text. Specifically, note 52 of Article 21.3 provides that "a finding in the most recent assessment proceeding that no duty is to be levied shall not by itself require the authorities to terminate the definitive duty". Thus, the current level of subsidization is not decisive as to whether subsidization is likely to recur. The EC's claim that a *de minimis* standard is required in the context of Article 21.3 sunset reviews would render note 52 meaningless.

5.65 The EC would also have the panel read into the use of the word "subsidization" in Article 21 an implicit reference to Article 11.9 because authorities must terminate an investigation if the amount of the subsidy is *de minimis*. However, nothing in the word "subsidization", as defined in the *SCM Agreement* implies anything about a *de minimis* standard. The term "subsidization" simply means the existence of a subsidy as defined in Article 1 of the SCM; Article 1 contains no *de minimis* standard.

5.66 In sum, giving the text of the Agreement its ordinary meaning, the only conclusion one can reach is that there is no obligation to apply the Article 11.9 *de minimis* standard in an Article 21.3 sunset review. The EC's arguments concerning the object and purpose of Article 21.3 fail to overcome the obvious lack of any textual support for their claim.

5.67 The EC argues that a sunset review is equivalent to an investigation because it could result in re-"*imposition*" of an order and, as such, the same *de minimis* standard is applicable in a sunset review. This argument completely ignores the fundamental difference between investigations, in which a *de minimis* standard is required under Article 11.9, and sunset reviews. In the context of Article 11.9, the function of the *de minimis* test is to determine whether foreign government subsidies warrant the imposition of a countervailing duty order in the first instance. For example, in an investigation, if the investigating authority found that a government programme had provided recurring subsidies at a rate of more than one per cent, imposition of a countervailing duty would be warranted if the subsidized imports were found to cause injury.

5.68 In contrast, the focus of the sunset review is the future. The mere continued existence of this same programme could warrant maintaining the duty beyond the five-year point, *even if* the amount of the subsidy was currently *zero*, as stated in footnote 52, because subsidization may be likely to recur absent the discipline of the duty. This distinction between the object and purpose of an investigation and the object and purpose of a sunset review supports the conclusion that, absent an express reference to the contrary, there is no basis to assume or infer an intent that the *de minimis* standard for investigations applies in sunset reviews.

5.69 In an attempt to bolster its non-existent textual argument, the EC cites the fact that the United States applies a *de minimis* standard in sunset reviews as "confirmation" of the requirement to apply a *de minimis* rule in the context of Article 21.3 sunset reviews. In addition, the EC argues that, given the provisions of Article 32.4, it had a "reasonable and legitimate expectation" that the United States would terminate the duty. The EC is wrong on both accounts.

5.70 The United States' *de minimis* "practice" is legally irrelevant. As demonstrated above, there is no *de minimis* standard in sunset reviews. Thus, Members are free to determine what, if any, *de minimis* standard they will apply. Furthermore, while Article 31.3(b) of the *Vienna Convention* permits consideration of "any subsequent practice in the application of the treaty which establishes the agreement of the parties regarding its interpretation," policy decisions made by one Member for purposes of its domestic legislation do not constitute "subsequent practice" within the meaning of Article 31.3(b).

5.71 In addition, the EC's only legitimate expectations with respect to Articles 32.4 and 21.3 are those reflected in the Agreement itself. As the Appellate Body, in *India Patent Protection*, stated: "[P]rinciples of interpretation neither require nor condone the imputation into a treaty of words that are not there or the importation into a treaty of concepts that were not intended."

5.72 In sum, applying customary rules of treaty interpretation, the Panel should find that there is no *de minimis* standard for sunset reviews in the *SCM Agreement* and, therefore, the United States' application of a 0.5 per cent *de minimis* standard in sunset reviews does not constitute a violation of its obligations under the *SCM Agreement*.

(c) Commerce Properly Determined that the Expiry of the Countervailing Duty Order would be likely to lead to Continuation or Recurrence of Subsidization Based upon an Appropriately Conducted review of all Relevant and Properly Submitted Facts

5.73 As demonstrated above, the United States' automatic self-initiation of sunset reviews and its application of a particular *de minimis* standard do not breach any provision of the *SCM Agreement*. The remaining claims raised by the EC concern Commerce's findings and procedural actions in this case. An "objective assessment" of Commerce's findings and actions, pursuant to Article 11 of the DSU, would focus on the consistency of the sunset review with the requirements of Articles 21.3 and 12.

5.74 As a starting point for making its likelihood determination in the sunset review, Commerce considered the countervailable subsidies and programmes used, and the amount of the subsidy determined, in the original investigation. As explained in

Commerce's preliminary sunset determination, the rationale for this approach is that the findings in the original investigation provide the only evidence reflecting the behaviour of the respondents without the discipline of countervailing measures in place. This approach makes sense given that, in a sunset review under the Article 21.3, an authority is considering whether, without the discipline of the duty, subsidization would likely continue or recur, *i.e.*, what would happen without the discipline of the order.

5.75 In the original investigation, Commerce determined that German producers of corrosion-resistant steel benefitted from five different subsidy programmes. In the sunset review, Commerce found that the benefit streams from non-recurring grants under the CIG programme will continue beyond the five-year mark; the Structural Improvement Aids and Special Subsidies for Companies in the Zonal Border Area programmes had been terminated; and the Aid for Closure of Steel Operations and ECSC Redeployment Aid Under Article 56(2)(b) programmes continue to exist. Significantly, the EC has not disputed or disproved these findings. As an initial matter, therefore, it was reasonable for Commerce to find likelihood given the continued existence and availability of countervailable subsidy programmes previously found to have been used by German producers of corrosion-resistant steel and the continuation of benefit streams from grants under the CIG programme.

5.76 Although the EC essentially concedes the continued existence of some benefits from the CIG programme, it claims that, based on routine amortization, Commerce should have considered the programme terminated without residual benefits to the German producers. With respect to non-recurring benefits (such as the benefits from the CIG programme), Commerce uses a "declining balance" formula to determine the amount of subsidization to be allocated in each period. An *ad valorem* subsidy rate, for a particular period, is derived by dividing a numerator – the subsidy benefit properly attributable to the subject merchandise – by a denominator – the value of the sales of the merchandise at issue (in the case of a domestic subsidy). Without knowing the sales volume, the *ad valorem* subsidy rate for any period cannot be determined despite the use of a "declining balance" methodology generally . The EC's claim, therefore, fails as a factual matter because there is no basis for its assumption that the sales volumes will remain constant.

5.77 The EC's amortization arguments, furthermore, are based in part on a calculation memorandum from the original countervailing duty investigation that is not part of the record considered in the sunset review (Exhibit EC-20). The request to submit this business confidential document was untimely submitted and Commerce properly declined to consider it. The German producers' request to submit this document also implicated Commerce's rules concerning treatment of confidential information ("business proprietary information" or "BPI" in US parlance). Pursuant to US law, release of that information is not permitted without the consent of the person that submitted it. Commerce could not ignore previous requests for confidential treatment and automatically place this information from the original 1993 investigation on the record of the sunset review. Further, other parties without prior access to the document would have been prejudiced by its untimely inclusion on the record.

5.78 Under these circumstances, Commerce did not consider it practicable or appropriate to consider the document. Commerce's decision to enforce procedural rules governing deadlines for submission of evidence and the release of confidential business information was proper and consistent with Article 12. (The evidentiary and procedural requirements of Article 12 are applicable to sunset reviews by virtue of Article 12.4.) As such, the Panel should find that Commerce appropriately declined to consider the information and that it is not this Panel's role to consider evidence which could have been timely presented to the decision maker but was not. Furthermore, even if the Panel should consider the document, it does not prove the EC's arguments. The calculation memorandum only provides the absolute subsidy amounts (*i.e.*, the numerator) – it does not shed any light on the value of the sales of the merchandise at issue (*i.e.*, the denominator). As demonstrated above, without a denominator, there is no way to calculate the *ad valorem* subsidy rate.

5.79 Consistent with the Appellate Body's ruling in *UK Lead Bar* and Article 21.3, Commerce properly considered that the existing benefit streams from the CIG programmes constituted evidence of the "continuation" of subsidization. Furthermore, the continued existence of other programmes previously found to be countervailable is not in dispute. As a result, Commerce's finding of likelihood of continuation or recurrence of subsidization is consistent with its obligations under Articles 21.3 and 12 of the *SCM Agreement*. In addition, as demonstrated below, Commerce's evidentiary and procedural actions also were consistent with its obligations under Article 12.

5.80 Article 12.1 requires domestic authorities to give interested Members and parties an ample opportunity to present in writing all evidence which they consider relevant to the proceeding. The facts do not support the EC's claims that Commerce failed to do so.

5.81 The *Sunset Regulations* describe specifically the information required to be provided by all interested parties in a sunset review, *i.e.*, they constitute the standard questionnaire. In addition, the *Sunset Regulations* specifically invite parties to submit, with the required information, "any other relevant information or arguments that the party would like [Commerce] to consider". Consistent with Article 12.1.1, Commerce's regulations also provide 30 days for parties to submit the required information and provide for extensions of time to meet this deadline. The EC and the German producers were on notice of the information requirements and options, as well as the applicable deadlines and extension options, over 15 months ahead of the scheduled date for initiation of the sunset review.

5.82 Yet over six months after the deadline for responding to the sunset questionnaire and submitting optional information, the German producers attempted to place new factual information on the record. The EC asserts that Commerce's rejection of these untimely submissions was contrary to their "right" under the *SCM Agreement* to have an "ample opportunity to present in writing all evidence which they consider relevant in respect of the sunset review". As a factual matter, however, the German producers and the German Government had ample time to submit factual information in the sunset review. Furthermore, as a legal matter, Commerce's filing deadlines and its decision not to accept late-filed information fully comport with its obligations under Article 12.

5.83 Specifically, the German producers had 30 days to respond to the questionnaire. In addition, Commerce's rejection of the German producers late-filed information was reasonable under the circumstances of this case, *i.e.*, the German producers attempted to file new factual information over six months after Commerce's deadline. Although an authority "should" grant extensions "whenever practicable", nothing required Commerce to find that it was practicable to accept and consider documents filed six months late, particularly given the fact that the EC and the German producers had over 15 months to gather any data they considered appropriate and to prepare their submission of required and optional information. Finally, the EC's argument, that Commerce arbitrarily applied its regulation to submissions from the various parties, ignores relevant factual distinctions between the submissions from the German producers rejected by Commerce and those submissions from the US producers and the German Government that were accepted by Commerce. In particular, the accepted submissions involved public documents containing no new factual information.

5.84 In sum, the Panel should dismiss the EC's claims with respect to treatment of evidence. Commerce followed reasonable, appropriate procedures that fully comply with the evidentiary and procedural requirements of Articles 21 and 12.

(d) The Panel should make a Preliminary Ruling that the EC's Claims Regarding the Expedited Sunset Review Procedure are not within the Panel's Terms of Reference

5.85 The United States requests that the Panel make a preliminary ruling that the EC's claims regarding the US expedited sunset review procedure are not properly before the Panel, because this procedure is not a measure within the Panel's terms of reference. Not until its first written submission to the Panel did the EC ever give any indication that it was complaining about this procedure.

5.86 In its initial request for consultations, the EC identified Commerce's determination in the *full* sunset review of the countervailing duty order on certain corrosion-resistant carbon steel flat products from Germany as the challenged measure, alleging that Commerce's determination is inconsistent with Articles 10, 11.9 and 21 of the *SCM Agreement*. In its second request for consultations, the EC identified Commerce's *procedures for initiation* of sunset reviews, both as applied by Commerce in the sunset determination in question and in general, as an additional challenged measure, alleging that such initiation procedures are inconsistent with Articles 21.1, 21.3 and 32.5 of the *SCM Agreement* and Article XIV:4 of the Marrakesh Agreement. The EC did not allege that any other sunset determination or procedure violated US WTO obligations. Furthermore, the parties did not discuss the expedited sunset review procedure at either the 8 December 2000, or 21 March 2001 consultations. Finally, there is no mention of the expedited sunset review procedure in the EC's request for the establishment of a panel.

5.87 Articles 4.7 and 6.2 of the DSU, therefore, preclude the EC's claims with respect to the expedited sunset review procedure, because the EC never identified this procedure as a measure in its consultation requests, in the consultations themselves, or in its panel request. It is well-established that a complaining party cannot add new measures after a panel's terms of reference have been established.

5. *Conclusion*

5.88 For the reasons set out in this submission, the United States respectfully requests that the Panel make the following findings:

(1) The US procedure for the automatic self-initiation of sunset reviews by Commerce is not inconsistent with the *SCM Agreement*;

(2) In not applying the 1 per cent *de minimis* standard of Article 11.9 of the *SCM Agreement* to sunset reviews, the United States has not acted inconsistently with its obligations under the *SCM Agreement*;

(3) The Commerce sunset review determination in certain corrosion-resistant carbon steel flat products from Germany is not inconsistent with United States obligations under the *SCM Agreement*.

5.89 In addition, the United States respectfully requests that the Panel make a preliminary ruling that the EC's claims with respect to the expedited sunset review procedure are not within the Panel's terms of reference.

C. *Oral Statement of the European Communities at the First Meeting of the Panel*

1. *Introduction*

5.90 The complaint concerns the decision of the US authorities to continue the countervailing duties on imports of corrosion-resistant carbon steel flat products from Germany (the product). The decision of the US authorities in this case is a result that is mandated by the basic US statute, the implementing legislation and administrative practice on sunset reviews of countervailing duty orders. For these reasons, the present proceeding covers certain aspects of the US basic sunset review legislation, their procedures and their implementation which led to the unlawful continuation of the countervailing duties in this case.[57]

5.91 The oral statement is organised as follows: (a) a presentation of the facts, (b) a review of the substantive legal claims, and (c) the issue of standard of review and the US request to make a preliminary ruling on expedited reviews.

5.92 The basic thrust of the EC case is that countervailing duty measures are exceptional, non-MFN measures that are permitted only and so long as it is necessary to offset injurious subsidies. This is true as regards both the original imposition of countervailing duties and their review under the sunset provisions of the *SCM Agreement*.

2. *Factual Background*

5.93 On 9 July 1993, DOC decided that exports of the product were subsidised. DOC countervailed *five* subsidy programmes (CVD rate 0.60 per cent). DOC found that *two* programmes, the Capital Investment Grants (CIG) (0.39 per cent) and the Aid for Closure of Steel Operations (0.06 per cent) were *non-recurring* grants and the benefit was allocated over a 15-year period. The other *three* programmes were found to be recurring subsidies (0.15 per cent of the total subsidy amount).

5.94 On 1 September 1999, DOC *automatically* initiated a sunset review of the definitive duties. On 20 March 2000, concluded that revocation of the CVD order was likely to lead to recurrence of continuation or recurrence of a countervailable subsidy at a net subsidy rate of *0.54 per cent*. DOC found that the CIG programme

---

57 These acts are: 1) Section 751(c) of the Tariff Act of 1930, as amended, (hereinafter "the Act") , 2) the Implementing Regulations on anti-dumping and countervailing duties issued by DOC, now Section 351 of Title 19 of the US Code of Federal Regulations (hereinafter the "*Sunset Regulations*") and 3)the DOC Policies Regarding the Conduct of Five-year ("Sunset") Reviews of Antidumping and Countervailing Duty Orders (so-called "*Sunset Policy Bulletin*").

would continue to confer a benefit beyond the end of the sunset review. The US simply took the subsidy rate from the original investigation in 1993 and deducted the amounts related to two programmes. On 2 August 2000, the DOC confirmed these findings in the *final* results.

3. *Legal Arguments*

(a) The US Standard of Initiation Applied to Sunset Reviews Leads Inevitably to a Violation of Article 21.3 of the *SCM Agreement*

5.95 Pursuant to Article 21.3 *SCM Agreement,* WTO Members have an obligation to terminate CVD measures no later than 5 years from their imposition, *unless* the authorities determine that the expiry of the duties would be likely to lead to continuation or recurrence of subsidisation and injury. The EC considers that Article 21.3 reinforces the requirement of Article 21.1 by creating an obligation to terminate duties not later than 5 years from their imposition. Therefore, the effect of these provisions is that the continuation of CVD measures beyond the five years period is the exception. Indeed, a proper interpretation of the provisions of Article 21.1 and of the terms "not later than" in Article 21.3 suggest clearly that a CVD should be terminated *even before 5 years*, if its application is *not necessary* to counteract injurious subsidisation. Therefore, the combined effect of these provisions is that the continuation of CVD measures beyond the five years period is an exceptional situation. This corresponds to the object and the purpose of the *SCM Agreement,* which – as explained above – is to guarantee that trade defence measures are to be imposed and maintained only if they are necessary to offset injurious subsidisation.

5.96 The EC considers that self-initiation without the necessary supporting evidence is in violation of the above principle. In this respect, self-initiation is justified only if the domestic authorities have an *equivalent level of evidence* that would be required in such a request from the domestic industry. Indeed, without requiring a *sufficient amount of evidence* of subsidisation and injury in sunset reviews, these become biased in favour of keeping in place unjustified CVD measures. It is clear that the investigating authority has the *burden of demonstrating* that subsidisation and injury *is* likely to continue or recur and cannot devise and apply a system that shifts this burden on the exporters and third countries.

5.97 The US attempts (at para. 63-66) to justify this inconsistency by reading the terms of Article 21.3 in "clinical isolation" and out of context, and without taking into account the proper object and purpose of these provisions. The US also draws (at para. 67) the wrong conclusions from the distinction between the *investigation* phase and the *review* phase of a CVD proceeding. Contrary to what the US argues in para. 67, it follows from Article 22.7, in conjunction with Article 21.1 and Article 11.6 of the *SCM Agreement*, that *without sufficient evidence* the authorities should not self-initiate automatically sunset reviews, but they should leave CVD orders to expire (unless a valid request is made by the domestic industry). Sunset reviews are not a neutral exercise and do not involve, as the US claims (at para. 58), "taking stock of the situation". Rather, in such cases there is a presumption of expiry of duties and the investigating authority is required to demonstrate that it has sufficient evidence when initiating the sunset review, and that the conditions for initially imposing the CVD measure would still be present in the absence of such measure. It is clear from the language of Article 21.3, read in context and in the light of the object and purpose of these provisions, that the investigating authority has the *burden of demonstrating* that subsidisation and injury *is* likely to continue or recur.

5.98 The EC submits that there is no difference as regards the object and purpose of the initial investigations and of sunset reviews. Their common objective is to determine if there is subsidisation and injury which will enable the application of CVD measures in principle for the next five years. It is generally admitted that every text, no matter how clear on its face it is claimed to be, as the US argues here of Article 21.3, requires to be scrutinised in its context and in the light of the object and purpose which is designed to serve. The US arguments throughout their written submission also run counter to the basic principle of good faith interpretation, because they lead unavoidably to results which are manifestly absurd and unreasonable[58] and, as explained above, would reduce parts of Article 21.3 to inutility. So, the question is not whether the Community proposes to read into Article 21.3 words which are not there, as the US now argues, but whether the interpretation it proposes makes sense in the light of the object and purpose of these provisions in their context.

5.99 The EC claim will be better understood if the automatic initiation under US law is examined in two situations: first, in the case of "expedited" sunset reviews, and, second, as applied to the facts in the present case.

5.100 Under the expedited procedure, if domestic interested parties file a "notice of intent to participate", the sunset procedure continues and interested foreign parties, i.e. exporters and the foreign government, are required to file substantive responses. This of course imposes serious economic and other costs on foreign exporters and other WTO Members. If the foreign government, or exporters accounting for at least 50 *per cent* of exports, do not file substantive responses for whatever reason, DOC will shorten the timeframe for the review and will normally presume without further investigation that subsidisation continues.[59] Therefore, the US procedure of expedited reviews, through automatic initiation and presumption of likelihood of continuation or recurrence, is applied so as to absolve the US authorities from their basic duty of investigation and demonstration of likely subsidisation and injury and, hence, is clearly biased towards continuation and perpetuation of countervailing duties, in violation of the duty to terminate them as set in Articles 21.3 and 21.1 of the *SCM Agreement*. It also enables the DOC, without any support in the *SCM Agreement*, to potentially ignore information submitted by a significant number of exporters.

(b) The Domestic Authorities are under an Obligation to "determine" the Likelihood of Continuation or Recurrence of Subsidisation

5.101 Article 21.3 *SCM Agreement* requires that the authorities *determine* that the expiry of the duty would be likely to lead to continuation or recurrence of subsidisation and injury. However, US law does not require a new investigation but requires in sunset reviews the DOC to consider only: (a) the net countervailable subsidy determined in the original investigation, and (b) whether there were any changes in the subsidies since the original investigation. In the EC's view, DOC's refusal to conduct

[58] See Sinclair, pp.116, 120.

[59] 19 C.F.R. §351.218(e)(1)(ii)(B) and (C).

any meaningful fresh investigation in a sunset review is in violation of the requirements of Article 21.3 of the *SCM Agreement.*

5.102 The EC considers that the DOC's refusal to conduct any meaningful fresh investigation in a sunset review is in violation of the requirements of Article 21.3 of the *SCM Agreement.* The US practice not only contravenes the duty placed by Article 21.3 on the domestic authorities to make a fresh "determination" about the likelihood of continuation or recurrence of a subsidy, but, by arguing that administrative reviews should have been requested, it also shifts the burden of proving a change in circumstances on the foreign exporters and at a previous stage of the procedure. Such reviews, however, are considered by the *SCM Agreement* as non-obligatory and are in any event overtaken by the sunset review. The fact that a party did not request an administrative review cannot, therefore, relieve in any way the domestic authorities from their basic and primary duty to "determine" the likelihood of continuation or recurrence of subsidisation [In the present case, the exporters could not request an administrative reviews, as no shipments to the US had been made since the original CVD order]. In fact, DOC sunset practice has been to consistently ignore reduced subsidy rates found in administrative reviews. At any rate, in the present case the German exporters did all they could to submit relevant information to DOC.

5.103 In this case, the German producers stated that the *CIG programme* had been terminated and could not provide any further benefits. DOC had already determined in the original investigation that this programme applied only to investments made prior to 1 January 1986. Despite this evidence, DOC stated that it was unable to determine whether any additional benefits under these programmes were received subsequent to the period of investigation. The US admits that DOC did not recalculate the rate but used the original subsidy rate for CIG. This violates Article 21.3 *SCM Agreement* because DOC did not take into consideration the termination of the CIG programme despite evidence on the record.

5.104 Despite this evidence, DOC rejected the claims of the German exporters. It stated that since no administrative reviews of these orders had been conducted, it was unable to determine whether any additional benefits under these programmes were received subsequent to the period of investigation. It should be stressed that, DOC had also the complete record from the original investigation, including the questionnaire responses and the calculation memoranda, and could have easily verified whether the benefits received by the German manufacturers of the subject merchandise under the CIG after 1 January 1986 were *de minimis.* The US now admits (at para. 40) that DOC did not recalculate the rate but referred back to the original subsidy rate for CIG. This violates Article 21.3 *SCM Agreement* because DOC did not take into consideration the termination of the CIG programme despite evidence on the record. Indeed, the grounds of the US explanation violate the "likely to lead" requirement in Article 21.3 and the "necessity" requirement laid down in Article 21.1 of the Agreement. It also runs counter to Article 21.4, in conjunction with Article 12.5, because the US authorities did not make any effort to satisfy themselves of the accuracy of the claims made by the German exporters. Therefore, the US failed to provide an adequate and reasonable explanation of how the facts support their decision in this case.

5.105 Moreover, DOC should have also reached the conclusion that the effects of the CIG programme had ended on the basis of its *declining balance methodology.*

5.106 As the Appellate Body held several times, the requirement to conduct an "objective assessment" of a claim imposes upon the Panel the obligation to review, first, whether the competent authorities have evaluated *all the relevant factors*[60] and, second, whether the authorities have provided a *reasoned and adequate explanation* of how the facts support their determination.[61] It follows that although panels are not entitled to conduct a *de novo* review of the evidence, nor to *substitute* their own conclusions for those of the competent authorities, this does *not* mean that panels must simply *accept* the conclusions of the competent authorities. Panels should instead examine the explanation offered in depth and in the light of all the facts before it.

5.107 It should further be stressed that in the present case, the calculation memorandum of the original investigation[62] shows that Thyssen last received payments under the CIG programme in 1989, and that the amount received after 1985 was so small that it would have been automatically expensed in the year of receipt under the DOC 0.5 per cent rule.[63] Therefore, in accordance with their obligations under Article 21.3 and 4, the DOC should have taken this into account.

5.108 The EC also considers that in the present case the US violated the standards of Article 21.3 *SCM Agreement* regarding the *treatment of evidence*. The German producers presented to DOC during the sunset review the reasons why the CIG programme should have been considered as terminated and as not providing any further benefits. Based upon this evidence, the German producers believed that DOC would find that subsidisation under the CIG programme would not be likely to continue or recur. However, in its preliminary results of 20 March 2000, DOC continued to assign a 0.39 per cent subsidy rate for this programme.

5.109 It follows from the above that DOC's refusal to conduct any fresh investigation in a sunset review and take into account all relevant and available evidence is in violation of the requirements of Article 21.3 of the *SCM Agreement*

(c) The *de minimis* rule under Article 21.3 of the *SCM Agreement*

5.110 The EC considers that the U.S. interpretation and application of the sunset provisions in Article 21.3 as regards the *de minimis* requirement is *inconsistent* with the *SCM Agreement*. The *de minims* requirements of Articles 11.9 of the *SCM Agreement* are applied by the US only to original investigations (but a 0.5 per cent *de minimis* rule is applied in sunset and administrative reviews under its domestic laws).

5.111 The EC believes that the *object and purpose* of the sunset reviews and of the original investigations is the same, i.e. the application of a CVD measure for the next five years and, therefore, the *de minimis* rule of 1 per cent in Article 11.9 should apply to sunset reviews.

5.112 Indeed, a systematic and good faith interpretation of Article 21.3 with Articles 21.1, 22.1, 22.7 and 11.9 of the *SCM Agreement*, would suggest clearly that the *de minimis* rule of 1 per cent should be applied also in sunset reviews. The US has

---

60 See Appellate Body Report in Korea – Definitive Safeguard Measure on Imports of Certain Dairy Products ("Korea – Dairy Safeguards"), WT/DS98/AB/R, adopted 12 January 2000, at para. 137.

61 See the Appellate Body Report in *Argentina – Safeguard Measures on Imports of Footwear ("Argentina – Footwear Safeguards")*, WT/DS121/AB/R, adopted 12 January 2000, at para. 121.

62 Exhibit EC-20.

63 See 19 C.F.R. § 351.524(b)(2).

failed to demonstrate so far how it is that essentially non-recurring and expensed subsidies of 0.60 per cent in the original investigation are likely to continue and cause injury in a sunset review.[64] The absurdity of the US approach is that a subsidy that, if examined in a new investigation after 1995, would have been found to be *de minimis* under Article 11.9 of the *SCM Agreement*, would now become not *de minimis* under a sunset review and would continue to be applied for 5 more years, even in the absence of a change of circumstances. It is therefore particularly revealing to examine the application of the US approach to the facts of the present case.

5.113 There is common agreement that of the five subsidy programmes examined in the original investigation, 2 have been terminated, i.e. the Structural Improvement Aids (0.05 per cent) and the Zonal Border Area (0.01 per cent). Two of the three programmes that, according to DOC, continued to exist, i.e. the Aid for Closure for Steel Operations (0.06 per cent) and the ECSC Redevelopment Aid (0.08 per cent) would have expired definitively in 2002. The last and most important programme, the Capital Investment Grants, was found by DOC to be non-recurring, and its original net subsidy rate of 0.39 per cent would have been reduced to 0.00234 per cent in accordance with the DOC's 15-year allocation period and calculation methodology. Because DOC only calculates subsidy rates to the second decimal point, a net rate of 0.00234 per cent would have been equivalent to zero. Therefore, on the basis of DOC's own calculation methods, the only 2 likely to continue subsidies would have provided a net amount of *0.14 per cent* (i.e. 0.06% + 0.08%).

5.114 The US provides now no credible explanation. In particular, we fail to see the reason for which the US cites (at para. 94) that there were 2 more programmes under the ECSC treaty which provided zero benefit to these products in the period of investigation, and the reason for which it states (at para. 34) that "domestic parties made allegations concerning new subsidy programmes providing benefits to the German steel industry", but later rejected these claims (at para. 40) because no administrative reviews had been conducted.[65] We cannot help but come to the conclusion that this is yet another ingenious way of DOC and the US to convey the impression (e.g., at paras. 95-96) that there were in place a number of important subsidy programmes ready to be re-deployed soon after the CVD order were to expire. One need only look carefully into the facts of this case to realise that this is absolutely not correct.

5.115 The US states that original investigations and sunset reviews are different and the *SCM Agreement* does not require recalculation of CVD in sunsets. However, there is nothing in Article 21.3 to *prevent* the US DOC from *recalculating* the amount of subsidy in a sunset by establishing a relevant investigation period and doing a recalculation. Moreover, it is required to *quantify* the amount of subsidy likely to prevail in the absence of measures. DOC should have based its quantification on the facts, and examine whether it can meet its burden of proof by positively

[64] In footnote 98, the US states that the EC is not challenging the injury determination in this proceeding but draws no conclusion. The EC in this proceeding is not challenging the injury requirement only for the purpose of verifying the accuracy of the ITC injury determination as such, but it is doing so for the purpose of the *de minimis* challenge, i.e. as a requirement that needs to be demonstrated in the context of a sunset review under Article 21.3 of the Agreement.

[65] Incidentally, the record shows that as regards new subsidy allegations DOC did not reject the petitioners' new subsidy allegations *because* no administrative reviews had been conducted. It rejected them because the petitioners failed to show good cause, i.e. their allegations were vague and unsupported by evidence. DOC should have investigated if the petitioners had indeed shown good cause.

demonstrating likelihood of continuation of subsidisation and injury. It has failed to do so in this case.

5.116 The US advanced further the argument that "the mere continued existence of the CIG programme could warrant maintaining the duty beyond the five-year point, *even if* the amount of the subsidy was currently *zero*, as stated in footnote 52, because subsidisation may be likely to recur absent the discipline of the duty" (at para. 81). Footnote 52 refers *only* to assessment proceedings, which are carried out annually on demand and involve *retrospective* calculations of the amount of subsidy for a particular period. Sunset reviews are completely different and involve an element of *prospective* analysis, i.e. whether subsidisation and injury is likely to recur. There is, consequently, no basis for the argument which the US is attempting to draw from the text of Footnote 52 of the *SCM Agreement*.

5.117 The US also alleges that the current level of subsidisation is not decisive as to whether subsidisation is likely to recur (at para. 74). Although the current *level* of subsidy might not be *decisive* as to whether a subsidy is likely to recur, it is nevertheless a very important factor. Especially in the case of a *non-recurring* subsidy which is already at *de minimis* level, because the future level of the subsidy is known and, under the US declining balance methodology, the subsidy amount will always go down in the future. In the present case, the CVD was based on *non*-recurring subsidies allocated over time (0.60 per cent). Because no new subsidies were granted and on the basis of all available facts in this case, the US should have terminated this measures as the level of subsidy likely to continue in this case was by far too low, even much lower than the 0.50 per cent applied unilaterally by the US domestically. The EC submitted that the 0.50 per cent *de minimis* threshold applied by the US domestically is not appropriate, and that since the rate of 0.54 per cent in the review is below the 1 per cent *de minimis* level which *should* apply in sunset reviews, the US was in breach of Article 21.3 in continuing the CVD measure.

(d) The Obligation to Bring its Law Into Conformity with the WTO Agreements

5.118 Article XVI:4 of the WTO Agreement and Article 32.5 of the *SCM Agreement* oblige Members to bring their domestic law into conformity with their obligations under the WTO Agreements. The EC has demonstrated that the basic US law, the accompanying regulations and practices relating to sunset reviews of countervailing duties and their concrete application to the facts of the present case are inconsistent with a number of provisions of the *SCM Agreement*, i.e. Articles 21, paragraphs 1, 3 and 4, Article 10 and Article 11.9. For those reasons, the EC submits that the US failed to bring its domestic law in conformity with WTO obligations and, thereby, violating Article 32.5 of the *SCM Agreement* and, consequently, Article XVI.4 of the WTO Agreement.

4. *Standard of Review*

5.119 The applicable standard is Article 11 DSU. However, the US claims that the panel cannot consider facts and evidence which were not considered by the US authorities in the sunset review. The EC disagrees based on Appellate Body decisions regarding Article 11 DSU. In *European Communities – Hormones*, it stated that "the applicable standard is neither *de novo* review as such, nor 'total deference', but rather the 'objective assessment of the facts'." In *Argentina – Footwear Safeguards*, the Appellate Body clarified the concept of "objective assessment". The requirement to conduct an "objective assessment" of a claim has thus two elements: a review of whether competent authorities have evaluated all the relevant factors and, second, a review of whether the authorities have provided a reasoned and adequate explanation of how the facts support their determination. The EC believes the US has failed to provide an adequate and reasonable explanation of how the facts support their decision in this case.

5.120 As with regard to requirement of a *reasonable and adequate explanation*, in the United States - *Lamb Safeguards* case, the Appellate Body held that panels must review whether the competent authorities' explanation fully addresses the nature, and, especially, the complexities, of the data, and responds to other plausible interpretations of that data.[66]

5.121 It follows also that although panels are not entitled to conduct a *de novo* review of the evidence, nor to *substitute* their own conclusions for those of the competent authorities, this does *not* mean that panels must simply *accept* the conclusions of the competent authorities. Panels should instead examine the explanation offered in depth and in the light of all the facts before it.

5. *US Request for Preliminary Ruling*

5.122 The EC consider without foundation the US request that the Panel issue a preliminary ruling that the EC's claims regarding the expedited sunset review procedure are not within its terms of reference.

5.123 This Panel was established by the DSB on 10 September 2001 with standard terms of reference. The matter referred to it is, therefore, the one described by the EC in its request for the establishment of the Panel (document WT/DS213/3). The EC referred explicitly to Section 751. c) of the Tariff Act of 1930, which sets out the procedures to conduct sunset reviews and this includes also expedited reviews. The expedited reviews have also been discussed explicitly or implicitly in the consultations, as the procedural and substantive requirements on evidence which foreign producers have to provide in all types of sunset reviews were indeed the subject of the consultations. The US was therefore not deprived of its rights of defence.

6. *Conclusions*

5.124 For these reasons, the EC respectfully requests that the Panel finds that the US basic countervailing duty law (Tariff Act of 1930), its accompanying regulations (sunset regulations) and policy practices (sunset policy bulletin), and their concrete application to imports of certain corrosion-resistant carbon steel flat products from Germany in the present case are inconsistent with Article 21 paragraphs 3, 1 and 4, Article 10 and Article 11.9 of the *SCM Agreement*. For the above reasons, the US countervailing duty law, regulations and practice should also be considered to be inconsistent with Article 32.5 of the *SCM Agreement* and, consequently, should be found to violate also Article XVI.4 of the *WTO Agreement*.

---

[66] Appellate Body Report, United-States – Safeguard Measures on Imports of Fresh Chilled or Frozen Lamb Meat from New Zealand and Australia ("United-States – Lamb Safeguards"), WT/DS177/AB/R, WT/DS178/AB/R, adopted 16 May 2001, para. 106.

D. *Oral Statement of the United States at the First Meeting of the Panel*

5.125 On behalf of the United States delegation, I would like to thank the Panel for this opportunity to comment on certain issues raised by the EC in its First Written Submission. We do not intend to offer a lengthy statement today; you have our written submission, and we will not repeat all of the comments that we made there. We will be pleased to receive any questions you may have at the conclusion of our statement.

5.126 Mr. Chairman, this proceeding presents three basic questions. The first is a purely legal question: Does the United States act inconsistently with Article 21.3 by self-initiating sunset reviews without regard to the evidentiary provisions of Article 11.6? The second is also a purely legal question: Does the United States act inconsistently with Article 21.3 by *not* applying the *de minimis* provisions of Article 11.9 in sunset reviews? The answer to both of these questions is no, for a simple, yet fundamental reason – it is impossible to act inconsistently with an obligation that does not exist.

5.127 I will return to these two issues in a moment, but first let me address the third question, which goes to the specific CVD determination at issue in this proceeding – Commerce's determination that expiry of the countervailing duty on certain corrosion-resistant carbon steel flat products from Germany would be likely to lead to continuation or recurrence of subsidization. The question here is whether Commerce's determination was based upon an appropriately conducted review of all relevant and properly submitted facts. An "objective assessment" of Commerce's findings and actions supports an answer in the affirmative.

1. *Commerce Properly Determined that Expiry of the Duty Would be Likely to Lead to Continuation or Recurrence of Subsidization*

5.128 Article 21.3 defines the point in time at which the authorities must take stock of or terminate a duty – that is every five years. Article 21.3 also defines the circumstances under which maintaining a duty may be considered "necessary" – that is when continuation or recurrence of subsidization and injury is likely. An authority's decision to maintain a duty must be supported by evidence of these requisite circumstances.

5.129 Setting aside the issue of injury, which is not being challenged in this case, what does it mean to determine likelihood of continuation or recurrence of subsidization?

5.130 First, we consider, individually, the words establishing the circumstances under which maintaining a duty may be considered necessary. The word "likely" carries with it the ordinary meaning of "probable". Where continuation or recurrence of subsidization is probable, this probability would then constitute a proper basis for entitlement to the continued imposition of a countervailing duty.

5.131 The word "continuation" expresses a temporal relationship between past and future. Something that happened in the past may continue in the future. An example might be where benefits from an untied, non-recurring financial contribution continue to flow.

5.132 The word "recurrence" also expresses a temporal relationship between past and future. Something that happened in the past may happen again in the future. An example might be where there was not a recent financial contribution under a particular subsidy programme, but the programme still exists and may be used in the future. In this situation, the existing programme is a source for new financial contributions – in other words, its continued existence enables recurrence of subsidization.

5.133 Considered together then, these words indicate that determining likelihood of continuation or recurrence requires a consideration of future, rather than present, circumstances. What are the prospects of subsidization in the future? Without the discipline of the duty, is subsidization likely to continue or recur? The analysis required in a sunset review, therefore, is necessarily prospective in nature.

5.134 Support for this proposition is found in the text of Article 21.3 itself. As discussed in our First Written Submission, note 52 provides that a finding in the most recent assessment proceeding that no duty is to be levied shall not by itself require the authorities to terminate the definitive duty. This indicates that the current level of subsidization is not decisive as to whether subsidization is likely to continue or recur.

5.135 In the sunset review involving German corrosion-resistant steel, Commerce found likelihood based on two unrefuted facts. The first fact is the continued existence and availability of countervailable subsidy programmes previously found to have been used by German producers. The second fact is the continued existence of benefit streams from a countervailable subsidy programme previously found to benefit German producers.

5.136 The EC argues that there are a number of factual and procedural flaws with Commerce's sunset determination, such that Commerce's determination is in violation of provisions of the *SCM Agreement*. In out First Written Submission, we address and rebut the EC's claims in greater detail. Today, I will only briefly touch upon the EC's two main claims. The first concerns the Capital Investment Grants, or CIG, Programme; the second concerns whether the German producers and the EC were afforded "ample opportunity" to participate in the underlying sunset review.

5.137 At the outset, I would note that rather than demonstrating that Commerce's findings or procedural actions were inconsistent with the *SCM Agreement*, the EC's claims present essentially another view of the facts. However, Article 11 of the DSU directs panels to make an "objective assessment" of the facts of the case and of the applicability and conformity with relevant agreements. This "objective assessment" must necessarily focus on the consistency of the sunset review with the requirements of Article 21.3 and Article 12.

5.138 With respect to the CIG Programme, the EC theorizes that, using Commerce's declining balance methodology, the benefits remaining from the programme would be *de minimis*. You will recall that in the original investigation, Commerce found that German producers of corrosion-resistant steel benefitted from non-recurring grants under this programme. In the sunset review, Commerce found that benefit streams from the CIG grants would continue beyond the five-year period. While the EC's declining balance theories are not unreasonable, they only address half of the equation. In particular, it is not possible to calculate a particular rate of subsidization using this methodology without information concerning sales of the subject merchandise. The EC's claim presumes that sales volumes have remained constant, a presumption for which there is no evidence in the record.

5.139 In addition, the EC's argument in this regard is based partly on a calculation memorandum which Commerce properly declined to consider in the sunset review below. As we demonstrate in our First Written Submission, it is not appropriate for the Panel to now consider this business confidential document. Nevertheless, even if this document were appropriately part of the record before the Panel, it does not prove the EC's argument. This is because the memorandum only provides absolute subsidy amounts; it does not contain the information on sales volumes necessary to calculate the *ad valorem* rate of subsidization.

5.140 Nothing in the *SCM Agreement* requires consideration of the magnitude of subsidization in determining the likelihood of continuation or recurrence of subsidization. Furthermore, as the Appellate Body recognized in *UK Lead Bar*, benefits from a non-recurring subsidy continue to flow. As a result, Commerce's "continuation of subsidization" finding with respect to the CIG programme is correct.

5.141 With respect to Commerce's procedural actions in the sunset review, the EC argues that Commerce did not provide an "ample opportunity" to present in writing all evidence which the parties considered relevant to the proceeding. As a factual matter, this assertion is simply incorrect.

5.142 Commerce's published *Sunset Regulations* contain the standard sunset questionnaire and provide an opportunity for parties to submit any argument and information they consider relevant to Commerce's sunset determination. Commerce's regulations also set a 30-day deadline for the submission of such information and provide for extensions of that 30-day deadline. The German Producers and the EC were on notice of these information requirements and options, as well as the applicable deadlines, at least *15 months* prior to the initiation date for the sunset review.

5.143 The EC has not demonstrated how Commerce's actions in this regard violate any of the evidentiary and procedural requirements of Article 12. Fifteen months certainly seems to provide "ample opportunity" to gather and present any evidence the German Producers and the EC considered pertinent to Commerce's sunset determination. I would also note that 15 months is longer than the normal deadline in Article 21.4 for the conduct and completion of sunset reviews. That the German Producers and the EC failed to avail themselves of the ample opportunity to present evidence is not a dereliction that can be ascribed to Commerce's procedural actions in this case.

2. *It is Impossible to Act Inconsistently with an Obligation that does not Exist*

5.144 I will turn now to the two purely legal claims raised by the EC. The first claim is that an authority must satisfy the evidentiary requirements of Article 11.6 before self-initiating a sunset review under Article 21.3. The second claim is that application of the Article 11.9 *de minimis* standard in a sunset review is required under the *SCM Agreement*. As set out more fully in our First Written Submission, there is no support in the *SCM Agreement* for these claims.

5.145 Article 31 of the *Vienna Convention* contain some very basic principles of treaty interpretation. As articulated by the Appellate Body, these principles "neither require nor condone the imputation into a treaty of words that are not there...." The EC's arguments in this case run afoul of this fundamental proposition.

5.146 With respect to the self-initiation issue, the EC argues that the Panel should read into Article 21.3, the requirements of Article 11.6 – the provision of the *SCM*

Agreement that deals with evidentiary requirements for self-initiation of an *investigation*. With respect to the *de minimis* issue, the EC argues that the Panel should read into Article 21.3, the requirements of Article 11.9 – the provision of the *SCM Agreement* that deals with the *de minimis* standard for an *investigation*. There is no support in the Agreement for the EC's theories.

5.147 With no textual foundation, the EC simply asserts that, under the *SCM Agreement*, sunset reviews are essentially nothing more than new investigations. It then takes that unsupported assertion and makes a further leap of logic to the conclusion that various provisions of Article 11 (addressing "Initiation and Subsequent Investigation") *must* therefore apply in sunset reviews carried out under Article 21 (addressing "Duration and Review of Countervailing Duties").

5.148 Japan, in its third party submission, makes an even more impressive leap of logic, arguing that Article 11 requirements are made applicable to Article 21.3 sunset reviews by virtue of the fact that Article 22 – which addresses "Public Notice and Explanation of Determinations" – applies to reviews under Article 21 (pursuant to paragraph 7 of Article 22). Apparently, according to Japan, the mere *mention* of Article 11 in Article 22.1 creates an obligation *to apply* Article 11 in Article 21.3 sunset reviews. I would also note that the provisions of Article 22 apply "*mutatis mutandis*" to reviews. This means that the public notice and explanation provisions are applicable to reviews, but with "necessary changes" or "changes as appropriate."

5.149 Mr. Chairman, it goes without saying that treaty interpretation does not work that way. One cannot create a new set of international obligations through unsupported theories and unfounded suppositions that ignore the very words of the treaty being interpreted. It is well-accepted that, under the *Vienna Convention*, the ordinary meaning of a treaty is the basis for interpreting that treaty. The fact that the EC and Japan have to try so hard to find a connection between Article 11 and Article 21 is itself evidence of the lack of the very connection that they seek. Put differently, the United States agrees with the EC and Japan that Article 11 provides context for purposes of interpreting Article 21.3; but it is context that disproves their assertions.

5.150 As discussed in our First Written Submission, the drafters clearly knew how to cross-reference a particular provision to make it applicable in the context of Article 21 reviews. For example, Article 21.4 expressly makes the evidentiary requirements of Article 12 applicable in Article 21 reviews. Even Japan's argument proves the point – Article 22.7 makes the public notice and explanation requirements of Article 22 applicable in Article 21 reviews on a *mutatis mutandis* basis.

5.151 The uncontested fact is that the drafters did not make the initiation and subsequent investigation requirements of Article 11 applicable in Article 21 reviews. And no amount of lawyering can override the plain text of the *SCM Agreement* or create an obligation that does not exist. The Article 11.6 evidentiary prerequisite simply does not apply to Article 21.3 sunset reviews; and neither does the Article 11.9 *de minimis* standard.

5.152 The EC makes claims based on its "reasonable and legitimate expectations" on these issues; yet it is the legitimate expectations of the Members as a whole, as expressed in the agreed text of the treaty, that are at risk of being infringed in this case. As the Appellate Body has stated in *India Patent Protection* at paragraph 45:

> The legitimate expectations of the parties to a treaty are reflected in the language of the treaty itself. The duty of a treaty interpreter is to examine the words of the treaty to determine the intentions of the par-

> ties. This should be done in accordance with the principles of treaty interpretation set out in Article 31 of the Vienna Convention. But these *principles of interpretation neither require nor condone the imputation into a treaty of words that are not there or the importation into a treaty of concepts that were not intended.*

(Emphasis added.) If the Members had actually agreed that various provisions of Article 11 should apply in sunset reviews carried out under Article 21, the text would reflect that agreement, just as it does with respect to the application of Article 12 to Article 21 reviews. The EC is improperly trying to have the Panel do what the negotiators did not.

5.153 The EC is asking the Panel to read into Article 21.3 words, and hence obligations, that are not there. For this reason, the EC's claims concerning self-initiation and *de minimis* must fail.

E. Responses of the European Communities to Questions from the Panel Following the First Meeting

Both parties

Q1. In your view:

(a) Is the *de minimis* standard contained in Article 11.9 of the Agreement on Subsidies and Countervailing Measures ("*SCM Agreement*" or "the Agreement") applicable to reviews under Article 21.2?

Reply

5.154 Article 21.2 deals with reviews during the lifetime of the measure with the aim of examining whether the continued imposition of the measure remains necessary (based on the principle set out in Article 21.1). In the EC's view, with regard to the US system, we should distinguish between two types of review under Article 21.2, i.e. duty assessment reviews (administrative reviews under US law) and reviews where the effective need for continued imposition of the measure is examined (changed circumstances review under US law). As regards a changed circumstances review, the *de minimis* standard under 11.9 is applicable because Article 21.2 requires that if the authorities determine that the countervailing duty is no longer warranted, it shall be terminated immediately. Changed circumstances reviews can thus affect the scope and, indeed, the continued imposition of the measure. Under Article 11.9 of the Agreement, the subsidy amount must be above 1 per cent to permit the imposition of a countervailing duty in the first place. It follows that if an interested party can show, in a changed circumstances review, that the subsidy amount will not rise above 1 per cent upon removal of the measure, the measure should be terminated immediately. It should be noted that virtually the same terminology "immediate termination" and "immediately terminated" is used in Articles 11.9 and 21.2 respectively.

5.155 On the other hand, a *de minimis* amount of subsidy found during a simple administrative review would not by itself oblige the authorities to terminate the proceeding, since the purpose of such a review is only to determine what amount of duty has to be collected. (Footnote 52 of the *SCM Agreement*). Thus, as the *Korea –*

DRAMS panel determined, simple administrative reviews have no effect on the scope and continued imposition of a measure and cannot lead to its termination. As the EC explained in its first submission, administrative reviews in the *SCM Agreement* appear to fall under Article 21.2 by default, whereas in the Anti-Dumping Agreement (Footnote 21) they are not considered to be reviews at all.

(b) Are the negligible import volume and injury standards contained in Article 11.9 and the negligible injury standard contained in Article 15.3 applicable to reviews under Article 21.2?

Reply

5.156 Negligible import volume and injury standards are provided for in the *SCM Agreement* because WTO members consider that such a small volume of imports can not be the cause of any injury sustained by the domestic industry. The use of the term "shall" indicates that this is *not* a refutable presumption. Therefore, if a certain volume of imports cannot cause injury at the initiation of an investigation, this irrefutable presumption applies to reviews under Article 21.2. in cases where it is demonstrated that the amount of the subsidy is less than 1 per cent ad valorem and is not going to increase above this level or that imports would not rise above *de minimis* upon removal of the measure. The terms, object and purpose of Article 21.2 in context compel such a conclusion.

(c) Are the negligible import volume and injury standards contained in Article 11.9 and the negligible injury standard contained in Article 15.3 applicable to reviews under Article 21.3?

Reply

5.157 Article 21.3 lays down clearly a presumption of termination ("shall be terminated"). The authorities are required, therefore, to show that the conditions for imposing the original measure would, in its absence, continue to exist or recur and it is for the domestic industry and the investigating authority to show that, if the measure were removed, imports would be likely to again rise above *de minimis*. For essentially the same reasons stated in the reply to the previous question above and those explained more detail in the first written submission of the EC, the EC considers that the standards contained in Articles 11.9 and 15.3 of the *SCM Agreement* are applicable to reviews under Article 21.3 thereof.

(d) Are the negligible import volume standards for developing countries set out in Article 27.10 applicable to reviews under Article 21 in general, and to reviews under Article 21.3 in particular? Is the 2 per cent *de minimis* standard for developing countries set out in Article 27.10(b) applicable to reviews under Article 21 in general, and to reviews under Article 21.3 in particular? And is the 3 per cent *de minimis* level for certain developing countries set out in Article 27.11 applicable to reviews under Article 21 in general, and to reviews under Article 21.3 in particular?

Please explain in detail.

Reply

5.158 The higher *de minimis* thresholds for developing countries are equally applicable to initial investigations and reviews examining the need for continued imposition of the CVD (under Article 21.2) and sunset reviews (under 21.3). The purpose of special *de minimis* thresholds for developing countries lies in Article 27.1 of the *SCM Agreement*. WTO members recognize that subsidies play an important role in the further economic development of developing countries and, therefore, agreed in Articles 27.10 and 27.11 to increase the minimum import volumes and subsidy amounts below which injury is presumed not to be caused. Likewise, this is an irrefutable presumption.

5.159 Article 27.10 states that "*Any* countervailing duty investigation of a product originating in a developing country Member shall be terminated as soon as the authorities determine...". It would be contrary to the explicit provisions of the *SCM Agreement* to grant certain exemptions because they are considered essential for development needs and only apply them to original countervailing investigations. It would also be contrary to the terms of Articles 27.10 and 27.11, read in conjunction with Articles 21.1, 21.2 and 21.3, not to apply them in reviews. Clearly the reference to "subsidization" in these Articles must be taken to refer to a level of subsidization which has been determined to be injurious with reference to the Member concerned.

5.160 An example may illustrate this point. Article 27.11 provides for a developing country Member, which eliminates export subsidies in less than eight years to benefit from an increased *de minimis* subsidy threshold of 3 per cent instead of 2 per cent. This provision aims to reward developing countries which have accelerated compliance with their obligations. Suppose a certain Member were able to benefit from this provision and the following year was involved in a US CVD sunset review involving one of its products. If the rate of subsidy likely to prevail was found to be 2.5 per cent, i.e. below the *de minimis* rate now applicable to the Member concerned, the US would continue to impose a CVD order and the Member involved would have obtained absolutely no benefit from its efforts to remove early the export subsidies.

European Communities

Q2. The Panel notes the European Communities' argument regarding the presumption of termination of all countervailing duties ("CVDs") contained in Article 21 of the *SCM Agreement* and the claim that the US law and statement of policy practice in reviews under Article 21.3 disregard this presumption through the automatic initiation of reviews under Article 21.3, and thereby violate Article 21.3. In what precise manner would the US law and statement of policy practice have had to be different for them to be WTO-consistent? Please respond in light of the phrase "in a review initiated ... on their own initiative" contained in Article 21.3 of the *SCM Agreement*.

Reply

5.161 The current US law requires the automatic initiation of sunset reviews *without any evidence*. This ignores the presumption of termination under Article 21.3 and reverses the burden of proof, which should be on the petitioners or the investigating authority to justify the initiation of a review and not on the exporters to justify the termination and the non-initiation of such a review.

5.162 The problem with US law is that it transforms the text and basic rationale of Article 21.3 and provides for self-initiation without taking account of the *standard of evidence required under Articles 21.3 and 4 to meet the burden of proof of either the petitioner or the investigating authority in conjunction with Articles 11.6, 22.1 and*

22.7 of the SCM Agreement. It follows that the investigating authority must be in possession of the same or an equivalent amount of sufficient evidence as the domestic industry at the time of initiating the review. The basic US law and its implementing regulations would have to provide for this in order to be WTO consistent. In particular, the US law will have to provide that:

- An applied CVD order shall terminate 5 years after its imposition and will not be reviewed unless the authorities, at the time of initiating the review, possess an amount of relevant evidence that is the same or equivalent to that required in original investigations;
- The burden of providing such evidence is placed on domestic industry or the authorities themselves;
- No reverse or negative inference is drawn from the fact that foreign exporters or producers or third countries do not participate at the initial call for the sunset review, except where Article 12.7 is applicable.

Q3. How, if at all, do the European Communities' own statutory and regulatory provisions in respect of the initiation of reviews under Article 21.3 give meaning to the presumption of termination of all CVDs that the European Communities considers is contained in Article 21 of the *SCM Agreement*?

Reply

5.163 Article 18 of Council Regulation (EC) No 2026/97 of 6 October 1997, the Community's basic CVD regulation, contains the relevant provisions on sunset reviews (known as "expiry reviews"). In accordance with Article 18.4, the Commission publishes a *notice of impending expiry* of a countervailing measure during the last year of its duration; our practice is to do this nine months before the date of expiry (the five-year anniversary date).

5.164 The notice of impending expiry states that *unless* a review is initiated, the measures will expire. In order for a review to be initiated, Community producers must, no later than three months before the expiry date, lodge a request containing *sufficient evidence* that the removal of the measures would be likely to result in continuation or recurrence of subsidy and injury. If the EU Commission considers that the request contains sufficient evidence, it initiates an expiry review. If there is no request, or if the request contains insufficient evidence, the Commission publishes a *notice of expiry* and the measures lapse on the five-year anniversary date. This notice of expiry is of purely declaratory nature.

5.165 There is consequently a presumption of termination, since in the absence of the provision of sufficient positive evidence by the Community producers justifying a review, the measures lapse automatically.

Q4. Does the European Communities consider self-initiation of reviews under Article 21.3 by investigating authorities to be in and of itself WTO-inconsistent?

Reply

5.166 No. Article 21.3 explicitly provides for the possibility of self-initiation, as does Article 18.1 of Regulation 2026/97. In fact, Article 21.3 provides for either self-initiation or initiation on the basis of a "duly motivated request" from the domestic industry. The Community's claim is that the investigating authority must be in possession of sufficient evidence, that is the same level or an equivalent amount of relevant evidence that would be required from the domestic industry if it initiates on its own initiative, as in the case in the initiation of new investigations (Articles 11.1 and 11.6). Otherwise, self-initiation would become the easy option and would lead to inconsistent results.

Q5. The Panel notes the European Communities' arguments contained in paragraph 15 of its oral statement at the first meeting of the Panel.

(a) Does the European Communities consider that there is a presumption in the *SCM Agreement* that *all* provisions of the Agreement are applicable to reviews under Article 21.3?

Reply

5.167 The EC believes that no provision of the *SCM Agreement* can be read in isolation, and that all provisions are potentially applicable *mutatis mutandis* to Article 21.3, to the extent that they are relevant to the issues covered by Article 21.3 and that their application to Article 21.3 does not create a situation of conflict or is not specifically excluded.

(b) In what circumstances might some provisions of the Agreement not apply to reviews under Article 21.3?

Reply

5.168 Subject to the above, there are provisions which clearly have no relevance to Article 21.3. As explained below, the provisions concerning multilateral subsidy disciplines, to the extent that they do not apply to countervailing duties at all, are not applicable to sunsets. Furthermore, a small number of provisions which concern countervailing duties cannot, for practical reasons, apply to sunsets. However, one has to be very careful before determining that a certain provision has no such relevance, since certain WTO Members may choose to take account of them in their own practice. For instance, the US, in its sunset practice, takes account of whether the subsidies fall under Articles 3 or 6.1 of the *SCM Agreement*, although neither of these provisions has any obvious relationship to countervailing duties.

(c) If there are particular provisions that, in the view of the European Communities, do not apply to reviews under Article 21.3, what are they, and why do they not apply?

Reply

5.169 The *SCM Agreement* contains two major divisions: multilateral obligations for WTO members and provisions regarding the conduct of countervailing investigations. It is obvious that certain provisions imposing multilateral obligations on WTO members by nature do not apply to countervailing investigations.

5.170 The EC will provide an overview of the different parts of the *SCM Agreement* and explain whether provisions apply to countervailing proceedings and reviews under Article 21.3 in particular.

Part I:

5.171 Article 1 applies to sunset reviews since only subsidies as defined in Article 1 could fall within the concept of "subsidization".

5.172 Article 2 regarding specificity applies equally to sunset reviews.

Part II:

5.173 Article 3: the prohibition of certain subsidies as such does not apply to CVD. However, read in conjunction with Article 2.3 *SCM Agreement*, the definition of prohibited subsidies plays a role for CVD and reviews under Article 21.3 because these subsidies are deemed to be specific.
5.174 Article 4: is not applicable for CVD and sunsets since it covers specific dispute settlement rules regarding those prohibited subsidies.

Part III:

5.175 This part deals with actionable subsidies and possible multilateral remedies against those subsidies. It does not apply to CVD and sunsets. In addition, Article 6.1 has now expired.

Part IV:

5.176 Expired pursuant to Article 31 *SCM Agreement* on 31.12.99. When applicable, it created a category of non-actionable subsidies which made them non-countervailable in all CVD actions, including sunsets. For example, a regional aid countervailed pre-1995 could have been green-lighted and found non-countervailable in a post-1995 sunset review.

Part V:

5.177 All provisions of Part V regarding countervailing investigations is in principle applicable *mutatis mutandis* to sunset reviews under 21.3. For Article 12, there is an explicit reference. For other provisions, e.g. Article 15 on injury, it is clear that the word "injury" in Article 21.3 can *only* be interpreted with reference to Article 15. The same is true for "domestic industry" with relation to Article 16.
5.178 In those cases where there is no *explicit reference* to a specific article or term in Article 21.3, the EC submits that all provisions are in principle applicable to Article 21.3. The only *exceptions* are provisions which cannot, for practical reasons, serve any purpose in a sunset review. For instance:

- *Article17* regarding provisional measures can only apply to new investigation, where no measure is yet in force. Provisional measures can be imposed when a preliminary determination is made that a subsidy exists and there is injury. It is mainly intended to prevent injury during the remainder of the investigation and also serves to provide interested parties with an opportunity to comment on the preliminary finding regarding subsidies and injury. It is obvious that this provision is not relevant to a sunset review, where a duty is already in force and can remain effective pending the outcome of the review.

- *Article 20* covers issues of retroactive collection of duties. This provides for the retroactive collection of provisional duties, and in critical circumstances, retroactive assessment for up to 90 days prior to the provisional stage. Since in a sunset review the duty is already in force this provision does not apply.

5.179 *Part VI* regards the establishment and the operation of the Committee on Subsidies and Countervailing Measures. As such, it does not have an impact on the conduct of countervailing proceedings including sunsets. However, the Committee may deal with issues regarding sunset investigations if a WTO Member puts a particular investigation on the agenda for discussion in the Committee.

5.180 *Part VII* deals with notifications and does not impact on the conduct of sunset reviews.

5.181 *Part VIII* deals with special and differential treatment for developing country members. Articles 27.10 to 27.12 refer to special CVD *de minimis* thresholds for developing countries, which are equally applicable to new investigations and sunset reviews (Question 1(d)). Article 27.15 deals with Committee review of any CVD measure, including the result of a sunset review. Article 27.1 is a declaratory provision which contributes to justifying the S&D provisions, including those relating to CVD.

5.182 *Part IX* does not apply to CVD since it covers some transitional multilateral obligations.

5.183 *Part X* concerning dispute settlement covers all aspects of the *SCM Agreement*. It also covers sunset reviews.

5.184 *Part XI.* Its provisions on "other final provisions" apply to sunsets.

5.185 Article 31. - The expiry of Article 8 removed the non-countervailable category of specific subsidies ; these are now countervailable in sunsets, even if, to reverse the example given under Part IV, the original subsidy had been green lighted in the first investigation.

5.186 Article 32 applies to sunsets (Article 32.4 explicitly).

Q6. With respect to reviews under Article 21.3, does the European Communities consider that:

(a) All the requirements of Articles 11.4, 11.5, and 11.11 apply to the initiation or self-initiation of reviews under Article 21.3? Why or why not?

Reply

5.187 The standing requirements in Article 11.4 apply to reviews initiated under Article 21.3. These two articles require that applications or requests must be made "by or on behalf of the domestic industry", which is defined in Article 11.4.

5.188 Article 11.5 also applies to both. There is no reason why Members should be required to avoid publicising *applications* under Article 11, but should be allowed to publicise review *requests* under Article 21.3. Applications under 11.5 and requests under 21.3 are aimed at securing the same objective, that is to avoid unjustified disruptions in international trade on the basis of allegations and claims that are manifestly incorrect. Article 11.11 does not apply to Article 21.3 reviews. Article 21.4 explicitly governs the timing and duration of all reviews under Article 21, and its provisions differ from those of Article 11.11.

(b) Article 13.1 applies to reviews under Article 21 in general, and to reviews under Article 21.3 in particular? Why or why not?

Reply

5.189 Article 13.1 refers explicitly to applications under Article 11 and "in any event before the initiation of any investigation". Footnote 44 refers to the fact that "no affirmative determination" shall be made without reasonable opportunity for consultations having been given. Such a determination may be made in either a new investigation or review, which implies that consultations should have been offered in the framework of a sunset. Thus, it would seem that Articles 13.1 and 13.2 would apply *mutatis mutandis* to Article 21.3 reviews.

(c) Article 19.4 applies to reviews under Article 21 in general, and to reviews under Article 21.3 in particular? Why or why not?

Reply

5.190 Yes, it applies to both types of reviews ("no countervailing duty..."). Moreover, this interpretation is in conformity with the overriding principles laid down in Articles 10 and 21.1 of the *SCM Agreement*.

Q7. The Panel notes the European Communities' arguments contained in paragraph 37 of its oral statement at the first meeting of the Panel.

(a) Could the European Communities explain its view that the object and purpose of reviews under Article 21.3 and original investigations is the same, in light of the fact that an original investigation determines the existence of subsidization and injury *ab initio*, while a review under Article 21.3 occurs in the context of the existence of a prior finding of subsidization and injury?

Reply

5.191 New investigations and Article 21.3 reviews with a positive outcome both have the same result – the application of a countervailing duty for a period of up to 5 years. In order for such duties to be imposed or maintained, the investigating authority must in both cases determine that the conditions for the imposition of a countervailing duty, as laid down in Article 19.1, are fulfilled. The only difference is that Article 21.3 reviews take place with a measure already in force, so that the investigating authority must determine whether, in the absence of that measure, the Article 19.1 conditions would be met. The difference in the wording of the provisions on new investigations and sunset reviews merely reflects the fact that, in the latter case, there is a need to take account of an existing measure in establishing whether the conditions still exist for applying countervailing measures; the object and purpose of both provisions, however, remains the same.

(b) Could the European Communities address specifically the difference, if any, between a finding of "the existence of and amount of the subsidy and that, through the effects of the subsidy, the subsidized imports are causing injury", so as to justify imposition of a CVD under Article 19.1, and a finding that "expiry of the duty would be likely to lead to continuation or recurrence of subsidization and injury" sufficient to justify continuation of the CVD under Article 21.3?

Reply

5.192 There are not differences except that in the case of Article 21.3 there are CVD measures already in force. The purpose of an Article 21.3 review is to determine whether, absent the measures in force, all the conditions for the imposition of a duty under Article 19.1 would still be present. Since an Article 21.3 review always takes place with a measure in force, this inevitably involves a certain element of prediction based on the facts presented of what would happen if the measures were left to expire. The investigating authorities are required to meet the "likely" standard, while applying the provisions of Article 21.1. However, the concepts of subsidization, causality and injury have to be interpreted in the same way in the context of both provisions. Moreover, it has to be based on *"evidence"*, not on pure conjecture and speculation. This follows from Article 21.4, which makes Article 12 relating to evidence applicable to reviews. Moreover, the requirement to re-establish the existence of the Article 19.1 conditions in a sunset review flows from the general presumption of termination in Article 21.3, in conjunction with the basic requirements of Article 21.1.

5.193 In this regard, it should be noted that, regardless of the presence or absence of measures, some factual situations are inherently more predictable than others. For example, while it may be relatively difficult to determine to what extent a company will resume dumping practices if a measure is dropped, sovereign States normally behave differently and in a more predictable way as regards the granting of subsidies. Moreover, a non-recurring subsidy in a CVD case (as is the case here) will always be predictable, since the benefit stream calculated is known for the whole allocation period of the subsidy. In such a case, it would be for the investigating authority to justify, on the basis of positive evidence, a finding that any other related factors, e.g. the denominator, would change.

Q8. The European Communities refers, in paragraph 3 of its oral statement at the first meeting of the Panel, to the fact that CVD measures are exceptional, non-MFN measures. The European Communities further relies on a characterization of continuation of a measure after a review as an "exception" in arguing that the provisions of Article 21.3 must be strictly interpreted.

(a) First, does the European Communities consider that this requirement of strict interpretation applies to the entirety of Part V of the *SCM Agreement*?

Reply

5.194 The EC considers that the provisions of Article 21.3 *SCM Agreement* relating to continuation of a CVD measure constitute an exception to the general rule which provides that CVD orders should in principle expire after 5 years. The exceptional character of continuation of the duty beyond the five-year period is reflected in the use of "unless" which introduces the exception. The EC considers that a number of provisions of the *SCM Agreement* (e.g. Articles 10, 11.3, 11.5, 11.9, 19.4, 21.1, etc.) provide implicit support for the proposition that CVD orders should be imposed after careful and strict interpretation of all the provisions of the *SCM Agreement*.

(b) Second, could the European Communities explain how, in its view, reading the text of Article 21.3 to include obligations not explicitly set out therein, but set out in Article 11.6 (or 11.9), is a "strict interpretation" of Article 21.3?

Reply

5.195 The phrase "strict interpretation" in this context simply stands for the proposition that the terms of Article 21.3 have to be interpreted also in light of their object and purpose and in context, which is the entire *SCM Agreement* and, in particular, Articles 11.6, 11.9 and 15.3 thereof. It is further meant to clarify the proposition that a subsidy which is found to be less than 1 per cent in the original investigation - before the entry into force of the *SCM Agreement* - would not benefit from a lenient or relaxed interpretation of Article 21.3 so as to permit its unjustified continuation even if it is likely to be below the 1 per cent *de minimis* rule in the sunset review. This relaxed interpretation is the basic US argument which proposes to read the terms of Article 21.3 in complete isolation of the rest of the Agreement.

Q9. What *precise* evidentiary standards does the European Communities consider as being required for the initiation of reviews under Article 21.3, particularly in light of the linkages the European Communities sees between Articles 21.3 and 11.6? In the view of the European Communities, is there any difference between the evidentiary standards required for the initiation of original investigations and those required for the initiation of reviews under Article 21.3?

Reply

5.196 When an investigating authority decides to initiate a review under Article 21.3, it should have sufficient evidence of subsidization, injury and a causal link between those requirements. The level of evidence required in a sunset review is the same or equivalent to the evidence required in an original investigation. Article 21.3 requires the investigating authority to make a determination of likelihood of continuation or recurrence of subsidization *and* injury. Therefore, before opening the sunset review there should be sufficient evidence of the two aspects which are likely to continue or recur. The final review determination should positively demonstrate both likelihood of subsidization causality and injury.

5.197 Article 11.6 requires that when an investigating authority self-initiates an original investigation, the standard of evidence is sufficient evidence. Since an original investigation and a sunset review have the same object and purpose, this standard should apply to self-initiated sunset reviews, as it is the practice under US law. Articles 22.1 and 22.7 confirm this proposition.

Q10. Please comment on the relevance, if any, of the retrospective and prospective nature of the assessment to be made, respectively, in original investigations and in reviews under Article 21.3. In particular, how is an assessment of the existence of injurious subsidization similar to and/or different from an assessment of the effects of the revocation of a duty in terms of injurious subsidization? How precisely would the European Communities suggest that the relevant subsidization rate for a review under Article 21.3 should be calculated?

Reply

5.198 Both types of investigation involve some retrospective and prospective assessment. This is because original investigations and sunset reviews are quite similar by nature and operation. The original investigation must necessarily involve *retrospective* calculations of the amount of subsidy for a particular period (an investigation period prior to the initiation of the case or the review). The purpose is to determine the amount of benefit granted to a particular company during a specific period of time. Likewise, sunset reviews also involve a retrospective analysis since the subsidization of the past years is often the basis for the sunset finding, especially when the subsidy is non-recurring. The retrospective analysis is consequently extrapolated for the five coming years (prospective nature).

5.199 In view of the prospective character of the measure which is the outcome of the original investigation and the sunset review, it is essential that a determination is made of the amount of subsidy. According to Article 19.1, an original investigation aims to measure the need for offsetting injury while in a sunset review the purpose is to examine in addition at what level subsidization will recur or continue if the measure were to be removed.

5.200 However, in a sunset review, as in an original investigation, the subsidy rate should be calculated exactly during the period of review since the investigating authority (particularly for non-recurring subsidies for which the benefit is known) should use this as the basis for establishing the level at which subsidization will continue or recur if the measure were to be removed. The "likelihood" element of the determination relates to the continuation or recurrence of the subsidy and injury, but if the amount found likely to continue or recur, on the basis of the amount found in the review period, is *de minimis*, the case should be terminated immediately.

Q11. Article 11.6 allows investigating authorities to proceed to initiation without having received a written application by or on behalf of a domestic industry "only if they have sufficient evidence of the existence of a subsidy, injury and causal link, as described in paragraph 2". Article 11.2 of the *SCM Agreement* sets out, in subparagraph (iii), that this evidence should include "evidence with regard to the existence, amount and nature of the subsidy in question". Could the European Communities comment on the proposition that the CVD order itself, or the results of the most recent review under Article 21.2, is evidence of the existence, amount, and nature of the subsidy in question, consistent with the requirements of Article 11.2(iii)?

Reply

5.201 The EC would agree that a sufficient amount of evidence on the existence, nature and amount of the subsidy is necessary for initiating a sunset review. However, the initial CVD order, dating from five or more years ago, is not by itself sufficient to meet the burden of proof for initiating a sunset review. There must be the same or equivalent evidence that the original subsidy is likely to continue to exist and to confer a benefit to the current exporters of the product, or there must be evidence of new subsidies.

5.202 The evidence of a more recent Article 21.2 review may in principle be more relevant, but it will not by itself be sufficient either. Furthermore, such evidence, as applied in the US system, must work both ways. For instance, if a recent administrative review shows that a subsidy amount is *de minimis* and the subsidy is non-recurring, this should confirm the presumption against initiating, unless compelling evidence of new subsidies is brought forward. Under the present US rules, the US takes no account of such factors when initiating reviews or when continuing CVD measures.

Q12. Please respond to the following:

In the view of the European Communities, is there any similarity between the evidentiary standards required for the self-initiation of reviews under Article 21.2 ("where warranted") and those required for the self-initiation of reviews under Article 21.3?

Reply

5.203 Subject to the kind of review that is to be carried out under Article 21.2, there is similarity to the extent that, in both cases, the investigating authority would need to be in possession of the same or equivalent amount of sufficient information required from an interested party ("positive information" in the case of a 21.2 review) or the domestic industry ("a duly motivated request" in the case of a 21.3 review). This similarity stems from the fact that in both cases the authorities are required to possess a sufficient amount of evidence in order to initiate review. This is because both types of review are *not* neutral, in the sense that both may impose costs on the parties involved and disrupt international trade.

(b) Could the European Communities explain its view – expressed in response to an oral question from the Panel at its first meeting – that the requirements for evidence necessary to justify self-initiation under Article 21.2 are lower than the requirements necessary to justify self-initiation under Article 21.3?

Reply

5.204 This will essentially depend on the type of review carried out under Article 21.2. In 21.2 reviews, the investigating authority, reflecting the burden of proof imposed on interested parties, would need to be convinced that the continued imposition of the duty was no longer necessary ("where warranted" in Article 21.2). Such a conviction **may** sometimes require a high standard of evidence but may sometimes be based on very simple evidence, for instance, the allocation period for a subsidy may have expired or domestic production in the country imposing the measure may have ceased. In addition, a 21.2 review may be limited to an examination of **either** subsidy or injury. Therefore, a 21.2 review may, in some circumstances, require a smaller amount of evidence.

5.205 In contrast, the purpose of sunset reviews under 21.3 is to rebut the presumption of termination of the measure. Such reviews **always** require a minimum (and rather high) standard of evidence to demonstrate that **both** subsidy and injury is likely to continue or recur if the measure were to be removed.

(c) Where in the *SCM Agreement* does the European Communities find the support for lower evidentiary standards applicable to self-initiation under Article 21.2?

Reply

5.206 See answer above. It will essentially depend on the kind of Article 21.2. reviews under consideration (i.e. administrative review, charge of circumstances reviews, etc.). The term "were warranted" can provide the basis for such a proposition.

(d) How is an assessment of the need for the continued imposition of the duty similar to and/or different from an assessment of the effects of the revocation of a duty in terms of injurious subsidization?

Reply

5.207 Leaving aside the situations where the authorities initiate the review, the assessment concerning the need for continued imposition (Article 21.2) and the effects of revocation of a duty (Article 21.3) are quite similar. Both examinations focus on the prospective nature of the exercise, i.e. would the removal of the duty lead to continued subsidization and injury. The main difference is the burden of proof. For example, in an Article 21.2 review, the burden of proof is essentially on the interested party (usually a foreign exporter) to justify that there is no need for continued imposition. In an Article 21.3 review, in contrast, the domestic industry must meet the burden of proof to rebut the presumption of expiry of a duty. In both cases, however, the authorities are required to make a positive determination about subsidization, causality and injury.

Q13. The European Communities argues that, "in order to initiate a sunset review on its own initiative, the domestic authorities should be in possession of the same level of evidence that would be required in a 'duly substantiated request' from the domestic industry".[67]

(a) What does the European Communities understand by the term "duly substantiated request"?

Reply

5.208 In the EC's view, therefore, a "duly substantiated request" is a request by or on behalf of the domestic industry that contains sufficient evidence that the expiry of the measures would be likely to result in a continuation or recurrence of subsidization and injury, in order to justify a review under Article 21.3. Such a likelihood may, for example, be indicated by evidence of continued subsidization and injury, or evidence that the removal of existing injury is due to the existence of measures. A "duly substantiated" request should normally, inter alia, contain information on:

- the volume and value of domestic production
- the volume and value of the production of petitioners
- volume and value of total imports
- volume and value of subsidized imports
- evidence with regard to the existence, amount and the nature of the subsidy, plus -evidence relating to its continuation or recurrence
- information regarding the effect of imports on prices, production, lost sales
- causality between subsidized imports and injury, and evidence of why such injury will continue or recur.

Although the exact content of a duly substantiated request under Article 21.3 will differ in some ways from the content of an application under Article 11.2, since an

67 First Written Submission of the European Communities, para. 65.

Article 21.3 request will relate to a situation where measures are in force and injurious subsidization has already been established, the elements contained in an Article 11.2 should normally be present.

(b) In the view of the European Communities, is there any difference between the evidentiary standards required for the initiation of reviews under Article 21.3 upon request from the domestic industry and those required for the self-initiation of reviews under Article 21.3 by investigating authorities?

Reply

5.209 The evidence required in a request from the industry and self-initiation should for all practical purposes be the same. The purpose of the evidentiary standard is to guarantee that genuine cases are brought which are backed-up by concrete evidence. If a different standard would apply to self-initiation, this would seriously alter the rights of affected parties and would allow circumvention of these mandatory provisions. This would open the door for situations where the domestic industry does not succeed in creating a prima facie case, but the investigating authority could circumvent it by self-initiating since the evidentiary standard would be different (i.e. lower).

5.210 The EC's point is that a correct interpretation of the purpose of Article 21.3 requires investigating authorities to self-initiate reviews only on the basis of sufficient evidentiary support. Where investigating authorities are free to initiate, as it is the case in the US, without any evidentiary support at all, a major distortion of the system as established by the *SCM agreement* was a parallel between the EC "automatic" notice of impending expiry and the US "automatic" notice of initiation of a CVD measure. The EC duly emphasized the fundamental difference between the "legal effect" attached to these notices: one (the EC) notifies that an expiry is impending, and placing the onus on the domestic industry to produce evidence, without putting any burden on the exporters; the other (the US) actually initiates an investigation without evidence and requires an important and burdensome action from exporters to produce evidence that the measure should not expire. This is a clear reversal of the burden of proof.

5.211 However, it should be noted that *de facto* the actual function and scope of the EC notice of impending expiry and the US notice of initiation is the same: to notify the domestic industry the imminent deadline. Actually, the two documents look quite alike and contain the same type of information. The substantial difference is that, under EC law, following a notice of impending expiry the domestic industry must produce a "duly substantiated request" in order to have the sunset review initiated, whereas under US law it is enough for one company to simply manifest its interest. Without such so-called "adequate response" from a domestic producer (which can be a two-line letter), DOC *must* terminate the sunset review by law.[68] This clearly shows that the automatic self-initiation by DOC is simply a device for lowering the level of evidence required from the domestic industry in order to initiate a sunset review.

[68] Section 751(c)3(A) of the Tariff Act 1930 states under the heading "No response": "*If no interested party responds to the notice of initiation under this subsection, the administering authority shall issue a final determination, within 90 days after the initiation of a review, revoking the order or terminating the suspended investigation to which such notice relates*".

Such is possible only if one admits that an investigating authority can initiate a sunset review automatically, i.e. by definition without any shred of evidence.

Q14. In paragraph 52 of its oral statement at the first meeting of the Panel, the European Communities comments that "a panel must not only revise the evidence submitted to it by the parties, but also all other evidence, including evidence it might consider necessary to get it [sic] itself under Article 13 DSU". Could the European Communities explain this view in light of the recent decision of the Appellate Body in *United States – Cotton Yarn*[69] concerning the evidence a panel may consider in reviewing a determination by a Member?

Reply

5.212 The EC agrees with the Appellate Body's findings in paragraphs 62-81 of the report in *United States – Cotton Yarn*. The Appellate Body has taken particular care to clarify that its findings in that case were limited only "to facts which predate the determination, but which was not in existence at the time the determination was made" by the competent authorities of a Member (at paragraphs 67 and 78). It also clarified that the evidence it was dealing with in that case was "evidence in the form of data that had not been compiled at the time of the determination and, hence, could not have been known." (at footnotes 39 and 51). It follows from the above description that the factual basis of the EC's claim in the present case is very different from the one examined by the Appellate Body in the *Cotton Yarn* case. The evidence the EC claims the US authorities should have taken into account is evidence that definitively existed at the time the determination made by the DOC and, moreover, it was well known to the US authorities since they were the actual authors of that evidence (which is also in the form of data on the declining balance methodology and the level of subsidization of the German exporters under the CIG programme). The accuracy of the above is not denied even by the DOC in its final determination in this case nor by the US's submissions to the Panel so far.

5.213 The EC also agrees with the summary of the "key elements" the Appellate Body laid down on the standard of review that panels should follow under Article 11 of the DSU (at para. 74). The EC notes that the Appellate Body cited with approval its previous finding that the national authorities "must undertake additional investigative steps, when the circumstances so require, in order to fulfil their obligation to evaluate all relevant factors" (at para. 73). That is why the EC considers that for the purpose of determining whether the US authorities have evaluated all relevant factors and examined all pertinent facts, the Panel can take advantage of the provision of Article 13 of the DSU. It is also noteworthy that in the view of the Appellate Body "in describing the duties of competent authorities, we simultaneously define the duties of panels in reviewing the investigations and determinations carried out by competent authorities" (at para. 73). Furthermore, the EC agrees that the standard of review laid down by the Appellate Body with respect to the Safeguards Agreement are equally applicable to the standard of review to be applied under the SCM *Agreement* (at para. 76).

---

[69] *United States – Transitional Safeguard Measure on Combed Cotton Yarn from Pakistan* ("*United States – Cotton Yarn*"), Report of the Appellate Body, WT/DS192/AB/R, adopted 5 November 2001, paras. 67-81.

5.214 What is particularly important is the finding by the Appellate Body that "a panel reviewing the due diligence exercised by a Member in making its determination ... has to put itself in the place of that Member at the time it makes its determination" (at para. 78). Application of this principle to the facts of the present case would clearly require the present Panel to consider the evidence that existed and was made available to the US DOC but which it refused to take into account on the erroneous allegation that it was submitted outside the time limit. This was not only relevant evidence but evidence indispensable for the proper conduct of the sunset review. The legal consequence of the US DOC's refusal to consider it should lead to the reversal of the DOC's findings. The EC does not request the Panel to carry out a *de novo* review in this case but simply to find that the DOC's determination is inconsistent with the US obligations under Article 21.3 of the *SCM Agreement* to determine subsidization, causality and injury, and because it refused to consider highly relevant evidence that existed at the time of the determination and of the existence of which they were fully aware at that time.

Q15. The Panel notes the following US statement: "As a starting point for making its likelihood determination in the sunset review, Commerce considered the countervailable subsidies and programmes used, and the amount of the subsidy determined, in the original investigation. As explained in Commerce's preliminary sunset determination, the rationale for this approach is that the findings in the original investigation provide the only evidence reflecting the behaviour of the respondents without the discipline of countervailing measures in place".[70] The Panel further notes the European Communities' arguments contained in paragraph 23 of its oral statement at the first meeting of the Panel. On what legal basis does the European Communities challenge the US Department of Commerce's ("DOC") use of the CVD rate from the original investigation (or a review under Article 21.2), and the rationale for the use of this rate?

Reply

5.215 The legal basis is Article 21.3, which imposes a clear obligation on the US authorities to make a fresh determination of likelihood of subsidization, causality and injury. The CVD rate from the original investigation may in some cases be an element to take into account in the fresh determination in a sunset review. However, the US law and practice is to use invariably this rate from the original investigation in sunset reviews, even in cases, such as the present one, where exporters and foreign governments have presented concrete and verifiable evidence to show that the subsidy has changed or ceased to exist.

5.216 The US argument that "...the findings in the original investigation provide the only evidence reflecting the behaviour of the respondents without the discipline of countervailing measures in place" is without merit, particularly in the case of a subsidy recognized by the US DOC to be a non-recurring one. In such a case, in the absence of new subsidies, it is definitively known that the amount of the subsidy will fall and is bound to disappear within the determined period of time in the original investigation.

---

[70] First Written Submission of the United States, para. 92 (footnote deleted).

5.217 The US DOC systematically refuses to change the original duty rate likely to prevail, even where administrative reviews have shown massive fall in non-recurring subsidies. In such cases, it always recommends the original rate, even if, as in some cases, this rate dates back to 15 years. For example, in the case of ***Certain carbon steel products from Sweden***, for which the expedited review was concluded on 29 March 2000, the US DOC alleged that the Swedish exporters will continue to benefit from two subsidy programmes beyond the end of the review. In light of this position, DOC has decided to confirm the original subsidy rate of 8.77 per cent, which dates from October 1985, even though in the most recent administrative review (covering the year 1997) the subsidy rate was determined to be only 0.72 per cent. Since the subsidies in question are long-term loans allocated over time, the future amounts of benefit are clearly predictable and are not going to increase. It is, therefore, hard to see how the subsidy amount will ever go beyond 0.72 per cent.

5.218 Similarly, in the case of ***Corrosion-resistant carbon flat steel products from France***, also concluded on 29 March 2000, the DOC has opted for the rate from the original investigation of 15.13 per cent, first imposed in 1993. Although no administrative reviews have been carried out in this case, a recent new countervailing duty investigation[71], presumably reflecting the level of subsidy without the discipline of an order in place, found a subsidy rate of 5.38 per cent for the company Usinor, the same exporter as in the above case. Given that the subsidies appear to be untied in both cases, there is no reason for the US DOC not to refer to sheet and strip rate in the context of the sunset review and to report a lower rate to the ITC. Furthermore, the US DOC appears to have much more flexibility when it comes to **increasing** the rate of a countervailing duty likely to prevail. In the ***Cut-To-Length Carbon Steel Plate from Belgium case (C-423-806),*** DOC increased the CVD rate which is likely to prevail from 0.96 per cent in the original investigation (of 1993) to 1.05 per cent in the sunset review. Although one administrative review was conducted by DOC in which the CVD rate was established at 0.69 per cent, DOC did not take these findings into account because it considers that all the subsidy programmes countervailed in the original investigation remained in place. Likewise, in the sunset review in the case of ***Sugar from the EC (C-408-046)***, a measure which dates from 1978, the CVD rate was increased from 10.8 cts/pound to 23.69 cts/pound.

5.219 If a final determination of likelihood of recurrence or continuation of subsidization and injury in a sunset review had to be based exclusively on evidence reflecting the behaviour of the exporters in the original investigation without taking into account the order in force, it is self-evident that a respondent will never succeed in getting rid of a CVD duty on such basis. As a matter of fact this is what happens in the US: DOC has never found until now that there was no likelihood of recurrence or continuation of subsidization in a CVD sunset review against EC exports.

5.220 There is, therefore, a need to understand what exactly the US means by using the terms "the findings in the original investigation provide the only evidence reflecting the behaviour of the respondents without the discipline of the countervailing measures in place". This reference to the so-called "discipline in place" in fact assimilates CVD orders to antidumping duties. The rationale of granting subsidies and imposing CVD orders are, however, drastically different from those pertaining to dumping and the imposition of AD duties. In the latter case there is one actor, the

[71] Stainless steel sheet and strip from France, July 1999.

individual exporter, who can swiftly decide the whole strategy of the company regarding when, where and at what price to export, if the AD duty were to expire. Conversely, in the case of subsidies the situation is not the same, because governments normally do not behave commercially in the same way as individual companies. For instance, in case of non-recurring subsidies, it is more reasonable to assume that governments will not rush again to grant a new subsidy if a CVD order were allowed to expire. The principle is that granting a new subsidy or increasing the level of an existing one is normally subject to rather different considerations (e.g. availability of funds, existence of social, regional, restructuring, environmental or other reasons in favour of continuing the subsidy, etc.), which distinguish them clearly from the natural desire of individual companies to swiftly divert exports in order to increase profits when an AD order is left to expire. Moreover, subsidies take normally time to be discussed and decided in national parliaments and this further distinguishes them from dumping practices. To speak of a "discipline in place", therefore, is to disregard completely the peculiarities and specificities of the reasons for which governments usually grant subsidies, compared to the risk of recurrence of dumping. It follows that as a matter of fact and law a CVD order is not a "discipline" in particular in case of non-recurring, declining subsidies, since such a subsidy has been given in the past, has been consumed for the period of time lapsed and is known that it will not recur in the future. It can, therefore, be said with confidence that in such cases the CVD order has no "disciplining" effect on exporters' behaviour. It also follows that applying again the rate of subsidy determined in the original investigation is a clear violation of Article 21.3 and the obligation to make a fresh determination on likelihood of subsidization, causality and injury.

Q16. Please respond to the following:

(a) Could the European Communities comment on the difficulty inherent in a review under Article 21.3 of making a forward-looking assessment, given that the data for the previous five years reflect government and exporter behaviour with "the discipline of countervailing measures in place"[72]?

Reply

5.221 First, as explained above, the EC contests the US assumption that there is "a discipline in place" which is likely to modify in any significant way the behaviour of governments and of the exporters in case a CVD order were allowed to expire. Second, a determination about the likelihood of continuation or recurrence of subsidization, causality and injury must necessarily be based on projections extrapolating from existing data. There is nothing unusual or especially difficult in this regard because governments are quite used to make this type of determinations in a number of situations. For example, in a different but, *mutatis mutandis*, comparable situation, the Appellate Body said in *United States – Lamb Safeguard* report the following:

> "*As facts, by their very nature, pertain to the present and the past, the occurrence of future events can never be definitively proven by facts.* There is, therefore, a tension between a future-oriented "threat" analysis, which, ultimately, calls for a degree of "conjecture" about the like-

[72] First Written Submission of the United States, para. 92.

> lihood of a future event, and the need for a fact-based determination. *Unavoidably, this tension must be resolved through the use of facts from the present and the past to justify the conclusion about the future, namely that serious injury is "clearly imminent"*.[73]

Had the US used facts from the present, and if necessary from the past, to justify its conclusions about the future in the present case, there should have been only one possible outcome, i.e. the termination of the CVD order in question because the level of the subsidy would have been clearly below the 1 per cent ad valorem *de minimis* rule applicable in reviews.[74] As explained time and time again, the CIG programme was determined by the US to be a non-recurring, declining subsidy. Applying the US's own calculation methodology, the amount that would have continued after 2000 is equivalent to zero. No new subsidies have been shown by DOC to exist or were likely to be granted in the period in question. There were, therefore, clearly no present or past facts that could justify a conclusion about the future different from the need to terminate immediately the CVD order applicable to the products in question.

5.222 The EC does not accept, therefore, the view that a review under Article 21.3 involves difficulties. Governments are used to this type of calculations and there can be no excuse to merely side step any need to undertake a fresh froward-looking determination in a sunset review on the basis of such alleged difficulties. Therefore, the EC considers that, as a general rule, the same elements, which the investigating authorities took into account in the original investigation in a retrospective manner, should be analysed in a prospective way during the sunset review.

(b) What range of factors needs to be taken into account, in the view of the European Communities, in making this forward-looking assessment?

Reply

5.223 As explained above, the EC considers that, as a general rule, the same elements and factors that the investigating authorities took into account in the original investigation in a retrospective manner should be analysed in a prospective way during the sunset review. These are laid down essentially in Articles 11, 12 and 15 of the *SCM Agreement*. However, the range of factors to be taken into account in making the forward-looking assessment necessary to establish the likelihood of recurrence or continuation of subsidization has to be evaluated on case by case basis, as it mainly depends on the kind of subsidy under examination. For example, if it is a recurring unemployment subsidy, the investigating authorities should consider the likelihood of lay-offs within the reasonable future. In the case at issue, however, the main subsidy was a non-recurring subsidy that by definition cannot recur. There could have been no continuation of benefits in such a case, if the US authorities were simply to take into consideration the calculation memorandum that was part of the file of the original investigation.

---

[73] See Appellate Body Report, *United States - Safeguard Measures on Imports of Fresh or Frozen Lamb Meat from New Zealand and Australia ("United States - Lamb Safeguard")*, WT/DS177/AB/R, WT/DS178/AB/R, adopted 16 May 2001, para. 136, emphasis added.

[74] Moreover, it would have also been below the 0.5 per cent ad valorem *de minimis* rule applied by the US under national law.

5.224 As noted above, an aspect to be considered in order to determine the likelihood of recurrence or continuation of subsidization may also be the CVD rate from the original investigation. But there are several other factors and some of them may be more relevant and important ones. For example, consideration should be given to old subsidy programmes now terminated, new subsidy programmes that did not exist at the time the original investigation was made, changes in existing programmes, economic situation of the exporting company, its production, etc. These are some very important factors to be taken into account in a sunset review, together with the expected behaviour of the foreign government. In a sunset review, the forward-looking aspect of the assessment, implied by the terms "would be likely to lead to", refers in particular to the continuation or recurrence of subsidization, causality and injury. Because this involves a certain amount of projections extrapolating from existing data, it may be argued that Article 21.3 somewhat "softens" the requirements in particular of Articles 11.2 and 11.3 of the *SCM Agreement* relating to the "existence" of subsidization and injury. However, a sunset review determination that is based only on the CVD rate established in the original investigation or one that does not apply the 1 per cent *de minimis* rule violates clearly the whole object and purpose of the *SCM Agreement*. The US, instead of conducting a fresh "determination" in the proper sense of this term, advance as excuse reasons pertaining to the difficulties in calculating the numerator or denominator in the formula used to calculate the subsidy. These are not exceptional nor insurmountable difficulties, however, and the US takes no concrete steps and does absolutely nothing positive to deal with them, other than simply acknowledge their existence.

(c) In this regard, the Panel notes the view of the European Communities – expressed in response to an oral question posed by the Panel at its first meeting – that the CVD rate from the original investigation can only be "a starting-point". Please explain in detail.

Reply

5.225 As explained above, the CVD rate from the original investigation may be just one of the factors to take into account in a sunset review. In this sense only it is a "starting point". For example, it is obvious that in a case of a non-recurring, declining subsidy the original CVD rate cannot be used as such, since the benefits of the subsidy are bound to expire.

5.226 On a more general plane, it should be noted that the text of Article 21.3 does not state expressly how exactly to conduct a sunset determination. However, there is nothing unusual in that, as other provisions of the same Agreement or of other WTO Agreements do not always laid down in detail provisions about their concrete application and implementation. This is because the applicable rules can be easily inferred. The identification of those rules is normally done on the basis of the customary rules of interpretation of public international law (Art. 3.2 DSU). One such recent example provides the Appellate Body report in *United States – Cotton Yarn* case, where the Appellate Body recognized the lack of explicit provisions on how to conduct a comparative analysis of the effects of imports under Article 6.4, second sentence, of the ATC Agreement (at paragraph 117), and resolved the issue by having recourse to the generally accepted rules of interpretation in the ensuing paragraphs (paras. 117-121) before turning to the specific provision of Article 6.4 and the facts of that case (at paras. 122-127).

5.227 This is what the EC proposes the Panel to do also in the present case. As explained above, as well as in the written and oral submissions, a sunset determination has, as a starting point, to take account of the same elements and factors that the investigating authorities took into account in the original investigation. This is, however, obviously not enough in the context of a sunset review for a number of reasons, e.g. because old subsidy programmes may now be terminated, new subsidy programmes may enter into force that did not exist at the time the original investigation was made, changes in existing programmes, economic situation of the exporting company, its production, etc. The non-recurring and declining nature of the subsidy is also a very important factor to take into account. To interpret the text of Article 21.3 otherwise would be to reduce the terms "shall determine" and the whole object and purpose of sunset reviews to inutility, as the Appellate Body said in the *United States – Cotton Yarn* case (at para. 121), because this will lead to the unjustified continuation of CVD measures for five more years. The US law and practice on sunset reviews provides a concrete example of such a flagrant violation of these basic principles of interpretation, because the US does not apply the 1 per cent *de minimis* rule in sunset reviews. The result is that a subsidy that was found to be below the 1 per cent *de minimis* rule in the original investigation will continue for five more years because the US uses in sunset reviews the CVD rate established in the original investigation.

Q17. Please explain what the European Communities understands by the term "total steel sales", contained in paragraph 5 of the European Communities' oral statement at the first meeting of the Panel, and how it applies to the calculation of likely ad valorem subsidy rates.

Reply

5.228 The term "total steel sales" contained in paragraph 5 of the EC's oral statement refers to the total sales of the respondent companies in 1991. Pursuant to its regulations, the US DOC calculates an ad valorem subsidy rate for domestic subsidies by dividing the amount of the benefit allocated to the period of investigation by the sales value of all products sold by the respondent during the period of investigation (19 C.F.R. § 351.525(a) & (b)(3)).

Q18. In the view of the European Communities, were the EC respondent parties given "ample opportunity [by the DOC] to present in writing all evidence which they consider[ed] relevant in respect of the investigation in question", within the meaning of Article 12.1:

(a) Prior to the DOC's determination of 20 October 1999 to conduct a full review under Article 21.3;

(b) Following such determination and prior to the DOC's preliminary determination of 27 March 2000; and

(c) Following such determination and prior to the DOC's final determination of 2 August 2000?

Why or why not?

Reply

5.229 As regards (a) above, the EC respondent parties were not given any opportunity, let alone an ample one, to present in writing "all evidence which they considered relevant in respect of the investigation in question". This is because the US authorities initiated automatically and of their initiative the sunset review. The US argument that the affected respondents had 15 months to prepare (e.g. para. 103 of 1st US written submission) is, therefore, totally misleading, false and irrelevant because the type of comments the respondents could and were allowed to submit before the initiation concerned only "the proposed schedule and grouping of reviews", not the substance of the conditions applicable for a sunset review (see Exhibit US-1, Federal Register/Vol. 63, No. 103/Friday, 29 May 1998/Notices, page 29373).

5.230 As regards (b) above, the US informed the respondents by letter of 26 August 1999, i.e. four days before the actual initiation of the reviews (1 September 1999) (See Exhibit US-2). This letter provided 15 days to file a "notice of intent to participate" and 30 more days therefrom to file "substantive responses". The rest of the information contained in the letter provided information on the formalities on such filings. The vague nature of the US DOC's information request, however, coupled with its refusal to accept any factual information after the initial 35 days of a sunset review proceeding violate the provisions of Article 12.1. Unlike in new countervailing duty investigations and administrative reviews, the US DOC does not issue questionnaires in a sunset review. Instead, the US DOC requires the interested parties to respond to a short list of questions contained in its regulations (see 19 C.F.R. § 351.218(d)(3)). Most of these questions are perfunctory in nature, seeking information concerning the name and address of the party's legal representative and the party's historic countervailing duty rates (see 19 C.F.R. § 351.218(d)(3)(ii)(A) & (iii)(A)). For example, with respect to the key issue of the likely continuation or recurrence of subsidization, the US DOC regulations simply request the interested party to provide a "statement regarding the likely effects of revocation of the order...under review, which must include any factual information, argument, and reason to support such statement." (see 19 C.F.R. § 351.218(d)(3)(ii)(F)).

5.231 In addition to this vague request for information, the US DOC regulations provide that "the Secretary normally will not accept or consider any additional information from a party after the time for filing rebuttals has expired." (see 19 C.F.R. § 351.218(d)(4)). Under the sunset regulations, rebuttals are required to be filed within 35 days of the publication of the notice of initiation in the Federal Register (see 19 C.F.R. § 351.218(d)(3) & (4)). Thus, under the US DOC's regulations, an interested party, guided only by the vague request to provide any factual information regarding the likely effects of revocation of the countervailing duty order, has merely 35 days to provide all of its factual information in the sunset review. Moreover, until the preliminary determination is made it knows completely nothing of the information possibly submitted by the other parties, the domestic industry or taken ex officio into account by DOC. In light of the fact that the sunset review statute provides DOC with 240 days in which to make its sunset review determination, there can be no justification for such a restrictively short period for providing factual information and to respond to the information submitted by the other interested parties (see 19 U.S.C. § 1675(c)(5)). Moreover, the fact that the US DOC's decision as to whether or not to conduct a full sunset review is not issued until 50 days after publication of the notice of initiation means that, even after the US DOC makes a determination to conduct a full sunset review, the parties will be given no additional opportunity whatsoever to submit factual information in this regard (see 19 C.F.R. § 351.218(e)(1)(ii)(C)(1)). The EC submits that in order to comply with the provisions of Article 12.1, the US DOC must inform the parties of the specific information it requires to complete its determination in the particular case, allow the parties access to the information submitted by the other interested parties and give all the parties ample opportunity to provide the information at a meaningful point in the proceedings. That is not done by the US in sunset reviews under the existing laws, regulations and practices and it was definitively not done in the present case.

5.232 As regards (c) above, the first time that the US DOC commented on the information submitted by the parties in this case was in its preliminary results of 20 March 2000. In its issues and decision memo, the US DOC ignore the evidence submitted by the Government of Germany and the German producers showing that the CIG programme applied only to investments made prior to 1 January 1986 and that the amount of Capital Investment Grants paid after 1986 was so small that no countervailable benefit would remain after the end of the sunset review (see Issues and Decision Memo at p. 24-25, Exhibit EC-7). The DOC simply stated that, because there was evidence that Capital Investment Grants were received as late as 1990, it would "determine that benefit streams from this programme continue beyond the end of this sunset review." (Ibidem, at 25). It is important to underline that the US DOC did not give the German respondents any opportunity to submit additional evidence to respond to its comments in the preliminary determination. As explained in our written and oral submissions, the US DOC even refused a request to review its own calculation memoranda from the original investigation to determine the exact amount of the original grant payments made after 1986. The EC believes that such a procedure that leaves respondents in complete darkness as to precisely what information an investigating authority requires until it is too late to provide the information cannot satisfy the requirements of Article 12.1. The US law and practice does not respect several provisions of Article 12 of the *SCM Agreement*, which by virtue of Article 21.4 is fully applicable to sunset reviews. In particular, Articles 12.1 and 12.1.1 lay down a general obligation to provide "ample opportunity" to exporters to present in writing all evidence they consider relevant. Article 12.2 allows also for the right to present information orally. Article 12.3 establishes in effect a procedure of mutual dialogue by providing that the affected exporters should be given timely opportunity "to see all information that is relevant to the presentation of their cases ... and to prepare presentations on the basis of this information". Moreover, Article 12.8 provides that before the final determination is made, disclosure should take place "in such sufficient time for the parties to defend their interests". The principle underlying Article 12 of the *SCM Agreement*, therefore, is that during all stages of the reviews the interested parties should be give ample opportunity to present evidence, to have access to the evidence presented by the other parties (except where confidentiality applies), to present counter-evidence and to defend their interests at all stages leading up to the final determination. As explained above, all these procedural rights and due process requirements are not respected by the US DOC in sunset reviews and in the present case.

Q19. Does the European Communities consider that a review under Article 21.3 must involve a *full* CVD investigation? Please explain.

Reply

5.233 In principle yes. As stated above in response to question 7, investigating authorities in a sunset review must determine that all the conditions for the imposition of a countervailing duty, as laid down in Article 19.1, will continue or recur if the duty is terminated. However, since a CVD measure is already in force, this cannot be entirely identical to a new countervailing duty investigation. However, the investigating authority must collect, consider and, where appropriate, verify all available and relevant evidence in making its sunset determination. As explained above, it must also allow parties access to and provide them with ample opportunity to comment and defend their interests at all stages of the review, as happens in an original investigation.

5.234 The US DOC failed to do this in the present sunset review. For example, with respect to the CIG programme, US DOC ignored evidence that the CIG programme applied only to investments made prior to 1 January 1986 and that the amount of Capital Investment Grants paid after 1986 was so small that no countervailable benefit would remain after the end of the sunset review. The US DOC made no attempt to actually measure the benefit that would remain under the CIG programme after the end of the sunset review or to adjust the subsidy rate for the grants that were made prior to the end of 1986, the benefit of which would have expired under the 15-year allocation period. The US DOC simply continued to apply the 0.39 per cent subsidy rate calculated for this programme for the 1991 period covered by the original investigation, as if the programme were likely to confer the same benefit in 2001 as it did ten years earlier in 1991. The US DOC even refused to consult its calculation memoranda from the original investigation to determine the amount of grants paid after 1986.

5.235 This irrefutable presumption that the benefit of the CIG programme remained unchanged since 1991 is directly contrary to the evidence presented in the case. Because the CIG programme applied only to investments made prior to 1 January 1986, there is no conceivable way that the benefit in 2001 would continue at the same level as in 1991. This is especially true in light of the evidence that the last grant payment under this programme was made in 1990. Even the US producers conceded that the CIG programme had expired (see Issues and Decision Memo at 25 n.36 (Exhibit EC-7)).

Q20. In the view of the European Communities, does the *SCM Agreement* require the record of the original investigation, in its entirety, to be made part of the record of the review under Article 21.3? Please explain in detail.

Reply

5.236 Yes. It is beyond doubt that Article 21.4 requires ("shall apply") the authorities to give parties in a sunset review access to the entire record (that is all information and evidence relevant to an investigation and not covered by the confidentiality provisions) in the same way as in the original investigation. For example, to the extent that the US DOC relies upon the rates calculated in its original investigation, it must, at minimum, make its original determination and all documents showing how the rates therein were calculated (i.e., the calculation memoranda) part of the record of the sunset review. Moreover, Article 12.2 requires that any decision must be based only on information what is in the record and which has been made available to all parties. Article 12.3 requires that all parties should be able to see all information that is relevant, and Article 12.8 requires that all essential facts should be made available in sufficient time for the parties to defend their interests.

5.237 It follows that the US DOC cannot evade this responsibility by claiming that it is somehow prohibited by US law from making the memoranda part of the record in the sunset review (see U.S. 1st written submission, at para. 104). The US International Trade Commission ("ITC") is subject to the same procedures regarding the treatment of business proprietary information as the US DOC. However, unlike DOC, the US ITC in its sunset reviews automatically makes the confidential version of its original determination, as well as the complete staff report from the original investigation, part of the record of the sunset review. This is done automatically right at the beginning of the review so that all parties will be able to use this information in preparing their arguments. The ITC simply provides the documents the same confidential status in the review that they enjoyed in the original investigation.

F. Responses of the United States to Questions from the Panel Following the First Meeting of the Panel

5.238 With respect to the Panel's question concerning the Article 11.9 *de minimis* standard and reviews under Article 21.2, for essentially the same reasons set forth in the United States' First Written Submission and Oral Statement, the *de minimis* standard contained in Article 11.9 is not applicable to reviews under Article 21.2. In particular, as is the case with respect to Article 21.3, there is no reference to Article 11.9 or any other *de minimis* standard in Article 21.2. It seems evident that had the drafters of the *SCM Agreement* wished such a reference, one could have been easily made. Furthermore, the panel in *Korea DRAMs* addressed this issue (albeit in the context of antidumping administrative reviews) and came to the same conclusion.

5.239 With respect to the Panel's question concerning negligible import volume and injury standards under Article 11.9 and the negligible injury standard under Article 15.3, and reviews under Article 21.2, with respect to Article 11.9, as stated above, Article 21.2 neither refers to nor incorporates any provisions of Article 11.9. With respect to Article 15.3, the United States directs the Panel's attention to the fact that this article does not refer to a "negligible *injury* standard." Rather, in connection with cumulation, Article 15.3 addresses the question of whether the *volume of imports* in an original investigation is negligible. Article 21.2 does not incorporate the provisions of Article 15.3.

5.240 With respect to the Panel's question concerning negligible import volume and injury standards under Article 11.9 and the negligible injury standard under Article 15.3, and reviews under Article 21.3, the negligibility provisions do not apply to Article 21.3 for the same reasons they do not apply to Article 21.2.

5.241 With respect to the Panel's questions concerning the applicability of the Article 27.10 negligible import volume standards and the Article 27.10(b) and Article 27.11 *de minimis* standards to reviews under Article 21, these negligibility provisions, like those contained in Articles 11.9 and 15.3, apply only to original investigations. Similarly, the *de minimis* standards for various developing countries, like the standard contained in Article 11.9, only apply to original investigations.

5.242 With respect to the Panel's questions concerning the impact of the large volume of "transition" orders on the genesis of the United States' sunset rules, on January 1, 1995, the date on which the WTO Agreement entered into force with respect to the United States, there were over 300 antidumping and countervailing duty orders in existence. Pursuant to its obligations under Article 32.4 of the *SCM Agreement* (and Article 18.3.2 of the AD Agreement), the United States deemed all of these "transition" orders to be imposed on January 1, 1995. Consequently, the United States was obligated to initiate sunset reviews of all of these transition orders no later than 1 January 2000, the *de jure* five-year anniversary date of the orders. In its First Written Submission, the United States described in detail the process it used to determine and publicly announce the schedule for the conduct of the sunset reviews of the transition orders.

5.243 When developing its procedures for sunset reviews, the United States certainly took into account the monumental task of initiating over 300 sunset reviews of transition orders. However, it is difficult to measure the extent to which the volume of the transition orders initially shaped both the procedural and substantive rules now in place. Procedurally, the rules with respect to sunset reviews of transition orders and those of non-transition orders differ very little. One notable difference that takes into account the volume of transition orders concerns Commerce's ability to extend its deadlines for its preliminary and final determinations. Substantively, Commerce's analysis is the same for transition orders and non-transition orders.

5.244 With respect to the Panel's question concerning when a sunset review is considered to be initiated, section 351.218(c)(1) of Commerce's *Sunset Regulations* provides that no later than 30 days before the fifth anniversary date of an order or suspension of an investigation, the Secretary will publish a notice of initiation of a sunset review. In order to provide to the public advance notice of the initiation of sunset reviews, Commerce provides on its website (http://ia.ita.doc.gov/sunset/schedule.htm) the schedule for sunset review initiations through calendar year 2005. With respect to the sunset reviews of transition orders, Commerce published its initiation schedule in the *Federal Register* on 28 May 1998.

5.245 With respect to the Panel's question concerning Commerce's adequacy determination and information collected after that determination, following normal procedures, Commerce promulgated its determination to conduct a full sunset review in the form of a decision memorandum issued and made public on October 20, 1999. The specific factual information needed to determine whether to conduct a full sunset review (*i.e.*, aggregate export figures) is only *a small part* of the information and argument contained in the original substantive responses submitted by the interested parties. Commerce normally does not collect additional information after it makes its adequacy determination. Commerce, therefore, did not collect any additional information between its 20 October 1999, adequacy determination and its 27 March 2000, preliminary determination. Between the time of its adequacy determination and its preliminary determination, Commerce analyzes and considers all of the remaining information and argument provided by the parties; *i.e.*, the bulk of the responses.

5.246 With respect to the Panel's questions concerning whether there is a "presumption" in the *SCM Agreement* that no provision of the Agreement is applicable to reviews under Article 21.3 unless specifically indicated, the United States considers that, in light of the text and context of Article 21.3, no provisions are applicable to reviews under Article 21.3, unless specifically indicated. In the view of the United

States, it is not a matter of there being a "presumption". Instead, it is a matter of what the text of Article 21.3 provides, as interpreted in accordance with the rules of Article 31 of the *Vienna Convention on the Law of Treaties*. There are several ways in which other provisions of the Agreement may be applicable to the provisions of Article 21.3. There could be a cross-reference between the two provisions, a reference in one provision to the other, or a general statement that a provision applies throughout the Agreement or throughout Part V of the Agreement. There are no such references with respect to the Article 11.6 evidentiary requirements for self-initiation or the Article 11.9 *de minimis* standard.

5.247 The United States considers that other provisions of the *SCM Agreement* would apply to reviews under Article 21.3 where the Agreement says they apply. Examples of other provisions that apply to Article 21.3 are: the definition of "subsidy" in Article 1 ("For the purpose of this Agreement"); the definition of "interested parties" in Article 12.9 ("for the purposes of this Agreement"); calculation of the amount of a subsidy under Article 14 ("For the purpose of Part V"); definition of "injury" under Article 15 and footnote 45 ("Under this Agreement"); definition of "like product" under footnote 46 ("Throughout this Agreement"); definition of domestic industry in Article 16 ("For the purposes of this Agreement"); definition of "levy" under footnote 51 ("As used in this Agreement").

5.248 With respect to the Panel's questions concerning the methodology for the calculation of the level of subsidization and the *ad valorem* rate in reviews under Article 21.3 versus in original investigations, the United States notes, as an initial matter, that the *SCM Agreement* does not specify a methodology for calculating the *ad valorem* rate. If Commerce were to calculate the level of subsidization in the context of reviews conducted under Article 21.3, it certainly would apply the same calculation methodology as it applies in original investigations conducted under Article 11. However, Commerce does not *calculate* the level of subsidization in sunset reviews. Article 21.3 does not require such a calculation. What Article 21.3 does require is that a countervailing duty be terminated not later that five years from the date upon which it is imposed, unless the authorities determine that expiry of the duty would be likely to lead to continuation or recurrence of subsidization and injury.

5.249 With respect to the Panel's question as to whether the injury test applicable to investigations is also applicable to reviews under Article 21.3, the Article 21.3 injury standard is not the same as the standard for injury in original investigations, although it contains some of the same elements. The injury determinations in original investigations are governed by the provisions of Article 15 of the *SCM Agreement* and Article VI of GATT 1994. Paragraph 6 of Article VI conditions the levying of countervailing duties on a determination that the effects of the subsidized imports are "such as to cause or threaten material injury to an established domestic industry, or [ ] such as to retard materially the establishment of a domestic industry." Article 15 of the *SCM Agreement* further specifies the factors that investigating authorities must consider in reaching "[a] determination of injury for purposes of Article VI of GATT 1994".

5.250 The aim of the Article 21.3 review is to determine whether revocation of the countervailing duty would be likely to lead to continuation or recurrence of injury. Footnote 45 to Article 15 indicates that the term *injury* as used throughout the Agreement "shall be interpreted in accordance with the provisions of this Article." In turn, Article 15 specifies three general criteria – volume, price effects and impact on the domestic industry – that are pertinent to any *injury* determination under the Agreement.

5.251 The focus of a review under Article 21.3, however, differs from that of an original investigation under Article 15. The nature and practicalities of the two types of inquiries demonstrate that the tests for the two cannot be identical. In an original investigation, the investigating authorities examine the condition of an industry that has been exposed to the effects of the subsidized imports. In that investigation, an authority examines the relationship between import-related factors (such as relative and absolute increases in import volumes and underselling and other price effects) to industry-related factors (such as trade, financial and employment data that have a bearing on the state of the industry and that may be indicative of present injury or imminent threat of injury). *See* Articles 15.5 and 15.7. Five years later, as a result of the countervailing duty order, subsidized imports may have either decreased or exited the market altogether, or if they maintain their presence in the market, may be priced higher than they were during the original investigation, when they were entering the market unencumbered by any additional duties. Thus, the inquiry contemplated in a review conducted pursuant to Article 21.3 is counterfactual in nature, and entails application of a somewhat different standard with respect to the volume, price and relevant industry factors. An authority must decide the likely impact of a prospective change in the status quo, *i.e.*, the revocation of the countervailing duty order and the elimination of its restraining effects on volumes and prices of imports.

5.252 With respect to the Panel's question as to whether, under US law, the Article 11.4 industry support provisions are applicable in a review under Article 21.3, the conditions of Article 11.4, with respect to industry support, are not required to be fulfilled in order for Commerce to conduct a sunset review under US law. Article 21.3 itself contains no requirement in this regard and contains no reference to Article 11.4 or the industry support requirements of that provision.

5.253 With respect to the Panel's question as to whether the Article 16 definition of domestic industry must be taken into account in the USITC's assessment of the likelihood of continuation or recurrence of injury in a review under Article 21.3, the answer is yes. Article 21.3 addresses the inquiry into whether revocation of the countervailing duty would be likely to lead to continuation or recurrence of *injury*. Footnote 45 to Article 15 of the *SCM Agreement* specifies that, "[u]nder this Agreement, the term 'injury' shall, unless otherwise specified, be taken to mean material injury *to a domestic industry*, threat of material injury *to a domestic industry*, or material retardation of the establishment *of such industry*...". (Emphasis added). Article 21.3 does not contain an exception to the general definition, and therefore, the *injury* referred to in that Article is relative to the condition of *the domestic industry*. Article 16 addresses the definition of the domestic industry "[f]or the purposes of this Agreement," and therefore applies in the context of addressing the continuation or recurrence of injury under Article 21.3.

5.254 With respect to the Panel's question as to what textual support exists in the *SCM Agreement* for the proposition that no *de minimis* standard is applicable to reviews under Article 21.3 as it is in original investigations, under Article 11.9, Members must apply a 1 per cent *de minimis* standard in countervailing duty *investigations*. Nothing in the text of Articles 11.9 or 21.3 requires application of the Article 11.9, 1 per cent *de minimis* standard in Article 21.3 sunset reviews, or any other type of review. As discussed above, there is no reference in Article 21.3 to a *de minimis* standard and the text of Article 11.9 makes no reference to Article 21.3.

5.255 With respect to the Panel's request that the United States respond to arguments in the EC's Oral Statement concerning the use and relevance of footnote 52, in its Oral Statement, the EC opined that the United States has confused the purposes of an administrative (*i.e.*, assessment) review and a sunset review and the application of footnote 52. It is the EC that is confused. Pursuant to Article 21.3 and footnote 52, the mere existence of a subsidy programme, even with a net countervailable subsidy rate of zero, could form the basis for a determination of likelihood of future subsidization in accordance with Article 21.3 and footnote 52. The United States agrees with the EC that footnote 52 refers to a situation where the authority determines that the subsidy rate for a particular time period is zero and that, in the United States, that determination takes place in the context of an administrative review. (Although not necessarily germane to the instant dispute, the United States does not agree with the EC's statement that footnote 52 refers to a situation where a subsidy is "*de minimis*" in an administrative review. Footnote 52 only discusses a finding in the most recent assessment proceeding that "no duty" is to be levied.) The EC seems to think, however, that footnote 52 serves no other purpose than to make a point about administrative reviews. The EC posits that "[s]unset reviews under Article 21.3 are completely different from administrative reviews". If that is so, why then did the Members include footnote 52 in Article 21.3, the provision governing sunset reviews? There must be a reason. The United States considers that footnote 52 means that the current level of subsidization is not decisive as to whether subsidization is likely to recur. The EC has not offered any alternative interpretation. The reason for this gap in the EC's argumentation is that the EC's claim that a *de minimis* standard is required in the context of Article 21.3 sunset reviews would render note 52 meaningless.

5.256 With respect to the Panel's question concerning the rationale for the United States' application of a 0.5 per cent *de minimis* standard in sunset reviews, as a matter of domestic policy, Commerce has long applied a 0.5 per cent *de minimis* standard in administrative (*i.e.*, assessment) reviews. The application of this standard pre-dates the Uruguay Round negotiations. The entry into force of the WTO Agreement did not require a change in this standard, because the Article 11.9 *de minimis* standard is only applicable to investigations. For this same reason, when the United States amended its law in 1994 to provide for sunset reviews, it chose to apply its long-standing 0.5 per cent *de minimis* standard to sunset reviews. The United States could have chosen to apply no *de minimis* standard to sunset reviews at all.

5.257 In a sunset review, the *de minimis* standard has particular application in several respects. For example, if Commerce determined in a sunset proceeding, based on the original investigation and any administrative reviews, that the existing countervailable subsidy programmes had been terminated and that the likely net countervailable rate of subsidization was *de minimis*, Commerce normally would determine that there was *no* likelihood of continuation or recurrence of subsidization. In addition, if the combined benefits of all programmes considered in the sunset review have never been above *de minimis* at any time the order was in effect, and there is no likelihood that the combined benefits of such programmes would be above *de minimis* in the event of removal of the duty, Commerce normally would determine that there is no likelihood of continuation or recurrence of subsidization.

5.258 In 1987, following a notice and comment rulemaking proceeding, Commerce published a final regulation codifying its long-standing practice of applying a 0.5 per cent *de minimis* standard in investigations and administrative reviews. In response to Commerce stated that "[t]he doctrine of *de minimis non curat lex*, that the law does not concern itself with trifles, is a basic tenet of Anglo-American jurisprudence, inherent in all US laws. With respect to the antidumping and countervailing duty laws, the Department has concluded that the potential benefits to domestic petitioners from orders on dumping margins or net subsidies below 0.5% are outweighed by the gains in productivity and efficiency provided by a *de minimis* rule.... [I]t would be unreasonable for the Department and the US Customs Service to squander their scarce resources administering orders for which the dumping margins or the net subsidies are below 0.5%". 52 FR at 30661.

5.259 With respect to the Panel's question concerning the relationship between duty assessment proceedings ("administrative reviews") and reviews under Article 21.3, the United States has a "retrospective" assessment system under which the amount of final liability for countervailing duties is determined after the subject merchandise is imported. The normal procedure used for determining the amount of final liability is the administrative review procedure. In contrast, a sunset review is not a procedure for determining the amount of final countervailing duty liability. The purpose of the sunset review is to determine the likelihood of the continuation or recurrence of subsidization in the event that the countervailing duty is revoked. Thus, a sunset review involves a prediction of a government's future behaviour without the discipline of an order in place. The focus of the analysis is predictive, as opposed to a focus on the present or the past.

5.260 With respect to the Panel's question concerning the ability of the German producers, the German government, and the EC Commission to request an administrative review of the countervailing duty order on certain steel flat products from Germany, Commerce's regulations provide no absolute requirement for shipments as a pre-requisite to an administrative review and provide Commerce with the discretion to conduct a "no shipment" administrative review of an order. Concerning the textual basis for this in the *SCM Agreement*, as discussed above, Commerce's regulations do not make the existence of shipments an absolute prerequisite for an administrative review. Instead, the regulations provide Commerce with the discretion to conduct a "no shipment" administrative review of an order. In this regard, Articles 19 and 21.2 of the *SCM Agreement* do not preclude no shipment administrative reviews.

5.261 In response to the Panel's question concerning the option of a changed circumstances review, yes, a "changed circumstances" review is discretionary and may be initiated when Commerce (or the USITC) determines that conditions warranting such a review exist. Such reviews normally are initiated based on a request from an interested party.

5.262 In response to the Panel's questions concerning the administrative record from the original investigation, no, the administrative record from Commerce's original countervailing duty investigation does not automatically become part of the administrative record of the sunset review. Under US law and Commerce regulations, each individual review (whether administrative, sunset, or changed circumstances) by Commerce is considered a separate segment of the proceeding, with a separate and distinct administrative record, and separately reviewable by domestic courts. Pursuant to section 751(c) of the Act and consistent with Article 21.3 of the *SCM Agree-*

ment, Commerce automatically self-initiates sunset reviews. Therefore, Commerce did not use any information from the original investigation to initiate the sunset review of the order on corrosion-resistant carbon steel flat products from Germany.

5.263 In response to the Panel's question concerning a particular calculation memorandum from the original investigation, yes, 13 April 2000 was the first time that the German exporters made a request to have the calculation memorandum placed on the administrative record of the sunset review. In response to the Panel's questions concerning other requests to place information from the administrative record in the original investigation on the administrative record of the sunset review, with respect to business confidential information, no other interested parties placed, or requested that Commerce place, such information on the administrative record during the sunset review. As discussed in the United States' First Written Submission, in the instant case, Commerce accepted and considered submissions or parts of submissions from the US producers and the German Government which included public information from the original investigation. Specifically, Commerce accepted a submission from the US producers dated 28 April and portions of a German government submission of 18 April.

5.264 In accepting the US producers' submission, Commerce considered that the submission contained the *public* version of Preussag's questionnaire response from the original investigation and that the US producers had submitted the document because the German producers had cited to the questionnaire response in one of their submissions prior to the deadline for factual information without submitting the document itself. Commerce also accepted portions of the German Government's 18 April submission. Commerce, however, only accepted those portions of the German Government's submission that were part of the original investigation, contained *no new factual information*, and were *publicly available*. None of the information accepted by Commerce in this instance was confidential information that would have been unavailable to other parties such as the US producers.

5.265 With respect to the Panel's question concerning the use of the word "determine" as used in Article 21.3, Article 21.3 establishes that in the context of the sunset review, Commerce is obligated to determine whether expiry of the countervailing duty would be likely to lead to continuation or recurrence of subsidization. The definition of "determine" in the context of Article 21.3 requires a decision about something. In *The New Shorter Oxford English Dictionary*, "determine" is defined as to "settle or decide (a dispute, controversy, etc., or a sentence, conclusion, issue, etc.) as a judge or arbiter." Further, this entry contains the notation "foll{owed} by simple obj{ect}, subord{inate} cl{ause} w{ith} *that, what, whether, etc.*" The United States considers that this is precisely the manner in which the word "determine" is used in Article 21.3. Article 21.3 requires the authorities to determine or decide something, *i.e.*, whether subsidization is likely to continue or recur. The United States considers that it may determine, in accordance with Article 21.3, whether subsidization is likely to continue or recur without conducting its own investigation, but, rather, by making its decision based on the evidentiary record developed during the sunset review because all parties, both foreign and domestic, have every opportunity under the US system to provide any information they deem relevant.

5.266 With respect to the Panel's question concerning the methodology used by the United States to determine the likelihood of continuation or recurrence of subsidization and injury, the substantive provisions governing likelihood of continuation or recurrence of subsidization are contained in Commerce's *Sunset Policy Bulletin*. In determining whether subsidization is likely to continue or recur, Commerce will consider the net countervailable subsidy determined in the investigation and subsequent reviews, and whether any change has occurred in programmes which gave rise to the net countervailable subsidy determined in the investigation and subsequent reviews. The USITC's regulations, at 19 CFR 207.60-207.69, address the procedures for conducting five-year review investigations to determine whether continuation of the countervailing duty would be likely to lead to continuation or recurrence of material injury.

5.267 With respect to the Panel's question as to whether, under the US system, original investigations and reviews under Article 21.3 are different segments of one proceeding, the answer is yes. Under the US system, a "proceeding" begins on the date of the filing of a petition and ends on, *inter alia*, the revocation of an order. A countervailing duty proceeding consists of one or more "segments". "Segment" refers to a portion of the proceeding that is separately judicially reviewable. For example, a countervailing duty investigation, an administrative review, or a sunset review each would constitute a segment of a proceeding. Each segment contains its own discrete administrative record. A final determination, and the discrete record upon which it is based, is subject to judicial review.

5.268 With respect to the Panel's questions concerning whether administrative reviews are prerequisites for conducting sunset reviews, under the US system, administrative reviews are not prerequisites for conducting full sunset reviews. However, as a starting point for making its likelihood determination in a sunset review, Commerce considers the countervailable subsidies and programmes found to be used, and the amount of the subsidy determined, in the original investigation. The rationale for this approach is that the findings in the original investigation provide the only evidence reflecting the behaviour of the respondents without the discipline of countervailing measures in place. This makes sense given that, in a sunset review under Article 21.3, an authority is considering whether, without the discipline of the duty, subsidization would likely continue or recur; *i.e.*, what would happen without the discipline of the duty. Commerce also considers its findings in administrative reviews subsequent to the original investigation because information developed during administrative reviews concerning subsidization – *e.g.*, additional subsidies and accompanying benefits granted after issuance of an order or programme terminations – may be an indicator of possible future subsidization or may demonstrate the cessation of subsidization. Finally, even if there has been no administrative review, Commerce will consider if is evidence demonstrating that programmes have been terminated with no residual benefits. In the instant case, even though no administrative review had been conducted, Commerce agreed with the EC and German producers that two programmes had been terminated with no residual benefits and adjusted the net subsidy rate accordingly.

5.269 With respect to the Panel's questions concerning a particular calculation memorandum and the use of this business confidential document in Commerce's sunset review, on 13 April 2000, the German producers in the sunset review sought to have *all* the calculation memoranda from the original investigation placed on the record of the sunset review. Commerce, however, could not move business confidential information from the record of one segment of the proceeding (*i.e.*, the investigation) to another separate segment of the proceeding (*i.e.*, the sunset review) without the express permission of the person who submitted the confidential information.

5.270 Article 12.4 of the *SCM Agreement* provides that confidential information shall not be disclosed without the specific permission of the party submitting it. Consistent with the obligations concerning the treatment of confidential information under Article 12, US law and Commerce regulations provide stringent requirements and safeguards regarding the disclosure and use of business confidential information in the context of countervailing duty proceedings under what is called an administrative protective order or "APO". The APOs granted during the original 1993 investigation would only have allowed for the disclosure of business confidential information in the context of that investigation, per the agreement of the party submitting the confidential information. As a result, Commerce could not accede to the German producers' request in the sunset review to move all the calculation memoranda from the record of the original investigation to the record of the sunset review without the permission of the parties who originally submitted the information. The request from the German producers in the sunset review contained no indication of such permission.

5.271 Under US law and regulations, certain information provided by interested parties in an administrative proceeding, whether an investigation or review, may be accorded business confidential treatment. Section 351.304 of Commerce's regulations sets forth the requirements for parties to claim that factual information should be considered business proprietary information and afforded protection from public disclosure. The claim for proprietary treatment must be made by the owner of the information, the information must be clearly identified, and the claim must be accompanied by an explanation why the information should be afforded proprietary treatment. The calculation memoranda from the original investigation would have contained the business confidential information of the three German producers of certain corrosion-resistant carbon steel flat products that were involved in the original investigation: Hoesch, Preussag, and Thyssen. These producers would have requested business confidential treatment for their data at the time they submitted the data during the original countervailing duty investigation in 1992-93. The German producers in the sunset review were Thyssen Krupp Stahl AG, Stahlwerke Bremen GmbH, EKO Stahl GmbH, and Salzgitter AG. The request from the German producers in the sunset review to move the business confidential information from the record of the original investigation to the record of the sunset review contains no indication that the German producers in the sunset review were authorized to permit the movement of such information. The particular document submitted by the EC in the instant case appears to contain business confidential information for Thyssen. In its First Written Submission, the EC itself notes that this exhibit contains business confidential information.

5.272 With respect to the Panel's questions concerning acceptance and consideration of certain evidence from respondent interested parties, section 351.218(d)(3)(v)(B) of Commerce's *Sunset Regulations* provides that interested parties may submit *any* relevant information or argument that the party would like Commerce to consider. Generally, therefore, Commerce will accept any evidence from foreign respondents, including evidence with respect to the issues set out in the Panel's question. In the context of a sunset review (or any other segment of a countervailing duty proceeding), Commerce considers all relevant evidence that is timely filed. Regarding the extent to which Commerce might base a particular determination on such evidence, it is difficult to say in the abstract. The relevance and probative value of a particular piece of evidence will vary from case to case. Suffice it to say that in the sunset review at issue in this dispute, Commerce considered information and argument from the EC and German producers in finding that two programmes had been terminated with no residual benefits. As a general proposition, Commerce's *Sunset Policy Bulletin* provides detailed guidance on analytical issues related to Commerce's determination of likelihood of continuation or recurrence of subsidization and the net countervailable subsidy rate likely to prevail if the duty were revoked.

5.273 With respect to the Panel's request for a schematic representation of the timing and information requirements under US law for sunset reviews, the United States provided copies of Annex VIII of Commerce's *Sunset Regulations*, which contains detailed schedules with timing and information requirements for Commerce sunset reviews, and Annex B of the ITC's *Sunset Regulations*, which provides a sample schedule for five-year reviews.

5.274 With respect to the Panel's request for certain figures concerning the United States' initiation and conduct of sunset reviews under Article 21.3, the United States indicated as follows: The number of sunset reviews under Article 21.3 initiated since 1 January 1995 is 56. The number of such reviews which resulted in revocation of the CVD order in question due to no filing by the domestic industry of a notice of intent to participate is 17. The number of expedited sunset reviews conducted since 1 January 1995 is 24. The number of such reviews which resulted in revocation of the CVD order in question, due to a finding of no likelihood of continuation or recurrence of subsidisation is 0, and due to a finding of no likelihood of continuation or recurrence of injury is 5. The number of full sunset reviews conducted since 1 January 1995 is 15. The number of such reviews which resulted in revocation of the CVD order in question, due to a finding of no likelihood of continuation or recurrence of subsidisation is 3, and due to a finding of no likelihood of continuation or recurrence of injury is 4.

G. *Responses of the United States to Questions from the European Communities Following the First Meeting of the Panel*

5.275 As an introductory matter, the United States observes that the EC in its questions makes various assumptions regarding the "purposes" of *SCM Agreement* provisions. In this regard, it is important to recall the explanation of the Appellate Body in *Japan – Alcoholic Beverages*: "the treaty's 'object and purpose' is to be referred to in determining the meaning of the 'terms of the treaty' and not as an independent basis for interpretation." In this dispute, the EC purports to find or discern various "purposes" without reference to the text of the *SCM Agreement*, and then refers to obligations not found in the text which presumably derive from these "purposes". This use of "purposes" is precisely the "independent basis for interpretation" which the Appellate Body described as incorrect, and operates to circumvent the requirement in DSU Article 3.2 that Dispute Settlement Body rulings cannot add to or diminish the rights and obligations provided in the covered agreements.

5.276 With respect to the EC's question concerning the meaning of "duly substantiated request", Article 21.3 of the *SCM Agreement* authorizes authorities to initiate a sunset review "on their own initiative *or* upon a duly substantiated request made by or on behalf of the domestic industry" (emphasis added). Under US law, Commerce automatically initiates a sunset review on its own initiative within five years of the date of publication of a countervailing duty order. US law does not contain a provision regarding initiation of sunset reviews based upon a "duly substantiated request".

5.277 With respect to the EC's question concerning "expression of interest" as applicable to initiation of sunset reviews, section 351.218(d)(1)(i) of Commerce's regulations provides for filing of a notice of intent to participate by domestic interested parties that intend to participate in a sunset review. Section 351.218(d)(1)(ii) sets forth the required contents of the notice of intent to participate, which includes, *inter alia*, information related to the identity of the domestic interested party and its legal counsel, whether the domestic interested party is related to foreign producers or exporters, the subject merchandise and country subject to the sunset review, and the applicable *Federal Register* citation. Section 351.303 of Commerce's regulations governs the filing, format, translation, service, and certification of documents, and applies to all persons submitting documents to Commerce for consideration in any segment of an antidumping or countervailing duty proceeding, including sunset reviews. All filings, including a notice of intent to participate in a sunset review, must be in writing in accordance with the provisions of section 351.303.

5.278 With respect to the EC's question concerning burden of proof in sunset reviews, Article 21.3 does not impose a burden of proof on US authorities. In order to withstand scrutiny under Article 11 of the DSU, however, an Article 21.3 sunset determination must be supported by sufficient evidence and be based on proper legal interpretations. The burden of proof is on the complaining party – in this instance, the EC – to demonstrate that Commerce's determination was not supported by adequate evidence or proper legal interpretations.

5.279 Article 21.3 does not contain the word "demonstrate". Instead, Article 21.3 provides for termination of a countervailing duty unless the authorities "determine" that the expiry of the duty would likely lead to continuation or recurrence of subsidization and injury. In the case at issue, Commerce determined that expiry of the countervailing duty on certain corrosion-resistant carbon steel flat products from Germany would be likely to lead to continuation or recurrence of subsidization. Commerce's determination is supported by adequate evidence and is based on a proper legal interpretation of the applicable provisions.

5.280 With respect to the EC's questions concerning the purpose and consequence of an investigation versus a sunset review, the purpose of a countervailing duty investigation is to determine the existence and degree of foreign government subsidization and whether the subsidized imports are causing injury. In contrast, the purpose of a sunset review is to determine whether revocation of a countervailing duty order would be likely to lead to continuation or recurrence of subsidization and injury. The consequence of an affirmative finding of subsidization and injury in an investigation is the imposition of a countervailing duty. The consequence of an affirmative finding of likelihood of continuation or recurrence of subsidization and injury in a sunset review is the continued maintenance of the countervailing duty. The completion of a sunset review does not trigger the assessment of duties or change cash deposit requirements.

5.281 With respect to the EC's questions concerning preliminary determinations under US system, the purpose of Commerce's preliminary determination in a full sunset review is to provide an explanation of Commerce's findings concerning the likelihood of continuation or recurrence of subsidization and the net countervailable subsidy likely to prevail if the countervailing duty were revoked. Commerce's preliminary determination takes into account the factual information and arguments submitted by the parties in their substantive responses and rebuttals.

5.282 Section 351.218(d)(3)(i) of Commerce's *Sunset Regulations* provide that substantive responses to a notice of initiation are due 30 days after the date of publication in the *Federal Register* of the notice of initiation. Rebuttal to a substantive response is due five days after the date the substantive response is filed. (Section 351.218(d)(4).) Section 351.218(d)(4) of the *Sunset Regulations* also provide that Commerce normally will not accept or consider any additional information from a party after the time for filing rebuttals has expired. Section 351.302(c), however, provides that a party may request an extension of a specific time limit. Unless expressly precluded by statute, Commerce may, for good cause, extend any time limit established by its regulations. (Section 351.302(b).) The US countervailing duty statute does not contain deadlines for submission of information in a sunset review.

5.283 The preliminary determination provides interested parties with an opportunity to review Commerce's analysis of the information on the record. Commerce issues preliminary determinations in investigations and administrative reviews as well. Preliminary determinations provide interested parties with an opportunity to comment, in case and rebuttal briefs, on Commerce's preliminary findings. Commerce is not precluded from requesting factual information after the issuance of a preliminary determination, but normally it does not do so.

5.284 With respect to the EC's questions concerning data collection periods, section 351.301(c)(2)(iii) of Commerce's regulations provides that interested parties will have at least 30 days from the date of receipt to respond to a questionnaire. This rule applies to original countervailing duty investigations. Similarly, section 351.218(d)(3)(i) provides for a 30-day deadline with respect to a response to the sunset questionnaire. Furthermore, as discussed above, a party may request an extension of a specific time limit.

5.285 With respect to the EC's question concerning Article 12, the United States agrees that Article 21.4 of the *SCM Agreement* expressly provides that the provisions of Article 12 – as opposed to the provisions of Article 11 – apply to these types of reviews.

5.286 With respect to the EC's questions concerning Commerce's application of a 0.5 per cent *de minimis* standard in sunset reviews, as well as its questions concerning the subsidy rate Commerce reports to the USITC, because Article 21 of the *SCM Agreement* does not contain any *de minimis* standard, these questions is not relevant to the issues raised in this dispute. Nevertheless, the United States notes that, as a matter of domestic policy, Commerce has applied a 0.5 per cent *de minimis* standard in administrative (*i.e.*, assessment) reviews. The application of this standard pre-dates the Uruguay Round negotiations. The entry into force of the WTO Agreement did not require a change in this standard, because the Article 11.9 *de minimis* standard is only applicable to investigations. For this same reason, when the United States amended its law in 1994 to provide for sunset reviews, it chose to apply its longstanding 0.5 per cent *de minimis* standard to sunset reviews. The United States could have chosen to apply no *de minimis* standard to sunset reviews at all.

5.287 Commerce's *de minimis* standard in reviews is different from its *de minimis* standard in investigations. Prior to the entry into force of the WTO Agreement, Commerce applied a 0.5 per cent *de minimis* standard in investigations. However, in order to conform to Article 11.9 of the *SCM Agreement*, Congress amended the US statute so as to require the use of a 1 per cent *de minimis* standard in investigations.

5.288 In a sunset review, the *de minimis* standard has particular application in several respects. For example, if Commerce determined in a sunset proceeding, based on the original investigation and any administrative reviews, that the existing countervailable subsidy programmes had been terminated and that the likely net countervailable rate of subsidization was *de minimis*, Commerce normally would determine that there was *no* likelihood of continuation or recurrence of subsidization.

5.289 In addition, the *Sunset Policy Bulletin* (section III.A.6.b) provides that, if the combined benefits of all programmes considered in the sunset review have never been above *de minimis* at any time the order was in effect, and there is no likelihood that the combined benefits of such programmes would be above *de minimis* in the event of removal of the duty, Commerce normally would determine that there is no likelihood of continuation or recurrence of subsidization.

5.290 In 1987, following a notice and comment rulemaking proceeding, Commerce published a final regulation codifying its long-standing practice of applying a 0.5 per cent *de minimis* standard in investigations and administrative reviews. 52 FR 30660 (17 August 1987). Pursuant to the regulation, net aggregate subsidies (and ad valorem dumping margins) of less than 0.5 per cent would be disregarded for purposes of publishing or revoking orders, setting cash deposit rates, or assessing countervailing duties. In response to comments regarding Commerce's decision to set 0.5 per cent as the *de minimis* threshold, Commerce stated as follows:

> The doctrine of *de minimis non curat lex*, that the law does not concern itself with trifles, is a basic tenet of Anglo-American jurisprudence, inherent in all US laws. With respect to the antidumping and countervailing duty laws, the Department has concluded that the potential benefits to domestic petitioners from orders on dumping margins or net subsidies below 0.5% are outweighed by the gains in productivity and efficiency provided by a *de minimis* rule. Even in price-sensitive markets, the effect of requiring a deposit or assessment of duty based on a rate of 0.5% *ad valorem* would be negligible. No party submitting comments has provided any information to support a different conclusion. Accordingly, it would be unreasonable for the Department and the US Customs Service to squander their scarce resources administering orders for which the dumping margins or the net subsidies are below 0.5%. The fact that the Department of Treasury and Commerce may not always have applied a uniform *de minimis* standard in the past is an additional reason supporting the adoption of a fixed standard which can be applied consistently in the future.

52 FR at 30661. In response to comments that the *de minimis* threshold be set at 1 per cent, Commerce also stated that,

> After many years of applying a 0.5 per cent *de minimis* threshold, the Department has developed no basis to conclude that 1 per cent represents a level of benefit not worth the expense of investigations or annual reviews....

5.291 As explained in the United States First Written Submission, Commerce starts with the total *ad valorem* rate determined in the original investigation and considers whether, since the investigation, it has found subsidy programmes to be terminated and/or new programmes to be countervailable. Based on findings, which normally are made in the context of administrative reviews, Commerce may adjust the rate determined in the original investigation to take these subsequent findings into account.

5.292 With respect to the EC's question concerning the amount of subsidy in the context of a sunset review, Article 21.3 provides for consideration of whether expiry of a countervailing duty would likely lead to a continuation or recurrence of subsidization and injury. Footnote 52 states that a finding, in the most recent administrative review, that no duty is to be levied shall not by itself require the authorities to terminate the definitive duty. This is consistent with the prospective nature of a sunset review. Thus, the level of subsidization at the time of a sunset review is not necessarily determinative of the outcome of a sunset review. However, if Commerce determined in a particular sunset review that there was no likelihood that the net countervailable subsidy rate would exceed 0.5 per cent *ad valorem* in the event of revocation of the countervailing duty, Commerce would determine that there was no likelihood of continuation or recurrence of subsidization and revoke the duty.

5.293 With respect to the EC's question concerning use of the 1 per cent, Article 11.9 *de minimis* standard, for the reasons set forth in the United States' First Written Submission and Oral Statement, the Article 11.9 *de minimis* standard does not apply to Article 21.3 sunset reviews. Article 21.3 does not contain any *de minimis* standard. Commerce does apply a 0.5 per cent *de minimis* standard in sunset reviews, but does not do so because of any obligation imposed by the *SCM Agreement*. In the final results of the full sunset review of corrosion resistant steel from Germany, Commerce determined that revocation of the order would be likely to lead to continuation or recurrence of a countervailable subsidy and found that the net countervailable subsidy likely to prevail if the order was revoked was 0.54 per cent *ad valorem*, which is above the *de minimis* standard under US law.

5.294 With respect to the EC's questions concerning calculation of a current rate of subsidization in a sunset review, Commerce normally does not determine the present net countervailable subsidy rate in a sunset review, and it did not calculate the level of subsidization present at the time of the sunset review in the corrosion-resistant steel from Germany case. Commerce did, however, adjust the net countervailable subsidy rate determined in the investigation to account for two programmes that the EC and German producers argued had been terminated with no continuing benefits. Nevertheless, nothing in Article 21.3 or any other provision of the *SCM Agreement* mandates a particular methodology for determining whether subsidization is likely to continue or recur if the duty were revoked.

5.295 The focus of a sunset review is necessarily on the possible future behaviour of foreign governments and exporters. The best evidence of that behaviour is the net countervailable subsidy rate determined in the original investigation because it is indicative of behaviour without the discipline of a countervailing duty in place. Starting with the net countervailable subsidy rate from the original investigation, Commerce may make adjustments, including adjustments for subsidies for which benefits were allocated over time, in accordance with the *Sunset Policy Bulletin*. (*See* section III.B.3.) Commerce, however, normally makes such determinations in the context of an annual administrative review where interested parties may submit, *inter alia*, information concerning the level of subsidization present during the period of review for Commerce's examination.

5.296 With respect to the EC's question regarding Commerce's declining balance methodology, as explained in the United States' First Written Submission, the *ad valorem* subsidy rate for any period cannot be determined without knowing the applicable sales volume.

5.297 With respect to the EC's questions concerning the rationale for the 1 per cent *de minimis* standard, the only *de minimis* standard found in the *SCM Agreement* is in Article 11.9 which, by its terms, is limited to investigations. Neither Article 11.9 nor any other provision of the *SCM Agreement* provides a rationale for the *de minimis* standard. This standard is a product of negotiations. As discussed in more detail above, when Commerce codified its own *de minimis* standard in its regulations, it considered several rationales, including administrative efficiency, as providing a basis for the standard.

5.298 With respect to the EC's questions concerning new countervailable subsidies granted since 1993, as discussed in Commerce's preliminary sunset determination, there were no administrative reviews of this order. As a result, Commerce had not considered whether German producers benefitted from additional subsidies granted since the original investigation. Commerce did not consider domestic interested parties' allegations concerning new subsidies in the context of the sunset review because US law intends that such allegations should normally be made in the context of administrative reviews and the lack of any administrative reviews, in and of itself, was not sufficient to constitute good cause to consider the petitioners' allegations in the context of the sunset review. Furthermore, once Commerce found likelihood based on previously investigated subsidies, a finding of additional new subsidies would not have changed its affirmative likelihood determination.

5.299 With respect to the EC's question concerning the application of footnote 52, footnote 52 stands for the proposition that an existing subsidy programme could be the basis for a determination in a sunset review that the expiry of the countervailing duty would likely lead to the continuation of subsidization even if Commerce found a net countervailable subsidy rate of *zero* attributable to that programme in the most recent administrative review. In other words, footnote 52 means that the current level of subsidization is not decisive as to whether subsidization is likely to recur.

5.300 With respect to the EC's questions concerning Commerce's findings in other sunset determinations, the dispute before this Panel involves Commerce's sunset determination concerning certain corrosion-resistant carbon steel flat products from Germany. As a general matter, Commerce sunset determinations involving other merchandise and other countries are available as public, published documents and can be found on Commerce's website, the website of the US Government Printing Office, or through commercial database services such as Lexis. We note, however, that to date, Commerce has found no likelihood of continuation or recurrence of subsidization in the following three full sunset reviews: C-122-404, Live Swine from Canada, 64 Fed. Reg. 60301 (November 4, 1999); C-333-401, Cotton Shop Towels from Peru, 64 Fed. Reg. 66884 (November 30, 1999); and C-201-505, POS Cookware from Mexico, 65 FR 284, (January 4, 2000).

5.301 With respect to the EC's question concerning the effect of the net subsidy rate on volume of exports, issues concerning the volume of exports to the United States are properly considered in the context of the USITC's injury determination, which has not been challenged by the EC in this dispute. Nevertheless, the United States would point out that the *ad valorem* countervailing duty rate determined in the investigation was 0.60 per cent and, according to the EC, the German producers stopped shipping to the United States once this 0.60 per cent countervailing duty was in place.

5.302 With respect to the EC's questions concerning amounts for certain denominators or numerators, Commerce's finding of likelihood of continuation or recurrence of subsidization is based on and supported by the administrative record of the sunset review. The EC's questions are not really questions. Rather, the EC is asking the United States to research and perform new calculations in the context of the EC's challenge to the United States' laws and regulations concerning sunset reviews and to a particular Commerce sunset determination. The United States does not believe it is appropriate to do so in this context.

H. Comments of the European Communities on the Responses of the United States to Questions from the Panel Following the First Meeting of the Panel

Introduction

5.303 The US points (para. 2) that the EC is not challenging the injury determination in this proceeding. However, the EC in this proceeding is not challenging the injury requirement only for the purpose of verifying the accuracy of the ITC injury determination as such, but it is doing so for the purpose of the *de minimis* challenge, i.e. as a requirement that needs to be demonstrated positively in the context of a sunset review under Article 21.3 of the *SCM Agreement* (see First Oral Statement of EC, footnote 27).

Question 1(a)

5.304 Throughout its responses to the questions from the Panel, the US espouses a formalistic interpretation of Article 21.3 *SCM Agreement* that would essentially strip Articles 21.1 and 21.3 of any practical effect. An example of this is the US's statement in paragraph 5 that Article 21.3 contains "no requirement to quantify the amount of subsidization likely to continue or recur". Article 21.3 permits the continuation of a countervailing duty order only if the authorities affirmatively determine that "the expiry of the duty would be likely to lead to continuation or recurrence of subsidization and injury". In turn, Article 15.5 defines "injury" as that injury caused by subsidized imports "through the effects of subsidies". Thus, an authority can only make a proper determination concerning the continuation or recurrence of injury if it considers the amount of subsidization that is likely to continue or recur if the duties were to expire. Under the US system, this means that DOC must provide the ITC with an accurate calculation of the amount of subsidization that is likely to continue or recur if the countervailing duty order were revoked. The US DOC has failed to do that in this case but simply continued to apply the countervailing duty rate calculated for 1991 despite the clear and indisputable evidence provided by the Government of Germany and the German producers establishing that this rate was no longer accurate.

5.305 As regards the references to paragraph 6.87 of the *Korea DRAMS* panel report, the US draws the wrong conclusions. In that report, the Panel had not dealt with a sunset review in the sense of Article 11.3 of the AD Agreement, but a claim for a duty assessment review under Article 9.3 of the AD Agreement. But there is no exact equivalent of Article 9.3 AD Agreement in the *SCM Agreement*. Such duty assessment reviews fall by default within the scope of Article 21.2 of the *SCM Agreement*. In addition, and more importantly, the basic reason for which that Panel interpreted Articles 5.8 and 9.3 of the AD Agreement in the way it did is stated in paragraph 6.90 of the report, to which the US omits to make any reference. There the Panel held that: "In the context of Article 9.3 duty assessment procedures, however, the function of any *de minimis* test applied by Members is to determine ***whether or not an exporter should pay a duty***. A *de minimis* test in the context of an Article 9.3 duty assessment procedure will ***not*** remove an exporter from the scope of the order." (emphasis added) This is clearly not the case of a CVD sunset review determination, because the basic principle laid down by Article 21.3 and 21.1 of the *SCM Agreement* is the termination of the CVD order unless a fresh, positive finding about likelihood of subsidization, injury and causality is made by the authorities.

Questions 1(b) and (c)

5.306 Contrary to the US responses, the US ITC does consider negligibility in its sunset review determinations. Under US law, cumulation is specifically prohibited in a sunset review if "imports are likely to have no discernable adverse impact on the domestic industry". 19 U.S.C. § 1675a(a)(7). This provision was added to US law by the Uruguay Round Agreements Act. In its report to that Act, the US Senate specifically stated that this cumulation provision was being added because Congress "believe[d] that it is appropriate to preclude cumulation where imports are likely to be negligible". S. Rep. No. 103-412, at 51 (1994). Similarly, the US ITC also considers differences in the "conditions of competition" in making its cumulation decision in a sunset review. *See Sugar from the European Union*, USITC Pub. No. 3238 at 15 (1999) <ftp://ftp.usitc.gov/pub/reports/ opinions/PUB3238.pdf>.

5.307 Moreover, for the reasons explained in the comment to the previous question, the combined effect of paragraphs 6.43-6.6.50 of the *Korea DRAMS* panel report supports the proposition that the standards of Article 11.9 and 15.3 should apply to Article 21.2 and to Article 21.3 reviews.

Questions 1(d)

5.308 Acceptance of the US position would render the provisions of Article 27, paragraphs 10 to 12, useless once the initial CVD order is in place. This position is totally unreasonable when proper consideration is given to the context, object, purpose and scope of special rules for developing country members laid down in the SCM and, more generally, the WTO Agreements.

Question 21

5.309 As the US readily admits, its rules apply with equal force to both "transition orders" and "non-transition" orders. Article 21.3 also makes no distinction between transition and non-transition orders and does not in any way permit an authority to apply a lower level of review or procedure with respect to transition orders.

Question 23

5.310 The US's response to this question reveals how its system of automatic self-initiation results in the conduct of a sunset review without the requirement that the domestic industry ever provide evidence substantiating the likelihood of the continuation or recurrence of subsidization. In paragraph 18, the US concedes that the "***only*** specific factual information" that it considers in making the decision as to whether to conduct a full sunset review is the "aggregate export figures provided by respondent interested parties". The other factual information submitted by the parties does not play any role in DOC's adequacy determination and is not discussed by DOC until its preliminary determination, which occurs after the time for submitting additional factual information has long expired (See EC Second Written Submission at paras. 41-42).

Question 24

5.311 The US arguments omit to mention another generally accepted principle of interpretation that "omissions in different contexts may have different meanings, and omission, in and of itself, is not necessarily dispositive". This is what the Appellate body has held in several cases. For example, in the *Canada – Automotive Industry* report, the Appellate Body held that the panel in that case had erred because it failed to examine the ordinary meaning of the terms in their relevant context and in light of the object and purpose of the entire *SCM Agreement* in order to identify the proper meaning of an omission in the text.[75] Another example provides the US reasoning in paragraph 48 of its response to question no 32(b) from the Panel, where it states that "Articles 19 and 21.2 of the *SCM Agreement* do not preclude no shipment administrative reviews". Without passing judgment on the substance of this US claim, what is important to note here is the ***reasoning by inference*** resorted to by the US, which is an accepted method of interpretation under the generally principles of public international law on treaty interpretation.

Question 25

5.312 In its response, the US concedes that it does not calculate the level of subsidization in a sunset review but simply reports to the US ITC the rate that was already calculated in the original investigation (at paras. 23-24). This in turn taints the US ITC injury determination because it is not based upon the level of subsidization that would be likely to continue or recur if the countervailing duties were terminated as required by Article 21.3. While the US contends that the rate from the original investigation is the "only calculated rate that reflects the behaviour of exporters and foreign governments without the discipline of an order in place", this reliance upon the rates from the original investigation cannot be applied as an irrefutable presumption. To do so would render the provisions of Articles 21.1 and 21.3, requiring the termination of countervailing duties after five years, meaningless because the fact that countervailing duties were originally imposed would be used as the justification for keeping those duties in place indefinitely.

5.313 The US's discussion (at para. 25) demonstrates a blatant violation of Article 12 *SCM Agreement* as made applicable to sunset reviews by virtue of Article 21.4. In paragraph 25 of its replies, the US states that, in making its determination in a sunset review, it "***only*** uses information developed in the original investigation or prior administrative proceedings" (emphasis added). The US tries to justify this practice by stating that "this information has been subject to the rigors of the administrative process in those proceedings, such as interested party briefing and onsite verifica-

[75] Appellate Body Report, *Canada – Certain Measures Affecting the Automotive Industry ("Canada – Automotive Industry")*, WT/DS139/AB/R, WT/DS142/AB/R, adopted 19 June 2000, paras. 138-143.

tion". In our view, what the US fails to discuss is that reviews under Article 21.3 are, by virtue of Article 21.4, subject to the same evidentiary and procedural requirements as investigations and administrative reviews, including the ability to conduct onsite verifications.

5.314 Moreover, DOC's stated preference for information developed in the original investigation cannot justify its refusal to adjust the subsidy determination for changes in the CIG programme. All of the information submitted by the Government of Germany and the German producers, showing the termination of the CIG programme with no significant residual benefit after 2000, comes directly from the original investigation and was subject to full briefing and verification in that case. The conditions and requirements of Article 12 are fully applicable to sunset reviews and no distinction is made therein whether the information is collected in the original investigation or in an Article 21.2 or an Article 21.3 review. Most importantly, what the US terms "***a relationship of ...convenience***" (at para. 25) under its domestic law cannot derogate from the basic principles of Articles 21.3 and 21.4 of the *SCM Agreement* to make a fresh, proper determination of likelihood of subsidization, injury and causality on the basis of positive evidence.

Question 26

5.315 While the United States concedes that the definition of injury contained in Article 15 applies throughout the *SCM Agreement*, it reads (at paras. 26-29) unduly restrictively Article 15, by applying only those provisions that it finds favourable. By doing so, however, it seems to contradict its previous replies to question 24 (a) and (b) from the Panel (at paras 19-21). Indeed, the reference in Footnote no 45 to "threat of material injury"[76] appears already to accommodate, albeit in a different context, the prospective nature of the analysis claimed by the US under the "likelihood" test of an Article 21.3 sunset review. Moreover, as stated in the comment to question 1(a) above, the definition of injury must include the element of causation. Article 15.3 also makes clear that the *de minimis* and negligibility provisions of Article 11.9 are an integral part to the definition of injury. As the *Korea DRAMS* panel has held, in the comparable situation of an Article 11.2 of the AD Agreement review, "*while mathematical certainty of recurrence of dumping is not required, the conclusions must still be demonstrable on the basis of the evidence adduced*" (at paras. 6.43 and 6.50 of the report). The obligation to adduce such "evidence" in a CVD sunset review is squarely place, by virtue of Article 21.4, on the authorities undertaking the review for the purpose of making a "determination" under 21.3.

Question 27

5.316 The US reply to question no 27(a) is another illustration of the isolationist interpretation of Article 21.3 advanced by it. There is indeed no valid reason to interpret the term "domestic industry" in Article 21.3 differently from that laid down in Article 11.4 in conjunction with Article 16 of the *SCM Agreement*. It follows that a request made by "at least one domestic interested party" is not a "duly" made request under Article 21.3 because it would not comply with the initiation requirements of Article 11.4.

---

[76] As this is defined in Article 15.7 of the *SCM Agreement*.

Question 28

5.317 Here the US appears to be placing undue importance on the use of the word "investigation" in Article 11.9, as opposed to the use of the word "*review*" in Article 21.3. The same undue reliance on the word "investigation" is shown by the US in its reply to question 1(d) above concerning Article 27.10. Although it is true that Article 11 lays down provisions on "initiation and subsequent investigation", the term "investigation" denotes the "process or an instance of investigating" or "a formal examination or study".[77] It follows that although this term encompasses a substantive exercise relating to this process of fact finding, it is more accurate to say that its scope is narrower than the scope of the term "determine" as this is used in a number of Articles in the Agreement, such as in Articles 19 or 21.3. Indeed, an investigation may lead to the imposition and collection of countervailing duties when the Member makes a final "determination" under the conditions laid down in Article 19. Therefore, what is particularly important in Article 11.9 is not the use of the term "investigation", as the US claims, but rather the use of the terms "***the authorities concerned are satisfied that***"[78], which is the equivalent to the concept of making a "***determination***" used in Article 19 or Articles 21.3 of the *SCM Agreement*. In other words, Article 11.9 comports an element of substantive determination, which, although made in the process of the original *investigation*, is not different from the substantive point of view of the finding that needs to be made in a sunset *determination* about likelihood of subsidization, injury and causality. What is significant, therefore, is the substantive determination that should be made by the authorities about the level of subsidization under both Articles 11.9 and 21.3, which must in both cases entail a determination on *de minimis* level of the subsidy, injury and causal link rather than the procedural process or stage at which this occurs. In other words, a determination in a sunset review requires the conduct of an investigation as much as an investigation is required prior to the original determination. Therefore, the fact that the word "investigation" does not appear in Article 21.3 makes no difference. Investigating authorities are not absolved of their obligation to **investigate** from the day after an original measure is imposed. This would amount to saying that authorities are entitled to apply a lower standard of examination to issues raised in reviews, compared to that which applies in original investigations. It follows that the US insistence only on the word "investigation" in Article 11.9 or 27.10 of the *SCM Agreement*, to exclude the application of the *de minimis* rule in sunset reviews, amounts to simply reading these provisions outside their context, object and purpose.

Questions 29 and 30

5.318 The US claims (at paras. 34-36) that the interpretation proposed by the EC would render Footnote 52 a nullity and asserts that there must be a reason for its inclusion in Article 21.3. This answer is rather puzzling. The EC does not dispute that "a finding in the most recent assessment procedure that no duty is to be levied shall not by itself require the authorities to terminate the definitive duty". Such a finding may be based on a finding on the zero subsidy or on some other reason. But Footnote 52 does not support the conclusion the US attempts to draw from it.

---

77 Oxford Concise English Dictionary, 9th ed. 1995.

78 The corresponding phrase in Article 5.8 of the AD Agreement is "the authorities ***determine*** that...".

5.319 The US argument is based on an understanding of the concept of *de minimis* in Article 11.9 that reflects the Latin proverb "*de minimis non curat lex*". As the US has explained in several places (e.g. in its reply to question 30 from the Panel and its reply to question 8 from the EC, respectively at paras. 41 and 16 of its replies), it applies voluntarily the *de minimis* rule of 0.50 per cent under domestic law for reasons of administrative efficiency because the US law is not supposed to "concern itself with trifles".

5.320 The preparatory history of Article 11.9 and the corresponding provision in the AD Agreement, however, indicate that the rationale of the *de minimis* rule in these Agreements is different from that on which the *de minimis* rule is applied in the US. In these two WTO Agreements, the level of 1 per cent ad valorem was agreed to be the *de minimis* threshold **not** for reasons of administrative efficiency but **because for imports below this level the causal link between subsidized imports and the material injury to domestic industry would not exist.**[79] This is a significantly different rationale, because it demonstrates that the US continued under its domestic law its old practice going back to 1980, as codified in the 1987 Guideline on the minimis rule (see Exhibit US-6). Based on that understanding of the *de minimis* rule, the US then extrapolates from Footnote 52 by making several illogical leaps: First, it argues that if a zero rate of subsidy cannot require the authorities to terminate the CVD duty, that means that the level of the subsidy, even if zero, is not relevant for deciding likelihood of continuation or recurrence of subsidization, injury and causality. Second, it draws the operational conclusion that it is not necessary to calculate the actual level of subsidy in a sunset review. Third, it does consider that the *de minimis* rule of Article 11.9 applies to Article 21.3 reviews.

5.321 The EC considers that the current level of subsidy is not always "determinative" of the outcome of a sunset review. However, the "prospective nature of a sunset review" is subject to the requirement for the authorities to positively determine that subsidization is likely to continue or recur. Thus, if the current level of subsidy is zero or de-minimis, this does not *by itself* end the measure, but it does require the US DOC to demonstrate what change of circumstances will lead to the subsidy increasing to a level above de-minimis, if it wishes to continue the measure. In the case of a non-recurring subsidy which is already de-minimis and subject to the US declining balance methodology, the DOC must adduce and rely on positive evidence of new subsidies or of a sharp fall in the denominator in order to find likelihood of subsidization, injury and causality.

5.322 Moreover, the US states that the "focus" of a sunset review is on the *possible* future behaviour of foreign governments and exporters. This is misleading. First, we do not see in what respect the behaviour of the **exports** would be relevant in this context. Second, a sunset review determination requires *positive* evidence to demonstrate that subsidization, injury and causality is *likely* to continue or recur. The review should therefore focus on "demonstrable evidence adduced by the authorities" rather than on pure speculation and conjecture derived by applying the level of subsidization from the original investigation. The US states that the "best evidence" of future behaviour of governments and exporters is the rate from the original investigation. However, in the case of *Corrosion-resistant steel from Germany*, how can this be?

[79] E.g., MTN.GNG/NG10/W/9/Rev. 3, point E, of 26 may 1988, and MTN.GNG/NG10/W/4, page 42.

The DOC has itself established that there are *no new subsidies* and that the non-recurring subsidies found in the original investigation, 9 years ago, have now declined to a level that is equivalent zero by its own calculation methodology.

5.323 There appears therefore to be only one reasonable conclusion: the US has modified its past practice after the WTO Agreements on AD and SCM entered into force only as regards determinations made in the initial investigation, but left its domestic legislation on sunset reviews unchanged by applying its 0.50 per cent *de minimis* rule based on a completely different rationale (i.e. administrative convenience and efficiency).

Question 30

5.324 In addition to what has been explained above, the US's response to question 30 again reveals its refusal to provide parties to a sunset review with the evidentiary and procedural rights established in Article 12. In paragraph 39, the US reiterates that its determination in a sunset review is "based on the original investigation and any administrative reviews". It states:

> "In a sunset review, the *de minimis* standard has particular application in several respects. For example, if Commerce determined in a sunset proceeding, based on the original investigation and any administrative reviews, that the existing countervailable subsidy programs had been terminated and that the likely net countervailable rate of subsidization was *de minimis*, ***Commerce normally would determine that there was no likelihood of continuation or recurrence of subsidization."*** (emphasis added)

5.325 A closer look into this statement reveals that the US's reasoning is, from a purely logical point of view, inherently contradictory. When the US DOC finds in a sunset review that the net subsidy rate is likely to be below its domestic 0.50 per cent rule, it makes a positive empirical finding that the subsidy is likely to continue at that level. But since this level of subsidy is not considered under US law worth pursuing, it draws the conclusion (which is literally a legal fiction) that there "will be no likelihood of continuation or recurrence of subsidization". In reality, however, this legal conclusion of no likelihood of continuation of subsidization is not empirically correct, because the subsidy will continue albeit at a level below the 0.50 per cent. Therefore, in reality this legal conclusion is equivalent to a finding that there is no causal link of material injury for the purposes of a sunset review under Article 21.3 of the *SCM Agreement*. For this reason as well, it simply makes no sense the US's refusal to recognize the need to apply in sunsets the 1 per cent *de minimis* rule of Article 11.9, but continue to apply a 0.50 per cent *de minimis* rule under its domestic law.

Question 31

5.326 The US's response to question 31 begs the issue. In paragraph 44, the US states that it "does not calculate the present rate [of subsidization in a sunset review] because the purpose of a sunset review is to determine the likelihood of the continuation or recurrence of subsidization" and that this "necessarily involves a prediction of a government's future behaviour without the discipline of a countervailing duty order in place". The issue is not whether DOC must determine the current level of subsidization rather than the likely future rate of subsidization in a sunset review. Instead, the issue is whether DOC may irrefutably presume that the likely level of future subsidization is the same as the rate of subsidization determined in the original investigation.

5.327 Moreover, the US does not answer the basic question why it can conduct on site verifications and apply the full rigors of an investigation in the context of an administrative review but cannot do or does not wish to do so in the context of a sunset review. Attempting to predict the future behaviour of a government in no way prevents the US authorities from conducting a proper, fresh, new investigation to find out about the numerator or denominator of the exporters' sales, the likelihood of the subsidy programme been modified or withdrawn or whether there is a non-recurring subsidy the amount of which has already been expensed and the remaining benefit flowing from it is nearly zero.

5.328 Furthermore, the US *Sunset Policy Bulletin* (see Exhibit EC-15) provides in Section III.A.5 some criteria about the way future government behaviour could be predicted. They include in particular the **legal method** by which the government granted or eliminated a programme, i.e. whether this is done by **administrative** action or through **legislative** action. The US *Sunset Policy Bulletin* proposes to the authorities to draw different conclusions depending on the legal method applied. This supports clearly the arguments the EC made in paragraph 34 of its Second Written Submission. This is all the more important here, as the programmes under review in the present case and, in particular the CIG programme, were granted by legislative action and could not as such be reinstated by administrative action only.

5.329 In addition, the improper nature of the irrefutable presumption used by the US DOC is clear from the facts of this case. In this proceeding, DOC determined that the CIG programme would continue to provide benefits after the end of the sunset review (*i.e.*, after 2000) in the same amount as was determined for the year 1991 in the original investigation (*i.e.*, 0.39 per cent). This determination that the CIG programme would continue to pay benefits in the future at the rate of 0.39 per cent is in direct conflict with all of the evidence submitted in the sunset review, showing that the CIG programme applied only to investments made prior to 1 January 1986 and that the amount of residual benefits that would continue after the year 2000 was close to zero by DOC's own calculation method.

5.330 The EC would also note the US admission, in its response to question 31, that, in a sunset review, it "***only*** uses information developed in the original investigation or prior administrative review". (at para. 45, emphasis added).

Question 32

5.331 While the US contends that its regulations theoretically permit "no shipment reviews", it readily admits that its "long-standing policy is to refrain from conducting administrative reviews where there have been no shipments of the subject merchandise" (at para. 47). In fact, the US points to no cases in which it has ever conducted a no-shipment administrative review of a countervailing duty order. The US DOC's uniform practice has always been to terminate any reviews in which it finds that no shipments were made during the administrative review.[80]

5.332 With respect the US's discussion of "change circumstances" reviews, it must be noted that DOC's determination whether or not to initiate a change circumstances

[80] See, e.g., *Certain Hot-Rolled Lead & Bismuth Carbon Steel Products from Germany*, 64 Fed. Reg. 44,489 (DOD 1999) (termination administrative review).

review is entirely discretionary. In addition, the *SCM Agreement* does not make a review under Article 21.3 in any way dependent upon a review under 21.2. Moreover, the complete evidentiary and procedural requirements contained in Article 12 apply in full to reviews under Article 21.3.

5.333 The EC would request the Panel to note the evasive nature of the US replies which stem in particular from the highly discretionary nature of the basic US law, regulations and practice. The US law does not provide any security or predictability to exporters and is, in addition, inconsistent with the relevant provisions of the *SCM Agreement*. The US cannot unilaterally decide simply not to conduct administrative reviews for reasons of administrative convenience in view of the very important legal consequences this refusal can give rise to, as in the present case.

Question 33

5.334 US law does not prohibit DOC from making confidential documents from the original investigation part of the confidential record in a sunset review. In fact, as discussed in the EC's second written submission, the US ITC automatically makes the confidential version of its original determination, as well as the complete staff report from the original investigation, part of the confidential record in a sunset review (EC Second Written Submission at para. 39). The US argument that these constitute "separate segments of the proceeding" is made exclusively for purposes of domestic US law which has no basis on the *SCM Agreement* and in particular Article 12 thereof (see EC Second Written Submission, at paras. 41-44).

Question 34(a)

5.335 In addition to the written request on April 13, 2000, the German producers in this case made several oral requests at the beginning of April 2000 (*i.e.*, directly after issuance of the preliminary results) that DOC make the calculation memoranda from the original investigation part of the record in the sunset review. These requests were prompted by DOC's failure in the preliminary determination to properly consider the evidence concerning the termination of the CIG programme timely submitted by the Government of Germany and the German Producers. **It must be clearly understood that, even without the calculation memoranda, the Government of Germany and the German producers submitted sufficient evidence to establish that the CIG programme had been terminated and ceased to pay any significant benefits after 1986.** There can be no dispute that under DOC's own allocation methodology, any nonrecurring subsidies received in 1986 would be fully amortized no later than 2000.[81]

Question 34(b)

5.336 The US DOC's regulation concerning the deadline for filing factual information does not make any distinction between confidential and public information. *See* 19 C.F.R. § 351.218(d)(4). Accordingly, the US DOC could not properly treat the German producers' request concerning the calculation memoranda as untimely but

[81] Under DOC's methodology, year one in the allocation period is always the year that the subsidy is received. *See* 19 C.F.R. § 351.524(d). Accordingly, using a fifteen-year allocation period as DOC did in this case, the benefit of any nonrecurring subsidies received in 1985 would have expired in 1999 and the benefit of any nonrecurring subsidies received in 1986 would have expired, at the latest, in 2000.

then accept factual information submitted by other parties after that date. Moreover, it is in this case necessary to conclude that the German producers, by making several specific requests to the DOC to place the data and memoranda from the original investigation into the sunset file, have renounced the confidential nature of the data, if any such confidentiality existed. It also follows that if the US DOC had any doubts about this, it should have taken positive steps and direct contact with the German producers to find out about this question instead of staying inactive until its final determination made in August 2000 by which it rejected it.

Question 35(a)

5.337 As discussed above in the comments to question 25, the sunset reviews conducted by DOC violate the provisions of Article 12 and, therefore, cannot be seen as a proper determination under Article 21.3. Moreover, the US's reasoning on this point is belied by the answers it has made to the Panel's other questions. The US claims at para. 58 that:

> "..it may determine, in accordance with the requirements of Article 21.3, whether subsidization is likely to continue or recur without conducting its own investigation, but, rather, by making its decision based on the evidentiary record developed during the sunset review because all parties, both foreign and domestic, have every opportunity under the US system to provide any information they deem relevant."

5.338 In numerous other places in its response, however, the US concedes that, in making its determination in a sunset review, it "***only*** uses information developed in the original investigation or prior administrative proceedings". (e.g., US Answers to Panel Questions at paras. 25, 45 & 75, emphasis added). Similarly, the US concedes that, in practice, any foreign producer that does not export subject merchandise to the US after imposition of countervailing duties would be prohibited from seeking an administrative review (*Ibid* at para. 47). Thus, the US's assertions that its determinations are "based on the evidentiary record developed during the sunset review" and that parties "have every opportunity under the US system to provide any information they deem relevant" are purely incorrect and misleading.

5.339 Moreover, accepting the US interpretation of the verb "determine" in Article 21.3 would entitle the US authorities and the national authorities of any WTO Member to become in reality passive observers and paper-collecting authorities as regards conducting an investigation and determining subsidization, material injury and causality (See EC First Written Submission, at paras. 67-71).

Question 35(b)

5.340 The US's response well demonstrates that its *Sunset Policy Bulletin* establishes a series of irrefutable presumptions that almost invariably lead to a determination that subsidization is likely to continue or recur. This is confirmed by the results of the available cases so far, as is explained below and in para. 17 of the EC Second Written Submission. As regards the US claims in paras. 62-65, the EC refers the Panel to its previous comments regarding the US replies to questions 28-31.

5.341 In paragraph 67, the US in fact admits that the rate it reports to the ITC for the injury determination is indeed the net countervailable subsidy determined by DOC.

Question 35(c)

5.342 As regards the US replies in paras. 69-70, the EC refers the Panel to its above comment to the US reply to question 33.

Question 36

5.343 The US's response is simply a matter of semantics. In paragraph 71, the US claims that, "[u]nder the US system, administrative reviews are not prerequisites for conducting full sunset reviews" but then, in paragraph 75, it concedes that, in a sunset review, it "only uses information developed in the original investigation or prior administrative proceedings". In addition, the US's statement in paragraph 73 that it makes adjustments to the net countervailable subsidy determined in the investigation when "there is evidence demonstrating that programmes have been terminated with no residual benefits" is proved wrong by the facts of this case. As detailed in the EC's written submissions, the Government of Germany and the German producers provided clear evidence that the CIG programme was terminated without any meaningful residual benefit continuing after the end of the sunset review (see EC First Written Submission at paras. 83-91, and EC Second Written Submission at paras. 38-44). Despite this evidence, the US DOC refused to adjust the rate from the original investigation to reflect this change.

5.344 Moreover, in para. 71 the US writes:

> "The rationale for this approach is that the findings in the original investigation provide the only evidence reflecting the behaviour of the respondents without the discipline of countervailing measures in place. This makes sense given that, in a sunset review under Article 21.3, an authority is considering whether, without the discipline of the duty, subsidization would likely continue or recur; *i.e.*, what would happen without the discipline of the duty."

5.345 The EC has replied to this argument in particular with its response to written question no 15 from the Panel (at pages 28-29 of its replies). In addition to those replies, the EC would like to draw the attention of the Panel to the fact that an amount of net countervailable subsidy of 0.60 per cent determined in the original determination or of 0.54 per cent determined in the sunset review **do not constitute nor do they put in place "a discipline"**. This is because a CVD order reflecting that rate is highly unlikely to discourage exporters from exporting to the US. There is as much admission of this reality in the US 1987 *De minimis* Guidelines (see Exhibit US-6, at page 30661) where it is accepted that:

> "Even in price-sensitive markets, the effect of requiring a deposit or assessment of duty based on a rate of a 0.50 per cent ad valorem would be negligible. No party submitted comments has provided any information to support a different conclusion".

5.346 In the same US 1987 *De minimis* Guidelines (see Exhibit US-6, at page 30661), "several parties suggested that the *de minimis* threshold be set at 1 per cent, on the basis that 1 per cent represents a level of benefit not worth the expense of an investigation or annual review". This also partly explains why the 1 per cent ad valorem rule was laid down in the *SCM Agreement*, although the rationale in this latter case is based on the fact that no causality exists between such a level of subsidization and material injury. Accordingly, there is no valid substantive reason to apply in sunset determinations a *de minimis* rule that is different from that applied in original determinations.

Question 37

5.347 The US's assertion that the parties to the sunset review were different than those in the original investigation and that "the record of the sunset review contains no indication that the German producers in the sunset review were authorized to permit the movement of [confidential] information" from the record of the original investigation to the record of the sunset review is patently false (*See* US Answers to Panel Questions at para. 83). In the substantive response of 1 October 1999, the German Producers carefully explained that Thyssen Krupp Stahl AG was the legal successor to Hoesch and Thyssen and that Salzgitter AG was the legal successor to Preussag (see the German Producers Substantive Response at 5 (1999), copy attached hereto as ***Exhibit EC-23***). Thus, there could have been no confusion over the authority of the German Producers to request that the calculation memoranda be placed on the record of the sunset review.

5.348 It must also be clearly understood that the German producers were not requesting that the memoranda be disclosed to the public. Their only request was that the memoranda be made part of the confidential record in the sunset review, thereby maintaining their confidential status. Accordingly, contrary to the United States' assertion, granting the German producers' request would not have violated the provisions of Article 12.4 (see US Answers to Panel Questions at para. 78). Moreover, as discussed above in the comment to question 33, US law does not prohibit the DOC from making confidential documents from the original investigation part of the confidential record in a sunset review. In fact, the US ITC automatically makes the confidential version of its original determination, as well as the complete staff report from the original investigation, part of the confidential record in a sunset review (see EC Second Written Submission at para. 39).

5.349 Moreover, paragraphs 77-79 of the US replies is a clear indication of how the US DOC perceives its role in sunset investigations and determinations, i.e. as a passive, paper-collecting authority. See in this regard the US reply to written question no 5 from the EC, at paras. 8-9 of the US replies.

5.350 As regards the US response in para. 82, this is confusing the EC claim and the level and venue of this proceeding.

Question 38

5.351 As discussed in the EC's Second Written Submission, DOC's vague request for "all relevant evidence" violates the requirements of Article 12 (see EC Second Written Submission at paras. 40-44). It is not until the preliminary results (*i.e.*, after the time for submitting evidence has already expired) that DOC comments upon the sufficiency of the evidence submitted by the parties (EC, *Ibid* at 42). Moreover, even when the DOC technically permits the submission of evidence, the presumptions dictated by the *Sunset Policy Bulletin* result in the evidence being either later excluded or given no weight (see EC Replies to the Panel Written Questions at question 19).

5.352 Moreover, the US in this case did not provide any rational explanation of its decision that the German producers' request about placing the data from the original investigation was untimely and how this would have affected DOC's decision making.

I. *Comments of the European Communities on the Responses of the United States to Questions from the European Communities Following the First Meeting of the Panel*

Question 3

5.353 The word "demonstrate" does not appear for example in Articles 11.1, 11.2, 11.9, Article 19.1, etc. Is the US suggesting that in all these instances the burden of demonstrating that subsidization, injury and causal link exist is upon the foreign producers and Members to establish? In the view of the EC, the US is confusing the two different level and venue of proceedings and misinterprets the established case law in the WTO on the burden of proof and burden of persuasion.

Question 4

5.354 The US does not draw the logical conclusions from its answer. As the EC says, the consequences of a CVD investigation and a positive sunset finding are the same – five more years of countervailing duties. The fact that a sunset review does not change the deposit rate is irrelevant; the important point is that duties continue to apply. In fact, the only real difference between a new investigation and an investigation in a sunset determination is a question of timing. The sunset takes place five years after the original investigation. If we accept the US argument that the sunset has a different purpose and consequence, we effectively reverse the presumption in favour of expiry in Article 21.3.

Question 6

5.355 The US misstates the length of the data collection period in original investigations. Pursuant to 19 C.F.R. § 351.301(b)(1), parties have until 7 days prior to verification to submit factual information. Because verification does not take place until after the preliminary determination, this gives parties well over 65 days in which to submit factual information. This compares to only 35 days in a sunset review although the time for completing a full sunset review is considerably longer than that for completing an original countervailing duty investigations (*i.e.*, 240 days in a sunset review compared to 140 days in an original investigation). *Compare* 19 C.F.R. § 351.218(f)(3)(i) *with* 19 C.F.R. § 351.210(b)(1). Moreover, the time to submit factual information in a sunset review expires long before issuance of the preliminary results so that a party can file no additional information in response to that determination. *See* 19 C.F.R. § 351.218(d)(4).

5.356 Moreover, the US approach seems to depend entirely on when a firm is investigated. This can be illustrated by the example of a new exporter or "new shipper" review under Article 19.3. In this situation, a firm which starts exporting after the original investigation period and therefore could not have participated during the original investigation even if it had wanted to, is entitled to an individual CVD rate. However, in such cases, the US will apply a 0.5 per cent *de minimis* threshold, while a firm investigated on exactly the same basis in an original investigation would have been subject to a 1 per cent *de minimis* level. There are simply no grounds for such a discrimination. In addition, in sunsets the US is asking the Panel to accept discrimination which is nowhere provided for in the *SCM Agreement*. It argues that it is entitled to determine the likelihood of continuation or recurrence of subsidization, but at only *half* the rate required at the stage of initiation.

Question 8

5.357 Again, the US comments are very revealing. The US, having rejected the introduction of a 1 per cent *de minimis* threshold in 1987 in favour of a 0.5 per cent rate, does not really accept the use of the *SCM Agreement*'s 1 per cent de-minimis threshold in countervailing duty investigations. It thus chooses to apply this threshold only in new investigations, and to attempt to make a spurious distinction between the purpose of such investigations and sunset reviews. It does this in order to cling on to its pre-Uruguay Round de-minimis rate, which it considers to be the "proper" level for *de minimis*. As well as depriving the EC of the benefit of the correct de-minimis level in sunsets, such an approach also deprives developing countries of the special and differential treatment embodied in the 2 per cent and 3 per cent de-minimis thresholds under Articles 27.10 and 27.11.

5.358 Moreover, the EC notes that in sunsets the DOC will take no notice of the progressive decline in the amount of non-recurring subsidies invariably found in administrative reviews.

Question 9

5.359 The US's response confirms the fact that it reverses the standard provided in Article 21.3 and requires foreign producers to prove "no likelihood" of continuation or recurrence of subsidization (see US Answers to EC Questions at para. 18). The proper standard under Article 21.3 requires the automatic termination of countervailing duties unless it is affirmatively determined that "the expiry of the duty would be *likely* to lead to continuation or recurrence of subsidization and injury" (Article 21.3 *SCM* (emphasis added).

Question 12

5.360 To the extent that DOC finds it necessary to have current sales information before it can calculate an *ad valorem* subsidy rate in a sunset review, it is incumbent upon DOC to request such information from the parties (see US Answers to EC Questions at para. 23). Although DOC's sunset regulations do request that foreign producers provide information on exports to the United States during the five years preceding initiation of the sunset review, the regulations do not request information on total sales (see 19 C.F.R. § 351.218(d)(3)(iii)(B)).

5.361 The US's statement that it must ignore the annual diminution in the value of nonrecurring subsidies under its declining balance methodology because it does not have revised sales information to use as the denominator in its calculation of an *ad valorem* subsidy rate is based upon faulty reasoning. The effect of the annual diminution in the value of a nonrecurring subsidy (*i.e.*, the numerator in the calculation of the *ad valorem* subsidy rate) can only be offset if there has been a significant decline in the value of total sales (*i.e.*, the denominator in the calculation of the *ad valorem* subsidy rate) since the original investigation. In this case, there is no evidence that total sales have declined. To the contrary, the sales information submitted by the German producers in their 15 October 1999 rebuttal reveals that the total sales of Preussag/Salzgitter more than doubled between 1991 and 1998 (*Compare* Exhibit

EC-18 at Appendix 1 *with* Exhibit EC-22 at p. 43). This dramatic increase in total sales would have resulted in an even greater decline in the *ad valorem* subsidy rate, pushing the rate even further below the *de minimis* level.

5.362 Finally, as the US DOC did with respect to the Structural Improvement Aids and Zonal Border Area programmes, it could have adjusted the subsidy rate calculated for the CIG programme by subtracting the benefit assigned to that programme without needing a revised value for total sales. As with the Structural Improvement Aids and Zonal Border Area programmes, the German producers submitted evidence demonstrating that the CIG programme had been terminated without any residual benefit accruing after the end of the sunset review.

Question 13

5.363 As regards the US statement in para. 24 about the possible rationales for including the *de minimis* rule of 1 per cent *ad valorem*, it states that there is no rationale for a de-minimis threshold in the *SCM Agreement*, and that the 1 per cent standard is the product of negotiations. Once again, the US makes little secret of its distaste for the 1 per cent de-minimis threshold. In fact, all provisions of WTO Agreements are the product of negotiations, but this does not mean that their appropriate application can simply be ignored. As regards the true rationale behind the *de minimis* rule of 1 per cent in the *SCM Agreement*, we refer the Panel to our comments in paragraphs 17-20 above on the US replies to questions 29-30 from the Panel.

Question 14

5.364 The US mischaracterize DOC's reason for rejecting the domestic interested parties' allegation of new subsidies (see US Answers to EC Questions at para. 25). The US DOC did not base its decision on the lack of administrative reviews alone. Instead, DOC made clear that the domestic interested parties failed to provide "concrete evidence" of new subsidies (see Final Results Decision Memo at 43, Exhibit EC-10).

Question 16

5.365 When one analyses the only 3 cases in which DOC found that a countervailing subsidy is not likely to continue or recur, it is evident that DOC applied very different procedures in those cases than the ones applied in this case. In *Live Swine from Canada*, DOC considered new information submitted by the Government of Nova Scotia specifically because foreign producers had been prevented from requesting administrative reviews due to a lack of US shipments. *Final Results of Full Sunset Review: Live Swine From Canada*, 64 Fed. Reg. 60301, 60304 (1999). In *Cotton Shop Towels from Peru*, parties were permitted to submit new evidence, and DOC even conducted verification. *Final Results of Full Sunset Review & Termination of Suspended Investigation: Cotton Shop Towels From Peru*, 64 Fed. Reg. 66894, 66895 (1999). Finally, unlike the present proceeding, *Porcelain-on-Steel Cooking Ware from Mexico*, exclusively involved recurring subsidies. *See Final Results of Full Sunset Review & Revocation of Countervailing Duty Order: Porcelain-on-Steel Cooking Ware from Mexico*, 65 Fed. Reg. 284 (2000). Accordingly, the DOC presumption concerning nonrecurring subsidies, under which DOC refused to treat the CIG programme as terminated, was not applicable in *Porcelain-on-Steel Cooking Ware from Mexico*.

Questions 18 and 19

5.366 The US is arguing that the EC's questions 18 and 19 are "not really questions", and suggests that the EC is asking the US to research and perform "new calculations", which were not on the record of the sunset review. The fact is that the DOC should have investigated both the projected denominator and the remaining amount of subsidy, in order to make a determination under 21.3. It is therefore saying that it was not required to look at these factors in a sunset. The EC would request the Panel to take due note of this statement.

J. Comments of the United States on the Responses of the European Communities to Questions from the Panel Following the First Meeting of the Panel

5.367 The United States does not intend to comment on every response by the EC to the Panel's questions, particularly where the issues raised have been addressed in prior written submissions of the United States. Instead, the United States will comment briefly on those specific responses where additional points or emphasis is warranted. First, however, there are several overarching theories or assumptions in the EC's answers that are best addressed in general.

5.368 In particular, the United States observes that the EC in its answers espouses a general principle that any provision of the *SCM Agreement* is potentially applicable *mutatis mutandis* to any other provision of the *SCM Agreement*.[82] According to the EC, the only limitation on this free-for-all application is that a provision must be "relevant to the issues" covered by another Article and that its application "does not create a situation of conflict or is not specifically excluded". The EC's approach to treaty interpretation turns the customary rule of treaty interpretation on its head.

5.369 Article 31 of the *Vienna Convention* reflects the basic principle of treaty interpretation. In particular, Article 31(1) provides that a "treaty shall be interpreted in good faith in accordance with the ordinary meaning to be given to the *terms* of the treaty in their *context* and in the light of its *object and purpose*". (Emphasis added). The EC's approach to treaty interpretation is the very antithesis of this customary rule. Rather than reading the words of a provision and interpreting them "in light of the object and purpose" of the Agreement, the EC would require Members to interpret the object and purpose and then, regardless of the plain meaning of the words, interpret those words in light of the "object and purpose" as divined by the Member. This runs afoul of the Appellate Body's admonition in *Japan – Alcoholic Beverages*, that "the treaty's 'object and purpose' is to be referred to in determining the meaning of the 'terms of the treaty' and not as an independent basis for interpretation."[83]

5.370 In its answers to the Panel's questions, the EC makes various assumptions regarding the "purposes" of various provisions of the *SCM Agreement* without reference to the text of the *SCM Agreement*, and then refers to obligations not found in the text which presumably derive from these "purposes". This use of "purposes" is precisely the "independent basis for interpretation" which the Appellate Body has de-

[82] *See, e.g.*, EC responses to Panel Questions 5(a) and (b).

[83] *Japan – Taxes on Alcoholic Beverages*, p.11, n.20 ("[T]he treaty's 'object and purpose' is to be referred to in determining the meaning of the 'terms of the treaty' and not as an independent basis for interpretation.").

scribed as incorrect, and operates to circumvent the requirement in DSU Article 3.2 that Dispute Settlement Body rulings cannot add to or diminish the rights and obligations provided in the covered agreements. If every "relevant" *SCM Agreement* provision applied to every other *SCM Agreement* provision (*mutatis mutandis*) unless the application created "a situation of conflict", the purely theoretical questions of what is "relevant" and what creates "a situation of conflict" would become the focus of every WTO dispute. The EC's approach ignores a fundamental tenet that where the Members wished to have explicit obligations set forth in one provision apply in another context, they did so expressly.[84] If accepted, the EC's approach would result in the nullification the Members' expectations as *explicitly* expressed in the *SCM Agreement*.[85]

5.371 Turning now to the EC's answers to specific questions, with respect to Question 1(a), the EC has applied its treaty interpretation approach to the Panel's question as to whether the Article 11.9 *de minimis* standard applies to reviews under Article 21.2. The result is that, according to the EC, sometimes Article 11.9 is applicable to reviews under Article 21.2 and sometimes Article 11.9 is not applicable to reviews under Article 21.2. According to the EC, whether Article 11.9 is relevant in Article 21.2 reviews is dependent on the purpose of the review. This type of analysis combines the worst of the EC's relevance- and purpose-based treaty interpretation approach and results in what is certain to be the standard answer to this type of inquiry based on the EC's approach: it depends.[86]

5.372 With respect to Questions 1(b) and (c), the EC's answers reflect reliance on assumptions concerning the purpose of the negligibility standards and its interpretation theory that every provision can be considered applicable to every other provision barring explicit conflict. However, as the United States demonstrated in its responses to the Panel's questions, neither the text of the *SCM Agreement* nor the practicalities associated with conducting a five-year review support the EC's view that a negligibility test is required under Article 21.3. Furthermore, even under the EC's proposed approach towards negligibility, the EC recognizes that there must be a demonstration that the amount of the subsidy "is not going to increase above [the current] level or that imports would not rise above *de minimis* upon removal of the measure". Thus, the EC and the United States are in concurrence that current subsidy or volume levels by themselves, without a prospective inquiry into likely future levels, are not sufficient to require termination of an order.

5.373 The EC's answer to Question 1(d) relies upon what it claims is "an irrefutable presumption" as to the purpose of the *de minimis* and negligible import standards.

---

[84] Article 21 itself illustrates this point in paragraph 4, which makes the provisions of Article 12 applicable to Article 21.3 reviews, and in paragraph 5, which expressly makes the provisions of Article 21 applicable to Article 18 undertakings. Examples of provisions that apply in other contexts include: the definition of "subsidy" in Article 1 ("For the purpose of this Agreement"); the definition of "interested parties" in Article 12.9 ("for the purposes of this Agreement"); calculation of the amount of a subsidy under Article 14 ("For the purpose of Part V"); definition of "injury" under Article 15 and footnote 45 ("Under this Agreement"); definition of "like product" under footnote 46 ("Throughout this Agreement"); definition of domestic industry in Article 16 ("For the purposes of this Agreement"); definition of "levy" under footnote 51 ("As used in this Agreement").

[85] *See Japan - Taxes on Alcoholic Beverages* ("*Japan Taxes*"), page 19 (discussing how the "omission" in Article III:2 of GATT 1994 to the general principle in Article III:1 "must have some meaning").

[86] *See also* EC's response to Panel Question 12(c).

The EC again purports to discern a purpose without reference to the text of the *SCM Agreement*. The EC then refers to obligations not found in the text which presumably derive from this "purpose" (*i.e.*, according to the EC, these standards must apply in sunset reviews under Article 21.3). As the United States demonstrated in its answers to the Panel's questions, by their very terms, Articles 27.10 and 27.11 apply only in investigations. The EC's use of "purposes" as an independent basis for interpretation in this case is incorrect and results in imputation into the *SCM Agreement* of "words that are not there.[87]

5.374 With respect to the EC's answers to Questions 2, 4, 9, and 13(b), the United States notes that the EC's responses fail to address the phrase "in a review initiated ... on their own initiative" contained in Article 21.3. The EC merely restates its argument that the evidentiary prerequisites of Article 11.6 apply to sunset reviews under Article 21.3. As demonstrated in the United States First Written Submission (paras. 60-62), the right of an authority to initiate a sunset review on its own initiative, as explicitly stated in Article 21.3, is unqualified. Whether a Member chooses to initiate a sunset review in every case through self-initiation or to initiate a review only in response to a "duly substantiated request" from the domestic industry is a decision that the plain text of Article 21.3 leaves to the Members.

5.375 With respect to the EC's answers to Questions 3, 11, and 13(b), the EC's answers either assume or specifically claim that Commerce self-initiates sunset reviews "without any shred of evidence". The EC is wrong. The results of the original countervailing duty order and of the most recent administrative reviews, if any, in general can be considered evidence of the existence of subsidization. The EC's argument that something more is required prior to initiation of a sunset review amounts to an argument that an authority must conduct the review before it initiates the review.

5.376 With respect to the EC's answers to Questions 5 and 6, the United States demonstrated above that the EC's approach to treaty interpretation (*i.e.*, any provision is in principle applicable *mutatis mutandis* to any other provision) is not consistent with customary rules of treaty interpretation. At the very least, the EC's response to these questions demonstrates the futility of relying on the EC's approach to interpret the meaning of the words contained in Article 21.3. According to the EC, Members may not rely on the plain text of the *SCM Agreement* to determine their obligations. Instead, the "object and purpose" of the *SCM Agreement* – as identified, of course, by the EC – trump the text of the Agreement.

5.377 In the *US Shrimp* case, the Appellate Body rejected this type of unconventional approach to treaty interpretation, stating as follows:[88]

> A treaty interpreter must begin with, and focus upon, the text of the particular provision to be interpreted. It is in the words constituting that provision, read in their context, that the object and purpose of the states parties to the treaty must first be sought. Where the meaning imparted by the text itself is equivocal or inconclusive, or where confirmation of the correctness of the reading of the text itself is desired, light from the object and purpose of the treaty as a whole may usefully be sought.

---

[87] *See India Patent Protection*, para. 45.

[88] *United States - Import Prohibition of Certain Shrimp and Shrimp Products*, WT/DS58/AB/R, Report of the Appellate Body adopted 6 November 1998, para. 114 (footnote omitted).

Thus, while the object and purpose of an agreement can be instructive in interpreting the text, the object and purpose cannot be used to override the text. In other words, object and purpose cannot be used to write into the text "words that are not there".[89]

5.378 In its response to Question 14, the EC suggests that Commerce did not exercise due diligence in refusing to consider the calculation memorandum from the original investigation. As the United States demonstrated in its First Written Submission (paras. 102-105), the calculation memorandum was not on the administrative record of the sunset review because the German producers failed to place it there in a timely fashion. Although cited by the EC as such, the Appellate Body's decision in *Pakistan Yarn* does not stand for the proposition that "new" evidence should be considered by a Panel in a dispute. The EC emphasizes that in *Pakistan Yarn* the Appellate Body addressed only the question of whether the Panel should have considered extra-record evidence consisting of facts that were not in existence at the time the administrative determination was made and hence could not have been known. However, that was because the United States specifically limited its appeal to the issue of whether a panel can consider evidence that was not in existence at the time of the national authority's determination. As the United States demonstrated in its First Written Submission (paras. 49-51), similar restrictions apply with respect to a panel's review of other types of extra-record information. Nothing in *Pakistan Yarn* or other Appellate Body or adopted Panel reports suggests that the restrictions on a Panel's review of evidence would not likewise apply with respect to properly-rejected information that had existed at the time the authorities made their determination.

5.379 In response to Question 15, the EC asserts that Commerce systematically "refuses" to change the rate from the original subsidy rate determined in the investigation. The EC is wrong. In the instant case, Commerce in fact agreed with the EC and the German producers that two programmes had been terminated with no continuing benefits. Commerce, therefore, adjusted the net countervailable subsidy rate accordingly.[90] More importantly however, the United States would point out that, as demonstrated in our First Written Submission (70-87), nothing in the *SCM Agreement* requires consideration of the magnitude of subsidization in determining the likelihood of continuation or recurrence of subsidization.

5.380 Question 18 addresses the evidentiary and procedural aspects of Commerce's sunset review. The EC's response to this question is disingenuous and misleading. As a general matter, and as discussed in greater detail in the United States' First Written Submission (paras. 14-23, 109-116), Commerce's sunset review followed reasonable, appropriate procedures that fully comply with the evidentiary and procedural requirements of Articles 21 and 12. The EC is wrong when it claims that the respondent interested parties, including the German producers, "were not given *any* opportunity" to present all evidence which they considered relevant in the sunset review. (Emphasis added). If the respondent interested parties failed to *gather and prepare* evidence during the 15 months prior to the scheduled initiation of the sunset review,

---

[89] As another blatant example of the EC's efforts to rewrite the text of the Agreement, the United States notes that throughout its responses (*e.g., EC Responses to Questions 9, 12, 14, 15, 16(a) and 16(b)),* the EC misquotes the text of the Agreement by inserting a "causality" test into Article 21.3. Aside from the EC's obvious misquoting of the Agreement, the United States finds this particularly troublesome given that the injury-related aspects of the United States' action are not within the terms of reference in this dispute.

[90] *See Sunset Calculation Memorandum*, p.1 (Exhibit EC-8).

they have only themselves to blame. Contrary to the EC's response, the United States never suggested that respondent interested parties could *submit* this information prior to initiation of the sunset review.

5.381 The EC's assertion that sunset information requirements were "vague" or "perfunctory" is also wrong. Fifteen months before initiation of the sunset review, the statutory requirements, the regulatory requirements (including the standard questionnaire), and Commerce's extensive *Sunset Policy Bulletin*, providing detailed guidance on methodological and analytical issues not explicitly addressed by the statute and regulations, were all available to respondent interested parties. Again, if the parties' failed to review and consider the guidance provided in these documents in preparation of their submissions, they have only themselves to blame. Finally, the EC's assertion that the respondent interested parties did not have access to the evidence presented by the other parties in the sunset review is simply false. Commerce's regulations require service of all submissions on all parties to the proceeding; there is no evidence that the parties did not do so in this case.

K. Second Written Submission of the European Communities

1. Introduction

5.382 The European Communities ("EC") will concentrate in this submission on responding to and commenting on the facts and arguments submitted by the US so far, in particular those that emerged in the oral statements to the first meeting of the Panel and in the questions from the Panel.

5.383 It is interesting to see how little the US has had to offer in terms of justifying its position. This may be summarised as follows: Article 21.3 of the *SCM Agreement* has to be read in a literal, formalistic way, without regard to its object and purpose and in complete isolation from the remaining provisions of the *SCM Agreement*.

5.384 At this stage, the EC would also like to point out that it respectfully disagrees with the preliminary ruling issued by the Panel at its first meeting with the Parties on its terms of reference and expedited sunset reviews. Having not yet seen the actual reasoning of the Panel, the EC is obliged to reserve its right in this respect for the remaining stages of the proceeding. The EC is firmly of the view that the Panel's ruling on this point is an error in law. For those reasons, the EC will clarify, to the extent still necessary, only the factual aspects of its argument relating to expedited reviews, as this may be necessary in subsequent adjudication of this matter.

2. Standard of Review

5.385 The EC agrees with the summary of the "key elements" of the report in the *United States – Cotton Yarn* case,[91] where Appellate Body laid down the standard of review that panels should follow under Article 11 of the DSU (at para. 74). The EC notes that the Appellate Body cited there with approval its previous finding that the national authorities "must undertake additional investigative steps, when the circumstances so require, in order to fulfil their obligation to evaluate all relevant factors" (at para. 73). Indeed, this echoes the Appellate Body's finding in particular in the *United States – Lamb Safeguard* case, where it held that:

---

[91] Appellate Body Report, *United States – Transitional Safeguard Measure on Combed Cotton Yarn from Pakistan*, WT/DS192/AB/R, circulated 8 October 2001, paras. 66-81.

"...competent authorities have an *independent* duty of investigation and that they cannot "remain[] passive in the face of possible shortcomings in the *evidence* submitted, and *views* expressed, by the *interested parties*."[92] (emphasis added) In short, competent authorities are obliged, in some circumstances, to go beyond the arguments that were advanced by the interested parties during the investigation. As *competent authorities* themselves are obliged, in some circumstances, to go beyond the arguments of the interested parties in reaching their own determinations, so too, we believe, *panels* are not limited to the arguments submitted by the interested parties to the competent authorities in reviewing those determinations in WTO dispute settlement."[93]

5.386 That is why the EC considers that for the purpose of determining whether the US authorities have evaluated all relevant factors and examined all pertinent facts, the Panel can take advantage of the provision of Article 13 of the DSU. It is also noteworthy that in the view of the Appellate Body "in describing the duties of competent authorities, we simultaneously define the duties of panels in reviewing the investigations and determinations carried out by competent authorities" (at para. 73). Furthermore, the EC agrees that the standard of review laid down by the Appellate Body with respect to the Safeguards Agreement is equally applicable to the standard of review to be applied under the *SCM Agreement* (at para. 76).

5.387 What is particularly important is the finding by the Appellate Body that "a panel reviewing the due diligence exercised by a Member in making its determination...has to put itself in the place of that Member at the time it makes its determination" (at para. 78). Application of this principle to the facts of the present case would clearly require the present Panel to consider the evidence that existed and was made available to the US DOC but which it refused to take into account on the erroneous allegation that it was submitted outside the time limit. The evidence the EC claims the US authorities should have taken into account is evidence that definitively existed at the time the DOC made the determination. Moreover, it was well known to the US authorities since they were the actual authors of that evidence. As in the *Cotton Yarn* case, this evidence is in the form of data on the declining balance methodology and the level of subsidisation of the German exporters under the CIG programme. The accuracy of the above is not denied even by DOC in its final determination in this case nor by the US's submissions to the Panel so far. It follows that this was not only relevant evidence but evidence indispensable for the proper conduct of the sunset review. The legal consequence of the DOC's refusal to consider it should lead to the reversal of the DOC's findings.

5.388 The EC does not request the Panel to carry out a *de novo* review in this case but simply to find that the DOC's determination is inconsistent with the US obligations under Article 21.3 of the *SCM Agreement* "to determine" subsidisation, causality and injury, also because it refused to consider highly relevant evidence that existed at the time of the determination and of the existence of which they were fully aware at that time.

---

[92] *Ibid.*, para. 55.

[93] Appellate Body Report, United-States – Safeguard Measures on Imports of Freshn Chilled or Frozen Lamb Meat from New Zealand and Australia ("United-States – Lamb Safeguards"), WT/DS177/AB/R, WT/DS178/AB/R, adopted 16 May 2001, para. 114.

3. *Article 21.3 of the SCM Agreement*

5.389 The text of Article 21.3 of the *SCM Agreement* mandates that WTO Members *shall terminate* any countervailing duty on a date *not later than five years* from its imposition (or from the date of a most recent review that has covered both subsidisation and injury, or of a sunset review). Thus, the obligation clearly spelt out in the text of this Article is that of an ending in the life of any countervailing duty after five years.

5.390 The text of Article 21.3 then proceeds to envisage one possible exception to this obligation, which is that a countervailing duty could be continued if the domestic authorities (1) initiate a review before the five years' deadline on the domestic authorities' own initiative or on the request of domestic industry prior to the five years deadline; and (2) determine that the expiry of the duty would be likely to lead to continuation or recurrence of subsidisation and injury.

5.391 The second of the above requirements reflects the *ratio* of the obligation and of its limited exception. These are to be found in the first paragraph of Article 21, which provides that "a countervailing duty shall remain in force only as long as and to the extent necessary to prevent subsidisation that is causing injury". In other words, as a countervailing duty is a trade defence measure which hinders trade, it can only be justified for a limited period of time – as long as necessary or, at the most, 5 years – *unless* the elements which had justified its imposition in the first place (i.e. subsidisation, causality and injury) are likely to continue or recur. In order to ascertain the likelihood of continuation or recurrence of these elements, a determination should be conducted as laid down in Article 21.3, as well as a series of other procedural and substantive requirements as laid down in other provisions of the *SCM Agreement* must be undertaken. These other provisions constitute therefore the necessary context of Article 21.3 and it is necessary to take them into account in order to give proper meaning and apply correctly its provisions.

5.392 In order to ascertain the likelihood of continuation or recurrence of these elements, a determination should be made as laid down in Article 21.3, and a series of other procedural and substantive requirements as laid down in other provisions of the *SCM Agreement* must be undertaken. For the purposes of this specific case, Article 21.3 should therefore be read in conjunction with the other relevant provisions of the *SCM Agreement*, in particular on initiation and subsequent investigation (Article 11) and the *de minimis* rule (Article 11.9).

4. *Initiation of Sunset Reviews*

(a) By Automatically Initiating Sunset Reviews the US Acts Inconsistently with the Obligation of Termination Laid Down in Article 21.3 of the *SCM Agreement*.

5.393 US law, by requiring that sunset reviews be automatically initiated, violates Article 21.3 of the *SCM Agreement* because it transforms an exception into a general rule. This is not only contrary to the letter and the object and purpose of the *SCM Agreement* but, coupled with the other characteristics of US procedure that will be analysed below, leads to the automatic continuation and perpetuation of countervailing duties.

5.394 As a matter of fact, a simple look at the outcome of the sunset reviews conducted by the DOC proves the above point. It seems that since July 1998, DOC conducted 204 full sunset reviews of Anti-Dumping and CVD duty orders. It appears that as far as Anti-Dumping duty orders were concerned, in only 3 out of about 150 cases, the DOC found that there was no likelihood of recurrence or continuation of dumping. On the other hand, with regard to CVD orders, of the 54 sunset reviews conducted, DOC did not find likelihood of recurrence or continuation of subsidisation and injury only in 3 cases after a full review. In 2 more cases DOC found likelihood of recurrence or continuation of subsidisation on *de minimis* grounds. These data provide clear evidence of the fact that the US law and regulations are biased in favour of keeping and perpetuating unjustified CVD orders.

5.395 Even when DOC "conducts" a full sunset review, the evidentiary presumptions that it applies are so unyielding that a foreign respondent has no chance of succeeding in the sunset review. For example, as detailed below, DOC irrefutably presumes that, if the allocation period of a non-recurring subsidy has not expired before the end of the sunset review, then the benefit of the programme will continue undiminished at the same level calculated during the original investigation. Because DOC normally applies a 15-year allocation period in cases involving steel, application of this presumption means that, if a foreign company receives a non-recurring subsidy during the original period of investigation that results in the assessment of countervailing duties, DOC will automatically find a likelihood of continuation of subsidisation for the next 15 years regardless of the time period that has lapsed in the meantime and of any other changes in that subsidy programme. US law is clearly biased towards the unjustified continuation and perpetuation of countervailing duties, in violation of the undisputed duty to terminate them laid down in Article 21 of the *SCM Agreement*.

(b) The Self-Initiation of Sunset Reviews Requires Sufficient Evidence of the Likelihood of Continuation or Recurrence of Subsidisation, Causality and Injury.

5.396 Under US law, sunset reviews are always self-initiated by DOC not later than 30 days before the fifth anniversary of an order. Therefore, as the US has admitted at the first meeting of the Panel, the possibility of waiting for a request of the domestic industry has just not been implemented in US law.

5.397 The purpose and effect of new investigations (under Article 11 of the *SCM Agreement*) and sunset reviews (under Article 21.3) are essentially the same. Under Article 11, the self-initiation of an original investigation by domestic authorities is an exceptional hypothesis, which is justified only if the domestic authorities have sufficient evidence of subsidisation, injury and causal link. Thus, without sufficient evidence the domestic authorities should not initiate an investigation. As Article 21.3 requires the investigating authority to make a determination of likelihood of continuation or recurrence of subsidisation and injury, it is reasonable to require that the domestic authorities, in order to initiate a sunset review on their own initiative, should be in possession of a level of evidence that is also sufficient as regards likelihood of continuation or recurrence of subsidisation, causality and injury. Articles 22.1 and 22.7 provide further support for this proposition.

5.398 The response of the US to this claim is essentially that the EC purports to read into Article 21.3 language that is not there. In other words, the US is proposing a interpretation of the terms of Article 21.3 which is formalistic and in complete isolation of its object, purpose and context. As the EC has already explained with its previous submissions, all the US arguments in defence should be rejected. The Appellate Body has held several times that "omissions in different contexts may have different meanings, and omission, in and of itself, is not necessarily dispositive".[94] For example, in the *Canada – Automotive Industry* report, the Appellate Body held that the panel in that case had erred because it failed to examine the ordinary meaning of the terms in their relevant context and in light of the object and purpose of the entire *SCM Agreement*.[95]

5.399 The EC submits that the US arguments in this case suffer from the same defect. The fact that US law requires sunset reviews to be automatically self-initiated, without the need that sufficient evidence of likelihood of continuation or recurrence of subsidisation and injury be present, violate Article 21.3, read in conjunction with Article 21.1, Article 11, Article 12, Article 15 and Article 22, because it leads to continuation of CVD measures that are not necessary to counteract subsidisation and injury.

5. *US Law, Regulations and Administrative Practices are Inconsistent with the Obligation to "determine" the Likelihood of Continuation or Recurrence of Subsidization and Injury*

5.400 As set out at length in the EC's first written submission[96], the second requirement that Article 21.3 of the *SCM Agreement* imposes in order to allow a derogation from the presumption of termination of countervailing duties is that the domestic authorities *determine*, i.e. make a positive finding on subsidisation, causality and injury.[97]

5.401 This requirement is reinforced by the overall object and purpose of Article 21.3 of the *SCM Agreement* as laid down in Article 21.1: that countervailing duties should remain in force only as long as and to the extent necessary to counteract injurious subsidisation. In other words, Article 21.1 of the *SCM Agreement* permits a countervailing duty to continue after five years *only if* it is established in a proper fresh determination that injurious subsidisation is likely to continue if the order were to expire. As the Appellate Body held in the comparable case *Korea DRAMS,* the continued imposition of the duty "must be essentially dependent on, and therefore assignable to, a foundation of positive evidence that the circumstances demand it. In

---

[94] Appellate Body Report, Canada – Certain Measures Affecting the Automotive Industry ("Canada – Automotive Industry"), WT/DS139/AB/R, WT/DS142/AB/R, adopted 19 June 2000, para. 138.

[95] *Ibid.*, paras. 139-143.

[96] EC first written submission, paras. 67-71.

[97] Appellate Body Report, United States – Imposition of Countervailing Duties on Certain Hot-Rolled Lead and Bismuth Carbon Steel Products Originating in the United Kingdom ("United States – Leaded Bars"), WT/DS138/AB/R, adopted 7 June 2000, at para. 54.

other words, the need for the continued imposition of the duty must be demonstrable on the basis of the evidence adduced"[98].

5.402 Under US law, Section 751(c), in conjunction with Section 752, mandates the DOC to consider only: (a) the net countervailable subsidy determined in the original investigation, and (b) whether there were any changes in the subsidies since the original investigation that may affect the countervailing duty. The EC does not deny that the CVD rate from the original investigation, which the DOC normally selects on the basis that it is the only rate that "reflects the behaviour of governments and exporters without the discipline of an order in place", may in some cases be a factor to take into account. However, as it has been explained, the object and purpose of the terms of Article 21.3 in context clearly require domestic authorities to make a new, proper "determination". This is because CVD orders can only be maintained for a limited period of time *unless it is demonstrated* that the elements which had justified their imposition in the first place, i.e. subsidisation, causality and injury, are likely to continue or recur in the absence of the order.

5.403 The US admitted in its first written submission and in the oral hearing that no fresh investigation is ever conducted in a sunset review[99]. This practice is in violation of the requirements of Article 21.3 of the *SCM Agreement* to make a new "determination" about the likelihood of continuation or recurrence of subsidisation and injury. Moreover, by in fact requiring that likelihood of continuation or recurrence of a subsidy be undertaken in previous *administrative reviews,* it in reality shifts the burden of proving a change in circumstances on the foreign exporters. Administrative reviews are considered by the *SCM Agreement* as non-obligatory. Therefore, the fact that a party did not request an administrative review cannot relieve in any way the domestic authorities from their basic and primary duty to make a fresh determination about the likelihood of continuation or recurrence of subsidisation under Article 21.3 sunset reviews.

5.404 Moreover, in the case of a *non-recurring subsidy*, maintaining that "the findings in the original investigation provide the only evidence reflecting the behaviour of the respondents without the discipline of countervailing measures in place" is misleading. In such a case, it is positively known that, in the absence of new subsidies or other evidence, the amount of the subsidy is diminishing and is bound to disappear in accordance with DOC's method of calculation. For example, in the present case, the main subsidy, the CIG programme, was a non-recurring subsidy. Thus, the continuation or not of its benefits was easy to establish by taking into account DOC's calculation memorandum, which was part of the file of the original investigation. DOC was the actual author of this memorandum and it was fully aware of its existence and relevance in determining that there could be no "likelihood" of continuation or recurrence of subsidisation and injury in this case[100].

---

[98] Panel Report, United States - Anti-Dumping Duty on Dynamic Random Access Memory Semiconductors (DRAMS) of One Megabit or Above from Korea ("United States – DRAMS"), WT/DS99/R, adopted 19 March 1999, para. 6.41.

[99] At pp. 21-22.

[100] A copy of the calculation memorandum that DOC prepared for Preussag in the original investigation is attached to this submission as Exhibit EC-22. As shown, this memorandum confirms the evidence submitted by the Government of Germany and the German producers during the sunset review demonstrating that no meaningful amount of subsidies were paid under the CIG programme after 1986.

5.405 If a final determination of likelihood of recurrence or continuation of subsidisation in a sunset review had to be based exclusively on evidence reflecting the behaviour of the respondents without the order in force, it is self-evident that a respondent will never get rid of a CVD duty on such basis. For those reasons, the EC considers that, as a general rule, the same elements and factors that the investigating authorities took into account in the original investigation in a retrospective manner can be analysed in a prospective way during a sunset review. These are laid down essentially in Articles 11, 12 and 15 of the *SCM Agreement*. However, the range of factors to be taken into account in making the forward-looking assessment necessary to establish the likelihood of recurrence or continuation of subsidisation has to be evaluated on case by case basis, as it mainly depends on the kind of subsidy under examination. For example, if it is a recurring unemployment subsidy, the investigating authorities should consider the likelihood of lay-offs within the reasonable future. In the case at issue, however, the main subsidy was a non-recurring subsidy that by definition cannot recur. There could have been no continuation of benefits in such a case, if the US authorities were simply to take into consideration the calculation memorandum that was part of the file of the original investigation.

5.406 The US argues that "...the findings in the original investigation provide the only evidence reflecting the behaviour of the respondents without the discipline of countervailing measures in place". There is, therefore, a need to understand what exactly the US means by using the terms "discipline in place". The EC submits that this reference in fact assimilates CVD orders to antidumping duties. The rationale of granting subsidies and imposing CVD orders are, however, drastically different from those pertaining to dumping and the imposition of AD duties. In the latter case there is one actor, the individual exporter, who can swiftly decide the whole strategy of the company regarding when, where and at what price to export, if the AD duty were to expire. Conversely, in the case of subsidies the situation is not the same, because governments normally do not behave commercially in the same way as individual companies. For instance, in case of non-recurring subsidies, it is more reasonable to assume that governments will not rush again to grant a new subsidy soon after a CVD order were allowed to expire. To speak of a "discipline in place", therefore, is to disregard completely the peculiarities and specificities of the reasons for which governments usually grant subsidies, compared to the risk of recurrence of dumping. It follows that, as a matter of fact and law, a CVD order is not a "discipline" in particular in case of non-recurring, declining subsidies, since such a subsidy has been given in the past, has been consumed for the period of time lapsed and is known that it will not recur in the future. It can, therefore, be said that in such cases the CVD order has no "disciplining" effect on exporters' behaviour. It also follows that applying again the rate of subsidy determined in the original investigation is a clear violation of Article 21.3 and the obligation to make a fresh determination on likelihood of subsidisation, causality and injury.

5.407 It follows that the US defence is without merit, particularly in the case of a subsidy recognised by the US DOC to be a non-recurring one. In such a case, in the absence of new subsidies, it is definitively known that the amount of the subsidy will fall and is bound to disappear within the determined period of time in the original investigation. The EC does not accept, therefore, the view that a review under Article 21.3 involves difficulties. Governments are used to this type of calculations and there can be no excuse to merely side step any need to undertake a fresh forward-looking determination in a sunset review on the basis of such alleged difficulties.

5.408 In a sunset review, the forward-looking aspect of the assessment, implied by the terms "would be likely to lead to", refers in particular to the continuation or recurrence of subsidisation, causality and injury. Because this involves a certain amount of projections extrapolating from existing data, it may be argued that Article 21.3 somewhat "softens" the requirements in particular of Article 11.2 and 11.3 of the *SCM Agreement* relating to the "existence" of subsidy, injury and causal link. However, a sunset review determination that is based only on the CVD rate established in the original investigation or one that does not apply the 1 per cent *de minimis* rule violates clearly the whole object and purpose of the *SCM Agreement*. The US, instead of conducting a fresh "determination" in the proper sense of this term, advance as excuses reasons pertaining to the difficulties in calculating the numerator or denominator in the formula used to calculate the subsidy. These are neither exceptional nor insurmountable difficulties, however, and the US takes no concrete steps and does absolutely nothing positive to deal with them, other than simply acknowledging their existence. Article 21.3 does not provide a particular methodology to be followed in making the "likelihood" determination. However, this is nothing exceptional or unusual as other WTO Agreements are equally short in providing all the details about the application and implementation of comparable provisions.[101] For example, the Appellate Body has found recently with regard to Articles 4.1(b) and 4.2(a) of the Agreement on Safeguards that:

> "As facts, by their very nature, pertain to the present and the past, the occurrence of future events can never be definitively proven by facts. There is, therefore, a tension between a future-oriented "threat" analysis, which, ultimately, calls for a degree of "conjecture" about the likelihood of a future event, and the need for a fact-based determination. Unavoidably, this tension must be resolved through the use of facts from the present and the past to justify the conclusion about the future, namely that serious injury is "clearly imminent".[102]

5.409 As the Appellate Body has stressed in both the *Thailand – H-Beams* and in the *United States – Lamb Safeguard* reports, omissions in the text of WTO Agreements are not dispositive and the true meaning of the provision in question should be examined in the light of its object and purpose in the appropriate context. In the present case, by virtue of Article 21.4, the determination of "likelihood" of continuation or recurrence of subsidisation and injury has to be made on the basis of "evidence", as this is defined in Article 12 of the *SCM Agreement*. Moreover, the term "likelihood" means "the state or fact of being likely".[103] Therefore, the domestic authorities in a sunset review cannot base their determination on mere conjecture or speculation in total disregard of the factual record and evidence available. In addition, the domestic authorities cannot escape of their duty to conduct a fresh, proper determination, on the ground that this is a difficult exercise or that some factors, as the US argues about the numerator or denominator in this case, are missing or difficult to calculate.

---

[101] See Appellate Body Report, United States – Safeguard Measures on Imports of Fresh, Chilled or Frozen Lamb Meat from New Zealand and Australia ("United States – Lamb Safeguard"), WT/DS177/AB/R, WT/DS178/AB/R, adopted 16 May 2001, para. 137.

[102] See *United States – Lamb Safeguard*, para. 136, emphasis added.

[103] Concise Oxford English Dictionary, 1995.

5.410 In this regard, the Panel should take account of the fact that DOC even refused to consult its own calculation memoranda from the original investigation to determine the amount of grants paid under the CIG programme after 1986. In fact, to the extent DOC relied upon the rates calculated in its original investigation, the duty of investigation laid down in Article 21.3 of the *SCM Agreement* would also require at a minimum that DOC made all documents showing how the rates were calculated in the original investigation also part of the record in the sunset review.

5.411 The US DOC cannot hide behind the argument that it is prohibited by US law from making the memoranda of the original investigation part of the record in the sunset review[104]. The US International Trade Commission ("ITC") is subject to the same procedures regarding the treatment of business proprietary information as DOC. However, unlike DOC, the ITC in its sunset reviews automatically makes the confidential version of its original determination, as well as the complete staff report from the original investigation, part of the record of the sunset review. This is done automatically right at the beginning of the sunset review so that all parties will be able to use this information in preparing their arguments. The ITC simply provides the documents the same confidential status in the review that they enjoyed in the original investigation.

5.412 Furthermore, the US DOC did not give to the EC respondent parties "ample opportunity" to present in writing all evidence to present in writing all evidence which they consider[ed] relevant in respect of the investigation in question", as required by Article 21.3, in conjunction with Articles 12.1 and 21.4, of the *SCM Agreement*.

5.413 Before DOC's determines to conduct a full review under Article 21.3, interested parties are only requested to provide responses to the notice of initiation. The vague nature of the US DOC's information request, however, coupled with its refusal to accept any factual information after the initial 35 days of a sunset review proceeding violate the provisions of Article 12.1. In addition to this vague request for information, the US DOC regulations provide that "the Secretary normally will not accept or consider any additional information from a party after the time for filing rebuttals has expired."[105] Under the sunset regulations, rebuttals are required to be filed within 35 days of the publication of the notice of initiation in the Federal Register.[106] Thus, under the US DOC's regulations, an interested party, guided only by the vague request to provide any factual information regarding the likely effects of revocation of the countervailing duty order, has merely 35 days to provide all of its factual information in the sunset review, despite that fact that the sunset review statute provides DOC with up to 240 days to make its determination. Moreover, the fact that the US DOC's decision as to whether or not to conduct a full sunset review is not issued until 50 days after publication of the notice of initiation means that, even after the US DOC makes a determination to conduct a full sunset review, the parties will be given no additional opportunity whatsoever to submit factual information in this regard.[107]

5.414 With regards to the rights of defence and provision of information in the present case, the first time that the US DOC commented on the information submitted by the parties was in its preliminary results of 20 March 2000. In its issues and deci-

[104] See US First Written Submission at para. 104.

[105] 19 C.F.R. § 351.218(d)(4).

[106] 19 C.F.R. § 351.218(d)(3) & (4).

[107] 19 C.F.R. § 351.218(e)(1)(ii)(C)(1).

sion memo, the US DOC ignored the evidence submitted by the Government of Germany and the German producers showing that the Capital Investment Grants ("CIG") programme applied only to investments made prior to 1 January 1986 and that the amount of CIG paid after 1986 was so small that no countervailable benefit would remain after the end of the sunset review.[108] The DOC simply stated that, because there was evidence that CIG funds were received as late as 1990, it would "determine that benefit streams from this programme continue beyond the end of this sunset review."[109] It is important to underline that the US DOC did not give the German respondents any opportunity to submit additional evidence to respond to its comments in the preliminary determination. As explained in our written and oral submissions, the US DOC even refused a request to review its own calculation memoranda from the original investigation to determine the exact amount of the original grant payments made after 1986.

5.415 The EC believes that such a procedure that leaves respondents in complete darkness as to precisely what information an investigating authority requires until it is too late to provide the information cannot satisfy the requirements of Article 12.1. The US law and practice does not respect several provisions of Article 12 of the *SCM Agreement*, which by virtue of Article 21.4 is fully applicable to sunset reviews. In particular, Articles 12.1 and 12.1.1 lay down a general obligation to provide "ample opportunity" to exporters to present in writing all evidence they consider relevant. Article 12.2 allows also for the right to present information orally. Article 12.3 establishes in effect a procedure of mutual dialogue by providing that the affected exporters should be given timely opportunity "to see all information that is relevant to the presentation of their cases…and to prepare presentations on the basis of this information". Moreover, Article 12.8 provides that before the final determination is made, disclosure should take place "in such sufficient time for the parties to defend their interests". The principle underlying Article 12 of the *SCM Agreement*, therefore, is that during all stages of the reviews the interested parties should be given ample opportunity to present evidence, to have access to the evidence presented by the other parties (except where confidentiality applies), to present counter-evidence and to defend their interests at all stages leading up to the final determination. As explained above, none of these procedural rights and due process requirements are respected by the US DOC in sunset reviews and in the present case.

6. *The de minimis Rule Requirement*

5.416 US law does not provide for the application of *de minimis* requirement for CVD reviews. Section 703(b)(4)(a) of the Act, in fact, establishes a 1 per cent *de minimis* rule only for the initial determination of a countervailable subsidy. It is in Section 351.106(c)(1) of the *Sunset Regulations* and in Section III.A.6.(b) of the *Sunset Policy Bulletin* that a general rule requiring to apply a 0.5 per cent *de minimis* rule in all reviews, including sunset reviews, is to be found.

5.417 As explained at length in its first written submission[110] and oral statement[111], the EC considers that the 0.5 per cent *de minimis* threshold applied by the US in sun-

---

[108] Issues and Decision Memo, at p. 24-25, Exhibit EC-7.

[109] *Ibid.*, at 25.

[110] See under Heading 6.3.

[111] See paragraphs 35-46.

sets differs from the 1 per cent *de minimis* level which *should* apply in sunset reviews, and thus is in breach of Article 21.3, in conjunction with Article 11.9. The US response to this claim is again that the EC purports to read into Article 21.3 language that is not there. In other words, the US is proposing again a formalistic interpretation of the terms of Article 21.3 and in complete isolation of its object, purpose and context. As the EC has already explained with its previous submissions, all the US arguments in defence should be rejected. The Appellate Body has held several times that "omissions in different contexts may have different meanings, and omission, in and of itself, is not necessarily dispositive".[112]

5.418 Article 21.3 of the *SCM Agreement* clearly establishes a presumption of termination. It is only where the domestic authorities establish likelihood of the continued existence of an injurious subsidy that the countervailing duty under review can be maintained in place. However, in the *SCM Agreement* a subsidy level of less than 1 per cent is irrefutably presumed not to cause injury. This practice is codified in Article 11.9 of the *SCM Agreement*, which prevents the authorities from making a finding on subsidisation and injury on the basis of an amount of subsidy that is less than 1 per cent *ad valorem*. The EC sees no valid reason to depart from the application of the definition of injurious subsidisation under Article 11.9 in the context of sunset reviews under Article 21.3. Indeed, there appears to be no reason in the *SCM Agreement* that would plead in favour of a different interpretation. The ordinary meaning of the terms "subsidisation" and "injury" in context, taking also into account the object and purpose of the *SCM Agreement* as a whole, suggests that if there can be no "subsidisation" and "injury" finding in case of a *de minimis* amount of subsidy in an original investigation, the same must hold true *a fortiori* in the case of sunset reviews. Indeed, holding otherwise would run contrary to the very object and purpose of the *SCM Agreement* and would most likely lead to contradictory results and unjustified protectionism. It would also violate the text of Articles 21.3 and 21.1 of the *SCM Agreement* because it would allow the continuation of countervailing duties for five more years without there being any real need to counter subsidisation which is likely to cause injury.

5.419 The US has been arguing until now that it is being generous in applying the 0.5 per cent *de minimis* threshold under domestic law in sunsets. However, the absurdity of the US approach is that a subsidy that, if examined in a new investigation after 1995, would have been found to be *de minimis* under Article 11.9 of the *SCM Agreement*, would now become not *de minimis* under a sunset review and would continue to be applied for 5 more years. This is contrary not only to the text, context, and object and purpose of Article 21.3, but also to the WTO report *Brazil – Desiccated Coconut* where Article 21.3 was interpreted as the means by which, ultimately, even measures taken prior to the entry into force of the *WTO Agreement* will be brought in line with the disciplines of the *SCM Agreement*.[113]

7. *Conclusion*

5.420 In conclusion, the EC requests the Panel to find that the US basic countervailing duty law (Section 751(c), as complemented by Section 752, of the Act), its accompanying regulations (*Sunset Regulations*) and policy practices (*Sunset Policy*

[112] Appellate Body Report, *Canada – Automotive Industry* cit. supra, para. 138.

[113] Panel Report, *Brazil - Desiccated Coconut*, cit. supra.

Bulletin), and their concrete application to imports of certain corrosion-resistant steel products from Germany in the present case are inconsistent with Article 21 paragraphs 3, 1 and 4, Article 10 and Article 11.9 of the *SCM Agreement*.
5.421 The US countervailing duty law, regulations and practice should also be considered to be inconsistent with Article 32.5 of the *SCM Agreement* and, consequently, should be found to violate also Article XVI.4 of the WTO Agreement.

L. Second Written Submission of the United States

1. Introduction

5.422 We are now midway through this very straightforward dispute. The questions generated by the Panel after the first meeting address most of the issues arising in this case, and the United States' answers to those questions are separately provided together with this submission. Given the comprehensive nature of the Panel's questions, the United States intends to use this second submission to highlight the major legal and factual errors underlying the EC's claims.
5.423 At the outset, the United States reiterates that most of the EC's claims can be disposed of merely by applying fundamental principles of treaty interpretation. With respect to the EC's systemic challenge to US sunset review procedures, the EC asserts that the initiation standards and *de minimis* requirement of Article 11 must be read into Article 21.3. The EC's assertion, however, finds no support in the *SCM Agreement* and runs afoul of basic principles of treaty interpretation reflected in Article 31 of the *Vienna Convention on the Law of Treaties* ("*Vienna Convention*"), which "neither require nor condone the imputation into a treaty of words that are not there ... ."[114] The Panel should reject the EC's assertion and refuse to impute into Article 21.3 of the *SCM Agreement* "words that are not there."
5.424 The EC also is wrong with respect to its case-specific claims regarding the sunset determination by the US Department of Commerce ("Commerce") in corrosion-resistant carbon steel flat products from Germany. Commerce's determination that the expiry of the countervailing duty order would be likely to lead to the continuation or recurrence of subsidization is based on the continued existence and availability of the two programmes[115] previously found to have been used by German producers and the continued existence of benefit streams from the CIG programme previously found to benefit German producers. The EC has not disputed or refuted these facts. Thus, the Panel should reject the EC's claims concerning Commerce's sunset determination.
5.425 With this overview of the case as background, the United States will now briefly discuss some of the specific issues that have been raised in the case.

[114] *India - Patent Protection for Pharmaceutical and Agricultural Chemical Products* ("*India Patent Protection*"), WT/DS50/AB/R, Report of the Appellate Body adopted 16 January 1998, para. 45.
[115] The two programmes are the Aid for Closure of Steel Operations and the ECSC Redeployment Aid under Article 56(2)(b). Both of these programmes still exist. Furthermore, during the sunset review, the German Government, the EC, and German producers admitted that both of these programmes continued to provide some benefits. *See Commerce Sunset Preliminary Decision Memorandum*, p.12-14 (Exhibit EC-7).

2. *With Respect to its Claims Concerning US Sunset Review Procedures, the EC Has Failed to Demonstrate that the United States Has Acted Inconsistently with Any Obligation under the SCM Agreement*

5.426 As noted, the Panel can dispose of the EC's claims concerning US sunset review procedures simply by applying basic rules of treaty interpretation. Article 3.2 of the DSU directs panels to "clarify" WTO provisions "in accordance with customary rules of interpretation of public international law." The Appellate Body has recognized that Article 31 of the *Vienna Convention* reflects customary rules of interpretation. Article 31(1) provides that a "treaty shall be interpreted in good faith in accordance with the ordinary meaning to be given to the *terms* of the treaty in their *context* and in the light of its *object and purpose*." (Emphasis added). In applying Article 31, however, the Appellate Body has cautioned that an interpreter's role is limited to the words and concepts used in the treaty, and that the principles of interpretation set out in Article 31 "neither require nor condone the imputation into a treaty of words that are not there ... ."[116] It goes without saying that a panel cannot "clarify" a treaty provision that does not exist.

(a) Automatic Self-Initiation of Sunset Reviews is Consistent with the *SCM Agreement* because Article 21.3 Explicitly Authorizes Authorities to Initiate Sunset Reviews on their Own Initiative

5.427 The EC alleges that the provisions of US law providing for the automatic self-initiation of sunset reviews by Commerce are inconsistent with Article 21.3 of the *SCM Agreement*. For purposes of evaluating the EC's claims, customary rules of treaty interpretation dictate that the words of a treaty form the starting point for the process of interpretation. Therefore, the analysis begins with the text of Article 21.3, which provides:

> Notwithstanding the provisions of paragraphs 1[[117]] and 2[[118]], any definitive countervailing duty shall be terminated on a date not later than five years from its imposition ..., unless the authorities determine, in a review initiated before that date on their own initiative or upon a duly substantiated request made by or on behalf of the domestic industry within a reasonable period of time prior to that date, that the expiry of the duty would be likely to lead to continuation or recurrence of subsidization and injury.[52] The duty may remain in force pending the outcome of such a review.

---

[116] *India Patent Protection*, para. 45; *see also United States - Definitive Safeguard Measures on Imports of Circular Welded Carbon Quality Line Pipe from Korea*, WT/DS202/AB/R, Report of the Appellate Body circulated 15 February 2002 (unadopted) ("[W]ords must not be read into the Agreement that are not there.").

[117] Paragraph 1 of Article 21 provides that "[a] countervailing duty shall remain in force only as long as and to the extent necessary to counteract subsidization which is causing injury."

[118] Paragraph 2 of Article 21 is relevant to types of reviews, other than sunset reviews, such as countervailing duty assessment reviews. *See, e.g., United States - Imposition of Countervailing Duties on Certain Hot-Rolled Lead and Bismuth Carbon Steel Products Originating in the United Kingdom* ("*UK Lead Bar*"), WT/DS138/AB/R, Report of the Appellate Body adopted 7 June 2000, para. 53.

> [52] When the amount of the countervailing duty is assessed on a retrospective basis, a finding in the most recent assessment proceeding that no duty is to be levied shall not by itself require the authorities to terminate the definitive duty.

5.428 The plain text of Article 21.3 clearly and unambiguously permits authorities to initiate a review on "their own initiative." Notwithstanding this clear and unqualified text, the EC argues that authorities should not be able to self-initiate sunset reviews unless they have first satisfied the evidentiary requirements for the initiation of an investigation under Article 11. The EC believes that this is so because, according to the EC, a "parallelism" exists between the investigation and sunset review provisions of the *SCM Agreement.*[119] The EC's parallelism theory is just that – a theory. Under customary rules of treaty interpretation, a theory cannot overcome the ordinary meaning of the words of a treaty, taking into account their "context" and the "object and purpose" of the agreement.

5.429 If, as the EC posits, the *SCM Agreement* implicitly incorporates a parallelism between investigation and sunset review provisions, why then did the Members feel it necessary to provide *explicitly* that the evidentiary and procedural requirements for conduct of an investigation in Article 12 are made applicable in the conduct of sunset reviews *pursuant to Article 21.4*? Where Members wished to have an obligation set forth in one provision apply in another context, they did so expressly. The fact is that the Members chose not to incorporate the evidentiary requirements of Article 11.6 for the self-initiation of sunset reviews. The Panel should decline the EC's request to create an evidentiary obligation for self-initiation under Article 21.3 where no textual support exists for such an interpretation.

(b) There is no *de minimis* Standard for Sunset Reviews in the *SCM Agreement*

5.430 The other systemic challenge by the EC involves its claim that the *de minimis* standard of Article 11.9 applies to sunset reviews under Article 21.3. As the United States demonstrated in its First Written Submission and Oral Statement, nothing in Article 21.3 or elsewhere in the Agreement establishes a *de minimis* standard for sunset reviews. Furthermore, a contextual analysis of Article 21.3, in light of the object and purpose of the *SCM Agreement* and the particular provisions at issue, provides no support for the EC's claim that the Article 11.9 *de minimis* standard is applicable in sunset reviews under Article 21.3. Once again, the EC is asking the Panel to read into Article 21.3 "words that are not there."

5.431 The EC has failed to refute the United States' textual and contextual arguments. Instead, the EC attempts to commingle its factual, case-specific claims regarding the Commerce sunset determination on corrosion-resistant steel with the separate, purely legal issue of whether the Article 11.9 *de minimis* standard applies to sunset determinations under Article 21.3.[120] The factual and the legal issues are distinct, however, and the United States has addressed them separately in significant detail in its First Written Submission and Oral Statement. In addition, the United States addresses certain of the EC's factual claims in more detail below.

---

[119] EC Oral Statement, paras. 13-15.

[120] *See* EC Oral Statement, para. 38.

5.432 With respect to the purely legal issue, the EC merely reiterates its previous argument that the *de minimis* standard for investigations contained in Article 11.9 "should" apply in sunset reviews conducted pursuant to Article 21.3 because investigations and sunset reviews serve the same purpose.[121] The United States disagrees. The purpose of an investigation is to determine whether and to what extent subsidization exists. In this context, the function of the one percent *de minimis* standard contained in Article 11.9 is to determine whether foreign government subsidies warrant the imposition of a countervailing duty in the first instance. Using the example given in our First Written Submission (para. 80), if the investigating authority found that a government programme had provided recurring subsidies at a rate of more than one percent, imposition of a countervailing duty would be warranted if the subsidized imports were found to cause injury. In contrast, the focus of a sunset review is the future, *i.e.*, whether subsidization is likely to continue or recur. Therefore, the mere continued existence of a subsidy programme could warrant maintaining the duty beyond the five-year point, *even if the amount of the subsidy were currently zero*, because subsidization may be likely to recur absent the discipline of the countervailing duty. To read a particular *de minimis requirement* for sunset reviews into the Agreement would render footnote 52 a nullity.

5.433 In its Oral Statement, the EC opined that the United States has confused the purposes of an administrative (*i.e.*, assessment) review and a sunset review and the application of footnote 52.[122] It is the EC that is confused. Pursuant to Article 21.3 and footnote 52, the mere existence of a subsidy programme, even with a net countervailable subsidy rate of zero, could form the basis for a determination of likelihood of future subsidization in accordance with Article 21.3 and footnote 52. The United States agrees with the EC that footnote 52 refers to a situation where the authority determines that the subsidy rate for a particular time period is zero and that, in the United States, that determination takes place in the context of an administrative review.[123] The EC seems to think, however, that footnote 52 serves no other purpose than to make a point about administrative reviews. The EC posits that "[s]unset reviews under Article 21.3 are completely different from administrative reviews." If that is so, why did the Members include footnote 52 in Article 21.3, the provision governing sunset reviews? There must be a reason.

5.434 The United States considers that footnote 52 means that the current level of subsidization is not decisive as to whether subsidization is likely to recur. The EC has not offered any alternative interpretation. The reason for this gap in the EC's argumentation is that the EC's claim that a *de minimis* standard is required in the context of Article 21.3 sunset reviews would, if accepted, render note 52 meaningless.

5.435 In sum, the EC's claim that a *de minimis* standard exists for sunset reviews under Article 21.3 is without merit. Applying customary rules of treaty interpretation, the Panel should find that there is no *de minimis* standard for sunset reviews in the *SCM Agreement*.

---

121 EC Oral Statement, para. 37.

122 EC First Oral Statement, para.44.

123 EC Oral Statement, para. 44. Although not germane to the instant dispute, the United States does not agree with the EC's statement that footnote 52 refers to a situation where a subsidy is "*de minimis*" in an administrative review. Footnote 52 only discusses a finding in the most recent assessment proceeding that "no duty" is to be levied.

3. *With Respect to Commerce's Sunset Determination Involving Corrosion-Resistant Steel from Germany, the EC Has Failed to Demonstrate that the United States Acted Inconsistently with Any Obligation under the SCM Agreement*

5.436 In the original countervailing duty investigation, Commerce determined that German producers of corrosion-resistant steel benefitted from five different subsidy programmes. In the sunset review, Commerce made the following findings with respect to these five programmes:[124]

1. *Capital Investment Grants ("CIG")*. The benefit streams from non-recurring grants will continue beyond the five-year mark.
2. *Structural Improvement Aids*. The programme has been terminated.
3. *Special Subsidies for Companies in the Zonal Border Area*. The programme has been terminated.
4. *Aid for Closure of Steel Operations*. The programme continues to exist.
5. *ECSC Redeployment Aid Under Article 56(2)(b)*. The programme continues to exist.

5.437 Commerce also found that two additional subsidy programmes which were found to provide a zero-benefit to corrosion-resistant products in the period of investigation still existed: ECSC Article 54 Long-Term Loans, and Interest Rebates on ECSC Article 54 Loans.[125]

5.438 Significantly, the EC has not disputed the facts which form the basis for Commerce's sunset determination. On the contrary, the EC admits in its Oral Statement that payments under the CIG programme were made as late as February 1990.[126] The EC also admits in its Oral Statement that the Aid for Closure of Steel Operations and the ECSC Redeployment Aid under Article 56(2)(b) programmes continue to exist.[127] Also, during the sunset review itself, the German Government, the EC, and German producers admitted that both of these programmes continued to provide some benefits.[128]

5.439 The EC, however, continues to assert that Commerce acted inconsistently with the *SCM Agreement* by failing to consider the CIG programme terminated and its benefits expired based on the EC's theory that a *de minimis* standard of one percent is required in sunset reviews. Based on this theory, the EC argues that Commerce should have terminated the countervailing duty.

---

[124] *Commerce Sunset Preliminary Decision Memorandum*, pp.24-29 (Exhibit EC-7); *Commerce Sunset Final Decision Memorandum* (Exhibit EC-10).

[125] *Commerce Sunset Preliminary Decision Memorandum*, p.29 (Exhibit EC-7); *Commerce Sunset Final Decision Memorandum* (Exhibit EC-10). In the investigation, Commerce determined that long-term loans under ECSC Article 54 had been provided to the following German producers of corrosion-resistant carbon steel flat products: Hoesch, Preussag, and Thyssen. Commerce also determined that Preussag and Thyssen received interest rebates with respect to interest expenses incurred on ECSC Article 54 loans. *See Commerce Investigation Final*, 58 FR at 37316-21 (Exhibit EC-2).

[126] EC First Oral Statement, para. 26. Using the 15-year allocation period, the benefit stream from subsidies received after 1985 would continue past the five-year mark (*i.e.*, 1 January 2000).

[127] EC First Oral Statement, para. 39.

[128] *See Commerce Sunset Preliminary Decision Memorandum*, p.12-14 (Exhibit EC-7).

5.440 In advocating this position, the EC misconstrued, in its Oral Statement, the United States' position with respect to the CIG programme and the effect of footnote 52.[129] Concerning the CIG programme, Commerce determined that benefits from the non-recurring grants would continue beyond the five-year mark.

5.441 With respect to the effect of footnote 52 in sunset determinations, the United States stated in its First Written Submission that "[t]he mere continued existence of this same programme could warrant maintaining a duty beyond the five-year point, *even if* the amount of the subsidy was currently *zero*, as stated in footnote 52, because subsidization may recur absent the discipline of the duty."[130] *The reference to the "same programme" was not to the CIG programme, per se*, but to a hypothetical programme discussed by the United States as an example in the preceding paragraph 80 in drawing a distinction between the object and purpose of an investigation versus the object and purpose of a review.[131] In its sunset determination, Commerce found that the CIG programme was terminated, but its benefit stream continued past the sunset review period. In paragraph 81, however, the United States was explaining that footnote 52 stands for the proposition that an existing subsidy programme could be the basis for a determination in a sunset review that the expiry of the countervailing duty would likely lead to the continuation of subsidization even if Commerce found a net countervailable subsidy rate of *zero* attributable to that programme in the most recent administrative review.

5.442 Article 11 of the DSU directs panels to make an "objective assessment" of the facts of the case. The facts in this case include the continuation of benefit streams and the continued existence and availability of countervailable subsidy programmes previously found to have been used by German producers of corrosion-resistant steel. The Panel's objective assessment of these facts should result in a finding that Commerce's determination was not inconsistent with the *SCM Agreement*.

4. *Conclusion*

5.443 Based on the foregoing, the United States renews its request that the Panel make the findings described in paragraph 127 of its First Written Submission.

M. *Oral Statement of the European Communities at the Second Meeting of the Panel*

1. *Introduction*

5.444 The European Communities ("EC") presentation aims at responding at the basic US arguments by focusing mainly on four issues: (1) the proper interpretation of Article 21.3 of the *SCM Agreement* as regards the obligation to conduct a sunset review and to apply the *de minimis* rule of 1 per cent *ad valorem*; (2) what does it mean to determine in a sunset review whether the expiry of the duty is likely to lead to continuation or recurrence of subsidisation and injury; (3) the meaning and scope of Footnote 52 in sunset reviews; (4) the extent to which the Opinion of the US Court of International Trade (CIT) of 28 February 2002 has clarified some legal issues raised also in this Panel proceedings (Exhibit EC-24).

---

[129] EC First Oral Statement, para. 44.

[130] US First Submission, para. 81 (emphasis in original).

[131] US First Submission, para. 80.

5.445 The US has offered very little to justify its laws, regulations and practices in the present case and even this very little explanation has now been substantially disapproved by the Opinion of the US CIT of 28 February 2002. Unfortunately, the CIT had to interpret the case on the basis of the US law, which is inconsistent with the *SCM Agreement*, and therefore it could not go as far as the EC would have liked it to go in clarifying the legal situation. Moreover, the judgement is not final and it does not ensure that the underlying dispute in the present case will be resolved in a way that is consistent with the US obligations under the WTO and *SCM Agreements*.

2. *Interpretation of Article 21.2 SCM Agreement*

(a) Generally Accepted Rules on Treaty Interpretation

5.446 Whilst the US pretends to agree that the principles laid down in Articles 31 and 32 of the Vienna Convention should be used to interpret the terms of Article 21.3, in reality it quotes the Appellate Body report in *India - Patent* to rely on *one* criterion only, the wording of Article 21.3. The US pays *no* attention at all to the context and to the object and purpose of the *SCM Agreement*. However, as it is evident from the whole of paragraph 45 of the *India - Patent* and from the recent report in *US - Safeguard of Line Pipe from Korea*, the Appellate Body maintains that its customary approach is to seek the meaning of the terms of a provision in their context and in the light of the object and purpose of the Agreement (at para. 251). This is what the EC proposes the Panel to do in the present case, i.e. to read the terms of Article 21.3 in their context, and in light of the object and purpose of the *SCM Agreement*.
5.447 On the contrary, the US interpretation does not conform to the object and purpose of the *SCM Agreement* - which is to allow a CVD only as long as and to the extent necessary to counteract subsidisation and injury - as it is also evident by the clear terms of Article 21. In particular, it does not explain how is that a subsidy rate of less than 1 per cent would lead to subsidisation, injury and causality in a sunset review, when the same rate found in the original investigation would lead to automatic termination. If an interpretation is incompatible with the object and purpose of a treaty, this interpretation may well be wrong (Oppenheim, p. 1273).
5.448 The strict textual and isolationist interpretation proposed by the US runs also counter to the basic principle of good faith interpretation, because they will lead unavoidably to results which are manifestly absurd and unreasonable and would reduce Article 21.3 to inutility (Sinclair, p. 116, 120), and to the principle of effectiveness, according to which the parties to a treaty are assumed to intend its provisions to have the fullest value and effect and not to be meaningless (Oppenheim, p. 1281).
5.449 "Good interpretation is often no more that the application of common sense" (Aust, p. 202). Indeed, although it is normally not for an international tribunal to revise a treaty by reading into it provisions which it does not contain, it is nevertheless sometimes necessary to interpret its terms as implying such a term (Aust, p. 201). The EC provided several examples of panel and Appellate Body reports which, despite an identified omission in the relevant text, interpreted the provisions in the light of the object and purpose of the WTO Agreement in question so as not to render it a nullity (e.g. AB report in *US - Safeguard of Line pipe from Korea*, the AB report in *Brazil - Desiccated Coconut*, the AB report in *Argentina - Footwear Safeguards*, the AB report in *Korea - Dairy Safeguards*, the AB report in *US - Section 211 Omni-*

bus Appropriations Act). This well established case law suggests that the determination of the ordinary meaning cannot be done in the abstract, but only in the context of the treaty and in the light of its object and purpose. The task of interpreting a treaty is one of ascertaining "the logic inherent in the treaty" (Aust, p. 185) in its entirety. The interpretation proposed by the EC of the terms of Article 21.3 is consistent with the above principles and with the preparatory history.

(b) Initiation of a Sunset Review and Interpretation of the Term "to determine" the Likelihood of Continuation or Recurrence of Subsidisation and Injury

5.450 The US argues that it does not have to conduct its own investigation in order "to determine" whether the expiry of the duty is likely to lead to continuation or recurrence of subsidisation and injury. The EC submits that this interpretation is inconsistent with the *SCM Agreement*, which places upon the national authorities the clear obligation *to conduct an investigation and to determine on the basis of positive evidence* whether expiry of the duty is likely to lead to continuation or recurrence of subsidisation and injury. The duty "to determine" entails the obligation to carry out a new, fresh *investigation* on continuation or recurrence and provide a rational explanation why this is likely to lead to subsidisation and injury.
5.451 The US CIT opinion of 28 February 2002 confirmed that the DOC (even under US law) did not fulfil its obligations pursuant to a full sunset review, because "it failed to consider adequately the evidence on the record, or to seek additional evidence necessary to make its determination".

(c) Article 21.3 and Likelihood of Continuation of Subsidisation and Injury

5.452 The US argument has constantly been that it "does not calculate the present rate of subsidization in a sunset review because the purpose of a sunset review is to determine the likelihood of the continuation or recurrence of subsidization", and that this "necessarily involves a prediction of a government's future behaviour without the discipline of a countervailing duty order in place". For this reason, the US "uses only information developed in the original investigation or prior administrative reviews because this information has been subject to the rigors of the administrative process in those proceedings". The EC respectfully disagrees with these propositions.
5.453 The EC agrees that there is a forward-looking aspect to a sunset review, but submits that a sunset review determination that is based only on the CVD rate established in the original investigation or one that does not apply the 1 per cent *de minimis* rule violates clearly the whole object and purpose of the *SCM Agreement*.
5.454 The determination of "likelihood" of continuation of subsidisation and injury has to be made on the basis of "evidence", as this is defined by Articles 21.4 and 12 of the *SCM Agreement*. The domestic authorities cannot escape of their duty to conduct a fresh, proper investigation, on the ground that this is a difficult or time consuming exercise or that some factors, as the US argues about the numerator or denominator in this case, are missing or difficult to calculate.
5.455 The US argues that "the findings in the original investigation provide the only evidence reflecting the behaviour of the respondents without the discipline of coun-

tervailing measures in place". There is, therefore, a need to understand what exactly the US means by using the terms "discipline in place". The EC submits that this reference in fact assimilates CVD orders to antidumping duties. The rationale of granting subsidies and imposing CVD orders are, however, substantially different from those pertaining to dumping and the imposition of AD duties. In the latter case there is one actor, the exporter, who can swiftly decide the whole strategy of the company regarding when, where and at what price to export, if the AD duty were to expire. In the case of subsidies the situation is not the same as AD, because governments normally do not behave commercially in the same way as individual companies. For instance, in case of non-recurring subsidies, it is more reasonable to assume that governments will not rush to grant again a new subsidy soon after a CVD order were allowed to expire. The principle is that granting a new subsidy increasing the level of an existing one is normally subject to rather different considerations which distinguish them clearly from the natural desire of individual companies to swiftly divert exports in order to increase profits when an AD order is left to expire. Moreover, subsidies take normally time to be discussed and decided in national parliaments, depending also on the type of procedure to be followed, and this further distinguishes them from dumping practices. To speak of a "discipline in place", therefore, is to disregard completely the peculiarities and specificities of the reasons for which governments usually grant subsidies, compared to the risk of recurrence of dumping.

5.456 Moreover, as the CIT Opinion clarified, the US does not answer the basic question why it can conduct on site verifications and apply the full rigors of an investigation in the context of an administrative review, but claims that it cannot do so in the context of a sunset review. Attempting to predict the future behaviour of a government in no way prevents the US authorities from conducting a proper, fresh, new investigation. In this regard, the Panel should take account of the fact that DOC even refused to consult its own calculation memoranda from the original investigation to determine the amount of grants paid under the CIG programme after 1986.

5.457 The above proposition is as much acknowledged by the US law and regulations in place, which lay down the following criteria in deciding continuation or recurrence. The US *Sunset Policy Bulletin* (see Exhibit EC-15) provides, in Section III.A.5, some criteria about the way future government behaviour could be predicted. They include in particular the *legal method* by which the government granted or eliminated a programme, i.e. whether this is done by *administrative* action or through *legislative* action. The US *Sunset Policy Bulletin* proposes to the authorities to draw different conclusions depending on the legal method applied. This is all the more important here, as the programmes under review in the present case and, in particular the CIG programme, were granted by legislative action and could not as such be reinstated by administrative action only.

5.458 It follows that a CVD order is not a "discipline in place" in the sense these terms are used by the US, in particular in case of a non-recurring, declining subsidy, since such a subsidy has been given in the past, has been largely consumed for the period of time up to the sunset review, and is known that it will not recur in the future. The US law that allows the DOC to use the subsidy rate determined in the original determination, unless a programme is terminated, is inconsistent with the provisions of Article 21.3 of the *SCM Agreement*.

5.459 Moreover, as the CIT Opinion clarified, the US does not answer the basic question why it can conduct on site verifications and apply the full rigors of an investigation in the context of an administrative review, but claims that it cannot do so in the context of a sunset review. Attempting to predict the future behaviour of a government in no way prevents the US authorities from conducting a proper, fresh, new investigation to find out about the numerator or denominator of the exporters' sales, the likelihood of the subsidy programme been modified or withdrawn or whether there is a non-recurring subsidy the amount of which has already been expensed and the remaining benefit flowing from it is nearly zero. As the US CIT has put it:

> Commerce cannot justify its failure to consider Plaintiffs arguments based on its conjecture that this information might be unavailable or otherwise incapable of being verified Presumably, sales values since 1993 would be readily available to commerce had it requested submissions regarding this information.[132]

(d) Need to Conduct Prior Administrative Reviews, Timely Submission of Data, and Obligation to Consider the Record from the Original Investigation

5.460 The US claims that "under the US system, administrative reviews are not prerequisites for conducting full sunset reviews" but then it concedes that, in a sunset review, it "only uses information developed in the original investigation or prior administrative proceedings." This is just one typical example of how fluid and sometimes contradictory is the US law and practice on sunset reviews, characterised by the use of terms such as "normally", "as a general rule", etc. In addition, the US argues that "normally" it makes adjustments to the net countervailable subsidy determined in the investigation when "there is evidence demonstrating that programmes have been terminated with no residual benefits". However, this apparent flexibility of US law in sunsets is not borne out in practice. Moreover, this flexibility and plasticity of US law are not virtues but serious legal defects, because they eliminate legal security and predictability in the interpretation and application of the US law on sunset reviews to the detriment of foreign exporters and international trade. In this case, the Government of Germany and the German producers provided clear evidence that the CIG programme was terminated without any meaningful residual benefit continuing after the end of the sunset review. Despite this evidence, the US DOC refused to adjust the rate from the original investigation to reflect this change. There could have been no continuation of benefits in such a case, if the US authorities had simply taken into consideration the calculation memorandum that was part of the file of the original investigation.

5.461 The US has been claiming that the German exporters had 15 months to prepare for the sunset review and that they are alone to blame if they did not submit in time the evidence regarding the calculation memoranda from the original investigation. This has been a particularly ingenious attempt by the US to exclude crucial evidence from the sunset review. The US CIT Opinion now lends support to the EC's claims in this regard. The CIT said:

> The record from the original investigation may be incorporated into the record for purposes of the sunset review ... Further, in the past, even in an expedited sunset review Commerce apparently has accepted untimely submissions relating to "important factual informa-

[132] Exhibit EC-24, at page 25 and footnote 22 thereto.

> tion that is already on the record of this [sunset review] proceeding, i.e., in the [prior] administrative review segment."...Thus, it is sufficient that Plaintiffs alerted the agency in their substantive response or rebuttal to the other interested parties' substantive response that the countervailable benefits accruing from the nonrecurring subsidies would be *de minimis* ... The court finds that the issue was raised with sufficient clarity to put Commerce reasonably on notice in a timely manner that it needed to consider the data underlying the calculation of the original CVD rate ... To the extent Commerce needed information beyond these calculation memoranda, it could have requested the information from the parties or from a third source ... Accordingly, Commerce shall consider the calculation memoranda as part of the record in this proceeding.[133]

5.462 For those reasons, the EC considers that under the *SCM Agreement*, as a general rule, the same elements and factors that the investigating authorities took into account in the original investigation in a retrospective manner can be analysed in a prospective way during a sunset review. These are laid down essentially in Articles 11, 12 and 15 of the *SCM Agreement*. However, the range of factors to be taken into account in making the forward-looking assessment necessary to establish the likelihood of recurrence or continuation of subsidisation has to be evaluated on case by case basis, as it mainly depends on the kind of subsidy under examination. For example, if it is a recurring unemployment subsidy, the investigating authorities should consider the likelihood of lay-offs within the reasonable future. In the case at issue, however, the main subsidy was a non-recurring subsidy that by definition cannot recur. There could have been no continuation of benefits in such a case, if the US authorities had simply taken into consideration the calculation memorandum that was part of the file of the original investigation.

(e) The *de minimis* Rule in Sunset Reviews and the Meaning and Scope of Footnote 52

5.463 The US argues that there is no rationale for including the 1 per cent *de minimis* rule in sunset reviews. This proposition does not explain, however, why the US considers useful to apply the 0.50 per cent *de minimis* rule under its domestic law; nor has the US offered any credible explanation for doing so.

5.464 The EC submits that Article 21.3 of the *SCM Agreement* clearly establishes a presumption of termination, and sees no valid reason to depart from the application of the definition of injurious subsidisation under Article 11.9 (that a subsidy of less than 1 per cent cannot cause injury) in the context of sunset reviews under Article 21.3. The preparatory history of Article 11.9 indicates that the *de-minimis* rule is based on a presumption that levels below *de-minimis* do not cause injury, rather than, as the US suggests, reasons of administrative efficiency. Exhibit EC-25 demonstrates that other WTO Members have also understood the preparatory history and the inter-

---

[133] Exhibit EC-24, at pages 17-18, references and footnotes omitted. Moreover, the UC CIT found on page 24 of its Opinion that "Commerce does not dispute that the information in the calculation memoranda and Preussag's questionnaire had been verified in the original investigation". The CIT also clarified (on page 38) that: "Commerce ignores the statutory provision that it may seek an extension of time for "extraordinarily complicated" sunset reviews."

pretation to be given to Article 21.3 as regards *de minimis* in the same way as the one proposed here to the Panel by the EC.

5.465 The US claims that the interpretation proposed by the EC would render Footnote 52 a nullity. It also asserts that there must be a reason for the inclusion of Footnote 52 in Article 21.3. These suggestions are puzzling. The EC does not dispute the essential function of this Footnote. A determination not to terminate the CVD order may indeed be compatible with a finding of zero subsidy rate in the most recent administrative review or be based on some other reason. But Footnote 52 does not support the extrapolation made of it by the US in order to reach the conclusion that there is no *de minimis* rule of 1 per cent *ad valorem* in sunset reviews. Furthermore, based on that understanding of the *de minimis* rule, the US then extrapolates from Footnote 52 by making several illogical leaps. First, it argues that a zero rate of subsidy cannot require the authorities to terminate the CVD duty. That means that the level of the subsidy, even if zero, is not relevant for deciding likelihood of continuation or recurrence of subsidisation, injury and causality. Second, it draws the operational conclusion that it is not necessary to calculate the actual level of subsidy in a sunset review. Third, it does consider that the *de minimis* rule of Article 11.9 does not apply to Article 21.3 reviews.

5.466 The preparatory history of Article 11.9 and the corresponding provision in the AD Agreement, however, indicate that the rationale of the *de minimis* rule in these Agreements is different from that on which the *de minimis* rule is applied in the US. In these two WTO Agreements, the level of 1 per cent *ad valorem* was agreed to be the *de minimis* threshold not for reasons of administrative efficiency but because for imports below this level the causal link between subsidised imports and the material injury to domestic industry would not exist.[134] This is a significantly different rationale, because it demonstrates that the US wrongly continued under its domestic law its old practice going back to 1980, as codified in the 1987 Guideline on *the minimis* rule (see Exhibit US-6).

5.467 The EC considers that the current level of subsidy is not always dispositive of the outcome of a sunset review. If the current level of subsidy is zero or *de minimis*, this does not *by itself* end the measure, but it does require the US DOC to demonstrate what change of circumstances will lead to the subsidy increasing to a level above *de minimis*, if it wishes to continue the measure. In the case of a non-recurring subsidy, which is already *de minimis*, and subject to the US declining balance methodology, the DOC must adduce and rely on positive evidence of new subsidies or of a sharp fall in the denominator in order to find likelihood of subsidisation, injury and causality.

5.468 Moreover, the US states that the "focus" of a sunset review is on the *possible* future behaviour of foreign governments and exporters. This is misleading. First, as already explained, a sunset review determination requires *positive* evidence to demonstrate that subsidisation, injury and causality is *likely* to continue or recur. The US keeps repeating that the "best evidence" of future behaviour of governments and exporters is the rate from the original investigation. However, in the case of *Corrosion-resistant steel from Germany*, how can this be? The DOC has itself established that there are *no new subsidies* and that the non-recurring subsidies found in the original

[134] E.g., MTN.GNG/NG10/W/9/Rev. 3, point E, of 26 may 1988, and MTN.GNG/NG10/W/4, page 42.

investigation, 9 years ago, have now declined to a level that is equivalent zero by its own calculation methodology.

5.469 The US has modified its past practice after the WTO Agreements on AD and SCM entered into force only as regards determinations made in the initial investigation, but left its domestic legislation on sunset reviews unchanged by applying its 0.50 per cent *de minimis* rule based on a completely different rationale (i.e. administrative convenience and efficiency).

3. Conclusions

5.470 The EC considers that not only the application of the basic US laws, regulations and policy guidelines in the present case are inconsistent with the US obligations under the WTO and *SCM Agreement*, but these US laws, regulations and guidelines are in themselves incompatible with the WTO and the *SCM Agreement.*

5.471 As the US CIT Opinion of 28 February 2002 put it, the DOC cannot act irrationally and arbitrarily. The DOC cannot accept domestic parties' "late" submissions and reject those of respondents. It cannot make some adjustments to an original CVD rate and then state it will not consider evidence of other adjustments because all adjustments are barred. It cannot avoid applying changes in the law because it is burdensome or inconvenient. It must conduct meaningful sunset reviews. It cannot erect barriers simply to avoid considering complicated problems.

5.472 In conclusion, the EC respectfully asks the Panel to find in accordance with our request as stated in the conclusions of our first written submission.

N. Oral Statement of the United States at the Second Meeting of the Panel

5.473 On behalf of the United States delegation, I would like to thank the Panel for this opportunity to comment on certain issues raised in this proceeding. We do not intend to offer a lengthy statement today. Instead, we will focus briefly on the central issues in this dispute.

5.474 Mr. Chairman, as we stated in our Oral Statement at the First Meeting of the Panel, this proceeding presents three basic questions. The first question is, does the United States act inconsistently with Article 21.3 of the *Agreement on Implementation of Article VI of the General Agreement on Tariffs and Trade 1994* ("Anti-Dumping Agreement") by self-initiating sunset reviews without regard to the evidentiary provisions of Article 11.6? The second question is, does the United States act inconsistently with Article 21.3 by *not* applying the *de minimis* provisions of Article 11.9 in sunset reviews? The third question is, whether Commerce's determination in the sunset review on corrosion-resistant steel was based upon an appropriately conducted review of all relevant and properly submitted facts?

5.475 The purely legal issues – can an authority automatically self-initiate a sunset review? is there a *de minimis* standard applicable to sunset reviews? what are the evidentiary and procedural requirements applicable to sunset reviews? – are all addressed in the *SCM Agreement*. This, of course, is no great revelation to any of us. Where the United States and the EC diverge, however, is on how the Panel should interpret what the *SCM Agreement* says on these issues.

5.476 Consistent with accepted WTO jurisprudence, the United States has argued that the Panel should interpret the *SCM Agreement*, and in particular Article 21.3, in accordance with the ordinary meaning of the terms of the Agreement in their context and in light of their object and purpose. This should be a straightforward exercise because the terms themselves are straightforward.

5.477 Simply put, Article 21.3 provides that a definitive countervailing duty must be terminated unless the requisite finding – likelihood of continuation or recurrence of subsidization and injury – is made. This likelihood finding is made in the context of a sunset review that, according to the explicit terms of Article 21.3, may be initiated on one of two bases – on an authority's "own initiative" *or* upon a "duly substantiated request" by or on the behalf of the domestic industry. There is no requirement in Article 21.3 or elsewhere in the Agreement to consider the magnitude of current subsidization in determining the likelihood that, absent the countervailing duty, subsidization would be likely to continue or recur. Finally, under the terms of Article 21.4, a sunset review must be conducted in accordance with the evidentiary and procedural requirements of Article 12. Commerce's sunset determination in corrosion-resistant steel comports with all of these terms of the *SCM Agreement*.

5.478 In contrast to the United States' text-based analysis, the EC makes various assumptions regarding the "purposes" of various provisions of the *SCM Agreement without* reference to the text of the *SCM Agreement*, and then refers to obligations not found in the text which presumably derive from these "purposes." According to the EC, the Panel should derive the object and purpose of the *SCM Agreement* and then ignore the plain meaning of the words in order to achieve that object and purpose. This, of course, is the very antithesis of the basic principles of treaty interpretation reflected in Article 31 of the *Vienna Convention*.

5.479 For example, despite the plain text permitting initiation of a sunset review on an authority's "own initiative," the EC argues that the Article 11.6 evidentiary prerequisites for self-initiation of investigations must be satisfied in sunset reviews as well. Similarly, the EC reads a *de minimis* requirement into Article 21.3, notwithstanding that no such obligation exists. In both instances, the EC's arguments are based on its assumptions as to the purpose of investigations and sunset reviews. This approach to treaty interpretation runs afoul of the Appellate Body's admonition in *Japan - Alcoholic Beverages*, that "the treaty's object and purpose is to be referred to in determining the meaning of the 'terms of the treaty' and not as an independent basis for interpretation."[135]

5.480 In the *US Shrimp* case, the Appellate Body rejected the EC's type of unconventional approach to treaty interpretation, stating that "[a] treaty interpreter must begin with, and focus upon, the text of the particular provision to be interpreted. It is in the words constituting that provision, read in their context, that the object and purpose of the states parties to the treaty must first be sought."[136]

5.481 The Appellate Body went on to say that "[w]here the meaning imparted by the text itself is equivocal or inconclusive ... light from the object and purpose of the treaty as a whole may usefully be sought". The United States submits that the meaning imparted by the text of Article 21.3 is neither equivocal nor inconclusive. Article 21.3 states unequivocally, and without qualification, that authorities may initiate sunset reviews on "their own initiative." There is not a shred of textual support for the notion that some sort of evidentiary prerequisite applies to this explicit right. Simi-

[135] Japan - Alcoholic Beverages, p.11, n.20.

[136] US Shrimp, para. 114 (footnote omitted).

larly, Article 11.9 states unequivocally that the one percent *de minimis* standard applies in investigations. Again, there is not a shred of textual support for the notion that this standard *must* be applied in sunset reviews as well.

5.482 The Appellate Body in *US Shrimp* also stated that "where confirmation of the correctness of the reading of the text itself is desired, light from the object and purpose of the treaty as a whole may usefully be sought." So let us consider for a moment whether the object and purpose of the treaty as a whole confirms the correctness of the United States' reading of the text.

5.483 The United States submits that the object and purpose of the *SCM Agreement* as a whole is to define certain trade distorting practices, that is, subsidies, and to establish a framework for addressing such practices, for example, application of countervailing measures. Both the definitions and the framework reflect a carefully negotiated balance of obligations and rights – obligations to, for example, eliminate certain types of subsidies, and rights to, for example, take countervailing measures against certain types of subsidies.

5.484 The United States' reading of the text of Article 21.3 – that it permits automatic self-initiation of a sunset review and that it contains no explicit requirement to quantify the current rate of subsidization when considering the likelihood of continuation or recurrence of subsidization – is consistent with the notion that the *SCM Agreement* sets out an agreed upon framework for addressing trade distorting practices. In other words, the *SCM Agreement* recognizes that it is appropriate to continue to apply countervailing measures where trade distorting practices are likely to continue or recur absent that countervailing measure.

5.485 In addition to the general legal issues just discussed, the EC also has made case-specific claims regarding Commerce's sunset determination involving corrosion-resistant carbon steel flat products from Germany. Commerce's determination – that the expiry of the countervailing duty order would be likely to lead to the continuation or recurrence of subsidization – is based on the *continued existence and availability* of programmes previously found to have been used by German producers and the continued existence of benefit streams from programmes previously found to benefit German producers.

5.486 The EC has focused almost exclusively on the Capital Investments Grant, or CIG, programme, arguing that the benefit stream that continues to exist after the five-year mark is very small. The United States has already demonstrated that there is no *de minimis* standard in the Agreement with respect to sunset reviews and the fact that a benefit stream continues after the five-year mark can be a basis for finding likelihood of continuation of subsidization. As important in Commerce's likelihood determination, however, are its findings concerning the continued existence and availability of subsidy programmes previously found to have been used by the German producers.

5.487 In particular, Commerce determined that the Aid for Closure of Steel Operations and the ECSC Redeployment Aid under Article 56(2)(b) programmes continue to exist. The EC has admitted as much in its Oral Statement. In addition, during the sunset review itself, the German Government, the EC, and German producers admitted that both of these programmes continued to provide some benefits. Commerce's findings regarding these programmes remain undisputed and unrefuted by the EC. Thus, with or without the CIG programme, an "objective assessment" of Commerce's determination supports its finding of likelihood of continuation or recurrence of subsidization beyond the five-year mark.

5.488 Finally, we would like make a few points with respect to the 28 February ruling of the US domestic court mentioned in the EC's March 4th letter to the Panel. A WTO panel is required to construe the meaning of a treaty provision and the consistency of, for example, a US statutory provision, with that treaty provision. In contrast, a US domestic court is required to interpret the US statutory provision itself. The United States' domestic court in the *Dillinger* case did just that; it did not interpret the WTO *SCM Agreement* or the consistency of US statutory provisions with the *SCM Agreement*.

5.489 Second, the decision is interlocutory. In other words, it is not a final court decision. The Court has remanded the case back to the US Department of Commerce to consider the Court's ruling and issue a new administrative determination. The Department of Commerce is in the process of doing just that in order to issue a redetermination on remand.

5.490 Third, although we are in the process of analyzing the Court's ruling, as an initial matter we believe that the Court's ruling is wrong as a matter of US law on a number of issues.

5.491 Finally, we note that the US Government, and private parties, have the right to appeal a Court of International Trade ruling and frequently do so. As a result, decisions of the Court of International Trade are often reversed by the appellate court. Thus the EC's desire for the Panel to consider and be guided by the US domestic court's interlocutory ruling is misplaced.

5.492 The United States would like to highlight and respond to two points in the oral statement of the EC today. Of course highlighting these two points is not to imply agreement with the other points contained in that statement.

5.493 First, in paragraph 5 of that statement, the EC says that the interpretation advanced by the United States in this proceeding "is not a good faith interpretation." The United States is quite surprised to see such a statement and takes sharp exception to this characterization. It should be obvious by now that the US interpretation is offered in good faith. It is completely inappropriate for the EC to make such a claim.

5.494 Second, the United States notes that the EC has referred to "uncertainty and predictability" in its oral statement, for example in paragraph 41 and elsewhere. In paragraph 41 the EC has said that the US measures at issue are inconsistent with the WTO because they "create uncertainty and unpredictability in international trade." The EC is again reading words into the text. The EC apparently is confusing the language in Article 3.2 of the DSU, which is a narrative statement that the WTO *dispute settlement system* is a central element in providing security and predictability to the multilateral trading system, with some obligation on *Members* to provide security and predictability in international trade through their measures. There of course is no such vague obligation in the WTO.

5.495 This concludes our presentation today. We will be pleased, of course, to answer any questions you may wish to pose. Thank you.

O. *Responses of the European Communities to Questions from the Panel Following the Second Meeting of the Panel*

Both parties

Q41. Do you consider it *impossible* that the drafters might have intended there to be different rules for sunset reviews from those for investigations? In other words, in your view, would it have been *irrational* for the drafters to establish a set of disciplines in respect of investigations, and intend some of them apply to sunset reviews and others not? If so, what might be the reasons for such differences? If not, why not?

Reply

5.496 The EC looked into the preparatory history of the *SCM Agreement*, and in particular Article 21.3 thereof, in order to verify what was the intention of the drafters on these issues. To the extent use can be made of the available texts, they seem to confirm the interpretation of Article 21.3 proposed by the EC. This interpretation is based on the terms of Article 21.3 in their context and takes also into account the object and purpose of the *SCM Agreement* (and the WTO Agreement) as a whole. In the context of a legal interpretation of texts, it is probably more appropriate to speak in terms of *unreasonable* rather than *impossible* or *irrational (see Article 32 of 1969 Vienna Convention).*

5.497 The EC has explained in its submissions (e.g., EC comments on the US answer to question no 28 from the Panel) why the US proposition, that in sunset reviews a proper, fresh investigation is not required, seems unreasonable. A systematic interpretation of Articles 21.3, 21.4, 22.1, 22.7, 12 and 11 of the *SCM Agreement* does not support the suggestion that some elements or requirements in the conduct of an original investigation are not required in the context of sunset reviews. Unless Article 21.3 excludes explicitly such elements, the most reasonable and generally accepted interpretation is to consider that they are all applicable. This is in conformity with a more classic way of drafting and interpreting treaties. The use of the word "determine" also supports this view, because the determination must necessarily entail the conduct of an investigation by the domestic authorities (or how else could they determine?). Article 10 also confirms the above view because it clearly states that to impose any type of CV duties, i.e. whether in the context of an initial determination or in the context of sunset determination, the conduct of an investigation is required. In this regard, as the EC has noted before, the effect of new investigations and sunset reviews is the same, i.e. they may both lead to the imposition of a countervailing duty for up to 5 years. Therefore, if the drafters of the *SCM Agreement* had wished to exclude in sunset reviews certain elements from the set of the disciplines from the original investigations they would have explicitly said so, as they did for instance in Article 21.4 as regards the 12 months period for the completion of a sunset review. It follows that the domestic authorities have to demonstrate in their sunset investigation and determination that expiry of the duty is likely to lead to continuation or recurrence of subsidization and injury. Consequently, in sunset determinations the only notable difference with determinations made in original investigations, as the EC has explained (e.g. with its answers to written question no 16(b) of the Panel and in para. 36 of its second written submission), is that in the former it is not the existence but only the "likelihood" of continuation or recurrence of subsidization and injury that is required to be demonstrated. Moreover, because the terms subsidization and injury need to be interpreted consistently throughout the Agreement, it follows that a rate of subsidy that is below 1 per cent *ad valorem* is not countervailable because it is irrefutably presumed not to cause injury whether in an original or sunset determination. This is further confirmed by the text of Article 15, in particular paragraph 5, of the *SCM Agreement*.

Q42. Footnote 37 to the *SCM Agreement* states:

> The term "initiated" as used hereinafter means procedural action by which a Member formally commences an investigation as provided in Article 11.

Please comment on the meaning of this footnote in the context of the issues in this dispute.

Reply

5.498 This footnote provides further support to the position advocated by the EC in the present dispute. Indeed, the placing of this footnote in the *SCM Agreement* and the ordinary meaning of its terms suggest that: first, an investigation is obligatory before any kind of CV duties can be imposed (i.e. whether following an original or sunset determination); second, the term "initiated" has to be understood in the same way throughout the entire *SCM Agreement*, that is as provided (i.e. laid down) in Article 11; third, the term "initiated" refers to the commencement rather than to the actual conduct of an investigation, as the text of Article 10 clearly distinguished these two terms. Therefore, in addition to Article 11, other provisions of the *SCM Agreement* have also to be applied in the conduct of any kind of investigation, such as Articles 12 or 22.

5.499 Finally, one of the claims of the EC in the present case is that the US laws, regulations and practices as such and as applied to the present case violate also Article 10, including footnote 37, because:

- they permit the automatic initiation of a sunset review without the authorities having a sufficient amount of evidence in their possession or even the slightest amount of evidence as in the case of expedited reviews; and
- they shift the burden of proof on foreign exporters and governments to demonstrate no likelihood of continuation or recurrence of subsidization and injury in violation of Articles 21.1 and 21.3, which require termination of CVD unless the domestic authorities demonstrate the opposite.

Q43. What textual support, if any, is there, in your view, for the proposition that the term "investigation" includes sunset reviews? Please comment, in particular, on the relevance, if any, of footnote 37 to and Article 32.3 of the *SCM Agreement*.

Reply

5.500 As explained with the answer to the previous question, footnote 37 and accompanying text provide clear support for the proposition that a determination in a sunset review requires the conduct of a proper, fresh investigation. The same can be said of Article 32.3, whose text clearly states that the provisions of the entire *SCM Agreement* apply to investigations and reviews of existing measures initiated on or after the entry into force of the WTO Agreements. In addition, both these provisions provide relevant context for the purpose of interpreting the terms of Article 21.3, as the EC has explained with its submissions to the Panel.

Q44. Please explain why, in your view, the drafters established a *de minimis* standard for investigations, providing support from the text and/or the negotiating history of the *SCM Agreement*. Do the mandatory nature and the strong language of the statement in Article 11.9 ("There shall be immediate termination in cases where the amount of a subsidy is *de minimis* ... ") indicate anything about the rationale for this standard?

Reply

5.501 The EC has already explained in detail the reasons for which it considers that a *de minimis* standard was established in investigations (see, e.g., paragraphs 114-117 of the first EC written submission; paragraphs 37-40 of EC oral statement in first substantive meeting of the Panel with the parties; paragraph 47 of the second EC written submission; EC replies to written questions no 1(b) and (c) from the Panel; EC comments on US responses to written questions no 28, 29 and 30 from the Panel; and paragraphs 32-40, in particular paragraph 36, of the EC oral statement in the second substantive meeting of the Panel with the parties).

5.502 To summarize the arguments again, the *de minimis* threshold was introduced in the Uruguay Round negotiations. The EC considers that the rational for this introduction was that a certain level of subsidization could not be the cause of any injury sustained by the domestic industry, in the sense the term injury is given in the Agreement. For this reason, it was clearly written into the text of the *SCM Agreement* as an irrefutable presumption ("shall be immediate termination").

5.503 This rationale was clearly spelled out in the negotiating history of the *SCM Agreement*. Thus, in the Checklist of issues for negotiation in the Uruguay Round, the Secretariat prepared in 1987 a paper stating:

> "Article 2:12 of the Code provides that an investigation shall be terminated when the investigating authorities are satisfied either that no subsidy exists or that the effect of the alleged subsidy on the industry is not such as to cause injury. It stands to reason that in case of a *de minimis* subsidy, a causal link does not exist between subsidized imports and material injury to a domestic industry. It would be useful to reach agreement on the level below which a subsidy should be deemed to be *de minimis*."[137]

5.504 Moreover, later in the negotiations, the rationale of introducing a *de minimis* threshold was further discussed. What it emerges from this preparatory history is that the rationale of the *de minimis* rule in the *SCM Agreement* is different from that on which the *de minimis* rule is applied in the US. In the *SCM Agreement*, the level of 1 per cent *ad valorem* was agreed to be the *de minimis* threshold not for reasons of administrative efficiency but because for imports below this level the causal link between subsidized imports and the material injury to domestic industry would not

[137] Negotiating Group on Subsidies and Countervailing Measures, Checklist of issues for negotiations, Note by the Secretariat, MTN.GNG/GNG/NG10/W/9/Rev.2, 2 December 1987.

exist.[138] This is a significantly different rationale from that claimed to be applied by the US domestically, because it demonstrates that the US wrongly continued under its domestic law its old practice going back to 1980, as codified in the 1987 Guideline on *the minimis* rule (see Exhibit US-6). The preparatory history, therefore, appears to confirm the view that the rationale for introducing *de minimis* standards was exclusively the effect of low subsidization on injury, and not reasons of administrative efficiency or convenience as suggested by the US. Norway and Japan who submitted third party submissions in the present case appear to read in the same way the preparatory history on this point. Administrative efficiency is something left to the discretion of Members and is not normally the basis for international trade provisions, such as Article 11.9 of the *SCM Agreement*. For instance, some WTO Members find it inefficient or unnecessary to have any countervailing or anti-dumping laws at all.

5.505 Further support for this interpretation can be found in the text of Article 15.5 *SCM Agreement*, which states that it must be demonstrated that subsidized imports are, through the effects of subsidies, causing injury. It should be stressed that this provision was already present in the Tokyo Round Subsidies Code (Article 6) and the Uruguay Round drafters reproduced in the *SCM Agreement*. The EU is of the view that there is clear link between Article 15.5 and Article 11.9 *SCM Agreement*. The "effects" of a subsidy necessarily include the level of subsidization. The terms of those Articles and the preparatory history make, therefore, plainly clear that a subsidy can only impact on the injury if it reaches a certain level. Footnote 45 defines injury as "material", which means that injury must reach a certain level before it becomes material. Therefore, this provision further implies that a low level of subsidization cannot produce the required effect as provided for in Article 15.5 of the *SCM Agreement*.

5.506 There is even more evidence elsewhere in the *SCM Agreement* that the drafters intended the amount of subsidy to be linked to the extent of the injury. In Article 6.1(a), subsidies which exceed 5 per cent ad valorem are *deemed* to cause serious prejudice, which means that it is for the subsidizing country to rebut this presumption under Article 6.2. This provision, which the preparatory history indicates that it was inserted at the insistence of the US, is based on the argument that subsidization above a certain amount triggers a presumption of injury. Although the application of the provision of Article 6.1(a) expired on 31 December 1999 (See Article 31), it is nevertheless supports the argument that the level of the subsidy, by itself, creates certain presumptions regarding injury.

5.507 Still another example is Article 6.3(c) of the Agreement. This relates to cases where serious prejudice must be demonstrated and covers, for example, the situation where "the effect of the subsidy is a significant price undercutting". This language suggests that the "effect" of a subsidy can only be "significant" price undercutting if the amount of the subsidy is itself significant. This implies that a certain minimum level of subsidy is required to lead to a serious prejudice and, by analogy, material injury.

Q45. Assuming for the sake of argument, and without prejudice to the outcome in the matter before the Panel, that a *de minimis* standard applies in respect of subsidiza-

---

[138] E.g., MTN.GNG/NG10/W/9/Rev. 3, point E, of 26 may 1988, and MTN.GNG/NG10/W/4, page 42.

tion to sunset reviews, would this *de minimis* standard be based on: (i) the rate of subsidization during the period of application of the countervailing duty ("CVD"); (ii) the rate of subsidization at the time of sunset review; or (iii) the rate at which subsidization is likely to continue or recur? How would you calculate that rate of subsidization on which the *de minimis* standard would be based?

Reply

5.508 The rate that should determine the outcome of a sunset review is the third one, i.e. the rate likely to continue or recur if the CVD measure were allowed to expire. Article 21.3 permits the continuation of a countervailing duty only if it is demonstrated, on the basis of positive evidence, that if the CVD measure were left to expire this is likely to lead to continuation or occurrence of subsidization, injury and causality. Some guidance may be drawn, *inter alia*, from the rate of subsidization applicable at the time of the sunset review, the existence of new programmes or the elimination of existing ones, the nature of the subsidies in question, etc., for the purpose of making the likelihood determination. However, subsidization does not exist in the abstract, and quantification of the rate at which continuation or recurrence of subsidization is likely to continue or recur in the future should always be feasible. The US DOC does much the same when it reports the rate to the US ITC under its domestic rule of 0.50 per cent, but it now claims that this is done on an autonomous, voluntary basis!

5.509 As to the method of calculation, it is acknowledged that it is for the investigating authorities to establish the level of subsidy likely to continue or recur, on a verifiable and reasonable basis and taking account of relevant evidence and data obtained in the course of the sunset review. If the amount of subsidy is currently below the 1 per cent *de minimis* threshold, it is for the investigating authorities to show that it will rise above the *de minimis* threshold in the near future. In the case of a non-recurring subsidy, the amount of which is declining year by year, this means showing that the denominator will fall sufficiently to take the *ad valorem* level of the subsidy above the *de minimis* threshold. In the case of a recurring subsidy, this means showing that circumstances will change sufficiently enough for the subsidy to go above the *de minimis* threshold. The US has demonstrated none of the above in the present case.

European Communities

Q46. The European Communities states:

> [T]he US law and practice to automatically self-initiate sunset reviews violate Articles [sic] 21.3 of the *SCM Agreement*, as complemented by Article 11.[139]

Is the Panel correct in understanding that the European Communities is making a claim that the evidentiary standards of Article 11.6 are incorporated into Article 21.3, or is it the European Communities' claim that these standards apply to sunset reviews on the face of Article 11.6?

[139] First Written Submission of the European Communities, para. 66.

Reply

5.510 It is not entirely clear what the Panel means by the terms "apply in the face of" as opposed to "incorporated". As to their practical legal effects, however, it does not appear to the EC that there is much of a difference between the two. The EC follows the generally accepted rules on treaty interpretation. The EC claim is that an interpretation of Article 21.3 should be made in context and in the light of the object and purpose of Article 21.3 and of the *SCM Agreement*. Articles 21.1, 22.1, 22.7, 10 and 11.6 provide relevant context and help define its object and purpose. Such an interpretation, in particular of the terms"...unless the authorities determine, in a review initiated..."in Article 21.3, requires that the evidentiary standards of Article 11.6 should be implied, and hence applied, also to the evidentiary requirements in sunset reviews.

Q47. The European Communities states:

> [S]ince 0.53 per cent [sic] is below the 1 per cent *de minimis* level which should apply in sunset reviews, the US was in breach of Article 21.3, in conjunction with Article 11.9, in continuing the measure[140].

Is the Panel correct in understanding that the European Communities is making a claim that the *de minimis* standard of Article 11.9 is incorporated into Article 21.3, or is it the European Communities' claim that this standard applies to sunset reviews on the face of Article 11.9?

Reply

5.511 As with the previous question, it is not entirely clear what the Panel means by the terms "apply in the face of" as opposed to "incorporated". As to their practical legal effects, however, it does not appear to the EC that there is much of a difference between the two. The EC follows the generally accepted rules on treaty interpretation. The EC claim is that an interpretation of the terms of Article 21.3 should be made in context and in the light of the object and purpose of Article 21.3 and of the *SCM Agreement*. Articles 21.1, 11.9, 15 and 10 provide relevant context and help define its object and purpose. Such an interpretation, in particular of the terms "would be likely to lead to continuation or recurrence of subsidization and injury" in Article 21.3, requires that the 1 per cent *de minimis* level of Article 11.9 should be implied, and hence applied, also to investigations and determinations made in sunset reviews.

Q48. Please provide the Panel the relevant statutory, regulatory, or other texts, including internal guidelines, if any, which set out the European Communities' methodology in respect of the determination of likelihood of continuation or recurrence of subsidization and injury in a sunset review, including calculation of the relevant rate of subsidization and application of any *de minimis* standard.

Reply

5.512 The relevant statutory provision is Article 18 of Council Regulation (EC) 2026/97 of 6 October 1997 (see Exhibit EC-26).[141] This provision reflects the rele-

[140] First Written Submission of the European Communities, para. 119.

vant provisions of the *SCM Agreement*, in particular Article 21.3. Paragraphs 1 and 2 of Article 18 of Council Regulation (EC) 2026/97 provide:

> "1. A definitive countervailing duty shall expire 5 years from its imposition or 5 years from the most recent review which has both covered subsidization and injury, unless it is determined in a review that the expiry of the duty would be likely to lead to continuation or recurrence of subsidization and injury. Such an expiry review shall be initiated on the initiative of the Commission or upon a request made by or on behalf of the Community producers, an the measure shall remain in force pending the outcome of such a review.
>
> 2. An expiry review shall be initiated where the request contains sufficient evidence that the expiry of the measures would be likely to result in a continuation or recurrence of subsidization and injury. Such a likelihood may, for example, be indicated by evidence of continued subsidization and injury or evidence that the removal of injury is partly or solely due to the existence of measures or evidence that the circumstances of the exporters, or market conditions, are such that they would indicate the likelihood of further injurious subsidization."

5.513 There are no other regulatory or administrative texts or guidelines concerning the conduct of countervailing duty expiry reviews in the EC. However, it should be noted that the EC has conducted one countervailing duty expiry review since the entry into force of the WTO *SCM Agreement*, which clearly demonstrates the EC's practice in expiry reviews.

5.514 This investigation concerned imports of polyester fibres and polyester yarns originating in Turkey (Exhibit EC-27).[142] This investigation was terminated on 12 June 1998 because the amount of subsidization was found to be *de minimis*, i.e. less than 2 per cent (as Turkey was considered to be a developing country). Following the publication of a notice of impending expiry, the investigation was initiated on 21 September 1996, on the basis of a duly substantiated request by the Community industry alleging that the repeal of the measures would be likely to result in a continuation or recurrence of injury. Following the initiation of the investigation, the European Commission sent questionnaires to the Community producers, exporting producers in Turkey and the Turkish government. After the examination of the questionnaire responses and verification visits in the Community and Turkey (see preambular paragraph 6, Exhibit EC-27), the European Commission found that the levels of subsidization lied between 0.55 per cent and 1.15 per cent. It concluded that the level of benefit for all producers was *de minimis* and, consequently, terminated the proceeding (see preambular paragraph 34, Exhibit EC-27).

Q49. The European Communities states:

> In that case [United States – Imposition of Countervailing Duties on Certain Hot-Rolled Lead and Bismuth Carbon Steel Products Originating in the United Kingdom], the Appellate Body considered that *a*

---

[141] Council Regulation (EC) 2020/97 of 6 October 1997 on the protection against subsidized imports of countries not members of the European Community, OJ L 288, 21.10.1997, p.1.

[142] Commission Decision of 12 June 1998 terminating the countervailing duty proceeding concerning imports of polyester fibres and polyester yarns originating in Turkey, O.J. L168, 1.6.1998, p.46.

> *finding* on the part of the domestic authority was needed for the purposes of reviews under Article 21.2 of the *SCM Agreement*. If this is true for a review under Article 21.2, which is not obligatory and takes place during the life time of the original countervailing duty, a fortiori a positive finding that all the conditions are fulfilled is necessary in the context of an Article 21.3 investigation, where the basic obligation is the termination of the original duty and the possibility of continuing a duty following a sunset review represents only an exception.[143]

Could the European Communities explain in what sense it uses the term *a fortiori* and why a fortiori reasoning applies here.

Reply

5.515 The EC uses the terms *a fortiori* here to mean *all the more so*. Indeed, if a positive finding on subsidization is necessary for an interim review under Article 21.2, it should all the more so apply to an Article 21.3 review. In an article 21.2 review, there is no presumption of termination. It is for the exporters or the foreign government to allege that circumstances have changed sufficiently to warrant the removal of the measures or, in the case of an administrative review, a reduction in the level of duty payable. Conversely, the finding on likelihood of continuation or recurrence of subsidization and injury is deviating from the general presumption laid down in Article 21.3, which is termination of the CVD. Of course, although a positive finding on subsidization is necessary under both paragraphs, the actual content of what is required to be determined or found is different. Under Article 21.3 what is required to be determined is whether expiry of the duty "would be likely to lead to continuation ...of subsidization...", whereas under Article 21.2 demonstration of the actual existence of subsidization is required.

Q50. The European Communities states:

> The EC in this proceeding is not challenging the injury requirement only for the purpose of verifying the accuracy of the ITC injury determination as such, but it is doing so for the purpose of the *de minimis* challenge, i.e. as a requirement that needs to be demonstrated in the context of a sunset review under Article 21.3 of the Agreement.[144]

Please explain in detail.

Reply

5.516 In a sunset review under Article 21.3 the domestic authorities have to establish that expiry of the CV duty would be likely to lead to continuation or recurrence of subsidization ***and injury***. In the request for consultations and in the request for the establishment of the Panel, the EC has clearly based its claims on Article 21.3 in its entirety and explained that a subsidy rate below the 1 per cent *de minimis* rule can never cause injury. This was clearly discussed during the consultations held with the US. The EC claim, therefore, is that the US laws, regulations and practices as such and their concrete application to the facts of the present case are inconsistent with Article 21.3 because there cannot be injurious subsidization of a subsidy rate likely to

[143] First Written Submission of the European Communities, para. 70 (emphasis in original).

[144] Oral Statement of the European Communities at the First Meeting of the Panel, footnote 27.

be below the 1 per cent *ad valorem* threshold. Because the US does not contest that the rate of subsidy likely to continue in this case is below 1 per cent (indeed DOC found that the rate of subsidization likely to continue here is 0.53 per cent), the EC considers that it is not necessary at this stage to initiate separate panel proceedings in order to verify whether the US ITC has correctly followed all the procedural and substantive requirements and accurately concluded that this level of subsidy is likely to cause injury to US industry. As said, such proceedings against the actual ITC findings are not necessary for the time being because the EC's point of departure and claim is that there can never be injurious subsidization, in the sense of Article 21.3, from the subsidy found likely to continue in this case by the US DOC. The US has never contested before the EC claim on this point, nor does it deny that a condition necessary in a sunset review determination is to establish whether injurious subsidization is likely to continue or recur.

Q51. In the context of its argument that "[t]he domestic authorities are under an obligation to 'determine' the likelihood of continuation or recurrence of subsidization", the European Communities claims:

> [T]he EC considers that Section 751(c) of the Act, as complemented by Section 752 and by US regulations and administrative practices, establishes a standard of investigation for sunset reviews that violates the requirements of the *SCM Agreement*.[145]

Is the Panel to understand that the European Communities is making a claim that US law as such violates the *SCM Agreement* in respect of the obligation to "'determine' the likelihood of continuation or recurrence of subsidization" contained in Article 21.3?

Reply

5.517 Yes. The US law as such is a web of provisions (basic law, regulations and guidelines) which permit the authorities to maintain CVD measures without there being any need to counter injurious subsidization. The US law as such allows the authorities to reach this result by laying down a standard of investigation in a sunset determination which is inconsistent with Article 21.3 of the *SCM Agreement*.

Q52. The European Communities states:

> In fact, to the extent DOC relied upon the rates calculated in its original investigation, the duty of investigation laid down in Article 21.3 of the *SCM Agreement* would also require at a minimum that DOC made all documents showing how the rates were calculated in the original investigation also part of the record in the sunset review.[146]

Please explain this argument.

Reply

5.518 The EC has explained with its written and oral submissions that the relevant authority in a sunset review must determine that all the conditions for the continued imposition of the countervailing duty are fulfilled. For that purpose, the relevant au-

[145] First Written Submission of the European Communities, para. 76.

[146] Oral Statement of the European Communities at the Second Meeting of the Panel, para. 26.

thority must carry out an investigation so as to collect, consider and verify all available and relevant evidence that is necessary in making the sunset determination. It must also allow parties access to and provide them with ample opportunity to comment on and defend their interests at all stages of the review, as happens in an original investigation.

5.519 It is beyond doubt that Article 21.4 makes the application of Article 12 obligatory ("shall apply"). Thus, in a sunset review the interested parties must have access to the entire record on the basis of which the sunset determination is made, that is all the information and evidence relevant to an investigation, in the same way as in the original investigation (Article 12.1). For example, to the extent that the US DOC relies upon the rates calculated in its original investigation, it must, at minimum, make its original determination and all documents showing how the rates therein were calculated (i.e., the calculation memoranda) part of the record of the sunset review. This is a basic requirement of due process and respect of the rights of defence. Indeed, Article 12.2 requires that any decision must be based only on information what is in the record and which has been made available to all parties. Article 12.3 requires that all parties should be able to see all information that is relevant, and Article 12.8 requires that all essential facts should be made available in sufficient time for the parties to defend properly their interests. It follows that the US DOC cannot evade this responsibility by claiming that it is somehow prohibited by US law from making the memoranda part of the record in the sunset review or that they are confidential. The US International Trade Commission ("ITC") is subject to the same procedures regarding the treatment of business proprietary information as the US DOC. However, unlike DOC, the US ITC in its sunset reviews automatically makes the confidential version of its original determination, as well as the complete staff report from the original investigation, part of the record of the sunset review. This is done automatically right at the beginning of the review so that all parties will be able to use this information in preparing their arguments. The ITC simply provides the documents the same confidential status in the review that they enjoyed in the original investigation.

Q53. The European Communities states:

> [T]his flexibility and plasticity of US law are not virtues but serious legal defects, because they eliminate legal security and predictability in the interpretation and application of the US law on sunset reviews to the detriment of foreign exporters and international trade.[147]

Please explain why, in the view of the European Communities this "flexibility and plasticity" are inconsistent with the *SCM Agreement*, and the textual basis for this assertion.

Reply

5.520 The WTO lays down certain rights and obligations and provides the means to ensure that they are observed. The WTO Agreement states, in its last preambular paragraph, that the Members are "determined to preserve the basic principles and to further the objectives underlying this multilateral trading system". Security and predictability in international trade have been recognized both under the previous GATT

[147] Oral Statement of the European Communities at the Second Meeting of the Panel, para. 29.

47 and the new WTO system to constitute part of the pursued objectives.[148] It should also be noted that one of the objectives of any system of law, including that of the WTO, is to lay down rules that are clear and enforceable. Discretion in the interpretation and application of the WTO provisions is tolerated as long as it does not undermine the rights and obligations of the Members.[149] This principle underlies also the DSU, which in Article 3.2 states: "The dispute settlement system of the WTO is a central element in providing security and predictability to the multilateral trading system." For this reason, too, Article 3.2 and Article 19.2 of the DSU provide that: "Recommendations and rulings of the DSB cannot add to or diminish the rights and obligations provided in the covered agreements".

5.521 More specifically, the *SCM Agreement*, in particular Articles 10, 19 and 21 thereof, lay down the basic principle that no countervailing duty shall be imposed or remain in force if it is not necessary to counteract subsidization that is causing injury. This basic obligation is bound to be frustrated if a Member does not interpret in good faith the provisions of the *SCM Agreement*, as laid down in Articles 31 and 32 of the 1969 Vienna Convention. The argument of the Community quoted by the Panel in this question aims to underscore this basic premise and objective. The basic US laws, regulations and administrative guidelines on the issue of sunset reviews are as such incompatible for the additional reason that they leave too much of a discretion and room for interpretation in their application to the relevant authorities which is inconsistent with the provisions of the Article 21.3 as interpreted by the EC, that is in context and in light of its object and purpose.

Q54. In the context of a discussion of the deadline for the submission of information by a party to the United States Department of Commerce ("DOC") in a sunset review, the European Communities states:

> Such a short deadline violates the provisions of Article 21.3, in conjunction with Articles 12.1 and 21.4, of the *SCM Agreement* because it fails to afford the producers with an 'ample opportunity' to present in writing all evidence which they consider relevant in respect of the sunset review[150].

Is the Panel to understand, from this statement, that the European Communities is making a claim that the US law as such violates the *SCM Agreement* in respect of the obligation to "give[] [interested Members and all interested parties] ... ample opportunity to present in writing all evidence which [the authorities] consider relevant in respect of the investigation in question" contained in Article 12.1?

---

[148] As the Appellate Body has clarified in the *Shrimps* case: "Maintaining, rather than undermining, the multilateral trading system is necessarily a fundamental and pervasive premise underlying the WTO Agreement; but it is not a right or an obligation, nor is it an interpretative rule which can be employed in the appraisal of a given measure under the chapeau of Article XX". See Appellate Body report in *United States - Import Prohibition of certain Shrimp and Shrimp Products*, AB-1998-4, WT/DS58/AB/R, 12 October 1998, at para. 116.

[149] A related aspect of this proposition is that under the WTO system, as under the previous GATT 47, even non-mandatory provisions of a Member, such as an administrative guidance, may qualify as a measure the consistency of which with the WTO Agreements can be examined and has indeed been found in some cases to violate certain provisions of such Agreements.

[150] First Written Submission of the European Communities, para. 99.

Reply

5.522 Yes, the EC has explained in detail (e.g., in paras. 40-44 of its second written submission) that the US law as such violates Articles 21.3 and 4 and Article 12, in particular paragraph 1 thereof. The EC claim is that in order to comply with the provisions of Article 12.1, the US DOC must inform the parties of the specific information it requires to complete its determination in the particular case, allow the parties access to the information submitted by the other interested parties and give all the parties ample opportunity to provide the information at a meaningful point in the proceedings. Article 12.2 allows also for the right to present information orally. Article 12.3 establishes in effect a procedure of mutual dialogue by providing that the affected exporters should be given timely opportunity "to see all information that is relevant to the presentation of their cases...and to prepare presentations on the basis of this information". Moreover, Article 12.8 provides that before the final determination is made, disclosure should take place "in such sufficient time for the parties to defend their interests". The principle underlying Article 12 of the *SCM Agreement*, therefore, is that during all stages of the reviews the interested parties should be given ample opportunity to present evidence, to have access to the evidence presented by the other parties (except where confidentiality applies), to present counter-evidence and to defend their interests at all stages leading up to the final determination. All these due process and rights of defence requirements should take place before the final determination is made in a sunset review. As explained above, all these procedural rights and due process requirements are not respected by the US DOC in sunset reviews under the existing laws, regulations and practices and were definitively not respected in the present case. The EC submits that a law or regulation that is open in fact to any type of interpretation by, or leaves too much of unbounded discretion to, the administrative authorities violates as such the provisions of the *SCM Agreement* in question.

P. Responses of the United States to Questions from the Panel Following the Second Meeting of the Panel

Questions to Both Parties

Q41. Do you consider it *impossible* that the drafters might have intended there to be different rules for sunset reviews from those for investigations? In other words, in your view, would it have been *irrational* for the drafters to establish a set of disciplines in respect of investigations, and intend some of them apply to sunset reviews and others not? If so, what might be the reasons for such differences? If not, why not?

Reply

5.523 As the United States previously discussed in response to the Panel's first set of questions, applying the customary rules of interpretation of public international law to Article 21.3 of the *Agreement on Subsidies and Countervailing Measures* ("*SCM Agreement*"), the United States considers that no provisions of the *SCM Agreement* are required to be applied to reviews under Article 21.3 unless expressly indicated.[151] Where the drafters intended to require that the rules for sunset reviews and investigations be the same, they made an express provision to that effect.[152] As a result, it is both possible and rational that the drafters intended there to be different rules for sunset reviews and investigations.[153]

5.524 The reason for such differences is straightforward – investigations and sunset reviews serve different functions and, in essence, gauge different things. The purpose of an investigation is to determine whether the conditions necessary for the *imposition* of a countervailing duty currently exist; *i.e.*, injury caused by subsidized imports. The purpose of a sunset review is to determine whether the conditions necessary for *continued imposition* of a countervailing duty exist; *i.e.*, expiry of the duty would be likely to lead to continuation or recurrence of subsidization and injury. The focus of a sunset review under Article 21.3 is likely future behaviour if the remedial measure is removed, not whether or to what extent subsidization currently exists, which is the focus of an investigation.

Q42. Footnote 37 to the *SCM Agreement* states:

> The term "initiated" as used hereinafter means procedural action by which a Member formally commences an investigation as provided in Article 11.

Please comment on the meaning of this footnote in the context of the issues in this dispute.

Reply

5.525 Footnote 37 defines the term "initiated" as used initially in Article 10 in the context of investigations. Article 10 provides that countervailing duties "may only be imposed pursuant to investigations initiated" in accordance with the *SCM Agreement*. Footnote 37 defines "initiated" in this context to mean "procedural action by which a Member formally commences an investigation as provided in Article 11". The term "initiated" in Article 21.3 is used in a different context, one to which footnote 37 does not apply. "Initiated" in Article 21.3 cannot be a reference to an "investigation as provided in Article 11" because sunset reviews are not "an investigation as provided in Article 11", and Article 21.3 states that the administering authority, on its own initiative, may "initiate" a "review" to determine the likelihood of continuation or recurrence of subsidization and injury. Thus, the definition of "initiated" in footnote 37 is limited to those instances where it refers to a procedural action - an investigation - "as provided in Article 11".

---

[151] Answers of the United States to Questions from the Panel ("US Answers"), 21 February 2002, paras. 19-21.

[152] *Ibid.*, paras. 19 and 21, providing examples of provisions that apply to both investigations and sunset reviews.

[153] Of course, the United States is mindful that it is problematic to speculate on the intent of the drafters of treaty text and that the text itself is the best evidence of the drafters' intent.

Q43. What textual support, if any, is there, in your view, for the proposition that the term "investigation" includes sunset reviews? Please comment, in particular, on the relevance, if any, of footnote 37 to and Article 32.3 of the *SCM Agreement*.

Reply

5.526 There is no textual support in the *SCM Agreement* for the proposition that the term "investigation" includes Article 21.3 sunset reviews.

5.527 The *SCM Agreement* distinguishes between the investigatory phase and the review phase of a countervailing duty proceeding. Article 11 deals with investigations, while Article 21 deals with reviews. This structure is reflected in other provisions of the *SCM Agreement*. For example, Articles 22.1 through 22.6 set forth obligations concerning the contents of public notices issued during an investigation, while Article 22.7 sets forth comparable obligations with respect to reviews. As the panel in *Korea DRAMs* concluded, "the term 'investigation' means the investigative phase leading up to the final determination of the investigating authority".[154]

5.528 Article 32.3, which is a transition rule, also distinguishes between "investigations" and "reviews of existing measures". In *Brazil Desiccated Coconut*, the Appellate Body specifically recognized this distinction between the initial investigation and the post-investigation phase, noting that the imposition of "definitive" duties (an "order" in US parlance) ends the investigative phase.[155]

5.529 As discussed in response to Question 42 above, footnote 37 defines the term "initiated" as used in the context of the commencement of an investigation under Article 11. Footnote 37 has no application to reviews under Article 21.

Q44. Please explain why, in your view, the drafters established a *de minimis* standard for investigations, providing support from the text and/or the negotiating history of the *SCM Agreement*. Do the mandatory nature and the strong language of the statement in Article 11.9 ("There shall be immediate termination in cases where the amount of a subsidy is *de minimis* ...") indicate anything about the rationale for this standard?

Reply

5.530 As demonstrated in the United States' previous submissions in this case, an analysis of the text and context of Article 21.3 and the object and purpose of the *SCM Agreement* leads to the conclusion that the Article 11.9 *de minimis* standard does not apply to reviews under Article 21, including sunset reviews under Article 21.3. This should be the end of the analysis. However, the EC has brought up the negotiating history of the *SCM Agreement* in a vain attempt to overcome the conclusion to which the text, context, and object and purpose inexorably lead. Significantly, in its attempted reliance on negotiating history, the EC does not explain how its invocation of negotiating history is justified under the customary rule of treaty interpretation reflected in Article 32 of the *Vienna Convention*, which permits recourse to supplementary means of interpretation:

---

[154] United States - Anti-Dumping Duty on Dynamic Random Access Memory Semiconductors (DRAMS) of One Megabit or Above from Korea, WT/DS99/R, Report of the Panel adopted 19 March 1999, para. 6.48, note 494.

[155] Brazil - Measures Affecting Desiccated Coconut, WT/DS22/AB/R, Report of the Appellate Body adopted 20 March 1997, p. 9.

in order to confirm the meaning resulting from the application of Article 31, or to determine the meaning when the interpretation according to Article 31:

(a) leaves the meaning ambiguous or obscure; or

(b) leads to a result which is manifestly absurd or unreasonable.

5.531 Nothing in the *SCM Agreement* with respect to the Article 11.9 *de minimis* standard is ambiguous or obscure. Under Article 11.9, Members must apply a one per cent *de minimis* standard in countervailing duty *investigations*. Nothing in Article 21.3 or elsewhere in the Agreement sets a *de minimis* standard for sunset reviews. Nothing in the Agreement requires Members to quantify an amount of subsidization when determining likelihood of continuation or recurrence of subsidization.

5.532 Furthermore, this absence of a *de minimis* standard or quantification requirement for sunset reviews does not lead to a manifestly absurd or unreasonable result. Determining likelihood of continuation or recurrence of subsidization requires a consideration of future, rather than present circumstances. What are the prospects of subsidization in the future? Without the discipline of the duty, is subsidization likely to continue or recur? The analysis required in a sunset review, therefore, is necessarily prospective and predictive in nature.

5.533 In the context of an investigation, the function of the Article 11.9 *de minimis* test is to determine whether foreign government subsidies warrant the imposition of a countervailing duty order in the first instance. For example, in an investigation, if the investigating authority found that a government programme had provided recurring subsidies at a rate of more than one per cent, imposition of a countervailing duty would be warranted if the subsidized imports were found to cause injury. In contrast, the focus of the sunset review is the future. The mere continued existence of this same programme could warrant maintaining the duty beyond the five-year point, *even if* the amount of the subsidy was currently *zero*, as stated in footnote 52, because subsidization and injury may be likely to recur absent the discipline of the duty. This distinction between the object and purpose of an investigation and the object and purpose of a sunset review supports the conclusion that, absent an express reference to the contrary, there is no basis to assume or infer an intent that the *de minimis* standard for investigations applies in sunset reviews.

5.534 Moreover, contrary to the EC's claim in its Second Oral Statement (para. 36), the negotiating history of the *SCM Agreement* reveals not one, but *two* theoretical justifications for the *de minimis* concept. The EC's claim is all the more astonishing given that the document it cites explicitly sets out both theories as follows:

There are two alternative (and not mutually exclusive) theoretical justifications for the *de minimis* concept.

- The first view holds that countervailing duty actions and measures may be taken only when the trade distorting effect of the subsidy and its effects on the industry in the importing country so require. Thus, no action should be taken where it would be clearly out of proportion to the objective sought, or as Article 2:12 states, 'where the effect of the subsidy on the industry in the importing country is not such as to cause material injury'.

– The second theory treats the issue of de minimis subsidy as a completely separate issue from the determination of injury in an investigation. If it can be established that the totality of subsidies on the product investigated are minimal (so small per unit that they are practically non-existent), the investigating authorities may determine that, as Article 2:12 states, 'no subsidy exists'. Thus, as the maxim states, 'de minimis non curat lex': the law does not take notice of minimal matters."[[156]]

In other words, one of the two plausible and recognized theories, which is similar to the justification under US law for a *de minimis* standard, is unrelated to the subject of injury and merely considers that the law should not concern itself with subsidization that is of a trifling amount.

5.535 Thus, the only thing the negotiating history demonstrates is that there was *no* consensus or single reason why the drafters established a *de minimis* standard for investigations. Furthermore, under either theoretical justification for a *de minimis* standard, there is no magic or empirical economic logic in the choice of the one per cent standard currently set forth in Article 11.9. Rather, the one per cent standard is simply a negotiated number. The negotiating history itself reflects that the original proposal for the *de minimis* standard set the threshold at 2.5 per cent.[157] The negotiators did not agree to include a *de minimis* standard in Article 21.3 for sunset reviews.

5.536 In addition, it is difficult to reconcile the EC's assertion that the *de minimis* standard relates to the question of whether there is injury when the *SCM Agreement* reflects not one, but three different, *de minimis* standards.[158] Furthermore, the *de minimis* standard in these provisions depends on the economic level of development *of the exporting country*. It is difficult to see how the injury in the importing Member from subsidized imports depends on the level of economic development in the exporting Member.

Q45. Assuming for the sake of argument, and without prejudice to the outcome in the matter before the Panel, that a *de minimis* standard applies in respect of subsidization to sunset reviews, would this *de minimis* standard be based on: (i) the rate of subsidization during the period of application of the countervailing duty ("CVD"); (ii) the rate of subsidization at the time of sunset review; or (iii) the rate at which subsidization is likely to continue or recur? How would you calculate that rate of subsidization on which the *de minimis* standard would be based?

Reply

5.537 There is no obligation under the *SCM Agreement* to quantify an amount of subsidization in the context of a sunset review. All three of the options posited in this question demonstrate the error in suggesting that there is a requirement to do so. Indeed, just the fact that it is necessary to ask the question as to the relevant time period demonstrates that there was no agreement to include a *de minimis* standard - these are

[156] MTN.GNG/NG10/W/4 (28 April 1987), page 51 (emphasis added) (copy attached as Exhibit US-7). This document, prepared by the Secretariat, was a reference paper which reproduced existing GATT rules on countervailing measures and subsidies and which summarized the status of the discussions concerning possible modifications of those rules.

[157] *Ibid.* page 50 (Exhibit US-7).

[158] See *SCM Agreement*, Articles 11.9, 27.10(a), and 27.11.

the types of questions that would have had to have been asked and negotiated at the time.

5.538 The consideration in a sunset review is whether subsidization and injury are likely to *continue or recur* in the absence of the duty. The rate of subsidization during the period of the application of the duty (option i), if above zero, would certainly demonstrate that subsidization continued with the discipline of the duty in effect and that, therefore, one could find a likelihood that subsidization would *continue* were the duty removed – for example, if benefits were being received under a recurring subsidy programme or the benefit stream from a non-recurring subsidy would continue. The same logic would apply if the rate of subsidization at the time of the sunset review (option ii) also was above zero. Nevertheless, even if the rate of subsidization were zero under either of these options, one might find a likelihood of *recurrence* of subsidization[159] – for example, if subsidy programs, whether providing recurring or non-recurring benefits, originally found to benefit exporters still exist. With respect to the rate at which subsidization is likely to continue or recur (option iii), one could never *calculate* a future rate of subsidization for obvious reasons, although it may be possible to infer a future rate based on past rates (which is in essence what the US Department of Commerce does under US law).

5.539 In sum, all of these options might inform a determination of the likelihood of continuation or recurrence of subsidization – but they just as easily might not. The only obligation in a sunset review under Article 21.3 is to determine whether expiry of the duty would be likely to lead to the continuation or recurrence of subsidization and injury. This is an inherently predictive exercise which may call for a reliance upon findings made in the original investigation or subsequent administrative (assessment) reviews, if any. However, nothing in the *SCM Agreement requires* a consideration of the magnitude of subsidization in determining the likelihood of continuation or recurrence of subsidization and injury.

Questions to the EC

5.540 Consistent with the Panel's instructions, the United States intends to file comments on the EC's answers to questions 46-54 on Tuesday, 9 April 2002.

Questions to the United States

Q55. The European Communities states:

> In fact, to the extent DOC relied upon the rates calculated in its original investigation, the duty of investigation laid down in Article 21.3 of the *SCM Agreement* would also require at a minimum that DOC made all documents showing how the rates were calculated in the original investigation also part of the record in the sunset review.
>
> Please respond to this argument.

Reply

5.541 There is no "duty of investigation" contained in Article 21.3, nor has the EC demonstrated that any such obligation exits. Article 21.3 requires that the administer-

[159] See US First Submission, para. 81; US Second Submission, paras. 11-12 and 19; and US Answers, paras. 34-36.

ing authority "determine" whether the expiry of the duty would likely lead to a continuation or recurrence of subsidization and injury. The United States considers that an appropriate definition for the term "determine" as used in Article 21.3 is "to decide" something – namely, that the administering authority is required to decide the likelihood issue in the affirmative or terminate the duty.[160] This is the only obligation under Article 21.3. Nothing in the *SCM Agreement requires* consideration of the magnitude of subsidization in determining the likelihood of continuation or recurrence of subsidization and injury.

5.542 In conducting sunset reviews, the US Department of Commerce determines whether the expiry of the duty would be likely to lead to the continuation or recurrence of subsidization and, if so, the level of that subsidization. The US Department of Commerce's likelihood determination does not "rely" on any particular *level* of subsidization. The US Department of Commerce does not *calculate* the level of subsidization in the context of the sunset review. Rather, as explained in the US Department of Commerce's *Sunset Policy Bulletin* (Section III.B)[161], the US Department of Commerce relies on rates previously calculated in the original investigation. These rates are contained in public, published determinations in the *Federal Register*. If the EC and the German producers believed that the data and documents underlying these public, published figures were germane to their arguments in the sunset review, they had ample opportunity to place such information on the sunset review record.

Q56. Could the United States point to the statutory or regulatory provisions, if any, of US law which provide an indication to interested Members and parties as to the parts of the record of a CVD investigation that would normally be expected to be made part of the record of the sunset review of any resulting CVD order. Please also point to any such provisions of US law in respect of the parts of the record of a duty assessment proceeding as well as the parts of the record of a review under Article 21.2 that would normally be expected to be made part of the record of the sunset review of the CVD order in question. Please provide the relevant statutory or regulatory texts, if any.

Reply

5.543 As the United States has explained previously[162], under the US system, a "proceeding" begins on the date of the filing of a petition and ends on, *inter alia*, the revocation of an order.[163] A countervailing duty proceeding consists of one or more "segments".[164] "Segment" refers to a portion of the proceeding that is separately judicially reviewable. For example, a countervailing duty investigation, an administrative review, or a sunset review each would constitute a segment of a proceeding.[165]

5.544 Under the US statute and the US Department of Commerce regulations, the administrative record from one segment of a proceeding never automatically becomes part of the administrative record of another segment of the proceeding. In

160 See US Answers, paras. 57-58.

161 Exhibit EC-15.

162 US Answers, paras. 69-70.

163 19 CFR 351.102 (definition of "proceeding"). A copy of section 351.102 and other regulatory provisions discussed herein is attached as Exhibit US-8.

164 19 CFR 351.102 (definition of "segment of proceeding") (Exhibit US-8).

165 See 19 CFR 351.102 (definition of "segment of proceeding", examples under para. 2) (Exhibit US-8).

other words, the administrative record from the investigation (one segment) or an administrative (duty assessment) review (another segment), never automatically become parts of the administrative record of a sunset review (yet another segment). Each segment of a proceeding contains its own discrete administrative record. Each final determination is based solely on the information placed upon and contained in the administrative record for that segment. Each final determination made in a particular segment, and the discrete record upon which it is based, is subject to judicial review.

Q57. The United States indicated, in response to an oral question from the Panel at the second meeting of the Panel, that the DOC's final determination in a CVD investigation is not made part of the record of the sunset review of any resulting CVD order, because that final determination is published and, therefore, publicly available. Is the Panel to understand, from this statement, that the DOC only makes part of the record of a sunset review information/documents which are not publicly available? If so, is the Panel to understand that the DOC may base its determination in a sunset review on publicly available information without making that information part of the record of the sunset review? Please explain in detail.

Reply

5.545 The administrative record of a sunset review (or any other segment of a proceeding) before the US Department of Commerce consists of all factual information, written argument, or other material developed by, presented to, or obtained by the US Department of Commerce during the course of the sunset review.[166] This record may include public as well as business proprietary information.[167] However, a relevant public, published decision, such as a prior US Department of Commerce determination (*e.g.*, the final determination in the original investigation which is published in the *Federal Register*) or a decision from a US court, need not be placed on the record to be considered by the US Department of Commerce in making its determination. This is simply a generally accepted precept of US administrative law.

Q58. The Panel notes the following comment in the Statement of Administrative Action accompanying the Uruguay Round Agreements Act:

> [The DOC] normally will select ... net countervailable subsidies determined in the original investigation or in a prior review

The Panel further notes that the United States indicated, in response to an oral question from the Panel at the second meeting of the Panel, that no information/documents from the record of a CVD investigation are automatically made part of the record of the sunset review of any resulting CVD order. Is the Panel to understand, from this statement, that the DOC relies in a sunset review on the net countervailable subsidy determined in the original investigation, where there have been no prior reviews, without taking into account the information / documents underlying the calculation of such subsidy? If so, could the United States explain how the DOC does so. In particular, how does the DOC make any appropriate adjustments to the subsidy without reliance on such information/documents? Please explain in detail.

---

[166] See 19 CFR 351.104 (record of proceedings) (Exhibit US-8).

[167] *Ibid.*

Reply

5.546 There is no obligation under the *SCM Agreement* to quantify an amount of subsidization in the context of a sunset review. Under US law, however, the USITC has the discretion to consider the magnitude of the net countervailable subsidy that is likely to prevail if the order is invoked.[168] As reflected in the portion of the SAA quoted by the Panel, the US Department of Commerce determines the likely magnitude in order to report it to the Commission.[169]

5.547 In determining the magnitude of the net countervailable subsidy, the US Department of Commerce begins with the net countervailable subsidy rate determined in the investigation. As explained in prior US submissions to the Panel, the US Department of Commerce begins with this rate because it is the only evidence reflecting the behaviour of the respondents without the discipline of countervailing measures in place. The US Department of Commerce may make adjustments to the net countervailable subsidy in accordance with the guidance contained in the *Sunset Policy Bulletin*.[170] However, a sunset review is not a procedure for determining the amount of final countervailing duty liability. Instead, a sunset review is conducted to determine the likelihood of the continuation or recurrence of subsidization and injury in the event that the countervailing duty order is revoked. Consequently, the US Department of Commerce does not *calculate* the net countervailable rate of subsidization in a sunset review. Rather, the US Department of Commerce starts with the rate determined in the investigation and may adjust that rate by simple subtraction or addition – for example, if, since the investigation a programme has been terminated without residual benefits, the US Department of Commerce will subtract the rate determined for that particular programme from the total rate determined for all programmes. This is, in fact, what happened in this case. The mechanics of this kind of adjustment are set forth in Exhibit EC-8.

Q59. The Panel notes the following statement of the DOC in its final determination in the sunset review on carbon steel:

> With respect to Dillinger's contention that the [DOC] should have included in the record of these sunset reviews the calculation memoranda the [DOC] prepared in the original investigation, we disagree. Insofar as Dillinger could have submitted some version of the memoranda in the sunset reviews, we determined that, in these sunset reviews, Dillinger did not file the information in a timely manner.

Did the DOC communicate to Dillinger, or any other German producer, notably Hoesch, Preussag, or Thyssen, prior to publication of this final determination, the DOC's refusal to include in the record of these sunset reviews the calculation memoranda the DOC prepared in the original investigation and its reasons therefor? If so, please indicate when and provide a copy of this communication.

Reply

5.548 On 13 April 2000, the German producers in the sunset review – Thyssen Krupp Stahl AG, Stahlwerke Bremen GmbH, EKO Stahl GmbH, and Salzgitter AG –

168 Section 752(a)(6) of the Act.

169 Section 752(b)(3) of the Act.

170 See US Answers, paras. 59-66.

sought to have *all* the calculation memoranda from the original investigation placed on the record of the sunset review. Three German producers of certain corrosion-resistant carbon steel flat products were involved in the original investigation: Hoesch Stahl AG (Hoesch), Preussag Stahl AG (Preussag), and Thyssen Stahl AG (Thyssen). Prior to the issuance of the final determination in the sunset review, the US Department of Commerce did not communicate to Dillinger (who was not a party in the corrosion-resistant case) or any other German producer that the request to have all calculation memoranda placed on the record of the sunset review was determined to be untimely submitted.

Q60. Does the DOC make the full record of a sunset review available to parties (including under administrative protective orders) prior to or after the publication of its preliminary determination? Is this a matter of law or policy? If the former, please point to the relevant statutory or regulatory provisions of US law, and provide the statutory or regulatory texts. Did the DOC make the full record of the sunset review on carbon steel available to parties? If so, when?

Reply

5.549 Under the US statute and the US Department of Commerce regulations, the public portion of the record of the sunset review, updated on a daily basis as information is placed on the record, is maintained in the US Department of Commerce's Central Record Unit, which is open to the public during normal business hours.[171] Under the US statute and the US Department of Commerce regulations, the business proprietary portion of the record of the sunset review is available to any person covered by, and subject to, an Administrative Protective Order ("APO") for the sunset review segment of the proceeding.[172] All documents submitted by interested parties must be served on all other interested parties at the same time as they are filed with the US Department of Commerce. This includes service of public documents on all parties and service of business proprietary documents on all parties under APO.[173] A copy of the proprietary portion of the record of the sunset review also is kept in the US Department of Commerce's Central Records Unit.[174] The respondents in the sunset review on carbon steel had continuous access to the administrative record as it was continuously updated.

Q61. Please respond to paragraphs 34 and 46 of the European Communities' comments on the responses of the United States to the questions from the Panel following the first meeting of the Panel, regarding the use - as opposed to disclosure - by the DOC of confidential information/documents in sunset reviews.

Reply

5.550 In paragraph 34, the EC suggests that the US Department of Commerce could have placed the proprietary calculation memoranda from the investigation on the

[171] See section 777(a)(4) of the Act. A copy of section 777(a)(4) and certain other provisions of the US statute discussed herein is attached as Exhibit US-9. See also 19 CFR 351.103 and 351.104(b) (Exhibit US-8).

[172] See section 777(c)(1) of the Act (Exhibit US-9); 19 CFR 351.305 (Exhibit US-8).

[173] See section 777(d) of the Act (Exhibit US-9); 19 CFR 351.303(f) (Exhibit US-8).

[174] See 19 CFR 351.103 and 351.104(a) (Exhibit US-8).

record of the sunset review because, by making requests to place such data on the sunset review record, the German producers have "renounced the confidential nature of the data". There is no merit to the EC's argument.

5.551 Article 12.4 of the *SCM Agreement* provides that business confidential information "shall not be disclosed without specific permission of the party submitting it". In other words, before business confidential may be disclosed: 1) the party submitting it, 2) must have given specific permission. Notwithstanding the EC's assertions, neither of those factors is present in this case. Furthermore, on such an extremely serious matter as the protection of business proprietary information, it is irresponsible to suggest that an administering authority simply should *infer* that a particular party has given the requisite permission.

5.552 Consistent with Article 12.4, the US statute provides that information submitted to the US Department of Commerce "which is designated as proprietary by the person submitting the information shall not be disclosed to any person without the consent of the person submitting the information ... ."[175] The parties that submitted the business proprietary information in the original investigation were Hoesch Stahl AG, Preussag Stahl AG, and Thyssen Stahl AG. The German producers in the sunset review were Thyssen Krupp Stahl AG, Stahlwerke Bremen GmbH, EKO Stahl GmbH, and Salzgitter AG. In the record of the sunset review, there is no evidence of express consent to move the information from the record of one segment of the proceeding to another, nor is there any explicit claim that the parties in the sunset review had the authority to give such consent.

5.553 There is no distinction between "use" and "disclosure" on this issue. Any information used by the US Department of Commerce as a basis for a determination is subject to disclosure. If the information is public, it must be disclosed to the public; if the information is business proprietary, it must be disclosed to any party under APO. The concern is not, as the EC asserts in paragraph 46, that placing the business proprietary information from the investigation on the record of the sunset review might result in public disclosure. Business proprietary information remains proprietary unless and until the submitter explicitly indicates otherwise. Rather, the issue in this case is that the original submitter of the business proprietary information relied upon the fact that its proprietary information would only be used during the investigation phase and would be subject to disclosure only to parties under APO involved in the investigation phase for their use during that phase. The EC's suggested cavalier treatment of business proprietary information is not consistent with either US law or Members' obligations under the *SCM Agreement*.

Q. Comments of the European Communities on the Responses of the United States to Questions from the Panel Following the Second Meeting of the Panel

US response to Panel's question 44

5.554 In paragraph 13 of its responses, the US affirms that the Uruguay Round negotiators did not agree on the inclusion of a *de minimis* standard for sunset reviews. The European Communities contests this statement. There is nothing in the legisla-

[175] Section 777(b)(1)(A) of the Act (Exhibit US-9).

tive history of the *SCM Agreement* that suggests such a conclusion. A *de minimis* threshold was simply not expressly included in Article 21.3 because it is clear from the overall context and object and purpose of the Agreement that this requirement applies to initial as well as sunset investigations alike.

5.555 Furthermore, in paragraph 14 of its responses, the US contests the EC's position that the *de minimis* standard is related to injury on the basis that the *SCM Agreement* contains three different *de minimis* standards.

5.556 The increased *de minimis* thresholds, established respectively by Articles 27.10(a) and 27.11 *SCM Agreement* for developing (2 per cent) and least developed (3 per cent) countries, do not affect the inherent relationship between *de minimis* level of subsidization and injury. They are, in fact, part of the special development package included in Article 27 of the *SCM Agreement* together with a number of concessions granted to developing countries in order to meet their development needs. An increased *de minimis* threshold does therefore not alter the ratio legis of the *de minimis* principle. For example, developing country members were also entitled to maintain export subsidies for a period of eight years (Article 27.2). This does not alter the principle that export subsidies are prohibited because they are presumed to be trade distorting. It is simply a relaxation of, an exemption to WTO requirements, as there are many in the WTO Agreements, granted in order to meet the development needs of specific WTO members.

5.557 Incidentally, if the US logic that the different *de minimis* thresholds of Article 27 have not to be interpreted as exceptions has to be followed, it appears difficult to reconcile these thresholds with the rationale of administrative efficiency put forward by the US for the *de minimis* rule. It is, in fact, difficult to understand how the administrative efficiency of collecting a countervailing duty at the border can depend on the origin of a product.

US response to Panel's question 45

5.558 In paragraph 16 of its responses, the US claims that a finding of likelihood of continuation or recurrence of a subsidy could be made if benefits were being received under a recurring subsidy programme or the benefit stream of a non-recurring programme would continue. The EC does not dispute that fact but the US argument evades the basic argumentation of the EC. Indeed, the US has to demonstrate the subsidization is likely to continue or recur *above the de minimis threshold* set out in Article 11.9 *SCM Agreement*. In the corrosion-resistant steel case from Germany, it was clear that subsidization (originally found at 0.54 per cent in 1993) could not continue or recur above the *de minimis* level of 1 per cent since a major proportion of the subsidy margin, i.e. the CIG programme, was based on a non-recurring subsidy programme where, in addition, the benefit stream is declining and would expire in the near future.

5.559 Likewise, if the rate of subsidization is zero, the investigating authority has to demonstrate how this zero-rate will increase above the *de minimis* threshold. A failure to do so results in a violation of Article 21.3 *SCM Agreement*. With regard to subsidy programmes, it is not sufficient to show that they "still exist". The investigating authority, in a sunset review, must demonstrate that such programmes are likely to be used, and explain why. In addition, it is not sufficient to "infer a future rate" of subsidy; a sunset review requires a determination of subsidization, and subsidization does not exist in the abstract.

Question 55

5.560 In its response, the US forgets that the conditions and requirements of Article 12 *SCM Agreement* are fully applicable to sunset reviews. Accordingly, the same rules regarding the disclosure of evidence that applies to investigations would also apply to sunset reviews.

Question 56

5.561 The response of the US to this question points to no statutory provision and discusses only two general regulatory provisions dealing with "segments" of a proceeding. From the conduct of the US ITC in similar sunset review proceedings, it is clear that US law does not prohibit automatic inclusion of key documents, even confidential documents, from the original investigation in the record of these sunset reviews.

Questions 57 & 58

5.562 It must be noted that the US' statement that there is no obligation under the *SCM Agreement* to quantify an amount of subsidization in the context of a sunset review is erroneous. This statement is also belied by the DOC's own policy bulletin, which makes it clear that "the purpose of the net countervailable subsidy in the context of sunset reviews is to provide the Commission with a rate which represents the countervailable rate that is likely to prevail if the order is revoked or the suspended investigation is terminated." DOC Sunset Policy Bulletin at para. III B3 (Exhibit EC -15). It is contradictory for the US to put so much importance on the rates from the original investigation and claim that they are the best evidence of the conduct of foreign producers and governments but then staunchly refuse to place DOC's own calculation memoranda on the record, showing how these rates were calculated. DOC's refusal to place the calculation memoranda on the record of this case was found to be unlawful by the US Court of International Trade. *AG der Dillinger Hüttenwerke v. United States*, Slip Op. 02-25 at 16-18 (Exhibit EC-24). It must be remembered that, under the US legal system, this decision has the force and effect of law and must be followed by the DOC. The decision is presumed correct unless later overturned by a court of competent jurisdiction.

Question 59

5.563 As previously explained by the EC, the parties to the corrosion-resistant sunset review were the legal successors to the parties in the original investigation (EC Comments to US responses after the first meeting with the Panel, at para. 45). Accordingly, there can be no dispute but that the parties to the review were authorized to request placement of the calculation memoranda from the original investigation on the record of the review. Indeed, during the sunset review, DOC never questioned the parties' authority to make their request concerning the memoranda.

Question 60

5.564 The problem faced by the German Producers was not that DOC did not make the record of the sunset review available to the parties prior to the preliminary determination. The German Producers timely submitted substantial evidence showing that subsidization was not likely to continue or recur if the countervailing duty order were revoked. The German Producers also timely submitted evidence rebutting all of the claims made by the US producers.

5.565 The problem was that the preliminary determination was the first time that the DOC made any statements concerning the adequacy of this evidence. Thus, despite the fact that the German Producers submitted evidence to rebut the claims of the US producers on every point, DOC claimed that it required even more evidence to confirm the German Producers' arguments. DOC, however, then proceeded to reject all additional evidence from the German Producers or even consult its own calculation memoranda from the original investigation, claiming that such information was untimely. DOC made this claim despite the fact that it had accepted additional information from other parties. The US Court of International Trade strongly rebuked DOC for this conduct, stating that "Commerce cannot act irrationally and arbitrarily." (*Dillinger v. United States*, at 41).

Question 61

5.566 Throughout this proceeding, the US has continually changed its rationale for refusing to make the calculation memoranda from the original investigation part of the record of the sunset review. In the final results of the sunset review, DOC stated simply that the request to make the calculation memoranda part of the record was untimely. At the beginning of this proceeding, the US stated that it was prohibited from granting the request because it could not disclose confidential information. Now the US claims that it is not a question of disclosing confidential information but one of "moving" confidential information from one segment of the proceeding to another segment without the party's consent. As stated above in the comments to question 59, the US completely ignores the fact that the parties to the sunset review were the legal successors to the parties in the original investigation. In their 1 October 1999 substantive response, the German Producers carefully explained that Thyssen Krupp Stahl AG was the legal successor to Hoesch and Thyssen and that Salzgitter AG was the legal successor to Preussag. (German Producers Substantive Response at 5 (1999), submitted as Exhibit EC-23). Thus, there could have been no confusion over the authority of the German Producers to request that the calculation memoranda be placed on the record of the sunset review.

5.567 The EC is not suggesting any "cavalier" treatment of business proprietary information as claimed by the US. The EC is merely arguing that confidential information from the original investigation that is necessary to the determination in the sunset review should have been made part of the confidential record in the sunset review. This is precisely what is done by the US ITC in its sunset review and therefore is clearly not inconsistent with US law. This procedure would also be fully consistent with Article 12.4 *SCM Agreement*.

R. Comments of the United States on the Responses of the European Communities to Questions from the Panel Following the Second Meeting of the Panel

5.568 The United States does not intend to comment on every response by the European Communities ("EC") to the Panel's second set of questions, particularly where the issues raised have been addressed in prior written submissions of the United States. Instead, the United States will comment briefly on those specific responses where additional points or emphasis is warranted.

5.569 At the outset, however, the United States notes the faulty assumption underlying many of the EC's arguments. In its answers, the EC discusses the *SCM Agreement* as if the text issued from a body of drafters that shared a common vision. In fact, the text was drafted by countries that did not agree on a lot of things. It is a *negotiated* text. As such, it simply reflects those areas where countries did manage to agree on something. For example, the negotiators agreed on a 1 per cent *de minimis* standard for investigations, but the negotiating history reveals no agreement on the theory underlying this negotiated rule.[176]

5.570 As the United States previously has demonstrated, if one applies customary rules of treaty interpretation, the issues in this case are fairly straightforward. In response, the EC has proposed an approach to treaty interpretation – what it alleges is "a more classic way of drafting and interpreting treaties"[177] – that is contradicted by numerous Appellate Body reports. The EC's approach in fact simply attempts to impute into the *SCM Agreement* words and obligations that are not there.

5.571 Turning now to the EC's answers to specific questions, with respect to Question 41, the EC's answer reflects a reliance on assumptions that: (1) the purpose of a sunset review is the same as that of an initial investigation; and (2) every provision of the *SCM Agreement* automatically should be considered applicable to every other provision. As the United States previously has demonstrated, these assumptions simply are incorrect.[178]

5.572 Furthermore, the EC's approach ignores the fact that where the drafters wished to have obligations set forth in one provision apply in another context, they did so expressly. *Article 21 itself illustrates this point.* Paragraph 4 of Article 21 makes the provisions of Article 12 applicable to Article 21.3 reviews. If, as the EC argues, the drafters intended that the provisions of other articles apply to Article 21, why did they bother with the first sentence of Article 21.4? Under the EC approach, the first sentence becomes superfluous, an outcome which violates the principle of effectiveness of treaty interpretation.[179]

5.573 With respect to Question 42, the EC's assertion that it has made a "claim" with respect to an alleged shifting of the burden of proof under the US system is incorrect. In its panel request (which established the terms of reference in this proceeding), the EC's "claim" was that, under Article 21.3, the United States cannot automatically self-initiate a sunset review.[180] In making this claim, the EC panel request included only an *argument* that automatic initiation somehow shifted the burden of

[176] See Responses of the United States of America to the Questions from the Panel Following the Second Meeting ("US Second Responses"), April 2, 2002, paras. 12-13.

[177] Replies of the European Communities to the second set of written questions from the Panel at the Second Substantive Meeting with the Parties ("EC Replies"), 2 April 2002, page 2.

[178] With respect to the purpose of a sunset review, see US First Submission, paras. 79-81; US Second Responses, para. 2; and Answers of the United States of American to Question from the European Communities, February 21, 2002, para. 6. With respect to the EC's approach to treaty interpretation, see Answers of the United States of America to Questions from the Panel, February 21, 2002, paras. 19-21; and Comments of the United States of America on the EC's Answers to Questions from the Panel, February 28, 2002, paras. 2-4 and 10-11.

[179] See, e.g., United States - Standards for Reformulated and Conventional Gasoline, WT/DS2/AB/R, Report of the Appellate Body adopted 20 May 1996, page 23 ("[I]nterpretation must give meaning and effect to all the terms of a treaty.").

[180] WT/DS213/3 (10 August 2001).

proof. Accordingly, the Panel should treat the EC's discussion of burden of proof as an *argument*, not as a separate and independent *claim*.

5.574 Moreover, as a substantive matter, the EC is wrong when it asserts that the United States imposes a burden of proof on foreign exporters and governments to demonstrate no likelihood of continued or recurring subsidization and injury.[181] As a matter of US administrative law, there is no burden of proof – in the sense of the ultimate burden of persuasion – imposed on either foreign exporters/governments or the US industry. Instead, the burden is on Commerce to make a determination that can withstand review by a domestic court.

5.575 With respect to the EC's answer to Question 44, the EC omits any explanation – let alone a demonstration – as to how its invocation of negotiating history is justified under the customary rules of treaty interpretation reflected in Article 32 of the *Vienna Convention*.[182] Nevertheless, as the United States has demonstrated, the only thing the negotiating history demonstrates is that there was *no* consensus or single reason why the drafters established a *de minimis* standard.[183] More importantly, however, an analysis of the text and context of Article 21.3 and the object and purpose of the *SCM Agreement* leads to the conclusion that the Article 11.9 *de minimis* standard does not apply to reviews under Article 21, including sunset reviews under Article 21.3.

5.576 With respect to the EC's answer to Question 49, by using the terms "presumption" and "all the more so", the EC seems to suggest that a sunset review is some sort of exceptional procedure that warrants a stricter interpretation of Article 21.3, as opposed to Article 21.2. Articles 21.2 and 21.3, however, are specific implementations of the general rule, found in Article 21.1, that a countervailing duty order shall remain in force only as long as and to the extent necessary to counteract subsidization that is causing injury. Nothing in the general rule found in Article 21.1 suggests any presumption concerning how long countervailing duties may continue to be necessary. Article 21.3 simply defines the point in time (*i.e.*, after five years) at which the authorities must do one of two things: automatically terminate the countervailing duty or take stock of the situation by conducting a review to determine whether continuation or recurrence of subsidization and injury is likely. If so, the duty may be maintained; if not, the duty must be terminated. As the Appellate Body has stated, "describing [or] characterizing a treaty provision as an 'exception' does not by itself justify a 'stricter' or 'narrower' interpretation of that provision than would be warranted by ... applying the normal rules of treaty interpretation."[184]

5.577 In its answers to Questions 50-54, the EC asserts new claims that were not included in its panel request. Because these claims were not included in the Panel's terms of reference, the Panel should dismiss them.

---

[181] EC Replies, page 3.

[182] As discussed in the US Second Responses, para. 8, Article 32 permits recourse to supplementary means of interpretation to confirm the meaning resulting from the application of Article 31, or to determine the meaning when the interpretation according to Article 31: (a) leaves the meaning ambiguous or obscure; or (b) leads to a result which is manifestly absurd or unreasonable. See also US Second Responses, paras. 9-10.

[183] US Second Responses, paras. 12-13.

[184] European Communities - Measures Concerning Meat and Meat Products (Hormones), WT/DS26/AB/R, WT/DS48/AB/R, Report of the Appellate Body adopted 13 February 1998, para. 104.

5.578 With respect to Question 50, the EC's asserts that it has made a "claim" that there can never be "injurious subsidization" as a result of a subsidy rate below1 per cent. This is incorrect. There is no mention of "injury" or "injurious subsidization" in the EC's panel request. Rather, the EC's claim in its panel request was that the Article 11.9 *de minimis* standard for investigations applies also in sunset reviews. Thus, the EC's new claim with respect to non-injurious subsidization is not within the Panel's terms of reference, but instead is at most an argument in support of the EC's claim.

5.579 Furthermore, as the United States has demonstrated in prior submissions, nothing in the text of Article 11.9 or 21.3 requires the application of the Article 11.9 one per cent *de minimis* standard in Article 21.3 sunset reviews, or any other type of review. Finally, the provision of a *de minimis* standard in Article 11.9 is not reflective of the EC's theory that subsidization below one per cent is non-injurious. Rather, the *de minimis* standard for investigations under Article 11 is a creature of negotiation.[185]

5.580 With respect to Question 51, the EC now asserts that it has made a "claim" that US law as such violates the *SCM Agreement* in respect of the obligation to "determine" the likelihood of continuation or recurrence of subsidization. The EC now argues that US law is equivalent to a "web of provisions (basic law, regulations and guidelines)" which allegedly violate the obligations of the *SCM Agreement.*

5.581 It is impossible to read the EC's panel request as articulating this type of claim. In its panel request, the EC essentially challenged three things: (1) the US system of automatic self-initiated sunset reviews, as such; (2) the US failure to apply a 1 per cent *de minimis* standard in sunset reviews, as such; and (3) Commerce's application of the principles described in (1) and (2) in the sunset review on corrosion-resistant steel from Germany. The EC's new claims concerning the definition of "determine" and the issue of "injurious subsidization" are simply not within the terms of reference of this dispute.

5.582 With respect to Question 52, the EC now alleges that by not making certain documents part of the record of the sunset review, Commerce violated various provisions of Article 12 of the *SCM Agreement.* However, Article 12 is nowhere mentioned in the EC's panel request, nor does the panel request refer to the alleged inadequacy of the record of Commerce's sunset review. Thus, once again, the EC appears to be advancing claims that are not within the Panel's terms of reference. Accordingly, the Panel should dismiss these new and improper claims.

5.583 In any event, the EC's statement that the USITC is "subject to the same procedures regarding the treatment of business proprietary information as the US DOC" is patently false. Commerce and the USITC each have practices and regulations which govern the collection, protection, and use of business proprietary information. There are significant differences between Commerce and USITC practices and regulations. One of those differences is that the USITC automatically makes certain parts of the record of the original investigation part of the record of the sunset review;[186] Commerce, by regulation, can not and does not automatically do the same. The EC is

---

[185] US Second Responses, paras. 12-13.

[186] See USITC's Notice of Proposed Amendments to Rules of Practice and Procedure, 62 FR 55185, 55190 (October 23, 1997) ; and USITC's Rules of Practice and Procedure, 63 FR 30599, 30606 (June 5, 1998) (final rulemaking) ("[T]he material from the record of the original investigation that the Commission will release to the parties will include the Commission opinion(s) in the original investigation and staff reports and non-privileged memoranda, where available.").

well aware of the fact that Commerce and the USITC have distinct roles in the United States' conduct of sunset reviews and that the two agencies have distinct sets of practices and regulations on this issue in particular.

5.584 In its response to Question 53, the EC appears to advance a new claim that US law violates the *SCM Agreement* because it provides too much discretion to Commerce in making a sunset determination, thereby allegedly eliminating "legal security and predictability" in the review "to the detriment of foreign exporters and international trade." It is not entirely clear from the EC answer which provisions of the *SCM Agreement* allegedly have been violated by the existence of "too much discretion", but the Panel need not concern itself with the lack of precision in the EC's answer. Here, too, the Panel should dismiss the EC's claim, because the claim was not included in the EC's panel request.

5.585 Nevertheless, the United States notes that it has statutory provisions (sections 751(c) and 752 of the Tariff Act) governing sunset reviews which provide the basic legal and procedural requirements for the conduct of a sunset review. In addition, Commerce has promulgated regulatory provisions (*e.g.*, portions of sections 351.102, 351.104, 351.218, 351.221-222, 351.308-310), primarily procedural in nature, to formalize the sunset review process and provide guidance for effective participation in sunset reviews. Commerce also has issued its *Sunset Policy Bulletin* which outlines the methodology Commerce will employ in making its sunset determination. These provisions provide parties with all the information on the procedural and substantive requirements necessary to participate meaningfully in a sunset review.

5.586 By contrast, the EC provides extremely limited guidance under its own system with respect to the conduct of sunset reviews. As explained in its answer to Panel Question 48, the EC has promulgated a Council Regulation which governs sunset reviews (Exhibit EC-26). This regulation does little more than mirror Article 21. The EC then admits that it has "no other regulatory or administrative texts or guidelines concerning the conduct of countervailing duty expiry reviews" and cites a single sunset review to illustrate the EC's "practice" in sunset reviews. Thus, while the United States provides expansive guidance on its conduct of sunset reviews, through statutory, regulatory and policy provisions, the EC provides no guidance beyond the limited language of the Council Regulation and the single instance where the EC has made a final countervailing duty sunset determination. Therefore, it would seem that if, *arguendo*, the EC's assertions regarding the US system were correct (and within the Panel's terms of reference), it must follow automatically that the EC system also violates the *SCM Agreement*. Also in violation would be those Members who have chosen to implement their obligations by simply incorporating the *SCM Agreement* into their domestic law.

5.587 In its response to Question 53, the EC also asserts that the "flexibility and plasticity" of US law eliminates security and predictability in the interpretation and application of that law, and thereby violates the *SCM Agreement*. Again, however, the EC is reading words into the text of the *SCM Agreement* that are not there. The EC apparently is confusing the language in Article 3.2 of the DSU, which is a narrative statement that the WTO *dispute settlement system* is a central element in providing security and predictability to the multilateral trading system, with some obligation on *Members* to provide security and predictability in international trade through their measures. Of course, there is no such vague obligation in the WTO.

5.588 Finally, with respect to Question 54, the EC states that it is alleging violations of various provisions of Article 12 of the *SCM Agreement* relating to what it describes as "due process and rights of defense requirements". Of course, in its panel request, the EC does not reference Article 12 at all (let alone any particular paragraph of Article 12) or the fact pattern which the EC believes gives rise to a violation of Article 12 (allegedly short deadlines for submissions). While the EC's panel request does mention Article 21, the only reference to particular paragraphs of Article 21 are to paragraphs 1 and 3.

5.589 This new claim comes nowhere close to satisfying the standards of Article 6.2 of the DSU, which requires that panel requests "identify the specific measures at issue and provide a brief summary of the legal basis of the complaint sufficient to present the problem clearly." No objective person could read the EC's panel request and discern that the EC had a problem concerning the deadline for submissions in Commerce sunset reviews. Accordingly, the Panel should dismiss this new EC claim.

VI. ARGUMENTS OF THE THIRD PARTIES

6.1 The arguments presented by the third parties – Japan and Norway – in their written submissions and oral statements are reflected below.

A. *Third-Party Submission of Japan*

1. *Introduction*

6.2 The WTO Agreement, in particular the Agreement on Subsidies and Countervailing Measures (hereinafter referred to as "the *SCM Agreement*"), permits the use of countervailing duty measures, to offset prohibited subsidies only under strict conditions. A Member must adhere strictly to the rules of the *SCM Agreement* when initiating a countervailing duty investigation or a sunset review of a previous investigation. The Government of Japan (hereinafter "Japan") has increasingly become concerned with how the United States (hereinafter "US"), and particularly the US Department of Commerce (hereinafter "DOC"), has conducted sunset reviews pursuant to its interpretation and application of the *SCM Agreement*.

6.3 The Government of Japan supports the European Communities' (hereinafter "EC") position in this case. Japan believes the proper interpretation of the *SCM Agreement* has broader implications for the WTO Agreements as a whole. The facts of this case illustrate the extent to which the DOC will go to maintain import restrictions under Title VII of the Tariff Act of 1930 (hereinafter "Title VII") that are directly contrary to US obligations under the *SCM Agreement*.

6.4 We believe the EC submission appropriately summarizes the key facts of this case. Before turning to our analysis of the legal issues in this case, we simply wish to note the rather extreme facts in this case. Continuing a CVD order at the level of 0.54 per cent - an order that never would have been imposed under the standards of the *SCM Agreement* - shows just how extreme the US has been in continuing orders regardless of the circumstances.

2. *Article 21.3 of the SCM Agreement*

(a) The Proper Scope of Article 21 of the *SCM Agreement*

(i) The provisions of Article 21 of the *SCM Agreement* must be read as an integrated part of the entire *SCM Agreement*

6.5 Article 31 of the *Vienna Convention on the Law of Treaties* ("*Vienna Convention*") provides that the words of a treaty must form the starting point for the process of interpretation. In this regard, words must be interpreted according to their "ordinary meaning" taking into account their "context" (*i.e.*, other provisions of the treaty) and the "object and purpose" of the agreement[187]. Although recourse to a treaty's object and purpose is permissible, it may not override the clear meaning of the text. As the Appellate Body in the *Japan Taxes* case recognized, a "treaty's 'object and purpose' is to be referred to in determining the meaning of the 'terms of the treaty' and not as an independent basis for interpretation".[188] All the provisions of the *SCM Agreement* must be given their ordinary meaning taking into account the context and purpose of the provision.

(ii) Article 21.3 of the *SCM Agreement* expressly requires the termination of the CVD duty after five years

6.6 The provisions of Article 21.3 of the *SCM Agreement* create a specific obligations that a countervailing duty ("CVD") order must be terminated five years after the date of its imposition. The Article states:

> Notwithstanding the provisions of paragraphs 1 and 2, any definitive countervailing duty ***shall*** be terminated on a date not later than five years from its imposition ... , ***unless*** the authorities ***determine***, in a review ... that the expiry of the duty would be likely to lead to continuation or recurrence of subsidization.[189]

6.7 This language stands for the proposition that termination of countervailing duties after five years is the rule, not the exception. First, the verb "shall" signals that termination is an obligation. Second, the term "[n]otwithstanding the provisions of paragraphs 1 and 2" sets forth that a CVD order shall be terminated even though continuation of the order would be justified under Articles 21.1 or 21.2. Finally, the ordinary meaning of the term "unless" means that the continuation of an CVD order is an exception of the general rule that a definitive countervailing duty must be terminated.

---

[187] *See, e.g., Competence of the General Assembly for the Admission of a State to the United Nations (Second Admissions Case)*, [1950], ICJ Rep., at 8 ("The Court considers it necessary to say that the first duty of a tribunal which is called upon to interpret and apply the provisions of a treaty, is to endeavour to give effect to them in their natural and ordinary meaning in the context in which they are occur.")

[188] *Appellate Body Report, Japan – Taxes on Alcoholic Beverages*, WT/DS8/AB/R, WT/DS10/AB/R, WT/DS11/AB/R, at 10 (1 November 1996).

[189] Agreement on Subsidies and Countervailing Measures, Art. 21.3 (emphasis added).

(iii) Article 21.3 requires that the administering authority must have sufficient evidence to initiate a sunset review before determining whether to continue the order

6.8 The language in Article 21.3 sets forth evidentiary standards that the administering authority must follow to initiate a sunset review. Article 21.3 also obliges the administering authority to establish with positive evidence that subsidization will continue or recur in the absence of the order. The mere possibility of continuation or recurrence of subsidization is not enough.

6.9 The EC correctly states that the self-initiation of sunset reviews requires sufficient evidence of the continuation or recurrence of subsidization.[190]

6.10 In addition to arguments made by the EC, Articles 22.1, 22.7, and 11.6 further clarify the point that Article 21 requires the authorities to satisfy themselves that sufficient evidence exists to self-initiate an investigation. Article 22.1 provides that, "[w]hen the authorities are satisfied that there is *sufficient evidence* to justify the initiation of an investigation pursuant to *Article 11*, the ... interested parties ... shall be notified and a public notice shall be given." (emphasis added) Article 22.7 provides that Article 22.1 "apply *mutatis mutandis* to the initiation and completion of reviews pursuant to Article 21". Thus, Article 22.1 obliges the authorities to give notice when initiating a sunset review. The Article further obliges the authorities to have sufficient evidence to justify the initiation of the sunset review pursuant to Article 11.

6.11 Paragraph 6 of Article 11 provides that the authorities "shall proceed only if they have sufficient evidence of the existence of a subsidy, injury and causal link ... to justify the initiation of an investigation". By operation of Article 22.1 and 22.7, therefore, the authorities are required to have sufficient evidence to self-initiate a sunset review under Article 21.3.

6.12 In addition to the "sufficient evidence" requirement to initiate sunset reviews, Article 21.3 further requires the authorities to have "positive evidence" on a prospective basis to warrant continuing a CVD order.

6.13 Article 21.3 requires the authorities to "determine" that the expiry of a CVD order would be likely to lead to continuation or recurrence of subsidization in the absence of the order. The plain and ordinary meaning of "determine" is to establish, or ascertain definitely.[191] The plain meaning of "determine" thus requires the authorities to make a new analysis, not simply repeat stale conclusions.

6.14 Previous Appellate Body and Panel decisions instruct that a determination of continued or recurrent subsidization must be based on positive evidence. In the context of Article 11.2 of the Anti-Dumping Agreement, the Panel in *United States - DRAMs,*[192] determined that "the continued imposition must, in our view, be essentially dependent on, and therefore assignable to, a foundation of positive evi-

---

[190] *See* EC Submission, at para 65.

[191] *See American Heritage Dictionary*, at 235 (3rd ed. 1994).

[192] *See Panel Report, United States - Anti-dumping Duty on Dynamic Random Access Memory Semiconductors (DRAMS) of one Megabit or Above from Korea*, ("United States - DRAMs"), WT/DS99/R, at para. 6.40 (29 Jan. 1999) (finding that Article 11.1 of the AD Agreement contains a general rule that anti-dumping duties shall remain in force only as long as and to the extent necessary to counteract dumping which is causing injury; this the general rule is implemented through Article 11.2 (and Article 11.3)).

dence".[193] Since both Article 11.2 and 11.3 of AD Agreement require the determination of necessity to continue an anti-dumping duty, the rationale in *DRAMs* also applies to Article 11.3 of AD Agreement. The rationale in *DRAMs* applies with equal force to the *SCM Agreement* because the language in Article 11 of the AD Agreement is nearly identical to the language in Article 21 in the *SCM Agreement*. Further, Vienna Convention Article 31 requires that these Articles must be given the same meaning because the object and purpose of both articles is the same.[194]

6.15 The Appellant Body in *United States - Leaded Bars* confirmed this textual interpretation where it found that, "in order to establish the continued need for countervailing duties, an investigating authority will have to make a finding on subsidization, i.e. whether or not the subsidy continues to exist".[195] The Appellant Body's finding therefore, lends further support to the interpretation in the *DRAM* panel.

6.16 Article 21.3 requires that the positive evidence of subsidization must be prospective, while current subsidization may be relevant. The panel in *DRAMs* found that the authorities need to establish "a status regarding the prospects of dumping"[196] in determining likely to continue or recur.[197] The Panel in *DRAMs* also noted that "there is nothing in the text of Article 11.2 of the AD Agreement that explicitly limits a Member to a 'present' analysis, and forecloses a prospective analysis".[198] Thus, the potential subsidization and the current CVD order are relevant to the determination in the sunset review.

6.17 In sum, Article 21.3 obliges the authorities to have sufficient evidence to initiate a sunset review. It also obliges the authorities to base their determination on positive evidence illustrating the likelihood of future subsidization. Indeed, the very purpose of a sunset review is to examine whether an injurious subsidy will continue for the next five years. The only proper way for the administering authority to determine whether or not subsidization will continue is to undertake a prospective analysis.

(b) Automatic Initiation by DOC of a Sunset Review Violates Article 21.3 of the *SCM Agreement*

6.18 The US statute and DOC practice of automatic initiation of sunset reviews is contrary to US obligations under the *SCM Agreement*.

6.19 Both the US. statute and DOC's practices mandate automatic initiation of a sunset review five years after imposition of the original order. Section 751(c)(2) of the Tariff Act of 1930 (hereinafter "the Act") mandates that DOC publish a "notice of

---

193 *See id.* at para. 6.42 ("In other words, the need for the continued imposition of the duty must be demonstrable on the basis of the evidence adduced.").

194 This fundamental principle was recognized by the Dispute Settlement Panel in *United States - DRAMs*. *See United States - DRAMS*, WT/DS99/R, at para. 4.65 - 4.67 (29 Jan. 1999) (citing the Vienna Convention on the Law of Treaties, art. 31.2 (23 May 1969)).

195 *Appellate Body Report, United States - Imposition of Countervailing Duties on Certain Hot-Rolled Lead and Bismuth Carbon Steel Products Originating in the United Kingdom*, ("United States - Leaded Bars") WT/DS138/AB/R, at para. 54 (7 June 2000) (finding that the US, in an administrative review regarding a non-recurring subsidy allocated over time, should have made a finding on subsidization).

196 *Ibid.* at para 6.28

197 As discussed above, the decision regarding ADA Article 11.2 is applicable to Article 11.3 of AD Agreement, and Article 21.3 of *SCM Agreement*.

198 *Ibid.* at para. 6.29.

initiation" in the Federal Register no later than 30 days before the fifth anniversary of the CVD order's publication.[199] DOC's regulations contain the identical obligation.[200] Section 351.218(c)(1) of DOC's regulations provides that, "no later than 30 days before the fifth anniversary date of an order ... the Secretary will publish a notice of initiation of a sunset review (see section 751(c)(2)." Finally, DOC published the initiation schedule of up coming sunset reviews based solely on the date of the original order.[201] DOC in fact initiated this case five years from the date of the imposition of the original order.[202] DOC has never showed sufficient evidence to initiate a sunset review. In fact, DOC initiates all sunset reviews without any evidence to justify initiation. The United States admitted as much in their 15 January submission.[203]

6.20 As we discuss above, however, the authorities must have sufficient evidence to justify the initiation of sunset reviews. The automatic initiation by the United States of sunset reviews thus does not satisfy the sufficient evidence requirement under Article 21.3.

6.21 Japan believes that the Panel should find the US statute, regulations, and practices to be inconsistent with the *SCM Agreement.*

(c) Failure to "Determine" the Likelihood of Continued Subsidization Based on Positive Evidence of Current and Prospective Subsidization Violates Article 21.3 of the *SCM Agreement*

6.22 The US determination of likelihood of continuation or recurrence of dumping is inconsistent with Article 21.3.

6.23 As discussed above, Article 21.3 requires the determination be based on a prospective analysis, with the presumption being termination of the duty. Also as discussed above, the obligations of Article 21.3 requires positive evidence to make the determination to continue CVD orders.

6.24 The US rules and practices do not satisfy these requirements. The SAA specifically states that:

> Commerce normally will select ... net countervailable subsidies determined in the original investigation or in a prior review .... Commerce normally will select the rate from the investigation, because that is the only calculated rate that reflects the behaviour or the exporters and foreign governments without the discipline of an order or suspension agreement in place.[204]

---

[199] 19 U.S.C. § 1675(c)(1).

[200] 19 C.F.R. § 351.218(c)(1).

[201] *See* 19 C.F.R. §351, Annex VIII-A-B-C; *see also Transition Orders; Final Schedule and Grouping of Five-Year Reviews, 63 Fed. Reg. 29372, 29380 (29 May 1998) ("Sunset Initiation Schedule"); Sunset Reviews - Upcoming Deadlines by Initiation Month, available at* www.ita.doc.gov/ia/ suncase.nsf/aeab85e5a579ee7a852568950050843d!OpenView (visited 17 January 2002).

[202] *Compare Countervailing Duty Order and Amendment to Final Determination of Certain Corrosion-Resistant Carbon Steel Flat Products from Germany*, 58 Fed. Reg. 43756 (17 Aug. 1993), *with Notice of Initiation of Five-Year ("Sunset") Reviews of Antidumping and Countervailing Duty Orders or Investigations of Carbon Steel Plates and Flat Products*, 64 Fed Reg. 47767 (1 Sep. 1999).

[203] United States - Countervailing Duties on Certain Corrosion-Resistant Carbon Steel Flat Products From Germany, First Written Submission of the United States of America, WTDS213, at para. 7 (15 January 2002).

[204] Statement of Administrative Action, at 890.

6.25 The United States admits, in its 15 January submission, that it based the sunset review determination in question on the CVD finding in the original investigation.

6.26 The SAA language and the United States' admission of its own practice are not based on positive evidence of continued or future subsidization as required by Article 21.3, as discussed above. Japan thus submits that the use of the out-dated information, instead of current or prospective CVD rates, is inconsistent with Article 21.3.

(d) The US *de minimis* Standard Applied in Sunset Review is Inconsistent with the *SCM Agreement*

6.27 Contrary to the US argument, the proper *de minimis* standard for the sunset review is 1 per cent *ad valorem* as provided in Article 11.9. The United States' application of the 0.5 per cent *de minimis* standard to the sunset review is inconsistent with the *SCM Agreement*.

(i) The US statute provides for two different *de minimis* standards: 1 per cent in an original investigation and 0.5 per cent in a sunset review

6.28 Section 703(b)(4)(a) of the Trade Act of 1930 states that in the original investigation US authorities shall regard a CVD rate of less than 1 per cent as *de minimis*.[205] The statute is silent, however, on the *de minimis* standard applicable to sunset reviews. The DOC regulations provide that a *de minimis* rate of less than 0.5 per cent ad valorem shall apply to sunset reviews.[206] The United States confirmed in its submission that it applied a 0.5 per cent *de minimis* standard to the sunset review in question.

(ii) The One Per cent de minimis Standard Must Apply to Sunset Reviews

6.29 The 1 per cent *de minimis* standard under Article 11.9 applies to both the original investigations and sunset reviews. The arguments of the United States on this issue should be rejected.

6.30 Evidentiary standards of the sunset review require that the 1 per cent *de minimis* standard of Article 11.9 apply to the sunset review. As discussed above, Article 21.3 requires the authorities to have sufficient evidence to initiate sunset reviews. Also as discussed above, Articles 22.1 and 22.7 set forth that the sufficient evidence rule under Article 11 applies to the initiation of sunset reviews. The sufficient evidence rule under Article 11 includes Article 11.9, which states that the sub-

---

205 *See* 19 U.S.C. § 1671b(b)(4)(A) "In making a determination under this subsection, the administering authority shall disregard any *de minimis* countervailable subsidy. [A] countervailable subsidy is *de minimis* if the administering authority determines that the aggregate of the net countervailable subsidies is less than 1 percent ad valorem or the equivalent specific rate for the subject merchandise." *Ibid.*

206 19 C.F.R. § 351.106(c)(1) ("In making any determination other than a preliminary or final antidumping or countervailing duty determination in an investigation ..., the Secretary will treat as *de minimis* any weighted-average dumping margin or countervailable subsidy rate that is less than 0.5 per cent ad valorem".).

sidy of less than 1 per cent *ad valorem* does not constitute sufficient evidence of subsidization. The authorities, therefore, may not initiate a sunset review if the evidence demonstrates that the subsidy is less than 1 per cent *ad valorem*.

6.31 In the same token, the positive evidence rule under Article 21.3, as discussed above, also prohibits the authorities from finding a likelihood of continuation or recurrence of subsidization when they have already found the subsidy to be less than the 1 per cent. These reasons are supported by Article 22.5, which requires the authorities to publish their "reasons for acceptance or rejection of relevant arguments" in the final determination. Article 22.7 states that these notice requirements *mutatis mutandis* apply to Article 21 reviews. The provisions of Article 11, referenced in Article 22.1, therefore fully apply to reviews under Article 21. Thus, the *de minimis* standard in Article 11.9 should apply to the sunset review under Article 21.3 .

6.32 Moreover, the purposes of the sunset review and the original investigation are essentially identical. The purpose of a sunset review under Article 21.3 is to determine whether CVD orders should be imposed for the next five years or should be terminated. The original investigation is also to determine whether or not a CVD order should be imposed for the next five year period.

6.33 Vienna Convention Article 31 requires that "a treaty shall be interpreted ... in light of its object and purpose".[207] The sunset review and the original investigation share the same object and purpose. Determinations in these two proceedings thus must apply the same standard.

6.34 Indeed, the underlying purpose provides no justification for a stricter standard for sunset reviews. The sunset review is not to determine a precise level of subsidization, as the United States does in annual reviews of countervailing duty orders called "administrative reviews". Rather, the sunset review addresses the continued existence of the order itself - precisely the same function served by the original investigation.

6.35 As such, the authorities are obliged not to initiate the sunset review, and not to determine continuation of the CVD order for the next five year in the sunset review, if the subsidy is less than the 1 per cent.

(iii) The Panel finding in *United States - DRAMs*, that different *de minimis* standards in Articles 5.8 and 9.3 of the AD Agreement do not violate the Agreement, is distinguishable

6.36 Contrary to the US argument, the Panel's finding in *United States - DRAMs*[208], regarding the applicability of Article 5.8 of the AD Agreement in fact supports our view that the *de minimis* standard for the original investigation also apply to the sunset review under Article 21.3 of the *SCM Agreement*.

6.37 The scope of the Panel's consideration of the non-applicability of Article 5.8 in DRAMs was limited to the retroactive duty assessment procedures under Article 9.3 of the AD Agreement. The Panel analyzed the term "case" in Article 5.8, and concluded that the *de minimis* standard in Article 5.8 of the AD Agreement did not apply to the duty assessment procedures.[209]

---

[207] *Vienna Convention on the Law of Treaties* ("*Vienna Convention*"), Articles 31 and 32, U.N. Doc. A/CONF.39/27* (23 May 1969).

[208] *United States - DRAMs*, WT/DS99/R, at para. 6.87 (29 Jan. 1999).

[209] *Ibid.* at para. 6.87.

6.38 A sunset review is clearly distinguishable from the duty assessment procedures. The duty assessment procedures determines the exact amount of antidumping (or countervailing) duty to be collected from importers for their *past* imports of subject merchandise. The US calls these procedures "administrative reviews". A sunset review, on the other hand, considers the prospect of *future* dumping or subsidization, not the past history thereof.

6.39 The Panel's construction of applicability of Article 5.8 to the duty assessment procedures thus does not apply to the sunset review.

6.40 To the contrary, the Panel in *DRAMs* in fact supports the point that Article 5.8 may apply to a sunset review. The Panel stated that:

> in the context of Article 5.8, the function of the *de minimis* test is to determine whether or not an exporter is subject to an anti-dumping order. In the context of Article 9.3 duty assessment procedures, however, the function of any *de minimis* test applied by Members is to determine whether or not an exporter should pay a duty.[210]

6.41 As discussed above, the function of the sunset review is, to determine whether or not an exporter should be subject to anti-dumping or countervailing duties for the next five years. The sunset review is thus analogous to the original investigation. The *DRAMs* Panel's logic thus supports our argument that Article 5.8 of the AD Agreement and its complementary Article 11.9 in the *SCM Agreement* apply to the sunset review.

6.42 In sum, the *de minimis* standard under Article 11.9 of *SCM Agreement* applies to the sunset review. Japan believes the Panel should find that the US practice of applying 0.5 per cent to sunset review proceedings is inconsistent with the *SCM Agreement.*

3. Conclusion

6.43 For the reasons stated above, Japan requests the Panel find that the US countervailing duty law (Section 751(c), as complemented by Section 752, of the Act), its accompanying regulations and policy practices (*Sunset Policy Bulletin*), and their concrete application to imports of certain corrosion-resistant steel products from Germany in the present case are inconsistent with Article 21 paragraphs 3, 1, and 4, Article 10, and Article 11.9 of the *SCM Agreement.*

B. Third-Party Submission of Norway

1. Introduction

6.44 The present case concerns whether the US basic countervailing duty law (Tariff Act of 1930, Sunset regulations) and policy practices (Sunset Policy Bulletin) and their concrete application to imports of certain corrosion-resistant steel products from Germany are inconsistent with the obligations of the United States under the WTO Agreement and annexed agreements.

6.45 Norway has systemic interests in the interpretation and application of the "sunset provisions" of the Agreement on subsidies and countervailing measures

---

[210] *Ibid.* at para. 6.90.

(SCM), and thus reserved its third party rights in the case during the Dispute Settlement Body meeting on 10 September 2001 (WT/DS213/3).

6.46 In deciding the case, Norway submits that the Panel should base its arguments on the following:

2. *The United States Department of Commerce (DOC) Initiation of the Sunset Review for Countervailing Duties on Import of Corrosion-Resistant Steel Products from Germany Has Infringed Article 21 of the Agreement on Subsidies and Countervailing Measures (SCM) in a Number of Ways*

(a) Automatic Reviews Infringe Articles 21.1 and 21.3 of the *SCM Agreement* and Article 10 of the *SCM Agreement* in Combination with Article VI of GATT 1994

6.47 Under Article 21.3 of the *SCM Agreement*, WTO Members are required to terminate countervailing measures on a date no later than five years from their imposition, unless it is determined in a review, that the expiry of the duties would be likely to lead to continuation or recurrence of subsidization and injury. This corresponds to the purpose of Article 21.1 of the *SCM Agreement*, which provides that a countervailing duty shall be maintained only as long as necessary and to the extent to counteract subsidization which is causing injury.

6.48 Article 10 of the *SCM Agreement* that refers to Article VI of GATT 1994 also sustains these provisions. Article VI paragraph 6 (a) of GATT 1994 provides that: No contracting party shall levy any anti-dumping or countervailing duty on the importation of any product of the territory of another contracting party unless it determines that the effect of anti dumping or subsidization, as the case may be, is such as to cause or threaten material injury to an established domestic industry, or is such as to retard materially the establishment of a domestic industry.

6.49 It follows from Article 21.3 that as a main rule countervailing duties shall be terminated no later than five years from their imposition - the presumption being that subsidization is counteracted after such period. A review is meant only to take place on exceptional occasions when there is a clear assumption based on the situation existing at the time of review that the expiry of the duty would be likely to lead to continuation or recurrence of both subsidization and injury.

6.50 Under US law sunset reviews are *automatically* initiated by DOC on its own initiative five years after the publication of the countervailing duty order. Regardless of the situation existing at the time of initiation of review, or the complete lack of information supporting an assumption that continuation or recurrence of both subsidization and injury will occur, a review is initiated.

6.51 In this way the United States transforms an exception into a general rule, thus infringing Articles 21.1 and 21.3 of the *SCM Agreement* and Article 10 of the *SCM Agreement* in conjunction with Article VI of GATT 1994.

(b) Expedited Reviews Are Biased Towards the Continuation of Countervailing Duties and Violate Article 21.3 of the *SCM Agreement*

6.52 The Norwegian Government is of the opinion that a sunset review has to be unbiased and independent of the original investigation. It follows from the letter of Article 21.3 of the *SCM Agreement* that if exception from the presumption of terminating countervailing duties after five years is to be made, the authorities have to *determine* in a review that the expiry of the duty would be likely to lead to continuation or recurrence of subsidization and injury.

6.53 It's our assertion that the US procedures of expedited sunset reviews are biased towards the continuation of countervailing duties. If domestic interested parties file a "notice of intent to participate" in the sunset review, the foreign government or exporters counting at least 50 per cent of exports are required to file substantive responses to the notice of initiation within a 30 days deadline. If no responses are given by those instances within 30 days, DOC will shorten the timeframe for the review and base the review on the facts available. This normally leads to a presumption of continued subsidization and thus to continuation of the countervailing duty.

6.54 This is also the case if the foreign respondents do not account for 50 percent or more of total exports of the subject product to the US. DOC then normally will conduct an expedited review and, not later than 120 days after the date of publication in the Federal Register of the notice of initiation, issue without further investigation, final results of review based on the facts available.

6.55 Norway considers that this represents a violation of the duty to terminate the countervailing measures set forth in Article 21.3 of the *SCM Agreement.*

(c) The Self-Initiation of Sunset Reviews by the Domestic Authorities does not Correspond to the Requirements Set Out in Article 21.3 as Complemented by Article 11.1 and 11.6 of the *SCM Agreement*

6.56 Article 21.3 of the *SCM Agreement* states that a review can be initiated either on the initiative of the domestic authorities or upon a duly substantiated request made by or on behalf of the industry. Norway considers that Article 11 on the initiation and conduct of the original subsidy investigation also applies to sunset reviews as referred to in Article 21.3 of the *SCM Agreement*. In fact also the procedures and procedural guarantees of the other articles of Chapter V of the *SCM Agreement* are meant to apply, and not to be disregarded in a sunset review context. The reference made to Article 12 in Article 21 is but one particular example of this. The contrary solution would otherwise create a "free for all" for the duty-imposing Member, and leave the foreign exporters without proper legal guarantees.

6.57 Article 11.1 of the *SCM Agreement* provides that the initiation of an investigation to determine the existence of subsidization should normally be based on the existence of a substantiated request made by or on behalf of the domestic industry. Self-initiation by domestic authorities constitutes on the other hand an exceptional measure, which is only to be accepted if domestic authorities have sufficient evidence of the existence of a subsidy, injury and causal link as described in Article 11.6[211].

6.58 In the United States, sunset reviews are *always* self-initiated by the domestic authorities. According to Section 751-(c) (1) and (2) of the Tariff Act of 1930 and of Section 351.218 of the Sunset regulations, DOC does not even have to wait for a request by the domestic industry before initiating sunset reviews.

6.59 Thus the United States hereby makes a general rule out of a clear exception, disregarding the requirement that sufficient evidence of continuation or recurrence of subsidization be present. Norway claims that this represents a violation of Article 21.3 in conjunction with Article 11.1 and 11.6 of the *SCM Agreement*.

3. *The US Standard of Investigation for Sunset Reviews Violates the Requirements of the SCM Agreement in Particular Article 21.3 Because:*

(a) Not Making a New Investigation in Sunset Reviews Represents an Infringement to Article 21.3 and 21.1 and the Purpose of Part V of the *SCM Agreement*

6.60 Article 21.3 of the *SCM Agreement* provides that:

> "..Any definitive countervailing duty shall be terminated on a date not later than five years from its imposition...*unless the authorities determine*, in a review initiated before that date on their own initiative or upon a duly substantiated request made by or on behalf of the domestic industry within a reasonable period of time prior to that date, *that the expiry of the duty would be likely to lead to continuation or recurrence of subsidization*". (emphasis added)

6.61 This represents a *positive obligation* upon the domestic authorities to "determine" the likelihood of continuation or recurrence of subsidization. In the case United States-Leaded Bars the Appellate Body considered that (in the context of a review under Article 21.2)[212]:

> "In order to establish the continued need for countervailing duties, an investigating authority will have to make a finding on *subsidization* i.e. whether or not the subsidy continues to exist".

6.62 When such requirements are applied to a review under Article 21.2, which is not obligatory and takes place during the life time of the original countervailing duty, it should be clear that a positive finding on subsidization is necessary also in the context of an Article 21.3 investigation.

---

[211] Article 11.6 reads:

> "If, in special circumstances, the authorities concerned decide to initiate an investigation without having received a written application by or on behalf of a domestic industry for the initiation of such investigation, they shall proceed only if they have sufficient evidence of the existence of a subsidy, injury and causal link, as described in paragraph 2, to justify the initiation of an investigation."

[212] See Panel Report, *United States – Imposition of Countervailing Duties on Certain Hot-Rolled Lead Bismuth Carbon Steel Products Originating in the United Kingdom ("United States – Leaded Bars")*, WT/DS138/R, adopted 7 June 2000, at para. 6.18, as upheld by the Appellate Body Report, WT/DS138/AB/R, adopted 7 June 2000, at para. 51.

6.63 In an Article 21.3 investigation the basic obligation is the termination of the original duty, while the possibility of continuing a duty following a sunset review constitutes the exception. In the opinion of the Norwegian government the latter requires an unbiased review independent of the results of the original investigation to be undertaken in full conformity with *all* the procedural and substantive requirements for an initial determination of subsidy and injury set forth in Articles 10 *et sec*. There is no reason to understand the requirement of "determination" of subsidization and injury differently in Article 21.3 as compared to *inter alia* Articles 11 and 15. This is also sustained/supported by Article 21.1 and the purpose of Part V of the *SCM Agreement*.

6.64 According to the written submission of the European Communities, the factual situation of the present case seems to be as follows: In determining whether any changes in the subsidies have occurred that may affect the countervailing duty, DOC normally selects the countervailing duty from the original investigation or a review, on the basis that it is the only rate that reflects the behaviour of governments and exporters without the discipline of an order in place. This means that no new investigation takes place during the sunset review. In the case of corrosion resistant steel from Germany no administrative reviews have taken place since the original investigation and the only (available) subsidization rate applied is the original 1993 subsidy rate. Even though German exporters have delivered concrete evidence, according to the first written submission of the EC, DOC refused during the sunset review, to consider changes/terminations of subsidy programmes. The reason for this decision given by the DOC was that no full investigation is conducted in a sunset review.

6.65 Norway considers that to the extent that United States' legislation or practice requires or implies that a full, objective and unbiased review is not undertaken, Article 21.3 of the *SCM Agreement* is violated.

(b) Not Requiring the Application of the 1 % *de minimis* Rule in Sunset Reviews is in Violation of Article 21 3. in Conjunction with Articles 21.1 and 11.9 of the *SCM Agreement*

6.66 Article 21.1 of the *SCM Agreement* provides:

> "A countervailing duty shall remain in force only as long as and to the extent necessary to counteract subsidization which is causing injury."

6.67 The purpose of the countervailing action is to counteract subsidization, which is causing injury. According to Article 21.3 of the *SCM Agreement* the authorities are obliged to "determine" if the expiry of the duty would be likely to lead to continuation or recurrence of subsidization and injury.

6.68 As stated above Norway considers that Article 11 of the *SCM Agreement* is applicable also for sunset reviews. Article 11.9 of the *SCM Agreement* provides in the context of original investigations:

> "[...] There shall be immediate termination in cases where the amount of a subsidy is *de minimis*.[...] For the purpose of this paragraph, the amount of a subsidy shall be considered to be the minimis if the subsidy is less than 1 per cent ad valorem. "

6.69 The Member States of the WTO have agreed that subsidization below this threshold does not permit a countervailing action. There is no exception to this rule, and immediate termination shall be the result in such cases.

6.70 The relevant US laws and administrative practice is to apply a 1 per cent *de minimis* rule in the initial determination of a countervailable subsidy as required by the *SCM Agreement*, but to apply, as a general rule, a 0.5 per cent *de minimis* rule in all reviews, including sunset reviews.

6.71 According to the facts submitted by the European Communities in its written submission, in the case of corrosion resistant steel from Germany, the countervailing duty rate determined in the original investigation was only 0.09 per cent above *de minimis* level of 0.50 per cent applied in the US before the entry into force of the WTO Agreements. The sunset review was conducted under the WTO rules and hence a *de minimis* level of 1 per cent. Despite finding that the subsidy rate likely to prevail would be 0.53 per cent, the US continued the measure because of their 0.5 per cent *de minimis* threshold in sunset reviews.

6.72 Reviewing the need for a duty to continue under Article 21.3, in conjunction with Articles 21.1 and 11.9 has the same implications as determining whether the original substantive conditions on the basis of which it was initially imposed continue to exist. The *de minimis* provision in the *SCM Agreement* is based on the fact that a subsidy level of less than 1 per cent is presumed not to cause injury. If this subsidy cannot cause injury in an original investigation, it is logically and legally unavoidable to conclude that it cannot cause injury in a sunset investigation. Consequently the United States should have lifted the countervailing duties and changed the *de minimis* threshold to 1 per cent in all review processes.

6.73 Based on the above, Norway submits that the 0,5% level used by the United States for sunset reviews represents a clear violation of Article 21.3 of the *SCM Agreement* read in conjunction with Article 11.9 of the *SCM Agreement*.

4. *US Countervailing Legislation is Inconsistent with Article 32.5 of the SCM Agreement and Article XVI:4 of the WTO Agreement*

6.74 Article 32.5 of the *SCM Agreement* provides that:

> "Each member shall take all necessary steps, of a general and particular character, to ensure not later than the date of entry into force of the WTO Agreement for it, the conformity of it laws, regulations and administrative procedures with the provisions of this Agreement as they may apply to the Member in question."

6.75 Furthermore, Article XVI:4 of the WTO Agreement requires that Each Member shall ensure the conformity of its laws, regulations and administrative procedures with its obligations as provided in the annexed Agreements.

6.76 Thus, by being inconsistent with Article 21 and related articles of the *SCM Agreement* as they apply to a sunset review, the US law, regulations and practices as such, and as applied to the products in question in this case, are also inconsistent with Article 32.5 of the *SCM Agreement* and Article XVI:4 of the WTO Agreement.

5. *Conclusion*

6.77 For the reasons stated in the submission, Norway respectfully requests the Panel to consider the US law, regulations and practices inconsistent with the obligations of the United States under Article 21 and related articles of the *SCM Agreement* as they apply to a sunset review, Article 32.5 of the *SCM Agreement* and Article XVI:4 of the WTO Agreement.

6.78 Finally, Norway respectfully requests the Panel to recommend that the United States bring its legislation into conformity with the corresponding covered agreements.

C. *Oral Statement of Japan at the First Meeting of the Panel*

6.79 The Government of Japan ("Japan") would like to appreciate this opportunity to express our views in this dispute.

6.80 Japan supports the European Communities' ("EC") position in this case. The facts of this case illustrate vividly the problem with the United States ("US") laws and practices. Continuing a CVD order at the negligible level of 0.54 per cent - an order that never would have been imposed in the first place under the standards of the Agreement on Subsidies and Countervailing Measures ("*SCM Agreement*")- shows problems with the current US system. We would like to briefly discuss today problems with the US system , focusing on the flaws in the US's argument.

6.81 First, the text of Article 21.3 expressly requires the termination of the CVD duty after five years. US fundamentally misinterprets Article 21.3. The text clearly states that any "definitive countervailing duty ***shall*** be terminated" not later than five years from its imposition ... "***unless*** the authorities determine" to continue the order. The terms "shall" and "unless" set forth a basic rule and an exception. The order may continue beyond the five years only if the authorities make an affirmative finding that subsidization will continue in the absence of the order, and follow all the rules and procedures for invoking the exception. In addition, Article 21.1 provides greater understanding to the object and purpose of Article 21.3. Article 21.1,states that the order "shall only remain in force *as long as* and *to the extent necessary* to counteract the subsidization which is causing injury." (emphasis added) For invoking the exception, there must be an affirmative finding based on positive evidence that subsidization is "likely" to continue or recur.

6.82 Second, Article 21.3 allows the US to self-initiate sunset reviews only *after* establishing the existence of sufficient evidence that subsidization will continue in the absence of the order. The US misunderstands the phrase "on their own initiative" in Article 21.3 to argue that it provides the necessary authority automatically to initiate a sunset review without any factual basis. As discussed in our submission, the appropriate contextual interpretation of Article 21.3 in the context of the SCM Agreement particularly Articles 22.1 and 22.7, requires the sufficient evidence standard of Article 11.6 to be applied to initiation of sunset reviews "on their own initiative".

6.83 Third, Article 21.3 requires the authority to conduct, at least to some degree, a new investigation into whether subsidization is likely to continue or recur. Use of the present tense verb "determine" in Article 21.3, followed by "likely to lead to continuation or recurrence of subsidization", requires independent prospective analysis of the future, not mechanical reference to the past. US's simple reference to stale conclusions would not justify a finding of continued subsidization or constitute a prospective determination.

6.84 The obligation to "determine" under Article 21.3 also must be read in light of "necessary" in Article 21.1. The Panel in *DRAMs* interpreted "necessary" to require a "foundation of positive evidence that circumstances" require continuation of the order(WT/DS99/R, para. 6.42). The Panel also stated that "mathematical certainty is not required, but the conclusions should be demonstrable on the basis of the evidence adduced."(WT/DS99/R, para. 6.43). The Panel's finding in *DRAMs* with regard to Article 11 of the AD Agreement provides analysis equally compelling with regard to the nearly identical language in the *SCM Agreement*. This reading of necessary means that an administering agency's "determination" must be based on a foundation of positive evidence. The US's practice of applying the original CVD rates to its sunset determination violates Article 21.3.

6.85 Finally, the US's application of 0.5 per cent *de minimis* standard to sunset reviews is inconsistent with the *SCM Agreement*. All of the arguments the US uses to support its inconsistent application of *de minimis* standards between the investigation and sunset review reflect flawed treaty interpretation. As discussed in our submission, the US's reading of the *SCM Agreement* ignores the textual references in Article 22 to the standards in Article 11 and their applicability to Article 21.3.

6.86 The US also erroneously asserts that the *DRAMs*' Panel found no support for extending the *de minimis* standard beyond the initial investigation. The Panel's finding in *DRAMs* in fact supports our view that the *de minimis* standard for the original investigation also applies to sunset reviews. The Panel of the DRAMs distinguishes proceedings to determine prospective application of antidumping duties from retroactive duty assessment procedures. The Panel then concluded that *de minimis* standard does not apply to the retroactive duty assessment procedures. Duty assessment procedures determine the exact amount of antidumping (or countervailing) duty to be collected from importers for their *past* imports of subject merchandise. A sunset review, on the other hand, is to determine whether or not an exporter should remain subject to the AD or CVD duty for the next five years. Therefore, the sunset review is analogous to the original investigation, and consequently, the same *de minimis* standard should apply to both.

6.87 Taking the US's interpretation to its logical conclusion leads to contradictory results. If an exporter found to have a 0.7 per cent net CVD rate in an original investigation would have been excluded from the original determination. However, if the investigation happened to be a sunset review, the same exporter would have been found to be receiving a countervailable subsidy. A proper contextual interpretation of Article 11.9 and 21.3 would not allow such an inconsistent application of the *de minimis* standard. If the order could not have been imposed in the first place it makes no sense for the order to be continued.

6.88 We would like to thank the Panel for their attention today. Japan believes that when the Panel examines the US's countervailing duty law, accompanying regulations and policy practices, it will find them to be inconsistent with the *SCM Agreement*.

D. *Oral Statement of Norway at the First Meeting of the Panel*

1. *Introduction*

6.89 The present case concerns whether the US basic countervailing duty law (Tariff Act of 1930, Sunset regulations) and policy practices (Sunset Policy Bulletin) and their concrete application to imports of certain corrosion-resistant steel products from Germany are inconsistent with the obligations of the United States under the WTO Agreement and annexed agreements.

6.90 Norway has systemic interests in the interpretation and application of the "sunset provisions" of the Agreement on subsidies and countervailing measures (SCM), and thus reserved its third party rights in the case during the Dispute Settlement Body meeting on 10 September 2001 (WT/DS213/3).

6.91 In deciding the case, Norway submits that the Panel should base its arguments on the following:

2. *The United States Department of Commerce (DOC) Initiation of the Sunset Review for Countervailing Duties on Import of Corrosion-Resistant Steel Products from Germany Has Infringed Article 21 of the Agreement on Subsidies and Countervailing Measures (SCM) in a Number of Ways*

(a) Automatic Reviews Infringe Articles 21.1 and 21.3 of the *SCM Agreement* and Article 10 of the *SCM Agreement* in Combination with Article VI of GATT 1994

6.92 Under Article 21.3 of the *SCM Agreement*, WTO Members are required to terminate countervailing measures on a date no later than five years from their imposition, unless it is determined in a review, that the expiry of the duties would be likely to lead to continuation or recurrence of subsidisation and injury. This corresponds to the purpose of Article 21.1 of the *SCM Agreement*, which provides that a countervailing duty shall be maintained only as long as necessary and to the extent to counteract subsidisation which is causing injury.

6.93 Article 10 of the *SCM Agreement* that refers to Article VI of GATT 1994 also sustains these provisions. Article VI paragraph 6 (a) of GATT 1994 provides that: No contracting party shall levy any anti-dumping or countervailing duty on the importation of any product of the territory of another contracting party unless it determines that the effect of dumping or subsidisation, as the case may be, is such as to cause or threaten material injury to an established domestic industry, or is such as to retard materially the establishment of a domestic industry.

6.94 It follows from Article 21.3 that as a main rule countervailing duties shall be terminated no later than five years from their imposition - the presumption being that subsidisation is counteracted after such period. A review is meant only to take place on exceptional occasions when there is a clear assumption based on the situation existing at the time of review that the expiry of the duty would be likely to lead to continuation or recurrence of both subsidisation and injury.

6.95 Under US law sunset reviews are *automatically* initiated by DOC on its own initiative five years after the publication of the countervailing duty order. Regardless of the situation existing at the time of initiation of review, or the complete lack of information supporting an assumption that continuation or recurrence of both subsidisation and injury will occur, a review is initiated.

6.96 In this way the United States transforms an exception into a general rule, thus infringing Articles 21.1 and 21.3 of the *SCM Agreement* and Article 10 of the *SCM Agreement* in conjunction with Article VI of GATT 1994.

(b) Expedited Reviews Are Biased Towards the Continuation of Countervailing Duties and Violate Article 21.3 of the *SCM Agreement*

6.97 The Norwegian government is of the opinion that a sunset review has to be unbiased and independent of the original investigation. It follows from the letter of Article 21.3 of the *SCM Agreement* that if exception from the presumption of terminating countervailing duties after five years is to be made, the authorities have to *determine* in a review that the expiry of the duty would be likely to lead to continuation or recurrence of subsidization and injury.

6.98 It's our assertion that the US procedures of expedited sunset reviews are biased towards the continuation of countervailing duties. If domestic interested parties file a "notice of intent to participate" in the sunset review, the foreign government or exporters counting at least 50 per cent of exports are required to file substantive responses to the notice of initiation within a 30 days deadline. If no responses are given by those instances within 30 days, DOC will shorten the timeframe for the review and base the review on the facts available. This normally leads to a presumption of continued subsidisation and thus to continuation of the countervailing duty.

6.99 This is also the case if the foreign respondents do not account for 50 per cent or more of total exports of the subject product to the US. DOC then normally will conduct an expedited review and, not later than 120 days after the date of publication in the Federal Register of the notice of initiation, issue without further investigation, final results of review based on the facts available.

6.100 Norway considers that this represents a violation of the duty to terminate the countervailing measures set forth in Article 21.3 of the *SCM Agreement*.

(c) The Self-Initiation of Sunset Reviews by the Domestic Authorities Does Not Correspond to the Requirements Set Out in Article 21.3 as Complemented by Article 11.1 and 11.6 of the *SCM Agreement*

6.101 Article 21.3 of the *SCM Agreement* states that a review can be initiated either on the initiative of the domestic authorities or upon a duly substantiated request made by or on behalf of the industry. Norway considers that Article 11 on the initiation and conduct of the original subsidy investigation also applies to sunset reviews as referred to in Article 21.3 of the *SCM Agreement*. In fact also the procedures and procedural guarantees of the other articles of Chapter V of the *SCM Agreement* are meant to apply, and not to be disregarded in a sunset review context. The reference made to Article 12 in Article 21 is but one particular example of this. The contrary solution would otherwise create a "free for all" for the duty-imposing Member, and leave the foreign exporters without proper legal guarantees.

6.102 Article 11.1 of the *SCM Agreement* provides that the initiation of an investigation to determine the existence of subsidisation should normally be based on the existence of a substantiated request made by or on behalf of the domestic industry. Self-initiation by domestic authorities constitutes on the other hand an exceptional measure, which is only to be accepted if domestic authorities have sufficient evidence of the existence of a subsidy, injury and causal link as described in Article 11.6.[213]

6.103 In the United States, sunset reviews are *always* self-initiated by the domestic authorities. According to Section 751-(c) (1) and (2) of the Tariff Act of 1930 and of Section 351.218 of the Sunset regulations, DOC does not even have to wait for a request by the domestic industry before initiating sunset reviews.

6.104 Thus the United States hereby makes a general rule out of a clear exception, disregarding the requirement that sufficient evidence of continuation or recurrence of subsidisation be present. Norway claims that this represents a violation of Article 21.3 in conjunction with Article 11.1 and 11.6 of the *SCM Agreement*.

3. *The US Standard of Investigation for Sunset Reviews Violates the Requirements of the SCM Agreement in Particular Article 21.3 Because:*

(a) Not Making a New Investigation in Sunset Reviews Represents an Infringement to Article 21.3 and 21.1 and the Purpose of Part V of the *SCM Agreement*

6.105 Article 21.3 of the *SCM Agreement* provides that:

> "..Any definitive countervailing duty shall be terminated on a date not later than five years from its imposition...*unless the authorities determine*, in a review initiated before that date on their own initiative or upon a duly substantiated request made by or on behalf of the domestic industry within a reasonable period of time prior to that date, *that the expiry of the duty would be likely to lead to continuation or recurrence of subsidisation*". (emphasis added)

6.106 This represents a *positive obligation* upon the domestic authorities to "determine" the likelihood of continuation or recurrence of subsidisation. In the case United States-Leaded Bars the Appellate Body considered that (in the context of a review under Article 21.2).[214]

---

[213] Article 11.6 reads:

"If, in special circumstances, the authorities concerned decide to initiate an investigation without having received a written application by or on behalf of a domestic industry for the initiation of such investigation, they shall proceed only if they have sufficient evidence of the existence of a subsidy, injury and causal link, as described in paragraph 2, to justify the initiation of an investigation."

[214] See Panel Report, *United States – Imposition of Countervailing Duties on Certain Hot-Rolled Lead Bismuth Carbon Steel Products Originating in the United Kingdom ("United States – Leaded Bars")*, WT/DS138/R, adopted 7 June 2000, at para. 6.18, as upheld by the Appellate Body Report, WT/DS138/AB/R, adopted 7 June 2000, at para. 51.

> "In order to establish the continued need for countervailing duties, an investigating authority will have to make a finding on *subsidisation* i.e. whether or not the subsidy continues to exist".

6.107 When such requirements are applied to a review under Article 21.2, which is not obligatory and takes place during the life time of the original countervailing duty, it should be clear that a positive finding on subsidization is necessary also in the context of an Article 21.3 investigation.

6.108 In an Article 21.3 investigation the basic obligation is the termination of the original duty, while the possibility of continuing a duty following a sunset review constitutes the exception. In the opinion of the Norwegian government the latter requires an unbiased review independent of the results of the original investigation to be undertaken in full conformity with *all* the procedural and substantive requirements for an initial determination of subsidy and injury set forth in Articles 10 *et sec.* There is no reason to understand the requirement of "determination" of subsidisation and injury differently in Article 21.3 as compared to *inter alia* Articles 11 and 15. This is also sustained/supported by Article 21.1 and the purpose of Part V of the *SCM Agreement.*

6.109 According to the written submission of the European Communities, the factual situation of the present case seems to be as follows: In determining whether any changes in the subsidies have occurred that may affect the countervailing duty, DOC normally selects the countervailing duty from the original investigation or a review, on the basis that it is the only rate that reflects the behaviour of governments and exporters without the discipline of an order in place. This means that no new investigation takes place during the sunset review. In the case of corrosion resistant steel from Germany no administrative reviews have taken place since the original investigation and the only (available) subsidisation rate applied is the original 1993 subsidy rate. Even though German exporters have delivered concrete evidence, according to the first written submission of the EC, DOC refused during the sunset review, to consider changes/terminations of subsidy programmes. The reason for this decision given by the DOC was that no full investigation is conducted in a sunset review.

6.110 Norway considers that to the extent that United States' legislation or practice requires or implies that a full, objective and unbiased review is not undertaken, Article 21.3 of the *SCM Agreement* is violated.

(b) Not Requiring the Application of the 1 Per Cent *de minimis* Rule in Sunset Reviews is in Violation of Article 21 3. in Conjunction with Articles 21.1 and 11.9 of the *SCM Agreement*

6.111 Article 21.1 of the *SCM Agreement* provides:

> "A countervailing duty shall remain in force only as long as and to the extent necessary to counteract subsidisation which is causing injury."

6.112 The purpose of the countervailing action is to counteract subsidisation, which is causing injury. According to Article 21.3 of the *SCM Agreement* the authorities are obliged to "determine" if the expiry of the duty would be likely to lead to continuation or recurrence of subsidisation and injury.

6.113 As stated above Norway considers that Article 11 of the *SCM Agreement* is applicable also for sunset reviews. Article 11.9 of the *SCM Agreement* provides in the context of original investigations:

> "[...] There shall be immediate termination in cases where the amount of a subsidy is *de minimis*.[...] For the purpose of this paragraph, the amount of a subsidy shall be considered to be the minimis if the subsidy is less than 1 per cent ad valorem. "

6.114 The Member States of the WTO have agreed that subsidisation below this threshold does not permit a countervailing action. There is no exception to this rule, and immediate termination shall be the result in such cases.

6.115 The relevant US laws and administrative practice is to apply a 1per cent *de minimis* rule in the initial determination of a countervailable subsidy as required by the *SCM Agreement*, but to apply, as a general rule, a 0.5 per cent *de minimis* rule in all reviews, including sunset reviews.

6.116 According to the facts submitted by the European Communities in its written submission, in the case of corrosion resistant steel from Germany, the countervailing duty rate determined in the original investigation was only 0.09 per cent above *de minimis* level of 0.50 per cent applied in the US before the entry into force of the WTO Agreements. The sunset review was conducted under the WTO rules and hence a *de minimis* level of 1 per cent. Despite finding that the subsidy rate likely to prevail would be 0.53 per cent, the US continued the measure because of their 0.5 per cent *de minimis* threshold in sunset reviews.

6.117 Reviewing the need for a duty to continue under Article 21.3, in conjunction with Articles 21.1 and 11.9 has the same implications as determining whether the original substantive conditions on the basis of which it was initially imposed continue to exist. The *de minimis* provision in the *SCM Agreement* is based on the fact that a subsidy level of less than 1 per cent is presumed not to cause injury. If this subsidy cannot cause injury in an original investigation, it is logically and legally unavoidable to conclude that it cannot cause injury in a sunset investigation. Consequently the United States should have lifted the countervailing duties and changed the *de minimis* threshold to 1 per cent in all review processes.

6.118 Based on the above, Norway submits that the 0.5 per cent level used by the United States for sunset reviews represents a clear violation of Article 21.3 of the *SCM Agreement* read in conjunction with Article 11.9 of the *SCM Agreement*.

4. *US Countervailing Legislation is Inconsistent with Article 32.5 of the SCM Agreement and Article XVI:4 of the WTO Agreement*

6.119 Article 32.5 of the *SCM Agreement* provides that:

> "Each member shall take all necessary steps, of a general and particular character, to ensure not later than the date of entry into force of the WTO Agreement for it, the conformity of it laws, regulations and administrative procedures with the provisions of this Agreement as they may apply to the Member in question."

6.120 Furthermore, Article XVI:4 of the WTO Agreement requires that Each Member shall ensure the conformity of its laws, regulations and administrative procedures with its obligations as provided in the annexed Agreements.

6.121 Thus, by being inconsistent with Article 21 and related articles of the *SCM Agreement* as they apply to a sunset review, the US law, regulations and practices as such, and as applied to the products in question in this case, are also inconsistent with Article 32.5 of the *SCM Agreement* and Article XVI:4 of the WTO Agreement.

5. *Conclusion*

6.122 For the reasons stated in the submission, Norway respectfully requests the Panel to consider the US law, regulations and practices inconsistent with the obligations of the United States under Article 21 and related articles of the *SCM Agreement* as they apply to a sunset review, Article 32.5 of the *SCM Agreement* and Article XVI:4 of the WTO Agreement.

6.123 Finally, Norway respectfully requests the Panel to recommend that the United States bring its legislation into conformity with the corresponding covered agreements.

VII. INTERIM REVIEW

7.1 On 23 May 2002, both parties submitted written requests for interim review by the Panel of particular aspects of the interim report issued on 14 May 2002. On 30 May 2002, each party provided written comments on the other party's request for interim review. Neither party requested an additional meeting with the Panel. The requests made by the parties are addressed below. In addition, certain clarifying changes were made to paragraphs 9.7, 9.30, 12.1, and 13.14 of the interim report (now paragraphs 8.57, 8.80, 9.1, and 10.15 respectively, *infra*). Finally, the Panel revised the numbering of certain sections of the interim report to reflect the format normally used in WTO panel reports.

A. *Request of the European Communities for Interim Review*

7.2 In respect of paragraph 7.4 of the interim report (now paragraph 8.4, *infra*), the European Communities requested the Panel to include the comment made by the European Communities on the preliminary ruling of the Panel – that the ruling misinterprets the relevant provisions of the DSU, appears to confuse the distinction between "claims" and "arguments", and is not in conformity with the established case law of the Appellate Body as summarised in the *Thailand – H-Beams* report. It is true that the European Communities did make this comment. It was, however, made in response to the Panel's preliminary ruling, and not the request of the United States for a preliminary ruling. Paragraph 7.4 – and indeed Section VII.A of the interim report (now Section V, *supra*) entitled "Arguments of the parties" – reflects only those arguments made *prior* to the ruling of the Panel. We therefore decline to include the statement requested by the European Communities.

7.3 In respect of paragraph 8.30 of the interim report (now paragraph 8.45, *infra*), the European Communities suggested that the rest of its response – edited out of the response cited by the Panel – would explain the confusion to which the Panel confessed. Our point in that paragraph is that merely the *correct* interpretation of Article 21.3 yields the result pointed to by the European Communities. The notion of a "strict" interpretation has no relevance to the analysis at hand. For the purpose of clarity, we have nonetheless quoted the European Communities' response in full, and revised this paragraph accordingly.

7.4 In respect of paragraphs 8.10-8.34 of the interim report (now paragraphs 8.22-8.49, *infra*), the European Communities submitted that the Panel did not address the European Communities' argument that automatic initiation in effect shifts the US burden of proof to foreign exporters or to other Members and thus leads to a violation of its obligation to determine continuation or recurrence of subsidisation. Accordingly, we have addressed this argument (*See* paragraphs 8.40-8.42, *infra*).

7.5 The European Communities drew the attention of the Panel to a typographical error in paragraph 9.5 of the interim report (now paragraph 8.55, *infra*), which we have corrected.

7.6 In respect of footnote 286 of the interim report (now footnote 293, *infra*), the European Communities argued that there is no distinction between the expressions Article 11.9 "itself applies" and Article 11.9 "is applicable" under Article 21.3, and suggests that the latter phrase be replaced by the phrase "is implied" in Article 21.3. In light of the fact that the European Communities characterises its claim as being that Article 11.9 "is implied" in Article 21.3, we have adopted the same characterisation and revised footnote 286 accordingly. We consider, however, that there *is* a distinction between the expressions Article 11.9 "itself applies" and Article 11.9 "is applicable" under Article 21.3, and we have revised footnotes 249, 286, and 356 accordingly (now footnotes 253, 293, and 365, respectively, *infra*). We have also made appropriate revisions to Sections VIII.B.2, VIII.C.1(b), VIII.C.2(b), and X, *infra*.

7.7 In respect of paragraph 9.12 of the interim report (now paragraph 8.62, *infra*), the European Communities considered that this paragraph was too long and not very easy to understand. We did not consider that this paragraph was unduly lengthy, or dense. We have therefore made no change to this paragraph.

7.8 In respect of paragraph 9.14 of the interim report (now paragraph 8.64, *infra*), the European Communities considered that the last two sentences of this paragraph might be further developed. We are of the view that the last two sentences are clear as drafted. We have nonetheless made a clarifying change to this paragraph.

7.9 In respect of paragraph 9.17 and footnote 314 of the interim report (now paragraph 8.67 and footnote 322, respectively, *infra*), the European Communities submitted that the Panel include the United States' argument that the European Communities' claim under Article 21.3 regarding application of a *de minimis* standard does not cover injury, as it is not within the Panel's terms of reference. We have revised footnote 314 accordingly.

7.10 In respect of paragraph 9.27 of the interim report (now paragraph 8.77, *infra*), the European Communities suggested that the words "among the most relevant factors" in the 9th line be replaced by the words "a relevant factor", as the latter language would be more consistent with the Panel's reasoning (presumably in the preceding paragraph). We have revised this paragraph accordingly.

7.11 In respect of paragraphs 9.7-9.29 of the interim report (now paragraphs 8.57-8.79, *infra*), the European Communities submitted that inclusion of its argument regarding the principle of effectiveness in the interpretation of Article 21.3 would strengthen the findings. We have provided the reasoning we consider appropriate in addressing this claim. We therefore decline to include the argument requested by the European Communities.

7.12 In respect of paragraphs 10.1-10.3 of the interim report (now paragraphs 8.85-8.87, *infra*), the European Communities submitted that the Panel might wish to include and address the European Communities' arguments regarding Article 22 in support of its claim under Article 21.3. We note that we are under no obligation to address each argument made by a party under a particular claim.[215] What matters is that we set out clearly what we consider the party's claim to be and provide a reasoned explanation for granting / rejecting the claim. We therefore decline to include and address the argument requested by the European Communities.

7.13 In respect of paragraph 10.7 of the interim report (now paragraph 8.91, *infra*), the European Communities submitted that the first sentence of this paragraph was not very clear. We have accordingly revised this sentence.

7.14 In respect of paragraph 10.21 of the interim report (now paragraph 8.105, *infra*), the European Communities argued that an expression of concern by a panel is insufficient to enable appellate review, and suggested that the Panel explain why it reached the conclusion of WTO-consistency in paragraph 10.22 (now paragraph 8.106, *infra*) in spite of the concern it expressed. We consider that the last sentence of paragraph 10.21 and the first two sentences of paragraph 10.22 do explain why we make a finding of WTO-consistency in paragraph 10.22 in spite of the concern we express. We have therefore made no change to this paragraph.

7.15 In respect of paragraph 10.28 of the interim report (now paragraph 8.113, *infra*), the European Communities requested that the Panel note that the parties do not dispute that some extremely small subsidy was paid after 1986 but because it was so small no countervailable benefit would have remained after the sunset review. We note, first, that the United States has never agreed with the European Communities that the amount of subsidy paid after 1986 was small, nor has the United States agreed that no countervailable benefit would have remained after completion of the sunset review. In fact, the US position is that the subsidy rate attributable to the CIG programme cannot be determined at present because the evidence necessary to calculate it was not on the record before the US DOC.[216] Second, the purpose of this paragraph is simply to provide the reader basic factual information about the CIG programme. Contrary to the suggestion of the European Communities, we are not at liberty to decide whether, given the amounts received by the German exporters after 1986, there would have remained any countervailable subsidy after completion of the sunset review. Any such assessment would constitute a *de novo* review, which would

---

[215] The Appellate Body has stated in this regard:

> Just as a panel has the discretion to address only those *claims* which must be addressed in order to dispose of the matter at issue in a dispute, so too does a panel have the discretion to address only those *arguments* it deems necessary to resolve a particular claim. So long as it is clear in a panel report that a panel has reasonably considered a claim, the fact that a particular argument relating to that claim is not specifically addressed in the "Findings" section of a panel report will not, in and of itself, lead to the conclusion that that panel has failed to make the "objective assessment of the matter before it" required by Article 11 of the DSU. (*European Communities – Measures Affecting the Importation of Certain Poultry Products*, Report of the Appellate Body, WT/DS69/AB/R, adopted 23 July 1998, para. 135) (emphasis in original)

[216] Comments of the United States on Request of the European Communities for Interim Review, p. 3.

run counter to the teachings of the Appellate Body.[217] We therefore decline to include the statement requested by the European Communities.

7.16 In respect of paragraphs 11.1-11.2 of the interim report (now paragraphs 8.120-8.121, *infra*), the European Communities submitted that its arguments should be reflected in further detail, and that the Panel's findings should address those arguments as such. In particular, the European Communities referred to the obligations that "flow from the requirement to provide ample opportunity as these are exemplified in the remaining paragraphs of this Article". We have accordingly elaborated on the European Communities' arguments (*See* paragraph 8.122, *infra*). We note, however, that we find the European Communities' claims in respect of the obligation to provide ample opportunity to be outside our terms of reference (*See* Section VIII.E, *infra*). We therefore do not address these arguments.

7.17 In respect of paragraph 12.1(b) of the interim report (now paragraph 9.1(b), *infra*), the European Communities argued that the Panel should justify further its finding of a violation of Article 32.5 of the *SCM Agreement* and Article XVI:4 of the WTO Agreement. We have accordingly added paragraph 8.81, *infra*. To ensure clarity and consistency in this respect throughout the findings, paragraphs 8.50, 8.107, and 10.14 have also been added, *infra*.

7.18 In respect of paragraphs 12.1(a), (d), and (f) of the interim report (the first two are now paragraphs 9.1(a) and (d), respectively, *infra*; paragraph 12.1(f) has been deleted in light of our findings in Section VIII.E, *infra*), the European Communities indicated that it disagreed with the Panel's findings in these paragraphs and the underlying reasoning. We consider that there is no request as such by the European Communities, and have therefore made no change to these paragraphs.

B. *Request of the United States for Interim Review*

7.19 In respect of Section IX and footnote 286 of the interim report (now Section VIII.C and footnote 293, respectively, *infra*), the United States considered that the European Communities' claim in respect of the application of a *de minimis* standard to sunset reviews is effectively that Article 11.9 itself applies to sunset reviews, and that the Panel's characterisation of this claim as being that Article 11.9 "is applicable under Article 21.3" was not a minor error. According to the United States, this misstatement of the Panel obscured the fact that the majority of the Panel effectively applied a provision to sunset reviews which the majority itself conceded cannot apply to sunset reviews. We consider that the changes made in response to the European Communities' request regarding its "is implied" claim address this request of the United States (*See* paragraph 7.6, *supra*).

7.20 In respect of Section X of the interim report (now Section VIII.D, *infra*), the United States submitted that the Panel should not have made any substantive findings regarding the consistency of US law as such with the "obligation to determine", because the European Communities' claims regarding this obligation were not set out in its request for establishment and are therefore not within the Panel's terms of refer-

[217] With respect to the issue of *de novo* review, the Appellate Body stated in *US – Cotton Yarn*:

> [P]anels must not conduct a *de novo* review of the evidence nor substitute their judgement for that of the competent authority. (*United States – Transitional Safeguard Measure on Combed Cotton Yarn from Pakistan* ("*US – Cotton Yarn*"), Report of the Appellate Body, WT/DS192/AB/R, adopted 5 November 2001, para. 74)

ence. Alternatively, the United States considered that the Panel should dismiss these claims due to the failure of the European Communities to provide in its request for establishment "a brief summary of the legal basis of the complaint sufficient to present the problem clearly", as required by Article 6.2 of the DSU.

7.21 We recall that paragraph 13 of our working procedures states that "[a] party shall submit any request for a preliminary ruling not later than its first submission to the Panel ... Exceptions to this procedure will be granted upon a showing of good cause". In this regard, while we note that the United States had raised its objection regarding the European Communities' claims in respect of the obligation to determine prior to interim review (in its comments on the responses of the European Communities to questions from the Panel following the second meeting of the Panel), we consider that the United States could reasonably have raised this objection by the time of its first written submission, as required by our working procedures. It was clear enough, in our view, from the first written submission of the European Communities that it was making a claim in respect of the obligation to determine, for the United States to be able to do so. Thus, we do not address this objection, and have made no change to Section X of the interim report.

7.22 In any event, we consider that the European Communities' request for establishment does contain a reference to the "obligation to determine" continuation or recurrence of subsidisation. We note that the request reads in relevant part:

> Under Article 21.3 of the *SCM Agreement*, [CVDs] have to be terminated after five years, unless the investigating authorities *determine that their expiry would be likely to lead to (i.e. cause), inter alia, the continuation or recurrence of subsidisation*. It is therefore for the DOC to make a *positive demonstration* to this effect. In fact, the DOC has not made such a demonstration; it has merely found that subsidies of less than the *de minimis* level provided for in Article 11.9 will continue. The European Communities do not consider that the presence of a level of subsidy which would automatically lead to the termination of a new investigation can be sufficient to warrant a further five years of countervailing measures in a sunset review, unless it can be demonstrated, on the basis of positive evidence, that there is a likelihood of the amount of subsidy increasing.[218]

7.23 We further note that paragraph 11 of the request summarises the European Communities' challenge as being to the US decision not to revoke CVDs in the review on carbon steel as well as to "certain aspects of the sunset review procedure which led to it". In our opinion, this paragraph includes US law in respect of the obligation to determine continuation or recurrence of subsidisation as such and as applied in the review on carbon steel. Articles 21.1 and 21.3 are clearly cited in this paragraph and, while the European Communities could certainly have been more forthcoming in its request for establishment, we are of the view that references to the US decision in carbon steel and the aspects of US law which led to it inherently include the requirements set out in Article 21.3 for the continuation of CVDs beyond the first five years of their application. We therefore do not consider that the European Communities' claims regarding the obligation to determine likelihood of continuation or recurrence of subsidisation are outside the Panel's terms of reference.

---

[218] WT/DS213/3, para. 6 (emphasis added).

7.24 In respect of Section XI of the interim report (now Section VIII.E, *infra*) – which originally contained substantive findings on the European Communities' claims in respect of the obligation to provide ample opportunity – the United States submitted that the Panel should not have made any substantive findings regarding this obligation, because the European Communities' claims regarding this obligation were not within the Panel's terms of reference because they did not meet the standards of Article 6.2 of the DSU. The European Communities argued that the reference in its request for establishment to Article 21 *in toto* would include Article 12, as paragraph 4 of Article 21 expressly indicates that Article 12 is applicable to sunset reviews. The European Communities further submitted that the obligation under Article 12 to provide ample opportunity to submit evidence in a sunset review is expressly mentioned in its first written submission. We have addressed these arguments and found that the European Communities' claims in respect of the obligation to provide ample opportunity are outside our terms of reference. Our reasons are set out below (*See* Section VIII.E.2, *infra*).
7.25 Finally, in respect of footnote 326 of the interim report (now footnote 334, *infra*), the United States pointed out that the citation contained therein was incorrect. We have accordingly corrected this footnote.

VIII. FINDINGS OF THE PANEL

A. *Request of the United States for a Preliminary Ruling*

1. *Arguments of the Parties*

(a) United States

8.1 The United States requests that the Panel make a preliminary ruling that the European Communities' claims with respect to the expedited sunset review procedure are not before the Panel because this procedure is not a measure within the Panel's terms of reference.[219]
8.2 The United States submits that the European Communities did not identify any measure or type of proceeding in consultations other than (i) the sunset review determination in carbon steel; (ii) the initiation of sunset reviews by the DOC; and (iii) the *de minimis* standard employed by the DOC in sunset reviews.[220] Nor, argues the United States, did the European Communities identify the expedited sunset review procedure in its request for consultations or in its request for the establishment of a panel.[221]

(b) European Communities

8.3 The European Communities considers the United States' request for a preliminary ruling to be without foundation. The European Communities submits that, in its request for establishment, it refers explicitly to Section 751(c) of the Tariff Act, which, among other things, sets out the procedures for the conduct of sunset reviews, including expedited reviews.[222]

---

219 First Written Submission of the United States, para. 122.
220 *Ibid.*, para. 125.
221 *Ibid.*, para. 126.
222 Oral Statement of the European Communities at the First Meeting of the Panel, para. 56.

8.4 The European Communities considers that whether the specific issue of the expedited review procedure was discussed during consultations is, therefore, irrelevant. In any event, the European Communities argues, the issue of the procedural and substantive requirements as to the evidence which foreign producers must provide in sunset reviews was also discussed in the consultations and, under US law, whether a full or an expedited review will take place depends precisely on the evidence provided by the foreign producers. Finally, the European Communities submits that expedited reviews were discussed, whether explicitly or implicitly, in consultations.[223]

2. *Findings of the Panel*[224]

8.5 We note that the United States does not make its request for a preliminary ruling on the basis of a particular provision of the DSU. We consider the relevant provisions of the DSU to be Article 7, covering the terms of reference of panels, and Article 6, covering the establishment of panels. Article 7 clearly indicates that the terms of reference of panels are contained in the request for the establishment of a panel[225]. With regard to the request for establishment, Article 6.2 of the DSU provides in part:

> The request for the establishment of a panel ... shall indicate whether consultations were held, identify the specific measures at issue and provide a brief summary of the legal basis of the complaint sufficient to present the problem clearly.

The Appellate Body has stated, in respect of the terms of reference of panels:

> Thus, "the matter referred to the DSB" for the purposes of Article 7 of the DSU and Article 17.4 of the *Anti-Dumping Agreement* must be the "matter" identified in the request for the establishment of a panel under Article 6.2 of the DSU. That provision requires the complaining Member, in a panel request, to "identify the *specific measures at issue* and provide a brief summary of the *legal basis of the complaint* sufficient to present the problem clearly." (emphasis added) The "*matter* referred to the DSB", therefore, consists of two elements: the specific *measures* at issue and the *legal basis of the complaint* (or the *claims*).[226]

---

[223] *Ibid.*

[224] The Chairman of the Panel made the following statement at the first meeting of the Panel with the parties:

> The Panel takes note of the United States' request for a preliminary ruling as set out in its first written submission and the European Communities' response to it as set out in its oral statement at the first meeting of the Panel.
>
> The Panel has considered the arguments of both parties, and has determined that the United States' expedited sunset review procedure is *not* within its terms of reference. We therefore grant the United States' request for a preliminary ruling, and will not be addressing the European Communities' claim in respect of the United States' expedited sunset review procedure in the present dispute. The reasons for this will be set out in full in our report.

[225] WT/DS213/3 in the present dispute.

[226] *Guatemala – Anti-Dumping Investigation Regarding Portland Cement from Mexico* ("*Guatemala – Cement I*"), Report of the Appellate Body, WT/DS60/AB/R, adopted 25 November 1998, para. 72 (emphasis in original).

Further, the Appellate Body has stated, in *European Communities – Bananas*:

> As a panel request is normally not subjected to detailed scrutiny by the DSB, it is incumbent upon a panel to examine the request for the establishment of the panel very carefully to ensure its compliance with both the letter and the spirit of Article 6.2 of the DSU. It is important that a panel request be sufficiently precise for two reasons: first, it often forms the basis for the terms of reference of the panel pursuant to Article 7 of the DSU; and, second, it informs the defending party and the third parties of the legal basis of the complaint.[227]

8.6 Thus, the United States' request raises two separate, but related, issues: (i) whether the US expedited sunset review procedure was identified in the request for establishment as a measure challenged by the European Communities and, if so, (ii) whether the European Communities' request for establishment provides "a brief summary of the legal basis of the complaint sufficient to present the problem clearly" and therefore satisfies the standard set out in Article 6.2 of the DSU.

8.7 We shall first examine the request for establishment to determine whether, on its face, the United States – and any other WTO Member – could have been reasonably expected to know that the expedited review procedure was part of "the matter referred to the DSB".

8.8 It is clear from the European Communities' request for establishment that the word "expedited" does not appear in that request. Nor does the request contain any all-encompassing reference to US procedures, generally, for sunset review. Paragraphs 1-2 of the request for establishment set out the procedural background to the request for establishment, paragraph 3 explains that the request relates particularly to the sunset review in carbon steel, paragraphs 4-7 set out the European Communities' claim in respect of the *de minimis* standard applied in that review, paragraphs 8-10 set out the European Communities' claim in respect of the evidentiary standards applied in relation to the initiation of that review, and paragraph 11 summarises the European Communities' challenge to the US decision in that review, as well as to "certain aspects of the sunset review procedure which led to it". This latter phrase could not be understood to include the expedited review procedure, as the sunset review in carbon steel was a full review.[228]

8.9 We note that the request for establishment further outlines the statutory and regulatory underpinnings of the US sunset review procedures as such, and as applied in the sunset review in carbon steel. These statutory and regulatory provisions also govern the expedited review procedure, as pointed out by the European Communi-

[227] *European Communities – Regime for the Importation, Sale and Distribution of Bananas* ("*European Communities – Bananas*"), Report of the Appellate Body, WT/DS27/AB/R, adopted 25 September 1997, para. 142.

[228] Indeed, while this has no legal relevance to our examination of the European Communities' request for establishment, we note that a similar phrase is used by the European Communities in its first written submission:

> The present proceeding concerns also certain aspects of the US basic sunset review legislation and procedure *which led to the continuation of the duties in this case* (First Written Submission of the European Communities, para. 30 (emphasis added)).

ties. We consider, however, that this fact alone is insufficient for us to conclude that the expedited review procedure is identified as a specific measure at issue.[229]

8.10 Having found that the expedited review procedure is not identified in the request for establishment, we shall consider whether that "measure" is sufficiently related to a measure or measures that *are* specifically identified so as to bring it within our terms of reference. We note the finding of the Panel in *Japan – Film*:

> The question thus becomes whether the ordinary meaning of the terms of Article 6.2, i.e., that "the specific measures at issue" be identified in the panel request, can be met if a "measure" is not explicitly described in the request. To fall within the terms of Article 6.2, it seems clear that a "measure" not explicitly described in a panel request must have a clear relationship to a "measure" that is specifically described therein, so that it can be said to be "included" in the specified "measure". In our view, the requirements of Article 6.2 would be met in the case of a "measure" that is subsidiary, or so closely related to a "measure" specifically identified, that the responding party can reasonably be found to have received adequate notice of the scope of the claims asserted by the complaining party. The two key elements – close relationship and notice – are inter-related: only if a "measure" is subsidiary or closely related to a specifically identified "measure" will notice be adequate.[230]

8.11 The United States explains that, upon automatic initiation by the DOC of a sunset review within five years of the date of publication of a CVD order, a review can follow one of three basic paths: (i) revocation of the order; (ii) an expedited sunset review; and (iii) a full sunset review.[231] We do not consider that the European Communities' general discussion of the automatic initiation of sunset reviews by the DOC is sufficient to put the United States – as well as other Members – on notice that the expedited review procedure was also under challenge. We note that the European Communities' request refers to "certain aspects of the sunset review procedure which led to [the DOC decision not to revoke the CVDs on carbon steel]". The challenge is thus apparently to those aspects of the sunset review procedure that have some relevance to the carbon steel case, which is not true of the expedited review procedure, because the carbon steel case involved a full, not expedited, review. We do not consider the expedited review procedure to be "a 'measure' that is subsidiary, or so closely related to" any of the measures specifically identified, "that the responding party can reasonably be found to have received adequate notice of the scope of the claims asserted by the complaining party". We, therefore, find that the expedited review procedure is not sufficiently related to a measure or measures that are specifically identified in the request for establishment as to properly bring it within our terms of reference.[232]

---

[229] We therefore need not, and do not, address the United States' arguments with regard to the measures identified by the European Communities in consultations, and the European Communities' response thereto (*See* paras. 8.2 and 8.4, *supra*).

[230] *Japan – Measures Affecting Consumer Photographic Film and Paper* ("*Japan – Film*"), Report of the Panel, WT/DS44/R, adopted 22 April 1998, para. 10.8.

[231] First Written Submission of the United States, paras. 7-10.

[232] Having concluded that the European Communities has not identified the expedited review procedure as a specific measure at issue in its request for establishment, we need not, and do not, con-

8.12 For the foregoing reasons, we consider that the European Communities has failed to set out a claim in its request for establishment with respect to the United States' expedited sunset review procedure, and this "measure" is, therefore, outside our terms of reference. Accordingly, we grant the United States' request for a preliminary ruling.

B. Whether US CVD Law as such is Inconsistent with the SCM Agreement in Respect of the Application of Evidentiary Standardsd for the Self-Initiation of Sunset Reviews

1. Arguments of the Parties

(a) European Communities

8.13 In the view of the European Communities, the non-application of evidentiary standards to the self-initiation of sunset reviews constitutes a violation of Article 21.3 of the *SCM Agreement*.

8.14 The European Communities considers that the ordinary meaning of the text of Article 21.3 establishes an unequivocal obligation on WTO Members to terminate any measure imposing CVDs on a date no later than five years from its imposition.[233] The European Communities explains that Article 21.3 thus renders effective the requirement in Article 21.1 that application of a CVD be limited to the time necessary to counteract injurious subsidisation, by establishing the presumption that this time elapses five years from the imposition of the CVD[234], "unless the authorities determine, in a review initiated before that date on their own initiative or upon a duly substantiated request made by or on behalf of the domestic industry within a reasonable period of time prior to that date, that the expiry of the duty would be likely to lead to continuation or recurrence of subsidisation and injury". Referring to this language, the European Communities explains that the ordinary meaning of the word "unless", which "introduces an exception to the presumption of termination, clearly conveys the notion that an exception to the basic rule is introduced"[235]. US law, by requiring that sunset reviews are automatically initiated for all existing CVD measures no later than 30 days before the fifth anniversary date of their imposition, "clearly transforms this exception into a rule"[236], thus infringing the letter and the spirit of Article 21, paragraphs 1 and 3, as well as Article 10, of the *SCM Agreement*. The European Communities further submits that the US statement of policy practices "confirms the disregard for the presumption of termination of all [CVDs]"[237] contained in Article 21 of the *SCM Agreement*.

8.15 The European Communities argues that, in order to initiate a sunset review on their own initiative, the domestic authority must be in possession of evidence, as would be required in order to initiate an investigation on their own initiative, thus

sider whether the European Communities has provided "a brief summary of the legal basis of the complaint sufficient to present the problem clearly" in that request for establishment (*See* paras. 8.5-8.6, *supra*).

[233] First Written Submission of the European Communities, para. 48.

[234] *Ibid.*, para. 51.

[235] *Ibid.*, para. 52.

[236] *Ibid.*, para. 53.

[237] *Ibid.*, para. 54.

imputing the principle of Article 11.6 into Article 21.3. It further argues that, in order to initiate a sunset review on their own initiative, the domestic authority should be in possession of the same level of evidence as would be required in a "duly substantiated request" from the domestic industry, thus equating the level of evidence required for self-initiation under Article 21.3 with that required for initiation upon request by the domestic industry under Article 21.3. It considers that, as the purpose and effect of initial investigations and of sunset reviews are the same, it is reasonable and coherent to apply the same standards as regards initiation and conduct of reviews in both instances. Otherwise, "self-initiation would become the easy option and would lead to inconsistent results"[238]. According to the European Communities, the purpose of the evidentiary standard is to guarantee that genuine cases are brought which are backed by concrete evidence. In the view of the European Communities, the automatic self-initiation of sunset reviews by the DOC is simply a device for lowering the level of evidence required from the domestic industry in order to initiate a sunset review[239].

8.16 In particular, the European Communities posits that a "duly substantiated request" should normally contain information, *inter alia*, on the:

- volume and value of domestic production
- volume and value of the production of petitioners
- volume and value of total imports
- volume and value of subsidised imports
- existence, amount, and nature of the subsidy, plus evidence relating to its continuation or recurrence
- effect of imports on prices, production, and sales
- causality between subsidised imports and injury, and evidence of why such injury will continue or recur[240]

8.17 More generally – and this is also relevant to the European Communities' claim that the *de minimis* standard is applicable to sunset reviews (*See* Section 0, infra) – the European Communities considers that "all provisions [of the *SCM Agreement*] are potentially applicable mutatis mutandis to Article 21.3, to the extent that they are relevant to the issues covered by Article 21.3 and that their application to Article 21.3 does not create a situation of conflict or is not specifically excluded"[241].

(b) United States

8.18 The United States points to one of the basic principles of treaty interpretation, that a treaty interpreter cannot read into a treaty "words that are not there"[242], which is precisely what, in the view of the United States, the European Communities is asking the Panel to do here by imputing into Article 21.3 the obligations contained in

---

[238] Response of the European Communities to Question 4 from the Panel.

[239] Response of the European Communities to Question 13(b) from the Panel.

[240] Response of the European Communities to Question 13(a) from the Panel.

[241] Response of the European Communities to Question 5(a) from the Panel.

[242] *India – Patent Protection for Pharmaceutical and Agricultural Chemical Products* ("*India – Patents (US)*"), Report of the Appellate Body, WT/DS50/AB/R, adopted 16 January 1998, para. 45.

Article 11.6.[243] The European Communities' claims must therefore fail, according to the United States. The United States characterises the European Communities' argument that a parallelism exists between the investigation and sunset review provisions of the *SCM Agreement* as a theory, and argues that a theory, under customary rules of treaty interpretation, cannot overcome the ordinary meaning of the words of a treaty, taking into account their context and the object and purpose of the agreement.[244] In particular, argues the United States, if the *SCM Agreement* implicitly incorporates this parallelism, why then did the Members find it necessary to provide explicitly in Article 21.4 that the requirements contained in Article 12 for the conduct of investigations are also applicable to the conduct of reviews, including sunset reviews?[245]

8.19 The United States considers that nothing in the text of Article 21.3, or Article 11.6, imposes any evidentiary requirements on authorities who initiate sunset reviews on their own initiative. The United States also emphasises the distinction between the investigatory phase and the review phase of a CVD proceeding, as reflected in the provisions of the *SCM Agreement*.[246] In this regard, the United States cites the finding, regarding the Anti-Dumping ("AD") Agreement, of the Panel in *United States – DRAMS*:

> [T]he term "investigation" means the investigative phase leading up to the final determination of the investigating authority.[247]

8.20 The United States does not consider sunset reviews to be an "exception" to a presumption of termination (or anything else), but instead merely one part of an overall balance of rights and obligations negotiated during the Uruguay Round.[248] In any event, submits the United States[249], even if one were to treat sunset reviews as an "exception" to something else, the European Communities' arguments run afoul of a different principle, that set out by the Appellate Body in *European Communities – Hormones*:

> [M]erely characterising a treaty provision as an "exception" does not by itself justify a "stricter" or " narrower" interpretation of that provision than would be warranted ... by applying the normal rules of treaty interpretation.[250]

8.21 More generally, the United States considers that "no provisions are applicable to reviews under Article 21.3, unless specifically indicated ... [I]t is a matter of what the text of Article 21.3 provides, as interpreted in accordance with the rules of [treaty interpretation] ... There could be a cross-reference between the two provisions, a reference in one provision to the other, or a general statement that a provision applies throughout the Agreement or throughout Part V of the Agreement"[251]. The United

243 First Written Submission of the United States, para. 2.

244 Second Written Submission of the United States, para. 6.

245 *Ibid.*, para. 7.

246 First Written Submission of the United States, paras. 67-68.

247 *United States – Anti-Dumping Duty on Dynamic Random Access Memory Semiconductors (DRAMS) of One Megabit or Above from Korea* ("*United States – DRAMS*"), Report of the Panel, WT/DS99/R, adopted 19 March 1999, footnote 519.

248 First Written Submission of the United States, para. 3.

249 *Ibid.*

250 *European Communities – Measures Concerning Meat and Meat Products (Hormones)* ("*European Communities – Hormones*"), Report of the Appellate Body, WT/DS26/AB/R-WT/DS48/AB/R, adopted 13 February 1998, para. 104.

251 Response of the United States to Question 24(a) from the Panel.

States considers that "other provisions of the *SCM Agreement* would apply where the Agreement says they apply"[252].

2. *Findings of the Panel*

8.22 We understand the European Communities' claim in respect of the US system of automatic self-initiation of sunset reviews to be the following: that the US system of automatic self-initiation of sunset reviews runs counter to the presumption of termination of all CVDs contained in Article 21.3, because it does not satisfy the evidentiary standards of Article 11.6 that the European Communities believes are implied in Article 21.3.[253] The thrust of the European Communities' argument is, therefore, that automatic self-initiation transforms an exception – possible continuation of a CVD – into a general rule, because self-initiation, coupled with other characteristics of US procedure, leads to the automatic continuation of CVDs.[254] Further, statistical data, according to the European Communities, "provide clear evidence of the fact that US law and regulations are biased in favour of keeping and perpetuating unjustified CVD orders"[255].

8.23 In response to a question from the Panel as to whether it considers the self-initiation of sunset reviews to be in and of itself WTO-inconsistent, the European Communities' states, "No ... The [European Communities'] claim is that the investigating authority must be in possession of sufficient evidence, that is the same level or an equivalent amount of relevant evidence that would be required from the domestic industry if it initiates on its own initiative, as in [sic] the case in the initiation of new investigations."[256] It is, therefore, the "automatic" nature of self-initiation in the US sunset review system – that is, the fact that the DOC is not required to have any evidence of likelihood of continuation or recurrence of injurious subsidisation to initiate sunset reviews – to which the European Communities objects, and not the self-initiation of sunset reviews itself.

8.24 With regard to the evidentiary standards to be met by authorities who initiate sunset reviews on their own initiative (or "self-initiate"), the European Communities draws a parallel between sunset reviews and investigations, submitting that the Panel should consider implied in Article 21.3 the requirements of Article 11.6. The princi-

---

252 Response of the United States to Question 24(b) from the Panel.

253 We do not understand the European Communities to be alleging a violation of Article 11.6, but of Article 21.3, of the *SCM Agreement*. In this regard, we note that the European Communities argues that "an interpretation of Article 21.3 should be made in context and in the light of the object and purpose of Article 21.3 and of the *SCM Agreement*. Articles 21.1, 22.1, 22.7, 10, and 11.6 provide relevant context and help define its object and purpose. Such an interpretation ... requires that the evidentiary standards of Article 11.6 should be *implied*, and hence applied, also to the evidentiary requirements in sunset reviews" (Response of the European Communities to Question 46 from the Panel (emphasis added)).

Nor could the European Communities successfully allege a violation of Article 11.6. Article 11 is entitled "Initiation and Subsequent Investigation", and clearly deals with investigations, such as that term is distinguished from reviews by the Agreement. This is also made clear in the text of Article 11.6 itself, which refers to investigations. We therefore consider whether Article 21.3 contains by implication the same type of obligation as Article 11.6, and whether the United States has violated Article 21.3 in this respect.

254 Second Written Submission of the European Communities, para. 16.

255 *Ibid.*, para. 17.

256 Response of the European Communities to Question 4 from the Panel.

pal question before us, therefore, is whether the text of Article 21.3 imposes any evidentiary requirements on authorities in the self-initiation of sunset reviews. In other words, is the European Communities correct in arguing that, as exceptions need to be strictly interpreted and applied, and the continuation of a duty past the initial five-year period is an exception to the presumption of termination and thus equivalent to a new imposition of the original duty, it follows that the self-initiation of sunset reviews must satisfy evidentiary requirements, as is required in Article 11.6 for the self-initiation of investigations?

8.25 Article 3.2 of the DSU indicates that Members recognise that the dispute settlement system serves to clarify the provisions of the covered agreements "in accordance with customary rules of interpretation of public international law". In this regard, the Appellate Body, in *United States – Gasoline*, refers to "a fundamental rule of treaty interpretation [which] has received its most authoritative and succinct expression in the *Vienna Convention on the Law of Treaties*"[257] ("Vienna Convention"), and cites Article 31.1 thereof, which reads as follows:

> Article 31
>
> *General rule of interpretation*
>
> 1. A treaty shall be interpreted in good faith in accordance with the ordinary meaning to be given to the terms of the treaty in their context and in the light of its object and purpose.[258]

The Appellate Body indicates that "[this] general rule of interpretation has attained the status of a rule of customary or general international law. As such, it forms part of the 'customary rules of interpretation of public international law'"[259]. We shall, therefore, begin our analysis of the European Communities' claim under Article 21.3 of the *SCM Agreement* on the basis of the text of that provision in its context and in light of the object and purpose of the Agreement.

8.26 We recall that Article 21.3 states:

> Notwithstanding the provisions of paragraphs 1 and 2, any definitive [CVD] shall be terminated on a date not later than five years from its imposition (or from the date of the most recent review under paragraph 2 if that review has covered both subsidisation and injury, or under this paragraph), unless the authorities determine, in a review initiated before that date on their own initiative or upon a duly substantiated request made by or on behalf of the domestic industry within a reasonable period of time prior to that date, that the expiry of the duty would be likely to lead to continuation or recurrence of subsidisation and injury. The duty may remain in force pending the outcome of such a review.[260]

We note, at the outset, that nothing in the text of Article 21.3 specifically provides that the evidentiary standards applicable to the initiation of investigations are also

---

[257] *United States – Standards for Reformulated and Conventional Gasoline* ("*United States – Gasoline*"), Report of the Appellate Body, WT/DS2/AB/R, adopted 20 May 1996, p. 16.

[258] (1969) 8 *International Legal Materials* 679.

[259] *United States – Gasoline*, Report of the Appellate Body, footnote 257, *supra*, p. 17 (footnote omitted).

[260] Footnote deleted.

applicable to the initiation of sunset reviews. We would expect that the drafters would have been able and chosen to include a clear indication to that effect, should that have been their intention. Indeed, we agree with the United States' argument that the absence of a clear indication, for instance, in the form of a cross-reference, is all the more significant given the context of Article 21.3 – that is, the fact that the drafters *did* provide explicit indications elsewhere in Article 21, in relation to Articles 12 and 18. It is clear that the drafters knew how to have obligations set forth in one provision apply in another context.[261] The most obvious inference we can draw from the absence of a clear indication, therefore, is that the Members chose not to imply in Article 21.3 the evidentiary requirements of Article 11.6. And we must first find that the provision contains such requirements before we can find that the United States violated the provision on the basis of its non-observance of such requirements.

8.27 We cannot, however, conclude on the basis of silence alone that the evidentiary standards of Article 11.6 necessarily do not apply to sunset reviews. Doing so would mean that the mere absence of an explicit statement as to the applicability of the evidentiary standards of Article 11.6 is conclusive. In our opinion, reading the text of Article 21.3 in its context and in light of the object and purpose of the treaty, as required by the customary rules of treaty interpretation reflected in the Vienna Convention, means that we cannot treat silence as to the applicability of Article 11.6 as conclusive. An explicit articulation of the scope of application of the evidentiary standards of Article 11.6 would certainly be conclusive, in that if the Agreement provided that they applied only in certain circumstances or did not apply in certain circumstances, such articulation would be determinative; we find it difficult, however, to consider that silence has the same dispositive value. While silence could be explained by the drafters' intention for the requirements of the provision not to apply in any other context, as suggested by the United States, silence could also be explained by the drafters' belief that it was obvious that it did. In other words, we are unable to conclude *solely* on the basis of silence that an evidentiary standard is not implied in Article 21.3. Rather, we believe that we must consider the context of Article 21.3 – that is, provisions of the *SCM Agreement* other than Article 21.3 – and the object and purpose of the *SCM Agreement* in reaching a conclusion.

8.28 Article 31 of the Vienna Convention does not, in our view, limit us to a literal reading of the provision in question. Were such a reading to be required, provisions such as Article 15.3 – which deals with the circumstances in which imports may be cumulated for purposes of injury determinations – and Article 19 – which deals with the imposition and collection of CVDs – would be limited in ways that would negatively affect the operation of the Agreement, particularly with respect to sunset reviews, something that cannot have been intended by the drafters.

8.29 Equally persuasive, we consider, is the case of Article 21.1, which reads:

[261] A number of provisions in the *SCM Agreement* also apply independently of cross-references in that they contain explicit statements of their scope of application: definition of "subsidy" in Article 1 ("For the purpose of this Agreement"); definition of "interested parties" in Article 12.9 ("for the purposes of this Agreement"); calculation of the amount of a subsidy under Article 14 ("For the purpose of Part V"); definition of "initiated" in footnote 37 ("as used hereinafter"); definition of "injury" under Article 15 and in footnote 45 ("Under this Agreement"); definition of "like product" in footnote 46 ("Throughout this Agreement"); definition of domestic industry in Article 16 ("For the purposes of this Agreement"); and definition of "levy" in footnote 51 ("As used in this Agreement").

> A [CVD] shall remain in force only as long as and to the extent necessary to counteract subsidisation which is causing injury.

Were this provision to be read literally, the words "is causing injury" would suggest that a CVD could only remain in place, including under Article 21.3, where there is likelihood of *continuation* of subsidisation and injury, not *recurrence*. The notion of recurrence contained in Article 21.3, therefore, has to be implied in Article 21.1, or it would be rendered meaningless. Finally, Article 32.3[262], if read literally, would apply only to investigations and reviews initiated pursuant to applications from the domestic industry, and not initiated on an ex officio basis. Again, this cannot be the case. These several instances of provisions in the Agreement that, if read literally, would yield irrational results, confirm our view that we are not limited to a literal reading of the text of Article 21.3.

8.30 We also recall certain statements of the Appellate Body in *Canada – Autos*. In addressing the Panel's finding that Article 3.1(b) of the *SCM Agreement* did not apply to subsidies contingent in fact upon the use of domestic over imported goods, the Appellate Body stated:

> As we have said [in *Japan – Alcohol*], and as the Panel [in *Canada – Autos*] recalled, "omission must have some meaning". *Yet omissions in different contexts may have different meanings, and omission, in and of itself, is not necessarily dispositive*. Moreover, while the Panel rightly looked to Article 3.1(a) as relevant context in interpreting Article 3.1(b), the Panel failed to examine other contextual elements for Article 3.1(b) and to consider the object and purpose of the *SCM Agreement*.[263]

We consider that these statements of the Appellate Body make it clear that silence – or omission – is not controlling, and that interpretation under Article 31 of the Vienna Convention does not require that silence must be controlling.

8.31 Accordingly, it is important that we first set out the legal framework within which Article 21.3 exists and operates. We recall that paragraph 6(a) of Article VI of the General Agreement on Tariffs and Trade ("GATT") 1994, which deals with anti-dumping and CVDs, states:

> No contracting party shall levy any anti-dumping or [CVD] on the importation of any product of the territory of another contracting party unless it determines that the effect of the dumping or subsidisation, as the case may be, is such as to cause or threaten material injury to an established domestic industry, or is such as to retard materially the establishment of a domestic industry.

Further, Article VI:3 states, in relevant part:

---

262 Article 32.3 provides:

> Subject to paragraph 4, the provisions of this Agreement shall apply to investigations, and reviews of existing measures, initiated pursuant to applications which have been made on or after the date of entry into force for a Member of the WTO Agreement.

263 *Canada – Certain Measures Affecting the Automotive Industry* ("*Canada – Autos* "), Report of the Appellate Body, WT/DS139/AB/R-WT/DS142/AB/R, adopted 19 June 2000, para. 138 (footnote deleted, emphasis added).

> The term "[CVD]" shall be understood to mean a special duty levied for the purpose of offsetting any bounty or subsidy bestowed, directly, or indirectly, upon the manufacture, production or export of any merchandise.[264]

This definition is confirmed for purposes of the *SCM Agreement* in footnote 36 to that Agreement, which reads:

> The term "[CVD]" shall be understood to mean a special duty levied for the purpose of offsetting any subsidy bestowed directly or indirectly upon the manufacture, production or export of any merchandise, as provided for in paragraph 3 of Article VI of GATT 1994.

The two GATT provisions, in our view, set out the purpose of CVDs and the general circumstances in which they may be levied as well as give some indication of the object and purpose of the *SCM Agreement*.

8.32 Part V of the *SCM Agreement* sets out the specific substantive and procedural conditions that must be met for the WTO-consistent imposition of CVDs. Particularly noteworthy are Articles 10 and 19.4, which read, respectively:

> Members shall take all necessary steps to ensure that the imposition of a [CVD] on any product of the territory of any Member imported into the territory of another Member is in accordance with the provisions of Article VI of GATT 1994 and the terms of this Agreement. [CVDs] may only be imposed pursuant to investigations initiated and conducted in accordance with the provisions of this Agreement and the Agreement on Agriculture.[265]

> No [CVD] shall be levied on any imported product in excess of the amount of the subsidy found to exist, calculated in terms of subsidisation per unit of the subsidised and exported product.[266]

Article VI of the GATT 1994 and Part V of the *SCM Agreement* must, thus, be seen as not only explaining the purpose of CVDs but also constituting the framework of rights and obligations within which CVDs exist. This complex framework of rights and obligations is the context in which we consider we must interpret Article 21.3.

8.33 Let us now situate Article 21.3 in its immediate context. We recall that Article 21.1 sets out a fundamental obligation, which relates to the above provisions of Article VI of the GATT 1994:

> A [CVD] shall remain in force only as long as and to the extent necessary to counteract subsidisation which is causing injury.

In other words, a Member must ensure that any CVD only remains in place under these circumstances. Articles 21.2 and 21.3 are, therefore, further articulations, in respect of certain specific scenarios, of the ongoing obligation contained in Article 21.1. Article 21.2 provides the modalities for compliance with this obligation during the period of application of a CVD, while Article 21.3 provides the modalities for compliance with this obligation upon expiry of that period. Both provisions emphasise the basic discipline on the imposition of CVDs, that they can only apply where subsidisation causes or is likely to cause injury.

---

264 Ad notes deleted.

265 Footnotes deleted.

266 Footnote deleted.

8.34 We now examine Article 11.6, the evidentiary standards of which the European Communities argues are implied in Article 21.3, and which provides:

> If, in special circumstances, the authorities concerned decide to initiate an investigation without having received a written application by or on behalf of a domestic industry for the initiation of such investigation, they shall proceed only if they have sufficient evidence of the existence of a subsidy, injury and causal link, as described in paragraph 2, to justify the initiation of an investigation.

Again, we recognise, at the outset, that nothing in the text of the provision provides for its evidentiary standards to be implied in Article 21.3. What is clear from this language, however, is that a CVD investigation cannot be self-initiated by an investigating authority unless the requirement of sufficient evidence of subsidisation, injury, and causation is met. Investigating authorities must ensure that they are in the possession of such evidence. The terms of the provision are unequivocal. Such mandatory and conditional ("in special circumstances"; "only if"; "to justify") language would suggest that the drafters had an important consideration in mind in drafting this provision, reflected in the precise choice of words. In particular, the mandatory nature and conditional language of the provision convey, in our view, that the drafters sought a particular outcome, to protect exporters and prevent trade harassment through initiation of groundless investigations.

8.35 It is in light of this rationale for the inclusion of evidentiary standards for self-initiation of CVD investigations and the requirement of sufficient evidence that we must address the European Communities' claim that such standards are implied in Article 21.3. In this regard, we must consider whether the rationale of protection of exporters is equally applicable to sunset reviews as it is to CVD investigations. It would seem to us that, while the initiation – whether upon application by a domestic industry or on the initiative of the investigating authorities – of a CVD investigation clearly has a chilling effect on trade in the product concerned, it is less clear that the initiation of a sunset review of an existing CVD has the same effect.

8.36 Essentially, we do not see how trade in a product subject to a CVD would suffer a chilling effect upon initiation of a sunset review *additional* to that already in existence. And this existing chilling effect would only be completely mitigated upon actual expiry of the CVD, not the possibility of its expiry, contrary to the suggestion of the European Communities. Certainly, the potential for impact on trade is less in case of the initiation of a sunset review than that of an investigation. If anything, the initiation of a sunset review while it might not allow for a positive impact that might otherwise have occurred through the expiry of the CVD, might also have a positive impact on trade flows (in the expectation of a possible expiry of the CVD), rather than have a negative impact per se. In sum, given the framework of disciplines that governs the imposition of CVDs and the role of the *SCM Agreement* in ensuring that CVDs do not unjustifiably impede international trade, we find it difficult to see how self-initiation of a CVD investigation could be considered comparable to self-initiation of a sunset review of a CVD.

8.37 While the European Communities is correct in stating that "[*a*]*pplications* under [Article] 11.5 [sic] and requests under [Article] 21.3 are aimed at securing the same objective, that is to avoid unjustified disruptions in international trade on the basis of allegations and claims that are manifestly incorrect"[267], there is no dispute over the evidentiary standards required to be fulfilled for initiation upon requests under Article 21.3 by the domestic industry. Rather, the focus of this claim is self-initiation, and the dispute is over whether, in the absence of language like that contained in Article 11.6 – which clearly characterises the self-initiation of investigations as something that occurs "in special circumstances" and sets out the requirement of "sufficient evidence of a subsidy, injury and causal link" before an investigating authority may self-initiate – Article 21.3 must in respect of self-initiation be understood to include a requirement of some degree of evidentiary support as well.

8.38 We recall that Article 11.2 of the Agreement sets out in detail the evidentiary standards to be met by written applications by or on behalf of a domestic industry, and Article 11.6 indicates that the investigating authorities must satisfy the same evidentiary standards before they can proceed to self-initiate. The marked difference between the terms of Articles 11.2 and 11.6, on the one hand, and those of Article 21.3, on the other, suggests that the drafters did *not* intend the self-initiation of sunset reviews to be held to the same evidentiary standards as the self-initiation of investigations or indeed to any evidentiary standards at all. To our minds, the terms of Article 21.3 ("in a review initiated ... on [the investigating authorities'] own initiative or upon a duly substantiated request made by or on behalf of the domestic industry") suggest that the drafters considered the self-initiation of sunset reviews to be simply one of two modalities for the initiation of sunset reviews – and not something that occurs "in special circumstances" – and it therefore follows that self-initiation does not require the fulfilment of particular evidentiary standards. It is simply one way for investigating authorities to commence a sunset review, something which must be undertaken to determine whether a CVD may remain in place past the five-year deadline set out in the Agreement.

8.39 Further, we note the Appellate Body's statement, in *EC – Computer Equipment*:

> The purpose of treaty interpretation under Article 31 of the *Vienna Convention* is to ascertain the *common* intentions of the parties.[268]

Given the marked difference between the terms of Articles 11.2 and 11.6, on the one hand, and those of Article 21.3, on the other, we cannot conclude that the "common intentions of the parties" were to have the evidentiary standards of Article 11.6 apply to sunset reviews. As the Appellate Body has stated, in *India – Patents (US)*:

> The duty of a treaty interpreter is to examine the words of the treaty to determine the intentions of the parties. This should be done in accordance with the principles of treaty interpretation set out in Article 31 of the *Vienna Convention*. But these principles of interpretation neither require nor condone the imputation into a treaty of words that are not there or the importation into a treaty of concepts that were not intended.[269]

8.40 We note that the European Communities argues:

---

[267] Response of the European Communities to Question 6(a) from the Panel.

[268] *European Communities – Customs Classification of Certain Computer Equipment* ("*EC – Computer Equipment*"), Report of the Appellate Body, WT/DS62/AB/R-WT/DS67/AB/R-WT/DS68/AB/R, adopted 22 June 1998, para. 84.

[269] *India – Patents (US)*, Report of the Appellate Body, footnote 242, *supra*, para. 45.

> The current US law requires the automatic initiation of sunset reviews *without any evidence*. This ignores the presumption of termination under Article 21.3 and reverses the burden of proof, which should be on the petitioners or the investigating authority to justify the initiation of a review and not on the exporters to justify the termination and the non-initiation of such a review.[270]

We find this argument to be rather circular. The claim we are deciding is made in respect of the application of evidentiary standards to the self-initiation of sunset reviews. The above argument presupposes that evidentiary standards do apply to the self-initiation of sunset reviews. We do not find that it provides further grounds for the application of evidentiary standards to the self-initiation of sunset reviews.

8.41 The European Communities also argues that US CVD law:

> "shift[s] the burden of proof on foreign exporters and governments to demonstrate no likelihood of continuation or recurrence of subsidisation and injury in violation of Articles 21.1 and 21.3, which require termination of [the] CVD unless the domestic authorities demonstrate the opposite".[271]

We recall that Article 21.3 requires that a CVD be terminated after five years unless the investigating authority determines that expiry of the duty would be likely to lead to continuation or recurrence of subsidisation and injury. What the European Communities characterises as "an important and burdensome action from exporters"[272] to produce evidence that the measure should expire does not, in our view, relieve the United States from – or run counter to – the obligation to make the determination required by Article 21.3 before the United States can extend application of a CVD beyond five years. It seems to us that, while the action of exporters may result in expiry of the measure, it may also result in a sunset review in which the United States would have to satisfy the conditions of Article 21.3 in order to take a decision not to revoke the measure.

8.42 Thus, while we neither adopt nor endorse the "shift[s] the burden of proof" language used by the European Communities – language not used by the Agreement itself – it is clear that, in the absence of an affirmative determination by an investigating authority, CVDs may not be maintained beyond a five-year period. It is also clear that any such determination must be correctly reasoned and based on positive evidence. We cannot, however, see how the automatic self-initiation of sunset reviews runs afoul of that obligation in any way. The initiation of a review is merely the beginning of a process leading to a determination as to whether or not subsidisation and injury are likely to continue or recur. The standards for the *initiation* of a review – whether on the initiative of an investigating authority or upon request by the domestic industry – in no way prejudge the standards applied by an investigating authority in reaching the *substantive determination* to be made in that review. In sum, it seems to us that the European Communities' argument is based upon an incorrect equation of the standards for the initiation of a review with those for the substantive determination to be made in a review.

---

270 Response of the European Communities to Question 2 from the Panel (emphasis in original).

271 Response of the European Communities to Question 42 from the Panel.

272 Response of the European Communities to Question 13(b) from the Panel.

8.43 We note that the European Communities posits that "the purpose and effect of initial investigations and of sunset reviews are the same" and "the object and purpose of both provisions ... remains the same". In the view of the European Communities, therefore, the requirement that certain evidentiary standards be fulfilled for the self-initiation of investigations must have its equivalent in the self-initiation of sunset reviews. We see no difficulty, however, with an interpretation under which investigating authorities may not self-initiate investigations without certain evidence, but may self-initiate sunset reviews without any evidence.[273] Given that evidentiary standards for the self-initiation of investigations are understood to exist for the purpose of avoiding trade harassment, the drafters could very reasonably have intended such standards to be inapplicable to the self-initiation of sunset reviews, as sunset reviews do not have the same potential for trade harassment as investigations, as discussed above (*See* paragraph 8.36, *supra*). We consider it perfectly rational for them to have established a set of disciplines in respect of investigations, and have some of them apply to sunset reviews and others not. To accept the European Communities' proposition would require us first to accept as fact that "the purpose and effect of initial investigations and of sunset reviews are the same", and then to conclude that this purpose and effect somehow override conclusions based on our reading of the text itself. We see no sound legal basis for the conclusion that the purpose and effect of proceedings governed by certain provisions trump textual analysis of those provisions in their context and in light of the object and purpose of the treaty.

8.44 Moreover, it is not a foregone conclusion that "the purpose and effect of initial investigations and of sunset reviews are the same". The European Communities argues, in respect of the substantive assessments to be made in each, "There are not [sic] differences except that in the case of Article 21.3 there are CVD measures already in force ... [T]his inevitably involves a certain element of prediction based on the facts presented of what would happen if the measures were left to expire"[274] ... "The difference in the wording of the provisions on new investigations and sunset reviews merely reflects the fact that, in the latter case, there is a need to take account of an existing measure in establishing whether the conditions still exist for applying [CVD] measures; the object and purpose of both provisions, however, remains the same"[275]. While it is factually correct that both types of proceedings (or both segments of the proceeding) have the same effect in that they can result in the imposition / continuation of CVDs for a period of five years, whether the purpose of, and the substantive assessment involved in, each is the same is certainly at least debatable.

8.45 The European Communities explains that "[CVD] measures are exceptional, non-MFN measures that are permitted only and so long as it is necessary to offset injurious subsidies. This is true as regards both the original imposition of [CVDs] and their review under the sunset provisions of the *SCM Agreement*[276] ... [T]he provisions of Article 21.3 [of the] *SCM Agreement* relating to continuation of a CVD

---

[273] We note, in this regard, that Article 21.2 – which sets out the obligation of investigating authorities to review the need for the continued imposition of a CVD – contains the phrase "where warranted". The marked difference between the terms of Articles 11.6 and 21.2, on the one hand, and those of Article 21.3, on the other, would support our view that self-initiation of various proceedings – or segments of a proceeding – do not necessarily require fulfilment of the same evidentiary standards, and that this situation was intended by the parties.

[274] Response of the European Communities to Question 7(b) from the Panel.

[275] Response of the European Communities to Question 7(a) from the Panel.

[276] Oral Statement of the European Communities at the First Meeting of the Panel, para. 3.

measure constitute an exception to the general rule which provides that CVD orders should in principle expire after 5 years[277] ... The phrase 'strict interpretation' in this context [reading the text of Article 21.3 to include obligations not explicitly set out therein] simply stands for the proposition that the terms of Article 21.3 have to be interpreted also in light of their object and purpose and in context, which is the entire *SCM Agreement* and, in particular, Articles 11.6, 11.9 and 15.3 thereof. It is further meant to clarify the proposition that a subsidy which is found to be less than 1% in the original investigation – before the entry into force of the *SCM Agreement* – would not benefit from a lenient or relaxed interpretation of Article 21.3 so as to permit its unjustified continuation even if it is likely to be below the 1% *de minimis* rule in the sunset review. This relaxed interpretation is the basic US argument which proposes to read the terms of Article 21.3 in complete isolation of the rest of the Agreement"[278]. In our view, the correct – whether or not "strict" – interpretation of the terms of Article 21.3 would involve precisely the type of analysis proposed by the European Communities. Moreover, the Appellate Body has stated, in *European Communities – Hormones*:

> [M]erely characterising a treaty provision as an "exception" does not by itself justify a "stricter" or " narrower" interpretation of that provision than would be warranted ... by applying the normal rules of treaty interpretation.[279]

8.46 It would seem to us that it is the very analysis characterised by the European Communities as "strict" – which we consider simply to be that outlined in Article 31 of the Vienna Convention – that the European Communities asks us to ignore by focusing on the notion that "the purpose and effect of initial investigations and of sunset reviews are the same" and "the object and purpose of both provisions ... remains the same". With regard to the object and purpose of parties to a treaty and of the treaty, we note that the Appellate Body has stated, in *US – Shrimp*:

> A treaty interpreter must begin with, and focus upon, the text of the particular provision to be interpreted. It is in the words constituting that provision, read in their context, that the object and purpose of the states parties to the treaty must first be sought. Where the meaning imparted by the text itself is equivocal or inconclusive, or where confirmation of the correctness of the reading of the text itself is desired, light from the object and purpose of the treaty as a whole may usefully be sought.[280]

The context of a particular provision and the object and purpose of a treaty – or of the provision at issue – do not override the plain meaning of the text of the provision; rather, the text is to be read *in* its context and *in light of* the object and purpose of the treaty. In sum, we do not find that the text of Article 21.3 lends itself to the interpretation proposed by the European Communities.

8.47 While we do not disagree that application of evidentiary standards to self-initiation of sunset reviews would ensure a certain balance between the disciplines

---

[277] Response of the European Communities to Question 8(a) from the Panel.

[278] Response of the European Communities to Question 8(b) from the Panel.

[279] *EC – Hormones*, Report of the Appellate Body, footnote 250, *supra*, para. 104.

[280] *United States – Import Prohibition of Certain Shrimp and Shrimp Products* ("*US – Shrimp*"), Report of the Appellate Body, WT/DS58/AB/R, adopted 6 November 1998, para. 114.

applicable to investigations and those applicable to sunset reviews, it is nonetheless difficult to conclude on that basis *alone* that the same evidentiary standards apply to self-initiation in both instances. As the Appellate Body has stated, in *EC – Hormones*:

> The fundamental rule of treaty interpretation requires a treaty interpreter to read and interpret the words *actually used* by the agreement under examination, not words the interpreter may feel *should have been used*.[281]

In our opinion, the conclusion to be reached in applying the customary rules of treaty interpretation to Article 21.3 is quite clear. Article 21.3 establishes no requirement that investigating authorities have any evidence before they may self-initiate sunset reviews.

8.48 Seeking to confirm the meaning resulting from the application of Article 31, as permitted by Article 32[282] of the Vienna Convention, we found that the negotiating history of the *SCM Agreement* does not provide guidance in respect of this question. An examination of the work of the Negotiating Group on Subsidies and Countervailing Measures and, in particular, of the discussion of a sunset clause, reveals no reference to evidentiary standards for the initiation of sunset reviews, whether for self-initiation or initiation upon request by the domestic industry.

8.49 We therefore find that no evidentiary standards are applicable to the self-initiation of sunset reviews under Article 21.3.[283] We thus conclude that US CVD law and the accompanying regulations are consistent with the *SCM Agreement* in respect of the automatic self-initiation of sunset reviews, and accordingly reject the European Communities' claim in this regard.

8.50 Further, we note that the European Communities claims that, owing to the lack of consistency with Article 21.3 of the *SCM Agreement* in respect of the application of evidentiary standards to the self-initiation of sunset reviews, US CVD law is also inconsistent with Article 32.5 of the *SCM Agreement* and Article XVI:4 of the WTO Agreement, which provisions require that Members ensure the WTO-conformity of their laws, regulations, and administrative procedures. Having found, however, that US CVD law and the accompanying regulations are consistent with Article 21.3 of the *SCM Agreement* in respect of the application of evidentiary standards to the self-initiation of sunset reviews, we need not, and do not, consider whether US CVD law and the accompanying regulations are inconsistent with Article 32.5 of the *SCM Agreement* and Article XVI:4 of the WTO Agreement.

---

[281] *EC – Hormones*, Report of the Appellate Body, footnote 250, *supra*, para. 181 (emphasis added).

[282] We recall that Article 32 of the Vienna Convention states:

Article 32

Supplementary means of interpretation

Recourse may be had to supplementary means of interpretation, including the preparatory work of the treaty and the circumstances of its conclusion, in order to confirm the meaning resulting from the application of article 31, or to determine the meaning when the interpretation according to article 31:

(a) leaves the meaning ambiguous or obscure; or

(b) leads to a result which is manifestly absurd or unreasonable. ((1969) 8 *International Legal Materials* 679)

[283] Having found that no evidentiary standards apply for the self-initiation of sunset reviews, we need not, and do not, consider the question of what those standards might be.

C. Whether US CVD Law as such and as Applied in the Instant Sunset Review are Inconsistent with the SCM Agreement in Respect of the Application of a de minimis Standard to Sunset Reviews

1. Whether US CVD Law as Such is Inconsistent with the SCM Agreement in Respect of the Application of a de minimis Standard to Sunset Reviews

(a) Arguments of the Parties

(i) European Communities

8.51 In the view of the European Communities, the non-application of a *de minimis* standard to sunset reviews constitutes a violation of Article 21.3 of the *SCM Agreement*. The European Communities considers that a *de minimis* standard is applicable to the likely future rate of subsidisation.

8.52 The European Communities submits that the ordinary meaning of the terms "subsidisation" and "injury" in context, taking also into account the object and purpose of the *SCM Agreement* as a whole, suggests that if there can be no "subsidisation" and "injury" finding in case of a *de minimis* amount of subsidy in an original investigation, the same must hold true *a fortiori* in the case of sunset reviews.[284] The European Communities focuses here on the various paragraphs of Article 21 that contain the word "review", that is, paragraphs 2, 3, and 4. It considers that reviewing the need for a CVD to be continued under Article 21.2 is equivalent to determining whether the original substantive conditions on the basis of which it was initially imposed (subsidisation causing injury) continue to exist.[285] It follows then, for the European Communities, that the same *de minimis* rule, applied in investigations – 1 per cent[286] – must also be applied in reviews under Article 21.2. This analysis, in the opinion of the European Communities, applies all the more so in the context of reviews under Article 21.3.

8.53 The European Communities argues that the *de minimis* provision in the *SCM Agreement* is based on the fact that a subsidy level of less than 1 per cent is presumed not to cause injury. If this subsidy level cannot cause injury in an investigation, it is logically and legally unavoidable, in the view of the European Communities, to conclude that it cannot cause injury in a sunset review.[287] According to the European Communities, holding otherwise would run contrary to the very object and purpose of the *SCM Agreement*, most likely lead to "contradictory results and unjustified protectionism"[288], and violate the text of Articles 21.3 and 21.1 because it would allow

---

[284] First Written Submission of the European Communities, para. 116.

[285] *Ibid.*, para. 111.

[286] We note, in this regard, that the European Communities recognises that this threshold does not apply to developing country Members in investigations, as such Members receive special and differential treatment in the form of higher *de minimis* thresholds. It considers that "[t]he higher *de minimis* thresholds for developing countries are equally applicable to initial investigations and reviews examining the need for continued imposition of the CVD (under Article 21.2) and sunset reviews (under Article 21.3)" (Response of the European Communities to Question 1(d) from the Panel).

[287] First Written Submission of the European Communities, para. 115.

[288] *Ibid.*, para. 116.

the continuation of CVDs for five more years "without there being any real need to counter subsidisation which is likely to cause injury"[289].

(ii) United States

8.54 The United States submits that there is no *de minimis* standard for sunset reviews, that nothing in Article 21.3 or elsewhere in the *SCM Agreement* sets a *de minimis* standard for sunset reviews, and that a contextual analysis of Article 21.3 in light of the object and purpose of the *SCM Agreement* provides no support for the European Communities' *de minimis* claims.

8.55 In particular, argues the United States, footnote 52 states that the mere continued existence of a subsidy programme could warrant maintaining the duty beyond the five-year point, even if the amount of the subsidy was currently zero, because subsidisation may be likely to recur absent the discipline of the duty.[290] The United States submits that the European Communities seems to think that footnote 52 serves no other purpose than to make a point about administrative reviews. If that is so, continues the United States, then why did the Members include footnote 52 in Article 21.3, the provision governing sunset reviews? The United States considers that footnote 52 means that the current level of subsidisation is not decisive as to whether subsidisation is likely to recur, and accepting the European Communities' claim in respect of a *de minimis* standard in the context of sunset reviews would render footnote 52 meaningless.[291]

8.56 The United States also submits that the focus of sunset reviews is future behaviour and, thus, mathematical certainty or precision as to the exact amount of likely future subsidisation is not necessarily practicable and certainly not required.[292]

(b) Findings of the Panel

8.57 Again, the overarching question before us is whether a specific obligation applicable to CVD investigations is also applicable to sunset reviews. In particular, we must consider whether, applying the customary rules of treaty interpretation – set out above (*See* para. 8.25 and footnote 282, *supra*) – to Article 21.3, we should consider implied in that provision the *de minimis* standard of Article 11.9.[293] In other

---

289 *Ibid.*

290 First Written Submission of the United States, para. 81.

291 Second Written Submission of the United States, para. 12.

292 First Written Submission of the United States, para. 70.

293 We do not understand the European Communities to be alleging a violation of Article 11.9, but of Article 21.3, of the *SCM Agreement*. In this regard, we note that the European Communities argues that "an interpretation of the terms of Article 21.3 should be made in context and in the light of the object and purpose of Article 21.3 and of the *SCM Agreement*. Articles 21.1, 11.9, 15, and 10 provide relevant context and help define its object and purpose. Such an interpretation ... requires that the 1 [per cent] *de minimis* level of Article 11.9 should be *implied*, and hence applied, also to investigations and determinations made in sunset reviews" (Response of the European Communities to Question 47 from the Panel (emphasis added)).

Further, the European Communities "objects to the [United States'] suggestion to use only the phrase 'Article 11.9 itself applies to sunset reviews'" (Comments of the European Communities on Request of the United States for Interim Review, para. 3). Indeed, the European Communities argues that it "has taken particular care to explain that there is an omission in Article 21.3 and that only a systematic interpretation can fill up [sic] this gap by *implying* the *de minimis* standard of Article 11.9" (Comments of the European Communities on Request of the United States for Interim Review, para. 3 (emphasis added)). Nor could the European Communities successfully allege a violation of

words, is the European Communities correct in arguing that, as reviewing the need for continuation of a CVD past the initial five-year period (involving consideration of whether expiry of that CVD would be likely to lead to continuation or recurrence of subsidisation and injury) is equivalent to considering the need for an original duty (involving consideration of whether subsidisation is causing or threatens to cause injury), it follows that the same *de minimis* standard must apply to sunset reviews as to investigations?[294]

8.58 We recall that Article 21.3 reads:

> Notwithstanding the provisions of paragraphs 1 and 2, any definitive [CVD] shall be terminated on a date not later than five years from its imposition (or from the date of the most recent review under paragraph 2 if that review has covered both subsidisation and injury, or under this paragraph), unless the authorities determine, in a review initiated before that date on their own initiative or upon a duly substantiated request made by or on behalf of the domestic industry within a reasonable period of time prior to that date, that the expiry of the duty would be likely to lead to continuation or recurrence of subsidisation and injury.[52] The duty may remain in force pending the outcome of such a review.

Article 11.9. Article 11 is entitled "Initiation and Subsequent Investigation", and clearly deals with investigations, such as that term is distinguished from reviews by the Agreement. This is also made clear in the text of Article 11.9 itself, which refers to investigations. We therefore consider whether Article 21.3 contains by implication the same type of obligation as Article 11.9, and whether the United States has violated Article 21.3 in this respect.

[294] We note that US CVD law and the accompanying regulations require the application of a 1 per cent *de minimis* standard to CVD investigations and a 0.5 per cent *de minimis* standard in reviews, including sunset reviews. Section 703(b)(4)(a) of the Tariff Act provides:

> In making a determination under this subsection, the administering authority shall disregard any *de minimis* countervailable subsidy. For purposes of the preceding sentence, a countervailable subsidy is *de minimis* if the administering authority determines that the aggregate of the net countervailable subsidies is less than 1 percent *ad valorem* or the equivalent specific rate for the subject merchandise (19 USC Section 1673a(b)(4)(B)).

Section 351.106(c)(1) of the *Sunset Regulations* provides:

> In making any determination other than a preliminary or final ... [CVD] determination in an investigation ..., the Secretary will treat as *de minimis* any ... countervailable subsidy rate that is less than 0.5 percent *ad valorem*, or the equivalent specific rate.

The SAA accompanying the URAA explains:

> The *de minimis* requirements of Articles 11.9, 27.10, and 27.11 of the Subsidies Agreement are applicable only to initial CVD investigations. Thus, under section 705(a)(3) these standards are not applicable to reviews of CVD orders. In such reviews, the Administration intends that Commerce will continue its present practice of waiving the collection of estimated deposits if the deposit rate is below 0.5 % *ad valorem*, the existing regulatory standard for *de minimis* (Exhibit EC-16, pp. 938-939).

We further note that the United States submits that "[t]he statute itself does not set forth the *de minimis* standard for reviews, but the [Statement of Administrative Action] clarifies the intent of Congress and the Administration that [the DOC] continue to apply to reviews the pre-URAA standard of 0.5 per cent *ad valorem*" (First Written Submission of the United States, para. 13).

> [52] When the amount of the [CVD] is assessed on a retrospective basis, a finding in the most recent assessment proceeding that no duty is to be levied shall not by itself require the authorities to terminate the definitive duty.

We recognise, at the outset, that nothing in the text of Article 21.3 specifically provides that the *de minimis* standard applicable to investigations is also applicable to sunset reviews. For the same reasons that we could not conclude on the basis of silence alone that the evidentiary standards of Article 11.6 necessarily do not apply to sunset reviews (*See* paragraphs 8.27-8.30, *supra*), however, we cannot conclude on the basis of silence alone that the *de minimis* standard of Article 11.9 necessarily does not apply to sunset reviews. Accordingly, we believe that we must consider the context of Article 21.3 – that is, provisions of the *SCM Agreement* other than Article 21.3 – and the object and purpose of the *SCM Agreement* in reaching a conclusion. In particular, we are of the view that we must interpret Article 21.3 in respect of the *de minimis* standard set out in Article 11.9 in the context of the same complex framework of rights and obligations as we did Article 21.3 in respect of the evidentiary standards set out in Article 11.6 (*See* paragraphs 8.31-8.33, *supra*).

8.59 We now examine Article 11.9, the *de minimis* standard of which the European Communities argues is implied in Article 21.3, and which provides:

> An application under paragraph 1 shall be rejected and an investigation shall be terminated promptly as soon as the authorities concerned are satisfied that there is not sufficient evidence of either subsidisation or of injury to justify proceeding with the case. There shall be immediate termination in cases where the amount of a subsidy is *de minimis*, or where the volume of subsidised imports, actual or potential, or the injury, is negligible. For the purpose of this paragraph, the amount of the subsidy shall be considered to be *de minimis* if the subsidy is less than 1 per cent ad valorem.

Again, we recognise, at the outset, that nothing in the text of the provision provides for its *de minimis* standard to be implied in Article 21.3. What is clear from this language, however, is that a *de minimis* subsidy cannot be countervailed, and that, upon a finding of a *de minimis* subsidy, the Agreement mandates but one outcome. Investigating authorities must not only terminate the investigation, but they must do so immediately. The terms of the provision are unequivocal. Such mandatory ("shall") and strong ("immediate") language would suggest that the drafters had an important consideration in mind in drafting this provision, reflected in the precise choice of words. In particular, the mandatory nature and strong language of the provision convey, in our view, that the drafters sought a particular outcome, to protect exporters under investigation and prevent trade harassment through continuation of an investigation of a *de minimis* subsidy.

8.60 Let us first consider the ordinary meaning of the Latin phrase "*de minimis*", which is defined in law dictionaries as "lacking significance or importance: so minor as to be disregarded"[295]. In the context of the *SCM Agreement*, we take this to mean that a *de minimis* level of subsidy lacks significance or importance because the effects attributable to it are so small as not to be material. In this regard, it is useful to consider the rationale for the application of a *de minimis* standard to investigations,

---

[295] Merriam-Webster's Dictionary of Law, Merriam-Webster, Inc., p. 131.

as reflected in a Note by the Secretariat prepared in April 1987 for the Uruguay Round Negotiating Group on Subsidies and Countervailing Measures. This note reads in relevant part:

> There are two alternative (and not mutually exclusive) theoretical justifications for the *de minimis* concept.
>
> - The first view holds that [CVD] actions and measures may be taken only when the trade distorting effect of the subsidy and its effects on the industry in the importing country so require. Thus, no action should be taken where it would be clearly out of proportion to the objective sought, or as Article 2:12 states, 'where the effect of the subsidy on the industry in the importing country is not such as to cause material injury'.
>
> - The second theory treats the issue of *de minimis* subsidy as a completely separate issue from the determination of injury in an investigation. If it can be established that the totality of subsidies on the product investigated are minimal (so small per unit that they are practically non-existent), the investigating authorities may determine that, as Article 2:12 states, 'no subsidy exists'. Thus, as the maxim states, '*de minimis non curat lex*': the law does not take notice of minimal matters.[296]

While it is not known which of the two rationales, if not both ("not mutually exclusive"), served as a basis for Article 11.9, the language of that provision suggests to us that it was the first rationale that was the basis for, or was at least paramount in, the drafting of that provision. Were the basis of Article 11.9, either solely or principally, simple administrative convenience, that would be a matter for investigating authorities to decide. There would arguably be no need for the Agreement to address the consequences of *de minimis* subsidisation. In that case, Article 11.9 might *permit* or *encourage* authorities to terminate an investigation in case of a finding of *de minimis* subsidisation, but would not need to *require* it, and immediately upon such finding.

8.61 Administrative convenience where a *de minimis* subsidy is concerned is, after all, a question of individual Members' policies vis-à-vis trade remedies and vis-à-vis allocation of resources to their trade remedy regimes, issues over which they should arguably have discretion. Why *require* Members to avail themselves of administrative convenience? We note, in this regard, that the above-cited discussion of the rationale of non-injurious subsidisation uses the phrase "no action should be taken" – suggesting the *desirability* of such an outcome – while discussion of the rationale of administrative convenience uses the phrase "the investigating authorities may determine" – suggesting the *possibility* of such an outcome. The clear difference between the two phrases would support our reasoning that the drafters considered a *de minimis* subsidy to be non-injurious, as the language of Article 11.9 mirrors the former phrase, that relating to the rationale of non-injurious subsidisation. For the foregoing reasons, we are of the view that the sole or principal rationale for the *de minimis* standard set out in Article 11.9 is that a *de minimis* subsidy is considered to be non-injurious.

8.62 We note that, in any event, both the rationale of non-injurious subsidisation and that of administrative convenience would be as relevant in the context of sunset

---

[296] MTN.GNG/NG10/W/4, p. 2 (emphasis in original).

reviews as in that of investigations. We do not see how it would be reasonable to hold the view, on the one hand, that a rate of subsidy that would be deemed to be non-injurious in investigations should be found to be so in sunset reviews as well, but not the view, on the other hand, that a rate of subsidy that would be found to be minimal in investigations should be deemed to be so in sunset reviews as well. In other words, we see no particular distinction between the two rationales that would suggest that, depending on which one served as the basis for Article 11.9, a *de minimis* standard might *not* apply to sunset reviews.

8.63 We note that Article 11.9 sets out certain other grounds for termination of CVD proceedings as well: (i) insufficient evidence of either subsidisation or of injury; (ii) negligible volume of subsidised imports; and (iii) negligible injury. It would seem clear to us that all three bases for termination are fundamentally grounded in the notion of, and seek to limit CVD proceedings to cases of, injurious subsidisation. We consider that all grounds for termination of CVD proceedings – including *de minimis* subsidisation – link expressly with the purpose of CVDs and with the object and purpose of the *SCM Agreement* as set out in Article VI of the GATT 1994. The recurrent theme, in our view, is that CVD proceedings serve to counter injurious subsidisation and therefore may not continue if injurious subsidisation does not (or is not likely to) exist. The nature of the other bases set out in Article 11.9 for termination of CVD proceedings supports our view that the rationale for the *de minimis* standard is that relating to non-injurious subsidisation.

8.64 It would also seem to us that the lack of reference to the term "*de minimis*" in Article 27.10 of the *SCM Agreement* – which sets out special and differential treatment for developing countries – is further recognition of the rationale that the *de minimis* standard relates to non-injurious subsidisation. As it is not possible to have different *de minimis* levels depending on the source of the subsidised imports, Article 27.10 simply provides for special and differential treatment for developing country Members. In this regard, we note that Article 11.9 includes the following sentence:

> For the purpose of this paragraph, the amount of the subsidy shall be considered to be *de minimis* if the subsidy is less than 1 per cent ad valorem.

The use of the phrase "[f]or the purpose of this paragraph" reflects, in our opinion, a desire to clarify that the termination requirement is triggered by a 1 per cent subsidy under this paragraph, as opposed to the differing percentage under Article 27.10. Accordingly, in our opinion, the language of Article 11.9 does not prevent its *de minimis* standard from being implied in Article 21.3.

8.65 It is in light of this rationale of non-injurious subsidisation for the inclusion of the *de minimis* standard and the requirement to terminate if *de minimis* subsidisation is found that we must address the European Communities' claim that such a standard is implied in Article 21.3. Given the framework of disciplines that governs the imposition of CVDs and the role of the *SCM Agreement* in ensuring that CVDs do not unjustifiably impede international trade, we find it difficult to see how *de minimis* rate of likely subsidisation could be considered injurious at the stage of sunset review and continuation of a CVD, when the same rate is considered non-injurious at the stage of investigation and imposition of a CVD.

8.66 An interpretation of Article 21.3 under which the *de minimis* standard set out in Article 11.9 does not apply to sunset reviews would, in our view, have serious implications for the operation of the *SCM Agreement* and the framework of disciplines it sets out in conjunction with Article VI of the GATT 1994. To hold that a threshold of *injurious* subsidisation that applies for the first five years of the life of a CVD becomes inapplicable for the remainder of its life, should the CVD be continued, would seem to us to run counter to the object and purpose of the Agreement, which is to provide Members a framework within which to offset *injurious* subsidisation.

8.67 In particular, we believe it would pave the way for Members to maintain CVDs indefinitely, when CVDs are typically measures which would otherwise be WTO-inconsistent and are therefore only permitted upon fulfilment of certain conditions set out in the *SCM Agreement*: subsidisation, injury, and causation. We fail to see why the threshold of injurious subsidisation – which we consider to be an important substantive criterion – would become inapplicable simply by virtue of the age of the CVD. We note, in this regard, that if an investigating authority were to revoke the CVD, but subsequently find the need to initiate a new investigation on the concerned product, this threshold would once again become applicable. A suspension of the *de minimis* standard that is triggered solely by the fact that the CVD is five years old does not, in our opinion, reconcile with the fundamental rationale of the *SCM Agreement* and thereby negates the operation of the Agreement.

8.68 One of the objectives of the *SCM Agreement* is to discipline the use of CVDs by Members through the establishment of a set of rules by which WTO Members must abide. Investigating authorities would therefore have to be bound by the substantive rules of the Agreement, including following imposition of a CVD. Under the US view, no *de minimis* standard would be implied in Article 21.2 either. In other words, the moment a CVD is imposed, no *de minimis* standard applies. A suspension of the *de minimis* standard is therefore triggered not by the fact that the CVD is five years old, but by its mere existence, whatever its age. We find it difficult to reconcile the suspension of a criterion relating to non-injurious subsidisation in the context of a regulatory framework that seeks to limit the use of CVDs to cases of injurious subsidisation.

8.69 Equally, as discussed above, an interpretation of Article 21.3 – on the basis of a literal reading of Article 21.3 – under which the *de minimis* standard set out in Article 11.9 does not apply to sunset reviews would render certain provisions of the *SCM Agreement* inapplicable to sunset reviews so as to undermine the object and purpose of the Agreement. Such an interpretation would also yield irrational results in respect of other provisions of the Agreement.

8.70 As earlier discussed, Article 31 of the Vienna Convention does not, in our view, limit us to a literal reading of the provision in question. Were such a reading to be required, provisions such as Article 15.3 – which deals with the circumstances in which imports may be cumulated for purposes of injury determinations – and Article 19 – which deals with the imposition and collection of CVDs – would be limited in ways that would negatively affect the operation of the Agreement, particularly with respect to sunset reviews, something that cannot have been intended by the drafters.

8.71 For the reasons outlined above, we consider equally persuasive the case of Article 21.1, which reads:

> A [CVD] shall remain in force only as long as and to the extent necessary to counteract subsidisation which is causing injury.

Were this provision to be read literally, the words "is causing injury" would suggest that a CVD could only remain in place, including under Article 21.3, where there is likelihood of *continuation* of subsidisation and injury, not *recurrence*. The notion of recurrence contained in Article 21.3 therefore has to be implied in Article 21.1, or that notion would be rendered meaningless. Finally, Article 32.3, if read literally, would apply only to investigations and reviews initiated pursuant to applications from the domestic industry, and not initiated on an ex officio basis. Again, this cannot be the case. These several instances of provisions in the Agreement that, if read literally, would yield irrational results, confirm our view that we are not limited to a literal reading of the text of Article 21.3.

8.72 We note that the United States is of the view that there is no obligation under the *SCM Agreement* to quantify an amount of subsidisation in the context of sunset reviews: "Indeed, just the fact that it is necessary to ask the question as to the relevant time period demonstrates that there was no agreement to include a *de minimis* standard – these are the types of questions that would have had to have been asked and negotiated at the time"[297]. We disagree. Nor are we persuaded by the US argument that, as there is no obligation to quantify subsidisation in sunset reviews, there can be no obligation to apply a *de minimis* standard. We consider that, because there is an obligation to apply a *de minimis* standard, and this cannot be done unless subsidisation is quantified, there is a consequential obligation to quantify the likely future rate of subsidisation.

8.73 The United States submits that the focus of a sunset review is the future behaviour of foreign exporters, and there is therefore no need or legal obligation to quantify the amount of subsidy during such reviews.[298] We note also the United States' argument that "nothing in the *SCM Agreement requires* a consideration of the magnitude of subsidisation in determining the likelihood of continuation or recurrence of subsidisation and injury"[299]. We consider, however, that investigating authorities are required to assess the rate at which subsidisation is likely to continue or recur for purposes of their assessment of likelihood of continuation or recurrence of injury which arises from the likely continuation or recurrence of subsidisation. Article 15 of the *SCM Agreement* sets out the substantive assessment that must go into making a determination of injury:

> A determination of injury for purposes of Article VI of GATT 1994 shall be based on positive evidence and involve an objective examination of both (a) the volume of the subsidised imports and the effect of the subsidised imports on prices in the domestic market for like products and (b) the consequent impact of these imports on the domestic producers of such products.[300]

Further, Article 15.5 states, in relevant part:

> It must be demonstrated that the subsidised imports are, through the effects[47] of subsidies, causing injury within the meaning of this Agreement.
>
> ---
>
> [47] As set forth in paragraphs 2 and 4.

---

[297] Response of the United States to Question 45 from the Panel.

[298] Response of the United States to Question 1(a) from the Panel.

[299] Response of the United States to Question 45 from the Panel.

[300] Footnote deleted.

We simply do not see how these provisions of Article 15 can be given meaning in an assessment of likelihood of continuation or recurrence of subsidisation and injury without assessment of a likely rate of subsidisation.[301]

8.74 The United States submits that "one could never *calculate* a future rate of subsidisation for obvious reasons, although it may be possible to infer a future rate based on past rates (which is in essence what the [US DOC] does under US law)"[302]. The European Communities, on the other hand, argues that "subsidisation does not exist in the abstract, and quantification of the rate at which continuation or recurrence of subsidisation is likely to continue or recur in the future should always be feasible"[303]. We agree. While we certainly acknowledge the difficulty of calculating a *precise* likely rate and we agree with the United States that it is perhaps better described as "inferred" rather than "calculated", we are of the view that quantification of the future rate of subsidisation is entirely feasible. We do not, in other words, see the difficulty of assessing a likely rate of subsidisation as being great enough to suggest that a *de minimis* standard could not possibly have been intended to apply to sunset reviews.

8.75 The issue of assessment of the rate of subsidisation brings up the related issue of footnote 52 to the *SCM Agreement*, which reads:

> When the amount of the [CVD] is assessed on a retrospective basis, a finding in the most recent assessment proceeding that no duty is to be levied shall not by itself require the authorities to terminate the definitive duty.

We note the United States' argument that the location of this footnote in the *SCM Agreement* – in a provision governing sunset reviews – indicates that it is relevant to the present question and suggests that no *de minimis* standard is applicable to sunset reviews. We note also the European Communities' response that this footnote refers only to duty assessment proceedings and therefore sheds no light on the possible existence of a *de minimis* standard as being applicable to sunset reviews. In our view, under both interpretations, footnote 52 has no implications for the question before us. We do not see how the results of duty assessment proceedings – which establish a level of duty for a prior period – could be *dispositive* of the likelihood of continuation or recurrence of subsidisation or of the rate at which subsidisation is likely to continue or recur. Thus, there is no inconsistency, in our opinion, between footnote 52 and the requirement to apply a *de minimis* standard to sunset reviews.

8.76 When asked by the Panel, supposing application of a *de minimis* standard to sunset reviews, whether this standard would be based on (i) the rate of subsidisation during the period of application of the CVD, (ii) the rate of subsidisation at the time of sunset review, or (iii) the rate at which subsidisation is likely to continue or recur, the European Communities argues that "[t]he rate that should determine the outcome of a sunset review is ... the rate likely to continue or recur if the CVD measure were allowed to expire"[304]. The United States, on the other hand, responds that "all of these options might inform a determination of the likelihood of continuation or recurrence

[301] We note, in this regard, that the US DOC is required, under US law, to send to the ITC the net countervailable subsidy that is likely to prevail if the CVD order is revoked (*See* Section 1675(a)(b)(3) of the Tariff Act (Exhibit EC-13)).

[302] Response of the United States to Question 45 from the Panel (emphasis in original).

[303] Response of the European Communities to Question 45 from the Panel.

[304] *Ibid.*

of subsidisation – but they just as easily might not"[305]. While we accept that, depending on the facts of the case before the investigating authorities, one, two, or all of the above-mentioned rates might be relevant to an *assessment of the likelihood of continuation or recurrence of subsidisation*, there is no doubt in our minds that the rate to which the *de minimis standard* is to be applied in sunset reviews is the likely future rate of subsidisation.

8.77 Whatever the rate of subsidisation at the time of sunset review, any *de minimis* standard could not be applicable to that rate, as such a practice would encourage deliberate diminution of subsidies at the time of sunset review with a view to ensuring that the rate falls below the *de minimis* threshold. Nor could a *de minimis* standard apply to the past rate of subsidisation – that during the period of application of the CVD – as that would mean that non-subsidisation during that period is determinative of the likelihood of continuation or recurrence, which cannot be the case. Such an interpretation would seriously call into question the notion of recurrence contained in Article 21.3. Of course this is not to suggest that the past level of subsidisation is not a relevant consideration in an assessment of likelihood of continuation or recurrence; it is without doubt a relevant factor in such an assessment. But the existence or absence of past subsidisation cannot be dispositive of the likelihood of continuation or recurrence of subsidisation. Accordingly, the *de minimis* standard applicable to sunset reviews could only be based on the rate at which subsidisation is likely to continue or recur. This also reflects the purpose and substance of a sunset review, i. e., an assessment of the likelihood of continuation or recurrence of subsidisation and injury.

8.78 The United States cites the decision of the Panel in *United States – DRAMS* as support for its argument that no *de minimis* standard is required by the Agreement in sunset reviews.[306] The Panel in that case held that the *de minimis* standard contained in Article 5.8 of the AD Agreement – the parallel provision to Article 11.9 of the *SCM Agreement* – did not apply beyond the investigative phase.[307] It is important to note, however, that that case did not address the question of whether the *de minimis* standard was applicable to sunset reviews, or even in reviews in general. Rather, the *United States – DRAMS* case addressed the question of whether a *de minimis* standard was applicable to duty assessment procedures under Article 9.3 of the AD Agreement. The retrospective calculation of a duty payable arguably has no relationship with the duration of the duty or the possible continuation of the duty. Retrospective calculation is a method of calculation used by some Members for purposes of calculating the amount of duty payable *during* the period of application of the duty. The issue before us is whether the *de minimis* standard is applicable to sunset reviews as it is to investigations. Calculating the amount of duty to be collected under an order which is not in and of itself being reviewed is different from reviewing whether an order may be continued. At least in principle, any amount of dumping (or subsidy) should lead to a collection of that amount of duty. That any, or less than the *de minimis*, level of subsidy should justify continuation of a CVD order would undermine the object and purpose as well as operation of the *SCM Agreement*.

8.79 In sum, we consider that the rationale for the *de minimis* standard set out in Article 11.9 is clearly that CVDs are to be used to counter injurious subsidisation,

305 Response of the United States to Question 45 from the Panel.

306 First Written Submission of the United States, para. 73.

307 *US – DRAMS*, Report of the Panel, footnote 247, *supra*, para. 6.87.

and the threshold set out in this provision demarcates the level below which subsidisation is deemed to be so small as to be non-injurious for purposes of the imposition of CVDs. Having found this to be the case, and having established that one of the objects and purposes of the *SCM Agreement* is to regulate the imposition of CVDs and to create a disciplinary framework therefor, we are of the view that the *de minimis* standard must be applicable to sunset reviews as it is to investigations. Finding otherwise would compromise the very object and purpose of the *SCM Agreement* and the disciplinary framework that the drafters sought to create through the Agreement.

8.80 We therefore find that the *de minimis* standard of Article 11.9 is implied in Article 21.3. We thus conclude that US CVD law and the accompanying regulations are inconsistent with the *SCM Agreement* in respect of the application of a *de minimis* standard to sunset reviews, and accordingly grant the European Communities' claim in this regard.

8.81 Further, we note that the European Communities claims that, owing to inconsistency with Article 21.3 of the *SCM Agreement* in respect of the *de minimis* standard applicable to sunset reviews, US CVD law is also inconsistent with Article 32.5 of the *SCM Agreement* and Article XVI:4 of the WTO Agreement, which provisions require that Members ensure the WTO-conformity of their laws, regulations, and administrative procedures. On the basis of our finding that US CVD law and the accompanying regulations are inconsistent with Article 21.3 of the *SCM Agreement* in respect of the *de minimis* standard applicable to sunset reviews, we find that US CVD law and the accompanying regulations are also inconsistent with Article 32.5 of the *SCM Agreement* and Article XVI:4 of the WTO Agreement, and accordingly grant the European Communities' claim in this regard.

2. *Whether US CVD Law as Applied in the Instant Sunset Review is Inconsistent with the SCM Agreement in Respect of the Application of a de minimis Standard to Sunset Reviews*

(a) Arguments of the Parties

(i) European Communities

8.82 The European Communities considers that the United States violated the *SCM Agreement* by failing to apply to the instant sunset review the *de minimis* standard applicable to investigations. The European Communities indicates that the United States, despite finding that the subsidy rate likely to prevail would be 0.53 per cent, nevertheless continued the CVD. The European Communities submits that, for the reasons stated above (*See* Section 0, *supra*), this threshold is not appropriate, and that since 0.53 per cent is below the 1 per cent *de minimis* level which *should* apply to sunset reviews, the United States was in breach of Article 21.3, in conjunction with Article 11.9, in continuing the CVD on carbon steel.[308]

(ii) United States

8.83 As stated above (*See* Section 0, *supra*), the United States argues that no *de minimis* is applicable to sunset reviews under Article 21.3 of the *SCM Agreement*.

[308] First Written Submission of the European Communities, para. 119.

The United States also asserts that the fact that it has in its domestic law a *de minimis* provision for sunset reviews is legally irrelevant because Members are free to go beyond their obligations under the Agreement.[309] In the view of the United States, therefore, the determination of the US DOC in the instant sunset review was not inconsistent with the Agreement in this respect.

(b) Findings of the Panel

8.84 We note the US argument, in respect of the previous claim of the European Communities, that applying the customary rules of treaty interpretation, the Panel should find that there is no *de minimis* standard applicable to sunset reviews in the *SCM Agreement* and, therefore, the United States' application of a 0.5 per cent *de minimis* standard in sunset reviews does not constitute a violation of its obligations under the *SCM Agreement*.[310] We note that the United States accordingly applied this standard – and not the 1 per cent threshold set out in Article 11.9 – in the instant sunset review.[311] Having found that the *de minimis* standard set out in Article 11.9 is applicable to sunset reviews and that US CVD law is inconsistent with the *SCM Agreement* in this respect, we find that the United States violated the *SCM Agreement* by failing to apply such a *de minimis* standard to the instant sunset review.

D. Whether US Law as such and as Applied in the Instant Sunset Review are Inconsistent with the SCM Agreement in Respect of the Investigating Authority's Obligation to Determine the Likelihood of Continuation or Recurrence of Subsidisation in a Sunset Review

1. Whether US Law as such is Inconsistent with the SCM Agreement in Respect of the Investigating Authority's Obligation to Determine the Likelihood of Continuation or Recurrence of Subsidisation in a Sunset Review

(a) Arguments of the Parties

(i) European Communities

8.85 The European Communities submits that US law as such is inconsistent with Article 21.3 of the *SCM Agreement* in respect of the investigating authorities' obligation to "determine" the likelihood of continuation or recurrence of subsidisation in a sunset review. In particular, the European Communities asserts that Section 751(c) of the Act, as complemented by Section 752 and by US regulations and administrative practices, runs counter to the requirements of Article 21.3 in this respect.[312]

8.86 According to the European Communities, Article 21.3 imposes a positive obligation on the investigating authorities to find whether subsidisation continues to exist or not.[313] This, argues the European Communities, needs to be a new, proper determination.[314] In the view of the European Communities therefore an investigating

309 First Written Submission of the United States, para. 83.
310 First Written Submission of the United States, para. 87.

312 First Written Submission of the European Communities, para. 76.
313 *Ibid.*, para. 68.
314 Second Written Submission of the European Communities, para. 29.

authority in a sunset review is required to play an active role in the process of gathering facts that the authority will use in its likelihood analysis.[315]

8.87 With respect to the determination of the likelihood of subsidisation, the European Communities argues that the same factors used by an investigating authority in an original CVD investigation in a retrospective manner should be analysed prospectively in the sunset review.[316] According to the European Communities, these factors are those set out in Articles 11, 12 and 15 of the *SCM Agreement*. However, the European Communities argues that the range of factors to be considered as part of the analysis of the likelihood of continuation or recurrence of subsidisation should be decided on a case by case basis, depending on the type of subsidy involved.[317]

(ii) United States

8.88 The United States points out that what an investigating authority is required to do in a sunset review under Article 21.3 is to determine whether subsidisation would be likely to continue or recur without the discipline of the duty in place.[318] This analysis, in the view of the United States, requires a consideration of future rather than present circumstances. Therefore the analysis required under Article 21.3, according to the United States, is prospective in nature.[319] Thus, in the view of the United States, there is no contradiction between the provisions of the *SCM Agreement* and US law in this respect.

b) Findings of the Panel

(i) Requirements of Article 21.3 of the *SCM Agreement* in respect of the investigating authority's obligation to determine the likelihood of continuation or recurrence of subsidisation in a sunset review

8.89 We now proceed to our analysis of Article 21.3 of the *SCM Agreement* in order to address the obligation to "determine" the likelihood of continuation or recurrence of subsidisation in a sunset review. The text of Article 21.3 reads:

> Notwithstanding the provisions of paragraphs 1 and 2, any definitive [CVD] shall be terminated on a date not later than five years from its imposition (or from the date of the most recent review under paragraph 2 if that review has covered both subsidisation and injury, or under this paragraph), unless the authorities determine, in a review initiated before that date on their own initiative or upon a duly substantiated request made by or on behalf of the domestic industry within a reasonable period of time prior to that date, that the expiry of the duty would be likely to lead to continuation or recurrence of subsidisation

315 First Written Submission of the European Communities, para. 71.

316 Second Written Submission of the European Communities, para. 32.

317 *Ibid.*

318 First Written Submission of the United States, para. 92.

319 First Oral Statement of the United States, para. 9.

and injury. The duty may remain in force pending the outcome of such a review.[320]

8.90 In accordance with customary rules of treaty interpretation as reflected in Article 31 of the Vienna Convention, we base our interpretation of Article 21.3 on its text read in context and in the light of the object and purpose of the *SCM Agreement*. Accordingly, we shall first consider the ordinary meaning of the word "determine". "Determine" is defined, *inter alia*, as "settle or decide (a dispute, controversy, etc., or a sentence, conclusion, issue, etc.) as a judge or arbiter"[321]. This definition would seem to fit the usage in Article 21.3, which requires termination of a CVD unless the authorities "determine ... that the expiry of the duty would be likely to lead to continuation or recurrence of subsidisation and injury".

8.91 Article 21.3 reflects the application of the general rule set out in Article 21.1 – that a CVD shall remain in place only as long as necessary – in the specific instance where five years have elapsed since the imposition of a CVD. Article 21.2 reflects the same general rule in a different circumstance, when a reasonable period has elapsed since the imposition of the duty, and it is deemed necessary to review the need for the continued imposition of the duty. We also note that one of the principal objects of the *SCM Agreement* is to regulate the imposition of CVD measures. Article 21.3 effectuates that purpose by providing that after five years, a CVD should be terminated unless the investigating authorities determine that there is a likelihood of continuation or recurrence of subsidisation and injury.

8.92 The question we must consider next is what it means to "determine" that subsidisation is likely to continue or recur.[322] In our opinion, although there is no specific language in the *SCM Agreement* to that effect, it goes without saying that any determination made by investigating authorities under the *SCM Agreement* must be properly substantiated in order for that determination to be legally justified. In this regard, the Appellate Body has stated in *US – Lamb*:

---

[320] Footnote deleted.

[321] The New Shorter Oxford English Dictionary, Oxford University Press, p. 651.

[322] The European Communities states that it is not challenging the injury determination of the US ITC *per se* in this dispute, but that it is doing so *as part of its claim regarding the application of a de minimis standard* (Oral Statement of the European Communities at the First Meeting of the Panel, footnote 27 (emphasis added)). The United States argues that the European Communities has not raised the claim of "non-injurious subsidisation" in its request for consultations nor in its request for the establishment. Therefore, according to the United States, the European Communities' "new claim with respect to non-injurious subsidization is not within the Panel's terms of reference, but instead is at most an argument in support of the [European Communities'] claim" (Comments of the United States on the Response of the European Communities to Question 50 from the Panel, paras. 10-11). We consider – and both parties agree that – the European Communities' argument relating to non-injurious subsidisation is an additional argument in support of its claim that the *de minimis* rule set forth in Article 11.9 also applies in sunset reviews. Therefore, in our view, the argument of the European Communities regarding non-injurious subsidisation raises no question in respect of the scope of our terms of reference because we are not, in this dispute, concerned with the question of whether the ITC properly determined that expiry of the duty was likely to lead to continuation or recurrence of injury, and do not address that issue.

> [C]ompetent authorities must have a sufficient factual basis to allow them to draw reasoned and adequate conclusions concerning the situation of the "domestic industry".[323]

We recognise that the Appellate Body's statement refers to the basis of an injury determination in a safeguard investigation. Yet, as far as the adequacy of the factual basis for a determination is concerned, we see no reason to distinguish between injury determinations in a safeguard investigation and a determination of the likelihood of continuation or recurrence of subsidisation in a CVD sunset review.

8.93 We also note the decision of the Panel in *US – DRAMS* in which the Panel stated:

> Accordingly, we must assess the essential character of the necessity involved in cases of continued imposition of an anti-dumping duty. We note that the necessity of the measure is a function of certain objective conditions being in place, *i.e.* whether circumstances require continued imposition of the anti-dumping duty. That being so, such continued imposition must, in our view, be essentially dependent on, and therefore assignable to, a foundation of positive evidence that circumstances demand it. In other words, the need for the continued imposition of the duty must be demonstrable on the basis of the evidence adduced.[324]

Although the decision of the Panel was made as part of a review under Article 11.2 of the AD Agreement we believe this excerpt provides helpful guidance for our case relative to the adequacy of the factual basis for a determination.

8.94 Based on the two foregoing decisions, we consider that a determination of likelihood under Article 21.3 must rest on a sufficient factual basis.

8.95 An investigating authority's determination of the likelihood of continuation or recurrence of subsidisation should rest on the evaluation of the evidence that it has gathered during the original investigation, the intervening reviews and finally the sunset review. In our view, a likelihood analysis based on this evidentiary framework would be consistent with the requirements of Article 21.3.

8.96 In our view, one of the components of the likelihood analysis in a sunset review under Article 21.3 is an assessment of the likely rate of subsidisation. We do not consider, however, that an investigating authority must, in a sunset review, use the same calculation of the rate of subsidisation as in an original investigation. What the investigating authority must do under Article 21.3 is to assess whether subsidisation is likely to continue or recur should the CVD be revoked. This is, obviously, an inherently prospective analysis. Nonetheless, it must itself have an adequate basis in fact. The facts necessary to assess the likelihood of subsidisation in the event of revocation may well be different from those which must be taken into account in an original investigation. Thus, in assessing the likelihood of subsidisation in the event of revocation of the CVD, an investigating authority in a sunset review may well consider, *inter alia*, the original level of subsidisation, any changes in the original subsidy programmes, any new subsidy programmes introduced after the imposition of the original CVD, any changes in

---

[323] *United States – Safeguard Measures on Imports of Fresh, Chilled or Frozen Lamb Meat from New Zealand and Australia* ("*US – Lamb*"), Report of the Appellate Body, WT/DS177/AB/R-WT/DS178/AB/R, adopted 16 May 2001, para. 131(emphasis in original).

[324] *US – DRAMS*, Report of the Panel, footnote 247, *supra*, para. 6.42.

government policy, and any changes in relevant socio-economic and political circumstances.

(ii) Is US CVD law as such consistent with the requirements of Article 21.3 of the *SCM Agreement* in respect of the investigating authority's obligation to determine the likelihood of continuation or recurrence of subsidisation in a sunset review?

8.97 Having addressed the substance of the obligation of investigating authorities to assess the likelihood of continuation or recurrence of subsidisation, we now turn to the question of whether US law is consistent with that obligation.

8.98 We recall that the European Communities argues that the governing provisions in US law (Section 751(c), as complemented by Section 752, of the Tariff Act[325], as amended, the Implementing Regulations[326], and the accompanying statement of policy practices[327]) preclude the US DOC from making the determination required under Article 21.3.

8.99 Turning to our analysis, we note that Section 751(c) of the Tariff Act reads, in relevant part:

> (b) Five-year review
>
> In general
>
> ... 5 years after the date of publication of —
>
> (A) a countervailing duty order ...
>
> the administering authority and the Commission shall conduct a review to determine...whether revocation of the countervailing...duty order...would be likely to lead to continuation or recurrence of ... a countervailable subsidy (as the case may be) and of material injury...[328]

8.100 Section 752 of the Tariff Act provides, in relevant part:

> (b) Determination of likelihood of continuation or recurrence of a countervailable subsidy
>
> (1) In general

[325] 19 U.S.C.A. Section 1675(c) (Exhibit EC-13).

[326] Procedures for Conducting Five-year ("Sunset") Reviews of Antidumping and Countervailing Duty Orders, or "Sunset Regulations". 63 FR 13516 (20 March 1998), codified in 19 CFR part 351 (Exhibit EC-14).

[327] 63 FR 18871 (16 April 1998) (Exhibit EC-15). The United States explains: "Under [US] law, the Sunset Policy Bulletin would be considered a non-binding statement, providing evidence of [the DOC's] understanding of sunset-related issues not explicitly addressed by the statute and regulations. In this regard, the Sunset Policy Bulletin has a legal status comparable to that of agency precedent ... As with its administrative precedent, [the DOC] normally would follow its policy bulletin or explain why it did not do so" (First Written Submission of the United States, footnote 37). In this context, the findings of the Panel in *United States – Export Restraints* in respect of the legal status of the measures challenged by the European Communities in that case may provide useful guidance. (*See United States – Measures Treating Exports Restraints as Subsidies* ("*United States – Export Restraints*"), Report of the Panel, WT/DS194/R and Corr.2, adopted 23 August 2001.)

[328] 19 U.S.C.A. Section 1675(c) (Exhibit EC-13).

> In a review... the administering authority shall determine whether revocation of a countervailing duty order... would be likely to lead to continuation or recurrence of a countervailable subsidy... The administering authority shall consider-
>
> (A) the net countervailable subsidy determined in the investigation and subsequent reviews, and
>
> (B) whether any change in the programme which gave rise to the net countervailable subsidy ... has occurred that is likely to affect that net countervailable subsidy.
>
> (2) Consideration of other factors
>
> If good cause is shown, the administering authority shall also consider-
>
> (A) programmes determined to provide countervailable subsidies in other investigations or reviews ...
>
> (B) programmes newly alleged to provide countervailable subsidies but only to the extent that the administering authority makes an affirmative countervailing duty determination with respect to such programmes and with respect to the exporters or producers subject to the review.
>
> (3) Net countervailable subsidy
>
> The administering authority shall provide to the Commission the net countervailable subsidy that is likely to prevail if the order is revoked or the suspended investigation is terminated.[329]

8.101 With respect to the DOC's obligation to "determine", the Sunset Regulations essentially repeat the language of the Statute. They provide, in relevant part:

> [T]he Secretary must determine whether dumping or countervailable subsidies would be likely to continue or resume if an order were revoked or a suspended investigation were terminated...
>
> Even where the Department conducts a full sunset review, only under the most extraordinary circumstances will the Secretary rely on a countervailing duty rate or a dumping margin other than those it calculated and published in its prior determinations...[330]

The Sunset Policy Bulletin and the Statement of Administrative Action[331] ("SAA") basically elaborate further on the provisions of the Statute and the Sunset Regulations within the limits set out in the Statute.

8.102 In this case, the question we must address is whether US law mandates WTO-inconsistent behaviour or gives rise to executive authority that can be exercised with discretion. If we find that US law provides the executive branch with discretionary authority, we will conclude that US law as such is not inconsistent with the *SCM*

---

329 19 U.S.C.A. Section 1675(a) (Exhibit EC-13).

330 19 CFR 351.218(a) (Exhibit EC-14).

331 We note that US law, 19 U.S.C. Section 3512(d), provides that "[t]he statement of administrative action approved by Congress under section 3511(a) of this title shall be regarded as an authoritative expression by the United States concerning the interpretation and application of the Uruguay Round Agreements and this Act in any judicial proceeding in which a question arises concerning such interpretation or application".

Agreement in respect of the investigating authorities' duty to "determine" the likelihood of continuation or recurrence of subsidisation. If, on the other hand, we find that US law mandates WTO-inconsistent behaviour, we will find that it violates Article 21.3 of the *SCM Agreement*. Our approach in this respect is consistent with the established jurisprudence of the Appellate Body that distinguishes between mandatory and discretionary legislation in proceedings where a Member's legislation as such is challenged before a WTO Panel.[332]

8.103 At the outset, we observe that the words of Section 751(c) of the Tariff Act reflect closely the language of Article 21.3 of the *SCM Agreement*. Indeed the operative language with which we are concerned is almost identical. The US DOC is required to "determine whether revocation" of a CVD would be likely to lead to the continuation or recurrence of subsidisation and injury in order to extend the application of a CVD beyond the initial five-year period. After setting out this general rule, Section 751(c) lays down further procedural rules that the investigating authorities have to follow in sunset reviews.[333]

8.104 Section 752 of the Tariff Act sets out, in subsection (b), rules on the consideration of the rate of subsidisation. Section 751(b) in subsection (1) states that the original rate of subsidisation – or the rate obtained in a later review – should be taken into account, together with subsequent changes that occurred in the original subsidy programmes, that affect the net countervailable subsidy. Section 751(b)(2) stipulates that potential new programmes shall be taken into account. Section 751(b)(3) states that the administering authority should report to the US ITC the rate of subsidisation that is likely to continue or recur should the existing measure be revoked.

8.105 We note, however, the following statement in the Sunset Regulations:

> Even where the Department conducts a full sunset review, only under the most extraordinary circumstances will the Secretary rely on a countervailing duty rate or a dumping margin other than those it calculated and published in its prior determinations...[334]

While this statement does not preclude the assessment and provision of a likely rate of subsidisation by the DOC to the ITC, the introduction of the additional criterion of "the most extraordinary circumstances" seems to us to be dubious. The language is strong, and apparently places the burden of proof to demonstrate "the most extraordinary circumstances" on the exporting parties. We consider that this criterion imposes fairly severe legal limitations on the ability of the DOC to come up with a new rate of subsidisation. While not requiring WTO-inconsistent behaviour in this regard, US law nonetheless curtails the discretion of the investigating authority such that, in the absence of information about what might constitute "the most extraordinary circumstances", we feel compelled to express some concern about the effect of this regulation.

8.106 We recall our finding in paragraph 8.102, *supra*, however, that unless US CVD law mandates WTO-inconsistent behaviour, we will find that it is not inconsis-

---

[332] For the most recent application of this test by the Appellate Body, *see*, *United States – Section 211 Omnibus Appropriations Act of 1998* ("*US – Section 211 Appropriations Act*"), Report of the Appellate Body, WT/DS176/AB/R, adopted 2 February 2002, para. 259.

[333] Subtitles under this section are: (1) In general, (2) Notice of initiation of review, (3) Responses to notice of initiation, (4) Inadequate response, (5) Conduct of review, (6) Special transition rules, and (7) Exclusions from computations.

[334] 19 CFR 351.218(e)(2)(i) (Exhibit EC-14).

tent with the *SCM Agreement*. Having considered the provisions challenged by the European Communities, we find no provision in US law that *mandates* WTO-inconsistent behaviour. We also note that the Regulations, the Sunset Policy Bulletin and the SAA do not contain any provision that changes US law in this respect. We therefore find that US law is not inconsistent with Article 21.3 of the *SCM Agreement* with respect to the obligation that the investigating authorities determine the likelihood of continuation or recurrence of subsidisation in a sunset review.

8.107 Further, we note that the European Communities claims that, owing to the lack of consistency with Article 21.3 of the *SCM Agreement* in respect of the obligation that the investigating authorities determine the likelihood of continuation or recurrence of subsidisation in a sunset review, US CVD law is also inconsistent with Article 32.5 of the *SCM Agreement* and Article XVI:4 of the WTO Agreement, which provisions require that Members ensure the WTO-conformity of their laws, regulations, and administrative procedures. Having found that US CVD law and the accompanying regulations are consistent with Article 21.3 of the *SCM Agreement* in respect of the obligation that the investigating authorities determine the likelihood of continuation or recurrence of subsidisation in a sunset review, we need not, and do not, consider whether US CVD law and the accompanying regulations are inconsistent with Article 32.5 of the *SCM Agreement* and Article XVI:4 of the WTO Agreement.

2. *Whether US CVD Law as Applied in the Instant Sunset Review is Inconsistent with the SCM Agreement in Respect of the Investigating Authority's Obligation to Determine the Likelihood of Continuation or Recurrence of Subsidisation in a Sunset Review*

(a) Arguments of the Parties

(i) European Communities

8.108 The European Communities argues that the DOC failed to "determine" the likelihood of continuation or recurrence of subsidisation in the instant case. The European Communities asserts that during the sunset review in question, the DOC refused to consider changes or terminations in the original subsidy programmes that occurred after the imposition of the original CVD order simply because no administrative review had been requested by the German exporters and conducted by the DOC during this period.[335]

8.109 According to the European Communities, the US DOC had in its possession the non-confidential version of the German exporters' responses to the questionnaires in the original investigation as well as the calculation memorandum as part of the record of the original investigation. Thus, the European Communities maintains the DOC could have easily determined whether the benefits received by the German exporters under the CIG programme after 1 January 1986 were *de minimis*.[336] According to the European Communities therefore the US DOC failed to fulfill its obligation to determine the likelihood of continuation or recurrence of subsidisation by

335 First Written Submission of the European Communities, para. 77.

336 *Ibid.*, para. 87.

declining to consider a document that allegedly contained information that could be relevant in its likelihood analysis.

(ii) United States

8.110 The United States points out that in the sunset review at issue, the DOC considered the subsidy programmes and the rate of subsidisation calculated in the original investigation. According to the United States, this approach conforms to the requirements of Article 21.3 because what that article requires an investigating authority to do in a sunset review is to determine the likelihood of continuation or recurrence of subsidisation.[337]

8.111 The United States also argues in this respect that even using the calculation memorandum that was part of the original CVD investigation would not shed light on the rate of subsidisation because that memorandum contained no information concerning the value of the German exporters' sales.[338]

(b) Findings of the Panel

8.112 Having found that US law as such is not inconsistent with the *SCM Agreement* in respect of the investigating authority's obligation to determine the likelihood of continuation or recurrence of subsidisation under Article 21.3, we now turn to the consistency of US CVD law as applied in the instant sunset review with the *SCM Agreement* in respect of the investigating authority's obligation to determine the likelihood of continuation or recurrence of subsidisation under Article 21.3.

8.113 We note that among all the subsidy programmes involved in this sunset review, the Capital Investment Grants ("CIG") programme had the highest share. The CIG programme was the major subsidy programme involved in the original CVD investigation. There is no dispute between the parties that this programme was terminated after the imposition of the original CVD order. It provided non-recurring subsidies and applied only to investments made prior to 1 January 1986.[339]

8.114 In this context, we will consider the analysis and explanation underlying the US DOC's determination that subsidisation was likely to continue or recur in this sunset review. US DOC stated in its final determination in the instant sunset review that it had determined that the revocation of the CVD order at issue would be likely to lead to the continuation or recurrence of subsidisation at the rate of 0.54 per cent.[340]

8.115 Thus, it appears that the US DOC made an assessment of the rate at which subsidisation was likely to continue or recur. We recall, however, our finding above that the determination of the investigating authority must rest on an adequate factual basis. We therefore consider whether the US DOC's assessment of the likelihood of whether subsidisation would continue or recur rested on an adequate factual basis, consistent with the requirements of Article 21.3. We consider that in the context of a sunset review under Article 21.3 of the *SCM Agreement*, an investigating authority should collect relevant facts and base its likelihood analysis on those facts. These

---

[337] First Written Submission of the United States, para. 92.

[338] *Ibid.*, para. 106.

[339] Final Affirmative Countervailing Duty Determinations: Certain Steel Products from Germany, 58 FR 37316 (9 July 1993) (Exhibit EC – 2).

[340] Final Results of Full Sunset Reviews, 65 FR 47407 (2 August 2000) (Exhibit EC – 9).

facts will include, among others, changes in the original subsidy programmes, any new subsidy programmes introduced following the imposition of the original CVD, potential subsidy programmes, and benefits that flow or may flow from these programmes to the exporters. Such relevant facts may be in the possession of either the investigating authorities or the interested parties. Article 12 of the Agreement, which governs, *inter alia*, the collection of evidence, is specifically incorporated into Article 21. Therefore, where necessary in sunset reviews, the investigating authorities may make use of the methods provided for in Article 12 for the collection of evidence, as they do in original investigations.

8.116 In the instant case, the DOC took the original CVD rate found in the original investigation as a starting-point and then subtracted from that rate the share of two subsidy programmes found to have been terminated after the imposition of the original CVD. Thus the factual basis of the DOC's determination was limited to the original rate of subsidisation and the fact that two of the original subsidy programmes were terminated after the imposition of the original CVD order.

8.117 In our view, the DOC's likelihood determination, which did not go beyond simple arithmetic calculation, lacks sufficient factual basis. In particular, we note that the US DOC refused to accept information that would have been relevant to the assessment of the likelihood of subsidisation. With respect to the obligations of the investigating authorities regarding the establishment of an adequate factual basis for their determinations, the Appellate Body, in the *US – Cotton Yarn* case, stated:

> [A]n investigation by a competent authority requires a proper degree of activity. Their "duties of investigation and evaluation preclude them from remaining passive in the face of possible shortcomings in the evidence submitted." They "must undertake additional investigative steps, when the circumstances so require, in order to fulfil their obligation to evaluate all relevant factors."[341]

8.118 In the instant sunset review, as discussed further below, the DOC declined the request made by the German exporters that the calculation memorandum from the original investigation be placed on the record of the sunset review on the grounds that the submission was untimely. In our view, and in light of the Appellate Body's ruling in *US – Cotton Yarn*, the investigating authorities are required to consider factual evidence already in their possession that is relevant to the assessment of the likelihood of continuation or recurrence of subsidisation, particularly where, as in this case, that information may be relevant to the assessment of the rate at which subsidisation is likely to continue or recur. Investigating authorities cannot remain completely passive and expect the exporters to formally submit information that is in the possession of the investigating authorities in connection with the original investigation. Applying that test to our case, the DOC's failure to accept the German exporters' request that the calculation memorandum be placed on the record of the sunset review indicates that the DOC did not even consider a document that was in its possession and that would have been relevant in its likelihood analysis, let alone taking additional steps.

8.119 In light of the foregoing, we conclude that the US DOC failed to properly determine the likelihood of continuation or recurrence of subsidisation in the instant sunset review because its decision regarding the rate at which subsidisation was likely to continue or recur lacked an adequate factual basis. Therefore, we conclude

---

[341] *US – Cotton Yarn*, footnote 217, *supra*, para. 73 (footnotes omitted, emphasis in original).

that US CVD law as applied in the instant sunset review is inconsistent with the *SCM Agreement* in respect of the investigating authority's obligation to determine the likelihood of continuation or recurrence of subsidisation under Article 21.3.

E. Whether US CVD Law as such and as Applied in the Instant Sunset Review are Inconsistent with the SCM Agreement in Respect of the Investigating Authority's Obligation to Provide Ample Opportunity to Interested Members and Parties to Submit Relevant Evidence in a Sunset Review

1. Arguments of the Parties

(a) European Communities

8.120 The European Communities argues that US law violates Article 12.1 of the *SCM Agreement* in that it fails to provide ample opportunity to the interested parties to present in writing all evidence which they consider relevant in respect of a sunset review. In particular, the European Communities refers to Section 351.218(d)(4) of the US Sunset Regulations – which, together with Section 351.218(d)(3), provides 35 days for the parties to respond to the questionnaires – and submits that this short deadline violates the provisions of Article 21.3, in conjunction with Articles 12.1 and 21.4, of the *SCM Agreement.*[342]

8.121 The European Communities also asserts that US CVD law is inconsistent with the *SCM Agreement* in that, under US CVD law, the DOC does not send questionnaires to interested parties in sunset reviews and requires them to respond only to a short list of questions which, in the European Communities' view, are perfunctory in nature.[343]

8.122 Further, the European Communities argues as follows:

> The US law and practice does [sic] not respect several provisions of Article 12 of the *SCM Agreement* ... In particular, Articles 12.1 and 12.1.1 lay down a general obligation to provide "ample opportunity" to exporters to present in writing all evidence they consider relevant. Article 12.2 allows also for the right to present information orally. Article 12.3 establishes in effect a procedure of mutual dialogue by providing that the affected exporters should be given timely opportunity "to see all information that is relevant to the presentation of their cases ... and to prepare presentations on the basis of this information". Moreover, Article 12.8 provides that before the final determination is made, disclosure should take place "in sufficient time for the parties to defend their interests". The principle underlying Article 12 of the *SCM Agreement*, therefore, is that during all stages of the reviews the interested parties should be given ample opportunity to present evidence, to have access to the evidence presented by the other parties (except where confidentiality applies), to present counter-evidence and to de-

342 First Written Submission of the European Communities, paras. 98-99.

343 Second Written Submission of the European Communities, para. 41.

fend their interests at all stages leading up to the final determination.[344]

8.123 The European Communities also submits that the United States acted inconsistently with Article 12.1 of the *SCM Agreement* by failing to consider in its likelihood analysis in the instant sunset review the calculation memorandum that was in the DOC's possession as part of the record of the original investigation. In the view of the European Communities, had the US DOC taken this memorandum into account in its sunset determination, it would have found no likelihood of continuation or recurrence of subsidisation.[345]

8.124 In response to the US DOC's argument that the calculation memorandum contained confidential information, the European Communities argues that this document was drafted by the DOC and that it did not contain confidential information that was not known to the DOC or the other interested parties in this sunset review.[346] Similarly, the European Communities counters the US arguments that the request made by the German exporters was untimely because, in the view of the European Communities, the US DOC could still conclude this sunset review in a timely manner had it taken this calculation memorandum into account.[347]

8.125 In its response to a question from the Panel following the second meeting of the Panel, the European Communities clarified that it was indeed making a *separate* claim regarding the obligation set out in Article 12.1 to provide ample opportunity to interested Members and parties to submit all relevant evidence.[348]

8.126 In its comments on the request of the United States for interim review (*See* paragraph 8.134, *infra*), the European Communities argued that the reference in its request for establishment to Article 21 *in toto* would include Article 12, as paragraph 4 of Article 21 expressly indicates that Article 12 is applicable to sunset reviews. The European Communities further submitted that the obligation to provide ample opportunity under Article 12 is expressly mentioned in its first written submission. The European Communities considered that it had fully complied with the standards of Article 6.2 of the DSU.

8.127 Finally, the European Communities argued that the United States was not only "somewhat foreclosed", following the first meeting of the Panel, from raising such an issue but that, in addition, the Panel had not proceeded "in any extension of its authority or jurisdiction". The European Communities based its objection on what it considered "the clear and verifiable evidence" that the United States was never in any doubt about the European Communities' claims under Article 12 throughout the consultations, request for establishment, and subsequent written and oral submissions of the European Communities. The European Communities indicated that it had "serious difficulties" in understanding the US argument that the United States only had the opportunity to raise this issue following the European Communities' responses to questions from the Panel following the second meeting of the Panel.

344 Second Written Submission of the European Communities, para. 44.
345 Second Written Submission of the European Communities, para. 32.
346 First Oral Statement of the European Communities, para. 33.
347 *Ibid.*, para. 33.
348 Response of the European Communities to Question 54 from the Panel.

(b) United States

8.128 In response to the European Communities' claim regarding "ample opportunity" under Article 12 of the Agreement, the United States first points out that, consistent with Article 12.1.1 of the Agreement, the US Sunset Regulations provide 30 days for the parties to submit the required information. The United States also points out that, also consistent with Article 12.1.1, the Sunset Regulations provide for the extension of this time-limit.[349]

8.129 With respect to the European Communities' argument concerning the US' failure to send questionnaires in sunset reviews, the United States submits that in addition to the information requirements set out in the Sunset Regulations – which constitute the standard questionnaire in US sunset reviews – the Sunset Regulations allow interested parties to submit additional information that they would like the DOC to consider.[350] In the view of the United States, therefore, the provisions of US law are fully consistent with Article 12 of the *SCM Agreement*.[351]

8.130 The United States counters the European Communities' arguments made in respect of the inclusion of the calculation memorandum from the original investigation basically on two grounds, i.e., lack of timeliness of the request and the confidential nature of the information contained therein.

8.131 The United States argues that the request made by the German exporters to have the calculation memorandum made part of the record of the sunset review was untimely because it was made over six months after the deadline for filing information in the instant sunset review.[352] The United States also points out that the German producers failed to file any request for the extension of this deadline although under US law they were entitled to do so.[353] Finally, the United States submits that the lack of timeliness of the German producers' request is all the more obvious given that they were on notice of the information requirements and applicable deadlines over fifteen months before the initiation of this sunset review.[354]

8.132 The United States asserts that another reason the US DOC declined to place this memorandum on the record of the sunset review was because it contained confidential information that could not be released without the consent of the person submitting it.[355] The United States argues in this respect that the DOC could not ignore previous requests for the confidential treatment of this document and automatically place it on the record of the sunset review.[356]

8.133 In its comments on the response of the European Communities to a question from the Panel following the second meeting of the Panel (*See* paragraph 8.125, *supra*), the United States submitted that the European Communities' claims under Article 12 were new, as the European Communities' request for establishment does not reference Article 12 or the fact pattern which the European Communities believes

349 First Written Submission of the United States, para. 111.
350 *Ibid.*, para.110.
351 *Ibid.*, para. 108.
352 First Written Submission of the United States, para. 103.
353 *Ibid.*
354 *Ibid.*
355 *Ibid.*, para. 104.
356 *Ibid.*

gives rise to a violation of Article 12.[357] The United States argued that the new claims did not satisfy the standards of Article 6.2 of the DSU, and requested the Panel to dismiss these new claims.

8.134 In its request for interim review, the United States again submitted, for the above reasons, that the Panel should not have made any substantive findings regarding the obligation to provide ample opportunity to interested members and parties to submit evidence in a sunset review, because the European Communities' claims regarding this obligation were not within the Panel's terms of reference.

2. *Findings of the Panel*

8.135 We recall that paragraph 13 of our working procedures states that "[a] party shall submit any request for a preliminary ruling not later than its first submission to the Panel ... Exceptions to this procedure will be granted upon a showing of good cause". In this regard, we note, at the outset, that, although it was in the course of interim review that we addressed the objection of the United States regarding the claims of the European Communities in respect of the investigating authority's obligation to provide ample opportunity, the United States had registered this objection prior to that time. The United States first presented this objection in its comments on the responses of the European Communities to questions from the Panel following the second meeting.

8.136 Further, as the European Communities had up to that point only discussed the obligation to provide ample opportunity in the context of the obligation to determine continuation or recurrence of subsidisation, it was not clear to us that the European Communities was making a *separate* claim in respect of the obligation to provide ample opportunity. It was on this basis that we posed a question to the European Communities following our second meeting with the parties, requesting clarification. And the United States made its objection known following the response by the European Communities that it was indeed making a separate claim in respect of this obligation. Therefore, this is not a situation in which we need to decide whether we can address an objection which could have been raised in a timely manner, but was not.

8.137 Thus, we have addressed the issue raised by the United States regarding the European Communities' claims in respect of the obligation to provide ample opportunity[358], and concluded that these claims are outside our terms of reference. Our reasons are set out below.

---

[357] Comments of the United States on Responses of the European Communities to Questions from the Panel following the Second Meeting of the Panel, paras. 21-22.

[358] *See also* the following ruling of the Appellate Body, in *United States – Anti-Dumping Act of 1916*:

> ... we also agree with the Panel's consideration that "some issues of jurisdiction may be of such a nature that they have to be addressed by the Panel at any time". We do not share the European Communities' view that objections to the jurisdiction of a panel are appropriately regarded as simply "procedural objections". The vesting of jurisdiction in a panel is a fundamental prerequisite for lawful panel proceedings. We, therefore, see no reason to accept the European Communities' argument that we must reject the United States' appeal because the United States did not raise its jurisdictional objection before the Panel in a timely manner. (*United States – Anti-Dumping Act of 1916* ("*US – 1916 Act*"), Report of the Appellate Body, WT/DS136/AB/R-WT/DS162/AB/R, adopted 26 September 2000, para. 54 (footnote omitted))

8.138 We note that Article 7 of the DSU covers the terms of reference of panels, and Article 6 the establishment of panels. Article 7 clearly indicates that the terms of reference of panels are contained in the request for the establishment of a panel[359]. With regard to the request for establishment, Article 6.2 of the DSU provides in part:

> The request for the establishment of a panel ... shall indicate whether consultations were held, identify the specific measures at issue and provide a brief summary of the legal basis of the complaint sufficient to present the problem clearly.

The Appellate Body has stated, in respect of the terms of reference of panels:

> Thus, "the matter referred to the DSB" for the purposes of Article 7 of the DSU and Article 17.4 of the *Anti-Dumping Agreement* must be the "matter" identified in the request for the establishment of a panel under Article 6.2 of the DSU. That provision requires the complaining Member, in a panel request, to "identify the *specific measures at issue* and provide a brief summary of the *legal basis of the complaint* sufficient to present the problem clearly." (emphasis added) The "*matter* referred to the DSB", therefore, consists of two elements: the specific *measures* at issue and the *legal basis of the complaint* (or the *claims*).[360]

Further, the Appellate Body has stated, in *European Communities – Bananas*:

> As a panel request is normally not subjected to detailed scrutiny by the DSB, it is incumbent upon a panel to examine the request for the establishment of the panel very carefully to ensure its compliance with both the letter and the spirit of Article 6.2 of the DSU. It is important that a panel request be sufficiently precise for two reasons: first, it often forms the basis for the terms of reference of the panel pursuant to Article 7 of the DSU; and, second, it informs the defending party and the third parties of the legal basis of the complaint.[361]

8.139 Thus, the United States' request raises two separate, but related, issues: (i) whether US CVD law in respect of the opportunity to submit evidence in a sunset review was identified in the request for establishment as a measure challenged by the European Communities and, if so, (ii) whether the European Communities' request for establishment provides "a brief summary of the legal basis of the complaint sufficient to present the problem clearly" and therefore satisfies the standard set out in Article 6.2 of the DSU.

8.140 We shall first examine the request for establishment to determine whether, on its face, the United States – and any other WTO Member – could have been reasonably expected to know that US CVD law in respect of the opportunity to submit evidence in a sunset review was part of "the matter referred to the DSB".

8.141 It is clear from the European Communities' request for establishment that the words "opportunity to submit evidence" or the like do not appear in that request. Nor, as we have noted above, does the request contain any all-encompassing reference to US procedures, generally, for sunset review. Paragraphs 1-2 of the request for estab-

---

[359] WT/DS213/3 in the present dispute.

[360] *Guatemala – Cement I*, Report of the Appellate Body, footnote 226, *supra*, para. 72 (emphasis in original).

[361] *European Communities – Bananas*, Report of the Appellate Body, footnote227, *supra*, para. 142.

lishment set out the procedural background to the request for establishment, paragraph 3 explains that the request relates particularly to the sunset review in carbon steel, paragraphs 4-7 set out the European Communities' claim in respect of the *de minimis* standard applied in that review, paragraphs 8-10 set out the European Communities' claim in respect of the evidentiary standards applied in relation to the initiation of that review, and paragraph 11 summarises the European Communities' challenge to the US decision in that review, as well as to "certain aspects of the sunset review procedure which led to it". This latter phrase could not be understood to include US CVD law in respect of the opportunity to submit evidence.

8.142 We note that the request for establishment further outlines the statutory and regulatory underpinnings of the US sunset review procedures as such, and as applied in the sunset review in carbon steel[362]. These statutory and regulatory provisions also govern the opportunity to submit evidence in a sunset review. We consider, however, that this fact alone is insufficient for us to conclude that US CVD law in respect of the opportunity to submit evidence in a sunset review is identified as a specific measure at issue.

8.143 Having found that US CVD law in respect of the opportunity to submit evidence in a sunset review is not identified in the request for establishment, we shall consider whether that "measure" is sufficiently related to a measure or measures that *are* specifically identified so as to bring it within our terms of reference. We note the finding of the Panel in *Japan – Film*:

> The question thus becomes whether the ordinary meaning of the terms of Article 6.2, i.e., that "the specific measures at issue" be identified in the panel request, can be met if a "measure" is not explicitly described in the request. To fall within the terms of Article 6.2, it seems clear that a "measure" not explicitly described in a panel request must have a clear relationship to a "measure" that is specifically described therein, so that it can be said to be "included" in the specified "measure". In our view, the requirements of Article 6.2 would be met in the case of a "measure" that is subsidiary, or so closely related to a "measure" specifically identified, that the responding party can reasonably be found to have received adequate notice of the scope of the claims asserted by the complaining party. The two key elements – close relationship and notice – are inter-related: only if a "measure" is subsidiary or closely related to a specifically identified "measure" will notice be adequate.[363]

8.144 We note that the European Communities' request refers to "certain aspects of the sunset review procedure which led to [the DOC decision not to revoke the CVDs on carbon steel]". We do not consider US CVD law in respect of the opportunity to submit evidence in a sunset review to be "a 'measure' that is subsidiary, or so closely related to" any of the measures specifically identified, "that the responding party can reasonably be found to have received adequate notice of the scope of the claims asserted by the complaining party". To consider otherwise would mean that the general sentence "certain aspects of the sunset review procedure which led to [the DOC decision not to revoke the CVDs on carbon steel]" put Members on notice that *any* aspect

[362] WT/DS213/3, para. 12.

[363] *Japan – Film*, Report of the Panel, footnote 230, *supra*, para. 10.8.

of US CVD law of relevance in the sunset review on carbon steel might be before the Panel. This cannot be, for that universe is potentially extremely large. We therefore find that US CVD law in respect of the opportunity to submit evidence in a sunset review is not sufficiently related to a measure or measures that are specifically identified in the request for establishment as to properly bring it within our terms of reference.[364]

8.145 For the foregoing reasons, we consider that the European Communities has failed to set out a claim in its request for establishment with respect to the United States' CVD law in respect of the investigating authority's obligation to provide ample opportunity to interested members and parties to submit relevant evidence in a sunset review. This "measure" is therefore outside our terms of reference. Accordingly, we do not address the European Communities' claims under Article 12 of the *SCM Agreement*.

IX. CONCLUSIONS AND RECOMMENDATIONS

9.1 In conclusion, we find that:

(a) US CVD law and the accompanying regulations are consistent with Article 21, paragraphs 1 and 3, and Article 10 of the *SCM Agreement* in respect of the application of evidentiary standards to the self-initiation of sunset reviews;

(b) US CVD law and the accompanying regulations are *inconsistent* with Article 21.3 of the *SCM Agreement* in respect of the application of a 0.5 per cent *de minimis* standard to sunset reviews, and therefore violate Article 32.5 of the *SCM Agreement* and, consequently, also Article XVI:4 of the WTO Agreement;

(c) the United States, in applying a 0.5 per cent *de minimis* standard to the instant sunset review, acted *in violation* of Article 21.3 of the *SCM Agreement*;

(d) US CVD law and the accompanying regulations and statement of policy practices are consistent with Article 21.3 of the *SCM Agreement* in respect of the obligation to determine the likelihood of continuation or recurrence of subsidisation in sunset reviews; and

(e) the United States, in failing to determine properly the likelihood of continuation or recurrence of subsidisation in the sunset review on carbon steel, acted *in violation* of Article 21.3 of the *SCM Agreement*.

9.2 We recommend that the Dispute Settlement Body request the United States to bring its measures mentioned in paragraph 9.1(b), (c), and (e) above into conformity with its obligations under the WTO Agreement.

---

[364] Having concluded that the European Communities has not identified US CVD law in respect of the opportunity to submit evidence in a sunset review as a specific measure at issue in its request for establishment, we need not, and do not, consider whether the European Communities has provided "a brief summary of the legal basis of the complaint sufficient to present the problem clearly" in that request for establishment (*See* paras. 8.5-8.6, *supra*).

X. DISSENTING OPINION OF ONE MEMBER OF THE PANEL ON THE ASSESSMENT OF THE PANEL RELATING TO THE APPLICATION OF A *DE MINIMIS* STANDARD TO SUNSET REVIEWS

10.1 One member of the Panel dissociated himself from the above assessment relating to the US CVD law as such and as applied in the sunset review on carbon steel in respect of application of a *de minimis* standard to sunset reviews (*See* Sections VIII.C.1(b) and VIII.C.2(b), *supra*) and expressed the following dissenting opinion[365]:

10.2 I agree with the statement of the majority of the Panel, that "nothing in the text of Article 21.3 specifically provides that the *de minimis* standard applicable to investigations is also applicable to sunset reviews"[366]. I do not, however, share the view of the majority that, such silence in the relevant provision as to the applicability of a *de minimis* standard to sunset reviews is *not* dispositive given an examination of the text of Article 21.3 in its context and in light of the object and purpose of the *SCM Agreement*, as required by Article 31 of the Vienna Convention. I consider that an examination of Article 21.3 pursuant to the customary rules of treaty interpretation yields the conclusion that no *de minimis* standard is applicable to sunset reviews.

10.3 In my view, the drafters would have been able and chosen to include a clear indication to the opposite effect, should that have been their intention. Indeed, I am persuaded by the United States' argument that the absence of a clear indication, for instance, in the form of a cross-reference, is all the more significant given the immediate context of Article 21.3 – that is, the fact that the drafters *did* provide explicit cross-references elsewhere in Article 21, to Articles 12 and 18. It is clear that the drafters knew how to have obligations set forth in one provision apply in another context. The most obvious inference one can draw from the absence of a cross-reference, therefore, is that the Members chose not to have the *de minimis* standard of Article 11.9 be implied in Article 21.3. There appears to me to be no textual basis to read Article 21.3 in the manner argued for by the European Communities. Given the

[365] Like the majority of the Panel, I do not understand the European Communities to be alleging a violation of Article 11.9, but of Article 21.3, of the *SCM Agreement*. In this regard, I note that the European Communities argues that "an interpretation of the terms of Article 21.3 should be made in context and in the light of the object and purpose of Article 21.3 and of the *SCM Agreement*. Articles 21.1, 11.9, 15, and 10 provide relevant context and help define its object and purpose. Such an interpretation ... requires that the 1 [per cent] *de minimis* level of Article 11.9 should be *implied*, and hence applied, also to investigations and determinations made in sunset reviews" (Response of the European Communities to Question 47 from the Panel (emphasis added)).

Further, the European Communities "objects to the [United States'] suggestion to use only the phrase 'Article 11.9 itself applies to sunset reviews'" (Comments of the European Communities on Request of the United States for Interim Review, para. 3). Indeed, the European Communities argues that it "has taken particular care to explain that there is an omission in Article 21.3 and that only a systematic interpretation can fill up [sic] this gap by *implying* the *de minimis* standard of Article 11.9" (Comments of the European Communities on Request of the United States for Interim Review, para. 3 (emphasis added)). Nor could the European Communities successfully allege a violation of Article 11.9. Article 11 is entitled "Initiation and Subsequent Investigation", and clearly deals with investigations, such as that term is distinguished from reviews by the Agreement. This is also made clear in the text of Article 11.9 itself, which refers to investigations. I therefore consider whether Article 21.3 contains by implication the same type of obligation as Article 11.9, and whether the United States has violated Article 21.3 in this respect.

[366] Para. 8.58, *supra*.

marked difference in the terms of Article 21.3 and those of other provisions of the *SCM Agreement* which do explicitly establish cross-cutting obligations, I cannot conclude that it was the drafters' intention to have Article 11.9 be implied in Article 21.3.

10.4 To consider the question of cross-references or other explicit statements of cross-application in the broader context of Article 21.3 – that is, provisions of the *SCM Agreement* other than Article 21 – I note that a number of provisions in the Agreement contain an explicit indication where the drafters wished to make their scope of application clear[367]. Take Article 11.9, which sets out the *de minimis* standard applicable to investigations (except for products originating in developing country Members). I agree with the statement of the majority of the Panel, that "nothing in the text of [Article 11.9] provides for its *de minimis* standard to be implied in Article 21.3"[368]. I therefore cannot conclude, given the explicit language elsewhere in the Agreement, and in the absence of such language in Article 11.9, that the *de minimis* standard set out in that provision must nonetheless be understood to be implied in Article 21.3.

10.5 I note the Appellate Body's statement, in *US – Gasoline*:

> One of the corollaries of the "general rule of interpretation" in the *Vienna Convention* is that interpretation must give meaning and effect to all the terms of the treaty. An interpreter is not free to adopt a reading that would result in reducing whole clauses or paragraphs of a treaty to redundancy or inutility.[369]

I am of the opinion that to consider provisions relating to investigations applicable by implication under provisions relating to sunset reviews does not give meaning and effect to the explicit statements of cross-application in the *SCM Agreement*, and effectively renders such statements redundant. In other words, if all provisions are applicable to sunset reviews, except perhaps where impracticable, then there would be no need for such explicit statements to exist.

10.6 I recall that Article 11.9 requires the termination of an investigation in cases of *de minimis* subsidisation, negligible volume of subsidised imports, or negligible actual or potential injury. It seems to me that, if the rationale for the inclusion of a *de minimis* subsidisation standard were that *de minimis* subsidisation is deemed to be non-injurious, as the majority of the Panel considers (*See* paragraphs 8.60-8.64), then there would be no need to include a further standard of negligible actual or potential injury. It should be noted, in this context, that negligible actual or potential injury is nonetheless *material* injury, as footnote 45 to the Agreement states that "[u]nder this Agreement the term 'injury' shall, unless otherwise specified, be taken to mean material injury to a domestic industry, threat of material injury to a domestic industry or material retardation of the establishment of such an industry".

10.7 I recall also that Article 27.10 reads:

---

367 The definition of "subsidy" in Article 1 ("For the purpose of this Agreement"); the definition of "interested parties" in Article 12.9 ("for the purposes of this Agreement"); the calculation of the amount of a subsidy under Article 14 ("For the purpose of Part V"); the definition of "injury" under Article 15 and footnote 45 ("Under this Agreement"); the definition of "like product" under footnote 46 ("Throughout this Agreement"); definition of domestic industry in Article 16 ("For the purposes of this Agreement"); and the definition of "levy" under footnote 51 ("As used in this Agreement").

368 Para. 8.59, *supra*.

369 *United States – Gasoline*, Report of the Appellate Body, footnote 257, *supra*, p. 23.

> Any [CVD] investigation of a product originating in a developing country Member shall be terminated as soon as the authorities concerned determine that:
>
> (a) the overall level of subsidies granted upon the product in question does not exceed 2 per cent of its value calculated on a per unit basis;
>
> ...

The use of the word "investigation" in this provision confirms, in my opinion, that the two *de minimis* subsidisation thresholds specified in the *SCM Agreement* apply only to investigations. Were the *de minimis* standard to apply to sunset reviews, the special and differential treatment provided to developing countries in the context of investigations would presumably have been extended to include sunset reviews. The word "investigation" in Article 27.10 clearly indicates that that is not the case. It is difficult to see why the drafters would intend the *de minimis* standard to apply to both investigations and sunset reviews, but provide special and differential treatment in this respect only in the context of investigations. In other words, the text of Article 27.10 suggests that no *de minimis* standard applies to sunset reviews.

10.8 I am of the view that the European Communities' argument is largely contextual; indeed, the European Communities has characterised its argument as a reading of Article 21.3 "in the context of" Article 11.9. It is not a given, however, that, because the negotiators agreed to certain standards for purposes of investigations, they necessarily agreed to the same for purposes of sunset reviews. The context of a legal provision – i.e., other paragraphs of the provision or related provisions elsewhere in the text – does not in and of itself create a legal obligation. The legal obligation must be found first and foremost in the text of the provision.[370] Otherwise, one would be forced to accept the view that consistency reasons may constitute sufficient grounds for the so-called "implication" of obligations.

10.9 While I do not disagree that application of the same *de minimis* standard to sunset reviews as to investigations would ensure a certain balance between the disciplines applicable to investigations and those applicable to sunset reviews, it is difficult to conclude on that basis *alone* that the same *de minimis* standard applies to both instances. Policy arguments alone are not sufficient for me to find that this is the case; rather, I would have to find that there is a proper *legal* basis for the European Communities' position, interpreting Article 21.3 pursuant to the customary rules of treaty interpretation.[371] While it would not be illogical – and it would reflect a degree of consistency in the treatment of investigations and sunset reviews – to apply the

---

370 In this regard, I recall the statement of the Appellate Body, in *Japan – Alcoholic Beverages II*:

> Article 31 of the *Vienna Convention* provides that the words of the treaty form the foundation for the interpretive process: "interpretation must be based above all upon the text of the treaty". (*Japan – Taxes on Alcoholic Beverages* ("*Japan – Alcoholic Beverages II*"), Report of the Appellate Body, WT/DS8/AB/R-WT/DS10/AB/R-WT/DS11/AB/R, adopted 1 November 1996, p. 12 (footnote deleted))

371 In this regard, I recall the statement of the Appellate Body, in EC – Hormones, that:

> The fundamental rule of treaty interpretation requires a treaty interpreter to read and interpret the words *actually used* by the agreement under examination, not words the interpreter may feel *should have been used*. (*EC – Hormones*, Report of the Appellate Body, footnote 250, *supra*, para. 181 (emphasis added))

same *de minimis* standard to sunset reviews as to investigations, I cannot conclude on those grounds alone that that is the case, and I consider that the *text* of the *SCM Agreement* does not require investigating authorities to do so. I consider that the text of Article 21.3 – literally *and* in its context – clearly fails to establish an obligation on investigating authorities to apply a *de minimis* standard to sunset reviews.

10.10 Nor do I consider it *impossible* that the drafters might have intended there to be different rules for sunset reviews from those for investigations. It is arguably perfectly rational for there to be different disciplines for sunset reviews than for investigations. For instance, the negotiators might well have considered that application of a *de minimis* standard in the form of a specific numeric threshold was not feasible in the context of sunset reviews because any assessment of the rate at which subsidisation is likely to continue or recur would be but an approximation. One important observation in this regard is that Article 19.1 of the Agreement requires investigating authorities to make a final determination of both the existence and the amount of the subsidy (and that the subsidised imports are causing injury) before they may impose a CVD. It is therefore entirely reasonable that a *de minimis* threshold of 1 per cent is set out in this respect in Article 11.9. There is, however, no language similar to that of Article 19.1 in Article 21.3. In other words, were the *de minimis* standard set out in Article 11.9 implied in Article 21.3, the drafters would have set out in Article 21.3 the requirement to make a determination of both the existence and the amount of the subsidy. I consider that there is nothing in a decision that the *de minimis* standard applicable to investigations does not apply to sunset reviews that would undermine the operation of the Agreement or the ability of investigating authorities to operate under the Agreement. I see the framework of CVD disciplines as supporting the conclusion that a *de minimis* standard is not required under Article 21.3. In other words, it is not necessary to – and there could be entirely rational reasons not to – have the *de minimis* standard of Article 11.9 be implied in Article 21.3 to make the latter, or another, provision functional or ensure that the basic framework of CVD disciplines is preserved.

10.11 Finally, I consider that it is worth noting that, while the negotiating history of the *SCM Agreement* does not specifically address the question of whether a *de minimis* standard should apply to reviews, the questions of definition of a subsidy, investigation, imposition of measures, and review of need for measures were negotiated as separate items. *De minimis* as a concept was addressed in the context of the question of the imposition of measures; it does not seem to have been addressed at all in the context of the discussion of the need for a sunset clause or review mechanism. I am of the view that this would tend to confirm the results of my textual analysis above.

10.12 In sum, I recognise that the negotiators may well have had differing views as to whether it was desirable to apply the same *de minimis* standard to sunset reviews as to investigations – and it is indeed likely that some of them believed it would be. I do not, however, see that a rigorous and faithful reading of Article 21.3 in its context and in light of the object and purpose of the *SCM Agreement* leads to the conclusion that they agreed to impose such an obligation on investigating authorities.

10.13 I therefore find that the *de minimis* standard of Article 11.9 is not implied in Article 21.3. I thus conclude that US CVD law and the accompanying regulations are consistent with the *SCM Agreement* in respect of the application of a *de minimis* standard to sunset reviews, and accordingly reject the claim of the European Communities in this regard.

10.14 Further, I note that the European Communities claims that, owing to the lack of consistency with Article 21.3 of the *SCM Agreement* in respect of the application of a *de minimis* standard to sunset reviews, US CVD law is also inconsistent with Article 32.5 of the *SCM Agreement* and Article XVI:4 of the WTO Agreement, which provisions require that Members ensure the WTO-conformity of their laws, regulations, and administrative procedures. Having found that US CVD law and the accompanying regulations are consistent with Article 21.3 of the *SCM Agreement* in respect of the application of a *de minimis* standard to sunset reviews, I need not, and do not, consider whether US CVD law and the accompanying regulations are inconsistent with Article 32.5 of the *SCM Agreement* and Article XVI:4 of the WTO Agreement.

10.15 Accordingly, in conclusion, in contrast with paragraphs 9.1(b) and 9.1(c), I find that:

(a) US CVD law and the accompanying regulations are *consistent* with Article 21.3 of the *SCM Agreement* in respect of the application of a 0.5 per cent *de minimis* standard to sunset reviews; and

(b) the United States, in applying a 0.5 per cent *de minimis* standard to the instant sunset review, did *not* act in violation of Article 21.3 of the *SCM Agreement*.

Cumulative Index of Published Disputes